OUTSTANDING A
SYLVIE SIMMONS AN

Best Biography of 2012—NP

"*I'm Your Man* is the major, soul-searching biography that Leonard Cohen deserves. . . . A mesmerizing labor of love."

—Janet Maslin, *New York Times*

"A thoughtful celebration of the artist's life. . . . Simmons has deftly narrated Cohen's evolution, bringing the past into the present and reminding us of the breadth of the journey. . . . In the end, this biography has the oddest effect: as soon as you finish reading it you feel an overwhelming impulse to go back and begin again, revisiting the story with what you've learned along the way."   —A. M. Homes, *New York Times Book Review*

"A new gold standard of Cohen bios."   —*Los Angeles Times*

"Simmons, throughout, is not just a skillful reporter but a blisteringly good writer. . . . Like all good music writing, this makes you eager to listen to the songs with your newly attuned ear. And she creates what ought to become the enduring snapshot of Cohen in the present tense, a man well into his seventies enjoying a rather miraculous late-stage career."   —*Boston Globe*

"This is the bio Cohen has long deserved, and it makes every prior Cohen book practically unnecessary."   —*Rolling Stone* (4½ stars)

"The book is a seductive tribute to a master seducer."

—The Onion A.V. Club

"The challenge in profiling an artist like this is to rise to their occasion and . . . Simmons . . . soars. The heart of this tale . . . is how Leonard fought that darkness through his work and how the light ultimately prevailed when he triumphantly toured the world for three years beginning in 2008. . . . 'You could hear the hairs stand up on people's arms,' writes Simmons of the hushed reverence of his audience. This book demands a similar reaction."   —*MOJO* (5 stars)

"Simmons is a wonderful writer. She describes events with engaging clarity and a command of language that oftentimes enthralls. . . . The book informs like carefully researched nonfiction, but engages like enchanting fiction. . . . Like listening to one of Cohen's songs, this complex, beautiful biography requires you to stay with it, to think about it. This book will stay with you. It will change the way you hear Leonard Cohen." —*Paste Magazine*

"A deep, enlightening book. . . . Simmons, a music journalist and short-story writer, knows how to research and write and keep a critical distance from Cohen, who opens up some but uses his usual weapons, politeness and self-deprecation, to maintain an air of mystery." —*Oregonian*

"Exquisitely researched and elegantly written." —*Dallas Morning News*

"Cohen is a complex man and Sylvie Simmons has captured every essence of it in her remarkable book. This is a deeply insightful portrait that is guaranteed to haunt the reader." —*Tucson Citizen*

"In *I'm Your Man*, we see not only the life of one man who was transformed by words, but how we ourselves may be transformed by them." —*New York Jewish Week*

"Simmons's rich, compelling and provocative book . . . is a star-studded but also frank account of how the music industry really works and, at the same time, a discerning portrait of one especially important musician." —*Los Angeles Jewish Journal*

"Compelling biography. . . . A must for anyone interested in one of the most influential songwriters of our time." —*Booklist* (starred review)

"An elegant, deeply researched life of the Canadian musician, poet and novelist. . . . He emerges in his full complexity, brimming with both seemingly boundless brilliance and abundant human imperfection. Taking on a looming subject with intelligence and wit, Simmons manages to take the full measure of her man." —*Kirkus Reviews* (starred review)

"[A] vibrant and enthusiastic chronicle. . . . Carefully weaving the threads of all of his songs and albums through the patterns of his life, Simmons craftily explores the themes that regularly mark Cohen's work: desire, regret, suffering, love, hope, and hamming it up." —*Publishers Weekly* (starred review)

"In this elegantly crafted biography, Simmons captures the artist, who, in spite of all his highs and lows, is still sharp at the edges, a wise old monk, a trouper offering up himself and his songs." —*BookPage*

I'm Your Man

The Life of Leonard Cohen

Sylvie Simmons

ecco

An Imprint of HarperCollinsPublishers

To N.A., in loving memory

The way you do anything is
the way you do everything.

—TOM WAITS

SECOND ECCO PAPERBACK EDITION PUBLISHED 2021

A hardcover edition of this book was published in 2012 by Ecco, an imprint of HarperCollins Publishers.

Designed by Leah Carlson-Stanisic

Library of Congress Cataloging-in-Publication Data has been applied for.

ISBN 978-0-06-6311490-6 (pbk.)

HB 08.15.2024

Contents

Prologue

He is a courtly man, elegant, with old-world manners. He bows when he meets you, stands when you leave, makes sure that you're comfortable and makes no mention of the fact he's not; the discreet stroking of the Greek worry beads he carries in his pocket gives the game away. By inclination he is a private man, rather shy, but if probing is required he'll put his feet in the stirrups with dignity and humor. He chooses his words carefully, like a poet, or a politician, with a habit of precision, an ear for their sound, and a talent and a taste for deflection and mystery. He has always liked smoke and mirrors. And yet there is something conspiratorial in the way he talks, as there is when he sings, as if he were imparting an intimate secret.

He is a trim man—there's no excess to him at all—and smaller than you might think. Shipshape. You imagine that he wouldn't find it hard to wear a uniform. Right now he is wearing a suit. It is dark, pin-striped, double-breasted, and if it's off-the-rack it doesn't look it.

"Darling," says Leonard, "I was born in a suit."[1]

One

Born in a Suit

When I'm with you
I want to be the kind of hero
I wanted to be
when I was seven years old
a perfect man
who kills

—"The Reason I Write," *Selected Poems 1956–1968*

The chauffeur turned off the main road by the synagogue, which took up most of the block, and headed past St. Matthias's Church on the opposite corner, and up the hill. In the back of the car was a woman—twenty-seven years old, attractive, strong featured, stylishly dressed—and her newborn baby son. The streets they passed were handsome and well-appointed, the trees arranged just so. Big houses of brick and stone you might have thought would collapse under the sheer weight of their self-importance appeared to float effortlessly up the slopes. Around halfway up, the driver took a side road and stopped outside a house at the end of the street, 599 Belmont Avenue. It was large, solid and formal-looking, English in style, its dark brick softened by a white-framed veranda at the front and at the back by Murray Hill Park, fourteen acres of lawns, trees and flower beds, with a sweeping view of the St. Lawrence River to one side and, on the other, downtown Montreal. The chauffeur stepped out of the car and opened the rear door, and Leonard was carried up the white front steps and into his family home.

Leonard Norman Cohen was born on September 21, 1934, in the Royal Victoria Hospital, a gray stone pile in Westmount, an affluent neighborhood of Montreal, Canada. According to the records, it was at six forty-five on a Friday morning. According to history, it was halfway between the Great Depression and World War II. Counting backward, Leonard was conceived between the end of Hanukkah and Christmas Day during one of the subarctic winters his hometown managed to deliver with both consistency and brio. He was raised in a house of suits.

Nathan Cohen, Leonard's father, was a prosperous Canadian Jew with a high-end clothing business. The Freedman Company was known for its formal wear, and Nathan liked to dress formally, even on informal occasions. In suits, as in houses, he favored the formal English style, which he wore with spats and tempered with a boutonniere and, when his bad health made it necessary, with a silver cane. Masha Cohen, Leonard's mother, was sixteen years younger than her husband, a Russian Jew, a rabbi's daughter and a recent immigrant to Canada. She and Nathan had married not long after her arrival in Montreal in 1927. Two years later she gave birth to the first of their two children, Leonard's sister, Esther.

Early photographs of Nathan and Masha show him to be a square-faced, square-shouldered, stocky man. Masha, slimmer and a head taller, is in contrast all circles and slopes. The expression on Masha's face is both girlish and regal, while Nathan's is rigid and taciturn. Even were this not the required camera pose for the head of a household at that time, Nathan was certainly more reserved, and more Anglicized, than his warm, emotional Russian wife. As a baby, Leonard, plump, compact and also square-faced, was the image of his father, but as he grew he took on his mother Masha's heart-shaped face, thick wavy hair and deep, dark, sloping eyes. From his father he acquired his height, his tidiness, his decency and his love of suits. From his mother he inherited her charisma, her melancholy and her music. Masha always sang as she went about the house, in Russian and Yiddish more than in English, the sentimental old folk songs she had learned as a child. In a good contralto voice, to imaginary violins, Masha would sing herself from joy to melancholy and back again. "Chekhovian" is how Leonard described his mother.[1] "She laughed and wept deeply,"[2] said Leonard, one emotion following the other in quick succession. Masha Cohen was not a nostalgic woman; she did not talk much about the country she had left. But she carried her past in songs.

The residents of Westmount were well-to-do, upper-middle-class Protestant English Canadians and second- or third-generation Canadian Jews. In a city that was all about division and separation, the Jews and Protestants had been filed together on the simple grounds of being neither French nor Catholic. Before the "Quiet Revolution" in Quebec in the sixties, and before French became the sole official language of the province, the only French in Westmount were the domestic help. The Cohens had a maid, Mary, although she was Irish Catholic. They also had a nanny, whom Leonard and his sister called "Nursie," and a gardener named Kerry, a black man, who doubled as the family chauffeur. (Kerry's brother held the same job with Nathan's younger brother Horace.) It is no secret that Leonard's background was privileged. Leonard has never denied being born on the right side of the tracks, has never renounced his upbringing, rejected his family, changed his name or pretended to be anything other than who he is. His family was well-off, although there were certainly wealthier families in Westmount. Unlike the mansions of Upper Belmont, the Cohens' house, though big, was semidetached, and their car, though chauffeur driven, was a Pontiac, not a Cadillac.

But what the Cohens had that very few others came close to matching was status. The family Leonard was born into was distinguished and important—one of the most prominent Jewish families in Montreal. Leonard's ancestors had built synagogues and founded newspapers in Canada. They had funded and presided over a lengthy list of Jewish philanthropic societies and associations. Leonard's great-grandfather Lazarus Cohen had been the first of the family to come to Canada. In Lithuania, which was part of Russia in the 1840s, when Lazarus was born, Lazarus had been a teacher in a rabbinical school in Wylkowyski, one of the most rigorous yeshivas in the country. In his twenties, he left his wife and their baby son behind to try for his fortune. After a brief stay in Scotland, he took a ship to Canada, stopping in Ontario in a small town called Maberly, where he worked his way up from lumber storeman to the owner of a coal company, L. Cohen and Son. The son was Lyon, Nathan's father, whom Lazarus sent for, along with his mother, two years later. The family eventually made their way to Montreal, where Lazarus became president of a brass foundry and started a successful dredging company.

When Lazarus Cohen first arrived in Canada in 1860, the country's Jewish population was tiny. In the middle of the nineteenth century there had been fewer than five hundred Jews in Montreal. By the mid-1880s, when Lazarus assumed the presidency of the synagogue Congregation Shaar Hashomayim, there were more than five thousand. The Russian pogroms had led to a wave of immigration, and by the end of the century the number of Jews in Canada had doubled. Montreal had become the seat of Canadian Jewry, and Lazarus, with his long, white, biblical beard and uncovered head, was a familiar figure among its community. Along with building a synagogue, Lazarus established and headed a number of organizations to aid Jewish settlers and would-be immigrants, even traveling to Palestine (where Lazarus bought land as early as 1884) on behalf of the Jewish Colonization Association of Montreal. Lazarus's younger brother Rabbi Tzvi Hirsch Cohen, who joined him in Canada soon after, would become chief rabbi of Montreal.

In 1914, when Lyon Cohen took over the presidency of Shaar Hashomayim from his father, the synagogue could claim the largest congregation in a city whose Jewish population now numbered around forty thousand. In 1922, having grown too big for its old premises, the synagogue relocated to a new building in Westmount, almost a block in length, just minutes down the hill from the house on Belmont Avenue. Twelve years later Nathan and Masha added their only son to the synagogue's "Register of Births of the Corporation of English, German and Polish Jews of Montreal," giving Leonard his Jewish name, Eliezer, meaning "God is help."

Lyon Cohen, like his father, had been a very successful businessman—clothing and insurance. He also followed Lazarus into community service, being appointed secretary of the Anglo-Jewish Association while still in his teens. He would go on to establish a Jewish community center and a sanatorium, and preside over relief efforts for victims of the pogroms. Lyon held top positions in the Baron de Hirsch Institute, the Jewish Colonization Association and Canada's first Zionist organization. He went to the Vatican on behalf of his community to talk to the pope. He cofounded the first Anglo-Jewish newspaper in Canada, the *Jewish Times*, to which he contributed the occasional article. Lyon had written a play when he was sixteen years old titled *Esther*, which he produced and in which he acted. Leonard never knew his grandfather—he was two years old when Lyon died—but there was a strong connection, which intensified as Leonard grew older. Lyon's principles, his work ethic and his belief in "the aristocracy of the intellect,"[3] as Lyon always referred to it, all sat well with Leonard's own persuasion.

Lyon was also a staunch Canadian patriot, and when World War I broke out he launched a recruitment drive to encourage Montreal's Jews to enlist in the Canadian Army. The first to sign up were his sons Nathan and Horace (the third son, Lawrence, was too young). Lieutenant Nathan Cohen, number 3080887, became one of the first Jewish commissioned officers in the Canadian Army. Leonard loved the photographs of his father in uniform. But after his return from the war, Nathan suffered recurring periods of ill health, which left him increasingly invalid. This might be why Nathan, although the oldest son of the oldest son, did not continue the family tradition of holding the presidency of the synagogue, nor of much else. Although on paper he was president of the Freedman Company, the business was largely run by his brother Horace. Neither was Nathan an intellectual nor a religious scholar like his forebears. The dark wooden bookshelves in the house on Belmont Avenue held an impressive leather-bound set of the great poets—Chaucer, Wordsworth, Byron—Nathan's bar mitzvah gift, but their spines remained uncracked until Leonard took them down to read. Nathan, Leonard said, preferred the *Reader's Digest*, but "his heart was cultured; he was a gentleman."[4] As to religion, Nathan was "a Conservative Jew, not fanatical, without ideology and dogma, whose life was purely made up of domestic habit and affiliations with the community." Religion was not something that was discussed in Nathan's house, or even thought about. "It was mentioned no more than a fish mentions the presence of water."[5] It was simply there, his tradition, his people.

Masha's father, Rabbi Solomon Klonitzki-Kline, was a noted religious scholar. He had been the principal of a school for Talmudic study in Kovno in Lithuania, some fifty miles from the town where Lazarus had been born. He was also an author, whose two books, *Lexicon of Hebrew Homonyms* and *Thesaurus of Talmudic Interpretations*, would earn him the sobriquet "Sar HaDikdook," the Prince of Grammarians. When the persecution of Jews made life in Lithuania untenable, he moved to the U.S., where one of his daughters lived and had married an American. Masha had gone to Canada, where she had taken a job as a nurse. When Masha's work permit expired, he turned to his American son-in-law for help, which led to his introduction to Lyon Cohen's resettlement committee. It was through the subsequent friendship of the rabbi and Lyon that Masha and Nathan met and married.

Leonard, as a young boy, heard about Grandfather Kline more than he saw him, since the rabbi spent much of his time in the U.S. Masha would tell Leonard stories about how people came hundreds of miles to hear his grandfather speak. He also had a reputation as a great horseman, she told him, and Leonard was particularly pleased with this information. He liked it that his was a family of important people, but he was a young boy and physical prowess trumped intellect. Leonard was planning to attend the military academy once he was old enough. Nathan told him he could. Leonard wanted to fight wars and win medals—like his father had done, before he became this invalid who sometimes found it hard to even walk up stairs, who would stay home from work, nursed by Leonard's mother. Through Leonard's early childhood, Nathan had often been ill. But the boy had proof that his father had been a warrior once. Nathan still had his gun from World War I, which he kept in his bedside cabinet. One day, when no one was around, Leonard slipped into his parents' bedroom. He opened the cabinet and took out the gun. It was a big gun, a .38, its barrel engraved with his father's name, rank and regiment. Cradling it in his small hand, Leonard shivered, awed by its heft and the feel of its cold metal on his skin.

Five ninety-nine Belmont Avenue was a busy house, a house of routine, well ordered, and the center of the young Leonard's universe. Anything the boy might need or want to do orbited closely around it. His uncles and cousins lived nearby. The synagogue, where Leonard went with the family on Saturday morning, and on Sunday for Sun-

day school, and to Hebrew school two afternoons a week, was a short
walk down the hill. So were his regular schools, Roslyn Elementary
School and, later, Westmount High. Murray Hill Park, where Leonard played in the summer and made snow angels in the winter, was
immediately below his bedroom window.

The Westmount Jewish community was a close-knit one. It was
also a minority community in an English Protestant neighborhood.
Which was itself a minority, if a powerful one, in a city and a province
largely populated by the Catholic French. Who were themselves a
minority in Canada. Everybody felt like some kind of outsider; everyone felt like they belonged to something important. It was "a romantic, conspiratorial mental environment," said Leonard, a place of
"blood and soil and destiny." "That is the landscape I grew up in," he
said, "and it's very natural to me."[6]

Leonard's community, half a city away from the working-class
immigrant Jewish neighborhood around Saint-Urbain (which formed
the backdrop to Mordecai Richler's novels) might have appeared to
be hermetically sealed, but of course it wasn't. The Cross on the
top of Mount Royal; Mary, the family maid, always crossing herself;
and the Easter and Christmas celebrations at school were part of the
young Leonard's landscape just as the Sabbath candles his mother lit
on Friday evenings were, and the imposing synagogue down the hill,
from whose walls Leonard's great-grandfather and grandfather stared
down at him in large, framed portraits, reminding him of the distinc-
tion of his blood.

As Leonard recalled it, it was "an intense family life."[7] The Cohens would get together regularly—at the synagogue, in the workplace and also once a week at Leonard's paternal grandmother's
home. "Every Saturday afternoon, at around four o'clock, Martha,
her devoted maid, would wheel in a tea trolley with tea and little
sandwiches and cakes and biscuits," says David Cohen, two years
older than Leonard and a cousin with whom Leonard was particu-

larly close. "You were never invited, and you never asked if you could go, but you knew that she was 'receiving.' It sounds very archaic, but it was quite something." Leonard's grandmother had a flat in one of the grand houses on Sherbrooke Street at Atwater, which was where all the parades that were held in Montreal would end up—"Saint Jean Baptiste," says David Cohen, "that was a big one, before it became a very tough political situation in Montreal, and we'd watch from inside from the big, beautiful window in her living room." Their grandmother was very much a Victorian lady, "but, though it sounds archaic and old-fashioned, she was a pretty hip lady too." She made quite an impression on Leonard, who would later describe her tea parties in his first novel, *The Favorite Game*.

In that same book, Leonard described the older men in his family as serious and formal. Not all of them were. Among the more colorful members of the family was Cousin Lazzy, David's older brother Lazarus. Leonard thought of Lazzy as "a man about town, familiar with the chorus girls and the nightclubs and the entertainers."[8] There was also a cousin of an older generation, Edgar, Nathan's cousin, a businessman with a literary bent. Many years later Edgar H. Cohen would go on to write *Mademoiselle Libertine: A Portrait of Ninon de Lanclos*, a biography published in 1970 of a seventeenth-century courtesan, writer and muse whose lovers included Voltaire and Molière, and who, after a period in a convent, emerged to establish a school where young French noblemen could learn erotic technique. Leonard and Edgar, says David Cohen, were "very close."

Leonard's was a comfortable, secure life during an uncomfortable, insecure time. Days before Leonard's fifth birthday, Germany invaded Poland and World War II began. Closer to home, in 1942 there was an anti-Semitic rally on St. Lawrence Boulevard—the Main, as locals called it—which was the traditional dividing line between English and French Montreal. It was led by Montreal's French Nationalist movement, which included supporters of the Vichy regime in France.

One particularly risible claim of the organization was that the Jews had taken over the clothing business in order to force modest young French-Canadian girls to wear "improper gowns in New York styles."[9] During the rally, the windows of several Jewish-owned shops and delis on the Main were broken and racist slurs painted on walls. But for a seven-year-old living in Westmount, sitting in his room reading his *Superman* comics, it was another world. "Europe, the war, the social war," Leonard said, "none of it seemed to touch us."[10]

He breezed through the early years of childhood, doing all that was required—clean hands, good manners, getting dressed for dinner, good school reports, making the hockey team, keeping his shoes polished and lined up tidily under his bed at night—without showing any worrying signs of sainthood or genius. Nor of melancholy. The home movies shot by Nathan, a keen amateur cameraman, show a happy little boy, beaming as he pedals his tricycle along the street, or walks hand in hand with his sister, or plays with his dog, a black Scottish terrier named Tinkie. His mother had originally given it the more dignified name of Tovarich, the Russian word for "ally," but it was vetoed by his father. Nathan was already aware that in this small, Anglicized, Canadian Jewish community, Masha's Russianness, her accent, her imperfect English and big personality, made her stand out. "It wasn't thought to be a good idea to be passionate about anything," said Leonard, or to draw attention. "We were taught," says cousin David, "to mind our P's and Q's."

Then in January 1944, at the age of fifty-two, Leonard's father died. Leonard was nine years old. Around fourteen years later, in two unpublished stories titled "Ceremonies" and "My Sister's Birthday,"[11] Leonard described what happened: "Nursie told us the news." Seated at the kitchen table, her hands folded in her lap, Leonard's nanny informed Leonard and Esther that they would not be going to school that morning because their father had died in the night. They should be quiet, she said, because their mother was still sleeping. The funeral would take place the following day. "Then the day dawned on me," Leonard wrote. "'But it can't be tomorrow, Nursie, it's my sister's birthday.'"

At nine o'clock the next morning, six men arrived and carried the coffin into the living room. They set it down alongside the leather chesterfield sofa. Masha had the maid soap all the mirrors in the house. By noon people started arriving, shaking the snow off their boots and topcoats—family, friends, people who worked at the factory. The coffin was open, and Leonard peered inside. Nathan was wrapped in a silver prayer shawl, his face white, his mustache black. His father, Leonard thought, looked annoyed. Uncle Horace, who ran the Freedman Company with Nathan and who had served alongside him in the Great War, whispered to Leonard, "We've got to be like soldiers." Later that night, when Esther asked Leonard if he had dared to look at their dead father, each confessed that they had, and agreed that it appeared that someone had dyed his mustache. Both of these stories ended with the same line: "Don't cry, I told her. I think it was my best moment. Please, it's your birthday."

A third version of the event appeared in *The Favorite Game*. It was a more poised account, partly due to Leonard's writing having matured considerably in the time between these abandoned stories and his first novel, and partly from the distance accorded by having ascribed it in the latter to a fictional character (although Leonard has confirmed that it happened as he wrote it in the book).[12] This time the episode concludes with the young boy taking one of his father's bow ties from his bedroom, slicing it open, and hiding a small piece of paper inside it on which he had written something. The next day, in his own private ceremony, the boy dug a hole and buried it in the garden under the snow. Leonard has since described this as the first thing he ever wrote. He has also said he has no recollection of what it was and that he had been "digging in the garden for years, looking for it. Maybe that's all I'm doing, looking for the note."[13]

The act is so weighty with symbolism—Leonard having for the first time in his life made a rite of his writing—that it is tempting to take these words from a 1980 interview at face value, even if it is more likely just another of the many good lines that Leonard always gave his interviewers. Children are often drawn to the mystical and to secret ceremonies. And if Leonard has also said that as a young child he had "no particular interest in religion," except for "a couple of times when we went to hear a choir,"[14] he was also well aware that he was a Kohen, one of a priestly caste, a patrilineal descendant of Moses's brother, Aaron, and born to officiate. "When they told me I was a Kohen, I believed it. I didn't think it was some auxiliary information," he said. "I wanted to live this world. I wanted to be the one who lifted up the Torah. . . . I was this little kid, and whatever they told me in these matters resonated."[15]

Still, as a child he showed little interest in the synagogue his ancestors founded. Hebrew school, he said, "bored" him, and Wilfred Shuchat, who was appointed rabbi of Shaar Hashomayim in 1948, appears to confirm this. Leonard "was okay" as a student, says the old rabbi, "but scholarship wasn't his real interest. It was his personality, the way he interpreted things. He was very creative."

Leonard did not cry at the death of his father; he wept more when his dog Tinkie died a few years later. "I didn't feel a profound sense of loss," he said in a 1991 interview, "maybe because he was very ill throughout my entire childhood. It seemed natural that he died. He was weak and he died. Maybe my heart is cold."[16]

It is true that since the previous summer Nathan had been in and out of the Royal Victoria Hospital. If it is also true that the loss of his father had no great effect on Leonard, he was not so young at nine years old that it would not have registered on him. Somewhere inside, something would have changed—an awareness for the first time of impermanence, perhaps, or a sad wisdom, a crack where the insecurity or the solitude came in. What Leonard has said, and written, that he was most aware of during this important episode of his childhood was the change of status it bestowed on him. While his father lay in the living room in the coffin, his uncle Horace took him aside and told him that he, Leonard, was the man of the house now, and that the women—his mother and his fourteen-year-old sister, Esther— were his responsibility. "This made me proud," Leonard wrote in "Ceremonies." "I felt like the consecrated young prince of some folk-beloved dynasty. I was the oldest son of the oldest son."[17]

Two

House of Women

___

In his early teens Leonard developed a keen interest in hypnosis. He acquired a slim, pocket-sized, anonymously written book with the lengthy title *25 Lessons in Hypnotism: How to Become an Expert Operator* and the extravagant claim of being "the most perfect, complete, easily learned and comprehensive COURSE in the world, embracing the Science of Magnetic Healing, Telepathy, Mind Reading, Clairvoyant Hypnosis, Mesmerism, Animal Magnetism and Kindred Sciences." On the front cover, beneath a crude sketch of a Victorian lady held spellbound by a wild-haired, mustached gentleman, Leonard wrote his name in ink in his best handwriting and set about his studies.

It turned out that Leonard had a natural talent for mesmerism. Finding instant success with domestic animals, he moved on to the domestic staff, recruiting as his first human subject the family maid. At his direction, the young woman sat on the chesterfield sofa. Leonard drew a chair alongside and, as the book instructed, told her in a slow gentle voice to relax her muscles and look into his eyes. Picking up a pencil, he moved it slowly in front of her face, back and forth, back and forth, and succeeded in putting her in a trance. Disregarding (or depending on one's interpretation, following) the author's directive that his teachings should be used only for educational purposes, Leonard instructed the maid to undress.

What a moment it must have been for the adolescent Leonard. This successful fusion of arcane wisdom and sexual longing. To sit beside a naked woman, in his own home, convinced that *he* made this happen, simply by talent, study, mastery of an art and imposition of his will. When he found it difficult to awaken her, Leonard started to panic. He was terrified his mother might come home and catch them—though one imagines this would have simply added a sense of impending doom, despair and loss to the heady mix that would make it even more exquisitely Leonard Cohenesque.

Chapter Two of the hypnotism manual might have been written as career advice to the singer and performer Leonard would become. It cautioned against any appearance of levity and instructed, "Your features should be set, firm and stern. Be quiet in all your actions. Let your voice grow lower, lower, till just above a whisper. Pause a moment or two. You will fail if you try to hurry."[1]

When Leonard re-created the episode in his twenties in *The Favorite Game*, he wrote, "He had never seen a woman so naked. . . . He was astonished, happy, and frightened before all the spiritual authorities of the universe. Then he sat back to stare. This is what he had waited for so long to see. He wasn't disappointed and never has been."[2] Although it is ascribed to his fictionalized alter ego, it is hard to imagine that these sentiments were not Leonard's own. Decades later he would still say, "I don't think a man ever gets over that first sight of the naked woman. I think that's Eve standing over him, that's the morning and the dew on the skin. And I think that's the major content of every man's imagination. All the sad adventures in pornography and love and song are just steps on the path toward that holy

vision."[3] The maid, incidentally, was a ukulele player, an instrument
his fictional alter ego took for a lute and the girl, by extension, for an
angel. And everybody knows that naked angels possess a portal to
the divine.

―――――

"Leonard always complained there were no girls. That he couldn't
get girls," says Mort Rosengarten. "And it was always a serious complaint." Rosengarten is a sculptor and Leonard's oldest friend. He is
the model for Krantz, the best friend of the protagonist of *The Favorite Game.* "You have to remember," Rosengarten says, his soft voice
barely audible over the whirr of the ventilator emphysema obliges him
to use, "that at that time we were raised in a totally segregated way.
At school the boys were in one part of the school and the girls were
in another and there was no interaction whatsoever, and because we
didn't fall in with the conventional Westmount society of our peers
in terms of our behavior, we didn't have access to those women either, because they were on a certain path. But I always thought that
Leonard was lucky, that he knew and understood something about
women, because he lived in a house of women, his sister, Esther, and
his mother. I knew nothing about women; I just had a brother, and
my mother wasn't giving any of her secrets away about what women
were about. So we always complained."

Rosengarten's home is a small, wonky, two-story terraced house
with a bathtub in the kitchen, near to the Parc du Portugal, off the
Main. When he moved here forty years ago, it was a blue-collar, immigrant neighborhood. Despite the signs of gentrification—the fancy
boutiques and cafés—the old Jewish delis with Formica tabletops
that Mort and Leonard used to frequent are still there. It was a world
away from their privileged Westmount origins. Mort grew up on Upper Belmont, five hundred yards and another economic stratum above
the Cohen family's Lower Belmont home. Though the money is long

gone now, the Rosengartens had been extremely wealthy; they had two Cadillacs and a country estate in the Eastern Townships, some sixty miles outside Montreal. Leonard and Mort met and became friends on neutral territory, when Mort was ten and Leonard nine years old. It was at summer camp in June 1944, five months after the death of Leonard's father.

The Cohens had long been accustomed to spending the season together at the seaside in Maine, in the U.S. But in the summers of 1940 and '41, when Canada was at war with Germany but America had not yet joined the battle, the U.S. imposition of currency restrictions made it more sensible for Canadians to take their holidays at home. A popular spot was the Laurentians, north of Montreal. The writer Mordecai Richler described it as "a veritable Jewish paradise, a minor-league Catskills,"[4] with hotels and inns where old men in yarmulkes gossiped in Yiddish across the road from the "Gentiles only" bowling green. For those at Leonard's end of the age spectrum there was a proliferation of summer camps along the lakes around Sainte-Agathe. Camp Hiawatha offered its young charges the usual menu of fresh air, cabin dorms, communal showers, arts and crafts, playing fields and biting insects, but "it was terrible," says Rosengarten, with feeling. "Their biggest concern was to reassure the parents that you would never get into any kind of adventure whatsoever. I was stuck there for a few years, though Leonard only went for one summer; his mother found a more sensible camp where they taught you to canoe and swim"—swimming being something Leonard did enthusiastically and well. An itemized bill from Camp Hiawatha in 1944 appears to confirm Rosengarten's dim view of the activities on offer: Leonard's allowance was spent on the tuck shop, stationery, stamps, a haircut and a train ticket home.[5]

Leonard and Mort had more in common than their prosperous Westmount Jewish backgrounds. Neither had much of a father figure in his life—Leonard's was dead and Mort's often absent—and each had a mother who, certainly by 1940s Westmount Jewish society standards, was unconventional. Mort's mother came from a working-class background and considered herself "modern." Leonard's was a Russian immigrant and had been considerably younger than her late husband. If Masha's accent and dramatic nature had not ensured a certain separateness from the other mothers in the young boys' small, insular community, being an attractive, strikingly dressed young widow most likely would. But Leonard and Mort's friendship would really deepen four years later, when they both attended the same junior high school.

Westmount High, a large gray stone building, with lush lawns and a crest with a Latin motto (*Dux Vitae Ratio*: "Reason Is Life's Guide"), looked like it had snuck out of Cambridge and onto a plane to Canada in the dead of night, having grown tired of spending centuries shaping the minds of well-bred British boys. In fact it was relatively young, a Protestant school founded in a far more modest building in 1873, although still among the oldest English-speaking schools in Quebec. At the time of Leonard's attendance, Jewish pupils made up between a quarter and a third of the school population. A general mood of religious tolerance, or indifference, reigned, and the two groups mixed and socialized, went to each other's parties. "We took our Jewish holidays when they came up and we celebrated the Christian holidays," says Rona Feldman, one of Leonard's classmates. "A lot of us were in the choir and the Christmas plays." Leonard's Catholic nanny, who walked him to school every morning—no matter, as Mort Rosengarten pointed out, that "it was a block away; Leonard's family was a very formal kind of scene"—had taken him to church with her in the past. "I love Jesus," Leonard said. "Always did, even as a kid." He added, "I kept it to myself; I didn't stand up in shul and say 'I love Jesus.'"[6]

At the age of thirteen, Leonard celebrated his bar mitzvah, his Jewish coming of age. Watched by his uncles and cousins, a battalion of Cohens, he climbed onto a footstool—it was the only way he could see—and read from the Torah for the first time in the synagogue his ancestors had founded and presided over. "There were lots of members of his family," recalls Rabbi Shuchat, with whom Leonard had taken his bar mitzvah class, "but it was very difficult for Leonard, because his father was not there" to speak the customary prayer of release. But since the war began, everyone seemed to have someone, or something, missing. "There was the rationing and coupons for certain things like meat," Rona Feldman remembers, "and they sold war savings stamps in the school and some of the classes competed with each other for who bought the most war savings stamps each week. There was a girl going to school with us who was part of a program of children sent to different places to keep them safe during the war, and we all knew families who had members overseas in the army or the air force." And when the war was over, there were the nightmarish photos of victims of the concentration camps. The war, said Mort Rosengarten, was "a very big thing for us," meaning Leonard and himself. "It was absolutely a very important factor in our sensibility."

The summer of 1948, the bridge between leaving Roslyn Elementary and starting at Westmount High, was once again spent at summer camp. Among the mementos from Camp Wabi-Kon in Leonard's archives are a swimming and water safety certificate, and a document written in a neat, child's hand and signed by Leonard and six other boys. A schoolboy pact, it read: "We should not fight and we must try to get along better. We should appreciate things better. We should be better sports and we should have more spirit. We shouldn't boss each other around. We must not use foul language."[7] They had even devised a list of penalties, ranging from missing supper to going to bed half an hour early.

The boyish earnestness and idealism had an almost Enid Blyton–like innocence to it. Back home in his bedroom on Belmont Avenue, though, Leonard was thinking about girls—cutting pictures of models from his mother's magazines and gazing out of the window as the wind whipped up the skirts of the women as they walked through Murray Hill Park or plastered them deliciously to their thighs. In the back pages of his comic books he would study the Charles Atlas ads that promised puny little boys like himself the kind of muscles it takes to woo a girl. Leonard was small for his age; a new use the adolescent had found for Kleenex was to wad it up and put it in his shoes to make lifts. It bothered Leonard that he was shorter than his friends—some of the girls in his high school class were a head taller—but he started to learn that girls could be won around "by stories and talk." In *The Favorite Game* his alter ego "began to think of himself as the Tiny Conspirator, the Cunning Dwarf."[8] In Rona Feldman's recollection, Leonard in fact was "extremely popular" with the girls in their class, although, due to his height, "most girls thought he was adorable more than a hunk. I just remember him being very sweet. He had that same kind of grin that he has now, a little bit of a half grin, kind of shy, and when he smiled it was so genuine, it was so satisfying to see him smile. I think he was very well liked."

Since the age of thirteen Leonard had taken to going out late at night, two or three nights a week, wandering alone through the seedier streets of Montreal. Before the Saint Lawrence Seaway was built the city was a major port, the place where all the cargo destined for central North America went to be offloaded from oceangoing freighters and put on canal boats and taken up to the Great Lakes or sent by rail to the West. At night the city swarmed with sailors, longshoremen and passengers from the cruise ships that docked in the harbor, and welcoming them were countless bars, which openly flouted the law requiring that they close at three A.M. The daily newspapers carried notices for shows on Saint Catherine Street that started at four in the morning and ended just before dawn. There were jazz clubs, blues clubs, movie houses, bars where the only thing they played was Quebecois country and western, and cafés with jukeboxes whose content Leonard came to know by heart.

Leonard wrote about his night ramblings in an unpublished, undated piece from the late fifties titled "The Juke-Box Heart: Excerpt From a Journal." "When I was about 13 yrs old I did the things my friends did until they went to bed, then I'd walk miles along Saint Catherine street, a night-lover, peeking into marble-tabled cafeterias where men wore overcoats even in the summer." There was a boyish innocence to his description of his early wanderings: peering into the windows of novelty shops "to catalogue the magic and tricks, rubber cockroaches, handshake buzzers." As he walked he would imagine he was a man in his twenties, "raincoated, battered hat pulled low above intense eyes, a history of injustice in his heart, a face too noble for revenge, walking the night along some wet boulevard, followed by the sympathy of countless audiences [. . .] loved by two or three beautiful women who could never have him." He might have been describing a character from one of the comic books he read or from one of the private eye movies he had seen; Leonard was by this time already a cinephile. But, after throwing a quote from Baudelaire into the mix, he was enough of a self-critic to add, "This writing embarrasses me. I am humorist enough to see a young man stepping out of Stendhal, given to self-dramatization, walking off a comfortless erection. Perhaps masturbation would have been more effective and less tiring."[9]

Leonard walked slowly past the working girls on the street, but in spite of the need and longing in his eyes the hookers looked over his head, calling out to the men who passed, offering them what Leonard had begun to want more than anything. The world of Leonard's imagination must have grown enormously during that time, and an exhilarating sense of possibility, but also a sense of isolation, an awareness of the blues. Says Mort Rosengarten, who after a time would join his friend on his late-night adventures, "Leonard looked young, and I did too. But you could get served in bars—girls at thirteen. It was very open back then and also very corrupt. A lot of these bars were controlled by the Mafia, you had to pay someone off to get a license, and it was the same with taverns, which were bars that sold only beer and only to men, no women allowed, and there were lots of those because they were the cheapest place to drink. At six in the morning you could go in and it would be full of people. Leonard didn't have to sneak out of the house; we both came from homes where nobody really worried about that or where we were. But the Westmount Jewish community was quite small and a very protected environment, with a very strong sense of group identity, these young people who all knew each other. So he went to Saint Catherine Street to experience what we had never seen or been allowed to do."

While this was going on, Leonard's musical boundaries were also starting to expand. At his mother's encouragement he had started taking piano lessons—not because he had shown any special interest or talent in that area but because his mother encouraged Leonard in almost everything and piano lessons were what one did. Piano was not Leonard's first musical instrument—in elementary school he had played a Bakelite Tonette, a kind of recorder—and he did not stick with it for long. He found practicing the exercises that his teacher, Miss MacDougal, sent him home with a dull and solitary business. He preferred the clarinet, which he played in the high school band alongside Mort, who had escaped his own piano lessons by taking up the trombone. Leonard was involved in a number of extracurricular school activities. He had been elected president of the student council and was also on the executive of the drama club, as well as on the board of publishers responsible for the high school yearbook, *Vox Ducum*—a periodical that might claim to have been the first to publish one of Leonard's stories. "Kill or Be Killed" appeared in its pages in 1950.

Rosengarten recalls, "Leonard was always very articulate and could address groups of people." A report from Camp Wabi-Kon dated August 1949 noted that "Lenny is the leader of the cabin and is looked up to by all members of the cabin. He is the most popular boy in the unit and is friendly with everyone [and] well-liked by the entire staff."* At the same time, school friends remembered Leonard as a shy boy, engaged in the solitary pursuit of writing poetry, someone who deflected attention more than courted it. Nancy Bacal, another close friend who has known Leonard from boyhood on, remembers him during that period as "someone special, but in a quiet way. That seeming contradiction: he moves into leadership naturally, except that he remains invisible at the same time. His intensity and power operates from below the surface." A curious mix, this public and private nature, but it appears to have been workable; certainly it stuck.

———————

The Big Bang of Leonard, the moment when poetry, music, sex and spiritual longing collided and fused in him for the first time, happened in 1950, between his fifteenth and sixteenth birthdays. Leonard was standing outside a secondhand book shop, browsing through the racks, when he happened upon *The Selected Poems of Federico Garcia Lorca*. Leafing through its pages, he stopped at "Gacela of the Morning Market."[10]

The poem made the hairs stand up on the back of his neck. Leonard had felt that sensation before, hearing the power and the beauty of the verses read aloud at the synagogue—another repository of secrets. Lorca was a Spaniard, a homosexual, an open anti-Fascist, who

———————

* The same report described Leonard's "personal and hygiene habits" as "neat and clean. He is careful about his clothes and always appears well dressed." It also made note of his interest and abilities in sailing—"one of the best skippers in the unit"—and his "fine sense of humor."

was executed by the Nationalist militia when Leonard was two years old. But "the universe he revealed seemed very familiar" to Leonard, his words illuminating "a landscape that you thought you alone walked on."[11] Part of that landscape was loneliness. As Leonard tried to explain more than three decades later, "When something was said in a certain kind of way, it seemed to embrace the cosmos. It's not just my heart, but every heart was involved, and the loneliness was dissolved, and you felt that you were this aching creature in the midst of an aching cosmos, and the ache was okay. Not only was it okay, but it was the way that you embraced the sun and the moon." He was, in his own words, "completely hooked."[12]

Lorca was a dramatist and a collector of old Spanish folk songs as well as a poet, and his poems were dark, melodious, elegiac and emotionally intense, honest and at the same time self-mythologizing. He wrote as if song and poetry were part of the same breath. Through his love for Gypsy culture and his depressive cast of mind he introduced Leonard to the sorrow, romance and dignity of flamenco. Through his political stance he introduced Leonard to the sorrow, romance and dignity of the Spanish Civil War. Leonard was very pleased to meet them both.

Leonard began writing poems in earnest. "I wanted to respond to these poems," he said. "Every poem that touches you is like a call that needs a response, one wants to respond with one's own story."[13] He did not try to copy Lorca—"I wouldn't dare," he said. But Lorca, he felt, had given him permission to find his own voice, and also an instruction on what to do with it, which was "never to lament casually."[14] Over the subsequent years, whenever interviewers would ask him what drew him to poetry, Leonard offered an earthier reason: getting women. Having someone confirm one's beauty in verse was a big attraction for women, and, before rock 'n' roll came along, poets had the monopoly. But in reality, for a boy of his age, generation and background, "everything was in my imagination," Leonard said.

"We were starved. It wasn't like today, you didn't sleep with your girlfriend. I just wanted to embrace someone."[15]

At the age of fifteen, at around the same time he discovered the poetry of Lorca, Leonard also bought a Spanish guitar for twelve Canadian dollars from a pawnshop on Craig Street. He found he could play some very rudimentary chords almost immediately on the top four strings, thanks to having previously owned (like the hypnotized maid in *The Favorite Game*) a ukulele. Leonard had taught himself to play ukulele—much as he had taught himself hypnosis—from an instruction manual, the famous 1928 book by Roy Smeck, the so-called "Wizard of the Strings." "I think I had mentioned it to cousin Lazzy, who was very kind to me after my father died—he would take me to the baseball games at the Montreal ballpark, the Montreal Royals, which was the first team that Jackie Robinson played in. He said, 'Roy Smeck is coming to El Morocco,' a nightclub in Montreal. 'Would you like to meet him?' I couldn't go hear him, because a child wasn't allowed in a nightclub, but he brought me to Roy Smeck's hotel room and I met the great Roy Smeck."[16]

In the summer of 1950, when Leonard left once again for summer camp—Camp Sunshine in Sainte-Marguerite—he took the guitar with him. Here he would begin playing folk songs, and discover for the first time the instrument's possibilities when it came to his social life.

You were still going to summer camp at age fifteen?

"I was a counselor. It was a Jewish Community Camp for kids that really couldn't afford the expensive summer camps and the director they had hired, an American, accidentally happened to be a Socialist. He was on the side of the North Koreans in the Korean War, which had just broken out. The Socialists at that time were the only people who were playing guitar and singing folk songs; they felt that they had an ideological obligation to learn the songs and repeat them. So a copy of The People's Songbook *appeared. Do you know it? A great songbook, with all the chords and tab-*

*lature, and I went through that book many, many times during that sum-
mer, with Alfie Magerman, who was the nephew of the director and had
Socialist credentials—his father was a union organizer—and a guitar.
I started learning the guitar, going through that songbook from beginning
to end many many times during that summer. I was very touched by those
lyrics. A lot of them were just ordinary folk songs rewritten—"His Truth
Goes Marching On"* was transformed by the Socialists into* 'In our hands
is placed a power / Greater than their hoarded gold / Greater than
the might of Adam / Multiplied a million-fold / We will give birth
to a new world / From the ashes of the old / For the union makes us
strong / Solidarity Forever / Solidarity Forever / Solidarity Forever /
For the union makes us strong.' *There were a lot of the Wobbly songs—I
don't know if you know that movement? A Socialist international workers
union. Wonderful songs.* 'There once was a union maid / Who never
was afraid / Of goons and ginks and company finks / And deputy
sheriffs that made the raid . . . No you can't scare me I'm stickin' with
the union.' *Great song.*"

If one can tell a man's enthusiasm by the length of an answer,
Leonard was clearly enthused. Some fifty years after his stay at Camp
Sunshine he could still sing the songbook by heart from beginning to
end.* In 1949, 1950, a guitar did not come attached to the immense
iconography and sexual magnetism it would later acquire, but Leonard learned quickly that playing one did not repel girls. A group photograph shot at summer camp shows the teenage Leonard, though
still short, slightly plump and wearing clothes no man should ever
wear in public—white shorts, white polo shirt, black shoes, white
socks—with the blondest, coolest-looking girl sitting next to him, her
knee touching his.

Back home in Westmount, Leonard continued his investigations

---

* Another song Leonard learned for the first time at Camp Sunshine was "The
Partisan," which would be the first song he recorded that was not his own.

into folk music—Woody Guthrie, Lead Belly, Canadian folksingers, Scottish border ballads, flamenco. He says, "That's when I started finding the music I loved."[17] In Murray Hill Park one day, he happened upon a young, black-haired man standing by the tennis courts, playing a lonely-sounding Spanish melody on an acoustic guitar. A cluster of women had gathered about the musician. Leonard could see that "he was courting them" with his music, in some mysterious way.[18] Leonard was also captivated. He stayed to listen and at the appropriate moment asked the young man if he would consider teaching him how to play. The young man, it turned out, was Spanish and did not understand English. Through a combination of gestures and broken French, Leonard gained the phone number of the boardinghouse downtown where the Spaniard was renting a room, and a promise that the Spaniard would come to 599 Belmont Avenue and give him a lesson.

On his first visit, the Spaniard picked up Leonard's guitar and inspected it. It wasn't bad, he said. Tuning it, he played a rapid flamenco progression, producing a sound on the instrument unlike anything Leonard had ever thought possible. He handed the guitar back to Leonard and indicated that it was his turn. Leonard had no desire after such a performance to play one of the folk songs he had learned and declined, professing that he did not know how. The young man placed Leonard's fingers on the frets and showed him how to make some chords. Then he left, promising to return the next day.

At the second lesson, the Spaniard started to teach Leonard the six-chord flamenco progression he had played the day before, and at the third lesson Leonard began learning the tremolo pattern. He practiced diligently, standing in front of a mirror, copying how the young man held the guitar when he played. His young teacher failed to arrive for their fourth lesson. When Leonard called the number of his boardinghouse, the landlady answered the phone. The guitar player was dead, she told him. He had committed suicide.

"I knew nothing about the man, why he came to Montreal, why he appeared in that tennis court, why he took his life," Leonard would say to an audience of dignitaries in Spain some sixty years later, "but it was those six chords, it was that guitar pattern, that has been the basis of all my songs, and of all my music."[19]

In Montreal in 1950, Leonard's home life had taken a new turn. His mother had remarried. Her new husband was Harry Ostrow, a pharmacist, "a very sweet, ineffectual man, a nice guy," as Leonard's cousin David Cohen recalls him, with whom Leonard seemed to have little more than a pleasant but distant relationship. By coincidence Masha's second husband would also be diagnosed with a grave illness. With his mother preoccupied with the prospect of nursing another sick man, and his sister, twenty years old now, with other things on her mind than her adolescent brother, Leonard was left to his own devices. When he was not in the classroom or involved in some after-school activity, he was in his bedroom, writing poems, or, increasingly, out cruising the streets of Montreal with Mort.

Sixteen and legally old enough to drive, Mort took one of the family's two Cadillacs and cruised down the hill to Leonard's house. "One of our favorite things was at four in the morning we would drive the streets of Montreal, especially the older part of Montreal, along the harbor and out to the east end where the oil refineries were," says Rosengarten. "We were looking for girls—on the street at four o'clock in the morning, these beautiful girls we thought would be walking around, waiting for us. Of course there was absolutely nobody." On nights when the snow was heavy and the streets were empty they would still drive, the heater on, heading east to the Townships or north to the Laurentians, the Cadillac with Mort at the wheel cutting a black line through the deep snowdrifts like Moses practicing for his trick with the Red Sea. And they would talk about girls, talk about everything.

"They were not bound to anything. They could sample all the

possibilities. They flashed by trees that took a hundred years to grow. They tore through towns where men lived their whole lives.... Back in the city their families were growing like vines. . . . They were flying from the majority, from the real bar mitzvah, the real initiation, the real and vicious circumcision which society was hovering to inflict through limits and dull routine," Leonard wrote, re-creating these night rides with Mort in fiction. "The highway was empty. They were the only two in flight and that knowledge made them deeper friends than ever."[20]

Three

Twenty Thousand Verses

———————

The streets around McGill University were named for august British men—Peel, Stanley, McTavish—its buildings constructed by solid, stony Scotsmen in solid Scottish stone. There was an Oxbridge air to the grand library and the grander Arts Building, on whose dome the McGill flag flew at half-mast when one of their number died. The spacious quadrangle was outlined by tall, thin trees whose posture remained perfectly erect even when weighed down by heavy snow. Beyond the iron gates there were Victorian mansions, some converted into boardinghouses where students lived. Had someone told you the British Empire was run from McGill, you'd be forgiven for believing them; in September 1951, when Leonard started at McGill on his seventeenth birthday, it was the most perfect nineteenth-century city-within-a-city in North America.

Three months earlier Leonard had graduated from Westmount High. *Vox Ducum*, the yearbook he had helped edit, contained two photos of him. One was a group shot in which the sixteen-year-old Leonard beamed from the center front row, above a caption that read, with unfamiliar familiarity, "Len Cohen, President of the Student Council." The other, more formal photograph, which accompanied his yearbook entry, showed Leonard wearing a suit and a faraway look. As yearbook tradition dictated, Leonard's entry opened with a stirring quote: "We cannot conquer fear yet we can yield to it in such a manner as to be greater than it." It went on to list his pet aversion ("the coke machine"), hobby ("photography"), pastimes ("leading sing-songs at intermissions") and ambition: "World Famous Orator." Under "Prototype" Leonard summed himself up as "the little man who is always there." It closed with an impressive list of his high school activities: presidency of the student council, a place on *Vox Ducum*'s publishing board, membership in the Menorah Club, the Art Club, the Current Events Club and the YMHA (Young Men's Hebrew Association) and cheerleader.[1] To all appearances this was a sixteen-year-old with a good deal of self-confidence, tempered with a large dollop of the requisite Canadian self-mockery. All in all, though, an achiever. It was only to be expected that the next step would be McGill, the foremost English-speaking university in the province.

During his first year at McGill, Leonard studied general arts, moving on to math, commerce, political science and law. More accurately, according to his own report, he read, drank, played music and missed as many lectures as possible. Judging by his average grade on graduation—56.4 percent—this was not one of his customary understatements. Leonard performed underwhelmingly in his favorite subject, English literature, and did no better in French—a class he took, according to his friend and fellow student (now chancellor of McGill) Arnold Steinberg, "because both of us had heard it was an easy course to pass. I failed the course and Leonard's French was certainly minimal. We never took it seriously." The curriculum offered no Baudelaire or Rimbaud; instead they spent the whole year studying a book about a young, aristocratic White Russian couple who had been forced to move to Paris after the revolution and work as servants for a French family. Written by the French dramatist Jacques Deval, it was titled *Tovarich*—the original name of Leonard's Scottish terrier Tinkie.*

This insensitivity to the language of half their hometown's population was by no means exclusive to Leonard and his friends. Montreal's Anglophones—particularly residents of a privileged enclave like Westmount, of which McGill was a privileged extension— had few dealings with the Francophone population other than the French-Canadian girls who had started pouring into the city from the countryside in the thirties, during the Great Depression, to get work as maids. The general attitude to bilingualism at that time was not a lot different, if less deity-specific, from that of the first female governor of Texas, Ma Ferguson: "If the English language was good enough for Jesus Christ, it's good enough for everybody." To English-speaking Montrealers of that time, French would have felt as much a foreign language as it did to any English schoolchild, and likewise would have been taught by an English-speaking teacher, because French-speaking teachers couldn't work in English-speaking schools (and vice versa).

"The French were invisible," says Mort Rosengarten. "At that time we had two school boards in Montreal, the Catholic, which was Francophone, and the Protestant, which was Anglophone, and the Jews—who had their own school board at one point—decided to throw in their lot with the Protestants. Not only were they in different schools, they had different school hours, so the kids were never on the street at the same time, so you never really had contact with them. It was very strange." Mort had already been at McGill for a year, studying art, and Steinberg studying commerce, when Leonard arrived. Where Leonard excelled at university, as he had at Westmount High, was in extracurricular activities. Like a trainee Grand-

---

* Tinkie was still alive at this time; he would expire during his sixteenth year after wandering off alone in a snowstorm.

father Lyon he amassed committee positions, society memberships and presidencies.

Along with his fellow McGill students, Leonard was enrolled automatically in the Debating Union. He shone in debate. He had a natural flair, as well as a taste, for using language with precision. He took easily to composing a statement that might or might not reflect his innermost thoughts but that, with his poet's ear, sounded convincing, or at the very least good, and could win over an audience. For a shy young man Leonard had no trouble getting onstage and talking in front of people; oration was the one subject at McGill for which he was awarded an A. In his first year at McGill Leonard won the Bovey Shield for his university's debating team; in the second year he was elected the Debating Union's secretary; in the third he rose to vice president and in his fourth and final year, president.

Leonard and Mort joined a Jewish fraternity house on the campus, Zeta Beta Tau, and Leonard became president of that too, and a good deal more swiftly. A certificate confirms his election date as January 31, 1952, only four months after his first day at McGill.[2] Like the other fraternities, ZBT had its own songbook—celebratory marching songs of the type improved by alcohol—and Leonard knew the words to all of them. Fraternities and presidencies might appear surprisingly pro-establishment for a youth who had shown himself to have Socialist tendencies and a poetic inclination, but Leonard, as Arnold Steinberg notes, "is not antiestablishment and never was, except that he has never done what the establishment does. But that doesn't make him antiestablishment. Leonard, of all the people I knew, was the most formal by far. Not formal vis-à-vis other people; he had a very winning way, very, very charming. But in his manners, his dress, his way of speaking, he had a very conventional approach to things."

Leonard's summer camp reports had described him as clean, tidy and polite, and he was. "That's how we were brought up," says David Cohen, Leonard's cousin. "We were always taught to be well mannered and say 'yes, sir,' 'thank you,' stand up when an adult came into the room and all that good stuff." As to his sartorial formality, Leonard had a reputation even then for being dressed to the nines (although, master of understatement that he was, he would have insisted he was dressed to the eights). Mort shared Leonard's love for a good suit. Both having families in the clothing business, they could indulge their tastes.

"We would design our own clothes in our teens and they were very distinctive," says Rosengarten, "and generally more conservative than the popular fashions at the time. I had access to a custom tailor who would make them according to my idea of what the suit should be and Leonard told them what he wanted. I even had my shirts made, but mostly because I had a very thin neck and couldn't get adult shirts in my size." David Cohen recalls seeing Mort hanging out in the pool room at the student union, cigarette dangling from the corner of his mouth, the sleeves of his made-to-measure shirt held up with armbands. "In some ways," Rosengarten continues, "the conformist part of the Westmount Jewish community were very hostile to the fact that we were artists and not conforming and doing the right things—but we always had a good suit. And Leonard was always impeccably dressed."

Leonard's unconventionality showed in other ways, Steinberg says. "He was always writing and drawing, even in his teens, and he never went anywhere without a notepad. He would draw sketches endlessly, but mostly he wrote. He would have ideas and he wrote them down, and he would write poems. Writing was his passion and so much a part of him. I remember sitting next to him in the French class on one of those double desk benches and there was an English woman named Shirley who we thought was the most beautiful girl. He was madly in love with this Shirley and he would write poems in class inspired by her."

Girls and writing tied for top place in Leonard's teenage preoccupations, and in each of these areas his performance showed marked improvement over Westmount High. One more markedly than the other: love was not yet the victory march he described in *The Favorite Game*, his alter ego walking home, exultant, from his first lover's arms, eager to brag about his conquest, piqued that the citizenry of Westmount hadn't risen from their beds to organize a ticker-tape parade. But this was the early fifties, a time when underwear white as a picket fence came up to the chest, where they met brassieres as impenetrable as fortresses. A boy's options were limited. "You could eventually hold a girl's hand," said Leonard. "Sometimes she would let you kiss her." Anything more was "forbidden."[3]

His writing had no such constraints and was quite promiscuous. Leonard wrote poems "all the time," Rosengarten recalls, "in a kind of journal he always carried with him, and which once in a while he would lose or leave somewhere and the next day he would frantically try to find it, very upset, because there was all this work in there and he had no copies." At home Leonard had started to use a manual typewriter, tapping away at the keys while his grandfather Rabbi Solomon Klonitzki-Kline wrote in the next room. Masha's father had moved in for the year, and he and Leonard would often sit together of an evening, going through the Book of Isaiah, which the rabbi knew by heart and which Leonard came to love for its poetry, imagery and prophecy. More than anything though, Leonard loved sitting with the old man, who would express "solidarity and pleasure"[4] that his grandson was a writer also.

Despite his poor showing in English classes (he did far better in math), it was at McGill that Leonard really became a poet—indeed was knighted a poet in a spontaneous ceremony by Louis Dudek, the Polish-Canadian Catholic poet, essayist and publisher. Dudek taught the thrice-weekly literature course that Leonard took during his third year. The class of fifty would meet Monday, Wednesday and Friday at five P.M. in the Arts Building; the curriculum included Goethe,

Schiller, Rousseau, Tolstoy, Chekhov, Thomas Mann, Dostoyevsky, Proust, T. S. Eliot, D. H. Lawrence, Ezra Pound and James Joyce.

Dudek's agenda, as described by Ruth Wisse, one of Leonard's fellow students and subsequently professor of Yiddish literature and comparative literature at Harvard, was to teach his students two important things: "The first was modern poetry and literature, which had evolved fully abroad but which had barely started in Canada, with small groups of poets having a limited audience. . . . The second program was the massive movement of European literature and thought since the eighteenth century, with its profound practical implications, which students' minds had still to experience, like buckets of cold water thrown at them from a high lectern." Leonard, she said, "was launched by the first." Confident even then of his inclusion in this world of modern Canadian poets, he "did not treat his teacher with [Wisse's] kind of deference but more like a colleague, on equal terms."[5] Leonard agreed. "Back then I was very self-confident. I had no doubts that my work would penetrate the world painlessly. I believed I was among the great."[6]

Lagging a little among Leonard's interests and pursuits, though still firmly in the race, was music. Intriguingly, considering his propensity for joining societies, Leonard was not a member of the McGill Music Club (despite the presence on the committee of an attractive blonde named Ann Peacock, whose name could also be found among the editorial staff of *The Forge*, a literary magazine). But in 1952, between his first and second years, Leonard formed his first band with two university friends, Mike Doddman and Terry Davis. The Buckskin Boys was a country and western trio (Mort had not yet taken up the banjo or it might have been a quartet), which set about cornering the Montreal square-dance market.

A square-dance band? What possessed you?

"Square dances were popular at the time. We would be hired for high school square dances and church square dances—those being the social oc-

casions that were affirmed and encouraged by the elders. There was really no slow dancing, not much touching, you just join arms and twist around for a while. Very decent. [A wry smile] And we all found out we had buckskin jackets—I had inherited mine from my father—so we called ourselves the Buckskin Boys."

The only Jewish country and western band in Montreal?

"It was actually an eclectic religious group. Mike was a neighbor of mine who played harmonica and Terry, who was a friend of Mike's, knew how to call the dances and played a bucket bass" (a washtub, rope and hockey stick). "We played the traditional songs, like 'Red River Valley' and 'Turkey in the Straw.' "

Were you any good?

"We never thought we were very hot, we were just happy that people hired us. I think if I heard the music now I would probably appreciate it. But there was never any sense that this would have any future, that there was anything but the moment. No sense of a career involved at all. The word 'career' always had an unattractive and burdensome resonance in my heart. My idea mostly was to avoid participating in that activity called career, and I've been pretty much able to avoid it."

The band would practice at the Davis family house, in the basement playroom. "They always seemed to have a great time together, with a lot of friendly kibitzing going on," remembers Dean Davis, the late Terry Davis's brother; Dean ran the phonograph at their shows and acted as soundman. "I know my parents thought of Leonard as being very polite and a gentleman for his age. My mother always thought it was pretty funny that their trio consisted of a Protestant, a Jew and a Catholic." Recalls Janet Davis, Terry's widow, "If she was giving them dinner, which happened to be pork on a Friday, she would say it was lamb if they asked."

Leonard also played in a second band, this time all Jewish, part of McGill's Jewish student society, Hillel. They provided the music for a play whose crew included Freda Guttman and Yafa "Bunny"

Lerner, two of Leonard's college-years girlfriends. Mostly, though, he played guitar—alone, in the quadrangle, at the frat house, or anywhere there was a party. It wasn't a performance; it was just something he did. Leonard with a guitar was as familiar a sight as Leonard with a notebook. Melvin Heft, who was at several of those teenage parties, says, "After a while, when he thought the mood was right, Leonard would take out his guitar and play songs and sing to us. He was not a braggart or trying to be a big shot—'I'm going to sing to you'—he just did it, no fuss at all; it was a natural thing for him. He was always there, singing. He was enjoying it and so were we."

On weekends the action might move to Mort's house in the Townships—half a dozen students piling into one car and heading for the countryside. Mort's parents weren't there and the place would be empty, except for a man who worked on the property and a woman who acted as concierge, neither of whom was in any position to stop their partying. The crowd might include Leonard; Arnold Steinberg; sometimes Yafa and Freda; Marvin Schulman, one of the first of their set to be openly gay; and Robert Hershorn, a close friend of Leonard's who came from an even wealthier family. They would sit around drinking and talking. When it got dark they would drive to the Ripplecove Inn on Ayer's Cliff, above Lake Massawippi, and drink and talk some more. At closing time they would go back to the house and put a record on the phonograph or play music themselves—Leonard on guitar, running through the folk songs he had learned at the Socialist camp or the pop songs he had absorbed from the jukeboxes of Saint Catherine Street.

"We used to listen to music a lot," says Rosengarten, "and Leonard, even before he started to write his own stuff, was relentless. He would play a song, whether it was 'Home on the Range' or whatever, over and over and over all day, play it on his guitar and sing it. When he was learning a song he would play it thousands of times, all day, for days and days and weeks, the same song, over and over, fast and slow, faster, this and that. It would drive you crazy. It was the same when he started to write his own stuff. He still works that way. It still takes him four years to write a lyric because he's written twenty thousand verses or something."

Sometimes the crowd would assemble at Leonard's family home on Belmont Avenue, although on these occasions his family would be there. Esther would drift in and out—mostly out; her little brother and his friends did not hold much interest—but Masha would preside over everything, making a fuss, making food, entertaining. "His mother was a dramatic lady," says Rosengarten. "She was Russian, and she could be very, very dramatically unhappy about something and then burst into laughter and send it all up. Sometimes we would be going downtown at about nine o'clock in the evening and Masha would have a fit and say that it was no time to be going out and get all upset, but other times, when we would leave a bar with eight friends at three in the morning and go to her house and start carrying on, and she would come downstairs and greet everyone and offer them food, totally at ease with it; there was no telling how she was going to react." Steinberg concurs: "Masha was very volatile, but everybody loved her because she was basically a lovely, warmhearted person and she adored Leonard. I don't think she mixed much with the other mothers, so she hadn't picked up the worrisome habits, and so it seemed to me that Leonard was very free. It was always fun just dropping in. I would sit there and listen and Leonard would play his guitar. He never thought of himself as a good musician or performer, but he was always playing, and always learning to play the guitar."

From the midfifties, the guests at Leonard's parties were starting to include poets and writers, older men, often teachers from McGill. "There were no barriers, no master/student relationships," Leonard said. "They liked our girlfriends."[7] Among the most influential of these teachers were Louis Dudek; Frank ("F. R.") Scott, McGill's dean of law, a poet and a Socialist; and Hugh MacLennan, author of

the celebrated 1945 book *Two Solitudes*, an allegory of the irrecon-
cilable differences between Canada's French- and English-speaking
populations. MacLennan joined McGill the same year as Leonard,
who took his classes in the modern novel and creative writing. But the
man who would prove the most crucial was an assistant political science teacher, a poet whom Leonard met in 1954 after inviting him to
read from his new work, *The Long Pea-Shooter*, at the fraternity house.
"There was Irving Layton and then there was the rest of us," Leonard
would say almost a lifetime later. "He is our greatest poet, our greatest
champion of poetry."[8] Irving Layton would have readily agreed, and
added even more laudatory adjectives of his own. Layton was larger,
and louder, than life, a bullish man who looked like he'd been hewn
from the same Scottish stone as McGill, only with less attention to
detail. Layton was a hothead; his eyes blazed, there was an inner fire.
Leonard, as did a succession of extraordinary women, loved him.

A dating agency would have been very unlikely to have introduced these two as potential life mates. Twenty-two years Leonard's senior, Layton's brazen, iconoclastic, self-promoting style could
hardly be more different from Leonard's modest, self-effacing de-
meanor. Layton, with his wild mane of hair and disheveled clothes,
looked like he had stepped out of a hurricane; Leonard looked like
his clothes had been sewn on him every morning by a team of personal tailors. Layton was proudly belligerent; Leonard, despite a long
attraction to machismo, wasn't. Layton had fought in the Canadian
Army, attaining the rank of lieutenant, the same as Leonard's father;
Leonard as a young child had hoped to go to military school, but that
dream had died with his father. Still, Leonard had his father's gun;
his mother had argued with him about it, but in the end, Leonard
won. Then there was the class difference. Layton was born in a small
town in Romania in 1912 (his name was Israel Lazarovitch before his
family emigrated to Canada) and raised in Saint-Urbain, Montreal's
working-class, Jewish immigrant neighborhood. Leonard's upper-

class Westmount background was at the opposite end of the Jewish social spectrum. What they had in common was a love of honesty, a taste for irony and a skill in the art of debate (in 1957, Layton appeared in a nationally televised debating series called *Fighting Words*, which he invariably won).

Layton openly despised bourgeois Canada and its puritanism, and so did Leonard, if more covertly—as befitted a man who considered his own family bourgeois—such as when he worked behind the scenes to overturn the rule banning women and alcohol from students' rooms at his fraternity house. Layton was powerfully sexual—which Leonard liked to think he was too, or might be, given half the chance—and so was Layton's poetry: flagrant, unabashed, happy to provide names and details. Layton was passionate about poetry and the beauty and melody of the word—as was Leonard. Layton had become a poet, he said, "to make music out of words." But he also wanted his poetry "to change the world," to which the idealist in Leonard related strongly.

As Rosengarten explains it, "The [Second World] War had been a very important factor on our sensibility; people you knew were going off and getting killed, and there was a possibility that we would lose the war and the Nazis would take over America or Canada. But the other thing was that, while this was going on, the word was that if we *did* win the war, because of the great sacrifice everybody had made, the world was going to become this wonderful utopian place, with all this collective energy that had been dissipated in the war directed toward its creation. I think for us it was somewhat disillusioning that, at the end of the war, the first thing they did was kind of repudiate the collective aspect of the society and maintain this idea that it was really good for business to produce things instead, and sell people products as substitutes for this collective spirit. And the enormous numbers of women who worked and did things during the war that were considered unfit for women were packed up after the war and sent back to the kitchen. Leonard and I, these were things we were shockingly aware of." That sense of a lost Eden, of something beautiful that did not work out or could not last, would be detectable in a good deal of Leonard's work.

"There was a very interesting poetry scene in Montreal," says Rosengarten, "and it was centered around Irving Layton and Louis Dudek, who were good friends at the time." (They fell out later; their feuds over poetry became famous.) "There were lots of parties where they would read, many of them at Irving's house in Côte-Saint-Luc," west of Montreal. It is a large suburb today, with a street named after Layton, but in the fifties the farmhouse in which Irving lived with his wife and two children stood alone, surrounded by farmland. "At these parties people would read their poems to one another and discuss them and criticize stuff; it was pretty intense, and it would go sometimes most of the way through the night. There were many times when Leonard and I might quit the bars downtown at three in the morning and go over there to Irving's, and there the scene would be going on. Leonard would show his poems at these parties. They took it seriously. They had a little magazine they mimeographed, two hundred and fifty copies, called *CIV/n*, because at that time the bookstores didn't carry Canadian poets, you couldn't buy a book with any of that contemporary poetry in a bookstore in Montreal; it was pretty grim. But, looking back on it, I realize now that that poetry scene had more influence on me in terms of aesthetics than all the art schools I attended in England with all these people who became important sculptors. I think the gang in Côte-Saint-Luc were way ahead of all of them."

"We really wanted to be great poets," said Leonard. "We thought every time we met it was a summit conference. We thought it was terribly important what we were doing."[9] He looked on these evenings as a kind of poetry boot camp, where "training was intense, rigorous, and taken very seriously." Leonard would always have an attraction to such regimens. "But the atmosphere was friendly. Once in a while there were tears, someone would leave in a rage, we would argue, but interest in the art of writing was at the center of our friendship." He considered it an apprenticeship and he was an enthusiastic learner. "Irving and I used to spend a lot of evenings studying poems by someone like Wallace Stevens. We would study the poem until we discovered the code, until we knew exactly what the author was trying to say and how he did it. That was our life; our life was poetry."[10] Layton became, if not Leonard's life coach, then his guide, his cheerleader and one of his dearest friends.

In March 1954 in the fifth issue of *CIV/n* Leonard made his debut as a published poet. Alongside poems by Layton and Dudek (who were on the editorial board) and others of the Montreal poetry scene were three works credited to Leonard Norman Cohen: "Le Vieux," "Folk Song" and "Satan in Westmount," the last of the three about a devil who quoted Dante and "sang fragments of austere Spanish songs."* The following year Leonard won first prize in McGill's Chester Macnaghten Literary Competition with his poems "Sparrows" and the four-part *Thoughts of a Landsman*, which included "For Wilf and His House," a poem that was published in 1955 in *The Forge*. A remarkably mature work, erudite and moving, it began,

> When young the Christians told me
> how we pinned Jesus
> like a lovely butterfly against the wood
> and I wept beside paintings of Calvary
> at velvet wounds
> and delicate twisted feet

and ended,

---

* Curiously, on the same page as Leonard's "Folk Song" was a line drawing, not by Leonard, of a bird on a wire.

Then let us compare mythologies.
I have learned my elaborate lie
of soaring crosses and poisoned thorns
and how my fathers nailed him
like a bat against a barn
to greet the autumn and late hungry ravens
as a hollow yellow sign.

Layton had started taking Leonard with him to his book readings, where Leonard reveled in his friend's showmanship, his grand
gestures and braggadocio, and the passion that his performance in-
duced in the audience, the women in particular. In the summer of '55
Layton brought Leonard along to the Canadian Writers Conference
in Kingston, Ontario, and invited Leonard onstage, where Leonard
read his own work and played a little guitar.

The guitar had done nothing to hurt Leonard's success with
women—and he could offer them hospitality now that he and
Mort had taken a room on Stanley Street. "We weren't really living there, we were just hanging out there, we'd have friends over,"
said Rosengarten of the old-fashioned double parlor in a Victorian
boardinghouse. Leonard's mother was not well pleased at this development, but she found it hard not to indulge him. Their relationship
appeared to be very involved, even beyond the usual mother-son
attachment, let alone an archetypal Jewish mother and son—and
Masha, according to no less an authority on Jewishness than Rabbi
Wilfred Shuchat at Shaar Hashomayim, was "very Jewish." When
Nathan died, Leonard became the object of her indulgence, castiga-
tion and utter devotion. She was a vital, passionate woman, with an
infirm husband, something of an outsider in Westmount circles, so it
was hardly surprising that her only son, her youngest child, became
her focus.

Leonard loved his mother. If she smothered him, he smiled or
made wisecracks. He learned to shrug off emotional blackmail and

her insistence on feeding him and his friends at all hours of the day and night. "My mother taught me well never to be cruel to women," Leonard wrote in an unpublished piece from the seventies. But what he also learned from Masha was to count on the devotion, support and nurturing of women and, if and when it became too intense, to have permission to leave—if not always completely, and rarely without conflicting emotions.

———

Aviva Layton, née Cantor, is a vivacious blond Australian, sharp as a pin. She was raised in a "small, stifling, middle-class Jewish community" in Sydney that she couldn't wait to leave, and the minute she turned twenty-one she did. She wanted to go to New York. When they wouldn't let her in, she went to Montreal. Friends had given her the name of someone to call, Fred Cogswell, the poet and editor of the Canadian literary magazine *Fiddlehead*. Cogswell, it turned out, lived in Nova Scotia, some eight hundred miles distant. "But," she says, "he told me there was a whole covey of Montreal poets that I should look up," and he gave her the names of half a dozen of them, including Dudek, Scott and Layton. The first person she called was Layton—"I wasn't going to look up anyone whose name sounded vaguely Jewish"—who invited her to come to the house in Côte-Saint-Luc where he lived with his second wife, the artist Betty Sutherland, and their children.

Aviva arrived to find he had company. "All the big names in Canadian literature were there," including those on Cogswell's list—"except they weren't big names then, they were a small fringe group. I thought, 'This is marvelous.'" She intended to become part of the group. This intention was thwarted when, soon afterward, she and Irving began an affair. It would last twenty years and produce a son, but its more immediate result was to cut her off from everyone. "I couldn't go back to his house. This was the fifties, and you had to be very careful about scandal; Irving was teaching in a parochial school and he could easily have lost his job. So I lived in Montreal mostly in isolation, with Irving coming to visit me two or three times a week. The only person Irving ever trusted to know about us was Leonard, and he brought him to my small, basement apartment.

"Irving was in his forties then, twenty-one years older than me, and Leonard was twenty, one year younger than me. I can see myself opening the door to that apartment and there was Leonard on the other side, looking very young, slightly chubby, but there was something absolutely special about him. Irving had said, 'Somebody called Leonard Cohen is going to come and have coffee with us and he is the real thing.' I'll never forget him saying that—and with Irving 'the real thing' meant he's a real poet. And this was late in 1955; *Let Us Compare Mythologies* was about to come out."

The three met up at Aviva's apartment on a regular basis. In spite of the large age difference between Leonard and Layton—Layton was old enough to be his father—they behaved, Aviva says, "like equals. A lot of people say Leonard was Irving's student—some think he was his actual, literal student, which is absolutely incorrect—or that Irving was his mentor. No. Leonard thought, and still does, that Irving was the great writer and poet and man in his life, as well as friend, but I would not say that Leonard was the junior partner in that enterprise."

Leonard, Layton said, "was a genius from the first moment I saw him. I have nothing to teach him. I have doors to open, which I did. . . . The doors of sexual expression, of freedom of expression and so on and so forth. Once the doors were opened, Leonard marched very confidently along a path . . . somewhat different from my own."[11] Says Aviva, "Leonard famously said that Irving taught him how to write poetry and he taught Irving how to dress. I think Leonard wrote better poetry and Irving was a better dresser, but they taught each other things." As to the class difference, she says, "That was interesting. Leonard came from the Bel Air of Montreal, absolutely exclusive, and Irving was born in the slums, but when Irving and I came to rent a house we went to as close to where Leonard had been brought up as possible, and when Leonard wanted to buy a house or rent or live, he came right back to Irving's old part of town. Irving wanted to be where Leonard wanted to escape from, and Leonard wanted to be where Irving wanted to escape from."

Irving would later say of Leonard that "he was able to find the sadness in Westmount. That takes genius. He was able to see that not all rich people, not all comfortable people, not all plutocrats, were happy." Genius, Layton said, is "the ability—it's a very rare ability—to see things as they actually are. You are not fooled."[12] Leonard had taken Irving and Aviva to Belmont Avenue on several occasions. "He used to go there frequently and still had his room there and lived there I think in between places. One time when Masha wasn't around we had a huge party, one of those mad parties you had in those days, and somebody vomited on her damask, heavy curtains. The place was an absolute shambles. I remember going in the kitchen with Leonard and he would open up the kitchen drawers and show us that Masha would keep every paper clip and nail and little bit of string that had ever come through the front door."*

When Aviva first met Leonard, he told her something, she says, "which he might not remember but which I remember absolutely clearly. He said he'd been studying law at McGill, and that one day while he was studying, he looked into the mirror and it was blank. He couldn't see his own reflection. And he knew then that the academic life in whatever form whatsoever was not for him." The following year, armed with a BA degree; another literary award, the Peterson

---

* The contents of the drawer, as described by Leonard in *The Favorite Game*, also included "candle-butts from years of Sabbath evenings," "brass keys to locks which have been changed," "toothpicks they never used" and a "broken pair of scissors."

Memorial Prize; a cover line on the March 1956 edition of *The Forge* and, at the top of the pile, his first published volume of poetry, *Let Us Compare Mythologies*, Leonard enrolled as a graduate student at Columbia University and left Montreal for Manhattan.

Four

I Had Begun to Shout

Let Us Compare Mythologies was published in May 1956. The slim hardback, containing forty-four poems written by Leonard between the ages of fifteen and twenty, was the inaugural release of a new imprint that aimed to introduce the public to new young writers of merit. It was funded by McGill University and edited by Louis Dudek. Leonard himself designed the book, which was illustrated by Freda Guttman, his artist girlfriend and the muse for several poems. Her mysterious pen-and-ink drawings are Edenic at times and at others tortured; the image on the front cover is of a cowed, misshapen human, who looks to be under attack from doves or miniature angels. On the back, in the author's photograph, the twenty-one-year-old Leonard gazes unflinchingly at the camera. In spite of the sober expression, the stubble and those deep lines running from nose to mouth, he looks very young. In the poems, by contrast, he appears a much older man—not just the maturity and authority of his language and his command of poetic technique, but the "raging and weeping"[1] of the kind that suggests a man who has lived long, seen much and lost something very precious. Leonard dedicated the book to the memory of Nathan Cohen. His father's death is the subject of the poem "Rites":

> *the family came to watch the eldest son,*
> *my father; and stood about his bed*
> *while he lay on a blood-sopped pillow*
> *his heart half-rotted*
> *and his throat dry with regret . . .*
> *but my uncles prophesied wildly*
> *promising life like frantic oracles;*
> *and they only stopped in the morning*
> *after he had died*
> *and I had begun to shout.*

The themes and content of much of the poetry would feel perfectly familiar to those who would come to know Leonard as a singer-songwriter. There are poems—some of them titled, in Lorcan fashion, "Song" or "Ballad"—about religion, myth, sex, inhumanity, humor, love, murder, sacrifice, Nazis and Jesus on the cross. There are echoes of Joan of Arc and the Holocaust in "Lovers," where a man has erotic feelings for a woman who is being led to the flames. Several poems contain naked women and wounded men, the two conditions not unrelated. In "Letter," a poet armed with only his pen and his indifference claims victory over the femme fatale fellating him:

> *I write this only to rob you*
> *that when one morning my head*
> *hangs dropping with the other generals*
> *from your house gate*
> *that all this was anticipated*
> *and so you will know that it meant nothing to me*

The poems have a sense of timelessness, or of multilayered time. Ancient wrongs are juxtaposed with modern-day atrocities, and archaic language—courtly, biblical, Romantic—with contemporary irony. Leonard employs both the traditional poetic form and prose poetry. Like a twentieth-century troubadour, or a nineteenth-century Romantic, he places his own inner experiences and feelings at the center—often feelings of failure and despair. The epigraph comes from William Faulkner's novel *The Bear* and refers to a comment a young man makes during a conversation on the meaning of Keats's "Ode on a Grecian Urn": "He had to talk about something." As Leonard explained later, when a writer "has some urgency to speak," the subject matter of what he writes "becomes almost irrelevant."[2] Leonard had that urgency.

The original print run for *Let Us Compare Mythologies* was around four hundred copies. Ruth Wisse, Leonard's fellow student in Louis Dudek's class and editor of the *McGill Daily*, took on the role of head of Leonard's sales team and sold half that number on campus. The book received a handful of reviews in Canada, largely positive. *Queen's Quarterly* called it "a brilliant beginning."[3] The *Canadian Forum*'s critic Milton Wilson wrote, "He knows how to turn a phrase, his poems at their best have a clean, uncluttered line, and he writes 'about something.' "[4] *Fiddlehead*'s Allan Donaldson found Leonard's virtues "considerable" but had problems with what he described as Leonard's greatest weakness, "an overuse of images of sex and violence, so that at its worst his work becomes a sort of poetic *reductio ad absurdum* of the Folies Bergères and of Madame Tussaud's Chamber of Horror. It was, I believe, Mr. Harry Truman who remarked of the Folies Bergères that there was nothing duller than the protracted spectacle of a large number of bare breasts."[5] Leonard and Truman would have disagreed. The criticism appeared to be less about the quality of the work and more a reflection of the conservatism and puritanism of Canadian literature, against which Irving Layton had so loudly raged. Leonard's book contained a poem to Layton, titled "To I.P.L.," in which he described his friend affectionately as

... depraved
hanging around street corners
entertaining hags in public places.

"I felt that what I wrote was beautiful and that beauty was the passport of all ideas," Leonard would say in 1991. "I thought that the objective, open-minded reader would understand that the juxtaposition of spirituality and sexuality justified itself entirely. I felt that it was that juxtaposition that created that particular beauty, that lyricism."[6] Later still, on the publication in 2006 of a fiftieth-anniversary facsimile edition, Leonard said, "There are some really good poems in that little book; it's been downhill ever since."[7] The coda might well be one of his familiar self-effacing tics—it is hard to argue that Leonard has not produced better work since. But there was something in this first book that Leonard would often, subsequently, seem to long for—the innocence, the confidence, the prolificacy and hunger of his youthful self.

Let Us Compare Mythologies won Leonard the McGill Literary Award. It also brought him attention from the Canadian media. The Canadian Broadcasting Company invited him to participate in a project titled *Six Montreal Poets*, a spoken-word album. The other five were Irving Layton, Louis Dudek, A. M. Klein, A. J. M. Smith and F. R. Scott, the leading members of the so-called Montreal Group—prestigious company for a new, young writer. The album, studio-recorded, was produced by Sam Gesser, a folklorist and impresario who founded and ran the Canadian division of the American label Folkways and promoted Pete Seeger's and the Weavers' first Montreal shows. Leonard made his first-ever appearance on record on side one, between Smith and Layton, reading eight poems from *Let*

Us Compare Mythologies: "For Wilf and His House," "Beside the Shepherd," "Poem," "Lovers," "The Sparrows," "Warning," "Les Vieux" and "Elegy." Listening to it today, Leonard's voice sounds high and forced, somewhat British. The last of these he blamed on "the influence in the [Canadian] universities" during that period. "That accent was meant to dignify the poem. The declamative style that the Beats introduced hadn't quite gotten there yet."[8]

It had, however, gotten to New York. In 1956, the same year that Leonard published *Let Us Compare Mythologies*, Allen Ginsberg, an American Jew and Columbia University graduate, published his visceral, personal poetry book *Howl*. In 1957, the same year that *Six Montreal Poets* was released in the U.S. on the Folkways label, Jack Kerouac, an American Catholic of Quebec ancestry who had gone to Columbia on a football scholarship, published his landmark autobiographical novel *On the Road*. These two books were sacred texts of the Beats, a literary movement dedicated to personal liberty, truth and self-expression and influenced by bebop jazz, Buddhism and experiments with drugs and sex. The Beats were hard-core. *Howl* had been banned for obscenity, before a celebrated court case put it back on the shelves, and Kerouac had conducted a private, backyard ceremony before sending out his first manuscript, in which he dug a hole, inserted his penis and mated with the earth. Though it was not quite the same as Leonard's interment of his first piece of writing in his father's bow tie, Leonard felt a kinship. In December 1957, when Kerouac made an appearance at the Village Vanguard in New York—a bohemian Greenwich Village speakeasy turned jazz club—Leonard was there. Kerouac, extremely drunk—he found drinking helped with his shyness—read to the accompaniment of jazz musicians. Leonard, who was also shy, and who claimed to have "never really liked poetry readings; I like to read poetry by myself,"[9] was impressed. If poems were to be delivered publicly, this was a fine way to do it.

Leonard liked the Beats. They did not return the sentiment. "I was writing very rhymed, polished verses and they were in open re-volt against that kind of form, which they associated with the op-pressive literary establishment. I felt close to those guys, and I later bumped into them here and there, although I can't describe myself remotely as part of that circle."[10] Neither did he have any desire to join it. "I thought that our little group in Montreal was wilder and freer and that we were on the right track, and we, in our provincial self-righteousness, felt that they were not on the right track and that they were getting some kind of free ride, that they weren't honoring the tradition as we felt we were."[11]

It is interesting that someone who in high school and university had seemed keen to sign up for, even lead, any number of groups should choose not to join this particular club at such a pivotal mo-ment for poetry. In the fifties, the Beats made poets the counter-culture spokesmen, the rock stars, if you like, of their generation. It's interesting too that although Leonard was younger than Ginsberg and Kerouac, they viewed him as part of the old guard. In the sixties, when rock stars would become the counterculture spokesmen and poets of their generation, Leonard would once again be considered old—if with better reason this time; he was in his thirties when he made his first album—and would feel himself to be an outsider.

Leonard did not appear at all troubled at his outsider status. In fact, a certain sense of isolation seems to have set in toward the end of his years at McGill and his first term at Columbia University, which seemed to coincide with Leonard's first bouts of serious depression. "What I mean by depression isn't just the blues, it's not just like a hangover from the weekend, the girl didn't show up or something like that," said Leonard, describing the paralyzing darkness and anx-iety he experienced. "It's a kind of mental violence which stops you from functioning properly from one moment to the next."[12] Leonard took to spending "a lot of time alone. Dying," he said. "Letting my-self slowly die."[13]

Leonard's first address in New York was International House, at 500 Riverside Drive, where Columbia billeted its foreign students. It was on the Upper West Side, a stone's throw from the Hudson River. At nights Leonard would head downtown, much as he had done in Montreal, and seek out the city's netherworlds, of which New York had many. Greenwich Village was a particular draw. Leonard's days were not devoted to studying; at Columbia, as at McGill, Leonard was not much interested in academic study. He was less interested in reading than in writing himself—or writing about himself, as he did when one professor, knowing when he was beaten, allowed Leonard to submit a term paper on *Let Us Compare Mythologies*.

In his room, sitting at the table by the window from which he could watch the sunset turn the gray river gold, he wrote a number of poems and short stories. One story, "The Shaving Ritual,"[14] was inspired by a piece of advice his mother had given him. Whenever things got bad, she said, he should stop what he was doing and have a shave, and he would feel better. It was counsel he found himself taking often, as the episodes of depression increased.

Leonard had gone to New York to be a writer—a serious writer, but also a popular writer. Even at this early stage, when the Canadian literary world was starting to talk about him as Canada's best young poet, he wanted his work to be read and liked by more than just Canadian literati, the small group that Irving Layton used to refer to as the "Canuckie Schmuckies." Enrolling at Columbia had really been a cover, something to keep Leonard's family happy. Going to America to do postgraduate studies at a renowned university was an acceptable activity for a young man from a conservative, upper-middle-class Montreal Jewish background; going to America to become a writer, not so much. Mort Rosengarten explains, "It was not, and still is not, encouraged by that community. They don't want their children becoming artists. They're very hostile to it. They don't want to know about themselves. But Leonard got away with it."

How Leonard got away with it had a lot to do with having lost his father when he was nine years old. "I never had to come up against that powerful male influence that a young man meets as he grows older,"[15] he says. The powerful influence in his childhood was female, his mother, who was "a generous Chekhovian spirit, very accepting in her way. She was alarmed when she saw me running around Montreal with a guitar under my arm, but she was very kind in her observations. She would occasionally roll her eyes, but that was about as far as it went."[16] His uncles would step in now and then with "indications and suggestions and advice and lunches held, but very subtly. Considering the tales one hears of the tyrannies of family, mine was very gentle in that respect."[17] Nevertheless, the other big reason for going to New York was to get away from Montreal, to put space between himself and the life his upper-class Montreal Jewish background mapped out for him: from Westmount to McGill, then on to studying law or commerce, and finally taking his place in the family business.

Leonard was writing in New York, but he was also floundering. After the euphoria of his first publication and the attention it brought him in Canada, now he was in a place where no one knew who he was, and if they did, they wouldn't have cared. For New Yorkers, Canadian literature was a dot on the cultural map barely visible to the naked eye. As a means of making contact with fellow writers— and having some status among them—Leonard founded a literary magazine, *The Phoenix*, but it was short-lived. Leonard was lonely. He missed his old crowd in Montreal; he really did believe that they were special. "Each time we met we felt that it was a landmark in the history of thinking. There was a great deal of fellowship and drinking. Montreal is tiny, it's a French city and the number of people writing in English is small; it didn't have any prestige prizes at the time, not even any girls. But a few of us were on fire and we would write for each other or any girl that would listen."[18]

And then, in New York, Leonard met a girl. Her name was Georgianna Sherman; Leonard called her Anne, or Annie. A year and a half older than Leonard, she had already been married once, briefly, at a very young age and was now working as the program coordinator at International House. Sherman was tall and very attractive, with long, dark hair, soulful eyes and a modulated, aristocratic voice. She came from a patrician New England family; her grandmother was a Daughter of the American Revolution. "Irving and I had heard so much from Leonard about this Annie and how beautiful she was," says Aviva Layton, "that she almost became a legend in our minds before we met her. But she really was exquisite, a beautiful soul, from very, very good American blood. She was an extremely cultivated young woman—great cook, wrote poetry, played piano—and here was this little Montreal Jew, Leonard. She had never met anyone like him before and he'd never met anyone like her, and they just fell for each other." Leonard moved into Sherman's upper Manhattan apartment.

"Annie was very, very important in Leonard's life at that time," says Aviva. "It was when he was just starting out on the enterprise of being a writer and he had moved to New York—this at a time when Canadians weren't crossing the border and going to the U.S. to make their careers—and Annie was in the thick of things in New York. She introduced him to a lot of people. And Leonard began to see that there was a whole other world outside of the world of Montreal."

In the summer of 1957, Leonard took Annie to Quebec to show her off to the Laytons, who had rented a summer cottage in the Laurentians. "Leonard and Annie would follow us, then find a lake and pitch an ordinary little tent and that was where they would stay. They would read to one another—they'd brought along lots and lots of poetry—and Leonard would play his guitar. They would go to bed when the sun went to bed and get up in the morning with the sun. Sometimes they'd row across the lake to us and spend a couple of days in our cottage. Annie was Leonard's first great love." She was also a muse, inspiring the poem "For Anne," in *The Spice-Box of Earth*, and the character Shell, the lover, in *The Favorite Game*.

The relationship did not last. It was Leonard who left; it had started to head down another path Leonard was keen to avoid in his life, which was marriage. As he wrote in *The Favorite Game*, "Supposing he went along with her toward living intimacy, toward comforting, incessant married talk. Wasn't he abandoning something more austere and ideal, even though he laughed at it, something which could apply her beauty to streets, traffic, mountains, ignite the landscape—which he could master if he were alone?" In other words, he had work to do, man's work. However much a woman's love might ease the loneliness and darkness, still it disturbed him, "as generals get uneasy during a protracted peace." The breakup was painful for Annie. It was for Leonard too. Being the one to end it did not mean that he did not miss her terribly. Years later, as he sat at a wooden table in a white house on a hill on a Greek island, staring out at the solid blue sky, he would write her letters, asking her to come and join him there. When she declined, he wrote her poems.

With Annie gone
Whose eyes to compare
With the morning sun?

Not that I did compare,
But I do compare
Now that she's gone.

"FOR ANNE," *SELECTED POEMS 1958–1968*

Annie went on to marry Count Orsini, the owner of Orsini's, the famous New York restaurant. In 2004 she published a book, *An Imperfect Lover: Poems and Watercolors*. In the poem "How I Came to Build the Bomb," she describes falling in love with "a wandering Jew" and learning that for "a traveling man, love / was a burden he couldn't take on."[19]

Having spent one year in New York, Leonard moved back to Montreal and into 599 Belmont Avenue. So did his grandfather Rabbi Klonitzki-Kline. The old man was suffering from Alzheimer's disease; once again Masha became the caregiver. To a fly on the wall it might have looked much like the old days—Masha in the kitchen, making food; Leonard tapping away on a manual typewriter; the old man poring over the dictionary he was trying to write from memory, and all the while his memory was disintegrating.

Leonard was working on a novel titled *A Ballet of Lepers*. It opened with: "My grandfather came to live with me. There was nowhere else for him to go. What had happened to all his children? Death, decay, exile—I hardly know. My own parents died of pain."[20] It was a depressing way to begin a book, and Leonard acknowledged this: "But I must not be too gloomy at the beginning or you will leave me, and that, I suppose, is what I dread most." After putting the novel through several drafts, Leonard sent it out to publishers in Canada. For a while it looked as if Ace Books might take it, but in the end, along with all the other publishers, they turned it down. *A Ballet of Lepers* was not, as some have thought, an early version of *The Favorite Game*. In Leonard's view it was "probably a better novel. But it never saw the light."[21] Leonard filed the manuscript away.

The rejection did not stop Leonard from writing. He continued to take a notebook with him everywhere. His friend from McGill Arnold Steinberg recalls, "Of all the things about Leonard, the first

thing that comes to mind was he was constantly, constantly writing—
writing and sketching. One always sensed that there was an inner
need—pushing out words and pictures, never ending, like a motor
running." Phil Cohen, a Montreal jazz musician and music professor,
remembers seeing Leonard sitting, writing at a table in the corner of
a drugstore at the intersection of Sherbrooke and Côte-des-Neiges.
"I'm guessing it was just a place where nobody knew him and he
could sit and do what he wanted. A couple of times he looked up,
and he looked like he was totally out of it—not drugged, just in a
totally different world, he was so into what he was doing. From my
experience of working with a lot of performers, there was this sense
of almost desperation that I picked up from the look on his face that
said, 'Don't disturb me.' I said to myself, 'This guy is very serious.'"

Leonard was finding it impossible to stay at his mother's house after having lived on his own, and with Annie. He found an apartment
on Mountain Street, and in order to pay the rent (and since he no longer had the excuse of studying in New York), he agreed to take a job
in one of the Cohen family firms. For a year Leonard worked at W. R.
Cuthbert & Company, the brass foundry that his uncle Lawrence
ran. A reference letter written by the foundry's personnel manager in
December 1957 stated: "Leonard Cohen was employed by us for the
period Dec 12th 1956 to Nov 29th 1957 in various capacities: Electro-
cycle turret lathe operator, Brass die-casting machine operator, Time
and motion study assistant. During the time of his employment, Mr
Cohen was known to be honest, capable and industrious. We have
no hesitation in recommending him for any sort of employment and
would like to express our regret at his departure."[22]

Leonard, who did not share this regret, was looking for work in
America. He applied to the U.S. Department of the Interior Bureau
of Indian Affairs in Washington, DC, for a teaching position on a
reservation. The bureau, oddly, had little use for a Jewish poet from
Montreal with electro-cycle turret lathe skills. (It would be nine more

years before Leonard would display his Native American scholarship in his second novel, *Beautiful Losers*.) So he moved on to another of the family firms, the Freedman clothing company, run by his uncle Horace. Leonard spent his days in the office, moving papers around, or in the factory, hanging the finished suits and coats on racks. His nights were spent in the clubs and bars of Montreal, which in the late fifties could still boast the liveliest nightlife in Canada—so lively that the military authorities had designated certain streets off-limits to its personnel because of the number of brothels. Montreal then was Canada's New York, the city that never slept; musicians who played in its many nightclubs were expected to keep on playing until the last drunk was carried out.

With the new decade, and Quebec's "Quiet Revolution," just two years away, it was hard not to notice there was a change in the air. "People of different backgrounds—linguistic, religious and the rest— were beginning to come forward and take chances," says Phil Cohen. Some of the clubs had started to feature more experimental musical acts. Among them was a jazz pianist named Maury Kaye. A small Montreal Jew whose goatee, thick black-framed glasses and unruly hair made him look like a beatnik, Kaye had become well-known on the Canadian jazz circuit as a big-band leader, a composer and a noted sideman who had played with Edith Piaf and Sammy Davis Jr. He also had a small, less mainstream jazz band that played late-night gigs at clubs like Dunn's Birdland on Saint Catherine Street, a jazz parlor above a popular smoked-meats delicatessen, which was reached by a flight of rickety stairs. One night in April 1958, at midnight, when Kaye came onstage with his band, Leonard was with them.

Among the audience of around fifty people was Henry Zemel, a math and physics student at McGill, who had no idea at that time who Leonard was, although in the sixties they would become close friends. "It was curious," remembers Zemel, "a little place with a small audience and a little stage. Leonard sang and he read some po-

etry but, as I remember, he sang more than he read poetry." Recalls
Aviva Layton, who went to Leonard's first night with Irving to give
moral support, "I don't remember him reading poetry, I remember
him singing and playing the guitar. He perched himself on a high,
three-legged stool and he sang—his own songs. That magic that he
had, whatever it was, you could see it there at these performances."

*"Maury Kaye was a very gifted pianist and jazz arranger. He would
play something, and I would improvise. That was probably the first time
that I . . ."*

Performed onstage as a singer?

*"Well, I was invited to read poetry now and then, but I never really
enjoyed it, I was never terribly interested in that kind of expression. But I
liked singing, chanting my lyrics, to this jazz group. It felt a lot easier and
I liked the environment better. [Smiles] You could drink."*

*Was it new to you, improvising? You're better known for a more studied
approach.*

*"Well, I would sit with friends on the steps of the place we were living
in when we were at college on Peel Street and calypso was popular in a
tiny corner of Montreal—there was a tiny black population and there were
some calypso clubs there that we started going down to quite a lot—and I
would improvise calypso lyrics about the people who were passing in the
street, things like that."*

Along with the Beat-style improvisations he had witnessed in
Greenwich Village, Leonard had prepared some set pieces, among
them "The Gift," a new poem that had its premiere on his first night
at Dunn's.* "They called it Poetry to Jazz," remembers David Cohen,
Leonard's cousin. "It was a very fifties-ish thing. Leonard wrote poetry and a little blues stuff and I remember him reading this poem
very seriously: 'She knelt to kiss my manhood,' or something like
that. I was cracking up, and all the young girls were going, 'Ooh, isn't

---

* "The Gift" was later published in *The Spice-Box of Earth*.

he something else?' Did it make Leonard popular with women? As the old expression goes, it didn't hurt." Leonard also ad-libbed and made jokes. Irving Layton, always his biggest cheerleader, declared him a natural comic.

Ever since Mort left Montreal to study sculpture in London, Leonard had increasingly come to rely on Layton for friendship and support. Several times a week he would go to Irving and Aviva's place for supper. Often, after they had eaten, they would "crack a poem." Aviva explains, "We would choose a poem—Wallace Stevens, Robert Frost, anyone—and we'd go through it line by line, image by image. How did this poet put together those images? What does this poem really mean? How do we crack this poem? Honestly, it was worth more than a PhD from Columbia." Some evenings they would go to the cinema—Leonard and Irving "both adored trashy movies," Aviva says—"and then we would sit up till dawn talking about the movie, analyzing the symbolism, and try and trip each other up on how many symbols we'd seen." On the nights they stayed in, they would "wheel in this old black and white television set with the rabbit ears on top and, while eating lots of candy—Leonard would always bring over a huge slab of his favorite, which was dyed sugar made to look like bacon—they would talk about what they'd seen until the cows came home."

Although Layton was still married to Betty Sutherland, he and Aviva had been living together openly for some time. The arrangement worked as well as such things could, until Aviva took a job as a teacher in a private girls' school—an institution not known for its sympathies toward alternative lifestyles. Irving and Aviva needed to marry. But Irving did not want to divorce his wife. Instead he proposed a solution: he would buy a wedding ring for Aviva and they would have a mock marriage ceremony—Leonard would be best man—and she could change her name legally to Layton. A date was set, and the three met at a bistro near Leonard's apartment for lunch and champagne, "Irving wearing some awful bottle-green coat, [Aviva] in a white, seersucker secondhand dress with curtain bobbles on the bottom, and Leonard, of course, the only one dressed beautifully." They headed off together to a small jewelry boutique on Mountain Street to buy the ring. "While I'm looking at the wedding rings," says Aviva, "all of a sudden I notice that Irving is on the other side of the shop saying, 'I've come to buy a bracelet for my wife. She's an artist.' Leonard, who just understood what I was going through, said, 'Aviva, I'm going to buy you a wedding ring,' and he did. He slipped it on my finger and said, 'Now you're married.' And I thought, who the hell am I supposed to be married to? I'm telling you this story because that is so part of Leonard. I'm sure he can be absolutely impossible if anyone wants a marriage kind of relationship with him, but he was, and always has been, impeccable—thoughtful, courtly, generous, really the most honorable man."

For detectives seeking to put together a picture of Leonard's activities and state of mind, a file in one of the stack of boxes in his archives in Toronto might provide some interesting clues. Or muddy the water entirely. Alongside Leonard's unpublished novel *A Ballet of Lepers* are a guitar string, a driving license, a vaccination certificate, a chest X-ray form, a leaflet marking the declaration of independence in Cuba and a library card. Whatever crime it was, the evidence pointed to its having been committed by a troubadour planning an overseas journey, likely somewhere exotic. There is also a number of forms filled out by Leonard requesting arcane publications. Several of these are for books and articles on the benefits, problems, philosophy and technique of fasting. These include "Notes of Some English Accounts of Miraculous Fasts," by Hyder Rollins, from the *Journal of American Folklore* in 1921, and the intriguingly titled "Individual and Sex Differences Brought Out by Fasting," by Howard Marsh, from a 1916 issue of *Psychological Review*. Leonard also requested the books *Mental Disorders in Urban Areas* by Robert E. Faris and *Venereal Disease Information* by E. G. Lion. On thin yellowed paper is a typewritten essay titled "Male Association Patterns." In it the author, Lionel Tiger, from the University of British Columbia—one of Leonard's fellow counselors at summer camp—discussed male homosexuality and the desire for same-sex companionship, as displayed in "sports teams, fraternities, criminal organizations like the Cosa Nostra, drinking groups, teenage gangs, etc. The list is long," Tiger wrote, "but the common factor is male homogeneity and the communal sense of maleness which prevails."

Fasting was something Leonard would pursue with enthusiasm in the coming years; he appeared as ardent about losing weight as Masha was to put it on him. As to homosexuality, by all accounts this was merely an intellectual curiosity, a subject that had been thrust into the zeitgeist by the Beats. When the British journalist Gavin Martin asked Leonard in 1993 if he'd ever had a gay relationship, Leonard answered, "No." Asked if he regretted this, Leonard said, "No, because I have had intimate relationships with men all my life and I still do have. I've seen men as beautiful. I've felt sexual stirrings toward men so I don't think I've missed out."[23] His friendships with his male friends were, and remain, deep and durable.

The summer of 1958 found Leonard back again in the Laurentians and at summer camp—as a counselor this time, at Pripstein's Camp Mishmar, which opened its doors to children with learning difficulties. Leonard took with him his guitar and a camera. He went home with a roll of film that contained a series of pictures of women he met there. Nudes. Now that he no longer lacked the female company he had so long craved, he was making up for lost time. "Leonard's always had yearnings for sainthood, [but] at the same time there's certainly been a strong streak of hedonism in him, as there is in almost every poet and every artist," said Irving Layton. "It's because the artist is dedicated to pleasure and bringing pleasure to others particularly. And if he takes a little bit himself in giving pleasure to others, so much the better."[24]

———————

While Leonard was at college in New York and Mort at art school in London, they sublet their room in the boardinghouse on Stanley Street to friends. When Mort returned to Montreal, he converted the double parlor into a sculpture studio for himself, and he and Leonard talked about turning it into an art gallery. The two put in long hours fixing up the place and planning how it should be. They did not want the hushed formality and office hours of the other Montreal galleries, which "would all close at five o'clock," says Rosengarten, "so if people were working they weren't free to go." The Four Penny Art Gallery, as they named it, was open every night until nine or ten, later on weekends, "and much later," says Rosengarten, "if we had a vernissage." Opening parties would carry on long into the night. Leonard immortalized one of these evenings in his poem "Last Dance at the Four Penny." In the poem, the room on Stanley Street and all its associations—art, friendship, freedom and nonconformity—became a fortress against the savagery of the world outside its walls, in Montreal and beyond.

> Layton, my friend Lazarovitch,
> no Jew was ever lost
> while we two dance joyously
> in this French province.

The artists they exhibited were those whom the Montreal establishment ignored, among them Layton's wife, Betty Sutherland. "We had some of the best young active artists at any given time, and it was very hard to find their work because the galleries were all stuck with their own rigid history and ideas," says Rosengarten. "We sold poetry books, because no one else would sell them, and ceramics, because no one else would sell them either." The Four Penny, says Nancy Bacal, became "a gathering place, a haven for art and music and poetry. On warm evenings we would all go up to the roof and sing folk songs and protest songs; Morton would play his banjo and Leonard would play his guitar."

"The gallery," Rosengarten says, "was starting to work. Starting to get the attention of the critics. And then in the dead of winter there was a huge fire and the building burned down. Completely. And that was the end of it, because we didn't have insurance. We had a huge show on at that time and there were paintings from floor to ceiling, all gone. I had a little wax sculpture, which survived the fire, which was amazing. It was such a remarkably delicate thing and the only thing to survive." The Four Penny was dead and cremated.

And Masha was in the hospital. Leonard's mother had been admitted to a psychiatric ward at the Allan Memorial Institute, suffering with depression. The Allan, as locals called it, was housed in a grand mansion at the top of McTavish Street in Mount Royal. From its immaculately kept grounds, the view across Montreal was even better than from the park behind Leonard's family home. "Loonies," wrote Leonard, revisiting the incident in *The Favorite Game*, "have the best view in town."*

It's not surprising that Masha, a woman with a leaning toward melancholy, would be seriously depressed, after her infirm second husband had moved out of the house on Belmont Avenue and gone to live in Florida and then her infirm father had moved in. Nor was it strange that she should lean so heavily on her only son when he visited her—which he dutifully did—berating him for having more time

---

* The Allan would later gain notoriety for its participation in Project MK-ULTRA, a covert CIA research program into mind control from 1957 to 1964, using drugs, abuse and sensory deprivation.

for his shiksas than for his mother and, in the next breath, worrying that he wasn't taking care of himself or eating properly.

It is also no surprise that Leonard would feel frustrated, helpless and angry—a multipurpose frustration, helplessness and anger that seemed to take in his own condition as well as Masha's. He knew by now that he had inherited her depressive tendency, and he was not at his happiest himself. Every weekday, from seven in the morning, he worked in his dead father's clothing company at a job he loathed, while the gallery he had helped create with Mort had literally gone up in smoke. But while Leonard soldiered on, uncomplaining—as Mort says, echoing the sentiments of many of Leonard's friends, "He wasn't the kind of moany-groany depressed person; he has a great sense of humor, and depression didn't stop him from being funny"— the woman who had always supported him and indulged him could lie around all day in a place that looked to Leonard like a country club. There must have been fear too—not just at seeing his sole parent helpless but at the responsibility that came with that, and the vision of what might await him if he stayed in Montreal. The city he had escaped New York to come back to had become uncomfortable, even threatening.

An article that appeared in the Canadian magazine *Culture*, written by Louis Dudek, must have been the final blow. Leonard's former teacher, publisher and champion criticized his writing as "a rag-bag of classical mythology" and a "confusion of symbolic images." Layton leapt to Leonard's defense immediately, branding Dudek "stupid" and declaring Leonard "one of the purest lyrical talents this country has ever produced." But the damage was done; although Leonard remained friendly with Dudek, he could no longer feel safe in his position as Montreal's golden boy of poetry. It was time to move. For which he needed money. But he could not bear to stay at the Freedman Company, and he knew he could not make a living as a poet. Leonard quit his job and devoted his energies to applying for scholarships and grants. In between working on poems, short stories and the occasional freelance review for the CBC, he and Layton sat together for hours on end, filling in applications and writing proposals. Leonard requested money to travel to the ancient capitals—London, Athens, Jerusalem, Rome—around which, he said, he would write a novel.

In the spring of 1959, two letters arrived from the Canada Council for the Arts: Leonard's and Irving's applications had been approved. Leonard was granted $2,000. Immediately, he applied for a passport. In December 1959, shortly after his return from a poetry reading at the 92nd Street Y in New York with Irving Layton and F. R. Scott, Leonard boarded a plane for London.

Five

A Man Who Speaks with a Tongue of Gold

It was a cold gray morning and starting to rain when Leonard walked down Hampstead High Street, clutching a suitcase and an address. It was just before Christmas and the windows of the little shops were bright with decorations. Tired from the long journey, Leonard knocked at the door of the boardinghouse. But there was no room at the inn. The only thing they could offer was a humble cot in the living room. Leonard, who had always said he had "a very messianic childhood," accepted the accommodation and the landlady's terms: that he get up every morning before the rest of the household, tidy up the room, get in the coal, light a fire and deliver three pages a day of the novel he told her he'd come to London to write. Mrs. Pullman ran a tight ship. Leonard, with his liking for neatness and order, happily accepted his duties. He had a wash and a shave, then went out to buy a typewriter, a green Olivetti, on which to write his masterpiece. On the way, he stopped in at Burberry on Regent Street, a clothing store favored by the English upper-middle classes, and bought a blue raincoat. The dismal English weather failed to depress him. Everything was as it should be; he was a writer, in a country where, unlike Canada, there were writers stretching back forever: Shakespeare, Milton, Wordsworth, Keats. Keats's house, where he wrote "Ode to a Nightingale" and love letters to Fanny Brawne, was just ten minutes' walk from the boardinghouse. Leonard felt at home.

Despite its proximity to the center of London, Hampstead had the air of a village—a village that crawled with writers and thinkers. Among the permanent residents in Highgate Cemetery, which was also a short walk away, were Karl Marx, Christina Rossetti, George Eliot and Radclyffe Hall. Back when London was shrouded in toxic smog, Hampstead, high on a hill, with eight hundred acres of heath land, drew consumptive poets and sensitive artists with its cleaner air. Mort had been the first among Leonard's crowd to stay there, renting a room from Jake and Stella Pullman while he was at art school in London. Next was Nancy Bacal, who had gone to London to study classical theater at the London Academy of Music and Dramatic Art, and stayed on to become a radio and television journalist. Nancy, like Leonard, had been given the "starter bed" and a hot-water bottle in the living room until Mort moved out and Mrs. Pullman, judging her worthy, allowed her to take over his room. Which is where she was when Leonard showed up in December 1959.

Bacal, a writer and teacher of writing, cannot remember a time when she did not know Leonard. Like him, she was born and raised in Westmount. They lived on the same street and went to the same Hebrew school and high school; her father was Leonard's pediatrician. "It was a very strong community, inbred in many ways, but in no way was he the usual person you'd find in the Westmount crowd. He was reading and writing poetry when people were more interested in who they were going to date for their Sunday school graduation. He pushed the borders from a very early age." What made it more curious was that Leonard was not openly rebellious; as Arnold Steinberg noted, he seemed conventional, respectful of his teachers, the least likely to rebel.

"Here you have the contradiction," says Bacal. "Leonard was embedded in religion, deeply connected with the shul through his grandfather, who was president of the synagogue, and because of his respect for the elders; I remember Leonard used to recount how his grandfather could put a pin through the Torah and be able to recite every word on each page it touched, and that impressed me enormously. But he was always prepared to ask the hard questions, break down the conventions, find his own way. Leonard was never a man to assault or attack or say bad things about anything or anyone. He was more interested in what was true or right." She recalls the endless talks she and Leonard would have in their youth about their community, "what was comfortable, where it left us wanting, where we felt people weren't penetrating to the truth." Their conversation had taken a break when Bacal left for London, but when Leonard moved into the Pullmans' house, it picked up where it left off.

Stella Pullman, unlike most residents of Hampstead, was working-class—"salt of the earth, very pragmatic, down-to-earth English" is Bacal's description. "She worked at an Irish dentist in the East End of London; took the tube there every day. Everyone who lived in the house used to schlep down there once a year and have their fillings done. She was very supportive—Leonard still credits her with being responsible for him finishing the book because she gave him a deadline, which made it happen—but she was not what you'd call impressed by him, or by any of us. 'Everyone has a book in them,' she'd say, 'so get on with it. I don't want you just hanging around.' She'd been through the war; she had no time for all that nonsense. Leonard was very comfortable there because there was no artifice about it. He and Stella got along very, very well. Stella liked him a lot—but secretly; she never wanted anyone to get, as she would say, 'too full of themselves.' " Leonard kept to his part of the agreement and wrote the required three pages a day of the novel he had begun to refer to as *Beauty at Close Quarters*. In March 1960, three months after his arrival, he had completed a first draft.

Late at night, after closing time at the King William IV pub, their local, Nancy and Leonard would explore London together. "To be in London in those times was a revelation. It was another culture, a kind of no-man's-land between World War II and the Beatles. It was dark, there wasn't much money and it was something we'd never experienced, London working class—and don't forget we'd started with Pete Seeger and all those workingman songs. We'd start out at one or two in the morning and wander way out to the East End and hang out with guys in caps with Cockney accents. We'd visit the night people in rough little places, having tea. We both loved the street life, street food, street activity, street manners and rituals"—the places and things Leonard had been drawn to in Montreal. "If you want to find Leonard," says Bacal, "go to some little coffee bar or hole in the wall. Once he finds a place, that's where he'll go, every night. He wasn't interested in what was 'happening'; he was interested in finding out what lay underneath it."

Through her broadcast work Bacal became familiar with London's West Indian community and started to frequent a cellar club on Wardour Street in Soho, the Flamingo. On Friday nights, after hours, it transformed into a club-within-a-club called the All-Nighter. It began at midnight, although anybody who was anybody knew it did not get going until two A.M. "It was, theoretically, a very dodgy place but it was actually magical," said Bacal. "There was so much weed in the air it was like walking into a painting of smoke." She and Harold Pascal, another of the Montreal set who was living in London, would go there most Friday nights. The music was good—calypso and white R & B–jazz acts like Zoot Money and Georgie Fame and the Blue Flames—and the crowd was fascinating. Quite unusually for the time, it was 50 percent black—Afro-Caribbeans and a handful of African-American GIs; the white half was made up of mobsters, hookers and hipsters.

On the first night Leonard went with Nancy to the club, there was a knife fight. "Somebody called the law. Everyone was stoned and dancing," she recalls, and then the police arrived. "I don't know if you've ever been to any of these sleazy joints, but you don't want to be there when they turn on the lights. Suddenly all the faces were white. The incident didn't last long, but we were all pretty shook up. I was worried about Leonard, but he was cool." Leonard loved the place. After a subsequent visit, Leonard wrote to his sister, Esther, saying, "It's the first time I've really enjoyed dancing. I sometimes even forget I belong to an inferior race. The Twist is the greatest ritual since circumcision—and there you can choose between the genius of two cultures. Myself I prefer the Twist."[1]

With the first draft of his novel finished, Leonard turned his attention to his second volume of poems. He had gathered the poems for *The Spice-Box of Earth* the year before and, at Irving Layton's recommendation, had given it to the Canadian publisher McClelland & Stewart. Literally. Driving to Toronto with a friend, Leonard handed his manuscript to Jack McClelland in person. McClelland had taken over his father's company in 1946 at the age of twenty-four and was, according to the writer Margaret Atwood, "a pioneer in Canadian publishing, at a time when many Canadians did not believe they had a literature, or if they did have one, it wasn't very good or interesting."[2] So impressed was McClelland by Leonard that he accepted his book on the spot.

Poets are not especially known for their salesman skills, but Leonard worked his book like a pro. He even instructed the publisher how it should be packaged and marketed. Instead of the usual slim hardback that poetry tended to come in—which was nice for pressing flowers in but expensive to print and therefore to buy—his should be a cheap colorful paperback, said Leonard, and he offered to design it. "I want an audience," he wrote in a letter to McClelland. "I am not interested in the Academy." He wanted to make his work accessible to "inner-directed adolescents, lovers in all degrees of anguish, disappointed Platonists, pornography-peepers, hair-handed monks and Popists, French-Canadian intellectuals, unpublished writers, curious musicians etc., all that holy following of my Art."[3] In all, a pretty astute, and remarkably enduring, inventory of his fan base.

Leonard was sent a list of revisions and edits and given a tentative publication date of March 1960, but the date passed.

In the same month, Leonard was in the East End of London, walking to the tube station from the dental surgery where Mrs. Pullman worked, where he had just had a wisdom tooth pulled. It was raining—Leonard would say "it rained almost every day in London," which sounds about right—but, that day, it rained even more heavily than usual, that cold, sideways, winter rain in which England specializes. He took shelter in a nearby building, which turned out to be a branch of the Bank of Greece. Leonard could not fail to notice that the teller wore a pair of sunglasses and had a tan. The man told Leonard that he was Greek and had recently been home; the weather, he said, was lovely there at this time of year.

There was nothing to keep Leonard in London. He had no project to complete or promote, which left him not only free but also vulnerable to the depression that the short, dark days of a London winter are so good at inducing. On his application for the Canada Council grant, Leonard had said he would go to all the old capitals—Athens, Jerusalem and Rome, as well as London. On Hampstead High Street he stopped in at a travel agent's and bought tickets to Israel and Greece.

Survival, in discussions of the mystery and motivations of Leonard Cohen, has tended to be left in the corner clutching an empty dance card while writers head for the more alluring sex, God and depression and haul them around the dance floor. There is no argument that between them these three have been a driving force in his life and work. But what served Leonard best was his survival instinct. Leonard had an instinct for self-protection that not all writers—or lovers, or depressives, or spiritual seekers, or any of those creative types that nature or nurture made raw and sensitive—possess. Leonard was a lover, but when it comes to survival he was also a fighter.

When Leonard's father died, what the nine-year-old boy wanted to keep of his was a knife and a service revolver; when Leonard was fourteen, the first story of his ever published (in his high school yearbook) bore the title "Kill or be Killed." Yes, young boys like guns and gangsters, and small Jewish boys who grow up during World War II have even more layers to add to the general chromosomal bias, but Leonard definitely has a fighting spirit. Asked who his hero was, he rattled off the names of spiritual leaders and poets—Roshi, Ramesh Balsekar, Lorca, Yeats—adding the caveat, "I admire many men and women but it's the designation 'hero' that I have difficulty with, because that implies some kind of reverence that is somewhat alien to my nature." But the following day Leonard sent an e-mail, having thought about the question. His message said, without qualification this time:

> i forgot
> my hero is muhammad ali
> as they say about the Timex in their ads
> takes a lickin'
> keeps on tickin'[4]

Leonard still is a fighter. Some years after this correspondence, when Leonard, in his seventies, discovered that his former manager had bled his retirement account dry, he dusted off his suit, put on his hat and set off around the world to win his fortune back. But the gods conspired to give him an instinct for flight as well as fight. When it came to survival, Leonard would often turn to the first of the two for, as he put it, "the health of my soul."[5]

Leonard was not entirely joking when he spoke about having had a "messianic" childhood. From an early age he had a strong sense that he was going to do something special and an expectation that he would "grow into manhood leading other men."[6] He had also known from an early age that he would be a writer—a serious writer. Of all the trades a sensitive and depressive man could follow, few are more hazardous than being a serious writer. Acting? Actors are on the front line, yes, but most of the damage occurs during auditions. Once they land a role, they have a mask to hide behind. But writing is about uncovering. "Not I, but the poet discovered the unconscious," said Freud, through what an analyst's analyst would recognize as the gritted teeth of envy. It's about allowing the mind to be as noisy and chaotic as it wants and leaping into the dark depths of this pandemonium in the hope of surfacing with something ordered and beautiful. The life of a serious writer requires long periods of solitary confinement; the life of a writer as serious, meticulous, self-critical and liable to depression as Leonard means solitary confinement in one's own personal Turkish prison, cornered by black dogs.

During childhood he had the comfort and kindness of women for protection. In his youth he had come to depend on having a community of like-minded, mostly (but not exclusively) male friends. He had no problem with leaving one place and moving to another—he traveled light and wasted little time on sentimentality. But wherever he lived, he liked to surround himself with a clan of fellow-thinkers: people who could hold a conversation, could hold a drink and knew how to hold their silence when he needed to be left alone to write. Athens couldn't provide that. But an acquaintance in London, Jacob Rothschild (the future fourth Baron Rothschild, young scion of a celebrated Jewish banking family), whom he had met at a party, had talked about a small Greek island named Hydra. Rothschild's mother, Barbara Hutchinson, was about to be remarried to a celebrated Greek painter named Nikos Hadjikyriakos-Ghikas, who had a mansion there. Rothschild suggested that Leonard go and visit them. The island's small population included a colony of artists and writers from around the globe. Henry Miller had lived there at the start of World War II and written in *The Colossus of Maroussi* about its "wild and naked perfection."

After leaving London, Leonard stopped first in Jerusalem. It was his first time in Israel. By day he toured the ancient sites and at night he went to Café Kasit in Tel Aviv, the haunt of "everybody that thought they were a writer."[7] Here he met the Israeli poet Natan Zach, who invited him to stay at his house. After a few days, Leonard took a plane to Athens. He stayed in the city one day, during which he saw the Acropolis. In the evening he took a cab to Piraeus and checked into a hotel down by the docks. Early the next morning, Leonard boarded a ferry to Hydra. In 1960, before they started using hydrofoils, it was a five-hour journey. But there was a bar on board. Leonard took his drink up on deck and sat in the sun, staring out at the rumpled blue sheet of sea, the smooth blue blanket of sky, as the ferry chugged slowly past the islands scattered like a broken necklace across the Aegean.

As soon as he set eyes on Hydra, in the distance, before the ferry even entered the port, Leonard liked it. Everything about it looked right: the natural, horseshoe-shaped harbor, the whitewashed buildings on the steep hills surrounding it. When he took off his sunglasses and squinted into the sun, the island looked like a Greek amphitheater, its houses like white-clad elders sitting upright in the tiers. The doors of the houses all faced down to the port, which was the stage on which a very ordinary drama unfolded: boats bobbing lazily on the water, cats sleeping on the rocks, young men unloading the day's catch of fish and sponges, old men tanned like leather sitting outside the bars arguing and talking. When Leonard walked through the town, he noticed that there were no cars. Instead there were donkeys, with a basket hung on either side, lumbering up and down the steep cobblestone streets between the port and the Monastery of the Prophet Elijah. It might have been an illustration from a children's Bible.

The place appeared to have been organized according to some ancient ideal of harmony, symmetry and simplicity. The island had just one real town, which was named, simply, Hydra Town. Its inhabitants had come to a tacit decision that just two basic colors would suffice—blue (the sea and the sky) and white (the houses, the sails and the seagulls circling over the fishing boats). "I really did feel I'd come home," Leonard said later. "I felt the village life was familiar, although I'd had no experience with village life."[8] What might have also given Hydra its feeling of familiarity was that it was the nearest thing Leonard had experienced to the utopia he and Mort used to discuss as boys in urban Montreal. It was sunny and warm and it was populated by writers, artists and thinkers from around the world.

The village chiefs of the expat community were George Johnston and Charmian Clift. Johnston, forty-eight years old, was a handsome Australian journalist who had been a war correspondent during World War II. Charmian, thirty-seven, also a journalist, was his attractive second wife. Both had written books and wanted to devote themselves to writing full-time. Since they had two children (a third arrived later), this necessitated finding a place to live where life was cheap but congenial. In 1954 they discovered Hydra. The couple were great self-mythologizers and natural leaders. They held court at Katsikas, a grocery store on the waterfront whose back room, with perfect Hydran simplicity, doubled as a small café and bar. The handful of tables outside overlooking the water made the ideal spot for the expats to gather and wait for the ferry, which arrived at noon, bringing the mail—all of them seemed to be waiting for a check—and a new batch of people, to watch, to talk to, or to take to bed. On a small island with few telephones and little electricity, therefore no television, the ferry provided their news and entertainment, and their contact with the outside world.

Leonard met George and Charmian almost as soon as he arrived. He was not the first young man they had seen walking from the port, carrying a suitcase and a guitar, but they took to him immediately, and he to them. Like Irving and Aviva Layton, George and Charmian were colorful, charismatic and antibourgeois. They had also been doing for years what Leonard had wanted to do, which was live as a writer without the necessity of taking regular work. They had very little money but on Hydra they could get by on it, even with three children to provide for, and the life they were living was by no means impoverished. They lunched on sardines fresh off the boat, washed down with retsina—which old man Katsikas let them put on a tab—and seemed to glow in the warmth and sun. Leonard accepted their invitation to stay the night. The next day they helped him rent one of the many empty houses on the hill and donated a bed, a chair and table and some pots and pans.

Although he had been brought up with so much, Leonard was happy with very little. He thrived in the Mediterranean climate. Every morning he would rise with the sun, just as the local workmen did, and start his work. After a few hours' writing he would walk down the narrow, winding streets, a towel flung over one shoulder, to swim in the sea. While the sun dried his hair, he walked to the market to buy fresh fruit and vegetables and climbed back up the hill. It was cool inside the old house. He would sit writing at George and Charmian's wooden table until it was too dark to see by the kerosene lamps and candles. At night he walked back again to the port, where there was always someone to talk to.

The ritual, routine and sparsity of this life satisfied him immensely.

It felt monastic somehow, except this was a monk with benefits; the Hydra arts colony had beaten the hippies to free love by half a decade. Leonard was also a monk who observed the Sabbath. On Friday nights he would light the candles and on Saturday, instead of working, he would put on his white suit and go down to the port to have coffee.

One afternoon, toward the end of the long, hot summer, a letter arrived by ferry for Leonard. It told him that his grandmother had died, leaving him $1,500. He already knew what he would do with it. On September 27, 1960, days after his twenty-sixth birthday, Leonard bought a house on Hydra. It was plain and white, three stories high, two hundred years old, one of a cluster of buildings on the saddle between Hydra Town and the next little village, Kamini. It was a quiet spot, if not entirely private—if he leaned out of the window he could almost touch the house across the alley, and he shared his garden wall with the neighbor next door. The house had no electricity, nor even plumbing—a cistern filled in spring when the rains came, and when that ran out he had to wait for the old man who came past his house every few days with a donkey weighted on both sides with containers of water. But the house had thick white walls that kept heat out in summer, a fireplace for the winter and a large terrace where Leonard smoked, birds sang and cats skulked in the hope that one might fall from its perch. A priest came and blessed the house, holding a burning candle above the front door and making a black cross in soot. An elderly neighbor, Kiria Sophia, came in early every morning to wash the dishes, sweep the floors, do his laundry, look after him. Leonard's new home gave him the pure pleasure of a child.

"One of the things I wanted to mention and which a lot of people haven't caught," says Steve Sanfield, a longtime close friend of Leonard, "is really how important those Greece years and the Greek sensi-

bility were to Leonard and his development and the things he carries
with him. Leonard likes Greek music and Greek food, he speaks
Greek pretty well for a foreigner, and there's no rushing with Leonard, it's, 'Well, let's have a cup of coffee and we'll talk about it.' He
and I both carry *komboloi*—Greek worry beads; only Greek men do
that. The beads have nothing to do with religion at all—in fact one of
the Ancient Greek meanings of the word is 'wisdom beads,' indicating that men once used them to meditate and contemplate."

Sanfield's friendship with Leonard began fifty years ago. He is
the "Steve" described in Leonard's poem "I See You on a Greek
Mattress" (from the 1966 book *Parasites of Heaven*), sitting in Leonard's house on Hydra, smoking hash and throwing the I Ching, and
the "great haiku master" named in Leonard's poem "Other Writers" (from the 2006 collection *Book of Longing*). He is also the man
who would introduce Leonard to his Zen master, Roshi Joshu Sasaki.
In 1961, when Sanfield boarded a ferry in Athens and, on a whim,
alighted at Hydra, he was "a young poet seeking adventure." Like
Leonard, he "fell in love" with the place. The people he met in the
bar at the port told him, "Wait until you meet Leonard Cohen, you're
both young Jewish poets, you'll like him." He did.

Sanfield's memories of Hydra are of light, sun, camaraderie, the
voluptuous simplicity of life and the special energy that emanated
from its community of artists and seekers. It was a small community, around fifty in number, although people would come and go.
The mainstays, the Johnstons, he says, "were vital in all of our lives.
They fought a lot, they sought revenge on each other a lot with their
sexuality, and things got very complicated, but they were really the
center of foreign life in the port." Among the other residents were
Anthony Kingsmill, a British painter, raconteur, and bon vivant, to
whom Leonard became close; Gordon Merrick, a former Broadway
actor and reporter whose first novel, *The Strumpet Wind*, about a gay
American spy, was published in 1947; Dr. Sheldon Cholst, an Ameri-

can poet, artist, radical and psychiatrist who set his flag somewhere between Timothy Leary and R. D. Laing; and a young Swedish author named Göran Tunström, who was writing his first novel and was the model for the character Lorenzo in Axel Jensen's 1961 novel *Joacim* (although many still believe Lorenzo was based on Leonard).

"A lot of people came through in those early years," says Sanfield, "like Allen Ginsberg and Gregory Corso"—the latter of whom was living on the neighboring island, coaching a softball team. Leonard met Ginsberg on a trip to Athens. Leonard was drinking a coffee in Saint Agnes Square when he spotted the poet at another table. "I went up to him, asked him if he was indeed Allen Ginsberg, and he came over and sat down with me and then he came and stayed in my house on Hydra, and we became friends. He introduced me to Corso," said Leonard, "and my association with the Beats became a little more intimate."[9]

Hydra in the early sixties was, according to Sanfield, "a golden age of artists. We weren't beatniks, and the hippies hadn't been invented yet, and we thought of ourselves as kind of international bohemians or travelers, because people came together from all over the world with an artistic intent. There was an atmosphere there that was very exciting and I think touched everyone who was there. There were revolutions going on in literature, and there was the sexual revolution, which we thought we'd won and we probably lost, and a number of us—George Lialios, Leonard and myself—began to examine different spiritual paths like Tibetan Buddhism and the I Ching."

George Lialios was a significant figure in Leonard's life on the island. Nine years older than Leonard, with a thick black mustache, bushy beard and bright, piercing eyes, he owned a seventeen-room mansion at the top of the hill. "He was a remarkable man and a mysterious man," says Sanfield, by various people's accounts a philosopher, a musician, a semiaristocrat and an intellectual. Lialios himself says that he was "from Patras, born in Munich, both parents Greek, the family returned to Athens from Germany in 1935. Studied law, did three years' military service during the so-called civil war, then followed studies of music and composition in Vienna, 1951–1960. An inclination toward philosophy is correct." His Greek father had been a composer and a diplomat who was in Germany during World War II. George was fluent in Greek as well as in German and English. Leonard spent many evenings on Hydra with Lialios, mostly at Leonard's house. Sometimes they would have deep conversations. Often they did not talk at all. They would sit together in silence in Leonard's barely furnished, white-walled room, much as Leonard would with Roshi in years to come.

Another expat islander who played a part in Leonard's life was Axel Jensen. A lean, intense Norwegian writer in his late twenties, he had already published three novels, one of which was made into a movie. The house where Jensen lived with his wife, Marianne, and their young child, also named Axel, was at the top of Leonard's hill. Sanfield stayed in the Jensens' house when he first arrived on Hydra; the family had rented it out while they were away. Its living room was carved out of the rock of the hillside. There were copies of the I Ching and *The Tibetan Book of the Dead* on the bookshelves.

When Marianne came back to the island, her husband was not with her. "She was the most beautiful woman I'd ever known," says Sanfield. "I was stunned by her beauty and so was everyone else." Leonard included. "She just glowed," said Sanfield, "this Scandinavian goddess with this little blond-haired boy, and Leonard was this dark Jewish guy. The contrast was striking."

Leonard had fallen in love with Hydra from the moment he saw it. It was a place, he said, where "everything you saw was beautiful, every corner, every lamp, everything you touched, everything." The same thing happened when he first saw Marianne. "Marianne," he wrote in a letter to Irving Layton, "is perfect."[10]

———

"It must be very hard to be famous. Everybody wants a bit of you," Marianne Ihlen says with a sigh. There were muses before Marianne in Leonard's poetry and song and there have been muses since, but if there were a contest, the winner, certainly the people's choice, would be Marianne. Only two of Leonard's nonmusician lovers have had their photographs on his album sleeves and Marianne was the first. On the back of the naked, intimate *Songs from a Room*, Leonard's second album, there she sat, in a plain white room, at his simple wooden writing table, her fingers brushing his typewriter, her head turned to smile shyly at the camera and wearing nothing but a small white towel. For many of the young people seeing that picture for the first time in 1969—a troubled year, particularly for young people—it captured a moment and a need and longing that has gnawed at them ever since.

Marianne at seventy-five years old has a kind, round face, deeply etched with lines. Like Leonard, she does not enjoy talking about herself but is too considerate to say no; one might imagine that is how she ended up with a Norwegian-language book about her life with Leonard, after agreeing to do an interview for a radio documentary.* She is as modest and apologetic about her English, which is very good, as she once was about her looks. Despite having been a model, she could never understand why Leonard would say she was the most beautiful woman he'd ever met. Fifty-three years before, "twenty-two, blond, young, naïve and in love," to the chagrin of her traditional Oslo family she had run off with Jensen, traveled around Europe, bought an old Volkswagen in Germany and driven it to Athens. An old woman invited them to stay and let them leave their car in her overgrown garden while they took a trip around the islands. On the ferry they met a fat, handsome Greek named Papas who lived in California, where he had a candy and cookie company that bore his name. They told him they were looking for an island. "He told us to get off at the first stop; it was Hydra."

---

* *So Long, Marianne: Ei Kjaerleikshistorie* by Kari Hesthamar.

It was mid-December, cold and raining hard. There was one café open at the port and they ran for it. It was neon-lit inside and warmed by a stove in the middle of the room. As they sat shivering beside it, a Greek man who spoke a little English came over. He told them of another foreign couple living on the island—George Johnston and Charmian Clift—and offered to take them to their house. And so it all began. Axel and Marianne rented a small house—no electricity, outside toilet—and stayed, Axel writing, Marianne taking care of him. When the season changed, Hydra came alive with visitors, and the two poor, young, beautiful Norwegians found themselves invited to cocktail parties in the mansions of the rich; Marianne recalls, "One of the first people that we met was Aristotle Onassis." During their time on Hydra, people of every kind drifted by. "There were couples, writers, famous people, homosexuals, people with lots of money who didn't have to work, young people on their way to India and coming from India, people running away from something or searching for something." And there was Leonard.

Much had happened in Marianne's life in the three years between her arrival on Hydra and Leonard's. She and Axel had broken up, made up, then married. With the advance for his third novel, they bought an old white house on top of the hill at the end of the Road to the Wells. When the rains came, the street became a river that rushed like rapids over the cobblestones down to the sea. Her life with Axel was turbulent. The locals talked about Axel's heavy drinking, how when he was drunk he would climb up the statue in the middle of the port and dive from the top, headfirst. Marianne, they said, was a hippie and an idealist. She was also pregnant. She went back to Oslo to give birth. When she returned to Hydra with their first child, a boy they named for her husband, she found Axel packing, getting ready to leave with an American woman he told Marianne he had fallen in love with. In the midst of all this, Leonard showed up.

She was shopping at Katsikas's when a man in the doorway said, "Will you come and join us? We're sitting outside." She could not see who it was—he had the sun behind him—but it was a voice, she says, that "somehow leaves no doubt what he means. It was direct and calm, honest and serious, but at the same time a fantastic sense of humor." She came out to find the man sitting at a table with George and Charmian, waiting for the boat with the mail. He was dressed in khaki trousers and a faded green shirt, "army colors," and the cheap brown sneakers they sold in Greece. "He looked like a gentleman, old-fashioned—but we were both old-fashioned," says Marianne. When she looked at his eyes, she knew she "had met someone very special. My grandmother, who I grew up with during the war, said to me, 'You are going to meet a man who speaks with a tongue of gold, Marianne.' At that moment she was right."

They did not become lovers immediately. "Though I loved him from the moment we met, it was a beautiful, slow movie." They started meeting in the daytime, Leonard, Marianne and little Axel, to go to the beach. Then they would walk back to Leonard's house, which was much closer than her own, for lunch and a nap. While Marianne and the baby slept, Leonard would sit watching them, their bodies sunburned, their hair white as bone. Sometimes he would read her his poems. In October, Marianne told Leonard that she was going back to Oslo; her divorce proceedings were under way. Leonard told her he would go with her. The three took the ferry to Athens and picked up her car, and Leonard drove them from Athens to Oslo, more than two thousand miles. They stopped off in Paris for a few days en route. Marianne remembers feeling like she was cracking up. Leonard, in turn, recalled "a feeling I think I've tried to re-create hundreds of times, unsuccessfully; just that feeling of being grown up, with somebody beautiful that you're happy to be beside, and all the world is in front of you, where your body is suntanned and you're going to get on a boat."[11]

From Oslo, Leonard flew to Montreal. If he was to stay on his Greek island, cheap as it was, he needed more money. From his rented apartment on Mountain Street he wrote to Marianne telling her of all his schemes. He had applied for another grant from the Canada Council and was confident of getting it. He was also "working very hard," he said, on some TV scripts with Irving Layton. "Our collaboration is perfect. We want to turn the medium into a real art form. If we begin selling them, and I think we will, there will be a lot of money. And once we make our contacts," he wrote, "we can write the plays anywhere." They'd talked about writing years ago, Leonard and Layton, when they sat on the couch with Aviva, watching TV, improvising their own dialogue and scribbling it down on yellow legal pads. Layton was in much the same bind as Leonard, having been fired from his teaching job for one revolutionary comment too far, so they were pursuing the project with particular enthusiasm. "Irving and I think that with three months of intense work we can make enough to last us at least a year. That gives us nine months for pure poetry," Leonard wrote. As for his second book of poetry, *The Spice-Box of Earth*, that would be published in the spring; the publicity might help them sell the screenplays. There would be a book tour too, he said, and he wanted Marianne to come with him. "Mahalia Jackson is on the record player, I'm right there with her, flying with you in that glory, pulling away the shrouds from the sun, making music out of everything." Man, he wrote a mean letter. The telegram he sent was shorter but equally effective: "Have a flat. All I need is my woman and her child." Marianne packed two suitcases and flew with little Axel to Montreal.[12]

Six

Enough of Fallen Heroes

It was not easy for Marianne in Montreal. But then, it had not been too easy anywhere for Marianne after one Axel arrived and the other Axel left. Marianne loved Leonard and loved Montreal and got along well with his mother, whom she describes as "a beautiful, strong woman, who was sweet to me and the child." But she knew no one in Montreal and had nothing to do, besides look after her son. Leonard on the other hand seemed to know everyone and had plenty to do. He and Irving Layton had completed two TV plays, *Enough of Fallen Heroes* and *Lights on the Black Water* (later retitled *Light on Dark Water*), which they submitted along with a play Leonard had written alone, titled *Trade*. They waited expectantly for the dollars and praise they were convinced would arrive by return of post. Nothing came.

Beauty at Close Quarters, the novel Leonard had written in London, fared little better. The editors at McClelland & Stewart, as Leonard reported in a letter he sent the writer and critic Desmond Pacey, judged it "disgusting," "tedious" and "a protracted love-affair with himself."[1] Jack McClelland appeared to be confused as to what his golden-boy poet had sent him; was it an autobiography? Leonard answered that everything in the book had happened in real life bar one incident (the death of the boy at the summer camp in part 2), but that the protagonist, Lawrence Breavman, wasn't Leonard. He and Breavman "did a lot of the same things," he wrote, "but we reacted differently to them and so we became different men."[2] McClelland rejected the novel but remained enthusiastic about Leonard's second volume of poetry. *The Spice-Box of Earth* had been scheduled for publication in the spring of 1961. On March 30, the galleys were at the publisher's, ready for Leonard to look at. Only Leonard wasn't in Canada, he was in Miami, boarding a plane to Havana.

It is no great surprise that Leonard should have wanted to see Cuba. Lorca, his favorite poet, had spent three months there when the country was America's playground, calling it "a paradise" and extolling its virtues and vices.[3] The recent revolution had made it even more irresistible to Leonard, with his interest in socialism, war and utopias. What was puzzling about the trip was the timing. Leonard had gone to Montreal to make money, not spend it; after a two-year wait his second book was at last coming out, with its attendant publicity; and he was leaving behind the woman who had only recently, at his behest, moved continents to be with him. It was a dangerous time to visit too. Relations between America and Cuba had been tense since Castro's forces ousted the U.S.-friendly Batista government. When Leonard checked into his room in the Hotel Siboney in Havana, Castro and President Kennedy were in a face-off. There was talk of war. But this only added to the attraction.

So, you went there looking for a war?

"*Yes, I did. Just because of the sense of cowardice that drives people to contradict their own deepest understanding of their own natures, they put themselves in dangerous situations.*"

As a test?

"*A kind of test, and hoping for some kind of contradiction about your own deepest conviction.*"

Sounds like a male thing.

"*Yeah. A stupid male treat.*"

In Havana Leonard dressed as a revolutionary soldier: baggy, mud-green trousers; khaki shirt; beret. In tribute to Che Guevara, he grew a beard. It was an incongruous look. In one of four poems Leonard wrote in Cuba, he described himself, with some justification, as the sole tourist in Havana ("The Only Tourist in Havana Turns His Thoughts Homeward" in *Flowers for Hitler*). In the song he wrote twelve years later about his Cuban experiences, "Field Commander Cohen," he described himself, with no justification whatever, as

our most important spy
wounded in the line of duty
parachuting acid into diplomatic cocktail parties.

He also began work on a new novel, to which he gave the title *The Famous Havana Diary*.

Two years into the new regime, the city was already fraying at the edges. There were broken windows in the modern offices of downtown Havana and cracks in the concrete through which weeds grew. The grand colonial houses where millionaires once lived were now home to peasants whose goats chewed lazily at brown stubble recognizable only to professional botanists as having once been lawn. But despite Castro's having overturned the moneylenders' tables, closed the casinos, rounded up the hookers and sent them off for retraining, there was still a nightlife in Havana and plenty of women to be found. Leonard found them. He drank into the early hours of the morning at La Bodeguita del Medio, one of Hemingway's favorite bars, and, following his routine in Montreal, New York and London, wandered the alleys of the old town, a notebook in one pocket, a hunting knife in the other.

Leonard spoke in an interview a year later of his "deep interest in violence." "I was very interested in what it really meant for a man to carry arms and kill other men," he said, "and how attracted I was exactly to that process. That's getting close to the truth. The real truth is I wanted to kill or be killed."[4] There was not much violence or killing to be had, but he did succeed in getting arrested by a small troop of armed Cuban soldiers on a day trip to the seaside town of Varadero. Dressed in his army fatigues, he was taken for part of an American invasion force. After finally persuading them of his Canadian-ness, his socialist credentials and his support for Cuban independence, he posed smiling with two of his captors for a photograph, which they gave him as a souvenir.

Like a good tourist, Leonard wrote postcards. In the card he sent Jack McClelland, he joked about how good it would be for publicity if he should be killed in Cuba. He sent three cards to Irving Layton, including one with a picture of Munch's *The Scream* and a quip about another man who had fled from a woman, screaming. If this was a reference to himself and Marianne it was a curious one, since it was he who had asked her to come to Montreal, and their relationship was not over. But if Leonard sometimes appeared to court domesticity, he also ran from it. It was so much more exquisite to long for somebody than to have her there beside him.

On April 15 a group of eight Cubans exiled in the U.S. led bomber raids on three Cuban airfields. A couple of days later, late at night, writing at the table beside the window in the room of his Havana hotel, Leonard was surprised by a knock at the door. In the corridor was a man wearing a dark suit. He told Leonard that his "presence was urgently requested at the Canadian embassy."[5] Leonard, still in his military khakis, accompanied the official; finally, Field Commander Cohen was being called to action.

At the embassy, Leonard was led into the vice consul's office. The vice consul did not seem impressed to see him. He told Leonard, "Your mother's very worried about you."[6] Having heard the reports of the bomb attacks and talk of war, Masha got on the phone to a cousin, a Canadian senator, and urged him to call the embassy in Cuba and have them track Leonard down and send him home. Of all the reasons for this summons that had gone through Leonard's mind on the drive to the embassy, this was not one of them. At twenty-six years old he was long past the age of having his mother tug at his leash. At the same time he was rather on the old side for swashbuckling and dressing up. It was understandable that Masha would be concerned; war held little romance for her, since she had witnessed one and nursed one wounded veteran, Leonard's father. But Leonard chose to stay.

He was in Havana on the day of the Bay of Pigs invasion, April 17, 1961. From his hotel room he could hear antiaircraft fire and see troops running through the streets. He did not leave the city until April 26. Although he admired the revolutionaries and had seen many happy Cubans, he had also seen the long lines of people waiting anxiously outside police headquarters, trying to get news of relatives who had been rounded up by Castro's forces and imprisoned, artists and writers among them. Nothing was straightforward; "I felt that I was defending the island against an American invasion and planning that invasion at the same time," he said. "I was behind everything. I couldn't see the megalomania that made up my perspective at that time."[7] He admitted that he had "no faith" in his political opinions and that "they changed often," saying, "I was never really passionate about my opinions even back then." He was attracted to Communist ideas, but in much the same way as he was "attracted to the messianic ideas in the Bible," he said: "the belief in a human brotherhood, in a compassionate society, in people who lived for something more than their own guilt." He had gone to Cuba feeling "that the whole world was functioning for the benefit of [his] personal observation and education."[8] Having observed, it was time to leave.

José Martí Airport swarmed with foreign nationals trying to get a seat on one of the few planes out of Havana. Leonard joined one

long queue after another, finally procuring a ticket. When he stood
in the last line at the departure gate, he heard his name called. He
was wanted at the security desk. Officials had gone through his bag
and found the photograph in which he posed with the revolutionary
soldiers. With his black hair and sun-darkened skin, perhaps they
thought he might have been a Cuban trying to escape. Leonard was
taken to a back room and left in the charge of a teenage guard with a
rifle. Leonard tried, unsuccessfully, to engage the young man in conversation. He told him he was Canadian and pleaded his case, but the
boy just looked bored—the kind of boredom that might possibly be
alleviated by shooting somebody. So Leonard sat quietly and stared
out of the window at the plane he was supposed to be on. All of a
sudden a tussle broke out on the runway. Armed guards rushed out
onto the tarmac, including Leonard's, who in his enthusiasm failed to
lock the door behind him. Leonard slipped out. Walking as calmly as
he could, he headed for the departure gate and, unchallenged, went
outside and up the steps into the plane.

———

Back in Canada, and back in civilian clothes, Leonard spent barely a
week in Montreal before taking off again, this time for Toronto. He
and Irving Layton had been invited to read at the Canadian Conference of the Arts on May 4. A clean-shaven Leonard read from *The
Spice-Box of Earth*. Three weeks later, at 599 Belmont Avenue, the
book was launched with a party over which Masha presided—a peace
offering to her from Leonard, perhaps, for the Cuban escapade.

   This was not the budget paperback Leonard had originally proposed to Jack McClelland but an elegant hardback, containing
eighty-eight poems. Six of them dated back to Leonard's Columbia
University days and had had their first printing in his literary magazine, *The Phoenix*. The book was dedicated jointly to the memory of
his maternal grandfather, Rabbi Kline, and his paternal grandmother,

Mrs. Lyon Cohen. On the dust jacket were comments from the literary critic H. N. Frye and the poet Douglas Lochhead, the first commenting that "his outstanding poetic quality, so far, is a gift for macabre ballad reminding one of Auden, but thoroughly original, in which the chronicles of tabloids are celebrated in the limpid rhythms of folksong," and the second describing Leonard's poetry as "strong, intense and masculine," with "a brawling spirit and energy." There was also a paragraph about Leonard that appeared to have been written by Leonard himself in the third person. It painted a romantic picture of the author, mentioning his trip to Cuba and the year he spent writing on a Greek island. He quoted himself saying, in his familiar partly humorous, partly truthful fashion, "I shouldn't be in Canada at all. I belong beside the Mediterranean. My ancestors made a terrible mistake. But I have to keep coming back to Montreal to renew my neurotic affiliations."[9] Clearly though, his roots were more important to him than that. He ended with an unexpected attack on the modern buildings that were taking over his favorite streets in Montreal. This might well have been ironic; Leonard knew his old neighborhood had more serious things to worry about, now that its grand residences had become the target of militant French separatists and mailbox bombs. But Leonard was genuinely fond of the old Victorian houses, and if, for now at least, he seemed to have soured on change, it was understandable so soon after his experience in Havana, where he saw for himself that life post-revolution was no less desperate than it had been before.

The position Leonard occupied on the conservative-modernist scale was an ambiguous one. A CBC TV presenter, curious to know where he thought he stood as a writer, asked Leonard if he considered himself a "modern poet." His answer was deflective. "I always describe myself as a writer rather than a poet, and the fact that the lines I write don't come to the end of the page doesn't qualify me as a poet. I think the term 'poet' is a very exalted term and should be applied to a man at the end of his work. When you look back over the body of his work and he has written poetry," Leonard said, "then let the verdict be that he's a poet."

The Spice-Box of Earth is the work of a major poet, profound, confident and beautifully written. The title makes reference to the ornate wooden box of fragrant spices used in the Jewish ceremony marking the end of the Sabbath and the beginning of the secular week, but this spice box is of earth. The poems dance back and forth across the border between the holy and the worldly, the elevated and the carnal. The opening poem, "A Kite Is a Victim," presents the poet as a man with some control over the heightened world but whose creative work is also subject to strictures and restraints, just as the kite, though it appears to fly freely, is tethered like a fish on a line. The poet makes a contract in the poem with both God and nature and keeps it throughout the book, which abounds in orchards, parks, rivers, flowers, fish, birds, insects. The killing of a man ("If It Were Spring") is romanticized through images from nature; "Beneath My Hands" likens Marianne's small breasts to upturned, fallen sparrows. In "Credo," the grasshoppers that rise from the spot where a man and his lover have just had sex leads to thoughts on biblical plagues. Sex and spirituality share a bed in several poems. In "Celebration," the orgasm from oral sex is likened to the gods falling when Samson pulled down their temples.

There are poems about lovers (Georgianna Sherman was the muse for "I Long to Hold Some Lady" and "For Anne," the latter singled out for praise by critics) and about angels, Solomon's adulterous wives and a sex doll made for an ancient king ("The Girl Toy"). Irving Layton, Marc Chagall and A. M. Klein are the subjects of other poems; Leonard's father and uncles appear in "Priests 1957." The masterful prose poem that ends the book, "Lines from My Grandfather's Journal," is one of three about Leonard's late grandfather. Rabbi Kline was a scholar and mystic, a holy man, a man of conviction; Leonard considered him the ideal Jew, someone who did not struggle with ambiguities as Leonard did. From Leonard's description of himself in "The Genius" ("For you / I will be a banker Jew . . . / For you / I will be a Broadway Jew," etc.) he was less sure what kind of Jew he was himself. And yet, in "Lines from My Grandfather's Journal," there are passages that might apply to Leonard as much as to his grandfather: "It is strange that even now prayer is my natural language. . . . The black, the loss of sun: it will always frighten me. It will always lead me to experiment. . . . O break down these walls with music. . . . Desolation means no angels to wrestle. . . . Let me never speak casually."

As in *Let Us Compare Mythologies*, there are poems that are called "songs." When Leonard became a songwriter, some of their content would be taken up in actual songs. Fans of his music will recognize King David and the bathing woman seen from the roof in "Before the Story" in the song "Hallelujah," the "turning into gold" in "Cuckold's Song" in the song "A Bunch of Lonesome Heroes," and the poem "As the Mist Leaves No Scar" as the song "True Love Leaves No Traces."

Critical reaction to *The Spice-Box of Earth* was for the most part very positive. Louis Dudek, who two years earlier had taken Leonard to task in print, applauded the volume unconditionally. Robert Weaver wrote in the *Toronto Daily Star* that Leonard was "probably the best young poet in English Canada right now."[10] Arnold Edinborough, reviewing for the *Canadian Churchman*, concurred, stating that Leonard had taken Irving Layton's crown as Canada's leading poet. Stephen Scobie would later describe the book in *The Canadian Encyclopedia* as the one that established Leonard's reputation as a lyric poet. There were a few barbs; David Bromige, in *Canadian Literature*, had problems with "the ornateness of the language" and felt that Leonard should "write less about love, and think about it longer," but concluded that "the afflictions mentioned here are curable, and once

Cohen has freed his sensibility from 'the thick glove of words' he will be able to sing as few of his contemporaries can."[11] The first edition of the book sold out in three months.

Looking back, it is curious to see how this mature, important book sat between two incongruously immature incidents. Just prior to publication there had been his adventure in Havana. Postpublication there was a stranger and even riskier episode, involving a junkie Beat novelist, a rescue mission and an opium overdose. Alexander Trocchi was a tall, charismatic Scotsman of Italian descent, nine years Leonard's senior. In the fifties he had moved into a cheap hotel in Paris, where he founded the literary magazine *Merlin*, published Sartre and Neruda, wrote pornographic novels and espoused his own Beat-meets-early-hippie interpretation of Situationism. An enthusiast for drugs, he turned his heroin addiction into Dadaist performance art; Trocchi, as Leonard would describe him in verse, was a "public junkie."

Trocchi moved to New York in 1956, the same year that Leonard went there to attend Columbia University, and took a job working on a tugboat on the Hudson River. He spent his nights, as Leonard did, in Greenwich Village, before taking over a corner of Alphabet City and founding the "Amphetamine University." "Trocchi and a bunch of his friends painted bits of driftwood, mainly, in psychedelic colors, really bright. With all this high-intensity speed going on, they were painting away in the most minute little detail," says the British author and sixties counterculture figure Barry Miles. "Allen Ginsberg took Norman Mailer there because it was just amazing to see." In this drab, run-down part of the Lower East Side, it looked like somebody had bombed a rainbow. Trocchi named these artworks "futiques"— antiques of the future. It's easy to see why Leonard was drawn to Trocchi.

In the spring of 1961, still a cheerleader for heroin, Trocchi gave some to a sixteen-year-old girl. "He wasn't a dealer; he had this absurd, fairly sick thing that he just loved turning people on to smack," explains Miles, "but it was a capital offense in New York." Trocchi was arrested. Facing the possibility of the electric chair, or at least a very long prison term, he went on the run. Nancy Bacal, whom Leonard introduced to Trocchi when she was making a program for CBC about drug use in London, says, "Alex was a strange, brilliant, one-of-a-kind person. Leonard was extremely fond of him." Evidently so. Leonard arranged to meet Trocchi at the Canadian border, then took him to Montreal and put him up in his apartment. The Scotsman did not like to visit empty-handed; he brought some opium with him and set to cooking it up on Leonard's stove. When he was done, he handed Leonard the pan with the leftovers. Apparently he left a little too much. When they set off on foot to find a place to eat, Leonard collapsed as they crossed Saint Catherine Street. He had gone blind. Trocchi dragged him out of the way of the passing cars. They sat together on the curb until Leonard came round. He seemed none the worse for wear. For the next four days Leonard played host to Trocchi until someone—some say George Plimpton, others Norman Mailer—came up with false papers for Trocchi to travel by ship from Montreal to Scotland. Alighting in Aberdeen, Trocchi made his way to London, where he registered as a heroin addict with the National Health Service and obtained his drug legally.

In his poem "Alexander Trocchi, Public Junkie, Priez Pour Nous," which would appear in Leonard's third book of poetry, *Flowers for Hitler*, Leonard wrote of the outlaw he helped rescue,

> *Who is purer*
> *more simple than you? . . .*
> *I'm apt to loaf*
> *in a coma of newspapers . . .*
> *I abandon plans for bloodshed in Canada. . . .*
> *You are at work*

> *in the bathrooms of the city*
> *changing the Law . . .*
> *Your purity drives me to work.*
> *I must get back to lust and microscopes*

The Spice-Box of Earth, despite its excellence and acclaim, failed to win the Governor General's Literary Award for poetry. According to Irving Layton, this hurt Leonard; whatever else might not work out the way he might like, Leonard could at least rely on being the darling of the Canadian poetry world. Then the Canada Council came through like the cavalry with a grant of $1,000. In August 1961, Leonard was back in Greece, writing.

"It was a good place to work," says Mort Rosengarten, who stayed with Leonard on Hydra for two months. "It was very special—no electricity, no telephone, no water. It was beautiful and, back then, very inexpensive, so it was the best place for him to be to write. We had a nice routine. We would go to sleep about three in the morning but we'd get up very early, six A.M., and work till noon. I started drawing—in fact the first time I really started drawing was there; I'd studied sculpture but I'd never drawn or painted—and he also got me a bag of plaster so I made some sculptures. At noon we would go down to the beach and swim, then come back, have lunch at the port, and then we would go up to the house, have a siesta for a couple of hours and then start happy hour. It was very good—a lot of fun and very productive. Leonard worked his ass off. But I couldn't—I'm sure neither of us could—maintain that schedule."

Leonard had the assistance, or at least the companionship, of a variety of drugs. He had a particular liking for Maxiton, generically dexamphetamine, a stimulant known outside of pharmaceutical circles as speed. He also had a fondness for its sweet counterpoint Mandrax, a hypnotic sedative, part happy pill, part aphrodisiac, very popular in the UK. They were as handsome a pair of pharmaceuticals as a hardworking writer could wish to meet; better yet, in Europe they could still be bought over the counter. Providing backup was a three-part harmony of hashish, opium and acid (the last of these three still legal at that time in Europe and most of North America).

Mandrax I get, but speed? Your songs don't sound like they come from a man on amphetamines.

"Well, my processes, mental and physical, are so slow that speed brought me up to the normal tempo."

And acid and the psychedelics?

"Oh, I looked into it quite thoroughly."

As in studied or dropped a few?

"Of course. A lot more than a few. Fortunately it upset my system, acid—I credit my poor stomach for preventing me from entering into any serious addiction, although I kept on taking it because the PR for it was so prevalent. I took trip after trip, sitting on my terrace in Greece, waiting to see God, but generally I ended up with a very bad hangover. I have a lot of acid stories, as everyone does. At the side of my house there was a kind of garbage heap that during the spring would sprout thousands of daisies, and I was convinced that I had a special communion with the daisies. It seems they would turn their little yellow faces to me whenever I started singing or addressing them in a tender way. They would all turn toward me and smile."

Is there a Leonard Cohen acid song or poem?

"My novel Beautiful Loser had a bit of acid in it, and a lot of speed."

"Did he tell you about the writing on the wall?" asks Marianne. "It was in gold paint and it said, 'I change, I am the same, I change, I am the same, I change, I am the same, I change, I am the same.' I think it was beautiful." Steve Sanfield remembers that they "smoked a lot of hashish and began to use LSD and psychotropic drugs more as a spiritual path than recreational." There was a variety of paths to follow. Hydra, says Richard Vick, a British poet and musician who lived on the island, "always had the odd shaman who came and went and would be the feature of the winter, who would be into the tarot or sandbox play or something." The I Ching and *The Tibetan Book of the Dead* were popular. George Lialios was also investigating Buddhism and Jung.

Leonard continued to fast, as he had in Montreal. The discipline of a week of fasting appealed to him, as did the spiritual element of purging and purification and the altered mental state that it produced. Fasting focused his mind for writing, but there was vanity in it also; it kept his body thin and his face gaunt and serious (although the amphetamines helped with that too). There seemed to be a deep need in Leonard for self-abnegation, self-control and hunger. In *Beautiful Losers* he would write, "Please make me empty, if I'm empty then I can receive, if I can receive it means it comes from somewhere outside of me, if it comes from outside of me I'm not alone. I cannot bear this loneliness. . . . Please let me be hungry. . . . Tomorrow I begin my fast." The hunger he wrote of appeared to be all-encompassing. In the *Spice-Box of Earth* poem "It Swings Jocko," a bebop song to his prick, he wrote,

> *I want to be hungry,*
> *hungry for food,*
> *for love, for flesh.*

Leonard abstained from eating meat, but he was less restrained when it came to his appetite "for the company of women and the sexual expression of friendship."[12] Sit in a taverna by the harbor in Hydra long enough and you could compile quite a catalog of who slept with whom and marvel at the complexity of it all and that so little blood was spilled. You might hear a tale of a woman, an expat, so distressed when Leonard left on the ferry that she threw herself into the sea after it, even though she could not swim; the man who dived in and rescued her, they say, became her new partner. "Everyone was in everyone else's bed," says Richard Vick. Leonard too, although compared to other islanders he was, according to Vick, "very discreet as a whole." Vick recalls one evening in a bar in Kamini where he was drinking with his then-girlfriend and her female friend. Leonard and Marianne showed up. During the course of the evening it came out that both of the women with Vick knew Leonard intimately. The women, says Vick, told Leonard genially, "You know, Leonard, we were never in love with you." Leonard replied equally genially, "Well, me too." "Those were innocent times," remarks Vick, but they could be difficult for Marianne. "Yes, he was a ladies' man," says Marianne. "I could feel my jealousy arousing. Everybody wanted a bit of my man. But he chose to live with me. I had nothing to worry about." It did not stop her worrying, but she was not one to complain, and she loved him.

———

In March 1962, two years after he had left London for Hydra, Leonard made the return journey and moved back into Mrs. Pullman's boardinghouse in Hampstead. He had found a London publisher—Secker & Warburg—for the novel he had begun writing there. At the publishers' urging, he was in London to revise it. For someone who described the writing process as being "scraped" and "torn from his heart," the cutting and revising of a manuscript he thought finished was torturous. He wrote to Irving Layton about wielding "a big scalpel" and how he had "torn apart orchestras to arrive at my straight melodic line."[13] The operation was performed with the aid of amphetamines and the pain eased by Mandrax and hashish. But still, it was difficult going back over something he'd been happy with, like being locked in a room with an old love he had once considered beautiful but could now see only her flaws. He wrote to friends about his dark dreams, his panic and depression. The flat gray sky over London did not help. The King William IV pub was not the Bodeguita del Medio, and Hampstead wasn't Hydra. He wrote a letter to

Marianne telling her how much he longed for her. In his novel he wrote how "he needed to be by himself so he could miss her, to get perspective."

As he had during his last stay in London, Leonard spent time with Nancy Bacal, who had since moved out of the Pullmans' house. Through Bacal, he came to know an Afro-Caribbean man from Trinidad named Michael X. Like Trocchi, Michael X was a complex, charismatic and troubled man. "Leonard was fascinated with Michael," says Nancy Bacal. "Everyone was. He was an intriguing man, all things to all people. He was a poet and rabble-rouser and a charmer and a bullshitter and a lovely, joyous, marvelous man and a potentially dangerous man. And so Leonard was drawn to him, as I was obviously." Before Nancy and Michael X became lovers in 1962, Michael de Freitas, as he was then named, had been a hustler whose résumé included working as an enforcer for Peter Rachman, a London slum landlord so notoriously iron-fisted that his last name has entered the lexicon.* Over time, Michael de Freitas had amassed his own little empire of music clubs and hookers. But Michael X, the man Bacal lived with, was a civil rights activist, an articulate man and a bridge between London's black underground and the white proto-hippie community. Together, Michael and Nancy founded the London Black Power Movement. They "churned out pamphlets on Xerox machines aimed to change the world for the better." On this and subsequent trips to London, Leonard got to know Michael "very well." He, Nancy, Michael and Robert Hershorn, when he was in London, would spend evenings in Indian restaurants, deep in discussions about art and politics.

"Michael said to me he was completely against arming the blacks in America," Leonard told a journalist in 1974. "He said it was crazy,

---

* Rachman also made the newspapers as the owner of the house that served as the place of business of Christine Keeler and Mandy Rice Davies, the call girls who almost brought down the British government in 1963 in the Profumo Affair.

they would never be able to resist that machine. They own the bullets and the armaments factories and the guns. So you give the blacks a few guns and have them against armies? He was even against knives. He said we should use our teeth, something everybody has. That was his view of the thing. It was a different kind of subversion. The subversion of real life to implant black fear."[14] Leonard recalled going to Michael's house and complimenting him on a drink he'd given him. "God, how do you make this?" Leonard asked. Michael replied, "You don't expect me to tell you. If you know the secrets of our food, you know the secrets of our race and the secrets of our strength."

As Bacal says, "These were very outrageous times. It was as if everything was and wasn't political. You never knew how far it would go or how dangerous it would get or how effective it would be or if it was just another flower [power] episode. Michael was one of these people who might say something as a joke but you never really knew what was truth and what wasn't—which made him fascinating, because we don't really know in life what is truth and what is fabrication or a dream. He just lived like that, openly. It was very lively."*

Rather too lively as it turned out. In 1967, when things started getting too dark, Bacal left Michael. That same year, her former partner became the first black person to be imprisoned under Britain's Race Relations Act—a statute originally passed to protect immigrants from racism—after calling for the shooting of any black woman seen with a white man; Bacal is white. On his release from prison, now using the name Michael Abdul Malik, he founded a Black Power commune run from a storefront in North London, supported and funded by wealthy, often celebrated white people. John Lennon and Yoko Ono donated a bag of their hair to auction. Lennon also paid Michael's bail when he was arrested for murder. The killing took place in Trinidad, Michael's home country, where he

---

* Bacal is in the process of writing a memoir of this period, *A Different Story*.

had returned to start another revolutionary commune. Two of the commune's members, one the daughter of a British politician, were found hacked to death, reportedly for disobeying Michael's orders to attack a police station.

In London Michael X had told Leonard—perhaps in jest, perhaps not—that he planned to take over the government of Trinidad. When he did, he said, he would appoint Leonard minister of tourism. An odd office, you might think, to choose for Leonard; he might have made a better minister of arts. "I thought it was rather odd too," said Bacal, "but for some reason Leonard thought it was marvelous." In some ways Michael X had him nailed; from Michael's point of view, as a black man in London involved in revolutionary politics, Leonard was a tourist, just as he had been in Havana. "I remember them shaking hands on it," said Bacal. "Leonard was very, very pleased and happy, and that was the end of that story." The end of De Freitas/X/ Malik's story came in 1975, when he was hanged for murder. The Trinidad government ignored pleas for clemency from people in the U.S., UK and Canada, many of them celebrities. They included Angela Davis, Dick Gregory, Judy Collins and Leonard Cohen.

In London in 1962, Leonard continued to turn out pages for Stella Pullman. He stayed in London for as long as he could stand to—four months, which was four weeks more than he managed the first time. He did not quite finish the revisions to his novel, but he was making great inroads into a new book of poetry. By the summer he was back in his house on Hydra, playing host to his mother. Masha still fretted that her boy wasn't looking after himself, but this time, rather than send in the consulate, she decided to go there and check on him herself. Marianne and little Axel moved in with a friend for the duration of her visit. Although Masha knew Marianne in Montreal and was aware that she was living with Leonard, there was a strong sense that she would not have been comfortable being under the same roof with her son and his Scandinavian, non-Jewish girlfriend.

Forsaken by one woman who loved him—if only temporarily and with his collusion—and engulfed by another, Leonard was unable to write. Masha stayed with him for a month. When she left, Leonard returned gratefully, joyfully, to his life with Marianne, little Axel and his Olivetti, and finished the novel he had variously retitled *The Mist Leaves No Scar*, *No Flesh So Perfect*, *Fields of Hair*, *The Perfect Jukebox* and, finally, *The Favorite Game*.

Seven

Please Find Me,
I Am Almost 30

"A biography is considered complete," Virginia Woolf wrote in *Orlando*, "if it merely accounts for six or seven selves, whereas a person may well have as many thousand." True, if not words to warm the heart of a biographer. Autobiographers have it easy; they can stand in front of the mirror and wear any mask they fancy. *The Favorite Game* is a sort of autobiography, though more accurately it's a sort of biography. A sort of biography of Leonard Cohen written, and at the same time ghostwritten, by Leonard Cohen. It recounts Leonard's life from childhood to early manhood through an alter ego named Lawrence Breavman, who looks like Leonard and has (name changes aside) the same family, friends, lovers and accumulation of experiences, to which he may or may not have reacted in the exact same way as Leonard did. Or as Leonard believed, or might like to think he did, autobiography, even sort of autobiography, can be one of the most fictional of genres. First novels often have a good deal of autobiography, but to complicate matters further, *The Favorite Game* was not technically Leonard's first novel. Before that there was the unpublished *Ballet of Lepers*, the unfinished *Famous Havana Diary*, and all those unpublished or unfinished, to some degree, autobiographical short stories, stacked up like mirror-lined Leonard Cohen Russian dolls reflecting, and deflecting, ad infinitum.

It is a beautifully written book and very funny in a dark, wry, incisive, exuberant, erotic, self-aware, playful, Cohenesque kind of way. It opens with scars: scars of beauty (his lover's pierced ear), scars of war (his father's battle wound), the scar from a fight with a boyhood friend over aesthetics (the correct style for a snowman's clothes). And it ends with a scar, the indelible memory of a game he played as a child and the mark a body leaves in the snow. In between, our self-inflated yet self-mocking, scarred hero chronologically contends with his father's death, Jewish summer camp, the synagogue, sexual longing, getting laid, and becoming a writer—"blackening pages," possibly the debut of Leonard's much-used line to describe his work. Although it irked Leonard that some reviewers dealt with the book as if it were autobiography, not a work of art, and though the contents of the novel might not stand up in court, it still provides useful evidence on Leonard's life for a biographer tired of digging in the trenches, who fancies a few hours in a comfy chair in the ivory tower.

The unconventional form in which Leonard arranges his "life" resembles a film more than a novel—more specifically an art-house coming-of-age film and a buddy movie, in which Breavman/Leonard and Krantz/Mort play the "two Talmudists delighting in their dialectic, which was a disguise for love." Each chapter of his account of how his life led to his becoming the writer of this story is presented as a separate scene, which he scripts, directs, stars in, and at the same time observes from the back row, smiling, while perfectly executing the popcorn-box trick on the girl in the next seat.

The Favorite Game was published in September 1963 in the UK by Secker & Warburg, and in the U.S. the following year by Viking. Reviews on both sides of the Atlantic were positive. The U.S. *Saturday Review* described it as "interior-picaresque, extraordinarily rich in language, sensibility and humour." The *Guardian* newspaper in the UK called it "a song of a book, a lyrical and exploratory bit of semiautobiography." It even made it into Britain's esteemed *Times Literary Supplement*, earning a short yet favorable critique in an "Other New Novels" roundup. The Canadian writer Michael Ondaatje praised its "tightly edited, elliptical poetic style"[1] and pointed out connections with James Joyce's *Portrait of an Artist*. (There were indeed several, and Leonard did study Joyce at McGill University with Louis Dudek.) Some years later, writer T. F. Rigelhof made comparisons with Hungarian-Canadian writer Stephen Vizinczey's *In Praise of Older Women*, likewise "poignant, hilarious and erotically-charged." Both novels, Rigelhof wrote, "were too brave and unbridled for Jack McClelland."[2] McClelland might have been slow to warm to a book that would become a cult classic, but he was by no means conservative in his tastes. According to the writer and editor Dennis Lee, who later worked for him, McClelland was a flamboyant man, "a real wild man, who kept pace with some of the wilder writers he was publishing." If he had an issue with Leonard's book, it was less likely to be its sexual content than that it was not poetry, and he had signed Leonard, personally and at first sight, as a poet. McClelland did eventually publish *The Favorite Game*, seven years behind the British. Until that time, Leonard's first novel was available in Canada only on import.

Still, life continued to lead Leonard back to Montreal, as it would for periods in the early and midsixties. "We didn't have any money so he went to Montreal. He left because he had to," said Marianne, who mostly stayed behind on Hydra, "not because he wanted to. He had to make money." The checks that arrived for him on the ferry rarely amounted to more than $20 at a time. Marianne helped out where she could. She sold her house at the top of the hill, took modeling assignments, and, when the annual dividend arrived from a small inheritance she had, she paid the tab that they had run up at Katsika's. Leonard and Marianne did not spend much on themselves, but there was the child to feed and clothe. They simply did not have enough. So, in order to keep the dream alive of living as a writer on an island for another year, Leonard hustled for money in Montreal. It became an increasingly tiring enterprise. It did not help when, in 1964, George Johnston and Charmian Clift, the first to show Leonard the possibility of leading such a life, decided to leave Hydra and move back to Australia. Johnston's latest book, *My Brother Jack*, was a bestseller—something that all the expat writers were hoping for to solve their financial problems.* But Johnston, in his fifties now, was suffering from tuberculosis. He wanted to go home for medical treatment and to capitalize on his success.

Leonard, no youngster himself by the standards of the sixties with his thirtieth birthday approaching, soldiered on, applying for grants and taking the odd job. He looked into the possibility of selling movie rights to *The Favorite Game*, but there were no takers until 2003, when the Canadian filmmaker Bernar Hébert made a film of it, curiously turning it into more of a conventional narrative on-screen than it was in the novel. Leonard also approached a Montreal book dealer with his archive of manuscripts, this time with more success. In 1964 the director of the Thomas Fisher Rare Book Library at the University of Toronto, Marian Brown, purchased the first of its collection of the Cohen papers.

It would be wrong though to picture Leonard plodding woefully through his hometown, black cloud above his head, begging bowl in hand. Although he often felt the need to escape from Montreal, he loved the place. Montreal for Leonard was much like Dublin was to

---

* Leonard was responsible for the title, according to Aviva Layton. "George said, 'I just don't know what to call it.' Leonard said, 'What's it about?' He said, 'My brother Jack,' Leonard said, 'There you are.'"

Joyce. He immersed himself in the city, luxuriating in the company of friends. Lovers also. Leonard was devoted to women, and they returned the sentiment in numbers that increased with his renown. As Leonard saw it, he had slaved for years trying to write "the perfect sonnet to attract the girl,"[3] then he had looked up from his "blackened pages" to find that women were making themselves sexually available. It had happened on Hydra, and now it was happening in Montreal. "It was terrific," he said. "It was a moment where everybody was giving to the other person what they wanted. The women knew that's what the men wanted."[4] Asked whether having so much of what he wanted devalued it for him, he said, "Nobody gets the right amount in terms of what they think their appetite deserves. But it lasted just a few moments, and then it was back to the old horror story. . . . I'll give you this if you give me that. You know, sealing the deal: what do I get, what do you get. It's a contract."[5] Leonard did not like contracts. He did not have one with McClelland; it was a handshake, a gentleman's agreement. It was not a question of loyalty for Leonard but of having freedom, control and an escape hatch.

Leonard had rented a furnished duplex in the west of Montreal, an old stagecoach house. Once again Marianne flew out to join him. The house was within walking distance of McGill University, and on warm days Leonard would go there and sit in the spot in front of the Arts Building where the grass curved down like a bowl and where people played guitar and sang. It was here that Erica Pomerance first saw him. Like most McGill art students, she knew who Leonard was and counted herself among the "circle of admirers" that surrounded him on the grass on the campus or in "the continental hipness of Le Bistro. If you were looking for Leonard," says Pomerance, "Le Bistro was the first place you would go."

Le Bistro looked like someone had smuggled it in from Paris, with its zinc-topped horseshoe bar, blackboard menu and long mirror along one wall. On another wall, Leonard had scribbled a poem:

MARITA
PLEASE FIND ME
I AM ALMOST 30

"MARITA," SELECTED POEMS 1956–1968

He had written it in response to having had his advances spurned by Marita La Fleche, a Montreal boutique owner, who told him to come back when he had grown up. Le Bistro was the meeting place of choice for both French- and English-speaking artists and intelligentsia, who would sit there, talking, long into the night, drinking red wine and smoking French cigarettes. On any given night you might see Leonard, Irving Layton, Mort Rosengarten, Derek May, Robert Hershorn, the sculptor Armand Vaillancourt and Pierre Trudeau, the socialist writer and law professor who would go on to become prime minister of Canada and whose beige Humphrey Bogart raincoat became as famous as Leonard's blue one.

Another regular haunt was the 5th Dimension, a coffee bar and folk club on Bleury Street. Leonard was with Hershorn the night he first met Pomerance there. Leonard remarked to Hershorn that she reminded him of Freda Guttman, his old girlfriend at McGill, and introduced himself. Pomerance says, "He was a ladies' man, an extremely magnetic personality, someone with a special aura, even before he burst on the music scene. I was eighteen and very impressed by these people. They were very sophisticated and very much into their own style in the way they dressed—black, very simple—and in what they talked about, art and literature mostly, not so much politics. They just seemed to have a handle on life. They were so sure of themselves and where they were going, and at the same time not too focused on any specific thing except creativity and art. As a younger girl I guess they were my ideal, particularly Leonard and Derek May. Leonard seemed to be the epitome of cool."

For a while, Leonard courted her. "He didn't seduce you in the typical way; he was very obtuse, very laid back. You felt drawn to him on some sort of spiritual level." He took her to the house on Belmont Avenue, where his mother still kept his bedroom. "There were photographs of his dad and of him as a boy. We smoked hash and he nearly seduced me in that room. But I was still a virgin, and I remember thinking that even though he was hard to resist I didn't want to make love for the very first time with someone who was living with another woman." She was referring to Marianne.

Leonard introduced the young woman to his mother. "A very attractive woman, very strong face, strong features, with steely gray hair and dressed like a high-class Westmount Jewish woman who had means," recalls Pomerance, herself a Montreal Jew. "She was halfway in the old world and halfway in the new. She ruled the roost; she was what you would call now a domineering mother. My feeling was that she was thirsty. She wanted to be let into Leonard's life and his successes." Leonard, though, "was like quicksilver, a free spirit who looked like he was doing just what he wanted and you couldn't tie him down anywhere. I think she would have liked to have had more of a piece of the pie in terms of having more time with him, but Leonard would come and go. When he'd enough of her he escaped, but he always remained close to her."

After dispensing with her virginity elsewhere, Pomerance "did not remain resistant forever" to Leonard's charms. "He took me to all the haunts where he took most of his paramours, like the Hotel de France, which was this seedy hotel which he loved, on Saint Laurent Street on the corner of Saint Catherine, and we went for walks in the mountains. At one point he took me to his house," she says, referring to where Leonard was living with Marianne. "That's where I heard him play guitar for the first time. We sat around and smoked a bit, because Leonard was into pot and hash, and we'd jam." Pomerance played guitar and sang. "I remember Leonard liking a western style of music."

Leonard also introduced her to Marianne. "She seemed so cool and beautiful and calm," says Pomerance. "Everything I wasn't was this woman. I think they must have had an understanding. He probably brought other women there he was having casual relationships with, and then when you were there it was obvious Marianne was his common-law wife, his muse, the queen, and that she had a tremendous amount of respect and they seemed to be on an equal footing. She was very nice and warm and very accepting—you didn't feel that she was jealous or anything—but I think that she probably put up with a lot to remain with him, because he was moody and he had his own rules and needed his freedom. I remember one day, it was his birthday, we went back to his room in his mother's house and he was lying down on his bed, and he had this yellow rose on his chest and he was just being very, very passive and Buddha-like, inviolable and untouchable, in some remote area.

"You could only get so much of him that he was willing to give at the moment. He was somebody who was not trying to fill up the spaces of silence with idle chatter; everything he did had to have meaning and importance. But on the other hand you got the feeling from him that time was seamless, that he didn't run on the same time or rhythm as other people. He didn't run after journalists, getting himself publicized; his magnetism is such that it's like a boat creating a wake and people are drawn to him and his ideas. For me what he emanated was model of creativity and freedom to explore and express."*

Throughout everything Leonard was writing, typing pages, filling notebooks. He was working on a new volume of poetry to follow up the successful *Spice-Box of Earth*, to which he had given the title *Opium and Hitler*. He sent the manuscript to Jack McClelland. His

---

* In 1968 Pomerance released her experimental debut album titled *You Used to Think*, which contained her song "To Leonard from Hospital." She went on to become a documentary filmmaker.

publisher objected to the title and, judging by the long correspondence between them, seemed not entirely convinced by the content.
Michael Ondaatje, who, like Leonard, was published by Jack Mc-
Clelland, wrote that McClelland was "uncertain of Cohen's being a
genius, yet rather delighted at its possibility, and so constantly presenting him to the public as one."[6]

This would have been a comfortable position for someone of
Leonard's sensibilities, able to float contentedly on a sea of praise
while all the time shrugging modestly. But Jack McClelland could
be far more critical in his letters to Leonard than he was when he
talked about him to other people. He told Leonard he would publish
his book anyway, "because you are Leonard Cohen"[7]—which was in
many ways the inverse of a famous incident that would occur twenty
years later, when the head of Leonard's U.S. record company, having
heard Leonard's seventh album, would tell him, "Leonard, we know
you're great, but we don't know if you're any good,"[8] and refused to
release it.

Leonard's reply to McClelland contained none of his usual humor
and mock braggadocio; it was angry, honest and sure of itself. He
knew his book to be "a masterpiece," he wrote. "There has never
been a book like this, prose or poetry, written in Canada." Yes he
could write another *Spice-Box* and make everyone happy, himself included, since he had nothing against flattering reviews. But he had
moved on. "I've never written easily: most of the time I detest the
process. So try and understand that I've never enjoyed the luxury of
being able to choose between the kinds of books I wanted to write,
or poems, or women I wanted to love, or lives to lead."[9]

Leonard also argued to keep the title. It would appeal, he wrote,
to "the diseased adolescents who compose my public."[10] But when it
came down to it, Leonard was a practical man. He agreed to many
of the revisions McClelland called for, saying, "I'll carve a little here
and there, as long as I don't touch the bone."[11] He ended up sending

McClelland fifty new poems. He also gave the book a new name, *Flowers for Hitler*, and removed the dedication, which McClelland had disliked:

> *With scorn, love, nausea, and above all,*
> *a paralysing sense of community*
> *this book is dedicated*
> *to the teachers, doctors, leaders of my parents' time:*
> *THE DACHAU GENERATION*

This bitter moniker had been taken from the poem Leonard wrote to Alexander Trocchi, his "public junkie" friend. In it, Leonard made excuses for his own inability to take such a committed stance:

> *I tend to get distracted . . .*
> *by Uncle's disapproval*
> *of my treachery*
> *to the men's clothing industry.*
> *I find myself . . .*
> *taking advice*
> *from the Dachau generation . . .*

Leonard had already felt his uncles' disapproval of *The Favorite Game;* they had been not well pleased, he said, with his description of them as having betrayed their priestly name of Cohen and pledged themselves only to financial success. (Nor for that matter had his uncles approved of his having written about Masha's stay in a mental hospital.)

The book was now dedicated not to the Dachau generation but to Marianne. He also wrote "A Note on the Title," which, like the original dedication, was arranged in the form of a poem:

A
while ago
this book would
have been called
SUNSHINE FOR NAPOLEON
and earlier still it
would have been
called
WALLS FOR GENGHIS KHAN

In turn, McClelland agreed to some of Leonard's requests, in particular that the original design for the front cover be scrapped—Leonard's face, superimposed on a woman's naked body. "Nobody is going to buy a book the cover of which is a female body with my face for tits," Leonard wrote in September 1964 in a long, heated letter to McClelland. "The picture is simply offensive. It is dirty in the worst sense. It hasn't the sincerity of a stag movie or the imagination of a filthy postcard or the energy of real surrealist humor." He told McClelland that he would not be returning to Canada to promote the book. "I'd really be ashamed to stand beside a stack of them at a cocktail party. . . . So why don't we forget about the whole thing? You never liked the book very much."[12]

Flowers for Hitler was published in the autumn of 1964. The dust jacket, which bore a different design, contained an excerpt from one of Leonard's letters to McClelland. "This book," it read, "moves me from the world of the golden-boy poet into the dung pile of the front-line writer. I didn't plan it this way. I loved the tender notices *Spice-Box* got but they embarrassed me a little. *Hitler* won't get the same hospitality from the papers. My sounds are too new, therefore people will say: this is derivative, this is slight, his power has failed. Well, I say that there has never been a book like this, prose or poetry, written in Canada. All I ask is that you put it in the hands of my generation and it will be recognized."[13]

Thematically, *Flowers for Hitler* "was not entirely new for Leonard; there had been sex, violence, murder and the Holocaust in his first two books of poems, as well as songs to lovers and celebrations of teachers and friends. What was different was its style. It was much less formal and its language freer and more contemporary, which made the darkness and torture it described seem more personal—self-torture, the darkness within—and the love it expressed, for Marianne, for Irving Layton, more heartfelt. As an epigraph Leonard chose the words of Primo Levi, a concentration camp survivor: "Take care not to suffer in your own homes what is inflicted on us here." A warning not so much that history can repeat itself but that history is not something frozen in some other place and time; it's the nature of humanity.

In a 1967 interview in the University of British Columbia student paper the *Ubyssey*, Leonard explained, "[Levi is] saying, what point is there to a political solution if, in the homes, these tortures and mutilations continue? That's what *Flowers for Hitler* is all about. It's taking the mythology of the concentration camps and bringing it into the living room and saying, 'This is what we do to each other.' We outlaw genocide and concentration camps and gas and that, but if a man leaves his wife or they are cruel to each other, then that cruelty is going to find a manifestation if he has a political capacity; and he has. There's no point in refusing to acknowledge the wrathful deities. That's like putting pants on the legs of pianos like the Victorians did. The fact is that we all succumb to lustful thoughts, to evil thoughts, to thoughts of torture."[14]

His interviewer, literary professor Sandra Djwa, asked Leonard if he wasn't mining the same seams as William Burroughs, Günter Grass and Jean-Paul Sartre in *Nausea*. He answered, "The only thing that differs in those writers and myself is that I hold out the idea of ecstasy as the solution. If only people get high, they can face the evil part. If a man feels in his heart it's only going to be a mundane confrontation with feelings, and he has to recite to himself Norman

Vincent Peale slogans, 'Be better, be good,' he hasn't had a taste of that madness. He's never soared, he's never let go of the silver thread and he doesn't know what it feels to be like a god. For him, all the stories about holiness and the temple of the body are meaningless. . . . The thing about Sartre is that he's never lost his mind. . . . The thing that people are interested in doing now is blowing their heads off and that's why the writing of schizophrenics like myself will be important."[15]

It was a curious answer. It appeared to be equal parts megalomania and madness, anti–New Age yet Newer Age, though with an Old Age patina. Or quite possibly he was high. Leonard clearly considered *Flowers for Hitler* an important book; in 1968 he would choose around half its content for his anthology *Selected Poems*. If Leonard truly believed, though, that *Flowers for Hitler* would prove too provocative for the literati and strip him of his "golden-boy poet" status, he would have been disappointed with the favorable reaction it received. It prompted the critic Milton Wilson to write in the *Toronto Quarterly* that Leonard was "potentially the most important writer that Canadian poetry has produced since 1950," adding, "not merely the most talented, but also, I would guess, the most professionally committed to making the most of his talent."[16] (Somewhat prophetic, since one of its poems, "New Step," would be staged as a theatrical ballet on CBC TV in 1972, and another poem, "Queen Victoria and Me," would become a song on his 1973 album *Live Songs*.)

Flowers for Hitler did little to heal relations between Leonard and the Montreal Jewish establishment, nor presumably with his uncles. In December 1963 at a symposium held in the city on the future of Judaism in Canada, Leonard had given an address titled "Loneliness and History," in which he castigated the Montreal Jewish community for abandoning the spiritual for the material. As he wrote in *The Favorite Game*, the men, like his uncles, who occupied the front pews at the synagogue were pledged only to their businesses; religious observance was an empty masquerade. "They did not believe their blood was consecrated. . . . They did not seem to realize how fragile the ceremony was. They participated in it blindly, as if it would last forever. . . . Their nobility was insecure because it rested on inheritance and not moment-to-moment creation in the face of annihilation."

Businessmen, Leonard told the assembly in the Montreal Jewish Public Library, had taken over and made a corporation of the religious community. Jews were "afraid to be lonely" and sought security in finance, neglecting their scholars and sages, their artists and prophets. "Jews must survive in their loneliness as witnesses," he told them. "Jews are the witness to monotheism and that is what they must continue to declare." Now that A. M. Klein, the great Canadian Jewish poet, a friend of Layton's and much admired by Leonard, had fallen silent—mental illness, attempted suicide and hospitalization had led Klein to stop writing—it remained to young Jewish writers and artists, Leonard said, to take on the responsibility of being the lonely witnesses and prophets. His indictment made the front page of the *Canadian Jewish Chronicle* with the headline POET-NOVELIST SAYS JUDAISM BETRAYED. The controversy was now national. Two months later, during an appearance at the University of British Columbia Jewish Community Center in Vancouver—part of a reading tour of Western Canada, which also included a Dunn's Birdland–style performance in Manitoba where Leonard was accompanied by jazz guitarist Lenny Breau and his band—Leonard was unapologetic. He seemed energized, manic almost, as he talked about his work. He announced that he planned to retreat from the world and consecrate himself to writing a liturgy and confessional that would take the form of a new novel.

Back in Montreal, the snow was falling thicker than ever. The cold of a Montreal winter was brutal. It mugged you. Leonard headed for his favorite sanctuary, Le Bistro. It was there, on a glacial night, that Leonard met Suzanne.

Suzanne Verdal has long black hair and wears long flowing skirts and ballet slippers. For years she has lived a gypsy life in a wooden caravan, with cats and planters of geraniums. It was built for her in the nineties and is towed by an old truck but otherwise seems straight out of a fairy tale. It is parked in Santa Monica, California, where Suzanne works as a masseuse and is writing her autobiography, by hand.

In the early sixties, when she and Leonard first met, Suzanne was a demure seventeen-year-old, "just out of an Ontario boarding school, with a future dream of bohemian heaven." She frequented the art galleries and the café scene, "making notes and observing the people; there was always some young artist passing through, to partake of long discussions on art or political issues." Suzanne wrote poetry, but her talent was as a dancer. She worked two jobs to pay for dance classes, and late at night, she would go to Le Vieux Moulin, one of the nightclubs Leonard and his friends frequented, where jazz was played into the early hours and Montrealers drank and danced their way through the glacial winter. One night, on the dance floor she met Armand Vaillancourt, a strikingly handsome man—long haired, bearded and fifteen years her senior. Vaillancourt, a friend of Leonard, was a Quebecois sculptor of some renown; he had a public sculpture on Durocher Street. Suzanne and Vaillancourt became dancing partners, then lovers, and then the parents of a baby girl. They lived in Vaillancourt's studio, an "uninsulated wooden shack" on Bleury Street.

The first time Suzanne met Leonard was at Le Bistro. She had seen him there on several occasions, sometimes sitting with Marianne at a small table under the long mirror on the wall. Suzanne could not recall what they talked about, but "more than conversation was our eye contact. It was the most intimate of touches and completely visceral. We were simultaneously witnessing the magical scenes unfolding at the time and, truly, it felt we were genuinely on each other's wavelength."

Suzanne had signed her first professional dance contract at the age of eighteen and, after spending a summer studying with Martha Graham in New York, had started her own modern dance company in Montreal, "experimenting with music such as John Cage and Edgar Varèse." They performed at the Beaux-Arts; at L'Association Espagnole, where flamenco was played long into the night; and also on television. She began to make a name as an avant-garde dancer and choreographer. Erica Pomerance says, "Suzanne was cool and creative and one of the beautiful people, an icon to dance like Leonard was to the poetry and artistic set. She would combine classical, modern and ethnic dance styles and she had a style about her that was the epitome of bohemianism, very New Age. She would design these sort of Gypsy clothes that she wore," sewn together from silks, brocades and old drapery she found in the Salvation Army store on Notre-Dame Street.

When her relationship with Vaillancourt ended, Suzanne would go for long walks along the harbor by the Saint Lawrence River. "I loved the huge ships that docked there and the taste of faraway travel," she says. "I related to the sounds of the slow-moving freight trains— hauntingly poetic and somehow soothing. I admired the centuries-old architecture and the grain elevators." She decided to rent a cheap apartment in one of its large, dilapidated buildings, becoming the first in their circle, she says, "to colonize Old Montreal." Today the area is fashionable; the half-abandoned rooming house from the 1850s where she lived with her child became a hotel charging $300 a night for a room. In the midsixties the only other occupants were "an elderly couple and an old British lady and her cat." The building reeked of old pipe tobacco and the floors were all crooked, but they were of fine old burnished wood, and there were stained-glass windows. Suzanne found the place "absolutely beautiful, inspirational."

There were few restaurants or cafés nearby, so her friends would come to the house. Suzanne would serve them "jasmine tea or Constant Comment and little mandarin oranges and lychee nuts from Chinatown," which was a short walk away. Among her visitors was Philippe Gingras, a poet friend "who wrote a beautiful homage to me way before Leonard did, in French, in a tome called *Quebec Underground*. When Philippe came I would light a candle to invoke the Spirit of Poetry—I called the flame Anastasia, don't ask me why." She performed the ceremony for Leonard. "I'm quite sure that Leonard observed that little ritual every time we sat and had tea together; that was a rarefied moment, a spiritual moment, because I would invite the Spirit of Poetry and quality conversation." They would walk through Old Montreal together, silently, "the click of his boots and the sound of [her] shoes almost like a synchronicity" as they went down to the river, past Notre-Dame-de-Bon-Secours, where the sailors went to be blessed before going to sea and where the Virgin, wearing a halo of stars, reached out to them across the harbor.

"We were definitely on the same wavelength," Suzanne says. "We could almost hear each other think at times and that was such a delight to us. I sensed a deep, philosophical side to Leonard that he seemed to see in me as well, and he got a kick out of it in that I was a sort of fledgling in a way, just emerging as a young artist." Leonard, though younger than Vaillancourt, was ten years older than Suzanne. On one visit, Leonard stayed overnight. "We didn't sleep together, although Leonard was a very seductive man. I didn't want to mar or contaminate that purity of my esteem for our relationship and for him and for myself."

In August 1967, Suzanne left Montreal for San Francisco. It was around this time, she says, that she learned from a mutual friend that Leonard had written a poem about her, titled "Suzanne." Not long afterward, when somebody played her a record of Judy Collins singing its words, she discovered it was also a song. The first time she heard it, she says she felt "cut to the core" and like someone was holding a magnifying glass to her life. When Suzanne returned to Montreal she was famous—not as a dancer, choreographer or designer but as the muse for a Leonard Cohen song that everyone seemed to be talking about.

Suzanne had been a muse for other men besides Leonard, but for nothing as iconic and ubiquitous as "Suzanne." It is possible that her view might have been more positive had "Suzanne" remained a poem, something more acceptably bohemian, or, since it had entered the world of commerce, if some of the financial benefits had come her way, since her own career had not taken off as conspicuously and successfully as Leonard's had done with this song that bore her name. Also, the song as Suzanne saw it concerned an intimacy, and in reality there was only distance. Leonard had moved on.

In a 2006 CBC television documentary on Suzanne Verdal, the professor of literature Edward Palumbo was asked if the muse is expendable. "I think in the case of Suzanne it appears she really is, or was" was his answer. "On the other hand, the muse is bigger than the poet, at least in the mythology. The muse is the source of what there is, the inspiration. Does the muse have a claim on anything more than that role?" His conclusion was that she did not.[17]

It was Jung's belief that the muse *was* the poet, or his anima anyway, his unconscious image of the Feminine. It was himself that Leonard saw in the mirror Suzanne held. Allan Showalter, a psychiatrist,[*] explains, "The key task of a muse is to allow the artist to see his own feminine aspect that is otherwise invisible to him and to be a screen that fits the artist's projections. What completes the artist isn't the intrinsic qualities of the romantic interest but the artist's own feminine archetype. So, to the extent that the artist's projections dominate or replace the muse's own qualities, the muse's soul is dissipated."

The relationship between artist and muse is invariably one-sided:

---

[*] Showalter is known in Leonard Cohen circles as the webmaster of 1heckofa guy.com.

photographers "steal" their subjects' souls; novelists shamelessly make
characters out of family and friends. Leonard the poet transformed
the physical Suzanne into the metaphysical "Suzanne" and made her
an angel. Leonard the magician sawed her down the middle, then
put the two parts back together—the carnal and the spiritual—and
made her more perfect than before. Leonard the composer made a
hallowed melody of her, both implausibly intimate and ineffably spacious. "Suzanne" is a weightless, mysterious song. The great songs,
the ones that keep drawing us back again and again, are mysteries.
We go to them not for familiarity and solace—although there is solace
in "Suzanne"—but for what is unknown, for something that's hidden
in them that continues to haunt us and makes us seekers.

Leonard has spoken about the song and its muse often over the
years; because it was his first, and, until "Hallelujah," best-known
song, interviewers have kept asking him about them. In the liner
notes for his 1975 *Greatest Hits* album, Leonard wrote, "Everything
happened just as it was put down. She was the wife of a man I knew.
Her hospitality was immaculate." To the filmmaker Harry Rasky in
1979 he elaborated: "An old friend of mine whose name was Suzanne
invited me down to her place near the river. . . . The purity of the
event was not compromised by any carnality. The song is almost a re-
portage. . . . But the song had been begun. It was as though she handed me the seed for the song." In a 1993 interview he generalized,
"I find there's usually somebody in my life from whom I'm drawing
enormous comfort and nourishment. . . . I always find there is someone in my life whom I can describe, without whom this wouldn't have
happened."[18]

In 1994 he spoke about it at some length in a BBC radio interview. "The song was begun, and the chord pattern was developed,
before a woman's name entered the song. And I knew it was a song
about Montreal, it seemed to come out of that landscape that I loved
very much in Montreal, which was the harbor, and the waterfront,

and the sailors' church there, called Notre-Dame-de-Bon-Secours, which stood out over the river. . . . I knew that vision." Into that picture came "the wife of a friend of mine. They were a stunning couple around Montreal at the time, physically stunning—everyone was in love with Suzanne Vaillancourt, and every woman was in love with Armand Vaillancourt. But one would not allow oneself to think of toiling at the seduction of Armand Vaillancourt's wife. First of all he was a friend, and second of all as a couple they were inviolate. I bumped into her one evening, and she invited me down to her place near the river . . . She served me Constant Comment tea, which has little bits of oranges in it. And the boats were going by, and I touched her perfect body with my mind, because there was no other opportunity. There was no other way that you could touch her perfect body under those circumstances. So she provided the name in the song."[19] In recent years he described "Suzanne" as "a kind of doorway. I have to open it carefully, otherwise what's beyond is not accessible to me. It was never about a particular woman. It was about the beginning of a different life for me, my life wandering alone in Montreal."[20]

In a letter sent by Suzanne following our interview there was a footnote: "Leonard has stated publicly that he did not attempt to seduce me. He forgets that, much later, when he had achieved great fame, I had the opportunity to visit him in an East End hotel on rue Saint-Laurent. I was back from one of my travels and wanted to wish him well. He clearly expressed his desire to have physical intimacy but I declined. I had cherished the sanctity of our connection. I felt that if I had shared a sexual encounter with him it would shift that vibration that once had inspired us both. Ours was a soul connection as far as I was concerned."

"I read somewhere that we don't originate a thought, that thoughts arrive spontaneously, then fractions of a second later we take possession of them. In that sense nobody has an original thought. But original thoughts arise and we claim them."

So you didn't write "Suzanne" or "So Long, Marianne" or "Sisters of Mercy" about women you knew, they were outside thoughts that you claimed the copyright on?

"Einstein was modest enough to say that his theory of relativity came from outside. We'd like to think that we make these things up but actually the thing arises and we explain it as our own."

Are you still in contact with these women who have inspired your songs?

"Except for Suzanne Vaillancourt, who I just haven't bumped into in the past thirty years, I'm in contact with most of my friends, both men and women."

———

Leonard's experiments with acid continued in Montreal. Says Aviva Layton, "The first-ever acid trip I ever went on was in 1964 in Leonard's apartment in Montreal. He gave me the acid on the end of his white handkerchief. It was from the very first batch from those professors from Harvard, Timothy Leary and Ram Dass. He sat with me for the entire day—which shows his generosity, because it's really boring to sit with somebody when they're on an acid trip." Three weeks later, at the Laytons' apartment, he did the same for Irving. "Irving resisted any drugs whatsoever, but Leonard persuaded him and I persuaded him, 'You've got to take acid.' Irving said, 'Acid will do nothing for me because I already live in an hallucinatory world.' Leonard gave him a little bit of blotting paper." For almost an hour they sat there, with Irving periodically interjecting, "See, nothing's happening." And then the drug kicked in. "Leonard saw Irving staring hard at the bookcases and Leonard said, 'What are you looking at?' Irving said, 'All the books are coming out one by one and bowing before me, every one of them.' We had tons and tons of books, a whole wall of them, each coming out and doing an obeisance in front of Irving, and then they all bowed in front of a painting of his mother." Irving never would admit that the drug had any effect on him. This, he told Leonard, was his "normal life."

In October '64, after receiving the Prix Litteraire du Quebec for *The Favorite Game*, Leonard and Irving Layton left with two other poets, Phyllis Gotlieb and Earle Birney, on a whirlwind reading tour of the university circuit—six schools and a library in one week. A filmmaker and sometime poet named Don Owen, an acquaintance of Leonard's, shot the performances for a purported National Film Board of Canada documentary—a project that was shelved when two of the poets proved less than engrossing on film. In the end, the footage would be employed in a documentary about just one of the poets. Right now that poet had gone to Greece; Leonard had a novel to write.

Leonard sat in his room in his house on the hill in Hydra, writing furiously. He was driven by an overpowering sense of urgency. He had the feeling, he said, of time running out. This was a strange sentiment for a thirty-year-old man, unless he were Jesus, or seriously ill, or thinking about suicide. "Around thirty or thirty-five is the traditional age for the suicide of the poet, did you know?" Leonard told Richard Goldstein of the *Village Voice* in 1967. "That's the age when you finally understand that the universe does not succumb to your command."[21]

It could be argued that the universe had done quite a good job of succumbing to Leonard. Within days of his thirtieth birthday he had been feted with a literary award and filmed on a poetry tour for a documentary, which would end up being entirely about him. He had good reviews and the respect of Canada's literati. He had a congregation of female admirers. He had won a grant that allowed him to live on a Greek island, where a beautiful woman kept house, put meals on his table and flowers on his desk, and allowed Leonard to do what he wanted to do, which was write his new novel, *Beautiful Losers*. "But when he worked," said Marianne, "sometimes it was torture to get it the way he wanted. Some of it came, *pouf!*, just like that, but he was a perfectionist, a man who demands much of himself."

Leonard went on to say that, in the process of writing *Beautiful Losers*, "I'd thought of myself as a loser. I was wiped out; I didn't like my life. I vowed I would just fill the pages with black or kill myself." He also said, "When you get wiped out . . . that's the moment, the REAL moment"—the true, ecstatic moment he had spoken of earlier, perhaps, which he said writers who hadn't been high or tasted madness could never know. Whether Leonard was high or mad during this period is debatable. He was unquestionably in an altered mental state while writing *Beautiful Losers*, smoking hash and taking acid and, above all, speed. A man can do a lot on amphetamine, and Leonard had given himself a great deal to do in his follow-up to *The Favorite Game*, with more mythologies to compare and another quest to undertake—or perhaps the same quest undertaken by another of his six or seven thousand selves.

Beautiful Losers is a prayer—at times a hysterically funny, filthy prayer—for the unity of the self, and a hymn to the loss of self through sainthood and transfiguration. Jesus might have nodded with fellow feeling; God might have finished it in six days instead of the nine months it took Leonard. It was "written in blood," Leonard said.[22] He was writing, at various points, ten, fifteen, twenty hours a day. He wrote on his terrace, in his basement room and "behind his house on a table set among the rocks, weeds and daisies."[23] He wrote with the Ray Charles album *The Genius Sings the Blues* for company, until the LP warped in the sun and then he turned on the radio, tuning it to the American Forces station, which mostly played country music. "It was a blazing hot summer. I never covered my head. What you have in your hands is more of a sunstroke than a book."[24] In a letter to Jack McClelland he talked his book up as "The Bhagavad-Gita of 1965"[25]; decades later, he talked it down in his foreword to the 2000 Chinese-language edition as an "odd collection of jazz-riffs, pop-art jokes, religious kitsch and muffled prayer." He told the press, "I think it's the best thing I've ever done."[26] It was all of the above.

When he finished typing the seven last words—"forever in your trip to the end"—Leonard went on a ten-day fast. He says, "I flipped out completely. It was my wildest trip. I hallucinated for a week. They took me to a hospital in Hydra." He was put on a protein drip. After they sent him home, he spent weeks in bed, hallucinating, he said, while Marianne took care of him. "I would like to say that it made me saintly," he said.[27]

It is tempting to suggest that Leonard was suffering manic-depression, a disorder thought to peak in men at the same age Leonard gave for poets committing suicide and whose indications include bouts of intense creative activity followed by paralysis, and a "messianic complex," a deep conviction of having something great or world-saving to do. On the other hand a similar effect might be achieved from taking large amounts of amphetamine, topped up with LSD, for long periods, working without a break and concluding all this with a ten-day fast. "Without a detailed set of observations by a witness on which to base a diagnosis," says Dr. Showalter, "I think the most one can claim would be that it is possible that Leonard Cohen's underlying diagnosis was bipolar disorder rather than major depressive disorder. But those symptoms could also result from a number of other disorders, including agitated psychotic state, intoxication, and various depressive and psychotic syndromes confounded by alcohol or drug abuse."

As Leonard told the story, one afternoon he looked up at the sky over Hydra and saw that it was "black with storks." The birds "alighted on all the churches and left in the morning." Leonard took this for a sign that he was better. "Then I decided to go to Nashville and become a songwriter."[28] Although he did not act on this decision immediately, music was certainly near the front of his consciousness during the writing of *Beautiful Losers*. One draft was subtitled *A Pop Novel*. Another included a section in which the narrative was set to guitar chords. In the published version, Leonard chose as an epigraph

"Somebody lift that bale," from the Kern-Hammerstein song "Ol'
Man River," in which a man tired of life and scared of death chooses
laughter over tears.

Leonard could not leave for Nashville at once because he was still
in time-limbo. He was coming down off speed and trying to adjust
to a place where time had already slowed down to a crawling pace,
a place where if you wanted to wash your face you might have to
wait for the water to come uphill on the back of a donkey. "Coming down is very bad," Leonard said. "It took me ten years to fully
recover. I had memory lapses. It was as if my insides were fried. I
couldn't get up anymore; I was in bed like a vegetable, incapable of
doing whatever for a long time."[29] He was exhausted. But he found
the wherewithal to send off copies of his manuscript to Viking in
New York and McClelland in Canada; the original was sold to the
Toronto University library that held his archive. He wrote a précis of
the book in which he spoke of a modern-day Montrealer "driven by
loneliness and despair" who "tries to heal himself by invoking the
name of Catherine Tekakwitha, an Iroquois girl whom the Jesuits
converted in the 17th century, and the first Indian maiden to take an
oath of Virginity."

"*Beautiful Losers*," he wrote, was "a love story, a psalm, a Black
Mass, a monument, a satire, a prayer, a shriek, a road map through the
wilderness, a joke, a tasteless affront, an hallucination, a bore, an irrelevant display of diseased virtuosity. In short," he concluded, it was
"a disagreeable religious epic of incomparable beauty."[30]

Eight

A Long Time Shaving

While Leonard was on Hydra, wasted and unglued, Marianne nursing him as Masha had nursed his father, in Canada two men were making a film that painted an entirely different picture. Its opening scene, shot in October 1964, showed a self-possessed young man who looked nothing like a speed freak, more like a well-bred, young Dustin Hoffman who still had a touch of baby fat. Standing onstage, entertaining a college audience with a story about visiting a friend in a Montreal mental hospital and being mistaken for an inmate, Leonard was droll, dry, self-deprecating and mannered, with the delivery and timing of a stand-up comic.

Ladies and Gentlemen . . . Mr. Leonard Cohen, which appeared in 1965, is a forty-four-minute, black-and-white documentary made up of footage shot by Don Owen on the previous year's four-poet university tour and new material shot by the National Film Board documentarian Donald Brittain. The latter depicts Leonard doing an assortment of cool-looking things in various cool-looking Montreal locations to a soundtrack of cool jazz. A voice-over describes him as "a singular talent with four books under his belt." (*Beautiful Losers* was finished but not yet published.) As affirmation of Leonard's celebrity in Canadian literature, this was several rungs up from the literary prizes and the *Six Montreal Poets* album.

It is a curious film, somewhere between a Leonard Cohen infomercial and a fly-on-the-wall study of Leonard at work and play. We observe him in Le Bistro and walking down the streets he used to roam as an adolescent, stopping to admire old movie posters outside a beautifully run-down cinema. We see him read a poem to a rapt audience of young women with teased hair and sixties makeup, then read the same poem to friends—Mort, Layton, Hershorn, May—only this time accompanying himself on guitar. We watch as he handles journalists and academics. We catch him unawares in his underpants in a cheap hotel room, which costs three dollars a night, we're told. We spy on him as he shaves, bathes, sleeps, expounds, ponders and sits writing at the small desk in his room, cigarette in one hand, pen in the other, while the streetlamp illuminates an overspilling ashtray and the lumps in the cheap wood-chip wallpaper.

Old home-movie footage underlines how much this contrasts with the life Leonard gave up for poetry: here's a cherubic little boy, standing by a car with the family's black chauffeur; here are his uncles, formally dressed in smart suits with boutonnieres; here are the grand houses of Westmount, whose residents, Leonard says, dream "of Jewish sex and bank careers." The path he chose, Leonard says, was "infinitely wide and without direction." His first concern when he wakes in the morning is "to discover if I am in a state of grace," which he defines as "the balance with which you ride the chaos around you." The film is full of the grand, ironic, playful and deflecting statements of the kind Leonard would come to employ in interviews throughout his career. Irving Layton was correct when he said on camera that Leonard's main concern really was "to preserve the self." Despite the appearance of vérité, much of the film is pure theater, as inscrutably and entertainingly fictionalized an account of Leonard's life as is *The Favorite Game.*

Being shown living in a run-down hotel in Montreal was better for the *poète maudit* image than the duplex Leonard rented near McGill, and it also guarded his privacy. Yet he was being truthful when he talked in the film about hotels being a "kind of a temple of refuge, a sanctuary of a temporary kind, so all the more delicious." Leonard would often seek out refuges and sanctuaries—spiritual, terrestrial and sexual—and show no inclination to want to linger too long in any. The hotel life might have been made for him. It was uncomplicated. The cheaper the hotel, the more uncomplicated it was: just the basics, no one bothering you, you're left alone to do what you want. And in a hotel, whatever you might do, the next morning your room will be cleaned, your sin expunged, leaving you free to start over or move on.

"Whenever I come into a hotel room," Leonard told the camera, "there is a moment after the door is shut and the lights you haven't turned on illumine a very comfortable, anonymous, subtly hostile environment, and you know that you've found the little place in the grass and the hounds are going to go by for three more hours and you're going to drink, light a cigarette and take a long time shaving." A good solution, as his mother advised him, when things got tough. Released on the cusp of Leonard's move into a music career, *Ladies and Gentlemen . . . Mr. Leonard Cohen* appears in retrospect less a portrait of a serious literary figure than of a pop/rock celebrity in training.

"Find a little saint and fuck her over and over in some pleasant part of heaven, get right into her plastic altar, dwell in her silver medal, fuck her until she tinkles like a souvenir music box . . . find one of these quaint impossible cunts and fuck her for your life, coming all over the sky, fuck her on the moon with a steel hourglass up your hole."

Beautiful Losers was published in the spring of 1966. There had been no book in Canada like it—nothing by Leonard Cohen like it either, even if some of its motifs (love, loneliness, friendship, God, ecstasy, the atrocities of modern life) might have had a familiar feel. The protagonist, whom we know only as "I," is an anthropologist, "an old scholar, wild with unspecific grief," who has fallen in love with a dead, young seventeenth-century Indian whose picture he happened upon while studying a near-extinct Native Canadian tribe. Catherine Tekakwitha, or "Kateri," is a martyr and a saint, the first Iroquois to take an oath of virginity, and an outsider, unable to live in the world she inhabited. "I" is an outsider too, and lonely, so lonely; despite its frenzied humor and bombast, this is one of the loneliest of Leonard's books.

I's wife, Edith, had committed suicide by sitting at the bottom of an elevator shaft, waiting quietly to be crushed. "F.," the protagonist's best friend, guru, masturbation buddy and sometimes lover (and Edith's lover too), is a madman, savant, Canadian separatist politician and, possibly, saint, who is in the hospital dying from syphilis, a martyr to Montreal but even more so to his cock. However, it's possible that F. is I, that all the characters might be the same person. There's a peyote quality to the book, its characters shape-shifting and dissolving. Sometimes they appear to be gods, but there's a comic earthiness too. *Beautiful Losers* is a prayer for both union and emptiness, and a quest for sexual and spiritual fulfillment. It's a satire on life in the sixties. It's also a treatise on the history of Canada: before the Jesuits came to the country, Catherine would have frolicked happily in the long grass with the boys of her tribe, at one with nature, the gods and man. Canada too had fallen from grace, with the vacuity of urban life and the "two solitudes," the schism between its English and French populations. Maybe it would set things right if he could go back in time and fuck this young saint, or if he could fuck like his old, sainted friend/teacher, or if he himself could be a modern saint, a celluloid Buddha.

Beautiful Losers is "a redemptive novel, an exercise to redeem the soul," Leonard said in a 1967 interview. "In that book I tried to wrestle with all the deities that are extant now—the idea of saintliness, purity, pop, McLuhanism, evil, the irrational—all the gods we set up for ourselves."[1] In a CBC television interview he said, "I was writing a liturgy, but using all the techniques of the modern novel. So there's this huge prayer using the conventional techniques of pornographic suspense, of humor, of plot, of character development and conventional intrigue."[2] He said he "was not interested in guarding anything," and he didn't. *Beautiful Losers* is excessive, manic, free— not tidied up into perfectly edited scenes like *The Favorite Game*. It mixes high and low art, poetry and Hollywood, lyrical beauty and the language of comic books. *The Favorite Game* had been considered a groundbreaking book; *Beautiful Losers* was truly groundbreaking. The *Globe and Mail* described it as "verbal masturbation"; the *Toronto Daily Star* called it "the most revolting book ever written in Canada," but also the "Canadian book of the year."

Leonard was most unhappy at how the book was received on publication and at how badly it sold in Canada—an understandable reaction given how intense the experience of writing the book had been. Word reached Jack McClelland that Leonard blamed his publisher, complaining about the book's price, its design, its poor distribution and lack of advertising. McClelland was angry. He felt that he had gone out on a limb to publish the book. When he had first read Leonard's manuscript in May 1965, McClelland found it "appalling, shocking, revolting, sick," but also "wild and incredible and marvellously well written." "I'm not going to pretend that I dig it, because I don't," he wrote to Leonard. "I'm sure it will end up in the courts, but that might be worth trying. You are a nice chap, Leonard, and it's lovely knowing you. All I have to decide now is whether I love you enough to spend the rest of my days in jail for you."[3] He had proven that he did, and now a year later, Leonard was "bitching because *Beautiful Losers* is not available in all stores. . . . Just what in hell did you expect?

You may be naïve but you are certainly not stupid. Booksellers have a perfect right to decide what they will sell and what they will not sell. Many stores have decided that they don't want to take the risk of handling this book." McClelland reminded Leonard that they had thrown a big promotional party for the book, whose value was "almost totally lost because you didn't think it suited your image or were unwilling to put yourself out. . . . I am beginning to think," McClelland concluded, "that the National Film Board did you no favor."[4] What McClelland was implying was that *Ladies and Gentlemen . . . Mr. Leonard Cohen* had gone to Leonard's head.

Beautiful Losers did not enjoy huge sales in the U.S. either (although one copy would be bought by a young Lou Reed), despite the review in the *Boston Globe* that declared, "James Joyce is not dead. He is living in Montreal." In 1970 the book was given its UK publication by Jonathan Cape. The publisher, Tom Maschler, was "amazed by *Beautiful Losers*." "I thought it quite wonderful," he says, "an original and important novel." The *Times Literary Supplement* ran a review whose length reflected Leonard's celebrity as a recording artist by that time:* "*Beautiful Losers* is an abstraction of all searches for a lost innocence. . . . [It] suffers badly from uncharacterised characters, cosmic desperations, unresolved even in the throes of frantic sex, the compulsively-listed paraphernalia of the environment and the iconographic employment of all the modern communications phenomena the author can manage to drag in. It's a novel that features wanking in a moving car, a masturbation machine that goes over to its own power supply, Brigitte Bardot and (you guessed) the Rolling Stones. It's a novel that's got everything, and that is exactly its trouble: with everything for a subject it has no subject and rounds itself out with

---

* The critic, Nicolas Walter, was clearly no fan of Leonard's music: "The impact on a young student of a song like 'Dress Rehearsal Rag' must be overwhelming," he wrote, "but in fact the song is merely an abstraction of all currently fashionable moods of doom, and in any case, overwhelming art is the kind you grow out of."

rhetoric like a bad poem trying to talk itself into shape. There is talent here, but no sense of limit."[5]

Leonard, said Irving Layton, "is one of the few writers who has voluntarily immersed himself in the destructive element, not once but many times, then walked back from the abyss with dignity to tell us what he saw, to put a frame around the wind. I see Leonard as the white mouse they put down into a submarine to see if the air is foul—he is the white mouse of civilisation who tests its foulness."[6]

The gospels diverge on exactly when and where Leonard decided to become a singer-songwriter. According to the journalist and socialite Barbara Amiel, it was in the summer of 1965, in Toronto, in a suite at the King Edward Hotel. Leonard was composing tunes on a harmonica and singing his poems to a female friend while elsewhere in the suite a naked couple were "getting it on." Leonard took this as a positive response. He announced, "I think I'm going to record myself singing my poems." His companion winced and said, "Please don't"[7]—though she was a touch too late, since Leonard had been filmed singing and playing guitar in *Ladies and Gentlemen . . . Mr. Leonard Cohen*. The song he performed was called "Chant"— he would later describe it as the first song he ever wrote.[8] It had a somewhat "Teachers"-like melody, over which Leonard chanted the words:

> *Hold me hard light, soft light hold me*
> *Moonlight in your mountains fold me*
> *Hold me hard light, soft light hold me*

Ira B. Nadel dated it to some six months later in his Cohen biography, at a poetry event presided over by F. R. Scott and attended by Irving Layton, Louis Dudek, Ralph Gustafson, A. J. M. Smith and Al Purdy. "Leonard played his guitar, sang, and raved about Dylan," and since no one in the room had ever heard of Dylan, Scott took off for a record shop, returning with *Bringing It All Back Home* and *Highway 61 Revisited*. He put the albums on, Nadel wrote, "to the chagrin of everyone" besides Leonard, who listened "intently, solemnly" and announced to the room "that *he* would become the Canadian Dylan."[9] But by Leonard's own account—in 1967 in the *Village Voice* and to any number of music journalists since, this biographer included—his intention was to write country songs, not to be a folk-rock singer-songwriter. He was more comfortable with country, given his history of being in the Buckskin Boys, than he was with folk or rock, genres with which he felt out of touch. Leonard himself dated his decision to a few weeks after the completion of *Beautiful Losers*, following a ten-day fast and a period in the wilderness.

Marianne Ihlen says that Leonard was talking about making records as far back as the early sixties. "We were sitting in one of these diners in Montreal where there are two leather couches and a table in the middle and on the wall was one of those little jukeboxes. Leonard said, 'Marianne, my dream is to have one of my songs in one of these boxes.' It was a long process. Leonard always had a guitar with him. If he sat at a table playing, suddenly there were twenty-five people standing around the table, so you could call it a performance, even though what he was doing was playing for us. You could hear in his voice that something was happening."

In the midsixties, Leonard's Montreal filmmaker friend Henry Zemel, who had heard him sing at Dunn's Birdland in 1958, recorded Leonard playing guitar and singing on an old Uher reel-to-reel at Zemel's house on Sherbrooke Street. The room had exceptional acoustics, Zemel says, and Leonard, Mort, Derek May and various musicians, including local folk band the Stormy Clovers, would come over to jam. The music on Zemel's tape sounds neither country nor folk. It is mostly instrumental, a mysterious mix of John Cage, Eastern music, flamenco and ancient field recordings, but one can hear

Leonard—accompanied by Zemel, improvising on tom-tom and Chinese flute—seeming to be working out his signature guitar sound. The last piece on Zemel's tape is an unknown and untitled song written by Leonard, on which he sings/intones, as if it were a dirge, the words "I can't wait." During this period Leonard also composed instrumental music for a short, experimental film made by his friend Derek May, titled *Angel*, in 1966. Leonard made an appearance in the film, conversing in a park with a woman with a dog who took it in turns to wear wings. His music was performed on the soundtrack by the Stormy Clovers.

So it happened by degrees, sometimes in public, more often in private, alone or with friends. In February 1966 in New York, appearing at the 92nd Street Y for a reading, Leonard closed by singing "The Stranger Song"—a little slower, his voice strained and plaintive, and with a handful of different words, but otherwise much as it would appear two years later on his first album. In 1968 Leonard told the *Montreal Gazette*, "I just see the singing as an extension of a voice I've been using ever since I can remember. This is just one aspect of its sound." In 1969 he told the *New York Times*, "There is no difference between a poem and a song. Some were songs first and some were poems first and some were situations. All of my writing has guitars behind it, even the novels."

But everybody, including Leonard, agrees on why he decided to be a singer-songwriter: economics.

"Well, I always played the guitar and sang. I'd been living in Greece for a number of years and it was a very good way of living, I could live in Greece for eleven hundred dollars a year, but I couldn't pay my grocery bill, so I would come back to Canada, get various jobs, get that money together plus the boat fare, come back to Greece and live for as long as that money lasted. I couldn't make a living as an author. My books weren't selling, they were receiving very good reviews, but my second novel Beautiful Losers *sold about three thousand copies worldwide. The only economic alternative*

was, I guess, going into teaching or university or getting a job in a bank, like the great Canadian poet Raymond Souster. But I always played the guitar and sang, so it was an economic solution to the problem of making a living and being a writer."

Hydra was cheap, and Leonard had a $750-a-year inheritance, but living there had proven impossible on a writer's income. *Beautiful Losers*, despite the controversy and attention, did not sell in significant numbers until Leonard became a recording artist and it was reissued in paperback. He published a fourth volume of poetry in 1966, which made no impact on his bank balance. The poems in *Parasites of Heaven*—some dating back to the late fifties—were also about love, loneliness and despair, but more conventional in structure than those of *Flowers for Hitler* and more personal, more like songs. Michael Ondaatje noted that while the poems in *Flowers for Hitler* "had a cast of thousands, these have a cast of one or two [and] the objects of his descriptions are not intense public tortures but private pain and quietness."[10] He could well have been describing a sensitive sixties singer-songwriter. And *Parasites of Heaven*, while it was generally treated by literary critics as an insubstantial work, was significant for fans of Leonard's music, as it included a number of his future songs: "Suzanne," "Master Song," "Teachers," "Avalanche" and "Fingerprints."

In the summer of 1966 CBC offered Leonard a position cohosting a new television show. His job would entail interviewing guests, making short films and commentating. Leonard accepted enthusiastically; he had often spoken about looking for an audience beyond the ivory tower—"I think the time is over when poets should sit on marble stairs with black capes"[11]—and this seemed a golden opportunity. He told the *Toronto Daily Star* that his intention was "to get close to the viewers, get them to participate in the show, even send in home movies"[12]—an interactive approach that was unusual in the middle sixties. But the TV show came to nothing. The producer Andrew Simon was reported as saying that Leonard changed his mind: "There was no fight. It was a personal-emotional thing. Leonard felt that God hadn't put him here to be a TV star." In the same article, though, Leonard said that he had no problem with the idea of a poet being on television: "I've always felt very different from other poets I've met. I've always felt that somehow they've made a decision against life. Most of them have closed a lot of doors. I never felt too much at home with those kind of people. I always felt more at home with musicians. I like to write songs and sing and that kind of stuff."[13]

All the signs were pointing to music. In 1966 Leonard borrowed some money from his friend Robert Hershorn and set off for Nashville.

Why Nashville and country music? There was a lot more interesting music going on and places to be in 1966.

"I listened to the Armed Forces Radio that came out of Athens and it had a lot of good country music on it. I had a few records there—Ray Charles, Edith Piaf, Nina Simone, Charlie and Inez Foxx, Sylvie Vartan; she did a Nashville record, in French; I don't know if you ever heard it, it's a great record—and I listened to those and to the radio. But I didn't know what was going on in America. Elvis Presley was the only guy that I was listening to, and the Shirelles, and the very early murmurings of Motown. I thought I would head down to Nashville and maybe get work down there. On the way down I stopped off in New York, and that's where I bumped into the so-called folk-song renaissance, which included Joan Baez and Dylan and Phil Ochs, Judy Collins, Joni Mitchell. This was the first time I'd heard their songs. I thought: I'd been writing those little songs for a while, just playing them for my friends, so I thought I'd try my hand at that and try presenting them to some kind of commercial institution who might be able to use them."

Stepping from the train at Pennsylvania Station, dressed in his blue raincoat, Leonard walked along Thirty-fourth Street to the Penn

Terminal Hotel, suitcase and guitar in hand. A New York noir movie of a hotel, it was cheap and it looked it: dark brown brick, dark narrow corridors, an elevator just big enough for a man and a corpse. The window in his oddly shaped room had been screwed into a position that was neither open nor closed; the radiator hissed like a steam train, to which the dripping tap in the brown-streaked washbasin added a slow, perpetual accompaniment. It was a terrible room, Leonard concluded with no real animosity—he would think that whenever he stayed at the Penn Terminal, which was fairly often, even when he could afford somewhere better. His clothes hung loosely on his 116-pound postamphetamine frame. When he looked at his reflection in the mirror he saw a man who looked like he had lived on a mountain for several years. Leonard had a shave and then he headed out. He had a woman to meet.

Robert Hershorn had told Leonard about Mary Martin. She had moved from her native Toronto to New York in 1962, finding her way to Greenwich Village. She had worked her way up from a hostess job at the Bitter End folk club to executive assistant to Albert Grossman, Bob Dylan's manager, then director of A & R at Warner Bros. and, in 1966, the head of her own artist management company. In the male-dominated music business of the early sixties—what few women there were were mostly behind a microphone: Joan Baez, Judy Henske, Carolyn Hester, Judy Collins—Martin was an exception. She had a track record of helping Canadian musicians: she had been instrumental in getting the Hawks, later known as the Band, the job as Dylan's backing band, and she also managed Leonard's acquaintances the Stormy Clovers. "A very enterprising and very sensitive woman," said Leonard, "and very supportive."[14] Leonard liked supportive women. He talked to Martin about his novels and his poetry and told her he had written a couple of things that he thought might be a song. Impressed with what she had heard, she told him she'd see what she could do. Then she called her friend Judy Collins.

Collins, then twenty-seven years old, was an aristocrat of the Greenwich Village scene: cool, elegant, with long straight hair and such remarkable blue eyes that Stephen Stills wrote a song about them.* She had begun as a classical pianist from Seattle, first performing with a symphony orchestra when she was thirteen, and then she discovered folk music. It led her to New York in 1961, where she moved into a two-dollar-a-night hotel, and barely had time to unpack before Jac Holzman, who owned and ran Elektra Records, saw her play at the Village Gate and offered her a record deal. Her first album, *A Maid of Constant Sorrow*—traditional folk—was released the same year. Holzman had previously tried without success to sign Joan Baez, who was the reigning queen of traditional folk and protest songs. He had been looking for his own Baez ever since, but it did not take him long to see that he had a quite different artist in Collins, who was musically much more experimental. This made her a more valuable commodity in the midsixties, at a time when traditional folk began its move into folk-rock.

When Leonard arrived in Manhattan in the summer of 1966, Collins was working on her sixth, and until then most innovative, album, *In My Life*. As well as the Beatles song of the title, she covered songs by Dylan, Donovan, Randy Newman, even Brecht and Weill. But Holzman, though he liked where she was heading, still thought there was something missing. "I told her, 'It doesn't fly yet, we need more songs,'" says Holzman. "Judy said, 'Where the hell am I going to get more songs?' I said, 'Put it out there that you're looking.' So she did, somewhat downheartedly. Then about ten days later I get a call from Judy saying, 'I've met the most wonderful writer.'"

Telling the story of the first time she met Leonard, Judy Collins laughs out loud. Two businessmen sitting at the next table in the

---

* "Suite: Judy Blue Eyes" was recorded with David Crosby and Graham Nash in 1969.

hushed hotel in Beverly Hills look up from their expense-account lunches to stare at this magnificent seventy-one-year-old with a long mane of pure white hair and dressed in a sharp rockabilly jacket.

It was early evening, she remembers, in early fall. She opened her door and there stood "a small man in a dark suit, good-looking, shy." He said Mary Martin had sent him and he had come to sing her his songs. "All the singers with new songs would come to me," she said, "because I had the record contract and I could get them out, and because I didn't write my own songs—not until 1967, and I only wrote them because Leonard said to me, 'Why aren't you writing your own songs?'" Mary Martin "would always talk about Leonard," Collins recalls. "It was 'Leonard this,' 'Leonard that.' She kept saying, 'Oh you've got to help him, you've got to hear the songs.' I liked and respected Mary so I said, 'Well what does he do?' She said, 'He writes poetry and he has written a novel, and he's written something he thinks is a song, and he wants to come down here and see you.' Most of the people in the Village would literally grab you on the street, throw you down on the floor and sing you the song before you'd even said hello. So I said, 'By all means, let him come.'

"He came to my house, we had some wine, and then we went to Tony's [a neighborhood Italian restaurant] for food, and then he left—no songs! We were having a conversation, you see, about things that mattered, and of course music matters, but not when you can have a really good conversation with someone. We talked about life, living in New York, Ibiza—Leonard had just come back from Ibiza and so had my lover Michael. And we talked about literature. By then I'd read of some of his poetry, and also *Beautiful Losers*. Michael was a writer also—he wrote a movie called *Scandal*, which is about the Profumo Affair—so we had a lot to talk about. When Leonard left I think I said, 'I've heard about these famous songs. Why don't you come back tomorrow?'"

Leonard returned the next day with his guitar. This time he sat in her living room and sang three songs: "Suzanne," "Dress Rehearsal Rag" and "The Stranger Song." Collins was "bowled over," she said, "particularly by 'Dress Rehearsal Rag.' Talk about dark: a song about suicide. I attempted suicide myself at fourteen, before I found folk music, so of course I loved it. We were desperately looking for something unusual for my album and when I heard 'Dress Rehearsal Rag,' that was it. 'The Stranger Song' I thought the least accessible of the three songs he sang—nowadays I love it and would do it in a second, but I was not there yet. Then Michael said, 'You have to do that "Suzanne" one too.' I thought about it and said, 'Yes, it has to be "Dress Rehearsal Rag" and "Suzanne" as well.'"

In accounts of the story elsewhere, Judy did not hear anything that day that she could use but told Leonard to keep in touch if he wrote any new songs, which reportedly he did, playing "Suzanne" to her over the phone from his mother's house in Montreal in December 1966. "Bullshit," says Collins. "We talked about my recording 'Dress Rehearsal Rag' right away and 'Suzanne' the next day." The evidence is in Collins's favor given that *In My Life*, which contained her covers of "Dress Rehearsal Rag" and "Suzanne," was released in November 1966. Jac Holzman confirms that Collins recorded the songs almost as soon as she heard them. "They were great," says Holzman, "the quality of the songs, the simple complexity, the internal rhymes—the lyrics are magical in their completeness. You finish listening to a song of Leonard's and you know he's said everything he had to say, he didn't let that song go until he's finished with it. Those two songs were the glue we needed to hold it all together." With the other songs ready to go and the photo for the front sleeve in place, it was a simple case of correcting the titles and credits before the record was in the stores and starting its climb into the Top 50.

"Suzanne" had its first airing on the New York radio station WBAI. "Judy Collins had a regular program," says disc jockey Bob

Fass. "It would be on for an hour, and she would sing herself and play records and have other musicians on; it was very popular. I was the engineer. Judy would give me her records a little in advance so I could play them on my program. She played me 'Suzanne' and I said, 'Judy, did you write that?' She said, 'No, Leonard Cohen.' 'Who's Leonard Cohen?' 'He's a Canadian poet.' Funny, after Judy Collins mentioned him, a young woman appeared at my door on Greenwich Avenue, climbed the steps and said, 'I'm here to talk about Leonard Cohen,' and we had some very pleasant hours together. I think she was a friend of his—I felt like I was being checked out. And I never saw her again. One of those mysteries."

Collins was so supportive of Leonard and sang his praises so generously that many assumed they were lovers. "We weren't," says Collins. "He's the kind of dangerous man that I would have gotten involved with and gotten into a lot of trouble with. He was charming and very intriguing, very deep, but I never had those feelings about him. I loved his songs and that was plenty. That was enough trouble." Collins laughs. "But his songs—there was nothing like them around. Nobody, including Dylan. Leonard was an unskilled, untrained musician, but because of his intelligence and sheer stubbornness, I suppose, he taught himself the guitar and he came up with songs which were very unusual—the melodic structure is not something that you would normally find and there are unexpected changes and twists and turns in every piece he does. They're brilliant, articulate, literary and utterly beyond. That's what hooked me. And the fact that a Jew from Canada can take the Bible to pieces and give the Catholics a run for their money on every story they ever thought they knew."

Leonard did continue to send Collins songs. "He was writing new songs all the time. By that time I was in so over my head with his material that I was ready to record anything he sent me. And as you know, I practically did—anything, everything. I think there was a Leonard song on practically every album after that"—three on her 1967 album and first Top 5 hit, *Wildflowers*: "Sisters of Mercy," "Priests" and "Hey, That's No Way to Say Goodbye," this last song composed to the sound of a radiator and dripping tap in a thin-walled hotel room on Thirty-fourth Street. It arose "from an over-used bed in the Penn Terminal Hotel in 1966," Leonard wrote in the liner notes to his 1975 *Greatest Hits* album. "The room is too hot. I can't open the windows. I am in the midst of a bitter quarrel with a blonde woman. The song is half-written in pencil but it protects us as we maneuver, each of us, for unconditional victory. I am in the wrong room. I am with the wrong woman."[15] This was not Marianne—though, when she saw the lyrics in his notebook, Leonard said she did ask whom it was about. Marianne was on Hydra. In the maelstrom of his life in New York, Hydra felt a million miles away.

Less than two months after arriving in Manhattan, Leonard had a manager and two songs on a major artist's album. He had discovered, to his joy, that he could write songs "on the run,"[16] that writing did not have to be the life-and-death ordeal it had been with *Beautiful Losers*. He had found that he could live in real life as he had on film: in a cheap hotel, unfettered and within arm's reach of an exit. Leonard put his plan to go to Nashville on hold. Instead, he packed his case and moved into the Henry Hudson Hotel on West Fifty-seventh Street. It was not, in the midsixties, the glamorous boutique hotel it is today; it was more like a low-rent version of the Chelsea Hotel, with the look and smell of a Victorian hospital for down-and-outs. If someone were taking a register of junkies, hustlers, drifters and penniless artists, many of its residents would have raised their hands.

Leonard's room, with its flowery curtain and threadbare counterpane, was barely twice the size of its single bed. But the window closed, at least, and there was a swimming pool in the hotel, as well as hashish and several young women willing to keep him warm at night. There was a tall Swedish woman who studied yoga and turned tricks; a pretty young writer, barely twenty years old, who was fighting a narcotics charge, with a little financial support from Leonard; and the lovely homeless artist whom Leonard invited in off the street and who, he found, shared his fascination with Saint Catherine Tekakwitha. Saint Catherine's image was embossed on a door of Saint Patrick's Cathedral on Fifth Avenue between Fiftieth and Fifty-first Streets. Leonard would go there and climb the stone steps, a pilgrim, and lay a flower at her feet.

Although it might not have won an arm-wrestling contest with Greenwich Village, the Montreal folk music scene was thriving. Penny Lang, a singer and guitar player, had been playing the city's coffeehouses since 1963. "If you liked folk music you didn't have to search for it, it seemed like it was everywhere. There were seven or eight coffeehouses but a lot of music happened spontaneously, in parks and other places. It felt very vibrant, as if a side of the city woke up which had been sleeping for a long time." Lang did not hear of Leonard ("I didn't read poetry") until 1966, when the Stormy Clovers started playing "Suzanne." "Then the song sort of passed down to the other singers around town and I learned it, and came up with a sort of different version. He's an exquisite writer, there was no one who writes as he does. And that's really all I knew about Leonard Cohen."

It was December and Leonard, back once again in Canada, was thinking hard about this music career into which he had made his first inroads. He wrote a letter to Marianne telling her that he knew what he must be, "a singer, a man who owns nothing. . . . I know now what I must train myself for."[17] He phoned Penny Lang. "It was the first time I'd ever spoken to him and he just called and said, 'Would you consider teaching me some guitar'?" says Lang. "But I was in very bad shape—I'm bipolar—and I said, 'No, I'm very depressed,' and that was the end of that. Later I realized that if anyone would have understood the word 'depression' at the time, it probably would have been Leonard." Lang would make her own way to New York a few months later, where a talent scout from Warner Bros. heard her play "Suzanne" at Gerde's in Greenwich Village and offered her a deal if she would record it with a rock band. "When 'rock band' came into the picture I said no." Lang did say yes to giving guitar lessons to Janis Joplin. Janis wanted to be able to accompany herself onstage when singing her version of Kris Kristofferson's "Me and Bobby McGee." "But it never happened, because Janis died." Leonard did not ask again. He practiced alone, playing in front of a full-length mirror to an audience of one, the only one whose opinion really mattered.

What was with the mirror?

"Through some version of narcissism, I always used to play in front of a mirror—I guess it was to figure out the best way to look while playing guitar, or maybe it was just where the chair was and the mirror in the room I happened to be living in. But I was very comfortable looking at myself playing."

The more he played, the more songs would come. It was as if his relatively minimal skills as a guitar player added a simplicity to the proceedings. "I was always interested by minimalism, even if we didn't use that term. I liked simple things, simple poetry, more than the decorative."[18] In the same way that the poetry he wrote had an implied melody, his melodies had an implied poetry. "I generally find the song arises out of the guitar playing, just fooling around on the guitar. Just trying different sequences of chords, really, just like playing guitar every day and singing until I make myself cry, then I stop. . . . I don't weep copiously, I just feel a little catch in my throat or something like that. Then I know that I am in contact with something that is just a little deeper than where I started when I picked the guitar up."[19]

Leonard's letter to Marianne closed with the words, "Darling, I hope we can repair the painful spaces where uncertainties have led us. I hope you can lead yourself out of despair and I hope I can help you."[20] The mailman arrived with a package for Leonard from New York: Judy Collins's new album. Carrying it carefully, by the edges, to the turntable, he placed the needle on track four. The snow was thick outside; in a few days baby Jesus would be reborn. Leonard, alone in his room in West Montreal, listened to Judy sing "Suzanne." When it was done playing he lifted the needle and put it back at the start of the track, over, and over, and over.

Nine

How to Court a Lady

The ad in the *Village Voice* read "Andy Warhol Presents Nico Singing to the Sounds of the Velvet Underground." It was February 1967 and Leonard, back in New York again, turned up the collar on his raincoat and walked through the East Village to the Dom. The cavernous room in a row of Victorian town houses on Saint Mark's Place had been a German immigrant community hall, a Polish restaurant and a music venue before Warhol had taken over the lease a year earlier and transformed it into an avant-garde circus-discotheque. It was the stage for his Exploding Plastic Inevitable performance art shows, offering experimental films (Warhol's and Paul Morrissey's), dancers (beauties and freaks from Warhol's Factory studio, like the socialite-turned-Warhol-film-star Edie Sedgwick and poet-photographer Gerard Malanga) and music. The house band was the Velvet Underground, whom Warhol managed. At his decree, their singer and songwriter Lou Reed, a short, young, Jewish New Yorker, shared the spotlight with a tall, blond German in her late twenties. Nico, said Lou Reed, "set some kind of standard for incredible-looking people."

Leonard happened upon Nico by chance. One night, during his last stay in New York, he had wandered into a nightclub and there she was, an ice queen, posed like Dietrich at the end of the bar. She had a chiseled face, porcelain skin, piercing eyes and a pretty-boy guitar player, who was her sole accompanist as she sang her songs in a strange, deep monotone. "I was completely taken," Leonard said. "I had been through the blonde trip; I had lived with a blonde girl and I had felt for a long time that I was living in a Nazi poster. This was a kind of repetition."[1] (Since he was presumably referring to Marianne, it might also have some bearing on why Marianne had to move out during Leonard's mother's visit.)

The woman who would become Leonard's next muse was born Christa Päffgen in Cologne in 1938, four years after Leonard was born and five years after Hitler came to power. She was a fashion model in Berlin and an actress who studied alongside Marilyn Monroe at Lee Strasberg's Method school in New York, and won a small role in Fellini's *La Dolce Vita* (1960) and a large one in Jacques Poitrenaud's *Strip-Tease* (1963). The first time she went into a recording studio was in Paris, with Serge Gainsbourg, to sing the title song for *Strip-Tease*, which he wrote. Her somber, death's-head voice was not to Gainsbourg's taste and a version by Juliette Gréco was used in its place.* Nico's second attempt at recording was more successful—in London this time, in 1965, with an equally celebrated producer, guitarist Jimmy Page. Her cover of Canadian folksinger Gordon Lightfoot's song "I'm Not Sayin'" was released as a single on Immediate Records, a label owned by Andrew Loog Oldham, the manager of the Rolling Stones; the Stones' guitar player Brian Jones was Nico's lover.

A liaison with Bob Dylan brought Nico back to New York. While Dylan was babysitting her son, Ari—the result of her brief affair with

---

* Nico's version was released posthumously on the compilation album *Le cinéma de Serge Gainsbourg* (2001).

the French movie star Alain Delon—Dylan wrote the song "I'll Keep It with Mine," which he gave to Nico. When his manager Albert Grossman sent her a plane ticket to New York, she assumed it was because Grossman wanted to manage her as a singer. He did not. But through the Dylan/Grossman connection she met Warhol, and Warhol thought her perfect. He put her in his films—most famously *Chelsea Girls*, in which Ari, then four years old, also appeared—and he put her in the Velvet Underground. Her bored, narcotic, gothic voice was featured on both sides of the band's first single, "All Tomorrow's Parties"/"I'll Be Your Mirror," which was released in October 1966, around the same time that Leonard was playing Judy Collins his songs. Leonard took to following Nico around New York, his unwitting tourist guide leading him from one haunt of the hip and demimonde to another.

"I remember walking into a club called Max's Kansas City that I'd heard was the place where everybody went—I didn't know anybody in New York—and I remember lingering by the bar, I was never good at that kind of hard work that's involved with socializing, and a young man came over to me and said, "You're Leonard Cohen, you wrote Beautiful Losers," *which nobody had read, it only sold a few copies in America. And it was Lou Reed. He brought me over to a table full of luminaries—Andy Warhol, Nico. I was suddenly sitting at this table with the great spirits of the time. [Laughs]"*

But you were more interested in talking to Nico. How did it go?

"I was among the multitudes that wanted Nico. A mysterious woman. I tried to talk to her, I introduced myself, but she wasn't interested."

Says Lou Reed, "*Beautiful Losers* is an incredible book, an amazing book, and on top of everything else, incredibly funny and very tricky. I remember later Leonard said to me he started writing songs after hearing 'I'll Be Your Mirror.' Who knows."[2] Leonard took a liking to Reed, at least in some part because Nico liked him.

You would imagine that Leonard and Warhol might get along, two men who believed in making their life their work, and their work their life. But, as with the Beats, Leonard claimed not to fit in. They made him feel provincial. According to Danny Fields, though, "There was no club that Leonard wasn't part of. We loved him, Nico loved him, I loved him, he was loved. His reputation then was fierce—and he was sexy. He didn't have to do very much except not vomit on the table." Fields was Elektra Records's New York A & R man, a close friend of Nico, who knew the midsixties Manhattan scene like the back of his hand. It was something else with Leonard, a kind of shyness, or a taste for being an outsider, or both, that turned the once-clubby youth into a man who really did not want to join any club, whether they wanted him or not.

Nico told Leonard she liked younger men and did not make an exception. Her young man du jour, her guitar player, was a fresh-faced singer-songwriter from Southern California, barely eighteen years old, named Jackson Browne. A surfer boy crossed with an angel, his natural good looks appeared unnatural alongside the cadaverous Warhol and his black-clad entourage. Browne had gone to New York on an adventure: some friends were driving cross-country and needed someone to split the bill; Browne grabbed his acoustic guitar and his mother's gas station credit card. When they rolled into Manhattan, Browne, looking up through the back window, saw "all these huge Nico posters everywhere, really beautiful, just amazing."[3] They were advertising her solo shows. Opening the show was Tim Buckley, a singer-songwriter Browne knew from the Orange County coffeehouse circuit. Buckley told him Nico was looking for a full-time electric guitarist and, since he "had his own thing going," he didn't want to do it. Browne borrowed an electric guitar.

Nico opened the door to her apartment. She looked him up and down with her famous stare. Liking what she saw, she invited him in. She sang the boy her songs, and he assured her he could play them. She asked him if he had any songs and he did, quite a lot of them;

although he did not yet have a record deal, Browne had a publishing contract. The first of his songs he played Nico was "These Days," an exquisite, pensive ballad he wrote when he was sixteen years old, after his second acid trip. Says Browne, "She said, 'I vill do zis song'—everybody did a Nico impersonation, she's fun to imitate."[4] She chose two more of Browne's songs and appointed him her new accompanist and lover, both effective immediately.

"Nico lived in this apartment with her little son who was about four years old. She had a roommate, a really big guy named Ronnie who wore big fur coats and had a lot of money and I don't know what he did, but I think that maybe he was a club owner or restaurateur or something. He was a very nice guy and amazingly he didn't seem to have any interest in her at all except as a friend; I thought, 'Wow, that's incredible.'" Browne laughs. "I remember Leonard used to come over to her house. I knew he had just become kind of very celebrated for 'Suzanne,' which Judy Collins covered, and he had this really great book he had written, *Beautiful Losers*, which he seemed to be embarrassed by for some reason, who knows. He used to also come to the club where we played. He'd just sit there at the front table and write and look at her."[5]

The picture he paints is somewhat reminiscent of *Death in Venice*—a solemn, love-struck old writer (at thirty-two years old, Leonard would have appeared quite old to the teenage Browne) mooning over a dangerous, unattainable beauty. Browne simply assumed that Leonard was "writing her a song," and in a way he was, although he was hoping for more than a cover. "She'd been given a song by Bob Dylan, one by Tim Hardin; she was gathering these great songs to interpret and they were songs that no one had ever heard of—sort of what Judy Collins was doing at the time, so if anybody cares to make the connection between Judy Collins and Nico, there it is."[6]

Leonard befriended the pair of them. "He would read us the poems he wrote while he watched her, very dreamy, and they were

amazing poems," says Browne. On a few occasions he would go with
the two of them to the Dom, before Browne broke up with Nico. "I
was into her," Browne says, "and it took me a while to realize I was
a fling. So I quit, but even though we weren't lovers anymore I was
working for her and seeing her every night. Then things got weird.
There was somebody calling and harassing her, a stalker, and she
accused me of making the calls and she kind of flipped." Browne
flew back to California—just in time for the Summer of Love. "Nico
was crazy and mysterious," says Browne. "She wouldn't tell anyone
where she was from—I don't think she wanted to be thought of as
German—and she had this ice-queen countenance. But she also had
this really girlish smile, and when she laughed she was like a little
kid, and she spent almost all her time with her son. There was this
side of Nico that I don't think many people know. I really dug her."[7]

So did Leonard. Although he never won her, he was "madly in love
with her."[8] Exclaims Danny Fields, "She didn't with Leonard? She
did it with Lou [Reed], God knows! And Nico *worshipped* Leonard.
She would call him up: 'Ohh, Lennhaarrrdt'—that's the way she said
his name, in that Germanic voice. 'Vat do you think, Lennhaarrrdt?'
'Would Lennhaarrrdt like my songs?' Nico was eager to ally herself
with creative people. Leonard was *very* important to her. She certainly was a girl of conflicted emotions." Though she was consistent
in her taste in men. After Jackson Browne, Nico moved on to Jim
Morrison and Jimi Hendrix, both in their early twenties.

*"I bumped into Jim Morrison a couple of times but I did not know him
well. And Hendrix—we actually jammed together one night in New York.
I forget the name of the club, but I was there and he was there and he knew
my song 'Suzanne,' so we kind of jammed on it."*

---

* Fields was responsible for signing, among others, Iggy Pop, the MC5 and the
Ramones. Iggy, whom Nico did not turn down, would go on to write an almost
Leonard Cohenesque song to her titled "Nazi Girlfriend"; its opening lines
were "I want to fuck her on the floor / Among my books of ancient lore."

You and Hendrix jammed on "Suzanne"? What did he do with it?

"He was very gentle. He didn't distort his guitar. It was just a lovely thing. I did bump into him again. I remember I was walking up Twenty-third Street, which is the street the Chelsea Hotel was on, and I was with Joni Mitchell, a very beautiful woman, and a big limousine pulled up and Jimi Hendrix was in the backseat, and he was chatting up Joni from the inside of the limo."

It didn't matter to him that she was with another man, specifically you?

"Well, you know, he was a very elegant man so it wasn't impolite."

Did Joni go off with him and leave you?

"No, she didn't. But Nico did. I went with Nico to hear Jim Morrison—I think he was playing for the first time in New York at a club—and Hendrix showed up and he was glorious, very beautiful, and I'd come with Nico and when it was time to go I said, 'Let's go,' and she said, 'I'm going to stay. You go.' [Laughs]"

Some years later, Leonard and Nico bumped into each other in the Spanish restaurant and bar El Quijote. When the bar closed, they wound up in Leonard's room in the Chelsea Hotel next door. It was one of the smaller guest rooms—Leonard was only passing through—and so they sat together on the bed, side by side, continuing the conversation they had begun downstairs. At one point, feeling encouraged, Leonard put a hand on her arm. Nico swung round and hit him so hard he levitated. "There are stories of her flare-ups and physical brutality," says Fields. "Her other brutality, the passive brutality, was just making you wonder what she was thinking, so much that people fell in love with her. Maybe it was a love punch, 'I don't vont to fall in love viz you'—*pow!* Maybe she wanted him to be a caveman conqueror, because men were so afraid of her. Nico loved Leonard. We all did."

But in 1967, feeling he "had no skill" and that he "had forgotten how to court a lady,"[9] Leonard went back alone to his hotel room. His thoughts full of Nico, he wrote "The Jewels in Your Shoulder" and

"Take This Longing," then titled "The Bells," both of which he later played and taught to Nico. She was the both "the tallest and blondest girl" in the song "Memories" and the muse for "Joan of Arc" ("This song was written for a German girl I used to know. She's a great singer, I love her songs. I recently read an interview where she was asked about me and my work. And she said I was 'completely unnecessary,'"[10] he told a Paris audience in 1974). She also inspired "One of Us Cannot Be Wrong." After one of the occasions on which Nico spurned him, Leonard went back to his room "and indulged [himself] in the black magic of candles"—the green candles he bought at a magic and voodoo shop—"and," he says, "I married these two wax candles, and I married the smoke of two cones of sandalwood and I did many bizarre and occult practices that resulted in nothing at all, except an enduring friendship."[11]

Leonard now lived in the Chelsea Hotel. An imposing redbrick Victorian at 222 West Twenty-third Street in what once was New York's theater district, it had four hundred rooms, a great many of which were occupied by artists, writers and bohemians. Mark Twain had stayed there; Arthur Miller lived there for six years, praising it as a place with "no vacuum cleaners, no rules, no shame." Dylan Thomas died there in his room and Sid Vicious killed his girlfriend Nancy Spungen in his. The hotel was the setting for Andy Warhol's film *The Chelsea Girls*.

The Chelsea was popular with Beat poets and equally popular with their successors, rock musicians—among them Bob Dylan, Jimi Hendrix, Janis Joplin and Patti Smith, who lived there with her photographer lover Robert Mapplethorpe. Smith described the hotel as "a doll's house in the Twilight Zone."[12] (Leonard had met Patti Smith the year before and taken her to dinner with Irving and Aviva Layton. "She was just a young kid then," says Aviva, "a skinny little waif, no breasts, and wearing rags, not feathers; I think she may have been living on the street—and Leonard told us, 'She's a genius, absolutely brilliant, she's going to be a real force.'")

The walls of the lobby of the Chelsea jostled with paintings, which had been given or hocked to Stanley Bard, the hotel manager, in lieu of rent. A door from the lobby led to the Spanish restaurant and bar next door, El Quijote. The slowest elevator in American hostelry crept up the twelve floors, opening out onto corridors painted yellow and a warren of rooms of various shapes, sizes and luxury. Leonard's, on the fourth floor, was lit by an overhead bulb and had a small black-and-white television, a hot plate and a washbasin where the water ran rust-brown until you counted to ten. More than half the hotel was taken up with long-term residents. Some gave the impression that they lived there for the sole purpose of getting an upgrade to a bigger, better room. It was "a big boho fraternity house," says the writer and journalist Thelma Blitz, and Leonard, the former fraternity house president, "felt entirely at home."

He had everything he needed in this latest version of home, including the succor of women. From the age of nine, when his father died, Leonard had been nurtured by women. During his infancy in the music business, those women were Mary Martin and Judy Collins. *In My Life* had been Collins's biggest-selling album to date, spending thirty-four weeks on the U.S. charts and getting a good deal of attention and radio play. "It was really the edge of the 'pop success' era," said Collins, "so it was partly that and the kind of promotion I was getting from Elektra." With "Suzanne" being such a powerful song and Collins such an evangelical cheerleader for its writer, Leonard was getting attention too, including from John Hammond, the leading A & R man at America's foremost record company, Columbia.

Hammond was a New York aristocrat—his mother was a Vanderbilt, his grandfather a Civil War general. His upbringing was extremely privileged, but, like Leonard, he chose a different path. Hammond aligned himself with the civil rights movement and became a jazz critic, a record producer and an A & R man with a remarkable résumé. Among the many greats Hammond signed and/or produced were Billie Holiday, Pete Seeger, Count Basie, Aretha Franklin and

Bob Dylan. "John Hammond was a genius," said Collins. "With Dylan he was able to see beyond his boring Woody Guthrie blues and signed him up for a three-record deal before 'Blowing in the Wind' ever happened. He was always carefully watching what was going on, and listening. He listened to what I was doing—he tried to sign me to Columbia, but I'd promised my hand to Elektra the week before—and that's where he heard Leonard, because there was nowhere else to hear him at that point." Mary Martin, meanwhile, was calling Hammond, talking Leonard up, sending him copies of Leonard's books and persuading him to go to CBC's New York office for a private screening of *Ladies and Gentlemen . . . Mr. Leonard Cohen.* She had Leonard record a demo tape of his songs, in her bathroom, sitting in the empty bathtub and singing into a borrowed Uher tape recorder. A copy was made for Garth Hudson, the keyboard player with the Band, to do the lead sheets of each of the songs, for publishing purposes. Another copy was delivered to Hammond personally at his office, Martin and her lawyer colleague E. Judith Berger having changed into their tiniest miniskirts.

Leonard received a phone call from Hammond inviting him to lunch at a nearby restaurant. Afterward, Hammond asked if he might come back to the Chelsea with Leonard and hear him play his songs in his room. Perched on the edge of the bed, beneath the overhead light, Leonard sang to him for an hour: songs including "Suzanne," "The Stranger Song," "Master Song," "Hey, That's No Way to Say Goodbye," "The Jewels in Your Shoulder," and a song he told Hammond he had just written that day, "Your Father Has Fallen." Hammond sat in the only chair, eyes closed, stone quiet. When Leonard finally stopped playing, Hammond opened his eyes and smiled. "You've got it," he said. Leonard, not entirely sure what it was he had, thanked him and showed him out. Back at Columbia Records, Hammond announced that he planned to sign Leonard. Not for the last time, this did not meet with universal enthusiasm at the label. The acting chief executive, Bill Gallagher, said, "A thirty-two-year-old poet? Are you crazy?"[13] He had a point; in 1967 rock was the new poetry, and the rock world did not trust a man over thirty. But Hammond persisted. Larry Cohen, former vice president of Columbia/Epic, who had the office next door to his, recalls Hammond telling him that "out of all the artists he had ever signed that Leonard was the most intelligent. That's saying something coming from John. If you knew John, he was not given to extraordinary platitudes. He thought very highly of Leonard Cohen."

On February 22, still unsigned, Leonard made his official live debut as a singer in New York. It was a benefit concert for WBAI, held in the Village Theatre on Sixth Street at Second Avenue, with an impressive lineup that included Pete Seeger, Tom Paxton and Judy Collins. It had been Bob Fass's suggestion that Collins bring him onstage and introduce him as a new artist, much as Joan Baez had once done with Dylan. Collins jumped at the idea but Leonard said no. "He said, 'I can't sing and I certainly can't perform,'" remembers Collins. "I said, 'Of course you can.' But Leonard never dreamed of being a performer. I said, 'Why don't you just come and sing "Suzanne"? Everyone will know the song so it'll be comfortable for you.' Finally he consented."

"Judy told me, 'I don't think he wants to,'" says Bob Fass, "then she called back again and said, 'He's changed his mind, he's going to come,' so we advertised him. On the night, Judy came onstage and sang a song, then called for Leonard to come out. And he came out, and he had trouble tuning his guitar and she finally gave him hers. He began to sing, but maybe it was in the wrong key or something or he couldn't hear, and his voice broke. He said, 'I can't go on,' and he left the stage. I thought, 'That's really too bad,' and went on with the show." Much later in the show, Collins told him Leonard would like to come back on. "And he did. I said, 'This man has balls.'" Says Collins, "Leonard was very, very nervous, shaking like a leaf. He hadn't sung in public like this before, only in these little clubs in New York where he read his poetry, and he started singing 'Suzanne' and about halfway through the song he stopped and walked off the stage. But everybody just adored him. So I went back and told him, 'You've got to come back and finish the song.' He said, 'I can't,' and I said, 'I'll come out and do it with you.' So I went onstage with him and we finished the song up together—and that was Leonard's debut."

In a letter to Marianne dated February 23, 1967, Leonard wrote, "Darling. I sang in New York for the first time last night, at a huge benefit concert. Every singer you've ever heard of was there performing. Judy Collins introduced me to the audience, over 3000 people." He described hitting a chord and finding his guitar "completely out of tune, tried to retune it, couldn't get more than a croak out of my throat." He managed to sing just four lines of "Suzanne," he said, his voice "unbelievably flat, then I broke off and said simply, 'Sorry, I just can't make it,' and walked off the stage, my fingers like rubber bands, the people baffled and my career in music dying among the coughs of the people backstage." He described to Marianne how he had stood and watched numbly from the wings while Collins played some more songs, and how he had finally come back on and managed to get through "Stranger Song," even though his voice and guitar continued to break down. "I finished somehow and I thought I'll just commit suicide. Nobody really knew what to do or say. I think that someone took my hand and led me off. Everybody backstage was very sorry for me and they couldn't believe how happy I was, how relieved I was that it had all come to nothing, that I had never been so free."[*]

Marianne says, "I was sitting in my mother's house in Oslo with little Axel at the time and something very strange happened. Suddenly my son stood up and said, 'Cohne died, Marianne'—he called

---

[*] Other accounts place Leonard's first appearance with Collins on April 30 at the Town Hall at a benefit concert for the National Committee for a Sane Nuclear Policy (SANE); the date on Leonard's letter belies that, as does an ad listing the participants in the SANE benefit.

Leonard 'Cohne' in those days—and, as Leonard told the story himself, he 'died' that night on the stage." Leonard's letter closed by saying that he would be back in Hydra in a month or two to start working on another book. "I hope you're feeling good, little friend of my life," he closed the letter. "Axel's card was beautiful, hug him from me. Goodnight darling. Leonard."[14]

Leonard was still talking about writing a book when he wrote to Marianne in April, three days after performing to a sold-out crowd at an arts festival at the State University of New York in Buffalo. He had been offered a forty-date tour of American colleges in the fall, he said, and, prior to that, the Newport Folk Festival and Expo 67 in Montreal, and he was "very anxious" to write a book before it started. But "it" had already started. A second recording artist, Buffy Sainte-Marie, was covering two of his songs, and Nico was planning to sing "The Jewels in Your Shoulder" on her debut solo album—all women. Yet he wrote to Marianne that he was "dead to lust, tired of ambition, a lazy student of my own pain." He told her that he had "given up plans for sainthood, revolution, redemptive visions, music mastery." What he wanted, he said, was to be with Marianne on Hydra.[15] Days later he wrote to Marianne again, this time describing the thin green candle he kept burning in his room that was "dedicated to St Jude Thaddeus, Patron Saint of Impossible Causes."[16] He made no mention of Nico in the letter. But clearly Nico was not the only lost cause on Leonard's mind.

John Hammond had not given up on Leonard. When Columbia Records appointed a new head, Clive Davis, Hammond persuaded him to give the go-ahead to sign Leonard. A contract dated April 26, 1967, naming Mary Martin Management Inc. as representative and Bob Johnston as producer, was delivered to Martin's Bleecker Street office. It offered four one-year options and an advance of $2,000, which would be paid within thirty days of his completing the recording of two sides of an LP. Leonard took out his pen and signed. He was a recording artist.

Columbia Studio E was on the sixth floor of the old lead-lined CBS Radio building on East Fifty-second Street. Stepping out of the elevator on May 19, 1967, his first day of recording, Leonard's eye was caught by a large canvas sign that read THE ARTHUR GODFREY SHOW. Godfrey, a popular radio personality, broadcast his daily program from a room next to the recording studio. Godfrey was known for his cheery persona; he even had his own line of plastic ukuleles and played one regularly on his shows. But the warmth did not spread to the freaks and long-haired musicians with whom he was obliged to share the floor.

Leonard, carrying a briefcase and a guitar, looking more like a college professor than a musician, pushed through the heavy door and into a room about thirty feet square with a nineteen-foot-high ceiling. Sitting on a couch in the control room, dressed in a suit and reading a newspaper, was John Hammond. Bob Johnston, the staff producer named on the contract, had been taken off the project. "I told Leonard I wanted to do it so bad," says Johnston, "and Leonard wanted me to do it, but they told me absolutely not because I had too many artists already—Dylan, Johnny Cash, Simon and Garfunkel." Six months earlier, the last of these had been in Studio E with Johnston recording their hit album *Parsley, Sage, Rosemary and Thyme.* John Hammond had decided to take over Leonard's album himself and brought along a small handful of session musicians.

In that first three-hour session, they recorded five takes of "Suzanne," six of "Stranger Song"—with guitar and organ, guitar and bass, and just guitar—and six of "Hey, That's No Way to Say Goodbye," five described as "rock versions" with the band and one "simple version," performed solo. Hammond, behind the glass, would call enthusiastically over the talk-back, "Watch out, Dylan!" Hammond "never said anything negative," said Leonard. "There were just degrees of his affirmation. Everything you did was 'good' but some things were 'very good.' " Over time Leonard came to learn that "if it was just 'good,' you knew you had to do another take."[17] At the second session he recorded four takes of "So Long, Marianne."

There was a lot of time in which to learn. Leonard often said that *Songs of Leonard Cohen* was a hard album to make, and job sheets found in Columbia's archives—handwritten cards that logged the dates, times and content of each recording session—back this up. Leonard recorded the album from May 19 until November 9, with two different producers in three different studios. For the fourth and fifth sessions in June, the operation shifted to Studio B, a penthouse in the old Columbia building on Seventh Avenue, where the elevators had operators who wore gray uniforms with brass buttons and piping. It was a smaller room at least, with a drab functional appearance that Leonard tried to alleviate with candles and incense. It made him no less uncomfortable.

"It's never come easily. I've never been particularly confident about the process and I was never able to exactly get what I wanted. I always had that sense, if I can just finish the damn thing! And you keep notching your standards down, degree by degree, until finally you say, 'I've finished, never mind.' Not, 'Is it going to be beautiful, is it going to be perfect, is it going to be immortal?' 'Can I finish?' became the urgent question."

As it was your first time, did you simply let Hammond get on with doing it the way he wanted to, or did you have any particular requirements?

"I asked them for a full-length mirror. That was my only requirement. And he had some very good ideas about how it should be done. He brought in a bass player whose name is on the tip of my tongue, a really fine bass player, and we just laid down a lot of the songs, just the two of us together. And he was a very sensitive player. I think those were the core tracks of at least half the songs on that record, just the guitar and bass."

Leonard knew how he wanted to sound, or at least how he did not want to, but as an untrained musician he lacked the language to explain it. He could not play as well as the session musicians, so he found them intimidating. "I didn't really know how to sing with a band, with really good, professional musicians that were really cooking, and I would tend to listen to the musicians rather than concentrate on what I was doing, because they were doing it so much more proficiently than I was."[18] Hammond, smartly, let the band go and had Leonard work with a single accompanist: Willie Ruff, a sophisticated, intuitive bass player who had played with Dizzy Gillespie, Count Basie and Louis Armstrong. Ruff did not care that Leonard could not read music or charts. "He supported the guitar playing so well. He could always anticipate my next move, he understood the song so thoroughly," said Leonard. "He was one of those rare musicians that play selflessly, and for pure and complete support. I couldn't have laid down those tracks without him."[19]

The location changed once again, this time to Studio C, a converted Greek-Armenian Orthodox church on Thirtieth Street where Miles Davis recorded *Kind of Blue*. By this point, Leonard was cutting his sixteenth take of "Suzanne" as well as a song titled "Come On, Marianne." "I thought it always was 'Come on, Marianne, it's time that we began to laugh and cry,'" says Marianne, "but—unless I'm dreaming—there was a group in California, maybe the Beach Boys, who had similar words in a song. When he wrote it, for me it was like, 'Come on, if we can just keep this boat afloat.' And then we found out that we could not."

Leonard had begun writing the song the year before, in Montreal, and finished it in the Chelsea Hotel, but he was still vacillating in the studio over these two words in the title and chorus that gave the song very different meanings. "I didn't think I was saying good-bye," said Leonard, "but I guess I was." He did not write it as a farewell song; it was almost as if the song made the decision for him. "There's a certain kind of writer that says hello to people in their songs and there's a certain kind of writer that says good-bye to people. And you know

I'm more a writer of elegies. . . . At least in that particular phase," he said in 1979. "I think for many writers the work has a prophetic quality, I don't mean in a cosmic or religious sense but just in terms of one's own life; you are generally writing about events that haven't taken place yet."[20] It was an interesting statement. The first half of it suggests that saying good-bye is a songwriting conceit, something that suited his taste and style; as to the second part, he was surely not so superstitious as to believe that the songs dictated his actions as they took form. When Leonard wrote a song, though, he did go deep, and it appears that what he found there was an urge to leave.

———————

In July, Leonard took a monthlong break from the studio; it felt like he'd been released from jail. So much had happened while he was in New York, wrapped up in his new music career. There had been a coup d'état in Greece, which was now ruled by a military junta, and in Israel there had been the Six-Day War. His friend Irving Layton had gone to the Israeli consulate to offer his services in the army. They were declined.[21] Leonard's duties, and the reason for the break, were a series of concerts he had to perform.

The first, on July 16, was at the famous Newport Folk Festival, for which once again he had Judy Collins to thank. Collins was on the festival's board of directors and, two years after Bob Dylan had been booed for going electric, was still fighting the traditionalists to acknowledge the new direction folk music, including hers, was taking, Collins wanted to stage a singer-songwriter workshop, and finally she got her way. Topping her list of participants were Leonard and another newcomer, an unsigned singer-songwriter named Joni Mitchell.

Says Collins, "I came to know Joni through Al Kooper," a rock musician friend who had played with Dylan in his historic Newport electric set. "He called me up, it was three in the morning, and he was hanging out with this girl who had told him she was a singer and writer, and he went home with her because he thought he could get laid, but he found out when he got to her house that she really *could* sing and write. He put her on the phone and had her sing me 'Both Sides Now,' which of course I had to record."

"Judy," says Danny Fields, "was a fountain of discovery. Leonard first turned up in my consciousness, as with many other people, with the song 'Suzanne' on Judy's 1966 album *In My Life*. After closing time at the Scene, a club where Hendrix and Tiny Tim became famous, a bunch of us who thought ourselves the cool rock 'n' roll crowd would go back to the owner Steve Paul's little house on Eighteenth Street and listen to that album. Then in early 1967 I started working at Elektra and Judy was one of my artists, and then came Leonard. But when I really met him was at Newport. I'd gone to the festival as representative of my record company and, like everybody, stayed at the Viking Hotel. It was beautiful and peaceful and I didn't have to drive so I took LSD. I was with Judy and Leonard and they said, 'Let's go back to Leonard's room.'"

Fields remembers "sitting on the floor, contemplating the carpet, while they sat on the two beds with their guitars. Leonard was teaching Judy 'Hey, That's No Way to Say Goodbye,' and that was the audio track to the universe and the eight dimensions of existence in the shag rug. When I woke up it was just predawn, they were still sitting on the two beds with the guitars, and Judy said, 'Oh, I think Danny looks as though he could use some fresh air, Leonard, let's take him for a walk,' and we went walking around the bay, where up on the cliffs the great robber baron palaces of Newport are, as the sun rose. It was wonderful. And when I flew back to New York, the next night Judy was doing the Central Park concert"—the Rheingold Festival—"and she brought Leonard up onstage with her to perform 'Suzanne.'"

The *New York Times* review of Leonard at Newport described him as an "extremely effective singer, building a hypnotic, spellbinding effect." Still, as he had been at the WBAI benefit, Leonard was terrified. "He told me he was *terribly* nervous," recalls Aviva Layton, who was in the audience in Central Park. "It was the middle of summer, the place was packed with people and the sun was setting, and Judy Collins said, 'I want to introduce to you a singer-songwriter, his name is Leonard Cohen.' Leonard came out with his guitar strapped on—and some people groaned, because they'd come to see Judy Collins, not this unknown Leonard Cohen. So he had to win over the crowd. He was facing thousands of people, standing packed like sardines, and he just said, very quietly, 'Tonight my guitar is full of tears and feathers.' And then he played 'Suzanne,' and that was it. Incredible." Leonard celebrated having made it through the performance, privately, in his Chelsea Hotel room. With him was his new inamorata, a woman he had met at Newport, a twenty-three-year-old, willowy blond singer-songwriter with a voice every bit as unique as Nico's.

Joni Mitchell, like Leonard, was from the East Coast of Canada. But their versions of Eastern Canada were vastly different—Leonard's urban and cosmopolitan, Joni's vast prairie skies. Joni, the daughter of a Canadian Air Force officer, had been raised in a small town in Saskatchewan. She was a talented painter, and when, as a child, she contracted polio (in the same epidemic in which her fellow small-town East Canadian Neil Young also contracted it), during her long, lonely convalescence she also discovered a talent for music. She taught herself to play the ukulele, then guitar, excelling at the latter and inventing her own sophisticated tunings and style. In 1964 Joni quit art school to be a folksinger, moving to Toronto and the coffee-houses around which the folk scene revolved. In February 1965 she gave birth to a daughter, the result of an affair with a photographer. A few weeks later she married folksinger Chuck Mitchell and gave the baby up for adoption. The marriage did not last. Joni left, taking his name with her, and moved into Greenwich Village, where she was living alone in a small hotel room when she met Leonard.

It was an intense romance. At the outset Joni played student to

Leonard's teacher. She asked him for a list of books she should read. "I remember thinking when I heard his songs for the first time that I was not worldly," she said. "My work seemed very young and naive in comparison."[22] Leonard gave her some suggestions, including Lorca, Camus and the I Ching. But he was quickly aware that Joni needed little help with anything, particularly her songwriting. They each wrote a (very different) song called "Winter Lady"—Joni's appears to have been written first—and Joni wrote two love songs referencing Leonard's song "Suzanne": "Wizard of Is," with an almost-identical melody and near-quoted lines ("You think that you may love him," she wrote of the man who speaks "in riddles") and "Chelsea Morning," set in a room with candles, incense and oranges, where the sun pours in "like butterscotch" instead of honey.

Leonard took Joni to Montreal. They stayed in his childhood home on Belmont Avenue. In her song "Rainy Night House" she described the "holy man" sitting up all night, watching her as she slept on his mother's bed. They painted each other's portraits. Leonard's was the face Joni drew on a map of Canada in her song "A Case of You," in which a man declares himself to be as "constant as a northern star." When it turned out he wasn't, Joni wrote about that too, in "That Song About the Midway" and in "The Gallery," in which a man who describes himself as a saint, and complains of her description of him as heartless, pleads with her to take him to her bed.

For the first time the tables were turned: Leonard was the muse for a woman. Not just any woman but one whom David Crosby—who also had an intense and short-lived love affair with Joni Mitchell in 1968—calls "the greatest singer-songwriter of our generation." Within a year Leonard and Joni's affair was over. Leonard told journalist Mark Ellen, "I remember we were spending some time together in Los Angeles years ago and someone said to me, 'How do you like living with Beethoven?'" How did Leonard like living with Beethoven? "I didn't like it," Leonard said, laughing, "because who would? She's prodigiously gifted. Great painter too."[23] As David Crosby says, "It was very easy to love her, but turbulent. Loving Joni is a little like falling into a cement mixer."

In later years Mitchell seemed keen to distance herself from Leonard artistically. "I briefly liked Leonard Cohen, though once I read Camus and Lorca I started to realize that he had taken a lot of lines from those books, which was disappointing to me," she said in 2005 of the man she had once described as "a mirror to my work," someone who "showed me how to plumb the depths of my experience." She would go on to describe him as "in many ways a boudoir poet"[24]—a grander term than "the Bard of the Bedsit," one of the nicknames the UK music press would later give him, but reductive nonetheless. Any close inspection of Mitchell's songs pre- and post-Leonard would seem to indicate that he had some effect on her work. Over the decades, Leonard and Joni have remained friends.

On July 22, 1967, Leonard was in Montreal, performing at Expo 67, the world's fair. It was an important concert. Canada, conscious of the eyes of the world on it, was treating the expo as a celebration of Canadian independence and, in the case of Quebec, harmony. As the Canadian journalist Robert Fulford wrote, its success marked "the end of Little Canada, a country afraid of its own future, frightened of great plans. Despite the spectre of French-Canadian separatism that haunted Canada through the early and middle 1960s, Expo seemed to suggest that we were now entering a new and happier period in our history."[25] Leonard, "*poète, chansonnier, écrivain,*" as he was described on the bill, would perform at the Youth Pavilion (being two months off thirty-three did not exclude him). It was one of the smaller marquees, set up like a nightclub with chairs and tables, and it was sold out.

Leonard had been nervous playing in Central Park, but this hometown performance terrified him. His family was there—his mother was in the front row—as were many of his friends. Erica Pomerance was there, along with "a flock of Leonard Cohen aficionados who were half friends, half admirers, basically fans of his poetry." Leonard had littered the small stage with candles. He told the audience to come forward and fetch a candle for their table so that he could sing. "He was tentative and earnest, very unpolished," says Montreal music critic Juan Rodriguez. Nancy Bacal concurs. "He was horrified, just frozen. He told me, looking out at these people, how could he just become this other person? How could he become this performer when they knew him, they'd known him all his life? It was just too hard for him."

There was one more summer festival for Leonard to play—the Mariposa Folk Festival, at Innis Lake, near Toronto—before going back to New York to continue work on his album. There were two more sessions with Hammond in August and then another three-week break, during which Leonard flew to L.A. Director John Boorman was talking about making a movie based on the song "Suzanne" and having Leonard score it. No one had ever paid his way across the continent before. There were even matchboxes with his name on them waiting for him in his room at the Landmark Hotel. Lighting a cigarette, Leonard sat at the desk and wrote a song called "Nine Years Old," which would become "The Story of Isaac." Nothing came of the film. At various times Leonard has said that he "couldn't relate" to the idea or that it was dropped when it was discovered he did not own the rights to the song. The rights to "Suzanne," "Master Song" and "Dress Rehearsal Rag," he said, had been "pilfered in New York City."[26] Leonard, assisted by his manager, had set up his own publishing company, Stranger Music. An arranger, producer and music publisher named Jeff Chase whom Mary Martin thought might prove helpful was brought in, and somewhere in the process Leonard appeared to have somehow signed over the songs to him.

Said Leonard, "My mother, who I always thought was kind of naive—she was Russian, her English was imperfect—said to me, 'Leonard, you be careful of those people down there. They're not like us.' And of course, I didn't say anything to disrespect, she was my mother, but in my mind I thought, 'Mother, you know, I'm not a child.' I was 32, I'd been around the block a few times. But she was right. She was right."*27

On September 8, in Studio B, Leonard recorded four more songs with Hammond. It would prove to be their last session together. Several reasons have been posited for Hammond's dropping out. Leonard always said that Hammond became ill, and certainly he had health problems: when he signed Leonard to Columbia it was shortly after he had taken time off following a heart attack, and in subsequent years he would suffer several more. Another reason given was the illness of Hammond's wife. In his autobiography, Hammond said nothing about illness and implied that there were musical differences. Leonard, he wrote, "got the jitters" at Hammond's simple production approach and "could not conceive of his voice being commercial enough to sell records. Simplicity was his greatest asset and we told him so. It was not what he wanted to hear. . . . I was overruled and another producer brought in."28

Hammond's recollections about signing Leonard admittedly include several errors, but Larry Cohen, his associate at Columbia, backs up what Hammond said about his production style. "John's MO, having known him for years, was not to change people or their sound, other than what they normally were, and what he did was bring out the best in people doing what they did. He didn't give Dylan any directions—Dylan came in with the things that he wanted to do and that's why John signed him and he let him do what he did."

Leonard himself said something once that suggested he wanted something more than just simple voice and guitar. "I was trying to find—I wanted a kind of 'found sound' background to a lot of my tunes. What I wanted running through 'The Stranger Song' was

---

* Chase and Cohen came to a settlement in 1987.

the sound of a tire on a wet pavement, a kind of harmonic hum.
[Hammond] was almost ready to let me take a recording device into
a car. He let me do the next best thing. I got in touch with mad sci-
entists around New York who had devices that would create sounds.
Unfortunately, he got sick in the middle of this operation."[29] Whatever the explanation, after four arduous months of work on his debut
album, nothing came of it. Leonard was back to square one.

Ten

The Dust of a Long Sleepless Night

So much had happened in the year since Leonard played Judy Collins his songs that the world itself seemed to be on speed. But some things had not happened—primarily, Leonard's album. It seemed to Leonard that this inability to make a record was a problem peculiar to him. Judy Collins had just finished her seventh LP, *Wildflowers*, which contained three more songs that Leonard had written but that he had not yet recorded himself. There was a second cover of "Suzanne" in the singles charts too, sung by Noel Harrison, an English actor, the same age as Leonard. It must have felt to Leonard that he had lost the rights to his song in more ways than one, and since "Suzanne" was by consensus his signature song, that he was losing himself as well. When the recording sessions stopped, Leonard behaved like a lost man. For a week he stayed shut in his hotel room, smoking a great deal of hashish. He had felt lost in New York once before, when he was attending Columbia University, and on that occasion he had left after a year and gone back home to Montreal and his friends. But with Columbia Records there was unfinished business, and so he stayed, turning to the nearest thing he had in New York to an artists' community: the Warhol set and the denizens of the Chelsea Hotel.

Occasionally the two would overlap. Edie Sedgwick, a gamine blond beauty and the most famous of Warhol's socialite starlets, had moved into the Chelsea, having accidentally burned down the apartment her mother bought for her. Edie had crawled along the floor and escaped with only a burned hand. Her new home at the Chelsea was on the fourth floor, down the hall from Leonard's room. Her friend Danny Fields, who was visiting Leonard, inquired if he had ever met Edie. Leonard said he had not. "Would you like to?" Fields asked. "She's a magical person that everyone falls in love with." Leonard said he would. Fields ran off to Edie's room. He found her there with Brigid Berlin, another of Warhol's renegade socialites. Plump and homely, Brigid might not have been blessed with looks but undeniably had personality—when Fields first set eyes on her, Brigid was climbing out of a yellow cab wearing nothing but a sarong around her waist, with a toy doctor's kit dangling between her naked breasts, and carrying the big fake doctor's bag that she took with her everywhere. It was filled with vials of "something she'd concocted like a mad scientist," its ingredients mostly liquid amphetamine and vitamin B. "She'd run around with a syringe, screaming, 'I'm going to get you!' and she did, injecting you in the butt right through your pants." It earned her the name Brigid Polk, as in "poke." Warhol gave her a starring role in *The Chelsea Girls*, alongside Edie and Nico.

When Fields walked into the room, he found the two women "pasting sequins one at a time in a coloring book," an activity pursued after the age of seven only if a person is on speed. "Brigid had fallen asleep on a tube of Ready Glue and she was stuck to the floor; she tried to turn around and gave up and was just lying there. There was the remnants of a fire in the fireplace and there were candles in candlesticks that she'd bought at the voodoo store where everybody went to get spells and unguents," Leonard included. "I said, 'Edie, Leonard Cohen the famous poet and songwriter is here and he'd like to meet you.' She said, 'Oh, bring him over, I'll just get made up.' When Edie put on makeup it could take three hours, literally. So I said, 'He's a simple guy, and anyway you look beautiful, I'm going to go get him.'"

Fields returned with Leonard. On entering the room, Leonard's eyes were immediately drawn to Edie's candles. He headed straight for them and stood there, staring. "The first thing Leonard said to her was, 'I'm wondering about these candles. Did you put them here in this order?' 'Order? Please! It's just candles.' And he said, 'No, it's a very unfortunate order that you've placed them in. It means bad luck or misfortune.' Edie giggled, and that was it, I left them alone with these candles. But wait. They caught fire soon afterward and the room was burned completely black. Edie got out a second time by crawling across the floor, and when she reached for the door handle, once again she burned her hand."

Brigid Polk was an artist. Among her best-known works was her series of "tit paintings," made by dipping her breasts in paint and pressing them onto paper. She also had a "Cock Book," a blank-paged book in which she asked people (women as well as men) to do a drawing of their penis. Among the participants were the painter Jean-Michel Basquiat, the actress Jane Fonda, and Leonard. Leonard, declining to illustrate his privates, wrote on a page, "Let me be the shy one in your book." He was involved and yet not involved—which described his general dealings with the Warhol set. They were more to his taste than the hippie scene on the West Coast that had begun to infiltrate New York: "There seemed to be something flabby about the hippie movement. They pulled flowers out of public gardens. They put them in guns, but they also left their campsites in a mess. No self-discipline," he said.[1] In addition, Warhol's Pop Art was an interesting study for Leonard as he made the shift from literature to pop music, from ivory tower to commercial art, and the models and starlets who surrounded Warhol were an interesting diversion and occasional indulgence. He was accidentally captured on film in the company of Warhol starlet Ivy Nicholson in *B.O.N.Y. (Boys of New York)*, made by a Texas film buff named Gregory Barrios, under Warhol's patronage. But in truth, Leonard was just passing through.*

He missed Marianne and Hydra. He took to eating alone in a Greek restaurant, drinking retsina, ordering from the menu in Greek, playing Greek records on the jukebox. He sent Marianne a long, tender poem he had written to her. It began,

> *This is for you*
> *it is the book I meant to read to you*
> *when we were old*
> *Now I am a shadow*
> *I am as restless as an empire*
> *You are the woman*
> *who released me.*

It ended,

> *I long for the boundaries*
> *of my wandering*
> *and I move*
> *with the energy of your prayer*
> *for you are kneeling*
> *like a bouquet*
> *in a cave of bone*

---

* This was Leonard's second movie appearance that year. He was filmed performing "The Stranger Song" in Canadian director Don Owen's *The Ernie Game*.

behind my forehead
and I move towards a love
you have dreamed for me.[2]

At Leonard's bidding, Marianne flew over to New York with little Axel. Leonard set about introducing Marianne to his life in the city, taking her, she says, to all the "funny little coffeehouses he loved." She would go and shop at the Puerto Rican magic store that Leonard and Edie frequented, buying candles and perfumed oils that made beautiful patterns on the water in Leonard's rust-stained hotel bathtub. They lunched at El Quijote, where Leonard introduced her to Buffy Sainte-Marie, whom Marianne liked. He also introduced her to Andy Warhol and to his fellow hotel residents, many of whom she found bizarre. It was "a strange scene," said Marianne. She couldn't help but contrast the dark, detached hedonism of his life in New York with their life on Hydra, when they were "barefoot, poor and in love." But it also became evident that Leonard really did not want her to live with him. While Leonard stayed on at the Chelsea, Marianne moved with Axel, who was now nine years old, into an apartment on Clinton Street, which she shared with Carol Zemel—the wife of Leonard's friend Henry Zemel—who was studying at Columbia.

During the daytime, while Axel was at school and Carol Zemel was at the university, Marianne would make little handicrafts, kittens made out of wool and steel. At night, while Carol kept an eye on the child, she sold them on the street outside clubs. It was not the best of neighborhoods, and Leonard asked her to stop, telling her that he worried about her, but she continued. The only time she encountered any trouble was when she was robbed of her earnings at knifepoint after leaving a cinema where she had gone alone to watch a Warhol film. Leonard and Marianne still saw each other; he took her to a Janis Joplin concert and introduced her to Joplin backstage. But the time he spent with Marianne grew less and less. She knew he was seeing other women. Things brightened for Marianne when Steve Sanfield, their friend from Hydra, showed up in New York on a mission to raise funds for Roshi's new Zen center, giving her someone else to talk to and see. She tried her best to make it work, staying for a year, but ultimately she was not happy in New York. When the school year was over, she went back to Europe.

Leonard packed his bags and moved out of the Chelsea, and back into the Henry Hudson Hotel, the dive on West Fifty-seventh Street. "It was a forbidding place, a hole and a holdout," says Danny Fields. "I thought maybe the Chelsea got a little too happy for him and he needed someplace more suitably grim and desolate."

Four weeks after Leonard's album had been put on hold, it was once again back on. Columbia had appointed a new producer. John Simon was twenty-six years old, "just another junior producer among many at Columbia Records—that is, until I made a lot of money for them with 'Red Rubber Ball.'" The song, cowritten by Paul Simon (no relation) and recorded by the Cyrkle, whom John Simon produced, was such a big hit that even Leonard was aware of it. ("I loved it," said Leonard, "still do.") As a result John Simon earned "an office with a window and some decent artists to produce," first Simon & Garfunkel, then Leonard Cohen.

John Simon knew nothing about Leonard or the album's troubled history. "Leonard told me that he'd been living in the Chelsea Hotel waiting for John Hammond to schedule a session, and, just as a recording date was approaching, John called him to put off the date for a month. Leonard, as I remember it, asked for a different producer because he was tired of waiting. As far as I know, Hammond was not ill. I visited with John in his office and he had nothing but praise for Leonard."

Simon started reading Leonard's poetry and, in order to get better acquainted, invited him to stay with him at his parents' empty house in Connecticut, where they could discuss the album in peace.

"I think Leonard saw a familiar milieu in that house; both our families were middle-class, intellectual Jews. I went to bed and when I woke up in the morning, I found Leonard poring through my father's books. He said he had stayed up all night." Simon listened to the "acoustic, demo-y" recordings that Leonard had done with Hammond, and they set a date to start work, October 11, 1967. This time, when Leonard arrived at Studio B for the first session, there were no musicians waiting for him, just his young producer and the two union-mandated engineers. ("Producers could only talk," says Simon. "Unless you were in the union, you were strictly forbidden from touching any equipment, mics, mixing board, etc.")

Leonard "appeared confident," says Simon, "and he was singing great—nice quality, great pitch." There was no full-length mirror this time; Leonard simply sat, played and sang. There were eleven sessions with Simon over the space of two months in Studios B and E. Steve Sanfield was still in town, so Leonard invited him along. "He laid down all of his songs, one after the other, and I was blown away by them," Sanfield remembers. "The producer seemed blown away too. He said, 'We're going to make a great album.'"

Sanfield was staying with a friend who lived in New York, Morton Breier, the author of *Masks, Mandalas and Meditation.* They had made plans to meet with a group of young Hasidic students—despite his deep involvement with Zen Buddhism, Sanfield had not lost interest in Judaism. Neither had Leonard, who accepted the invitation to go with them. On their way they happened upon a chanting circle—a group of Hare Krishnas, led by Swami Bhaktivedanta, who was on his first visit to the U.S. Allen Ginsberg was there, chanting with them. Leonard told Sanfield he wanted to stay and to go on without him. Sanfield, having found the meeting with the Hasidim unfulfilling, came back just as the chanting circle was breaking up. Leonard had not moved from where he had left him. "What do you think?" Sanfield asked him. Leonard answered, "Nice song."

Leonard was similarly unresponsive when Sanfield talked to him about his own teacher, Roshi Sasaki, and the effect he had had on his life. But that night Leonard came to Breier's apartment to see Sanfield and told him, "I need to tell you a story." Late into the night, says Sanfield, "he told me a long version of the tale of Sabbatai Sevi, the false Messiah. I said, 'Why did you tell me that?' He said, 'Well, I just thought you should hear it.' I think it was because I was talking in such superlative praise of my Roshi." Leonard was suspicious of holy men. "They know how to do it," he would explain three decades later, when he was living in Roshi's monastery. "They know how to get at people around them, that's what their gig is." The reason he understood was, as he said, "because *I* was able to do it in my own small way. I was a very good hypnotist when I was very young."[3]

It was four in the morning when Leonard and Sanfield left to get breakfast, "and who should come walking down the street," says Sanfield, "but Bhaktivedanta, in his robes." When the guru came close, Leonard asked him, "How does that tune go again?" Bhaktivedanta stopped and sang them "Hare Krishna," "and we picked it up, and continued walking down the streets, singing it ourselves."

Leonard was still finding it a struggle in the recording studio, but by the fourth late-night session with Simon he had succeeded in doing three final takes: "You Know Who I Am," "Winter Lady," and, after nineteen failed attempts at recording it, "Suzanne." Three weeks and four sessions later, Leonard nailed "So Long, Marianne," a song he had recorded more than a dozen times with two producers and with two different titles. In total, since May 1967 Leonard had recorded twenty-five original compositions with John Hammond and John Simon. Ten of these songs made it onto Leonard's debut album. Four would be revisited on his second and third albums, and two would appear as bonus tracks on the *Songs of Leonard Cohen* reissue in 2003 ("Store Room" and "Blessed Is the Memory").

The other nine songs Leonard recorded—almost enough for a

whole other album—were "The Jewels in Your Shoulder," "Just Two People" (a.k.a. "Anyone Can See"), "In the Middle of the Night," "The Sun Is My Son," "Beach of Idios," "Nobody Calls You But Me," "Love Is the Item," "Nancy, Where Have You Been Sleeping" and "Splinters." As of this writing, all of these songs appear to be unreleased. Leonard played "Jewels in Your Shoulder" at his performance in April 1967 at the university in Buffalo, New York, and somewhere in circulation there's a very rare acetate of early demos that includes "Love Is the Item." The rest remain on the shelf.

When Leonard had finished recording his vocals and guitar, John Simon took over. He came up with string arrangements and added backing vocals, the principal backing singer—uncredited on the album—being Nancy Priddy, Simon's then girlfriend. Simon also overdubbed other instruments onto Leonard's track. "What I welcomed, to satisfy my own creative impulse, was Leonard's allowing me some room with his arrangements," says Simon. "To this day, I'm real happy with the arrangements I did using women's voices instead of instruments." However, when Leonard heard what his producer had done, he was not happy. If he had indeed thought that Hammond's production was too raw, Simon's was not raw enough.

What exactly didn't you like about it?

"John Simon wrote some delightful arrangements like the one to 'Sisters of Mercy,' still based around my guitar playing. I wanted women's voices and he came up with some nice choirs of women. We did have a falling out over 'Suzanne'—he wanted a heavy piano syncopated, and maybe drums. That was my first requirement, that I didn't want drums on any of my songs, so that was a bone of contention. Also he was ready to substitute this heavy chordal structure under the song to give it forward movement and I didn't like that, I wanted it to be based on just my picking, and he felt it lacked bottom. And then where we had another falling out was 'So Long, Marianne,' in which there were certain tricky conventions of the time where a song would sometimes just stop and start again later, and I thought that

interrupted the song. But I do think he's a really fine producer and he did bring the project to completion. As my friend Leon Wieseltier said, 'It has the delicious quality of doneness.'"

Particularly delicious by that stage, I would imagine.

"Well, when John Hammond got sick it kind of threw me for a loop and I felt that I'd lost contact with the songs. I actually went to a hypnotist in New York—I wanted her to return me to the original impulse of the songs. It was a desperate measure but I thought I'd give it a shot. And it didn't work, I couldn't go under. [Laughs] The whole episode had a comic quality that I could not escape."

The disagreements continued until Simon finally threw up his hands. "He said, 'You mix it. I'm going on vacation,'" said Leonard, "and I did."[4] Leonard worked with the studio engineer, Warren Vincent. When Vincent asked Leonard what the trouble was, he answered that he disliked the arrangements: the orchestration on "Suzanne" was too big, and "Hey, That's No Way to Say Goodbye" sounded too soft. "I'm not that kind of guy," Leonard told him. "I don't believe that tenderness has to be weakness." Vincent said, "We'll see what we can do." "Well, if we can't," said Leonard, "I'll commit suicide."[5]

It happened that Nico was performing in New York that week at Steve Paul's the Scene, a cellar nightclub that was part cave and part labyrinth and was popular with both the rock crowd and high society. The series of shows was to promote Nico's solo debut *Chelsea Girl*, an album that included songs by Jackson Browne and Bob Dylan but ultimately nothing by Leonard. The house band at the Scene was a young West Coast psychedelic folk rock group called the Kaleidoscope; David Lindley, Chris Darrow, Solomon Feldthouse and Chester Crill were musical virtuosos who played a variety of stringed instruments of various ethnicities. It was their first East Coast tour and they were supposed to have been playing a series of shows at the Café Au Go Go, but, after the first night, the owner told them not to come back, that no one liked long-haired California hippies in New

York. Steve Paul took pity on them and offered them a three-week residency at his club.

"The Scene," says Chris Darrow, "was the heavy club in town at that time, and everybody who was anybody showed up the first night we played: Andy Warhol and all his people, Frank Zappa with the Mothers of Invention, the Cyrkle; Tiny Tim was the emcee. That was the night we met Leonard Cohen. He came up to me after our first set. In that light he looked like the palest human being I had ever met. He was wearing a black leather jacket and he was carrying a black briefcase—I remember this so particularly because he was out of place in terms of what a musician in 1967 looked like. My dad was a college professor and Leonard looked like a college professor—a real academic vibe. He appeared very confident, like he belonged there. He just walked right up to me and said, 'I'm doing an album for Columbia Records and I think you guys are really great. Would you be interested in playing on my album?'"

After the last set of the night, they met in the Greek hamburger joint above the club. Conversation turned to Greece and how much Leonard liked living there. As Chester Crill recalled, one thing Leonard said he liked about Greece was that he could get Ritalin there—a stimulant widely used for both narcolepsy and hyperactivity—without a prescription. Crill told Leonard that he had stopped taking acid since some of the manufacturers starting cutting it with Ritalin. "Leonard said, 'Oh, I really loved that.' He said it was very good for focus."

The following afternoon Leonard, carrying a briefcase and a guitar, met with the band at the Albert Hotel, where they shared a room. Sitting on a bed, the only place not taken up with one or another of their instruments, Leonard sang them his songs. "I didn't really know what to make of them," says Crill. "It sounded like it was probably an attempt at folk music, but kind of in the pop genre, but then the songs were a little unusual for pop, not your typical A-B, A-B." David Lindley says, "I liked them. I thought it was kind of an unusual approach, but in those days people did a lot of things that were unusual—every kind of approach. A lot of the words to the songs were great, and he had a real understated way of delivering them. And he really seemed to like us, so it was good." They agreed to come to the studio and play on his album. "I thought, 'Nothing's going to come of this,'" says Crill, "'but we're starving to death and we'll get enough money to eat and do our gigs in Boston then go home.' It really saved our asses."

The Kaleidoscope showed up at Studio E laden with stringed instruments, including harp guitar, bass, violin, mandolin and some of Feldtman's Middle Eastern assortment. Crill and Darrow found themselves sharing the elevator with Arthur Godfrey. "I remember listening to his radio show on the cab ride back with the guys and he was saying, 'I had to share the elevator with a bunch of those filthy hippies,'" recalls Crill. In the candlelit studio, Leonard was deep in discussion with the man behind the control desk, who was saying, "'We've spent all the money, it's already the most expensive album we've ever been associated with,' blah, blah, blah. Then they would play a track for us and the producer would come on the talk-back and say, 'We only have one track open so we can't put two instruments in here,' and a ten-minute argument would begin. Leonard, poor guy, would be, 'We don't want the glockenspiel'—because on every one of these tracks it sounded like there was two orchestras and a carousel. It was like a fruitcake, it was so full of stuff. Making the room for us to play on anything took more time than actually having us play, because of the old technology. And to go from a guy who was sitting in your room, just playing a guitar and singing a song in a nice quiet voice, to the Entrance of the Gladiators—Jesus! His songs weren't the kind that needed all that orchestration and women's voices to get them across. It sounded like Tiny Tim's first album. I felt really sorry for the guy."

In the studio, Leonard sang the songs as he had originally played them, before the overdubs. "He went through a lot of songs," says Chris Darrow, "basically trying to figure out if anybody had any ideas. I remember him playing the guitar and having a hard time myself trying to figure out what the groove was, because he had this sort of amorphous guitar style that was very circular. I think one of the problems that he was having was that he wanted something very specific and he understood what it was that he wanted, but I think he was having a hard time at that time either getting producers or other musicians to understand. I never remember him being disparaging about anybody else or anything, but it being his first record and him not being really known as a musician I think there were things he was having a hard time communicating."

There was no rehearsal. The band improvised, and Leonard told them when he liked something and if he wanted them to add another instrument. The latter would prompt a voice from the control room, over the talk-back, telling Leonard that he could only have one. When Leonard protested, Crill recalls, "he was told, 'We can't change it; we're locked into this.' It was horrible for him. It wasn't for us, because every minute we were getting more money for getting out of New York."

The Kaleidoscope did three Leonard Cohen sessions in all, two long and one short, playing on "So Long, Marianne," "Teachers," "Sisters of Mercy," "Winter Lady" and "The Stranger Song." They were not in the album credits, but neither were any of the other musicians; as Lindley points out, at that time "it was like dancing bears or performing seals"; you just did the job and moved on. John Simon too had moved on; he was now producing the band Blood, Sweat and Tears and, he said, pretty sure that he was not in the studio when Leonard and the Kaleidoscope played. Simon felt that he had done all he could for Leonard, and if Leonard wanted to change what he'd done, yes, he was disappointed—"But," he said, "it was *his* album. Plus he was older than I, so I was conditioned to back off graciously."

Talking to Simon more than forty years later, he still rhapsodizes about the album. "'Suzanne': fucking gorgeous, I love this track; the strings and the girls together with the rich vocal and guitar make a lush blanket of sound. 'Hey, That's No Way to Say Goodbye' is another of my favorites—this and 'Suzanne' both have a guitar line in thirds with the vocal. I like the girls' parts a lot—they're mine—and I love the instrument that sounds like a Brazilian *berimbau* or a low-pitched Jew's harp, which must be the Kaleidoscope. The mandolin on 'Sisters of Mercy' is probably the Kaleidoscope—talk about elaborate. 'So Long, Marianne': I heard somewhere that Leonard specified there be no drums on his album; well, there are drums on this. Incidentally, stereo was so new and strange to me—or to whomever mixed this; who knows at this point?—that I placed the bass and drums fully to one side of the stereo, a no-no. 'The Stranger Song' made me think about his lyrics. Although Bob Dylan paved the way for the lyricists who followed him, in that he got an audience to accept lyrics that were more thoughtful, less banal than the average pop lyric, Leonard's seem to show more finesse. His scansion is stricter, his rhymes truer, as a rule. Whereas Dylan's language had a connection to 'the people,' in the tradition of Woody Guthrie, blues and folk, Leonard's lyrics reveal a more educated, exposed, literate poet. But Leonard was not just a poet who strummed a little. What a marvel the speed of his finger-picking pattern is. I like the humor in the lyrics of 'One of Us Cannot Be Wrong,' they have an undercurrent of ardent young lust, but they're so funny at the same time. As for the questionable taste of the ending with the recorder, the whistle and Leonard screeching way up high, what can I say? We were young."

Said Leonard, "I always think of something Irving Layton said about the requirements for a young poet, and I think it goes for a young singer, too, or a beginning singer: 'The two qualities most important for a young poet are arrogance and inexperience.' It's only some very strong self-image that can keep you going in a world that conspires to silence everyone."[6]

Songs of Leonard Cohen was shipped on December 26, 1967, in the winter of the Summer of Love.* Leonard was thirty-three years old—by sixties standards antediluvian. He made no attempt to disguise his age in the photograph on the album's front sleeve, a head-shot, taken in a New York subway station photo booth. Sepia-toned and with a funereal black border, it showed a solemn man in a dark jacket and white shirt, unmistakably a grown-up; it might well have been the photo of a dead Spanish poet. Viewed alongside the head-shot on the back of *Let Us Compare Mythologies*, in which Leonard looked more buttoned-up, less defiant, it appeared that Leonard's bottomless eyes had seen too much in the eleven years between his first book and first LP. The back cover was taken up with a colorful drawing of a woman in flames—a Mexican saint picture Leonard found at the store where he bought his candles and spells. It was quite unlike any other album sleeve of its time.

Then, Leonard's album was like nothing of its time—or of any time, really. Its songs sounded both fresh and ancient, sung with the authority of a man used to being listened to, which he was. Their images and themes—war and betrayal, longing and despair, sexual and spiritual yearning, familiar to readers of his poetry—were in keeping with the rock music zeitgeist, but the words in which they were expressed were dense, serious and enigmatic. There is a hypnotic quality to the album—the cumulative effect of the pace and inflection, the circular guitar, Leonard's unhurried, authoritative voice—through which the songs are absorbed and trusted as much as understood.

There are characters in the songs as cryptic as those in Bob Dylan's, like the man with the sadism of a Nazi and the golden body of a god with whom the singer shares a lover in "Master Song." Dylan,

---

* Because of the holidays, the release date is generally considered January 1968.

in fact, was the name that came up most often in the reviews of *Songs of Leonard Cohen*, particularly in discussions of the lyrics. "One of Us Cannot Be Wrong," Leonard's wryly humorous song, inspired by Nico, about a man battered but unbroken by lust, shared a small patch of common ground with Dylan's "Leopard-Skin Pill-Box Hat." But the poetry of Leonard's lyrics was more honed and controlled, steeped in literary and rhetorical technique. In liturgy also.

"Suzanne," the opening song, appears to be a love song, but it is a most mysterious love song, in which the woman inspires a vision of Jesus, first walking on the water, then forsaken by his father, on the Cross. "So Long, Marianne," likewise, begins as a romance, until we learn that the woman who protects him from loneliness also distracts him from his prayers, thereby robbing him of divine protection. The two women in "Sisters of Mercy," since they are not his lovers, are portrayed as nuns. (Leonard wrote the song during a blizzard in Edmonton, Canada, after encountering two young girl backpackers in a doorway. He offered them his hotel bed and, when they fell straight to sleep, watched them from an armchair, writing, and played them the song the next morning when they woke.) Yet, however pure and holy, a sense of romantic possibility remains for a man who in *The Favorite Game* described the woman making up the hotel bed in which they had just made love as having "the hands of a nun." There are many lovers in these songs, but also teachers, masters and saviors. In the song titled "Teachers," the initiate is offered a variety to choose from, including a madman and a holy man who talks in riddles.

Perhaps the most cryptic track on the album is "The Stranger Song," a masterful, multilayered song about exile and moving on. It was born, Leonard said, "out of a thousand hotel rooms, ten thousand railway stations."[7] The Stranger might be the Jew, exiled by ancestry, perpetually on the run from his murderers and God; the troubadour, rootless by necessity; or the writer, whom domesticity would sap of his will to create. Here love is once again presented as something dangerous. We have Joseph, the good husband and Jew, searching for a place where his wife can give birth to a child who is not his, and whose existence will come to cause more problems for his people. In the "holy game of poker," it is of no use to sit around and wait in hope for a good hand of cards. The only way to win is to cheat, or to show no emotion, or to make sure to sit close to the exit door.

If Leonard had recorded just this one compelling album and disappeared, as Anthony DeCurtis, the American music critic, wrote in his liner notes to the 2003 reissue, "his stature as one of the most gifted songwriters of our time will still be secure." On its original release, the U.S. press was considerably more lukewarm. Arthur Schmidt in *Rolling Stone* wrote, "I don't think I could ever tolerate all of it. There are three brilliant songs, one good one, three qualified bummers, and three are the flaming shits. . . . Whether the man is a poet or not (and he is a brilliant poet) he is not necessarily a songwriter."[8] The *New York Times*'s Donal Henahan damned it with faint praise: "Mr. Cohen is a fair poet and a fair novelist, and now he has come through with a fair recording of his own songs." Leonard sounded "like a sad man cashing in on self-pity and adolescent loneliness," he wrote, placing him "somewhere between Schopenhauer and Bob Dylan" on the "alienation scale."[9]

In the UK the album was received positively. Tony Palmer praised it in the *Observer* newspaper.* *Melody Maker* critic Karl Dallas wrote, "I predict that the talk about him will become deafening. His songs are pretty complex things. No one could accuse him of underestimating his audiences."[10] The album failed to enter the charts in Canada. In America it scraped into the lower reaches of the Top 100, while in the UK it made it to No. 13 on the charts—a division of devotion that would continue throughout much of Leonard's musical career.

In interviews he gave in 1968 to promote the album, Leonard appeared to be feeling his way through this new pop music world he

---

* The same Tony Palmer would shoot the 1974 Leonard documentary *Bird on a Wire*.

had entered. He complained to the UK press that New York did not understand him: "[They] kept putting me in an intellectual bag, but that's not where I'm at. I never thought of myself as a Poet with a capital 'P,' I just want to make songs for people because I reckon that they can understand things that I understand. I want to write the sort of songs you hear on the car radio. I don't want to achieve any sort of virtuosity. I want to write lyrics that no one notices but they find themselves singing over a few days later without remembering where they heard them."[11] But despite his protestations that he wanted to be considered a popular artist, he had turned down "$15,000 worth of concerts," he said, "because I didn't want to do them," adding that "the presence of money in the whole enterprise has been having a sinister magical effect on me." Although money had been a big motivation for the shift from literature to the music business, he told *Melody Maker*, he was already thinking of giving music up. "Right now I feel like I did when I finished my novel [*Beautiful Losers*]. At the end of the book I knew I wouldn't write another because I'd put everything I had into that one."[12]

He talked about going back to Greece. But for now he stayed on the promotional treadmill and continued to try on masks to see how they fit. He described himself in *The Beat* as an anarchist "unable to throw the bomb."[13] He told the *New York Times*, "When I see a woman transformed by the orgasm we have together, then I know we've met. I really am for the matriarchy." He was also for the Cross: "The crucifixion will again be understood as a universal symbol, not just an experiment in sadism or masochism or arrogance."[14] In a 1968 *Playboy* article he said, "I had some things in common with the Beatniks and even more things with the hippies. The next thing may be even closer to where I am."[15] The headline of the *Playboy* article summed it up quite perfectly: RENAISSANCE MENSCH. The photo, shot on Hydra, made the melancholy Canadian New Yorker look curiously like a silent movie actor playing a Florida real estate salesman: wide-brimmed hat, thin mustache and villainous smile.

Leonard's U.S. record label changed its original advertisement for the album, which included a quote from the *Boston Globe* review, "James Joyce is not dead . . . ," to one with a quote from *Playboy:* "I've been on the outlaw scene since I was 15." They added a rather incongruous photo of a smiling, bestubbled Leonard, dressed in striped pajamas, lying alongside his somber self-portrait on the album sleeve. As part of a more sensible promotional campaign in the UK, CBS released in early 1968 a low-priced sampler album titled *The Rock Machine Turns You On*. Among tracks from Dylan, Simon & Garfunkel, Spirit, Tim Rose and Taj Mahal was Leonard, singing "Sisters of Mercy."

Leonard, meanwhile, was in a dreary room at the Henry Hudson, talking to a journalist from the *Montreal Gazette*, assuring him that his next album—the album that only weeks ago he was unsure he was going to make—would be a country and western record. As he had planned to do in the first place, he said, he was going to Tennessee.

Eleven

The Tao of Cowboy

He could ride a horse, he knew how to shoot a rifle and, for a man who claimed to have not a sentimental bone in his body, he could sing a Hank Williams song to break your heart. Out of all the thirtysome-thing urban sophisticates in New York City, the likeliest to survive being dropped from the sky into rural Tennessee was Leonard. But New York was not quite done with him yet. His American publisher, Viking, hitching a ride on the album's publicity campaign, issued a second edition of *Beautiful Losers* and was gearing up for the June 1968 release of a new poetry book, *Selected Poems 1956–1968.* The first of Leonard's poetry books to be published in the U.S. offered twenty new poems, including the one he once scrawled to Marita on Le Bistro's wall, along with a selection from earlier volumes. Many were handpicked by Marianne and the emphasis was on his lyrical and personal poems of love and loss. Although their love affair was all but over, eroded by time and distances and Leonard's ways in matters of domesticity and survival, there were still ties that bound.

---

* The UK edition appeared in 1969.

If there were good reasons not to leave New York, there were none to stay in the Henry Hudson Hotel. Leonard checked back into the Chelsea. Not many days passed before he noticed a woman who seemed to share his timetable, wandering the hotel at three in the morning looking for a drink and company. Janis Joplin had moved into the Chelsea while recording her second album with Big Brother & the Holding Company, which John Simon was producing. One night, as Leonard was on the way back to the hotel from the Bronco Burger and Janis from Studio E, they found themselves sharing the elevator, and then an unmade bed. In later years, after Leonard immortalized Janis's blow job in song—first in "Chelsea Hotel #1," which he sang live but never released, then "Chelsea Hotel #2," recorded on 1974's *New Skin for the Old Ceremony*—he polished the encounter into a stage anecdote. "She wasn't looking for me, she was looking for Kris Kristofferson; I wasn't looking for her, I was looking for Brigitte Bardot; but we fell into each other's arms through some process of elimination."[1] His words had the dark humor of both loneliness and honesty. Leonard's later refinements to the anecdote were less black, more stand-up comedy. He said he asked her who she was looking for and when she told him he quipped, "My dear lady, you're in luck, I am Kris Kristofferson."[2] Either way, she made an exception.

Interestingly, the anecdotes followed a similar pattern to the songs. "Chelsea Hotel #1" was the more open and emotional of the two:

A great surprise, lying with you baby
Making your sweet little sound. . .
See all your tickets
Torn on the ground
All of your clothes and
No piece to cover you
Shining your eyes in
My darkest corner.

The second was more guarded and unsentimental:

> *I can't keep track of each fallen robin. . . .*
> *I don't think of you that often*

making the encounter sound humdrum—particularly when compared with the extravagance in his poem "Celebration," where the
orgasm from oral sex felled the protagonist "like those gods on the
roof that Samson pulled down." Leonard expressed regret on several
occasions later at having named Joplin as the fellatrix and muse of the
song. "She would not have minded," he said. "My mother would have
minded."[3] Quite possibly, but really it was Leonard who minded—
not just this rare lack of good manners, but having revealed so much
of the mystery, shown how the trick was done. Janis was a one-night
stand and, it's safe to say, not the only woman in the Chelsea to have
given him head, yet something about her, or about what happened to
her—less than three years later, at the age of twenty-seven, in a hotel
room in Los Angeles, Janis Joplin OD'd and died—seemed to have
gotten under Leonard's skin.

David Crosby was in Miami, in the brief hiatus between being fired
by the Byrds and cofounding Crosby, Stills & Nash, when he first set
eyes on Joni Mitchell. She was singing alone in a coffeehouse and
Crosby was "smitten." He brought her back with him to Los Angeles
and she moved in with him. Crosby set about finding his new love
a record deal and appointed himself her album producer. "She was
magnificent and magical, and though I wasn't really a producer, I just
knew that somebody needed to keep the world from trying to translate what she did into a normal bass, drums and keyboards format,
because that would have been a fucking disaster." Despite his good
intentions, making an album with Joni "really wasn't fun"—working

with Beethoven was no easier than living with Beethoven. When it was done, and the blood washed from the walls, Joni surprised Crosby by suggesting that he produce her friend Leonard Cohen's second album.

Crosby knew nothing about Leonard, other than "Suzanne," Judy Collins's version; he thought it "one of the prettiest songs" he'd heard. But Joni was persuasive. Crosby booked two sessions, on May 17 and 18, at Columbia's Los Angeles studio, a large room in which he had previously worked with the Byrds, and Leonard, who appeared to have no objection to the plans Joni had made for him, flew to L.A. "I don't remember him saying anything about what he really wanted to have happen," says Crosby, "he just put himself in my hands. Poor fellow." On the first day, they recorded one song, "Lady Midnight." On the second they recorded two, "Bird on the Wire" and "Nothing to One."

"It really was not a happy experience," says Crosby. "It's an embarrassing story for me and a bitter pill to swallow because I could produce him now in a minute, but then I had no idea how to record him. I listened to him sing, and I'm a melodic singer, so I didn't know what to do with a voice like Leonard's. The only other singer vaguely like Leonard was Bob Dylan, and I couldn't have recorded Dylan either. When the Byrds tried to record Dylan songs, we changed them completely, gave them a beat, put harmonies to them, translated them completely from their original form. It was quite obvious that Leonard was one of the best poets and lyricists alive, so I imagined that the way to go about it was to take him in the direction that Dylan had gone and speak the lyrics more than sing them. It did not make him happy."

The Crosby-produced "Nothing to One" has Crosby singing harmony, while his production of "Bird on the Wire" has something of a solo, coffeehouse Byrds feel: folk rock with a touch of rhythmic pop. These two recordings were eventually unearthed as bonus tracks on the 2007 reissue of *Songs from a Room*. The Cohen-Crosby version of "Lady Midnight" remains in the vaults. "I've wondered over the years," says Crosby of the experience, "if Leonard forgave me. God knows he deserved somebody a bit smarter and more experienced than I was. But Bob Johnston knew *exactly* what he was doing."

Leonard ran into Bob Johnston in L.A. Normally Los Angeles is not a place to run into people, since they're all in cars inching along endless boulevards to some important meeting or other, but Johnston made a point of being the exception to the rule. Johnston, as Bob Dylan wrote of the man who produced many of his finest albums, was "unreal."[4] Like God, Johnston was everywhere, he had fire in his eyes, and heaven help you if you questioned his ways, particularly if you worked for a record company. Johnston was—still is at age eighty, at the time of writing this book—a maverick, a wiry, bearded redhead with a thick Texas accent and music in his blood. His great-grandfather was a classical pianist, his grandmother a songwriter, his mother won a songwriting Grammy at the age of ninety-two, and his wife, Joy Byers, had written songs that Elvis Presley covered. Johnston wrote songs too, but he was best known at that time as the producer of many of the era's greatest and most influential artists. Just four and a half months into 1968 he had recorded Bob Dylan's *John Wesley Harding*, Simon and Garfunkel's *Bookends*, Marty Robbins's *By the Time I Get to Phoenix*, Flatt & Scruggs's *The Story of Bonnie and Clyde* and Johnny Cash's *At Folsom Prison*, some of these albums still waiting their turn to come out, like buses in a depot. But having been thwarted the first time, he was still determined to produce a Leonard Cohen album.

"I had no plans to make another record," Leonard said. "I didn't think it was necessary. Then one day I met Bob Johnston and I liked the way he talked and how he understood my first album, exactly what was good and what was bad about it."[5] Johnston says, "Leonard said, 'Let's get together,' and I said, 'Fuck yeah.' I had just rented a farm, two thousand acres, Boudleaux Bryant's place"—Bryant and his wife, Felice, were successful Nashville songwriters, with hits that included "Love Hurts" and "All I Have to Do Is Dream"—"and I told Leonard about it. He said, 'Someday I'll have a farm like this and I'll write a couple of albums.' I said, 'Here, do it now,' and I gave him the key, and he moved in for two years."

But first Leonard went to Hydra. His affiliations with his second home were the opposite of his "neurotic affiliations" with Montreal. He wanted to sit in his shirtsleeves in the sun and smoke a cigarette and watch life crawl slowly by; he wanted to return to the simple life in the house on the hill with Marianne and her child. He was pleased to discover that the military junta had not had much tangible effect on the place. At first, when the new Greek government announced bans on long hair, miniskirts and a number of musicians and artists, the expats would gather in the tavernas at night, lock the doors, pull the shutters closed and play the outlawed music. But really the colonels hadn't noticed Hydra, or if they had, they did not much care. Still, there were some changes on the island that Leonard could not ignore. For one, George Johnston and Charmian Clift were no longer sitting at a table in the sun outside Katsikas, waiting for the ferry to arrive with its news and its newcomers. For another, at night the houses on the hills were lit up with electric lights.

It had been three years since Leonard had woken to find his house newly tethered to the twentieth century. Says Marianne, "Leonard got out of bed after a week of feeling lousy—he had been for a trip around the islands with Irving Layton and had some kind of flu. He came to his studio and he looked out and discovered that during the night they had put up all the new electric wires and they crossed in front of his window. He was sitting in this rocking chair that I brought from my little house. I brought him a cup of hot chocolate, and I took the guitar down which was hanging on the wall and it was totally out of tune. While we're sitting there, birds are landing on the wire like notes on a music sheet. I heard '*Like a bird—on the wire . . .*' So beautiful. But it took him three years before he felt the song was finished."

Finishing their relationship also took a long time. Leonard would say in 1970 (when introducing the song "So Long, Marianne" at a concert), "I lived with her for about eight years, about six months of the year, then the other six months I was stuck somewhere else. Then I found I was living with her four months of the year and then two months of the year and then about the eighth year I was living with her a couple of weeks of the year, and I thought it was time to write this particular song for her." But soon after starting the song he stopped singing and added, "I still live with her a couple of days of the year."[6]

All that Marianne will say about the end of the affair is, "To me he was still the same, he was a gentleman, and he had that stoic thing about him and that smile he will try to hide behind—'Am I serious now or is all this a joke?' We were in love and then the time was up. We were always friends, and he still is my dearest friend and I will always love him. I feel very lucky to have met Leonard at that time in my life. He taught me so much, and I hope I gave him a line or two."

From Hydra Leonard went to London, where that summer he made two appearances on the BBC: the radio show *Top Gear*, hosted by John Peel (the revered and influential British DJ was an early Leonard Cohen enthusiast) and a television concert in which he performed almost all the songs from his first album, along with three songs that would appear on later albums, and an improvised, self-deprecating, stoned-sounding sing-along titled "There's No Reason Why You Should Remember Me." Both shows were very well received. By now *Songs of Leonard Cohen* was in the Top 20 in the UK. He was to all intents and purposes a pop/rock star. There was some attention from the U.S. too. That summer, Leonard was featured in two different articles in the *New York Times:* one was an examination of the new singer-songwriter movement in pop; the other, illustrated with photographs of Leonard and Dylan, debated whether pop lyrics should be considered "poetry."

That Leonard's latest book of poetry, *Selected Poems*, was proving popular in America only muddied the waters. The dust-jacket blurb made an appeal to the pop/rock market by mentioning Leonard's album and the covers of his songs by Judy Collins, Buffy Sainte-Marie and Noel Harrison. It also appealed to the literary underground by recalling the outrage that greeted his novel *Beautiful Losers*, to critics and academics by calling him "a contemporary *Minnesinger*" (a singer-poet in the German chivalric tradition), and to sensitive souls with its description of him as "eclectic, searching, deeply personal."[7]

But the literati, particularly in Canada, did not take warmly to his move into the popular field. It made him a "personality," which brought with it the danger, as Michael Ondaatje wrote, that "our interest in Cohen makes the final judgement, not the quality of the writing."[8] Cohen and Dylan, Ondaatje said, were "public artists" who relied heavily "on their ability to be cynical about their egos or pop sainthood while at the same time continuing to build it up. They can con the media men who are their loudspeakers, yet keep their integrity and appear sincere to their audiences." It was a reasonable argument, although the media was often well aware of this game and interpreted Leonard as a work of fiction in action, where academics interpreted the words on the page. Leonard's words, thanks to the publicity and sales of his first album, had now started to sell in previously unimaginable quantities. Rock album numbers, not poetry book numbers. *Selected Poems* would sell two hundred thousand copies.

After his short promotional trip to London, Leonard returned to New York and the Chelsea. He checked into room 100 (which Sid Vicious and Nancy Spungen would later make notorious) and propped his guitar in the corner and put his typewriter on the desk. On the bedside table he put the books he was reading: Gore Vidal's *Myra Breckinridge* (a book that, like *Beautiful Losers*, had been deemed pornographic by several critics) and *Tales of the Hasidim: Later Masters* by

Martin Buber, stories about rabbis searching for enlightenment. As to this particular descendant of Aaron, he had started attending the Church of Scientology.

Scientology was a new religion, founded a decade and a half earlier by an American science fiction novelist named L. Ron Hubbard. It had some of the trappings of the old religions, like its eight-pointed cross and its sacred books. The first such book, *Dianetics*, an imaginative hodgepodge of, among other things, Eastern mysticism and Freud, read like an early self-help book and, like one, sold in enormous quantities. It claimed to heal the unconscious mind and, along with it, man's physical and psychological problems, resulting in liberation from pain and trauma, universal brotherhood, the end to war and oneness with the universe. Scientology, unsurprisingly, did good business in America in 1968, when there was no shortage of traumatized young people looking for some kind of answer. It was a year of turbulence and paranoia—the assassinations of Martin Luther King and Robert Kennedy, riots in the ghettos, protests in the universities, young Americans still being sent to Vietnam and coming home in caskets—and neither the drugs nor the old orthodoxies were working.

Hubbard's religion, in keeping with the times, had a slogan, "Scientology works," and spread the word through young adherents approaching other young people on the street. It also reflected its founder's origins in science fiction, coming with extraterrestrials, strange contraptions and its own language. Man's strongest urge, Hubbard wrote, was survival, but this survival was under attack by engrams, cellular memories of physical and mental pain that chain him to his past. The way to remove these charges was by auditing—revisiting past traumas under supervision with an auditor, a Scientology counselor, while wired to an e-meter, a device that resembled a couple of small tin cans and a dial. After a course of successful auditing, you go clear and are ready to take the next step toward becoming an Operating Thetan and living in a pain-free present. Leonard thought Scientology, for all its snake oil, had "very good data."⁹ He signed up for auditing.

At night the Chelsea Hotel came to life. People who rarely left their rooms by daylight emerged and came together, often in Harry Smith's room. Smith was an extraordinary man, a forty-five-year-old in the body of an eccentric old man: wild white hair, scraggly beard, towering forehead and oversized spectacles that magnified his bright, intelligent eyes. He lived with his pet birds in a dark, tiny, room with no bathroom on the eighth floor. It was crammed with curios: magic wands, Seminole Indian clothes, painted Ukrainian eggs, a collection of paper airplanes, esoteric books and weird old American records. In music circles Smith was renowned for his *Anthology of American Folk Music*, three double albums he compiled from his collection of old, raw folk, blues and gospel. The albums were an enormous influence on Dylan and the sixties folk revival. Smith was not only a musicologist but an anthropologist, an expert on Native America and shamanism, an experimental filmmaker, a raconteur and a mystic, who claimed to have learned the art of alchemy at around the same age Leonard was studying hypnotism. Little surprise that Leonard was drawn to him. Along with other assorted Chelsea residents and writers and music celebrities who were passing through, he would sit at Smith's feet and listen to his labyrinthine monologue.

"We saw Harry as a national monument and sardonic guru from whom even Leonard had something to learn," says Terese Coe, the author of the play *Harry Smith at the Chelsea*. "That's why Leonard was there. Harry could be expounding upon any number of intellectual, historical and artistic themes, he might be showing his paintings, talking about his recent misadventures in filmmaking, bewailing his financial disasters, insulting present guests in elliptical terms, playing Brecht-Weill or Woody or Arlo Guthrie—I never heard him play any Leonard Cohen songs. As far as anyone could tell, we were hanging out with a sage who was also at times an antihero, an amusement where anything could happen, but nothing truly decadent ever did in my experience. We were rather well behaved."

Leonard, noticeably more formally dressed than the others in the room, sat quietly, Coe recalls, and rarely said a word. She was a young poet and journalist for an underground newspaper when she met Leonard in Smith's room. She became the muse for two poems in *The Energy of Slaves* (1972): "It Takes a Long Time to See You Terez" and "Terez and Deanne." Says Coe, "I was a passing fancy and he made a fancy pass with provocative lines." She recognized him as "an incurable romantic. In that 'love and peace' era, many were caught in that conundrum. He wasn't one to speak about his philosophy of love in person. He kept his private life and friendships close to the vest. The answers are in his songs, and they are many and mercurial."

There were a number of regulars at Harry Smith's evenings. Peggy Biderman worked at the Museum of Modern Art and had a teenage daughter, Ann (now a successful TV screenwriter), whom Leonard saw for a while. Claude Pelieu and Mary Beach were collage artists who edited a magazine and translated Burroughs and Ginsberg into French. Stanley Amos ran an art gallery from his Chelsea room, complete with vernissages, and would come to Harry's room and read the tarot. Sandy Daley was a photographer, cinematographer and friend of Warhol and of Leonard. In 1970 Daley shot an underground film in her room, on the tenth floor, which was painted and decorated all in white. The film was called *Robert Having His Nipple Pierced*, the Robert being Mapplethorpe. The narrator of the film, Mapplethorpe's partner Patti Smith, was another close friend of Harry Smith. There was also Liberty, a beautiful blond poet and model, with whom Leonard had an affair. Liberty had sat for Salvador Dalí and was a muse for Richard Brautigan and Jerome Charyn, but she was also active in feminist politics, having left her Republican politician husband for the Yippies and the counterculture. After the gatherings everyone, Harry included, would meet up in El Quijote, at the large table at the back of the bar. Leonard would often discreetly pick up the tab for the whole crowd and leave before they discovered it had been paid. Being generous with money was one of the few things Leonard seemed to like about this new level of success.

September 21, 1968. The sun cast long shadows, three-quarters of the year had now passed and Leonard was still in New York. It was the eve of the most solemn day in the Jewish calendar, and Leonard's thirty-fourth birthday. To celebrate, he went by himself to a very crowded place, the Paradox, a macrobiotic restaurant in an East Village basement run by Scientologists. It was a hippie hangout, a place where a person could come to trip out and no one would bother them. If they had no money, they could work in the kitchen for food. Thelma Blitz, a young woman who worked as an ad agency copywriter, sat at one of the long, communal tables and looked up from her dinner to see the man sitting opposite looking deeply into her eyes.

"I didn't know him. He didn't look like a lot of the other people. He had short hair—everyone else there had long hair—and he looked kind of straight; he was dressed conservatively, not like a businessman, more like a college professor." And a lot like Dustin Hoffman, Blitz told him. "Leonard said, 'People often tell me that.'" They talked about all sorts of things—poetry, metaphysics, vegetarianism—with Leonard cordially taking the contrary position to everything she said. "It was a great debate. I didn't know until I read biographies of him that he was president of his debating club in college." They argued all night, until the Paradox closed and Leonard asked if she would like to walk with him. They strolled along Saint Mark's Place, where the freaks congregated. Leonard stopped to talk to a young man who was taking a large tortoise for a walk. "He asked him, 'What do you feed that thing?' and the young man said, 'Hamburger meat, speed and smack.'"

As they walked, Leonard told her that they were going to the Chelsea Hotel. "I didn't know what the Chelsea Hotel was so I said, 'What's there?' and he said, 'Nico.' I only had a vague idea then of Nico and Andy Warhol but he had a wistfulness in his voice when he said 'Nico,' which makes me think that was why he was there." At the hotel, Leonard went straight to the mail desk at the back of the lobby and gave them his name. "Which is how I found out who he was," says Blitz. "I freaked out a little bit, because I realized this man is important—his first album was in the window of the Saint Mark's bookstore—but I didn't recognize him, he didn't look anything like the picture on the cover. But instead of trying to floor me with his accomplishments, like the usual fellow who picks you up, he wouldn't even tell me who he was. He said, with a tinge of self-irony, downplaying his achievements, 'Well, I have some following in Canada.'"

He told Thelma that it was his birthday and they toasted it in El Quijote with a plate of celery and olives in place of alcohol. Then they went to Leonard's room on the first floor. "He took out a guitar and sang two songs to me that I didn't recognize until the second album came out, 'Bird on the Wire' and 'The Partisan Song' [*sic*]. When he sang, I saw this remoteness, and I noted in my journal that his mask of grief and remoteness deepened as he sang. He kept spacing out, coming back and forth, something like the nictitating membrane of a frog came over his eyes and he would seem not to be there. I thought, 'Am I boring him?' I told him I was sick of being an advertising writer, and he suggested starvation and several good books. He talked about teachers and masters and conquering pain, saying things like, 'The more we conquer pain, the more pain we incur on a higher level'—which sounds like the line from [the song] 'Avalanche,' '*You who wish to conquer pain.*' But there was a lot of pain at that time among the people who made up the counterculture: the pain of hating your culture, hating the system, being completely at odds with everything. Everybody was into something."

Leonard did not talk much to Blitz about Scientology, except "to say that it worked." She remembered his talking to her about money, saying that "he had a hundred thousand dollars and he didn't know what to do with it—buy land in Nova Scotia? I remember him looking kind of agonized as he talked about money." They spent the night together. The following morning, when Leonard walked her to the bus—she was off to spend the Jewish New Year with her family—he told her to call him when she got back. When she did, the operator at the Chelsea said he had checked out. He had gone to Tennessee.

––––––––––

Two years behind schedule, and three days before his first session for *Songs from a Room*, Leonard was finally in Nashville. His friend from Montreal Henry Zemel flew out with him. There at the gate to meet them was large man with long hair, a bandanna and a mustache. He was part hippie, bigger part good ol' boy. Since Bob Johnston was, as always, busy in the studio, he sent Charlie Daniels to pick them up. In 1968 Daniels wasn't the Opry-inducted, hard-core country star with the big beard and Stetson, but a songwriter and session musician—fiddle, guitar, bass and mandolin. Johnston first met Daniels in 1959 when he produced the Jaguars, the rock 'n' roll band Daniels fronted. They spent years playing the circuit, getting nowhere. One night Daniels called Johnston and asked if he could get him out of jail—it was advance planning; Daniels was about to get into a fistfight with a club owner. Johnston hollered down the phone that he should "get the fuck out to Nashville," and he did. Johnston had kept him busy ever since, playing on albums by Johnny Cash, Marty Robbins, Bob Dylan, and now Leonard Cohen.

For a city, Nashville felt like a suburb. On the drive from the hotel Leonard saw more men in suits than cowboy hats and more churches than bars. The town's biggest businesses were insurance and Bible publishing; Music Row was all dinky buildings and tidy lawns. But Nashville was the second-biggest music city in America behind New York, home of the Grand Ole Opry and a magnet to songwriters, Tin Pan Alley with twang. It was—like Leonard used to say on Hydra—where the money was. Nashville was chock-full of songwriters—most, like Leonard, hailing from anywhere but Nashville—and it was full of ghosts, of men who'd left wives and families in the mountains to sell their songs and wound up drinking away what little cash and dignity they had left. After checking into their hotel, Leonard and Zemel set off on foot, mapping out the city: the YMCA for a morning swim, the greasiest hole-in-the-wall diners and the dingiest, smokiest heartbreak bars.

On September 26, 1968, the pair arrived at Nashville's Columbia Studio A for the first session. Leonard was carrying a guitar and Zemel a lion tamer's whip. Looking around the room, Leonard took a deep breath: he would need a lot of candles to light up this place. It was enormous, large enough for a symphony orchestra with space left over for a football game. Bob Johnston was behind the glass, playing cheerleader, smiling and animated. But starting his second album couldn't help but bring back for Leonard unhappy memories of his first. Having his friend there helped. Zemel would crack the whip and keep him on task, which bemused the musicians almost as much as the Jew's harp he played on half the cuts. "I'm ready," Leonard said, a brave man facing the firing squad. "What do you want me to do?"

The first question Johnston would always ask the artists he worked with was, "What do *you* want to do?" This was quite a concept at a time when recording artists were more used to being told what to do. Johnston had a reputation for going into battle with record company executives to get what his artists wanted. But Johnston was smart enough to know that this question would not help Leonard. Instead he said, "Play a song." Leonard took out his guitar and started to sing.

As he did, Johnston stood up and announced, "Okay, we're going out to have a hamburger and a couple of beers." Leonard said, "Well, I was ready to do the song." Johnston said, "You can do it when you come back." They left to go to Crystal Burger. While they were gone, the engineer, Neil Wilburn, set up the mics the way Johnston liked them. Wilburn had worked with Johnston when he recorded Johnny Cash's prison albums and helped him get that deep, dark, jail-cell voice. For Leonard's album they used three microphones on his vocal, putting them through old echo plates for reverb.

"When we got back," says Johnston, "Leonard said, 'What'll I do?' I said again, 'Just play a song,' and he did." It was "The Partisan." "Then I played it back to him. His voice sounded like a goddamn mountain. When he heard it he said, 'Is that what I'm supposed to sound like?' I said, 'You're goddamn right.'" On that first day, starting at six in the evening and stopping at one in the morning, Johnston taped Leonard singing ten songs. Five would appear on *Songs from a Room;* one would be put aside for the third album, *Songs of Love and Hate;* and four have never as yet been released: "Baby I've Seen You," "Your Private Name," "Breakdown" and "Just Two People" (Leonard had also tried recording this last song with John Hammond for his debut).

For the same reason that Nashville teemed with songwriters, it also crawled with top-notch musicians. Johnston told Leonard he could have the cream of session men on his album, "but he said no, I want friends of yours, so they'll be friendly." Johnston put together a small team of outsiders, men who could play country music but weren't part of the mainstream "Nashvegas" system. As well as Charlie Daniels, there was Ron Cornelius on guitar, Charlie McCoy on bass and Elkin "Bubba" Fowler, a guitarist and banjo-playing preacher who had been half of a toga-wearing psychedelic pop duo called the Avant-Garde. There was no drummer—Johnston was of a mind with Leonard on this—and Johnston himself played keyboards.

Ron Cornelius, to whom Johnston had given the role of bandleader, played with a young, hippie, country rock/electric folk band from Northern California called West. They had come to Nashville in 1967 to work with Johnston on their debut album and returned in 1968 to have Johnston produce their second. West's members prided themselves on not taking outside gigs, but things weren't going well with the band's career when Johnston persuaded him to play on Leonard's album. When Johnston played him Leonard's songs, "I went, you've got to be kidding me," says Cornelius. "I was used to guitars, bass, drums, piano and loud, rock-out, amplified playing. I thought, 'Man, this is really weird stuff.' But then, I guess like anyone who becomes a Leonard Cohen fan, as soon as you get ankle-deep in the lyrics, you're 'Well, I don't care if I've never played anything like this in my life. This is very, very deep stuff.' "

The artist's cards for *Songs from a Room* are not as tidy or detailed as those for *Songs of Leonard Cohen;* Johnston did not have the time or inclination for paperwork. "Bob didn't fill out anything," says Cornelius, laughing. "He just rolled the tape and went to the airport." Johnston would rush off to New York in the morning, work with Simon & Garfunkel, fly back in the afternoon, record Dino Valenti, maybe slot in a session with Dylan or Cash or Dylan and Cash together, grab a beer and some burgers and an hour's nap in his red Eldorado and then work five or six hours with Leonard. The artist's cards list just ten studio sessions with Leonard—four in September, one in early October and, after a month's break, five in November—plus a few more sessions without him for Johnston to do overdubs.

Life in Nashville fell into as much of a routine as something revolving around the workaholic Johnston's schedule would allow: a morning swim at the Y, lunch at Bob and Joy Johnston's place on a workday, then in the evening, Studio A. While the engineers set up the room they would hang out in the basement, which Johnston had converted into a Ping-Pong room. It doubled as a vocals room, as did the broom closet, if there was a particular sound Johnston was going for. When the session was over Leonard and Zemel would go for bacon and eggs at their favorite diner—"Bright fluorescent lights, a blond floozy waitress and a short-order cook with tattoos who looked like he was on parole," says Zemel—and then a bar, where, unsurprisingly, they proved a success with several of Nashville's womenfolk.

Charlie Daniels recalls the recording as "very relaxed. All the candles were going and everything was so quiet. There were no charts—we changed things constantly—and nobody in the control room saying you need to do this or that. One of Bob Johnston's great strengths as a producer was that he stayed out of an artist's way and let the artist be who he was. He did it with every artist he produced, but it was very evident with people like Dylan and especially with Leonard Cohen. With Dylan it was a little different environment, because we used drums and electric instruments and it was more of a band concept. I remember one time, when Dylan wanted me to take a solo, Charlie McCoy said, 'Well how much do you want him to play?' and Dylan said 'All he can'—that was his attitude: 'Well, I'm doing what I do, you do what *you* do.' But Leonard is a very unique individual. The thing about Leonard is it's the lyrics, it's the melody and it's the way he tunes his guitar—I've never seen anybody that had that softness of touch that could play a gut-string guitar with the strings tuned down like that, almost flabby. He has a very unique kind of music, very fragile, that could very easily be bruised or destroyed by somebody being heavy-handed.

"Leonard would stand there with his guitar and sing a song and we would try and create something around it that would complement it. If there was a place that we felt needed enhancing, in one way or another that's what we tried to do. The main thing was being part of it but unobtrusive, very transparent, nothing that would distract from his lyric and melody. You could put something in there that would mess it up real quick. I learned a lot of things by working with Leonard that I probably wouldn't have known otherwise, that sometimes less is more. Because when you've got a studio full of musicians, everybody's going to want to play something, but with these songs it's more about what you leave out. And Bob was very good at keeping it together and letting you know when it fit or [saying] 'I think we need to go in a different direction on that.'"

Cornelius remembers, "It became a team. I'm sure that Leonard, when he first looked at Charlie Daniels and me, went, 'Oh brother, what have I got myself into here.' But then he saw that we got it, that we understood, musically, what he was doing and were in awe of him as a songwriter, and this was a project we thought about all day long, every day, until the album was over. And Bob Johnston is a very rare breed. He was born with a gift which I've never run into anywhere else, that he could make a stranger want to play or sing, right here tonight, better than they've ever sung or played in their life. Not by saying, 'Here's what I want you to play'; he just had a way of drawing out of a musician or a singer the best in them." Leonard would look up at the glass and see him swaying, sometimes dancing, lost in one of his songs. When he'd finished singing, Johnston would say, "Man! That is a fantastic song. We've got to have that on the album. My God, you've got to do that again," at the same time boosting Leonard's confidence and getting him to do another take he could capture live.

One song whose recording did not come easily was "Bird on the Wire." Leonard tried it over and over, in countless different ways, but every time he listened back, he thought it sounded dishonest somehow. Finally he told Johnston he was done, and the musicians were sent home. "Bob said, okay, let's forget it," said Leonard. "I went back to my hotel to think matters over, but got more and more depressed."[10] He was determined to get this song right. It was as if the song, as well as being a letter to Marianne, were personal treatise of sorts, a "My Way," but without the braggadocio (Leonard was never a big fan of Sinatra; he did have a fondness for Dean Martin, though). "In a way the history of that song on the record is my whole history," Leonard said. "I'd never sung the song true, never. I'd always had a kind of phony Nashville introduction that I was playing the song to, following a thousand models."[11]

Four days before his last recording session on November 25, 1968, Leonard asked everyone to leave except Zemel, McCoy and Johnston. "I just knew that at that moment something was going to take place. I just did the voice before I started the guitar and I heard myself sing that first phrase, '*Like a bird*,' and I knew the song was going to be true and new. I listened to myself singing, and it was a surprise. Then I heard the replay and I knew it was right."[12]

Another song Leonard was not entirely convinced by was "The Partisan," the song he had first learned to play at Camp Sunshine, from *The People's Song Book*, when he was fifteen years old. Johnston says, "He played it for me and it was beautiful, but Leonard wasn't happy with it. He was pacing up and down saying it would be great with some French voices. I said, 'I'll see you in a couple of days.' He said, 'Aren't we recording?' I said, 'Not right now.' The next day I flew to Paris and found three girl singers and an accordion player through some people I knew, and they came in and they did that, overdubbing Leonard's recording. I came back without saying anything to Leonard and I played it. He said 'They're good, they really sound French.' I said, 'That's because they are.'" Johnston laughs. "He was so mad at me for not taking him to France with me."

Hank Williams called country music "the white man's blues." By that definition you might say that, with *Songs from a Room*, Leonard succeeded in making his country album. The songs, like the raw, old country, folk and blues on Harry Smith's *Anthology*, are about God, death, love, loss, sin, redemption and soldiering on, and the sound is spare, much less ornamented than *Songs of Leonard Cohen*. "A lot of my friends who were musical purists had castigated me for the lushness and overproduction of my first record," said Leonard, "and I think that got to me somewhere and I was determined to do a very simple album. It's very stark."[13] But, aside from the jaunty "Tonight Will Be Fine" and "Bird on the Wire"—a song that Johnny Cash would cover many years later and whose sing-along melody Kris Kristofferson once compared with Lefty Frizzell's "Mom and Dad's Waltz"—these were not "Nashville" songs; you could not imagine singing them on a back porch or in a bar. Despite the chirping-cricket sound of the Jew's harp, its overall feel is less of wide, open rural America than small, plain, European or New York City rooms.

The album teems with killers: religious fanatics, revolutionaries and suicides. In the beautiful and mournful "Seems So Long Ago, Nancy," Leonard sings about a young woman he knew in Montreal, a judge's daughter, who shot herself when her illegitimate baby was taken away. In the haunting "Story of Isaac" Leonard takes the same biblical story Dylan referenced on "Highway 61 Revisited"—God commanding Abraham to sacrifice his son—and transforms it into a protest about violence and atrocities both ancient and modern, public and personal. The song has a novelist's eye for detail, the potency and elegy of his early poetry and also a touch of autobiography in the protagonist being a nine-year-old boy, Leonard's age when his father died. "The Butcher," raw acoustic blues, uses the Passover Haggadah to similar ancient/contemporary effect.

The reviews in the U.S. were not good. *Rolling Stone*'s Alec Dubro wrote, "In 'Story of Isaac,' he is matter of fact to the point of being dull. When he's not being matter of fact, but rather obscure, as he is in 'A Bunch of Lonesome Heroes,' he's just irritating. Other singer-poets are obscure, but generally the feeling comes through that an attempt is being made to reach to a heart of meaning. But Cohen sings with such lack of energy that it's pretty easy to conclude that if he's not going to get worked up about it, why should we."[14] The *New York Times*'s William Kloman was kinder, remarking that "as a story-teller Cohen is superb, even when he tacks self-effacing morals onto the end of his tales," but he disliked the album's more understated production and concluded, "Cohen's new songs are short on beauty."[15]

Released in April 1969, *Songs from a Room* performed better than its predecessor. It made it to No. 12 in Canada and No. 63 on the U.S. charts. In the UK, though it soared to No. 2, it was kept from the top position by a budget-priced compilation of hit singles titled *20 Dynamic Hits*, by artists from Deep Purple to Cilla Black. Reviewers across Europe all seemed to appreciate this new, unadorned production style. It was right that Leonard came to us naked, with very little baggage besides these strangely comforting songs that seemed to be written from a life led in the long dark hours before dawn, by someone whose word you could trust.

"I think that element of trust is critical. Certainly I think what draws anyone to a book or a poem or a song is that you trust the guy, the woman."

You too? Is that what draws you to others' work?

"I never put it that way but yes, I think that's so, I go for that feeling of trust. When I listen to somebody like George Jones, he's working with the best studio musicians in Nashville and it's an absolutely impeccable production, sometimes over the top, but it doesn't matter, you trust the voice."

Some thirty-five miles south of Nashville—the last half dozen of them down a winding dirt road from the outskirts of Franklin, the nearest town—was 5435 Big East Fork Road. The Bryants' two thousand acres encompassed forests, a creek, horses, herds of thoroughbred cattle, wild peafowl, chickens, four barns and a cabin. Stepping down from his new jeep, Leonard surveyed his new kingdom. He had sung in "Stories of the Street" about finding a farm—it was a common sentiment in the late sixties, going back to the land, since urban life had become increasingly dystopic—and here it was, his for two years for $75 a month. The cabin, in contrast to the rest of the place, was tiny. The front door opened straight into a living room, with a small kitchen at the back, two tiny bedrooms and a bathroom at the side. The back door opened onto the creek. It was plainly decorated and modestly furnished, a rural Tennessee version of his house on Hydra, only more isolated.

His nearest neighbor lived almost half a mile away, in a small tar-paper-roofed house raised up on cement blocks; out back there was an illegal still. Willie York was a toothless moonshiner who, along with his brother, had served eleven and a half years for the killing of a sheriff in 1944. The country singer Johnny Seay immortalized York in a song—"Willie's Drunk and Nellie's Dyin'," Nellie being his wife—which led to *Life* magazine descending on Big East Fork Road for the story. Leonard, who had had his own experience with *Life* when they came to Hydra to profile its expat artists, took a shine to York. Often at night he'd walk across the fields with a bottle of whiskey and visit.

Leonard bought pistols and a rifle at the army surplus store and a horse from a friend of York's, Ray "Kid" Marley, a champion rodeo rider from Texas who moved to Tennessee and trained horses. "Kid was truly one of a kind," says Ron Cornelius. "He was a big, big guy, a mountain of a man, who used to run with us [the band West] quite a bit when we were in town and stayed drunk all the time." Leonard said, "I thought I could ride—we used to ride at summer camp—but the horse Kid Marley sold me changed my idea of whether I could ride or not. I guess he saw this city slicker and it was a kind of practical joke of his to sell me this horse that I could rarely catch to saddle him up. This horse was mean." Leonard would later immortalize the horse in the song "Ballad of the Absent Mare,"* and would have done

* *Recent Songs,* 1979.

the same for Marley and York in "Chelsea Hotel," had the original version not been usurped by "Chelsea Hotel #2," which had quite different words.

"I was pretty much a bust as a cowboy. [Laughs] But I did have a rifle. During the winter there, there were these icicles that formed on this slate cliff a few hundred yards from my cabin, and I'd stand in the doorway and shoot icicles for a lot of the time so I got quite good."

Were you living alone in the cabin?

"I was living alone for much of the time but Suzanne would come down from time to time."

You liked it better on your own.

"Yeah, I've always liked that."

It is strange to think how different Leonard's life was now from nine months ago in New York. In Tennessee Leonard was Nature Boy. When Ron Cornelius took Bill Donovan—a close friend of Cornelius from San Francisco, who would become Leonard's and the band's tour manager—to the cabin to meet Leonard, "Leonard opened the door and he's stark naked," Donovan remembers. "He says, 'Welcome, friends, come in,' like it's nothing." Leonard offered them tea and declined a joint, "and he walked round the whole time naked," entirely unself-conscious and making friendly conversation.

"I thought," Leonard said, "I was living the life down there." In a poem written in the cabin and published in *The Energy of Slaves*, "I Try to Keep in Touch Wherever I Am," he wrote,

The sun comes in the skylight
My work calls to me
sweet as the sound of the creek

Twelve

O Make Me a Mask

The sixties had no intention of slipping out quietly. The last year of the decade witnessed the first man walk on the moon, while on Earth, in America, there was the Woodstock festival, the gathering of the hippie tribes, and also Charles Manson and Altamont, the death of the hippie dream. For Leonard too, 1969 would be a momentous year. It was the year in which he met the woman who would make him a father and the man who would make him a monk.

Joshu Sasaki Roshi is a short, round Japanese man, a Zen master of the Rinzai school—hard-core Buddhism—born on the first day of April 1907. In 1962, when Roshi was fifty-five, just a kid with a crazy dream, he left Japan for Los Angeles to establish the first Rinzai center in the U.S. Leonard first heard of Roshi through his friend Steve Sanfield, who studied with him and had lived for three years in the garage of his small, rented house in Gardena, an inexpensive Los Angeles suburb. Sanfield had fallen in love with another student's wife and Roshi had asked them to leave. Several months later, when the couple were expecting a child, Roshi told them to come back and he would marry them at the newly opened Zen Center on Cimarron Street. Sanfield wrote to Leonard in Nashville, asking him to be best man. There was no reply, but when he and his partner arrived for the wedding, Leonard was there, waiting.

Leonard appeared fascinated by the ceremony, particularly the Ten Vows of Buddhism, and how Roshi ignored the one about not indulging in drugs and alcohol by drinking an impressive amount of sake. Leonard and Roshi barely exchanged a word that day, which was fine with Leonard. Since becoming a music celebrity, Leonard seemed to have acquired a large number of "friends" he barely knew who wanted to talk to him. In his view, the ancient Japanese way, where men would meet and "bow to each other for as much as half an hour speaking words of greeting, gradually moving closer together, understanding the necessity of entering another's consciousness carefully,"[1] was a good one.

Some weeks later Leonard made another unannounced appearance, this time in Ottawa at a celebration thrown by Jack McClelland for the winners of the coveted Governor General's Award for literature. Leonard had won for *Selected Poems 1956–1968* but sent a telegram, declining to accept the award. This was most unusual. Only one other winner in the past had refused the honor and its $2,500 purse—a French separatist, who was making a political protest. Even more unusual, though, was turning down the prize and showing up at the party.

Mordecai Richler cornered Leonard and demanded to know his reasons; Leonard replied that he did not know what they were himself. In his telegram to the committee Leonard had written, "Much in me strives for this honour, but the poems themselves forbid it absolutely." Whether he meant that he had written books more deserving of the award than this anthology or that his poems had had it with being judged by anyone but himself is open to debate. Certainly since he had become a recording artist his work was receiving far more attention from far more critics. It had also brought a large increase in income, which meant that Leonard no longer depended on awards to help to pay the bills. However, to Canada's literary world, such behavior would have seemed nothing more than an expatriate pop celebrity rejecting his old country and his former life.

From Ottawa, Leonard traveled to Montreal, where he went to his old workplace, his uncle Horace's factory, to visit his cousin David. Over lunch in the factory cafeteria, David told Leonard, "You're famous, you're a big star." "I didn't mean it sarcastically," he recalls, "and he didn't take it that way. He just said, 'You get into Columbia's publicity mill and you cannot help but become very well-known. I'm no child, and I've seen it destroy a lot of young people who go from nothing to stardom. I've been through the mill. You can't escape it. Once you become an artist with them, that's it.'" When Leonard left Montreal for Nashville, once again he stopped off first in New York. After checking into the Chelsea Hotel, he went to the Scientology Center. There he met a woman.

"It was early spring in 1969. We both seemed to have signed up for a Scientology class the same day. He was getting into the elevator at the Scientology Center as I was coming out of it and our eyes locked. Some days later we both took seats near each other. Although I had another person I was living with, I left that relationship immediately for Leonard and moved into the Chelsea with him." Suzanne Elrod was a dark-haired beauty from Miami, Florida—some people in Montreal said she bore a resemblance to the Suzanne of Leonard's song. She was nineteen years old.

Leonard, at thirty-four, was fifteen years older than her—almost the same age difference as there was between his mother and father—but considerably younger than the wealthy man Suzanne was living with at the upscale Plaza Hotel. Suzanne declines to talk about her family background, which was secular Jewish. She had come to New York not for study or adventure or escape but as "a very young, naïve girl only armed with the typical romantic fantasies of my generation, wanting a family of my own. I had a river of love to give and found Leonard," she said. "I knew he was destined to be the father of my children and the love of my life, no matter what happened." When she told the man she lived with that she was leaving, he insisted on meeting "the poor poet" who had usurped him and organized a dinner for the three of them. Then, "he locked himself in one of the suites for hours and listened to the music and read the books he had his chauffeur go out and buy of Leonard's. He came out and said he at least felt I was leaving him for someone worthwhile."

Their life together in Leonard's room in the Chelsea was by Suzanne's account reclusive, with little partying or socializing. Leonard seemed as smitten with this headstrong, sexual young woman as she was with him. But he also appeared to have one eye on the door. In his passport was a folded sheet of motel notepaper containing a list of names and numbers of people all over the world,[2] among them Viva, one of Warhol's stars; folksinger Dave Van Ronk; folk rocker Julie Felix; Judy Collins; Marianne; and a "Jane" who lived at 41 West Street. Also on the list were the composer-conductor Leonard Bernstein and the Italian film director Franco Zeffirelli. In June 1969, not long after meeting Suzanne, Leonard joined Bernstein and Zeffirelli in Italy, where Zeffirelli was making a film on the life of Saint Francis. He took the two Leonards to Saint Francis's tomb and discussed the possibility of collaborating on the score. Nothing came of it, unfortunately; when *Brother Sun, Sister Moon* premiered in 1972, it featured a soundtrack by Donovan.

From Italy, Leonard went to Greece. Suzanne flew over and stayed with him in his little white house on Hydra. "My first impression was that the rooms were so small and run-down," Suzanne recalls. Over time she "changed many things, rebuilt the downstairs room and garden," but she says, "I kept the authenticity of the house, as that's what Leonard and I loved about it. I was very respectful of the spirit of the house. I liked it elegant, sparse and white, in all its Greek peasant simplicity."

While they were on the island, news came of the suicide of Charmian Clift. On July 8, on the eve of the publication of her husband's new novel, *Clean Straw for Nothing*, Clift took an overdose of barbiturates. (George Johnston would die a year later from tuberculosis.) Leonard mourned with the rest of the island, but on Hydra, as in New York, he and Suzanne kept mostly to themselves.

When he returned to his cabin in Tennessee, Leonard took Suzanne with him. He introduced her to Willie York and Kid Marley. The rodeo rider "would come by, uninvited and often drunk, to tell sometimes hilarious, sometimes insipid stories while he spat on the floor and dug his cowboy boot heels, spurs and all, into the wood floors, and slapped his hand on his knee saying, 'But ain't we having fun!' Sometimes he was fascinating," says Suzanne, "and we laughed and kept him drunk. Sometimes we got rid of him as fast as we could, politely, without being shot. They all had rifles in their back windows of their trucks. Did I mention the many Confederate flags that were still up down there 'in the holler'? It was an interesting place to visit and understand, but we lived there quietly, and briefly, thank goodness, as we lived everywhere else."

Leonard also took Suzanne to Montreal to meet his mother. For a short while, they stayed at Leonard's childhood home on Belmont Avenue, while he set about finding them a place of their own. Masha, said Suzanne in 1980, "was his most dreamy spiritual influence. The only thing that bothered me was that she always called me Marianne."[3] Leonard bought a cheap little cottage near the Parc du Portugal, off the Main, a neighborhood mostly populated by Portuguese and Greek immigrant families but that still retained the old Jewish delis with oilcloth-covered tables. The couple had barely moved in before they left for New York once again. In the city, Leonard revisited some of his old haunts—including the Gaslight, where he caught a show by Loudon Wainwright III—but this time with Suzanne. But Leonard no longer attended the Scientology Center. Disenchantment had set in, as well as anger that the organization had begun to exploit his name. Leonard had "gone clear"; he had a certificate confirming him as a "Senior Dianetic, Grade IV Release."[4] "I participated in all those investigations that engaged the imagination of my generation at that time," said Leonard. "I even danced and sang with the Hare Krishnas—no robe, I didn't join them, but I was trying everything."[5]

The dawn of the new decade found Leonard and Suzanne in their little house in Montreal until Suzanne could no longer take the cold and flew to Miami. Leonard in turn returned to Nashville. Bob Johnston was talking about a third album. And Columbia Records was talking even more loudly about a European tour.

Leonard had never really toured but he knew he did not like touring. Traveling wasn't the problem; "I tossed myself around like a cork," he said, "for most of my life."[6] But it was a different matter if someone else did the tossing, telling him where he had to be and when. Leonard's uncles would have been pleased to confirm his distaste for clock-punching, while his habit of becoming president of many of the clubs he joined might give some indication that Leonard did not much like following rules, unless they were his own. He also had a problem with stage fright—"I felt that the risks of humiliation were too wide"[7]—and had to psych himself up to perform. But mostly he was afraid for his songs. They had come to him in private, from somewhere pure and honest, and he had worked long and hard to make them sincere representations of the moment. He wanted to protect them, not parade and pimp them to paying strangers in an artificial intimacy. "My idea was to be able to make records only," he told Danny Fields. He said he had hoped his songs "would make their way through the world" on albums, audio equivalents of poetry books, without his having to get onstage and perform them.

Leonard called Bob Johnston. He told his producer that he would not tour unless Johnston agreed to manage him and play keyboards in his band. It was a good ruse. Johnston would have been the first to admit that he was not a musician, and the likelihood of Columbia letting the head of its Nashville division simply take off and go on tour would have seemed slim. Except that Johnston had just left Columbia to go independent. Celebrating with a trip around Europe, all expenses paid by his former employers, struck Johnston as a fine idea. As for management, he told Leonard that he would play in his band and look after him on the road, and not charge a dime for doing so, but that he would do better to talk to Marty Machat, the lawyer-manager who handled Johnston's business affairs. Machat had been the right-hand man of Allen Klein, who managed the Beatles and the Rolling Stones. Leonard and Johnston shook on it, and Johnston appointed Bill Donovan as tour manager and summoned the band for rehearsals—Cornelius, Daniels, Fowler and backing singers Susan Mussmano and Corlynn Hanney. Leonard, in turn, phoned Mort Rosengarten in Montreal and asked him to come to Tennessee.

"Leonard asked me to make a mask for him," says Rosengarten. "A theatrical mask. He said he wanted to wear it while he was performing. So I went out to his little place, down the dirt road, in the middle of nowhere." There was nowhere to buy materials, but they found a hobby shop in Franklin that sold "these little packages for model kits." "I bought them all," he says, "and Leonard came back from Nashville with a bag of plaster." While Leonard was in Nashville, rehearsing, Mort stayed in the cabin and worked on the mask. "With Leonard gone there was no one around except for this old guy who made moonshine and Kid Marley, who dressed like a cowboy and never went anywhere without his horse, which was in a trailer at the back of his pickup truck. One night he turned up at the cabin, drunk, and we were waiting for Leonard to come back, but then he decided to go back into town and get more booze. So I went with him and the horse came with us too, in the trailer."

The mask he made for Leonard to perform in was actually a mask of Leonard himself: a live death mask made from a plaster cast of his face, expressionless, with gaps for his mouth and eyes. Leonard clearly had enough self-regard that he did not want to operate behind someone else's face. The mask of himself would give him a thicker skin to cover his sensitivity and help protect his songs from contamination, but it also would make it obvious that the public Leonard was a performance and that he was well aware of the masquerade. As he wrote on the bathroom mirror in *Ladies and Gentlemen . . . Mr. Leonard Cohen*, "*caveat emptor*"—"Let the man watching me know," he said, "that this is not entirely devoid of the con." Leonard also knew his Dylan Thomas ("O make me a mask and a wall to shut from your spies / Of the sharp, enamelled eyes and the spectacled claws") and his Nietzsche ("Such a hidden nature, which instinctively employs speech for silence and concealment . . . desires and insists that a mask of himself shall occupy his place").

Rosengarten says, "Leonard felt it was helpful in deciding his persona onstage. A mask is neutral, it's the person that wears it that gives it life, the way you move your head and your eyes and all that stuff. It becomes very powerful." In the end Leonard decided not to wear the mask. He held on to it for decades though. Mort eventually had it cast for him in aluminum.

"Oh man," says Bob Johnston. "There was never anything like that tour." It began with nine shows in eight European cities in two weeks and was fuelled by LSD and Mandrax. Leonard, dressed in a khaki safari suit and wielding Henry Zemel's whip, was a quixotic General Patton leading his ragtag army. Or, at the Hamburg concert, more like cannon fodder. It was May 4, 1970, the day of the Kent

State massacre in the U.S., and, as some kind of convoluted anti-authority peace gesture, Leonard decided to start the second half of the show by clicking his heels twice and giving the Nazi salute. He had come back onstage to lighted matches and a long standing ovation, but the mood changed instantly.

The large crowd "went nuts," says Johnston, "cursing and throwing shit. One guy came running down the aisle with a gun. He was five feet from the stage when security wrestled him to the floor. Charlie Daniels turned to me and said, 'I'm out of here.' I said, 'Don't move, if they're going to kill someone it's Leonard.' But the crowd quieted when Leonard took up his guitar. He said, 'Are you finished, are you all through?' and they applauded as he started playing. But it was an old Yiddish song. And he started dancing on one leg across the stage like Jews do, singing '*Ai-eee, ai-eee,*' and they started cursing and throwing things again. Then he started one of his own songs and we all joined in, and it calmed down. Leonard was always pulling stunts like that, and getting away with it." The next morning at the hotel, though, Daniels told them he was quitting. "I've had it," he said, "I've got a wife and kid and you guys don't. I can't get shot out here over Leonard Cohen." It took the whole band to talk him into staying.

In London, Leonard gave a poetry reading at the ICA and played a concert at the Royal Albert Hall, which sold out almost the same moment it was announced; his first album had recently gone gold in the UK and the second was high on the charts. The *Guardian* reported, "The fashionably hippy audience cheered hysterically. But I hope they understood what Cohen is all about." If they didn't, the reviewer Robin Denselow explained that Leonard's songs reflected a "peculiarly Canadian wasteland" and that their message, with the poetry peeled off, was "self-obsession, cynicism, non-communication; it is two strangers frantically making love in a shadowy hotel bedroom."[8]

Leonard called Nico, who was also in London, but she turned

him down once again. He made the acquaintance of several women who were more generous with their affection. He bought a book for Suzanne titled *The Language of Flowers*, which he inscribed to her, writing that she was "a fragrant breath amid the foul storms of life."[9] Leonard took Cornelius, Johnston and Donovan to meet a friend in London who—he told them—had the best acid anywhere. "It was called Desert Dust and it was like LSD-plus," says Cornelius. "You had to take a needle—a pin was too big—and touch your tongue with this brown dust, and with as much as you could pick up on the end of that needle you were *gone*, sixteen hours, no reentry." Ample supplies were purchased and consumed; it would get to where the tour manager made them all hold hands at the airport as they walked to the plane so that he would not lose anyone—"a big conga line," Donovan says, "with everybody just singing along."

On the plane to Vienna the stewardess informed them that they had heard that there were around three hundred fans waiting for them at the airport. "Leonard said, 'Oh, they love me in Vienna,'" says Johnston, "but when we landed and he went out and waved to the crowd, they were all hollering, 'Where's Bubba?' Turned out Bubba Fowler had a big hit in Vienna but didn't know it." But the audiences across Europe loved Leonard, even when he provoked them—which could have been why he provoked them, although his pharmaceutical intake might have had something to do with it too. Much as Leonard claimed not to like performing, his feelings toward his audiences were of affection and gratitude. At the Amsterdam concert, he invited the entire crowd back to his hotel, which resulted in police action. At the Paris Olympia he invited the audience to come onstage, and once again the police were called.

It was his first real tour and he was still finding his way as a stage performer, but for a first tour it was quite remarkable. The band left France for New York in July, just as the Royal Winnipeg Ballet were getting ready to premiere *The Shining People of Leonard Cohen* in Paris.

Choreographed by a McGill University graduate named Brian Mac-
donald, who had met Leonard in 1964, it featured an electronic score
and the reading of several of Leonard's poems, among them the erotic "When I Uncovered Your Body" and "Celebration."

In the U.S. Leonard was booked to play at the Forest Hills folk
festival. To leave the grand opera houses and music halls of Europe
for a show at a tennis stadium put a dent in Leonard's mood, which
seemed to linger. Bob Dylan, who was also at the festival, had chosen
that day to meet Leonard. Dylan was not in the best of humor either,
having been barred from going to Leonard's dressing room by an official, who must have been the only man at a folk festival to fail to
recognize him. The official called Johnston over: "This guy says he's
Bob Dylan and he says he knows you." Johnston deadpanned, "I've
never seen the son of a bitch in my life. But okay, let him in." "Man,
that wasn't funny," said Dylan.

Leonard was backstage with Ron Cornelius, who was restring-
ing his guitar. Johnston put his head around the door saying, "Bob
Dylan's here."

"So?" said Leonard.

"He wants to meet you," said Johnston.

"Let him in, I guess," said Leonard. Dylan came into the room
and for a while he and Leonard just stood there, saying nothing.
Dylan broke the silence. "How're you doing here?" he said.

"Well you've got to be somewhere," Leonard answered.

"It was the strangest conversation," says Cornelius, who knew
Dylan and had worked with him in the past. "They were talking
between the sentences, if you know what I mean. You could see they
were communicating, however it really had nothing to do with the
words coming out of their mouth. It was one of the weirdest atmo-
spheres I've ever been in in my life—just a tiny bit hostile. But that
also goes along with the fact that we'd been playing in places where
Leonard was number one and Dylan was number two—Leonard

could sell out the Albert Hall in thirty-two minutes—and then we came to the U.S. and Bob Dylan is number one and nobody's ever heard of Leonard." However strange the encounter, Leonard and Dylan each left considering the other a friend. But Cornelius was correct about Leonard's lack of status in the U.S. A review of the show in *Billboard* described him as "nervous" and "lifeless." Wrote Nancy Erlich, "He works hard to achieve that bloodless vocal, that dull, humorless quality of a voice speaking after death. And the voice does not offer comfort or wisdom; it expresses total defeat. His art is oppressive."[10]

Leonard and the band still had two festivals left to play in Europe, so they flew straight back. The first festival was in the South of France, in the Provençal countryside six miles outside Aix. Their hotel was an old country lodge on the outskirts of the city. The hotel had stables and the band had the afternoon to themselves; they hired horses and rode through a landscape that looked like a Cézanne painting, singing cowboy songs. Unbeknownst to them, the three-day festival, whose bill included French bands and international acts—Mungo Jerry and Johnny Winter among them—had turned into a mini French Woodstock. More people had shown up than the organizers planned for, and many refused to pay fifty-five francs for a ticket and broke down fencing to get in. The local prefecture, concerned about the "hordes of destructive hippies in search of uproar and scandal" who were setting up makeshift camps in the meadow, dancing with the Hare Krishnas and basking stoned and naked in the sun, issued a ban on the festival and sent in the CRS—the French riot police. The show went on, by all accounts without any problems, apart from the demands from the more vociferous festivalgoers that the festival be free and the concerns of the organizers that they might not make enough to pay the acts.

Driving along the tree-lined road to the festival site, Leonard and the band found it completely blocked with parked and abandoned cars. There were still some miles to go—too far to walk, and they had instruments—and there was nowhere to call for help. Which was when Bob Johnston thought of the horses. Back at the inn, after negotiating terms through a translator, they set off again on horseback, taking the back route along narrow mountain roads, on a warm, starlit night, toward the distant lights.

"About halfway there," says Johnston, "Leonard said, 'We can't play the concert. We've run out of wine.' We were in the backwoods out there. I said, 'Leonard, don't worry.' Then about a mile down the road in the middle of nowhere we saw a bar called Texas." The good Lord had blessed and guided them to an unlikely Wild West theme bar. There was even a hitching post. They dismounted. In the bar, they hatched a plan to make their festival entrance by riding their horses onto the stage. It was the kind of decision that a large intake of wine mixed with the leadership style of Bob Johnston and the bravado the European tour had engendered might produce. When they rode into the backstage area, they headed toward the ramps and up onto the stage. "The stage was swinging up and down," says Johnston. "The French festival guys were all waving and screaming that it was going to collapse." This seemed a genuine possibility. The white stallion that Leonard was riding seemed to believe it and refused to move. In the end it was persuaded. "I gave it a kick on the ass," said Johnston, "and Leonard rode it up there into the middle of the stage, where it reared up, and Leonard saluted the audience."

At that moment, Leonard was the consummate showman, appearing to be in full control of both the spontaneity and the artifice. The only problem was that his grand entrance was greeted with hisses and boos. Hecklers began to shout insults: that Leonard was a diva, making such a grandiose entrance; that he was a capitalist and the tickets were so expensive because of his exorbitant fee; that he was a fascist sympathizer, having a house in Greece yet refusing to speak out against the military government. Leonard, as was his tendency, tried to engage "the Maoists"—as he called his detractors—in a debate in between songs. Their response was to throw bottles. At one point Leonard thought he heard gunshots, but it was only a stage light smashing. Still, whatever might happen, Leonard was not afraid. He was no longer Field Commander Cohen, he was Conquest, the white Horseman of the Apocalypse. He told the hecklers that if they wanted a fight they should come onstage: he and his men were ready to take them on. By the end of their performance, Leonard's band had an official name: the Army. Their next campaign would be to take a small island four miles off the coast of southern England, which had been invaded by six hundred thousand young people—ten times more than attended the Aix festival. But before landing in the Isle of Wight, Leonard went to a mental hospital.

———————

On August 28, two days before he was due to play the Isle of Wight Festival, a sedan pulled up outside the Henderson Hospital in Sutton, on the southern edge of London. Looking up, Leonard saw an old, imposing building with a tower with narrow windows. It had the look of an institution you might check into and never leave. Leonard went inside. Bill Donovan was there, telling him everything was set up for him in the tower. "Oh boy," said Leonard to Bob Johnston as the medical director of the hospital led them in, "I hope they like 'So Long, Marianne.'"

"Leonard said, 'I want to play mental asylums,'" says Johnston. And just like he'd done when Johnny Cash told him he wanted to play prisons, Johnston said, "Okay," and "booked a bunch of them." Despite appearances, the Henderson (closed now, due to funding cuts) was a pioneering hospital with an innovative approach to the treatment of personality disorders. It called itself a therapeutic community and the patients residents. "It was all talking therapy," says former charge nurse Ian Milne. "No medication, no 'zombies.'" Most of the patients were Leonard's age or younger, and so were the staff; to outsiders they would have been barely distinguishable. Both were at the morning Community Meeting where the medical director announced that he'd had a call saying, "Some guy wants to come and sing to us and run through his program for the Isle of Wight. His name's Leonard Cohen." Every mouth dropped; for once the talking stopped.

Ron Cornelius remembers the first time Leonard told the band of his intention to play at mental hospitals. "We were at the Mayfair Hotel and he said, 'We're going to enjoy this tour. We're going to see these cities and spend two or three days in them sometimes. And when we're not playing, I want to go and play mental institutions.' I went, 'What? I'm not going in a nuthouse to play. Yes, count me in for the Albert Hall, but count me out for the nuthouse.' Well they talked and talked and talked until Leonard finally said, 'Ron, just come one time.' After seeing what that music did for those people I ended up enjoying many of those, and we played a lot of them, all over Europe, Canada, even in America."

Leonard did not say why he wanted to play to mental patients and the band didn't ask, but Johnston recalls Leonard telling him once that "he had to go to the loony bin one time, when he wrote *Beautiful Losers* or something." As Johnston remembers it, Leonard said he had taken a lot of acid, gone out on a little boat and stared at the sun too long. He told journalist Steve Turner in 1974 that he was drawn to mental hospitals through "the feeling that the experience of a lot of people in mental hospitals would especially qualify them to be a receptive audience for my work. In a sense, when someone consents to go into a mental hospital or is committed he has already acknowledged a tremendous defeat. To put it another way, he has already made a choice. And it was my feeling that the elements of this choice, and the elements of this defeat, corresponded with certain elements that produced my songs, and that there would be an empathy between the people who had this experience and the experience as documented in my songs."[11]

So, fellow-feeling had something to do with it; in a 1969 interview he said, "I always loved the people the world used to call mad. I used to hang out and talk to those old men, or with the junkies. I was only 13 or 14, I never understood why I was down there except that I felt at home with those people." There was also something of "there but for fortune," given his own history and that of his mother. On a practical level, it was also a good place "to tighten the band up," says Donovan, "and blow their minds." Leonard did it at his own expense and without fanfare. Although there were two big Johnny Cash prison albums, there was no Leonard Cohen *At Henderson Hospital*. But a tape of the concert exists, and it's good. Milne, who was also an amateur sound recordist, captured it on his four-track stereo Stella reel-to-reel.

The concert started around seven P.M. in the high-ceilinged tower attic. There was a small stage, so crammed with the band and their regular concert equipment that Leonard had to play at floor level. He stood beneath one of the tall, narrow windows that gave the room the feel of a chapel. Around fifty residents made their way into one of a half dozen rows of folding chairs while the band did a quick sound check—"Arms of Regina," an unreleased song, sounding here like a midtempo country ballad with heart-tugging harmonies. To the audience Leonard said, "There was a fellow I spoke to last night, a doctor. I told him I was coming out here. He said, 'They are a tough bunch of young nuts.'" While playing the opening bars of "Bird on the Wire," Leonard stopped. "I feel like talking. Someone warned me downstairs that all you do here is talk. That's psychotic, it's contagious." Apparently so. Leonard spoke a lot during the eighty-minute concert, in between the eleven songs and one poem, and often more freely than at regular shows. He talked of how his affair with Marianne slowly faded and died and told the stories behind some of his songs: "You Know Who I Am" had "something to do with some three hundred acid trips I took" and "One of Us Cannot Be Wrong" "was written coming off amphetamine." "Tonight Will Be Fine" was played like a country hoedown, upbeat and raucous, and with extra verses. There were signs of "Tennesseefication" too in "Suzanne," where the lonely wooden tower became "lonesome." Here and there Leonard tried out different lyrics; in "Bird on the Wire," "*I have saved all my ribbons for thee*" was changed to the quite different "*I have broken all my sorrows on thee.*" There was no recognition or response from the audience when he added, "It was written in the Chelsea Hotel in New York City, a place where you never leave the elevator alone," but "Chelsea Hotel #2" and the Janis stories were still some years off.

There appeared to be quite a few Leonard Cohen fans in the audience. One called out a request for "Famous Blue Raincoat," "a song," he said, "that I didn't know anybody knew about, that we have only sung in concerts. It's a song that I wrote in New York when I was living on the east side of the East Side, and it's about sharing women, sharing men, and the idea of that if you hold on to somebody . . ." Leonard let the conclusion drift away. During the songs, the audience was silent, entranced. When the band stopped, the applause was loud and rapturous. "I really wanted to say that this is the audience that we've been looking for," said Leonard, who sounded moved and happy. "I've never felt so good playing before people." People who were mentally damaged seemed to make Leonard and his songs feel at home. They performed other mental hospital concerts later that year, "and those shows were one of the best things about the whole tour, every one of them," said Donovan, "just the way the audience locked in on what Leonard was doing and how he just interacted with them."

In early November 1970 they would play at the Napa State mental hospital, a colossal nineteenth-century Gothic pile set on 190 acres in California wine country. The band had a temporary new backing

singer in California, Michelle Phillips of the Mamas and the Papas.*
A few days earlier, on Halloween, Phillips had married the actor Dennis Hopper. Leonard, whom Hopper considered a friend, was at the ceremony. "So we dragged Hopper up to the hospital too," says Bill Donovan. "On the way he took some acid." It started to kick in just as the limo pulled into the grounds. As they started unloading, they could see the staff bringing the audience into the building in which they were to perform. Many of the patients were in wheelchairs; others lurched slowly on foot. The hospital housed many severely damaged and highly medicated patients; it also had a separate wing for the criminally insane. "When Hopper saw this," Donovan says, "he freaked out, like it was *The Night of the Living Dead* or something. Hopper ran back into the limo and locked the door and wouldn't come out." Leonard, performing for the patients, sang and played and talked a little, then jumped down among them with his guitar, "and anyone who could move followed him around the room and back and forward and over the stage."

In Montreal, when the band performed at a hospital there, a young woman patient told Leonard she was not crazy, and that her father had put her there because she had taken drugs. She begged him to help her get out. There was something in her story that brought to mind Nancy, the judge's daughter about whom Leonard wrote "Seems So Long Ago, Nancy." They formulated an escape plan. It did not succeed—fortunately, it seems, since they discovered that she did have a serious mental illness. "There are things that happened that would take your breath away," says Ron Cornelius. "At one show eight or nine people in wheelchairs all decided that at six o'clock exactly they would all shit their pants. They were marched out with their dirty gowns and they were all crying, because the mu-

---

* She sang at two official dates, the Berkeley Community Center and the Hollywood Bowl.

sic was doing something for them that they had never had. One kid
stood up with a triangle missing from his skull—you could see the
brain beating—and he started screaming at Leonard in the middle
of a song, to where we actually ground to a halt. The kid said, 'Okay,
okay, big-time poet, big-time artist, you come in here, you've got the
band with you, you've got the pretty girls with you, you're singing all
these pretty words and everything, well what I want to know, buddy,
is what do you think about me?' And Leonard just left the stage and
before you knew it he had the guy in his arms, hugging him."

On their way to the Isle of Wight, Leonard studied the music magazine that Johnston handed him. It was opened to a full-page ad for
his album, which pictured Leonard, dressed in a black polo-neck
sweater, gazing off to the left, as if trying to ignore what his record
company had written at the back of his head. It said, "Do you ever
get the feeling that you want to disengage yourself from life? To withdraw into some kind of solitary contemplation just to think about
everything for a while? Everything. You. Her. It. Them. Well that's
how a poet feels, because he's no different from everyone else. What
makes a poet different is that he takes time to put it all down on
paper. Beautifully. And what makes Leonard Cohen a very different
poet is that he turns his poetry into songs. He did it for *Songs of Leonard Cohen*. Then came *Songs from a Room*, the second Leonard Cohen
album for the growing number of people who have identified with
him. And what he feels. But don't have that rare poetic vision. There
could be millions of Leonard Cohens in the world. You may even,"
it ended, "be him yourself." If Mort had only mass-produced those
Leonard masks, they could have made a fortune. A slow, stoned smile
grew across Leonard's face, for which much of the credit went to his
drug of choice on this part of the tour. The Army had taken to calling
him Captain Mandrax.

The Isle of Wight, a four-mile ferry ride from England's south coast, is a placid little island, encircled by yachts and popular with retired naval officers and genteel holidaymakers. For five days in the summer of 1970, it was invaded by hundreds of thousands—six times the island's population—of young music lovers, hippies and militants. From the hill above the festival site in the west, on Afton Down, you could see dust rising from corrugated fences that had been trampled and the smoke rising from trucks and concession stands set on fire. Nicknamed Devastation Hill—for obvious reasons to anyone who was there—it had been taken over by ticketless squatters, some of whom were responsible for the disturbance. Off in the distance, crammed in front of the stage, were thousands of exhausted festivalgoers, who had spent days watching a bill that rivaled Woodstock. The artists who played that year included the Who, the Doors, Miles Davis, Donovan and Ten Years After. Leonard had the slot before last on the fifth and final day, after Jimi Hendrix and Joan Baez and before Richie Havens.

Tension had been rising at the festival for days. The promoters had expected a hundred and fifty thousand people but half a million more turned up, many with no intention of paying. Even after the promoters were forced to declare it a free festival, ill will remained. During a set by Kris Kristofferson, bottles were thrown and he was booed offstage. "They were booing everybody," says Kristofferson. "Except Leonard Cohen." As the day progressed, things only got worse. Baez offered to go on before Hendrix to try to calm things down; she said, "I knew that my music was a little more difficult to burn fires to."[12] During Hendrix's set, someone in the crowd threw a flare that set fire to the top of the stage. Flames shot up while Hendrix played on. Leonard and Johnston stood nearby and watched.

"Leonard wasn't worried," says Johnston. "Hendrix didn't care and neither did we. Leonard was always completely oblivious to anything like that. The only thing that upset him was when they told him that they didn't have a piano or an organ—I don't know, someone had set them on fire and pushed them off the stage—so I couldn't play with him. Leonard said, 'I'll be in the trailer taking a nap; come and get me when you've found a piano and an organ.'" He took some Mandrax. It was around two in the morning when they woke Leonard and brought him onstage, in his safari suit, his chin stubbled, hair long, eyes very stoned. As the Army took their places, he stood staring out into the pitch-black night.

Jeff Dexter, a well-known British DJ of that period who was onstage playing records between sets, made the introduction. He saw immediately that Leonard and the band "were totally Mandraxed; they were in such a state I could have fucked them all and they wouldn't have known it." He was worried for their safety. So was Murray Lerner, the American documentary filmmaker who was shooting the festival. "I thought, 'This is going to be a disaster,' and that what happened to Kristofferson would happen to him," says Lerner. "But he looked so calm." Johnston says, "He was calm, because of the Mandrax. That's what saved that show and saved the festival. It was the middle of the night, all those people had been sitting out there in the rain, after they'd set fire to Hendrix's stage, and nobody had slept for days"—all the ingredients for turning nasty. "But then Leonard, with the Mandrax in him, started out singing, very slowly—so slowly it took him ten minutes to sing it—'Like . . . a . . . bird.' And everybody in that audience was exactly with him. It was the most amazing thing I've ever heard." Charlie Daniels says, "If Leonard was in a zone with Mandrax, it certainly didn't cause any bad musical decisions. Crowds can be kind of funny and it was getting late and he just seemed to feel the mood. He just kind of laid it down, eased it down."

Before he sang, Leonard talked to the hundreds of thousands of people he could not see as if they were sitting together in a small, dark room. He told them—slowly, calmly—a story that sounded like a parable, worked like hypnotism, and at the same time tested the temperature of the crowd. He described how his father would take him to the circus as a child. Leonard didn't much like circuses, but he enjoyed it when a man stood up and asked everyone to light a match so they could locate each other. "Can I ask each of you to light a match," said Cohen, "so I can see where you all are?" There were few at the beginning, but as the show went on he could see flames flickering through the misty rain.

"He mesmerized them," says Lerner. "And I got mesmerized also." For the lovers in the audience, Leonard sang "Suzanne," saying, "Maybe this is good music to make love to," and for the fighters he sang "The Partisan," dedicating it to "Joan Baez and the work she is doing." Says Johnston, "It was magical. From the first moment to the last. I've never seen anything like it. He was just remarkable." Thirty-nine years later the spellbinding performance was released, along with Lerner's footage, on the CD/DVD *Leonard Cohen: Live at the Isle of Wight 1970*.

———

A month after the festival, Leonard, Johnston and the Army were back in Nashville's Columbia Studio A, recording Leonard's third album, *Songs of Love and Hate*. Work began on September 22, 1970, four days after Jimi Hendrix died at the age of twenty-seven in London, and continued daily until the twenty-sixth, eight days before Janis Joplin died at the same age in a Los Angeles hotel. The break from recording was to play a handful of U.S. and Canadian shows in November and December. The first was an anti–Vietnam War concert at a university in Madison, Wisconsin; a homemade bomb had gone off there that summer and Leonard was offered protection by the White Panthers, which he declined. He began the show with a song he had learned at Socialist summer camp, "Solidarity," and dedicated "Joan of Arc," a song written to Nico, to the memory of another muse, Janis.

When they reached Montreal on December 10 for the last show of

1970, the city was under martial law following the kidnappings of a
journalist and the British trade commissioner in Leonard's old neighborhood, Westmount. Canada's prime minister Pierre Trudeau—
Leonard's old friend from Le Bistro, he of the famous beige raincoat
to Leonard's famous blue one—was on CBC television, angrily telling the reporter, "There's a lot of bleeding hearts around who don't
like to see people with helmets and guns. All I can say is go on and
bleed." Meet the new decade, same as the old decade. In their little
house in the immigrant quarter, Leonard and Suzanne watched the
snow steadily fall and settle on the street, silently, whitewashing everything.

Thirteen

The Veins Stand Out
Like Highways

He smiled like a holy fool from the photo in the bottom corner of the album sleeve, which had been shot on tour—eyes ecstatic, face unshaven, his head dissolving into the black background. On the back cover, in place of song titles there was, written in white on black like a message on a madhouse chalkboard,

> *THEY LOCKED UP A MAN*
> *WHO WANTED TO RULE THE WORLD*
> *THE FOOLS*
> *THEY LOCKED UP THE WRONG MAN*

Critics had called *Songs from a Room* bleak; it wasn't, it was stark. *Songs of Love and Hate* was bleak: songs of pain and self-disgust of endless variation, including a hunchback, an immolation, a cuckold, a suicide, an abortion, broken limbs, a broken sky and a washed-up writer—"Last Year's Man"—who felt unable to move his hand and write the world back into being. Leonard was depressed and wasted. He'd had it. He had been backstage and he knew how they hid the rabbits in the hat. Those reviewers who had seen through the con and called his voice "weak and pitiful" and his songs "self-indulgent" had been right. There had been no victories. The medals were a sham. Almost four years had passed since he had written to Marianne describing his excruciating first stage appearance with Judy Collins and the freedom and beauty he felt from his "total failure." But now, living in the Tennessee cabin with Suzanne and contemplating a third album he did not want to make, didn't believe that he could make, but that his record contract required that he make, Leonard felt only "a deep, paralyzing anguish."[1]

Love, lust, the Bible Belt and the company of men, musicians, whom he trusted and admired might appear to an outsider to be the ideal Leonard Cohen setup. Then, they might have said the same thing about his life with Marianne in the little house on Hydra. Leonard's depression begged to differ. Says Suzanne, "Of course, it can feel like a dark room with no doors. It's a common experience of many people, especially with a creative nature, and the more spiritual the person, the closer to the tendency resembling what the church called *acedia*"—a sin that encompassed apathy in the practice of virtue and the loss of grace. "Maybe the biggest struggle—what permits the work to shine or lets you shine through the work—is the undressing, being only truly who you are, [and] tailoring the pathos, quieting the daily pettiness and ending the second-guessing, just in action"—knuckling down and getting on with it.

Leonard's contract with Columbia stipulated two more albums from him. He asked Bob Johnston if they could give the record company two live albums, since they'd recorded most of the shows on the last tour. Johnston said they might be able to get away with one live album, but not until they'd given the label a new studio album. So Leonard knuckled down and got on with it. He took a room in a hotel in Nashville, he swam in the pool at the Y twice a day and for five days straight he went to the studio. The recording was relatively painless at first; there was an easy familiarity with the road-honed band, the engineers and the studio. Charlie Daniels says, "We'd gotten used to each other and had much more of an idea of where we were going and what to do with his songs." And there were only eight songs, almost all of which Leonard had previously attempted to record on his first two albums and/or had performed with the band onstage. The version of "Sing Another Song, Boys" that appears on the album was in fact recorded live at the festival outside Aix.

After five days in Studio A, the band went their way and Leonard and Johnston took the master tape to London to do overdubs: Leonard's spoken-word part on "Joan of Arc," the children's choir on "Last Year's Man" and the string arrangements by Paul Buckmaster, a classical cellist and experimental rock bassist who had arranged Elton John's first two albums. They gave him "a free hand," Buckmaster said, but "Cohen's music is almost unarrangeable." His contribution was to add "little areas of emotional texture and color."[2]

Cornelius remembers, "It started out the way we recorded *Songs from a Room* but then it grew as things got deeper. 'Famous Blue Raincoat' kind of matured right before your eyes, and also 'Avalanche.' It's so easy to get too much going on, and yet at the same time without enough horsepower behind it that song would have never had the energy that it has. But it kind of grew into a monster." Cornelius and Leonard agreed there was something not quite right about the album. Leonard flew him to London. "For a while," says Cornelius, "with Bob [Johnston] and I, it was flat-out almost fistfights over things going in the record—fighting over wanting it to be the best for Leonard. There was tons of stuff that Buckmaster wrote that Leonard and I would finally just end up putting great big red X's through, because it would actually have been too much; but if you listen closely there's a heck of a lot on there."

"It was an odd sort of record," said Leonard.[3] There's barely a trace of Tennessee in it at all, except at a push the skewed back-porch rhythm of "Diamonds in the Mine," a snarling, screaming sing-along about the nothingness of it all. The album contains some of Leonard's blackest songs and also some of his most beautiful. The resigned eroticism of "Joan of Arc" and the serene bittersweetness of "Famous Blue Raincoat"—another of Leonard's triangle songs, this a letter written to a rival or friend or both in the dark hours before dawn—sound almost unbearably lovely alongside the dark, disturbing "Sing Another Song, Boys," "Dress Rehearsal Rag" (of which Leonard said, "I didn't write that song, I suffered it"[4]), and "Avalanche," the intense, compelling song with which the album opens. It is sung in the character of a hunchback, a grotesque creature with a mountain of gold lusting over women—a Nazi caricature of a Jew. Or from the depths of hell by a tormented man who longs for connection with the Divine. Or by a man who already has the woman but does not want her or the domesticity she offers. And/or it is sung by God—a gentle, New Testament Jesus, with the crumbs of the Last Supper on the table and a wound in his side, who turns out to be as hard and demanding as an Old Testament Jehovah. In these six verses, sung in a minor key, untempered by women's voices, there are layers upon layers, a whole house of mirrors, but the constants are a sense of loneliness and longing, depression and despair.

Songs of Love and Hate, along with the first two albums *Songs of Leonard Cohen* and *Songs from a Room,* make up a kind of trilogy wherein killers march alongside suicides, martyrs with soldiers, and gurus with Old Testamentarians, and men who long for love and their lovers march in opposite directions. As in Leonard's books of poetry, there are recurring themes and motifs, lessons learned and unlearned, joy becoming love becoming pain. Joan of Arc, whose picture was on the back sleeve of Leonard's first record, is the subject of a song in his third. Marianne Ihlen, pictured on the back of his second album, was the subject of a song on the first. "Dress Rehearsal Rag," a song written for the first album and recorded for the second, finally made it onto the third, three years after its appearance on the Judy Collins album that effectively launched Leonard's musical career.

When *Songs of Love and Hate* was released in March 1971, an imaginary whistle blew and the U.S. and UK ran to opposite ends of the playground. In Britain the album was a Top 5 hit. In America, despite a promotional campaign, it was an abject failure, not even making it into the Top 100. Canada did not take to it as warmly as to his last album, but Dalhousie University in Halifax was moved to award Leonard an honorary doctorate in the month that it came out. The citation read: "For many young people on both sides of the Atlantic, Leonard Cohen has become a symbol of their own anguish, alienation and uncertainty." It echoed the Columbia Records ad about there being millions of Leonard Cohens out there, disengaging themselves from life. "People were saying I was 'depressing a generation,'" said Leonard, "and 'they should give away razor blades with Leonard Cohen albums because it's music to slit your wrists by.'"[5] The UK press had taken to calling him "Laughing Len."

———

Spring in Montreal is a wonder. That after such prolonged abuse it still has the will to follow winter seems always little short of a miracle. The sun, no longer slacking on the job, got on with melting the snow. Tables and chairs sprouted outside cafés, where survivors, peeled of their winter armor, sat marveling at the flowers. The darkness had passed, for now. Leonard and Suzanne were installed in their little cottage near the Parc du Portugal. Suzanne had adopted "three adorable but constantly quacking ducklings, until Leonard said, 'It's me or the ducks, Suzanne.'" Leonard was trying to write. "He was al-

ways writing," says Suzanne, "even when he thought he wasn't. Continuously." Suzanne was writing too, a pornographic novel. "It was
an innocent ruse, catnip for a blank page, not only to amuse Leonard, but to get him to continue [to try] to write another novel again.
I believed—and still do—that he had another novel waiting to be
born, that I wished he would consecrate himself to. So I started this
book—pornographic, I suppose, for 1969/70, but in today's market it
would be just another modern sardonic/romantic novel—pretending
I was having the writer's block, not him. I asked him if I wrote a paragraph if he would write one, to push me along, and he did, and that's
how it began, playfully," each writing a page and reading it to the
other. "I never imagined I'd actually finish it, but I did"—it took Suzanne around two years. They sent it off to some publishing houses.
"We laughed as the rejection letters came in, because along with the
regrets they asked to meet me anyway."

Leonard completed his novel too, although not until the midseventies. It was accepted by his publisher, but at the proof stage, Leonard withdrew it. One friend to whom Leonard spoke of the book had
the impression it was an autobiography, in which Leonard discussed
the nature of fame and the sexuality of celebrity—what people expected of him and what they offered him now that they had not offered him before he became a music star. Another friend gathered
that it was fiction, largely autobiographical, and that he had written so
frankly about his family that he had second thoughts about making
it public—curious when Leonard wrote about his family with such
candor in *The Favorite Game*. A 1976 interview with *Melody Maker*[6]
appears to confirm the latter. He had written about his family, Leonard said, but he felt "that it wasn't honest enough. In other words, it
would hurt them but it didn't have the good side. So I took it back at
the last moment. But I feel good because it's written. Maybe there'd
be an appropriate time for it some time. But not for a while," and not
by the time of this book's publication.

In the summer a new film appeared in theaters featuring a soundtrack by Leonard Cohen. Robert Altman's *McCabe and Mrs. Miller* was a Western of sorts, starring Warren Beatty and Julie Christie as a gambler and prostitute who team up to run a bordello. Altman was a great fan of *Songs of Leonard Cohen*—he played it so often he wore more than one copy out, adding considerably to its U.S. sales. Altman called Leonard to ask if he might use it in his film; Leonard agreed, although given his experiences with directors he was not holding his breath. Then Altman called the production company, Warner Bros., to see if they could procure rights from Columbia. At the time the music department of Warner Bros.'s films division was run by Joe Boyd, an American who had made his name in Britain in the sixties, producing or launching the careers of artists such as Pink Floyd, Nick Drake and the Incredible String Band. Altman invited Boyd to a screening.

"The lights went down and onto the screen comes Beatty," says Boyd, "walking down a hill to the arpeggio guitar intro of 'The Stranger Song.' And then a couple of scenes with Julie Christie and Leonard Cohen's guitar and voice. I thought, 'Huh? That's a little wacky'; I didn't have any great feeling of 'Oh my god, Leonard Cohen's music, incredible.' But when the film finished and the lights came up, everyone else in the room—crew, editors—turned to Robert and said, 'Oh my God, Bob, that's *so* unbelievable, you're such a genius.'" So Boyd phoned Columbia Records. He ended up talking to Bob Johnston and asked him if he knew how they could get hold of the guitar tracks without the vocals. Although Johnston had not recorded that album, he knew that they could not have the guitar tracks, because the performances were recorded live in the studio, "the voice singing at the same time as the guitar was played." But they did find some instrumental passages that the Kaleidoscope had done without Leonard's vocals, which did not make it onto the album. Watching the movie in a cinema, Chris Darrow almost jumped

out of his seat when he recognized the instrumentation they had improvised to "Sisters of Mercy," "Winter Lady" and "The Stranger
Song." Chester Crill had much the same reaction. "When I heard it I
said, '*That's* the way the album was supposed to be mixed, stripped
down, with the instruments actually responding to Leonard's vocal.'"

That same year "Sisters of Mercy" would also feature five more of
Leonard's songs in the Rainer Werner Fassbinder film *Warnung vor
einer Heiligen Nutte—Beware of a Holy Whore*. (Fassbinder, an early
fan, would go on to employ Leonard's songs in several films.) Another
German film, Werner Herzog's *Fata Morgana*, used "Suzanne," "So
Long, Marianne" and "Hey, That's No Way to Say Goodbye." Others of Leonard's songs were also keeping busy. Tim Hardin covered
"Bird on a Wire" (one of several cover versions to substitute an "a"
for Leonard's "the"), and the ever-faithful Judy Collins included two
more Cohen songs on her new album *Living*, "Famous Blue Raincoat" and "Joan of Arc." A live recording from the Isle of Wight of
"Tonight Will Be Fine" turned up on a triple album, a compilation
titled *The First Great Rock Festivals of the Seventies: Isle of Wight/At-
lanta Pop Festival*, released in the summer of '71. Delighted that so
many of his songs were making a living without his having to perform
them, Leonard settled down to his writing. He was working on the
final edits of a new book of poetry, as well as on what he described to
Danny Fields as "a new big chunk of prose." It was called *The Woman
Being Born*—a title that was also given to an early draft of Leonard's
book *Death of a Lady's Man*.

Leonard had been in Montreal with Suzanne for six months now.
It had begun to feel like a very long time. He took a trip to London
in August, with the excuse that he was finding a UK publisher for an
anthology of Irving Layton's poems that Leonard wanted to release.
The following month, accompanied by a very attractive English girlfriend, an artist, he flew to Switzerland. He was there to meet his
friend Henry Zemel, who was making a documentary film about
Immanuel Velikovsky, the Russian psychoanalyst and catastrophist.

Leonard had first read about Velikovsky in *Reader's Digest*; the magazine had been a particular favorite of his father. In later years Leonard explored Velikovsky's writings on the sexuality of the gods and his theories that evolution, religion and myth were a response to real catastrophes of celestial origin—comets and colliding planets causing the biblical floods and plagues as well as a collective post-traumatic amnesia in mankind.

Having been dismissed as a kook by the science community, Velikovsky had agreed to take a teaching position at the University of the New World—a utopian educational experiment founded in Switzerland by the American political and behavioral scientist Alfred de Grazia, a former writer of psychological warfare manuals for the CIA. His fellow professors were to include William Burroughs and Ornette Coleman. When would-be student Brian Cullman, a writer and musician from New York, showed up in September 1971, "there was nothing, no campus, no buildings, just fifteen or twenty mostly rich kids who were using this as a way to avoid the draft and avoid college." Billeted in a resort hotel, they were given a small list of classes, including one on sexuality, which essentially consisted of "a sexy older woman with glasses and a lot of cleavage directing the students in sex games."

Then Velikovsky arrived, with Leonard and Zemel, and started giving lectures. Leonard attended them. He wanted, he told Cullman, to ask the professor about the sexuality that generated the first life on Earth. "I was really excited to meet Leonard," says Cullman, "but most people there, even the university kids, couldn't care less. One evening I sat around in the hotel lobby with Leonard and Henry, and Leonard had a guitar and played 'Bird on the Wire' and songs from *Songs of Love and Hate*. There were some very beautiful French girls in the lobby who had no idea who he was, and there was this long period of Henry talking Leonard up, Leonard talking himself down, then trying to talk himself back up again: 'Well have you heard of Charles Aznavour?' 'No.' 'Have you heard of Bob Dylan?' 'Yes.' 'Well,

I'm sort of this, sort of that,' and they weren't vaguely interested. He was putting on a show about not being concerned about the French girls, but clearly wounded that they had no idea who he was."

Leonard made an appearance in Zemel's film, near the end, asking Velikovsky questions. What effect would man's collective amnesia have on the future, what rituals might repeat the trauma and when would the next catastrophe happen? It would not stop happening, Velikovsky answered, while man continued to live "in a role that he created himself, in his arrogance, in his violence, in his misunderstanding of what happened in the past." The film, *Bonds of the Past*, was broadcast by CBC in February 1972—a month after the publication of Leonard's newest volume of poetry.

"I've just written a book called *The Energy of Slaves* and in there I say that I'm in pain," Leonard told journalist Paul Saltzman. "I don't say it in those words because I don't like those words, they don't represent the real situation. It took eighty poems to represent the situation of where I am right now. It's carefully worked on, you know. It's taken many years to write . . . and it's there . . . between hard covers. It's careful and controlled and it's what we call art."[7] The "real situation" appeared to be as savage and lost as it was on *Songs of Love and Hate*. He wrote,

> *I have no talent left*
> *I can't write a poem any more*
> *You can call me Len or Lennie now*
> *Like you always wanted*[8]

and elsewhere,

> *The poems don't love us anymore*
> *they don't want to love us . . .*
> *Do not summon us, they say*
> *We can't help you any longer*[9]

He was "one of the slaves," he wrote; "You are employers." Everybody wanted something from him that he no longer had the energy to give—the record company, his audience, and "all the flabby liars of the Aquarian age."[10] Even the women who had always been there for him, even though he was not always there for them, had started to become hard work.

> *You are almost always with someone else*
> *I'm going to burn down your house*
> *and fuck you in the ass . . .*
> *Why don't you come over to my table*
> *with no pants on*
> *I'm sick of surprising you*[11]

He was a celebrity now and women were his reward:

> *The 15 year old girls*
> *I wanted when I was 15*
> *I have them now . . .*
> *I advise you all*
> *to become rich and famous*[12]

THE ENERGY OF SLAVES

The review in the *Times Literary Supplement* sneered, "Teenyboppers of all ages will have the book on their shelves between the Bhagavad Gita and the unopened copy of the Cantos."[13] Other critics were not much kinder. Stephen Scobie, who was often Leonard's champion, described it as "blatantly bad . . . deliberately ugly, offensive, bitter, anti-romantic."[14] The last four words are hard to argue with, but Leonard was deliberately no longer writing for beauty, he said, but truth. He had been brutally honest in *Songs of Love and Hate* bar the one untruth in the song "Last Year's Man," in which he wrote that he was unable to write. Clearly he had found the clarity to finish the album.

The Energy of Slaves has a similar brutal honesty. Revisiting it today, it almost reads like punk poetry. The poem "How We Used to Approach the Book of Changes: 1966" strips all of Leonard's darkness down to a prayer, one he would return to in the turbulent coming year:

> *Good father, since I am broken down, no leader*
> *of the borning world, no saint for those in pain,*
> *no singer, no musician, no master of anything, no*
> *friend to my friends, no lover to those who love me*
> *only my greed remains to me, biting into every*
> *minute that has not come with my insane triumph*
> *show me the way now . . .*
> *. . . and let me be for a moment in*
> *this miserable and bewildering wretchedness, a happy*
> *animal.*

Columbia Records tugged on Leonard's chain. They needed him to play the places where people were buying his record: seventeen cities across Europe and two in Israel, all within the space of a month. It was nearly two years since his last tour—he must have thought he'd got away with never doing another—and he didn't have a band; the Army had been decommissioned more than a year before. Charlie Daniels was making a second album of his own and Bubba Fowler had left his wife and kids and run off with Susan Mussmano, one of the backing singers. The pair, who had become lovers on Leonard's 1970 tour, had no place to go, so Bob Johnston let them live on his boat—a cabin cruiser that had belonged to the country great Hank Snow, before Johnston bought it and paid another country great, though poor and unknown at the time, Kris Kristofferson, to work on it. Says Bill Donovan, "Leonard and I went out there a couple of times and saw them; and then they pulled out of the harbor, said they were going to take it out to the gulf, and we never heard or saw them again."*

Bill Donovan signed on for the second tour, as did Ron Cornelius and Bob Johnston, who put a new band together. Fowler and Daniels were replaced by two Californians, David O'Connor, a flamenco guitarist, and Peter Marshall, a jazz bassist, who was living at that time in Vienna. Johnston was still looking for backing singers as the three weeks of rehearsals began. "There was a redheaded girl who was gorgeous; she said, 'You'll be making the biggest mistake in the world if you don't take me with you,' and I said, 'I know it, I haven't heard anybody better yet.' Then the next day this girl came in—a horse face, big glasses and ragged from a trip from L.A." She told him she had sung in the musical *Hair* and made regular appearances on television in the Smothers Brothers' show. Johnston listened to her sing. "She was incredible—and she knew every song Leonard did. Though I hated to turn down the redheaded girl I told the horse-faced girl, 'You're going.'" Her name was Jennifer Warnes. The second female vocalist was another Los Angeleno, Donna Washburn, the daughter of the president of the 7-Up soft drinks company; her musical résumé included singing with Dillard & Clark and Joe Cocker.

Leonard was focusing all his efforts on holding it together and getting in shape for the campaign: yoga, swimming twice a day, fasting. He had a habit of fasting once a week, usually on a Friday if a tour did not get in the way. Brian Cullman recalls that when he and

---

* Susan Mussmano changed her name to Aileen Fowler, the one under which she is credited on the 1970 recordings on the *Live Songs* album. She and Fowler, who adopted the new name Elkin Thomas, finally left the boat for a farm in the North Texas prairies. They still live there, when not touring together as folk duo Aileen and Elkin Thomas. Leonard's second backing singer, Corlynn Hanney, went on to make spiritual albums.

Leonard talked in Switzerland, Leonard spoke more about fasting than he did poetry. "But even his fasting was elegant; while fasting, he would drink white grape juice with lemon and seltzer." Fasting was important to Leonard and had been ever since he began the task of chiseling away the softness that his old family photographs showed a tendency toward. He needed to keep the edges sharp.

Suzanne flew out to Nashville to join Leonard. She was there when Paul Saltzman interviewed Leonard in their hotel room. He noted how Leonard sat there quietly while Suzanne caressed his foot. Suzanne appeared to dote on Leonard, telling him at one point, "You've taught me most everything I know." They looked "so fine together," the journalist wrote, "warm and calm and loving."[15] Marty Machat was also working on ways to ease the pain of touring for him: they would take a filmmaker on the road with them, who would shoot and record every show. That way, once this tour was over, if anyone wanted to see Leonard in concert, here he was, on film.

The man Machat had in mind for the job was Tony Palmer, a young Londoner, who had made films on Frank Zappa, Gustav Mahler and the band Cream, all of which had won acclaim. Palmer was also a music critic with the *Observer*—"the first person," Palmer claims, "to review Leonard's first LP, and extremely favorably." Machat flew him to New York to meet Leonard. "We talked for three hours, Leonard was extremely self-effacing, humble, almost apologetic—he kept asking, did I think the songs were any good?—and he expressed a certain amount of dissatisfaction with the existing recordings, going back to the first album and 'Suzanne.' I asked him why and he said that they didn't really express the emotion that he'd felt when writing the songs; but probably, it was more complicated than that." He told Palmer "he didn't like filming, and gave [Palmer] all the reasons why he thought it was a bad idea," but added, "This will probably be the only tour I will make ever in my life. I'd like a proper record of what happens." "Then it was just a discussion about how I would do it," Palmer recalls. He signed a contract that gave him $35,000—"a low budget," says Palmer, since it had to cover a four-man crew, their travel expenses and their equipment; he paid himself £2,000—but it also gave him free range to shoot what he wanted, be it a butt-naked Leonard in a sauna, Leonard weeping onstage or Leonard taking acid before the show. Machat, Palmer says, told him he was putting up the money for the film himself, "so that Leonard doesn't have to worry about it."

"The impression one had was that he was very much a father figure for Leonard, his protective shield, who nursed him and looked after him. It was the same in the day-to-day life on the road: he was very solicitous, he'd always go and check out Leonard's room in the hotel first to see if it was okay and that Leonard felt comfortable. Leonard never wanted a grand suite on the top floor of the Ritz but he wanted the shower to be working." Leonard had told Johnston that on this tour, unlike the last, where their hotels were among the grandest in Europe, they were going to stay "in little rooms with a little bed and a table." He did not get his way. But that seemed to be happening a lot lately. When Leonard left with the band for Dublin, where the tour began on Saint Patrick's Day 1972, Suzanne was pregnant.

It was an extraordinary tour, all of it recorded by Palmer's camera, both the incandescent performances and the shambles, when the sound equipment, and on occasion Leonard, broke down. Palmer shot backstage too, and offstage, filming Leonard being interviewed by various European journalists asking much the same questions in different accents. Leonard would answer them patiently, sometimes candidly, more often evasively, or an inseparable mixture of the two. When asked by one reporter if he was a practicing Jew, he said, "I'm always practicing." He told a German journalist, "I can't say my childhood was in any way inconvenienced by [World War II but] I did have a sense of empathy for my race."

The Berlin concert was in the hall where Goebbels made his speech announcing total war. Leonard, echoing the Nazi salute on his last tour, decided to give the same speech. There were some boos and catcalls from the crowd, but mostly they loved him. The connection between Leonard and the audience at many of the concerts, as the film footage shows, was palpable, very physical. In Hamburg, Leonard jumped into the crowd and kissed a young woman—a deep, long kiss. "It just went on and on and on," Cornelius recalls. "It ended up with Leonard on the floor, and you wondered if they were going to start taking their clothes off now." Backstage Leonard told Palmer, "I've disgraced myself." The next night, in Frankfurt, he invited the audience onstage, and while the band played on, the fans pulled Leonard to the floor and lay on top of him. "There were people all over him, writhing like a pile of worms," says Cornelius. "He just lost it; he just got so sexually involved with the crowd that he took it to a new level."

A procession of women offered themselves. One woman, a beautiful actress, came backstage with her husband and, while her husband watched and Palmer kept filming, hit on Leonard. He turned her down. "There were numerous ladies he took a shine to," says Palmer. "I had thought at one point he was feeling very close to Jennifer [Warnes]. If they were they were very discreet, but we certainly filmed them looking very happy together." The camera also caught Leonard in crisis, debating with himself—and with his band, the fans, the media and Palmer—about performance and celebrity and their corruptive nature, the damage that they do to an artist. "One feels a sense of importance in one's heart that is absolutely fatal to the writing of poetry," he told an interviewer. "You can't feel important and write well."

He spoke of his humiliation at "not having delivered the goods," meaning the songs; it was always the songs. When Palmer remonstrated that "the audience was absolutely transfixed," Leonard said,

"There's no point in them being transfixed if I am not conveying my songs to them properly." At the Manchester concert, Leonard tried to explain to the audience that he was striving for more than "just the observance of a few 'museum' songs." He elaborated, "I wrote the songs to myself and to women several years ago and it is a curious thing to be trapped in that original effort, because here I wanted to tell one person one thing and now I am in a situation where I must repeat them like some parrot chained to his stand, night after night." He also called himself a "broken-down nightingale." At several shows he offered to give everyone their money back. Offstage, he recited his prayer-poem from *The Energy of Slaves* to the cameraman: *"Let me be for a moment in this miserable and bewildering wretchedness a happy animal."*

On the plane journey from Paris to Israel, Leonard was quiet. "He liked to sit near the front of an aeroplane, usually with me," says Palmer, "and, because he hated aeroplane food, he always had his little bowl of inexpensive caviar and lemons and a slice of brown bread. He was contemplative." He was looking forward to playing Israel. He was terrified of playing Israel. The day before he had played to doting crowds and he had gone on a date with Brigitte Bardot—he had invited Bill Donovan to come to lunch with them and meet her, but Donovan had to leave for Israel before the rest of them to make sure everything was set up for the shows.

Their first show, at the Yad Eliyahu Arena, was on the same day that Leonard and the band flew into Tel Aviv. Airport security was slow and grim, guns everywhere, but they arrived at the venue in good time. When they came out onstage though, the floor was completely empty. The audience was packed into the stands around the edges, like they were there to see an invisible basketball game. Security had been told to keep everyone off the floor, which had been newly varnished. When Leonard, disturbed by the distance between them, invited the audience to come down, they were set upon by armed guards in orange boiler suits. "They freaked out and started clubbing everybody, beating kids up," Donovan remembers. "Leonard jumped off the stage into the crowd and a guy ran up onstage and grabbed Ron's guitar and I knocked the guy offstage and then somebody hit me from behind and knocked me out. It ended up as sort of a riot." Peter Marshall says, "I was hiding behind my string bass and there was some guy raising a chair, like it was a movie, and he's going to hit me in the face, but somebody grabbed the chair from behind."

The band reconvened backstage. Jennifer Warnes said she was scared. Leonard wondered aloud, "Maybe I pushed it too hard." Then he led everyone back onstage. "I know you're trying to do your job, but you don't have to do it with your fists," he told the guards, then dedicated a song to them. He urged the audience to sit down and enjoy the concert. "Eventually," says Marshall, "he got everybody to calm down and he completed that show." As soon as it was done, they dashed out of the hall and into the tour bus—an Israeli street bus they had hired for the stay. As they drove toward Jerusalem, "the whole band drinking wine, playing music, having a grand old time," Marshall recalls, "there was this one Israeli soldier hitchhiking way out in the country. We pulled up. This guy thinks he's just getting on a regular bus and there's this gigantic party. We took his rifle and gave him whatever was going around"—pot, acid—"and the look on his face, I can still see it. Those guys had a tough life at that time."

The Binyanei Ha'uma hall in Jerusalem was small and new, with excellent acoustics. The audience were where they ought to be, sitting downstairs near the stage. In the dressing room, Bob Johnston handed around the LSD du tour, Desert Dust. "Think that stuff still works?" asked Leonard. "We'll be in serious trouble if it works—or it doesn't work." Standing at the microphone, looking out at the attentive, adoring crowd, he appeared even more affected than usual.

The connection he shared with them was more than just emotional; it encompassed their shared Jewish history and blood. Leonard's eyes were stoned and bright. He looked both energized and enervated, a tightrope walker who might fall any moment or be taken up out of his body into the sky. The songs sounded beautiful as he sang, and the band seemed to be wired into his nervous system. But Leonard felt that it was not good enough, that he was letting down this precious audience and these precious songs. He tried to explain this to them, but his explanation kept getting more and more complex.

"They become meditations for me and sometimes, you know, I just don't get high on it, I feel that I am cheating you, so I'll try it again, okay? If it doesn't work I'll stop. There's no reason why we should mutilate a song to save face. If it doesn't get any better we'll just end the concert and I'll refund your money. Some nights one is raised off the ground and some nights you just can't get off the ground and there's no point lying about it, and tonight we just haven't been getting off the ground. It says in the Kabbalah that if you can't get off the ground you should stay on the ground. It says in the Kabbalah that unless Adam and Eve face each other, God does not sit on his throne, and somehow the male and female part of me refuse to encounter one another tonight and God does not sit on his throne and this is a terrible thing to happen in Jerusalem. So listen, we're going to leave the stage now and try to profoundly meditate in the dressing room to try to get ourselves back into shape and if we can manage," Leonard said, "we'll be back."[16]

Backstage, Leonard was having a meltdown. He announced, "I'm splitting." He said he would give the fans their money back. But the fans didn't want their money back, they told him, the tickets weren't expensive, and some people had come two hundred miles for this show. Someone came to the dressing room door and told him that the audience was still out there, waiting, and that they wanted to sing Leonard a song. At first Leonard misunderstood. But then he heard them. They were singing him "Hevenu Shalom Aleichem," "We Bring You Peace." Marshall took Leonard aside. "We have to take care of business and finish the show or we might not get out of here in one piece." Leonard said, "I think what I need is a shave." That's what his mother had told him to do when things got bad. There was a mirror and a basin in the dressing room and someone fetched him a razor. Slowly, serenely, while the crowd clapped and sang in the auditorium, Leonard shaved. When he was done, he smiled. They went back onstage. As Leonard sang "So Long, Marianne," immersing himself in the song he'd written to a woman in a moment in a less complicated time, changing her description from "*pretty one*" to "*beautiful one*," tears began to stream down his face.

Backstage, when the show was over, everyone was crying. It was the last night of the tour; they were going home. Leonard picked up his guitar and started to sing "Bird on the Wire" in the style of a country song. Bob Johnston sang a verse and turned it into a gospel blues, and then the whole band joined in, making instruments with their voices, humming softly in the background, as sweet and comforting as a lullaby.

———————

Adam Cohen was born in Montreal on September 18, 1972—"not an *enfant du hasard*," said Suzanne, but "planned." If Leonard had planned on becoming a father, he did not behave that way. When Steve Sanfield showed up at the house with his wife and son to congratulate his friend on his first child, Suzanne was there, "very solemn," and Leonard was in New York. He was at the Chelsea, having what might have been a somber, one-man bachelor party. The hotel would have been the perfect setting, the Chelsea scene having become as fractured and dark at times as Leonard's state of mind.

"There were a lot of factions, a lot of drugs and trauma, a lot of rough stuff going on, a shooting," says Liberty, the model turned poet and feminist writer who lived in the Chelsea Hotel and who was Leonard's lover at one time. "I had a room with high ceilings, a fireplace and a wrought-iron balcony, but my next-door neighbors were cocaine dealers and pimps." If Leonard had gone back there to remind himself of a time when he was free and unencumbered, he did not strike Liberty as "someone [who was] reaching for freedom. . . . In some ways he seemed to carry the vestiges of a privileged middle-class background," particularly in the context of the early seventies and the Chelsea circle. She remembers him as "sweet and gentle" but "constrained." Liberty says, "I felt he hadn't yet gone through the looking glass, had not entered his own 'house of mystery,' or hadn't stayed there long enough—though, of course, Leonard survived. Many of the wild ones did not."

Even if Leonard were not wild, he clearly felt trapped. At the same time, his upbringing, his patriarchal roots, his sense of duty ensured that he could not shrug off fatherhood. He returned home, but reluctantly and impossibly weary. He was depressed. It was hard work, trying to find a way to keep going and not be pulled off course. Sanfield and his wife returned to the house for dinner. It was a "very uncomfortable" evening. Once they had eaten, says Sanfield, "Leonard said, 'Let's go,' and we got up and went to a couple of clubs. I was thinking, 'This guy just had a child; what are you doing, man?' Leonard said, 'It's tough, this life. It's just tough.'"

Later that year, when Sanfield was back in California, Leonard called him. "He said, 'Would you bring me to your teacher? He's been on my mind for a long time.'" Sanfield asked Leonard where he was. Montreal, he said; he was going to go to Tennessee and pick up his jeep and drive cross-country. It was more than two thousand miles from Tennessee to the Santa Barbara mountains and took several days. The mountain road was thick with snow when Leonard arrived at Sanfield's house. When they left together for L.A., the jeep got stuck on a back road and they had to hike through deep snow to find a pickup to pull them out. They stopped on the way in Fresno, where they took in an afternoon movie, then set off again for the Zen Center in L.A. "I brought Leonard to Roshi and we sat down and had tea," said Sanfield. "It was mostly silent. Then Roshi said, 'You bring friend to Mount Baldy.' So a couple of days later Leonard and I drove up there in his jeep, and Roshi said to Leonard, 'Okay, you stay here.'"

He stayed, but for barely a week. It was winter, it was Mount Baldy, it was a Buddhist boot camp, grim, with all these broken young people trudging through snow in walking meditation at three o'clock in the morning. Leonard came down from the frozen mountain and flew with Suzanne to Acapulco and the sun.

Fourteen

A Shield Against the Enemy

March 15, 1973: "Thank you for the knife and the good belt. I used them to scratch and choke her a little. While she suffers I have a chance to breathe the free air and look under the flab for my body." March 17: "Listening to gypsy violins, my jeep rusting in Tennessee, married as usual to the wrong woman. She loves the way I make love to her." March 19: "Lie down, there's no one watching you . . . the show is over."[1]

Leonard had given up the Tennessee cabin. He left his jeep in Bob Johnston's drive and went back to Montreal and Suzanne. He bought the house next door to his cottage—they were a matching pair, with a shared dividing wall—and designated the ground floor a sculpture studio for Mort and the upstairs his writing room. A place to escape to when domesticity became too much. To all appearances, a man not cut out for domesticity was making a real effort to make his domestic situation work. What Leonard was writing, though, did not give much cause for optimism.

In April, Columbia released Leonard's fourth album, *Live Songs*.

Although it failed to make even the UK charts, it was a contender for the most somber live album ever. The album contains nine songs recorded on the 1970 and 1972 tours and one that Leonard recorded alone, in the cabin, on a tape recorder borrowed from Johnston. It opens with "Minute Prologue," a despairing rumination on "dissension" and "pain," improvised over a slow solo guitar, and closes with the doleful cabin recording of "Queen Victoria," a poem from *Flowers for Hitler* ("*my love, she gone with other boys*") to which he had given minimal musical adornment. In between, alongside naked and emotional performances of songs from his first two albums, are "Please Don't Pass Me By (A Disgrace)," a thirteen-minute revival meeting sing-along with a Holocaust reference ("*I sing this for the Jews and the gypsies and the smoke that they made*"), "Passing Thru," performed as a weary country hymn, and "Improvisation," a mournful riff on the instrumental intro to "You Know Who I Am." The bleached-out photograph of Leonard on the front sleeve was taken by Suzanne. He is thin and blank faced, ashen, his hair shorn, his white-clad body fading like a ghost into the backdrop of white bathroom tiles.

The liner notes came from a letter to Leonard from a young British writer and artist named Daphne Richardson, with whom he had a correspondence. Richardson had first written to him about an experimental book she was working on, which included collages of Bob Dylan and Leonard Cohen poems. She asked for permission to use them, which (unlike Dylan) Leonard gave. Some time later Richardson, who had been in and out of mental hospitals, wrote to Leonard from a hospital, sending him a book she had written while she was there. Leonard had found it "shattering. A testimony of pain I've never read anything like."[2] When he was next in London, they arranged to meet; he found a "very attractive girl in her thirties" and a talented artist. He asked Richardson if she would like to illustrate *The Energy of Slaves*. During a period when he failed to check his mail, a pile of letters from her had accrued. She wrote, with growing desperation, that she had been readmitted to the hospital and had insisted on leaving because she had work to do on Leonard's book. They did not believe her, she said, and strapped her down. Leonard tried to get in contact, but he says, "I was just too late." She had killed herself three days before. Leonard was mentioned in her suicide note. He published her letter on the album sleeve, he said, because she had always wanted to be published and no one would do so.[3]

In February 1973, Leonard was back again in London, this time to meet with Tony Palmer and Marty Machat and see *Bird on a Wire*, Palmer's film of the previous year's tour. As he watched himself, there were tears in Leonard's eyes. "He wept for a good 50 percent of the film," Palmer says. "He kept saying, 'This is too true, this is too true,' repeating it like a mantra." Machat liked the film; "I'm very happy about this," he told Palmer. So did the BBC, who bought it on the spot, effectively covering 75 percent of what the film had cost to make. A week later, Machat called Palmer. There was a problem. Leonard thought the film "too confrontational." A meeting was set up during which, according to Palmer, a film editor named Humphrey Dixon, who had worked as his editing assistant on the film, stepped up and said that he could rescue it. "Go ahead," said Palmer, and the long, expensive business of remaking *Bird on a Wire* began. "I've read that, according to Leonard's testimony, a further half a million dollars was spent," Palmer says. "Marty looked at me somewhat wryly and said, 'Don't worry, it's not my money this time.'"

In an interview Leonard gave *Melody Maker*'s Roy Hollingworth while in London, he described the film as "totally unacceptable" and said that he was paying from his own pocket just to get it finished. When it was done, he said, he would "get out of the scene." Asked what he meant by that, Leonard answered, "Well, I'm leaving. I want to return to another rhythm. Somehow I haven't organised my life within rock very well. Somehow *it*—the rock life—became important rather than the thing that produced the song. I don't find myself leading a life that has many good moments in it. So I've decided to screw it, and go. Maybe the other life won't have many good moments either, but I know this one, and I don't want it." Throughout the interview, various people from Leonard's UK record company fussed about him. They had brought him a gold disc for UK sales of *Songs of Love and Hate*, which he had put on the floor, with no great regard for its well-being. By the end of the interview it was covered with trash, including an upturned coffee cup. "I've found myself not writing at all," he said, lighting another Turkish cigarette from the butt of the one he had just finished. "I feel that I'm no longer learning. I began to feel I was doing some of the songs a disservice. So I have to get into something else."[4]

Leonard hired Henry Zemel to work on *Bird on a Wire* with Dixon as coeditor; he needed someone he trusted to watch his back. Zemel, watching the footage from the tour, could see his friend's struggle with celebrity and how hard he worked at trying to maintain the sincerity of his engagement with both the audiences and his songs. He knew that Leonard felt that celebrity had taken a toll on his work. "He very much saw himself as a lyric poet," says Zemel, and "a lyric poet has a certain kind of innocence and naïveté and an uncompromising relationship with the world and with what they're doing. When something cracks that vision and idea of what the world could be and what they're devoted to making it be, can they ever put the pieces back together again? The quality of the work, the voice, is never the same."

Marianne was back on Hydra, in the house where she and Leonard had lived, when one day Suzanne appeared at the door. She had a baby in her arms who was crying loudly. She told Marianne, over her son's sobs, that she had been staying at a hotel and wanted to know when Marianne was moving out. Marianne packed her things and left. "That was a sad scene," says Marianne quietly. When Leonard heard about this he offered to buy Marianne a house—she had sold her own back in their impecunious days—or, if she wanted to stay, he would buy another house for Suzanne. "He was always very generous," says

Marianne, who declined his offer. It was time to return to Norway. When Leonard joined Suzanne and Adam in the little white house on the hill, it is hard to imagine that, as he tried to find his old rhythm, his thoughts did not turn now and then to life there with another woman and child in more innocent, nurturing times.

He resumed his old routine of a morning swim in the harbor. Afterward "he just hung around on the port, sitting on rocks and staring at people, for hours," says Terry Oldfield, a young composer and musician who had moved to Hydra in the early seventies; for a while he gave flute lessons to Marianne's son. Leonard was one of the first people Oldfield met on the island. Leonard, who struck Oldfield as being "in a very lucid state of mind," told him that he had recently been staying in a monastery.

On Hydra Leonard painted and also worked on the book of prose he had begun in Montreal, its title since changed from "The Woman Being Born" to "My Life in Art." Meanwhile, several of his old poems and songs were strutting the boards without him, sometimes in curious guises. "The New Step," from *Flowers for Hitler*, had been turned into a one-act ballet-drama of the same name, which was aired on CBC television, and an assortment of his lyrics and poems on the subject of women made up Gene Lesser's off-Broadway musical *Sisters of Mercy*. What Leonard was writing about women—or one particular woman—in "My Life in Art" was not pretty. "Fuck this marriage [and] your dead bed night after night."* He needed, he wrote, to "study the hatred I have for her and how it is transmuted into desire by solitude and distance."[5] He voiced the sentiment less savagely in a new song:

> *I live here with a woman and a child*
> *The situation makes me kind of nervous*

---

* These words would later appear in the prose poem "Death to This Book" in *Death of a Lady's Man* (1978).

The title he gave the song, which was in great part about his domestic situation, was "There Is a War."

On October 6, 1973, Egypt and Syria launched the attack on Israel that began the Yom Kippur War. The next day Leonard left Suzanne and Adam on Hydra and flew from Athens to Tel Aviv. His plan was to enlist in the Israeli Army: "I will go and stop Egypt's bullet. Trumpets and a curtain of razor blades," he wrote.[6] His motives, as these words might suggest, were complex: commitment to the cause certainly ("I've never disguised the fact that I'm Jewish and in any crisis in Israel I would be there," Leonard said in 1974. "I am committed to the survival of the Jewish people"[7]), but also bravado, narcissism and, near the top of the list, desperation to get away. "Women," he said, "only let you out of the house for two reasons: to make money or to fight a war,"[8] and in his present state of mind dying for a noble cause—any cause—was better than this life he was living as an indentured artist and a caged man.

Suzanne says, "I felt proud about Leonard's heroic actions and acts of generosity but fear about something happening—there was much hostility at that time—which turned into a fear of loss and dread of the worst. Knowing his mind couldn't be changed, I remember putting a blue ribbon inside his breast pocket without telling him, so that—in my mind—he'd be safe. And I was truly praying those first days." Leonard, on the other hand, sitting on the plane, heading for what he called his "myth home," felt free. He was "thin again and loose."[9] Shortly after arriving in Tel Aviv, Leonard met Oshik Levi, an Israeli singer. Levi was putting together a small team of performers to entertain the troops—Matti Caspi, Mordechai "Pupik" Arnon, Ilana Rovina—to which he was pleased to add Leonard. This was not what Leonard had in mind. He protested that his songs were sad and not known for their morale-boosting qualities. But Levi was persuasive and there had been no better offer from the Israeli Army. For the next few weeks Leonard traveled by truck, tank and jeep to outposts, encampments, aircraft hangars, field hospitals, anywhere they saw soldiers, and performed for them up to eight times a day. The soldiers would gather closely around—sometimes barely a dozen of them—and, if it was night and too dark to see, they would shine their flashlights on him as he played.

"Every unit we came to, he would ask what is the position of this or that soldier, and each and every time he wanted to join the forces and be one of them," Levi told the newspaper *Maariv*. "I used to tease him: 'Make up your mind, do you want to be a pilot, or an artillery man, or a naval commando diver? Each day you get excited by something else.'" The musicians would camp with the soldiers and talk to them all night long. "He was a modest person, with the soul of a philosopher, wondering about the meaning of human life," said Levi. "He had many talks with Arnon about philosophy, astrology and the Bible. He used to talk often about the essence of Judaism, and about his Hebrew name, Eliezer."[10]

In the notebook Leonard always carried with him, he made notes of what he had seen in Israel—the beauty of the desert, the kinship of the soldiers, the dead and wounded, who had made him weep. As he had in Cuba, he also wrote fantasies of glorious escapades, such as stealing a gun and killing the officer who bugged him "with relentless requests to sing 'Suzanne.'"[11] He wrote a song in Israel—miraculously quickly—called "Lover Lover Lover." Caspi remembered Leonard improvising it in front of the soldiers during their second performance.

May the spirit of this song
May it rise up pure and free
May it be a shield for you
A shield against the enemy

On his 1974 tour Leonard would introduce it as a song "written in the Sinai desert for soldiers of both sides."[12] That same year, when describing his experience to *ZigZag* magazine, he said, "War is wonderful. They'll never stamp it out. It's one of the few times people can act their best. It's so economical in terms of gesture and motion, every single gesture is precise, every effort is at its maximum. Nobody goofs off. There are opportunities to feel things that you simply cannot feel in modern city life"[13]—all of these, and the last in particular, having been things that had long exercised him.

From Israel he flew directly to Ethiopia, a country that was also on the brink of war. He appeared to be courting danger, tempting fate. Instead of attempting to take up arms, this time he took a room in the Imperial Hotel in Asmara. While the rain poured down outside, freed up, Leonard wrote. "I had my guitar with me and it was then I felt the songs emerging—at last, the conclusions that I had been carrying in manuscript form for the last four or five years, from hotel room to hotel room."[14] He refined "Lover Lover Lover," changing its opening line from "*I saw my brothers fighting in the desert*" to

> *I asked my father . . . "Change my name."*
> *The one I'm using now it's covered up*
> *With fear and filth and cowardice and shame*

In Ethiopia he also finally "broke the code" of "Take This Longing"—a song he had written years ago to Nico and that Buffy Sainte-Marie had recorded as "The Bells"—in order "to get a version for" himself.[15] He made final edits to the lyrics of "Chelsea Hotel #2," a second version of the song that described his sexual encounter in New York with Janis Joplin. Leonard and Ron Cornelius had written the music together on his last tour, on a transatlantic flight from Nashville to Ireland. "It was back when you could sit in the back of the plane and smoke," Cornelius remembers, "and for the best part of this eight-and-a-half-hour flight Leonard and I sat there smoking and worked on that song. When we finally landed in Shannon, it was complete." Leonard told Billy Donovan, the tour manager, that it was the first song he had ever cowritten. The other song that came together in Ethiopia was "Field Commander Cohen," an ironic account of his imagined heroic military exploits. But in reality, in traveling to these combat zones, Leonard was avoiding the war that awaited him at home with Suzanne.

He was weary, though, and ready to make peace. He had seen too much blood and death and hatred in Israel. He felt he should go back and tend this little garden whose seed he had planted and see if somehow he could make a success of family life. But first he went to the monastery to sit in retreat with Roshi. When he finally went home to Suzanne and Adam at the end of the year, peace reigned in the cottage in Montreal, long enough for Suzanne to become pregnant with their second child.

In July 1974 the new version of the concert film *Bird on a Wire* opened in London. It did not stay in circulation long. The BBC by this time had given up on broadcasting it. It was shown on German TV, but effectively it disappeared (bar the odd bootleg copy) for almost four decades. Leonard flew to London for the premiere. He seemed "very cheerful" to the journalist from *ZigZag* for whom he played three of his new songs—even while recounting that he'd had to give up his writing room, now that there was a new baby on the way, and he was obliged to go to the garden shed to write. This was quite a change in mood from his last visit to London, when his interviews suggested that he planned to quit the music business. "I don't want to give you the impression that I was very sick and have just come through it, that's not true," said Leonard. What had happened was that "two months ago I had a golden week, my guitar sounded good, a lot of unfinished songs suggested conclusions."[16]

Leonard had renewed his contract with Columbia Records. He

had spent most of the past month in a New York studio working on a new record called *New Skin for the Old Ceremony*. Drawing a line under his first four albums, on this one he was trying for a different sound, using all new musicians and a new, young producer. John Lissauer was fifteen years younger than Leonard and not long out of Yale music school, where he had studied classical music and jazz. They met by chance in Montreal, at the Nelson Hotel, where Lissauer performed in a band with Lewis Furey, whose first album Lissauer had just produced. Leonard was in the audience; he had known Furey since 1966, when Furey was a sixteen-year-old violin player and fledgling poet. He had asked Leonard to look at his poetry, which Leonard did, giving him homework—read Irving Layton; write a sonnet—and becoming his mentor.

After the show, Furey introduced Lissauer to Leonard. This impressed Lissauer's girlfriend, who was a big Leonard Cohen fan, rather more than it did Lissauer, who "wasn't really into the folk singer-songwriter thing." Leonard told Lissauer, "I like what you're doing; would you like to talk about recording?" Lissauer said, "Sure." He heard nothing more for some time until, out of the blue, Leonard called and told him he was at the Royalton Hotel in New York and ready to start work.

Lissauer lived in a large loft space in a four-floor walk-up on Eighteenth Street—it had been a Mafia after-hours club in the fifties—that was strewn with "every instrument known to man." Lissauer told Leonard to come over. He should ring the downstairs bell, then stand under the window, and Lissauer would throw down the front-door key. Some hours later, as Lissauer sat at the piano, playing quietly, listening for the doorbell, in walked Leonard, a large grin on his face. At the front door he had run into a pizza deliveryman with an order for Lissauer's neighbor. When she threw down her key, Leonard caught it, paid for the pizza and said he would take it up with him. "She was the biggest Leonard Cohen freak, so you can imagine, opening the door and having her pizza delivered by her idol. She screamed," says Lissauer. "It was nuts." He was beginning to get the idea that Leonard was popular with women.

Marty Machat, who had never heard of Lissauer, was not convinced by Leonard's choice of producer. He called John Hammond, Leonard's A & R man and first producer, who booked an afternoon session at Columbia Studio E. On June 14, 1974, Leonard and Lissauer arrived, accompanied by four musicians. Under the watchful eye of Leonard's doubting manager and Columbia's most celebrated executive, they recorded demos of "Lover Lover Lover," "There Is a War" and "Why Don't You Try." "I'd put together an Ethiopian, Middle Eastern kind of thing," says Lissauer. "Leonard had never had rhythm like this on any of his songs and it worked great." Hammond gave his endorsement: it was going to work, he told Leonard, he didn't need him there. Machat gave his more grudging assent. "I sensed that Marty didn't like me and I wasn't used to this because I'm easygoing and work hard and I get along with everybody. Maybe it was a possessive thing; Leonard was *his* guy and he was looking to me for stuff. Marty was obsessed with Leonard. Leonard was the only artist he cared about because he thought that by associating with Leonard he got some class and some humanity. I don't think he ever cheated Leonard—and it's legendary what a bad guy he was with other artists. But he did the right thing by Leonard. Whatever it was, it was not a comfortable situation."

Lissauer asked that the studio be closed to everyone—managers, record company, girlfriends—except Leonard, the musicians and himself. Sometimes Machat would come by to listen to the rough mixes, but for the most part Lissauer's request was granted. So too was his decision to record not in one of the Columbia studios but in a small, intimate studio called Sound Ideas. "It was much more comfortable, the engineers were younger and hipper and not in lab coats, looking things up in reference manuals." The team included a female

engineer—a rarity in the early seventies—named Leanne Ungar;
this album marked the beginning of one of Leonard's most enduring
musical associations. "The atmosphere in the studio was really fun
and really light" and the recording process "very experimental," Ungar says. "We tried lots of different instruments and different things."

Generally these ideas were Lissauer's. He would take home a
simple guitar-vocal demo of the song and "fool with it," Lissauer
remembers, "and then come back and say to Leonard, 'How about
we do it this way?' I wanted to take him out of the folk world. I
wanted the record to take the listener places, give them a little vi-
sual, cinematic trip. 'This is poetry,' I said to him. 'When you do a
straight-ahead singer-songwriter album like the last two, it becomes
easy to stop listening to the poetry and they're just songs.' I felt that
I was illustrating the poetry with these little touches here and there,
these unusual combinations of instruments." Onto Leonard's basic
guitar and vocal recording he added strings and brass from the New
York Philharmonic; woodwinds and piano, which Lissauer played;
a viola played by Lewis Furey and a Jew's harp played by Leonard. There were also banjo, mandolin, guitar, bass and—unusually
for a Leonard Cohen album—drums, played respectively by Jeff
Layton, John Miller, Roy Markowitz and Barry Lazarowitz. Singer-
songwriter Janis Ian, who happened to drop by the studio, sang
some backing vocals.

On this occasion Leonard, according to Lissauer, showed "no
insecurities about his singing. He felt he wasn't a 'singer' singer,
that he didn't have that pop tenor thing, but he knew that he carried musical attention and that he could communicate a story. We
never talked about pitch; what we talked about was, 'Have you
kept your line?' In other words, has the narrative stayed intact?
Do we believe this verse? That's all-important with Leonard. He
never hides behind vocal tricks; that's what you do when you don't
have anything to say. Sometimes he would say, 'Let me do that

again and see if I can get my energy up, see if I can find that line,' and use his finger to point the way. But for the most part, his vocals were effortless."

A quite different approach was taken to "Leaving Green Sleeves," the song that closed the album. Leonard's interpretation of the sixteenth-century English folk ballad was a live-in-the-studio recording with the band, "the product," Lissauer says, "of *ng ka pay*"—a sweet Korean liqueur with 70 percent alcohol content. Reportedly good for rheumatism, it was a favorite of Roshi, who was in the recording studio drinking with Leonard. An exception to the closed-studio rule had been made for him. Lissauer had found a place in Chinatown where *ng ka pay* could be bought, "and once in a while we would do a run and pick up a bottle. Hence some of the, shall we say, exotic vocals. On 'Leaving Green Sleeves,' we almost had to hold Leonard up to sing; he was *ng ka pay*'ed out of his mind."

While Leonard sang, his hands held up in front of him as if he were reading an invisible book, Roshi sat on the couch in his *tabi* socks, saying nothing. Lissauer remembers he was "just beaming and emanating good vibes."

What was Roshi doing in the studio?

"*He was nodding off most of the time; he was already an old man.*"

I meant, why was he there at all?

"*We had been traveling to Trappist monasteries—at that time there was a rapprochement between Catholicism and Zen under the tutelage of Thomas Merton, who was a Trappist monk who wrote beautiful books— and I would go with Roshi and he would lead these weeks of meditation at various monasteries. We happened to be in New York at the time I was recording. So he came to the studio.*"

Since everyone, even Zen masters, secretly want to be music critics, what did Roshi say about the songs and your performance?

"*The next morning when we were having breakfast I asked him what he thought and he said that I should sing 'more sad.'*"

A lot of Leonard Cohen fans would have bought him a drink and employed him as your musical director. What was your reaction?

"I thought, 'Not more sad, but you've got to go deeper.' "

To all appearances you were sad enough during that period. Because of your domestic situation?

"I don't think that was the case at all. Of course when this kind of condition prevails, it's almost impossible to sustain friendships."

When you're so busy torturing yourself?

"You don't have time for anybody else. It's time-consuming. And, although I think everyone lives their life as an emergency, the emergency is acute when you're just trying to figure out how to get from moment to moment and you don't know why, and there are no operative circumstances that seem to explain. Of course the circumstances become disagreeable because of the relationships that you can't sustain, but I don't think it's the other way round."

Did becoming a father make any difference to your depression, distracting it or shifting the focus in some way?

"It didn't happen in my case, although it's true that having kids gets you off center stage; you can't really feel exactly the same way about yourself ever after. But it didn't seem to mitigate that gloomy condition. I don't know what the problem was, still don't. I wish I did. But that was a component of my life and was the engine of most of my investigation into the various things I looked into: women, song, religion."

In August Leonard was back home in Montreal, doing an interview with an Israeli-Canadian writer and broadcaster named Malka Marom for the CBC program *The Entertainers.* The interview took place in his garden shed—his new writing room—which was illuminated by candles. Marom recalls, "He was very whimsical. Soon after I set up the recording equipment, Leonard's hand went right underneath my skirt. I said, 'What are you doing?' and he said, 'This is the real dialogue,' or something to that effect. I said, 'Well, aside from this physical thing, is there any other dialogue?' He said, 'It can only be expressed in poetry.' So I asked the most mundane things just to see how far the poetry would go, like 'When do you get up in the morning? What do you have for breakfast? Are you happily married?' and he answered everything with poems that he had not published."

She also asked him his views on marriage and monogamy, given the imminent arrival of his second child with Suzanne. "I think marrying is for very, very high-minded people," he said. "It is a discipline of extreme severity. To really turn your back on all the other possibilities and all the other experiences of love, of passion, of ecstasy, and to determine to find it within one embrace is a high and righteous notion. Marriage today is the monastery; the monastery today is freedom." He told Marom that he had arrived "at a more realistic vision" of himself. There was no "high purpose" in his activities. "I'm just going," he said, "so that I don't have to keep still."

In September, barely a month after the release of his new album, Suzanne gave birth to Leonard's second child, a girl. Leonard named his daughter Lorca, for the Spanish poet.

New Skin for the Old Ceremony was the first of Leonard's five albums not to include the word "songs" in the title, nor to have a picture of him on the sleeve.* Instead there was a drawing of a winged, naked couple copulating above the clouds. It was a woodcut from *Rosarium philosophorum*—the sixteenth-century alchemical text that had so fascinated Carl Jung—depicting the *coniunctio spirituum*, the holy union of the male-female principle. But the union described in these songs seems decidedly unholy. Their lyrics are caustic, mordant and black—blackly humorous at times but no less dark and brutal for that. The love he sings about is as violent as the war about which he also sings. His woman is *"the whore and the beast of Babylon."* Leonard, her poor beleaguered lover and servicer, is in various songs pierced,

---

* Except in the U.S., where a "modesty sleeve" with a photo covered the censored illustration.

hung, lashed, captive and—with a knee in the balls and a fist in the face—sentenced to death.

He was not without self-pity, this *"grateful faithful woman's singing millionaire . . . Working for the Yankee dollar."* His only power was in his contempt and in the brilliant cutting edge of his words. Even in his version of that most courtly of songs "Greensleeves," when he sees his woman *"naked in the early dawn,"* he hopes she will be *"someone new."* In "A Singer Must Die" he sings a scathing *"goodnight"* to his *"night after night, after night, after night, after night, after night."* "Why Don't You Try" is more vitriolic still:

> *You know this life is filled with many sweet companions,*
> *many satisfying one-night stands.*
> *Do you want to be the ditch around a tower?*

This barb is perfectly cruel in its encompassment of sex and captivity. Although his muse is not mentioned by name, never before had Leonard treated one quite so discourteously. The songs, aware of this, plead their case before courtrooms, his ancestors and his God.

What makes this album so different from its predecessors is that its dark poetry—every bit as dark as on *Songs of Love and Hate*—is often clad in sophisticated, unexpected musical arrangements, ranging from Afro-percussive to Brecht-Weill, to modern chamber music. Said Leonard, "It's good. I'm not ashamed of it and I'm ready to stand by it. Rather than think of it as a masterpiece, I prefer to look at it as a little gem."[17] The critical response was also generally favorable. In the UK, *Melody Maker* found it "more spirited than the past four,"[18] while *NME* described it as "an agreeable blend of vintage Cohen and some new textures. Armageddon has been postponed if only temporarily."[19] In the U.S., *Rolling Stone* took the middle ground, saying it was "not one of his best" but that it had some songs "which will not easily be forgotten by his admirers."[20]

The two most enduring songs on *New Skin* were quite different from one another. "Chelsea Hotel #2" was one of the album's most straightforward, singer-songwriter productions. "Who by Fire" had been directly inspired by a Hebrew prayer sung on the Day of Atonement when the Book of Life was opened and the names read aloud of who will die and how. Leonard said he had first heard it in the synagogue when he was five years old, "standing beside my uncles in their black suits."[21] His own liturgy ended with a question that his elders had never answered and whose answer Leonard still sought: what unseen force controls these things and who the hell is in charge?

New Skin for the Old Ceremony had not been a great commercial success outside of Germany and the UK, where it was certified silver. In the U.S. and Canada it completely bypassed the charts. But there was an album, ergo there had to be a tour. In September 1974—the month of Lorca's birth, Adam's second birthday and their father's fortieth—Leonard embarked on his biggest tour to date. Two months of concerts had been booked in Europe, including a performance at a CBS Records conference in Eastbourne, England, followed by two weeks in New York and L.A. in November and December. The first two months of 1975 were also taken up with concerts, bringing him back and forth between Canada, the U.S. and the UK.

As Bob Johnston had done in the past, Leonard's new producer put together his touring band—a small group of the multi-instrumentalists and singers who had played on the album: John Miller, Jeff Layton, Emily Bindiger and Erin Dickins. Also like Johnston, Lissauer joined him on the road, playing keyboards. It was "very different to his last tour with the country boys," says Lissauer. "We had a lot of artistic detail." Leonard's new band was very young. "We were all kids. I was twenty-two and I had never played a concert before such a big audience, and I've never been on tour with a guy who's revered like he was. In Europe Leonard was bigger than Dylan—all the shows were sold out—and he had the most sincere,

devoted, almost nuts following. Serious poetry lovers don't get violent but, boy, there was some suicide watches going on, on occasion.
There were people who Leonard meant life or death to. I'd see girls
in the front row"—women outnumbered men three to one in the audiences, by Lissauer's count—"openly weep for Leonard and they
would send back letters and packages. And invitations. We would see
people after the show—somebody intriguing or good-looking would
get backstage—and they'd say things like, 'I was suicidal and I put on
one of your records and you saved me.'"

The *Guardian* review of the Manchester show described Leonard
as having "the inspired and fragile air of a consumptive. He cut a
lonely and sensitive-looking figure centre-stage, wrapped around his
guitar, plucking away with an ill mustered resolve at what passed for
a melody line. Cohen generated an atmosphere of vulnerability and
regret, an odd sensation in pop. None of his songs showed a sense
of humor, none was bright and breezy. But the whole thing had a
gloomy warmth."[22]

The tour, particularly when compared with the last two, unfolded
largely without incident, apart from the bus breaking down on the
way to the Edinburgh show (they divided into pairs and hitchhiked
to the venue) and the showdown between Marty Machat and Her-
bert von Karajan in Berlin when the famed conductor, still rehearsing
the Berlin Philharmonic, refused to let them in to do their sound
check. "Marty's ego and von Karajan's ego—that was quite something," Lissauer recalls. Among the more memorable performances
was the Fête de l'Humanité in Paris. "Half a million people and all
these little communist factions had come together for a festival, and
they'd given us big limousines to take us there," Lissauer says. "We
dressed down for the occasion in fatigues and had them drop us off
half a mile from the site, where we got into a bunch of beat-up little
Renaults to drive up there, because we didn't want to be seen showing up [in the limos] because a lot of the people there were very fired

up. There was a lot of very passionate political talk and fatigues and berets and Gauloises. Leonard hung out with them and fit right in."

When the band arrived in New York for the November shows, Suzanne was there to meet Leonard. He took her along with him to his interview with Danny Fields.* He told Fields he had given up smoking, while elegantly eulogizing the beauty of the cigarette. He was no longer drinking either and tried to give Fields the bottle of vodka that had been given to him by Harry Smith. Fields asked him if his children were being raised as Jews. Leonard answered, "Unless I change my name, I will definitely raise them Jewish." Meaning yes. The pleas in the song "Lover Lover Lover" to his father/Father to change his name were rhetorical. "I never liked the idea of people changing their names. It's nice to know where you come from."[23]

In an interview around the same time with Larry "Ratso" Sloman, for *Rolling Stone*, Leonard complained, "I think I'm getting old. My nails are crumbling under the assault of the guitar strings. My throat is going. How many years more do I have of this?" But, far from giving up, he said he wanted to keep going "forever." Every man, he said, "should try to become an elder."[24]

In Los Angeles, a residency had been set up for Leonard at the Troubadour, the famous West Hollywood folk club where Tom Waits was discovered on an open mic night and where Joni Mitchell made her L.A. debut. "He did two shows a night, five nights, all sold out," says Paul Body, the Troubadour doorman. "I was the ticket-taker, so I remember Phil Spector coming in on the Sunday with Lenny Bruce's daughter, Kitty. Dylan also showed up one night. There were quite a few different celebrities—and tons of beautiful women. The only guy I've seen who drew better-looking women than Leonard Cohen was probably Charles Bukowski. These women were all dressed up

---

* The interview was intended for Andy Warhol's *Interview* magazine but at the last minute the editor decided Leonard "wasn't chic enough." It ran in *Soho Weekly* in December 1974.

in seventies style and hanging on Leonard's every word, during the show and afterwards." Leonard wore a gray suit—"He reminded me of the French actor Jean Gabin," says Body—and the band were all dressed in black. "The manager of the Troubadour, Robert Marchese, told me, 'You'd better check the bathroom for razor blades, because this stuff is real depressing.'"

Between sets, journalist Harvey Kubernik asked Leonard about the new album. "For a while I didn't think there was going to be another album. I pretty much felt that I was washed up as a songwriter because it wasn't coming any more," Leonard said. "Now I've entered into another phase, which is very new to me. That is, I began to collaborate with John on songs, which is something that I never expected, or intended, to do with anyone. It wasn't a matter of improvement, it was a matter of sharing the conception, with another man." His previous album, *Live Songs*, he said, represented "a very confused and directionless time. The thing I liked about it is that it documents this phase very clearly. I'm very interested in documentation."[25] Leonard was going to visit Dylan at his house in Malibu, he said, mentioning that Dylan had called him one of his favorite poets. Leonard also went to an Allen Ginsberg performance in Los Angeles and to dinner with Joni Mitchell. Kubernik, who accompanied Leonard, recalls a smiling Mitchell telling him off the cuff, "I'm only a groupie for Picasso and Leonard."

Aside from the New York and L.A. concerts, Leonard's U.S. tour earned a lukewarm reception at best. In a couple of places, tickets barely sold. "He was almost unknown," Lissauer says. "Leonard didn't really want to play the States, he didn't feel they understood him, and because they weren't putting out he wasn't putting out, so he had a nonaudience. This was distracting for me, as a record producer; I wanted to see him be big in the States. But on the Canadian tour he was mobbed, and some of those shows were really fabulous. We recorded a bunch of them."

While on the road, Leonard was already planning a new studio album. This time he wanted a full collaboration with Lissauer. "Leonard really liked my melodies, so we decided to write together. It was going really well, we wrote some really strong songs and worked on them on the road"—"Came So Far for Beauty," "Guerrero," "I Guess It's Time," "Beauty Salon" and "Traitor Song." They also worked on new and different versions of "Diamonds in the Mine," "Lover Lover Lover" and "There Is a War." When the tour was over, the two of them went to New York and straight to work on the album Leonard called *Songs for Rebecca*.

Leonard once again moved into the Royalton Hotel. Lissauer would meet him there and Leonard would give him some lyrics, which they discussed, before Lissauer took them home and started coming up with melodies. "Then we would get together at my loft," Lissauer remembers, "and work at the grand piano. Leonard didn't bring his guitar because my chord changes weren't, I think, the kind he naturally gravitated to. I mean, I was trying to write for him in a style that was comfortable—not just write a pop song and have him sing it—but I also lifted the melodies and structures a little out of his zone, which was mostly simple chords, no extended chords or inversions, that kind of thing. Also, he tended not to want to sing leaps, he liked to sing notes close together, almost speak-sing like a French *chanteur*. But I think he was tired of writing the same kinds of songs and wanted to break out of it, and he trusted me enough." Lissauer made demos of the songs so that they could evaluate what they had. Leonard seemed happy with where it was going. Then he decided to leave for Greece.

On Hydra the songs were put to one side. Leonard went back to working on "My Life in Art." "It was pretty bad ten years ago, before the world knew me, but now it's a lot worse," he wrote; he was going to have to "overthrow [his] life with fresh love."[26] There were a number of liaisons. He continued to live with Suzanne, but what he wrote about her was vituperative. Suzanne, by her own account, did not take this personally: "Living with a writer, you feel that it's all a white page, that it's all a rehearsal, that the author has the right to pause, erase, repeat, vary and repeat again. So I let him. Leonard found solace, purpose and comfort in the deconstruction and complaint of daily woes. I wanted to be a good audience and company, not just the reactive wife, although the last was inevitable at times of course."

When Leonard returned to America in the fall, it was to spend more time with Roshi. In an unpublished piece with the pessimistic title "The End of My Life in Art," he wrote: "I saw Roshi early this morning. His room was warm and fragrant. . . . Destroy particular self and absolute appears. He spoke to me gently. I waited for the rebuke. It didn't come. I waited because there is a rebuke in every other voice but his. He rang his bell. I bowed and left. I visited him again after several disagreeable hours in the mirror. . . . I was so hungry for his seriousness after the moronic frivolity and despair of hours in the mirror."[27] Leonard was also hungry for hunger. This domestic life had caused him to put on weight and what he needed was to be empty. As he wrote in *Beautiful Losers*, "If I'm empty then I can receive, if I can receive it means it comes from somewhere outside of me, if it comes from outside of me I'm not alone. I cannot bear this loneliness . . ."—a loneliness deeper than anything that the ongoing presence of a woman and children could relieve.

Lissauer flew to L.A. to meet Leonard and they resumed work on *Songs for Rebecca*. "We took a couple of rooms at the Chateau Marmont with an outdoor patio and rented an electric piano. We worked on these songs and got them happening and I taught him some chords for a couple of the songs so he could play his guitar. And then he and Marty said, 'Let's go back out on tour.'" A week of concerts had been booked in the U.S. Leonard's American record label was releasing a *Best Of* album, presumably having figured that *New Skin for the Old Ceremony*, which failed to even make it into the U.S. Top 200, was a dead horse no longer worth flogging. The compilation album was released under the title *Greatest Hits* on the other side of the Atlantic, where Leonard actually had hits—*New Skin* had made it to No. 24 on the UK charts. Leonard picked the songs for the compilation himself and wrote the liner notes.

For this tour Lissauer put a new band together, which this time included a drummer. They set off on the road in November, taking with them the new cowritten songs, adding them to the regular set. "Leonard was thrilled, I was thrilled, even Marty seemed to be happier than expected given that he didn't want Leonard to collaborate with me in the first place," Lissauer says. After the last concert, Leonard and Lissauer went into the studio—first Sound Ideas in New York, then A & M in Los Angeles. They recorded all the new collaboratively written songs and their new version of "Diamonds in the Mine." "And then the faucet shut off. Leonard disappeared. Marty wouldn't take my calls, I said, 'What the hell's going on?' It just evaporated. Without a word from anyone."

It was December 1975 and Leonard had gone home to Montreal. It turned out that Bob Dylan was also in Montreal, on his Rolling Thunder tour—a traveling rock revue whose guests included Joni Mitchell, Joan Baez, Roger McGuinn, Ronee Blakley, Bobby Neuwirth, Ramblin' Jack Elliott and Allen Ginsberg. Dylan was keen to add Leonard to the lineup. Ratso Sloman, who was traveling with the tour as a reporter,* remembers, "Bob was incredibly intent on getting Leonard to come. He was obviously a fan of Leonard's work, and vice versa. Dylan was proud of what he was doing on Rolling Thunder because those performances were intense and enthralling, and Montreal was Leonard's town, so it meant a lot to him for Leonard to be there. Bob was hounding me—'Make sure he comes'—and he dispatched me to Leonard's house."

When the car pulled up outside a "crazy little bungalow" off Saint Dominique Street, Sloman double-checked the address. It did not

---

* His account of the tour became the 1978 book *On the Road with Bob Dylan*.

give the appearance of a celebrity's house. When Suzanne let him in, Sloman ducked instinctively, the beamed ceiling was so low. The floor sloped and the walls were crammed with shelves filled with books, framed pictures and dusty tchotchkes. It looked like a fairy-tale grandmother's gingerbread house. Leonard was inside with a bunch of his friends, who were all playing music, Mort Rosengarten playing spoons to Leonard's harmonica. Suzanne took Sloman upstairs to see the children. "They looked so sweet, these little angels in their cribs in this ramshackle little room, and Suzanne was so patient. It looked like a very tranquil domestic scene."

It was hard work persuading Leonard to leave the house and come with him to the Forum. When he finally succeeded, Leonard insisted on taking his friends and his harmonica along with him. Everyone piled into the car and sang old French folk songs along the way. When they pulled up at the venue, Dylan came right out to greet Leonard. He told him that if he wanted to come up and play a couple of songs, it would be fine by him. Ronee Blakley, Bobby Neuwirth, and Ramblin' Jack came over too, as well as Dylan's wife Sara and Joni Mitchell. Leonard addressed Mitchell as "my little Joni," and the two appeared very relaxed around each other. Joni joined Sara in asking Leonard to sing something in the revue, but Leonard declined. "It's too obvious," he said. Leonard, Sloman surmised, was "a bit of a control freak, in the sense of controlling his own music, of presenting the songs and the context. He doesn't strike me as someone who jams with the band, unless it's his friends, at home." Although Leonard did not participate, Dylan dedicated a song to him—"a song about marriage," "Isis," whose lyrics included the sentiment "What drives me to you is what drives me insane." "This is for Leonard," said Dylan, "if he is still here."

Leonard was still trying to make his relationship with Suzanne work. He bought a small apartment building across the road from the Montreal cottages in order to have more space. A nanny had moved into his writing room in the cottage, and since it was too cold to use the shed, he worked in the kitchen. "I loved hearing him in the background playing the guitar, quietly singing or writing," says Suzanne. "When he wanted to enjoy the children he did. I never put pressure on him or made it an obligation, there was no domestic tyranny, but he was a loving, solid, dutiful father. He sung them lullabies and the normal tender gestures."

Come the spring, Leonard left once again on another European tour. This one was considerably longer, with more than fifty dates, starting in Berlin in April 1976 and ending in July in London. John Miller replaced Lissauer as musical director, the rest of the band consisting of Sid McGinnis, Fred Thaylor and Luther Rix. Leonard's new backing singers were Cheryl Barnes (who three years later would appear in the film of the musical *Hair*) and a nineteen-year-old Laura Branigan (who three years later would sign to Atlantic and become a successful solo pop artist). The set list this time included some new—or, technically, old—songs: "Store Room" was an outtake from Leonard's first album, "Everybody's Child" was an unreleased track from the second album, and "Die Gedanken Sind Frei," a German folk song about freedom of thought, had been written in the nineteenth century. A live review in *Melody Maker* noted how cheerful Leonard appeared onstage. "Gone is the doom and gloom, [he's] at his funkiest and wittiest."

After the final concert Leonard went to Hydra. Suzanne and the children were there and Irving and Aviva Layton were visiting. Leonard was eager to show Irving what he had been writing. "They always read to each other what they'd written," says Aviva. Irving was as effusive as ever about his friend's work. "The only time I ever heard Irving even mildly criticize Leonard was when Leonard went through a very religious, sort of mystical, semi-Judaic, semi-Christian stage and that was very much not Irving's sensibility. But that was all; Leonard loved Irving's poetry and Irving loved his."

When the Laytons left, Leonard spent hours with Anthony Kingsmill, the painter who lived on Hydra. Richard Vick remembers Kingsmill as "an incredibly witty and quite wise little man, as well as something of a drinker, [who] had quite a strong influence on Leonard. I remember an occasion at one of the places at the port where people would gather at dawn, after having gone around the bars during the night. Leonard was there, strumming a few chords, and Anthony, who was in his cups, got very frenetic and said, 'And who do you think *you're* fooling, Leonard?'" Leonard appeared to ponder the question deeply. He continued pondering after he left Hydra for the U.S.

Leonard rented a house in Brentwood, on the west side of Los Angeles, just off Sunset Boulevard. His reason for living in L.A. was that Roshi lived there, and Leonard was spending a great deal of time with Roshi, at the Zen Center in Los Angeles and on Mount Baldy, often acting as his chauffeur and driving him between the two. Roshi told Leonard that he should move to Mount Baldy with Suzanne and the children—there were family quarters at the monastery as well as individual monks' cabins—and stay there and study. It was tempting—at least it was to Leonard. Suzanne had accompanied him on one retreat but found that "sitting all through the night was an austerity [she] couldn't share." Leonard was also spending a lot of time in L.A. with a record producer with whom he was cowriting songs—not John Lissauer but Phil Spector. These days Spector is an inmate of a California state prison, serving nineteen years to life for second-degree murder, but at that time Spector lived in a mansion in Beverly Hills.

"So," says John Lissauer, "the famous missing album. I have the rough mixes but the master tapes just disappeared. Marty culled the two-inch tapes from both studios. He never returned my calls and Leonard didn't return my calls. Maybe he was embarrassed. I didn't find out what happened for twenty-five years. I heard this from a couple of different sources. Marty managed Phil Spector and Spector had not delivered on this big Warner Bros. deal; they got a huge advance, two million dollars, and Marty took his rather hefty percentage, but Phil didn't produce any albums. So Warner Bros. go to Marty, 'He comes up with an album or we get our money back.' So Marty said, 'I know what to do. Screw this Lissauer project, I'll put Phil and Leonard together.'" Which is what he did.

Fifteen

I Love You, Leonard

Phil Spector was thirty-six years old, five years younger than Leonard, a small, fastidious man with bright eyes and a receding hairline and chin. In matters of dress Spector favored bespoke suits and ruffled shirts, or sometimes a cape and wig. Between them they reflected his status as "the first Tycoon of Teen" (as Tom Wolfe dubbed him) and, for many years, the Emperor of Pop. Spector had been nineteen years old when he wrote and recorded his first No. 1 in 1958, a song called "To Know Him Is to Love Him," its title taken from the words on his father's tombstone. In 1960 Spector became a record producer, then the head of his own record label. During the first half of the sixties he turned out more than two dozen hits.

There had been record producers before Phil Spector but there was nobody like him. Other producers worked behind the scenes; Spector was up front, flamboyant, eccentric and more famous than many of the acts whom he recorded. His records were "Phil Spec-tor" records, the artists and musicians merely bricks in his celebrated "Wall of Sound"—the name that was given to Spector's epic production style. It required battalions of musicians all playing at the same time—horns bleeding into drums bleeding into strings bleeding into guitars—magnified through tape echo. With this technique Spector transformed pop ballads and R & B songs, like "Be My Baby," "Da Doo Ron Ron" and "Unchained Melody" into dense, clamorous, delirious minisymphonies that captured in two and a half exquisite minutes the joy and pain of teenage love.

Leonard was not a teenager. It is quite possible he never was a teenager. Leonard's songs, like his poetry, were a grown-up's songs. His lyrics were sophisticated and his melodies uncluttered, which gave his words room to breathe and resonate. His delivery was plain and his taste in production, as in most everything else, was subtle and understated. Other than finding themselves the last two left at a key party, it is hard to picture Leonard Cohen and Phil Spector ever ending up as musical bedfellows. But by the grace of Marty Machat they did. Machat's logic was simple. He had a client—Spector— who was one of the best-known names in American pop, but who had hit a rough patch and was about to lose them a lot of money if he didn't give Warner Bros. an album soon. And he had another client—Leonard—who was revered almost everywhere but America, who was cowriting songs with a producer far less celebrated than Spector—Lissauer—and whose last album with Leonard did nothing to get him onto the U.S. charts. Spector had seen Leonard play at the Troubadour and told Machat he had been "entranced." Leonard had confessed to being a fan of Spector's early records, considering them "so expressive I wouldn't mind being his Bernie Taupin."[1] So why not put them together and have Leonard do the lyrics and Spector the music? It would solve the Spector problem, and perhaps even Leonard's problem too.

As it turned out, Leonard and Spector had more in common than one might think, besides both being East Coast Jews who shared a manager. Spector and Leonard had both lost their fathers when they were nine years old—Spector's committed suicide—and had very close relationships with their mothers. Each deeply loved the sound of women's singing voices—Spector, who often wrote for women, had put together several sixties girl groups. Both were very serious about and protective of their work. They were also both subject to black moods and, in 1976, when they began working together, were in disintegrating relationships and drinking heavily. So began the extraordinary story of *Death of a Ladies' Man*.

Spector lived in a twenty-room mansion, a Spanish–Beverly Hills movie star hacienda built in the early twenties. There was a fountain in the front, a swimming pool in the back and, all around, lush gardens. The property was ringed with a barbed fence hung with "Keep Out" signs. Should someone choose to ignore the warning, there were armed guards. When Leonard first walked up its front steps, Suzanne beside him, the maid who answered the door led them past an antique suit of armor and walls hung with old oil paintings and framed photographs—Lenny Bruce, Muhammad Ali, Martin Luther King, John Lennon, Spector's heroes and friends—to the living room. Like the rest of the house, it was cold and dimly lit; there was more light coming from the aquarium and the jukebox than from the grand chandelier overhead.

Spector had invited the couple to dinner. It was a small gathering and Spector turned out to be a charming host—smart, funny and convivial. But as the night wore into morning and the empty bottles piled up, Spector became increasingly animated. One by one the guests took their leave; only Leonard and Suzanne remained. When they finally got up to go, Spector shouted to his staff to lock the doors. "He wouldn't let us out of his house," Suzanne says. Leonard suggested that if they were going to stay all night, they might find something more interesting to do than shout at the servants. By the next day, when the door was unlocked and Leonard and Suzanne were allowed to go home, Leonard and Spector had worked up a new arrangement of country singer Patti Page's "I Went to Your Wedding" and had made the first forays into cowriting songs.

Over the coming weeks, Leonard was a regular visitor to the mansion. Spector was a night owl, so it would be afternoon before Leonard would drive the short distance from his rented house in Brentwood. Leonard was dressed for work, wearing a suit and carrying a briefcase. He looked, Dan Kessel recalls, "like a suave, continental Dustin Hoffman." The maid would take Leonard to the living room, where the thick velvet curtains were firmly drawn against the bright California sun and an air conditioner blasted icy air, and leave him there alone, giving his eyes time to adjust to the round-the-clock twilight. A few minutes later Spector would make his entrance, flanked by Dan and David Kessel. The Kessel brothers had known Spector since childhood; their father, the jazz guitarist Barney Kessel, was a close friend of Spector who had played on a number of his hit records. His sons, who were also guitar players, had in turn appeared on several Spector records, including John Lennon's *Rock 'n' Roll* album, which Spector produced.

An antique silver cart was rolled in, laden with drinks and food. While the Kessel brothers retired to the adjoining room, Spector's office, Leonard and Phil hung out for a while and chatted before getting to work. Sometimes they would pick a song to listen to from Spector's jukebox, which was stacked with obscure R & B and rock 'n' roll as well as old hit singles: Elvis, Dion, Dylan, Sun-era Johnny Cash, Frankie Laine. Then they would start work on the songwriting, sitting together at the piano on the long mahogany bench. The Kessel brothers would listen in on the studio monitors in the office, giving an opinion when Spector asked for it and, when their services were required, coming in and playing guitar. The rest of the time they shot pool.

"All day and into the night, every day, they would work for a while,

break for a while, work for a while, break for a while," says David
Kessel. "Suggestions went back and forth between them. Leonard
had notes with him and Phil would say, 'Well okay, that story line
goes on this kind of a music track,' or Phil would have the music track
and Leonard would go, 'Hey, man, that kind of brings to mind this
for me.' Many times during breaks I sat outside with Leonard by the
fountain and he would go, 'Wow, this is different.' 'This is interesting.' 'This should be quite something.' 'I've never done this like this.'
He would use us as sounding boards: could we give him any insights
as to where this was headed or what he could expect? All Phil said
about it was, 'This is cool, it's going to be interesting; I want to see
how it comes out and hopefully it'll come out pretty good.'" Dan
Kessel remembers, "Leonard was notoriously slow and deliberate;
Phil got straight on it and got it done. Even so, or maybe because
of that, they complemented each other as songwriters. There was
plenty of laughter." When Doc Pomus, the blues singer-songwriter,
Spector's friend, came by the house one day to visit Spector, they
were "like two drunks," he said, "staggering around."[2]

Among the papers Leonard carried in his briefcase were lyrics of
some of the songs he had worked on with John Lissauer for *Songs for
Rebecca*—"Guerrero" and "Beauty Salon," given different melodies
and arrangements, would become "Iodine" and "Don't Go Home
with Your Hard-On." Leonard also brought along an unfinished song
called "Paper-Thin Hotel," which he had begun writing on the *New
Skin* tour. The song "Memories," though, was written at the piano
in Spector's mansion. Introducing it at a concert in Tel Aviv in 1980,
Leonard called it a "vulgar ditty that I wrote some time ago with
another Jew in Hollywood, in which I have placed my most irrelevant
and banal adolescent recollections."[3] Leonard's lyrics recalled, in an
almost Spectorian fashion, his high school days and the near-terminal
case of sexual longing with which he was plagued. At times it also
evokes his failed seduction of Nico:

I pinned an Iron Cross to my lapel
I walked up to the tallest
and the blondest girl
I said . . . Won't you let me see
Your naked body

In less than a month, they had around a dozen songs ready to go. In January and February 1977—plus one last session in June—they recorded nine of them: the eight songs that made it onto the final album plus one that didn't, another of the *Songs for Rebecca* songs, "I Guess It's Time." Recording began in Gold Star, a small, dark studio in the shabby heart of Hollywood. Spector's favorite place to record, its old tube equipment gave the studio its rich, expansive sound, as well as a distinctive smell of burning dust when the tubes in the mixing board started heating up. "It also had a famous echo chamber," says Hal Blaine, "like a cement casket running the length of the studio; an amazing sound. We did so many hits with Phil at Gold Star." Blaine, a drummer, was a linchpin of the loose group of top-notch, versatile L.A. studio musicians nicknamed the Wrecking Crew. Spector would always hire them when he needed a band; *Death of a Ladies' Man*, says Blaine, "was just another job. We never knew what we were going to do until we got there and did it."

On January 24, 1977, Leonard arrived at Gold Star for the first session dressed in pale slacks and a dark blue blazer, "looking," as David Kessel recalls, "like he was entertaining a date on the Riviera." Walking into the studio, Leonard was taken aback. The room was crammed with people, instruments and microphone stands. There was barely space to move. He counted forty musicians, including two drummers, assorted percussionists, half a dozen guitarists, a horn section, a handful of female backing singers and a flock of keyboard players. "It blew his mind," says David Kessel. "He was kind of disoriented, like, 'Whoa. Okay. Is this how he normally does it? What are we doing here? Can you help me figure it out?' This was a different thing for him." Spector, who was up in the control room and even more sharply dressed than Leonard, in an expensive black suit, green shirt and Cuban-heeled boots, called over the studio monitor, "Anybody laid-back in this room, get the fuck out of here."[4] On the console was a bottle of Manischewitz Concord grape wine. Spector picked it up, poured it into a Tweetie Pie glass and sucked it through a plastic straw.

There was another face in the room Leonard recognized: Ronee Blakley, the vivacious folksinger he had met in Montreal on Dylan's Rolling Thunder tour. Blakley, who had recently become famous for her portrayal of a fragile country star in Robert Altman's 1975 film *Nashville*, was a friend of Spector. "I wasn't his girlfriend," says Blakley, "but I went around with him a little bit. Phil has a very, very dear, sweet side to him." Spector had asked her to come and sing duets with Leonard on "Iodine"—the first track they recorded—a song about failure, loss and the wounds of love, which had been given a beguiling Nino Tempo arrangement. She also sang with him on the album's bittersweet opening track, "True Love Leaves No Traces," which was based on the poem "As the Mist Leaves No Scar" from Leonard's 1961 book *The Spice-Box of Earth*, and "Memories," a rambunctious burlesque number whose lyrics make wry reference to the kind of teen-angst pop in which Spector specialized and whose chorus was made for drunks in midnight choirs to sing along with.

It seemed to be the first time Leonard had heard anything about duets, but he raised no objection. "He was an elegant man, soft-spoken and thoughtful and kind," Blakley says. "He was not mean, not sharp, never 'I'm intelligent and I have a way with language and I know how to make a remark that may sound fine but has a cruel edge to it.'" There were no rehearsals or charts; they simply sang the song through together once or twice and Blakley made up her part. She remembers that "it wasn't that easy." As Hal Blaine points out, Leonard's "weren't regular rock 'n' roll songs. These were songs written by a poet for a rock 'n' roll record and kind of off the wall. Leonard was in a whole other world." The other problem was that Leonard seemed insecure about his singing. Says Blakley, "He really believed that he doesn't have a great voice, although it's amazing—so sensitive and vulnerable. It trembles at times, but at the same time it almost rumbles, it has that biblical quality. I think it's a voice that female voices work with especially well."

The sun was starting to come up by the time the first recording session ended. The Kessels checked that the tapes had been correctly cataloged and oversaw the loading of them onto a dolly, which was wheeled out to Spector's car after every session under armed guard—Spector's bodyguard George. "Phil always took his tapes home," says Dan Kessel. "He didn't single Leonard out, that's just the way Phil conducted his business. Studios don't protect your tapes with the same stringency you do." George was a retired U.S. federal marshal. Like Spector, he wore a gun in his shoulder holster. The difference, says Dan Kessel, was that "the bodyguard's gun was always loaded. Phil's never was." Leonard joked about getting his own armed bodyguard and having a shoot-out on Sunset Boulevard. He asked Malka Marom, who was visiting him in L.A., to come to the studio with him. He told her that Spector was afraid of her because he thought she was an Israeli soldier. Marom agreed to go to the studio. She found the atmosphere "very scary—because Phil Spector was sitting there with bottles of Manischewitz wine and a gun on the table. I said to Leonard, 'Why are you recording with this madman?' He said, 'Because he's really very good at what he does.'"

Harvey Kubernik, who had been given the job of food runner—Spector or Marty Machat, who would come by the studio with his girlfriend Avril, would dispatch him to Canter's deli to bring back chopped liver and corned beef sandwiches—had witnessed Spector in the studio before. Compared with other albums, he recalls, Spector's sessions with Leonard were "not too chaotic." But for Leonard, says David Kessel, "it was a bit of a whirlwind."

It was late on the second night of recording when Bob Dylan showed up at the studio. "He comes in through the back door," says David Kessel, "and he's got each arm around a different woman. In his right hand, around the woman, he's got a bottle of whiskey and he's drinking the whiskey straight." Allen Ginsberg followed close behind with his lover, the poet Peter Orlovsky. Seeing them, Spector jumped up and hailed them over the monitor. There were so many Jews in the room they could have a bar mitzvah, he joked. Work stopped while Spector came down to socialize. There was much hugging and drinking, then, as happened to anyone who came into Spector's studio, the visitors were put to work.

Leonard was recording "Don't Go Home with Your Hard-On," a boisterous commentary on domestic bliss. Dylan, who was in the process of being divorced by his wife, Sara, seemed to have no problem entering into the spirit of the song. Ginsberg said later that "Spector was in a total tizzy, ordering everybody around, including Dylan: 'Get over there! Stay off the microphone!' "[5] Dan Kessel remembers, "He was very animated. He was behind the console, then with us in the studio, back and forth, interacting with everyone and conducting us." Says Blaine, "It was like he was conducting the philharmonic, and it went on for hours. But that's the way we worked with Phil; he wasn't trying to run us into the ground, he was looking for that feeling. That magic."

The session had turned into a boozy party. By daylight, when most of the revelers had gone, Spector and Leonard listened to the tape through the big studio speakers, the volume up, the music ferocious. "This," said Spector, sipping at his Manischewitz, "is *punk rock*, motherfucker!" Leonard poured himself a glass of Cuervo Gold. "Everybody will now know," said Leonard, "that inside this serene, Buddha-like exterior beats an adolescent heart."[6]

At Dan Kessel's suggestion, the next session was moved to Whitney Studios in Glendale. A new building in a more sedate neighborhood, with all new, state-of-the-art equipment, it was owned by the Church of Latter-Day Saints; Frank Zappa and Captain Beefheart had recorded there. "One night," says Dan Kessel, "Phil was monitoring at supersonic levels—Leonard had to put his hands up over his ears—and suddenly one of the two huge playback speakers completely blew out, rattling the three-paned soundproof glass window separating the studio room from the control booth. The roar of the Wall of Sound at high volume can do that." While the speaker was being fixed, the recording moved again, this time to Devonshire Sound Studio in the San Fernando Valley.

Leonard could not say precisely when he lost control of the album, but he knew that he had. "It definitely wasn't hippie or mellow, but Leonard was very together, very dignified and professional," says David Kessel. "Then it got a little freaky for him." The "entire enterprise," as Leonard described it, was as "an ordeal." Spector, as painstaking at getting the instruments and sound right as Leonard was with his endless rewriting, would often make him wait until two, three, even four in the morning to sing, at which point Leonard was exhausted and his nerves were shot. "It was just one of those periods where my chops were impaired and I wasn't in the right kind of condition to resist Phil's very strong influence on the record and eventual takeover of the record," Leonard said.[7] In the early hours of morning, after watching Spector's car drive away, taking the tapes of the day's recording to his mansion, Leonard drove back to his rented house in a foreign city, to a family on the verge of breaking up.

"I'd lost control of my family, of my work and my life, and it was a very, very dark period," Leonard said. "I was flipped out at the time and [Spector] certainly was flipped out." Where Leonard's darkness manifested as "withdrawal and melancholy," with Spector it was "megalomania and insanity, and the kind of devotion to armaments that was really intolerable. People were armed to the teeth, all his friends, his bodyguards, and everybody was drunk or intoxicated on other items, so you were slipping over bullets, and you were biting into revolvers in your hamburger. There were guns everywhere. Phil was beyond control." During one session, at four o'clock in the morning, as Leonard was finally getting to sing, Spector came down from the control room. In his left hand was a half-empty bottle of Manischewitz and in his right hand a gun. Spector wrapped an arm around Leonard's shoulder in a comradely manner. Then he pushed the nuzzle of the gun into Leonard's neck. "Leonard, I love you," he said, cocking the trigger. "I hope you do, Phil," Leonard replied.[8]

"Bullets all over the floor is an exaggeration," David Kessel says, and in all likelihood that is true; the more media interviews a person does, the more an incident gets polished and hyperbolized. "There weren't bullets on the studio floor," Kessel continues. "He's probably talking about Phil's house. By the way, there are a lot of Americans who have firearms for whatever purpose, and the Constitution says you can have that." Dan Kessel says, "Leonard seemed intrigued with the whole Spector milieu and often made witty comments and observations about us, but I never got the feeling he was uneasy about the guns or anything else. On the contrary, in his own low-key way, he seemed to enjoy himself during the production."

Stan Ross, the assistant engineer and co-owner of Gold Star, took an opposite view. "My main memory of that whole episode was that Phil and Leonard were both very unhappy with what was coming off and I think rightly so."[9] Devra Robitaille, Spector's assistant and, until recently, girlfriend, who played synthesizer on the album, agreed with Ross. She told Spector biographer Mick Brown that Leonard and Spector "didn't see eye to eye at all. There were a lot of creative differences. It was always very tense, very uncomfortable." And unpredictable. Spector "could be in a great mood or he could be a raving lunatic. A lot of it was the drinking. Someone would say something, or he'd just get in a mood and stalk off. Everybody would be hanging around and then tempers would start to build and it's five o'clock in the morning and everyone's exhausted. . . . There were a couple of times when he would pass out drunk and Larry [Levine] and I would have to haul him back into his chair and revive him, and sometimes he'd somehow rally and that would be the brilliant take, the moment of genius."[10] Even Levine, Spector's longtime engineer and friend, had to say that Phil was "not at his best" and Leonard "deserved better than he got."[11]

The fiddle player who had a gun pulled on him during the recording was Bobby Bruce. It was late, and he was doing a solo on "Fingerprints," a countrified song about a man in love losing his identity, and Spector, Dan Kessel remembers, "wanted Bobby to do it again with a certain feeling. 'Do it this way, Bobby. No, more like that.'" The atmosphere in the studio was tense and, in an attempt to lighten it, Bobby started affecting an effeminate manner: "Why of course, Phillip, I'm just mayonnaise in your hands," says Don Kessel. "Ordinarily Phil might have laughed but he wasn't in a lighthearted mood." Spector pulled out his gun. Levine stepped in to try to calm things down, but Spector refused to put away the gun. The engineer had to threaten to turn off the equipment and go home if he did not. "He finally realized I was serious and put the gun away," said Levine. "I loved Phil. I knew that wasn't the real Phil."[12] Bruce quietly shut his fiddle in its case and quit.

For the recording of the album's title track at Whitney Studios, Leonard brought along his own protection: Roshi. Dan Kessel remembers, "Leonard's Zen master was nice and friendly and spoke quietly. He was wearing proper monk's garb." Says Ronee Blakley, "He was the kind of man you wanted to be around, funny, kind and disciplined—special. Leonard was also serving as Roshi's driver. It was—I hope I'm not saying this wrong—a lesson in humility. He was learning to serve." Leonard had tried to persuade Ronee to go to

Mount Baldy and sit with Roshi. "He told me," she says, "that it had saved his life."

The session started as usual at seven thirty P.M. but by three thirty A.M. they had still not played "Death of a Ladies' Man" all the way through; Spector had the musicians play no more than six bars at a time. At four A.M., Spector stood at the window of the control room and clapped his hands, and Leonard began singing his nine-minute meditation on love, marriage, emasculation and the emptiness left behind when *"the great affair is over."* The enormous studio room had a cathedral pipe organ in it, which Spector told Dan Kessel to play. Kessel had never played one before. "I turned on the power switch, sat down and quickly experimented with the stops till I got the hugest sound I could find." Then Spector "began leading us like a symphony orchestra conductor and Leonard came in at the perfect moment and started singing his heart out, while forty musicians came in together with sensitive attention to every breath of Leonard's vocal. Miraculously, without a chart and with no rehearsal, we all managed to glide in together for a smooth landing. We were all exhilarated when we wrapped," says Dan Kessel, "and no one more so than Leonard."

Four months after the last Whitney session in February, during which "Fingerprints" and "I Guess It's Time" were recorded, there was one session in June, back in Gold Star, for "Paper-Thin Hotel." The song, with the familiar Leonard Cohen themes of separation, cuckolding and surrender, had been given a bittersweet, romantic arrangement with choirs, pianos and pedal steel. And that was it. Spector took home the tapes under armed guard, as he always did, and went to work mixing them in a secret location.

No one appeared to have told Leonard that the album was finished. He believed that the exhausted parts he sang in the early hours of the morning were rough vocals that he would have the chance to redo. They were not. When Leonard listened to the playback of the finished album, he flinched. What he heard coming out of the large speakers was a spent man, a punch-drunk singer, lost in the tracks. "I thought he had taken the guts out of the record and I sent him a telegram to that effect," Leonard said.[13] He asked Spector if they might go back into the studio so that he could sing his parts again, but Spector demurred. "In the final moment," Leonard said, "Phil couldn't resist annihilating me. I don't think he can tolerate any other shadows in his darkness."[14]

Leonard told the *New York Times* that he liked nothing about the album. "The music in some places is very powerful but, by and large, I think it's too loud, too aggressive. The arrangements got in my way. I wasn't able to convey the meaning of the songs"[15]—songs that feature some of Leonard's most powerful lyrics about desperate, suffocating, true, faithless, tender, but more often murderous, love. Yet, however he felt about *Death of a Ladies' Man*, it would be hard to deny that Spector had captured Leonard's own sense of annihilation during that period of his life. Leonard *was* lost and spent, and there *was* nothing left. Suzanne had left him. Leonard's mother was in the process of leaving too.

Masha was in the late stages of leukemia. Leonard had been flying back and forth to Montreal, jet-lagged and heavyhearted. While all this was going on, he was also making the final edits to a new book, titled *Death of a Lady's Man*. Marty Machat, meanwhile, had recruited his son Steven, just out of law school, to persuade Warner Bros. to release the record. Mo Ostin, the head of the label, wanted nothing to do with it. Neither, for that matter, did Leonard's label, Columbia.

"That record," says Steven Machat, "was two drunks being no different than any other boys, making an album about picking up girls and getting laid. It was the most honest album Leonard Cohen has ever made." Steven Machat succeeded in winning over a Warner Bros. product manager, and from there he "got the deal done for [his] father." He made it clear that he did not do it for Leonard, for whom he has no great affection, although there may have been some satisfaction in knowing that Leonard "didn't want the album to see daylight." In his book *Gods, Gangsters and Honor* Steven Machat wrote that Leonard told him, "This album is junk. It's your father's masturbation. I love Marty, he's my brother. But I never want to see that man Spector again. He is the worst human being I have ever met."

"At home Phil was delightful—except for the air-conditioning and the fact that he wouldn't let you leave. When it was just the two of us it was a very agreeable time. You know Phil, he has something endearing about him; it's impossible not to be fond of him. It was only when there was a large audience that a kind of performance that he's famous for would arise."

What changed when you went in the studio?

"He got into a kind of Wagnerian mood. There were lots of guns in the studio and lots of liquor. It was a somewhat dangerous atmosphere. There were a lot of guns around. He liked guns. I liked guns too but I generally don't carry one."

Were the guns being fired?

"No firing, but it's hard to ignore a .45 lying on the console. The more people in the room, the wilder Phil would get. I couldn't help but admire the extravagance of his performance. But my personal life was chaotic, I wasn't in good shape at the time mentally, and I couldn't really hold my own in there."

Death of a Ladies' Man was released in November 1977, credited in large letters, front and back, to "Spector & Cohen." It was not surprising that Spector should have given himself equal billing, but for the producer to put his name ahead of the artist's was a curious outcome for an album that Leonard told Harvey Kubernik was "the most autobiographical album of [his] career."[16] Its gatefold sleeve opens out to a panoramic, sepia-tinged photograph shot in a restaurant in L.A., where Leonard sits at a table, flanked by Suzanne and her woman friend, looking like a deer in the headlights, the expression on his face some unidentifiable place between stoned and stunned. The moment the picture captures could hardly be more different from the only other Leonard Cohen album sleeve with a photo of one of his nonmusician lovers—*Songs from a Room*, where Marianne, dressed only in a towel, sits at his writing table in their house on Hydra, smiling shyly.

Critics seemed unsure what to make of the album; it was such a departure from what one had come to expect from Leonard. Yet the reviews were not particularly savage. In the U.S., in fact, they were quite positive, particularly in comparison with those for Leonard's earlier albums. The *New York Times* wrote, "This record may be one of the most bizarre, slowly satisfying hybrids pop music has ever produced."[17] Robert Hilburn of the *Los Angeles Times* was "convinced it's *the* album of '77. Everything is done with an ear for intensity and nerve-edged emotion." Paul Nelson wrote in *Rolling Stone*, "It's either greatly flawed or great *and* flawed, and I'm betting on the latter," noting that in spite of their differences ("the world's most flamboyant extrovert producing the world's most fatalistic introvert") Spector and Cohen had a lot in common, such as both being members of "that select club of lone-wolf poets," and each painfully aware of "what fame and longing are."[18]

In the UK, the music paper *Sounds* compared the album with Dylan's *Desire* and the title track with John Lennon's "Imagine" and John Cale's "Hedda Gabler," while adding, "Diehard acolytes need not worry; it still sounds like [Cohen] but with a much wider appeal."[19] It did turn out to be a durable album. Many who disliked it intensely for its incongruous bombast would warm to it in later years. Leonard also became less negative toward it in time, although, with the exception of "Memories," he would rarely play songs from it in concert. The album did nothing to help Leonard's standing in the U.S.; it did not enter the charts. But had he wanted proof of how much he was loved overseas, it made it to No. 35 in the UK.

With Suzanne gone, Leonard moved out of the house in Brentwood and back to Montreal. He wanted to be close to his mother
for whatever time she might have left. When she was taken into the
hospital, Leonard visited her every day and sat by her bed. One time
Mort Rosengarten came with him and they smuggled in a bottle of
alcohol so that they could all raise a glass together, like the old days.
He phoned Suzanne and told her Masha was dying. "The last phone
call convinced me to come home immediately," Suzanne says. She
flew to Montreal with the children. In February 1978, Leonard's
mother died. Shortly before her death, someone broke into the house
on Belmont Avenue; the one thing that was stolen was Leonard's father's gun.

———

*You ask me how I write. This is how I write. I get rid of the lizard.
I eschew the philosopher's stone. I bury my girlfriend. I remove my
personality from the line so that I am permitted to use the first person as often as I wish without offending my appetite for modesty.
Then I resign. I do errands for my mother, or someone like her. I eat
too much. I blame those closest to me for ruining my talent. Then
you come to me. The joyous news is mine.*

"I BURY MY GIRLFRIEND," *DEATH OF A LADY'S MAN*

Death of a Lady's Man, Leonard's new book, which he dedicated "to
Masha Cohen, the memory of my mother," was published in the autumn of 1978. Although the title was almost identical to that of his
new album, there was a small but telling difference. Here it referred
to one woman in particular. The illustration on the front and back
cover—the *coniunctio spirituum*, symbol of the union of the male and
female principle—was the same as on the sleeve of his album before
last, *New Skin for the Old Ceremony*. "I thought I'd confuse the public

as much as I was confused myself," Leonard said.[20] Its ninety-six poems and prose poems had been written largely over a period of ten years—the span of Leonard's "marriage" to Suzanne—in a number of places, including Hydra, Mount Baldy, Montreal, the Tennessee cabin and Los Angeles. Some of them had been reworked from the novel Leonard had withdrawn from publication, which at various junctures had been titled "The Woman Being Born," "My Life in Art" and "Final Revision of My Life in Art."

At the core of *Death of a Lady's Man* is the story of a marriage and the capacity of this particular union—whose rise and fall are digested in the poem "Death of a Lady's Man," much as they were in the album's title song "Death of a Ladies' Man"—to both heal and wound. The discussion extends beyond man-woman union to a man's relationship with God and the world, and a writer's relationship with his words, but in all cases war and peace, victory and defeat, seem to be separated by a paper-thin wall. Leonard's intention had been to publish the book before the album's release. He had submitted the manuscript in 1976, but at the last minute he withdrew it. He wanted to write a series of companion pieces to its contents to—as he put it—"confront the book," go back through it page by page, and write his reaction to what he read.

Leonard's commentaries appear on the facing page of eighty-three of the poems. The device gives *Death of a Lady's Man* the appearance of a school textbook, crib notes to *Death of a Ladies' Man* or a Leonard Cohen I Ching. The commentaries take on a variety of forms. In some Leonard offers critiques of his poems—at various times serious, playful, critical, laudatory, ironic, enlightening and obfuscating. Some commentaries are prose poems in themselves. On several occasions the poems appear to be in an ongoing debate with their companion piece. Some commentaries, adding a further layer, are made not in the voice of the author but of a character in the poem. In others, like a professor teaching a course on the writings of Leonard Cohen, he tells us what meaning we should take from the poems, referring the student to the unpublished "My Life in Art," "Final Revision of My Life in Art" and "the Nashville Notebooks of 1969," which of course the reader is unable to consult. His commentary to a poem titled "My Life in Art" offers a Buddhist teaching: "Destroy particular self and absolute appears." The commentary on "Death to this Book"—the book is full of deaths and births—makes a close study of the poem's angry, brutal rant and declares, "It will become clear that I am the stylist of my era and the only honest man in town." The last poem in the book, just five lines long, is "Final Examination":

> *I am almost 90*
> *Everyone I know has died off*
> *except Leonard*
> *He can still be seen*
> *hobbling with his love*

The commentary questions the accuracy of this ending to the story and, after raising more questions than it answers, concludes with a declaration of union: "Long live the marriage of men and women. Long live the one heart."

Death of a Lady's Man is a remarkable book, as tightly structured as Leonard's first novel, *The Favorite Game*, and as complex, puzzling and ambiguous as his second, *Beautiful Losers*. It is a mirror, a hall of mirrors, and smoke and mirrors, all of its many layers bleeding into each other like, well, a Phil Spector production. It was not Leonard's most popular book of poems but, particularly when coupled with *Death of a Ladies' Man*, it is one of his most wide ranging and fully realized. Leonard thought the book "good" and "funny" and felt "very warm" toward it, but it was "very coldly received in all circles. It got no respect." Hardly anyone reviewed it, he said, and when they did they "dismissed it uniformly . . . And that was it. That was the end of the book."[21]

A month after Masha's death, Leonard was back in L.A. with Suzanne and the children. Suzanne never could stand the Montreal cold. They were renting a new place in the Hollywood Hills. Then, when spring arrived, Suzanne "abruptly left." "I loved him one day and said good-bye that evening," Suzanne says. "It was the story of 'the mouse that roared' and shocked both of us." Although they were never legally married, in 1979 Leonard and Suzanne divorced. Steven Machat took care of the arrangements. "They both came in and they told me everything they owned and they told me the deal that they'd made and I drew up the deal. What I was told," says Machat, "was he honored every single clause in it."

Sixteen

A Sacred Kind
of Conversation

In November 1978, in Montreal, Leonard was in a studio, recording. He worked by himself, no musicians, no producer. It felt good
to be alone. It felt bad to be alone. It was Leonard's first summer
in a decade without Suzanne. Suzanne was in Leonard's house on
Hydra with her lover. Leonard was in his house in Montreal with
Adam and Lorca. Barbara Amiel was there, interviewing Leonard for
Maclean's magazine, when the telephone rang. It was Suzanne, calling
long-distance from the police station on Hydra. After locals had complained about "commotions" at the house, she and her boyfriend had
been arrested for possession of drugs. The combination of the Kama
Sutra woodcuts she had hung on the walls and the absence of the
beloved patriarch had, it seemed, proven too much for the locals to
bear. Leonard told Amiel that he had warned Suzanne that her new
decor would offend the cleaning lady. The case against Suzanne and
her friend was dropped, but at the cost of several thousand dollars to

Leonard. "These days," he told Amiel, "I work to support my wife, my children and my responsibilities."[1]

When Suzanne returned to Montreal, she took the children and moved with them to France, renting a house in Roussillon, in the Vaucluse. If Leonard wanted to see them—and he did; after his initial misgivings about fatherhood he had taken to it seriously, and his friends say he was grief-stricken at being separated from them—there were negotiations to be made. Leonard had chosen not to tour with *Death of a Ladies' Man*, saying, "I didn't really feel I could be behind it."[2] Aside from its having been such a volatile and enervating experience, the large-scale, sometimes brawling, songs that resulted would have to be seriously de-Spectorized for him to sing them onstage. Not touring also gave Leonard more time to negotiate this new, long-distance family life, which would involve spending even more time on transatlantic flights. Leonard chose, somewhat curiously, to move back to Los Angeles, making the journey to France considerably longer than from Montreal. He bought, along with two fellow students of Roshi, another cheap house in an inexpensive neighborhood. The duplex was a short drive from the Cimarron Zen Center. Every morning at the same time, Leonard would go to the Zen Center to meditate. From there he would go to the gym, before returning to his sparsely furnished part of the house to write. His life without Suzanne and the children was, it seemed, more structured, not less.

Leonard's old friend Nancy Bacal was also living in Los Angeles. When Leonard showed up at the door of her home in the Hollywood Hills, she had recently suffered a terrible loss; her fiancé had been killed in a motorcycle accident. Bacal was "devastated," she remembers. "I could barely breathe. Leonard looked at me, smiled his sweet wry smile and said quietly, 'Welcome to life.'" He urged her to come with him to Mount Baldy and sit with Roshi, saying, "It's perfect for you. It's for the truly lost." That Leonard clearly considered himself among that congregation was evidenced by the central role that Roshi and his austere form of Zen Buddhism played in his life at this time. When Leonard was not at the Zen Center in L.A., you might find him in the monastery on Mount Baldy—a "hospital for the broken-hearted," as he called it[3]—or accompanying Roshi to various monasteries of other religious denominations around the U.S.

Leonard also became a contributing editor of a new Buddhist magazine called *Zero*, which had been founded a year earlier and was named for Roshi's fondness for mathematical terms—zero, to Roshi, was the place where all the pluses and minuses equated in God, the absence of self, and true love. Steve Sanfield had been one of its first editors. Each issue contained some words from Roshi, interviews with artists such as Joni Mitchell and John Cage, articles by scholars and poems by, among others, Allen Ginsberg, John Ashbery and Leonard Cohen.

In spite of his deep involvement with Buddhism, Leonard insisted to anyone who asked that he remained a Jew. "I have a perfectly good religion," he said, and pointed out that Roshi had never made any attempt to give him a new one.[4] When Bob Dylan went public with his conversion to Christianity in 1979 "it seriously rocked [Leonard's] world," said Jennifer Warnes, who was staying at that time at Leonard's house. He would "wander around the house, wringing his hands saying, 'I don't get it. I just don't get this. Why would he go for Jesus at a late time like this? I don't get the Jesus part.'"[5]

In the summer of 1979 Leonard began work on a new album to which he had given the working title *The Smokey Life*. Still smarting from his experience with Phil Spector, he planned to produce, or at least coproduce, it himself. He had been thinking about working with John Lissauer again, but Lissauer was in New York and Roshi was in L.A. and Leonard did not feel ready to leave him. Joni Mitchell, with whom Leonard had remained friends, suggested that he work with her longtime engineer-producer, Henry Lewy. Since Leonard had ignored her last recommendation—that he not work with Phil

Spector—at his peril, he agreed. Leonard met Lewy, a soft-spoken man in his fifties, and liked him immediately. Lewy was born in Germany and had been in his teens when World War II broke out and his family had bribed their way out of the country. His background was as a radio man and a studio engineer, which made him more interested than the average record producer in simply getting things done, rather than having them done his way.

Leonard played Lewy the new songs he had recorded in Montreal, including "Misty Blue," a cover of a country-soul song from the sixties written by Bob Montgomery, and "The Smokey Life," which Leonard had recorded in some form with both Lissauer and Spector (with the latter under the title "I Guess It's Time"). Lewy liked what he heard and suggested they book a studio and make some demos—very informal, just the two of them. The place Lewy chose was Kitchen Sync, a small eight-track studio in East Hollywood that was popular with L.A. punk bands. Harvey Kubernik, who was in Kitchen Sync recording *Voices of the Angels*, an album of punk artists reading poetry, "was startled," he says, to see Leonard, "a guy who's been in the biggest studios in the world," recording there. "This was Bukowski land, the only place where you'd get hit on by a hooker and she'd say, 'I've got change for a fifty,'" says Kubernik. When he asked Leonard what he was doing there. Leonard answered, "My friend Henry Lewy and I are doing some exploratory navigation."

As work on Leonard's album continued, Lewy suggested they bring in a bass player. The man he had in mind was Roscoe Beck. Beck was a member of a young jazz-rock band based in Austin, Texas, named Passenger. They had come to L.A. because Joni Mitchell was looking for a backing band for her tour and Lewy had put their name forward. The tour failed to materialize. Lewy called Beck and booked a session. Beck says, "I went to the studio, met Leonard, shook his hand, and we sat down one-on-one to record. He showed me, on guitar, the two songs we did that day, 'The Smokey Life' and

'Misty Blue,' and Henry pushed 'record' on the tape machine and that was that." Leonard, dressed in a dark gray suit, a tie and black cowboy boots, "had a very gentlemanly manner about him and a lot of charisma," Beck remembers. "I was really struck by that. I had the immediate feeling that it was the beginning of something." Noting how pleased Leonard had been with the session, Lewy said, "He has a whole band, you know." Leonard said, "Well, great, next time bring them all."

The album, retitled *Recent Songs*, was recorded at A & M, a major studio situated on Charlie Chaplin's old lot in Hollywood. There were no guns, no bodyguards, not even any alcohol in the studio that anyone can recall. Lewy "created an extremely hospitable atmosphere where things could just happen," Leonard said. "He had that great quality that Bob Johnston had: he had a lot of faith in the singer, as he did with Joni. And he just let it happen."[6] Mitchell was actually at A & M herself, working in a studio down the hall on her album *Mingus*, which Lewy was producing at the same time as he was making Leonard's. Sometimes she would drop by Leonard's sessions. It was all very easygoing. "Henry's spirit was just lovely," says Beck, "and 'lovely' was a word he used a lot. You would finish a take and Henry would hit the talk-back and say, 'That was just lovely.' I don't recall ever hearing a negative word out of Henry's mouth."

After laying down the tracks with Passenger—augmented on "Our Lady of Solitude" by Garth Hudson, the keyboard player with the Band—Leonard brought in Jennifer Warnes as his main backing vocalist. He also hired John Bilezikjian and Raffi Hakopian to play oud and violin solos on "The Window," "The Guests," "The Traitor" and "The Gypsy's Wife." Another thing in Lewy's favor was that, since he was not a musician—he was an engineer—he worked best with artists who had their own strong vision of what they wanted to do. "The musical ideas were specifically mine," said Leonard. "I'd always wanted to combine those Middle Eastern or Eastern European sounds with the rhythmic possibilities of a five- or six-piece jazz band or rock 'n' roll rhythm section."[7]

In his album credits, Leonard thanked his mother for reminding him, "shortly before she died, of the kind of music she liked." When he had played her his last album, *Death of a Ladies' Man,* she had asked why he didn't make songs like the ones they used to sing together around the house, many of these being old Russian and Jewish songs, whose sentimental melodies were often played on the violin. So Leonard did. He found the classical violinist Bilezikjian through a mutual acquaintance, Stuart Brotman.* When Bilezikjian came to the studio, he also brought with him his oud. Leonard was so taken with his improvisations on it that he had him switch instruments, hiring Bilezikjian's friend and fellow Armenian Hakopian to play the violin.

That the album would include a mariachi band was a spontaneous idea of Leonard's. He and the band had taken to enjoying a post-session burrito and margarita at El Compadre, a Mexican restaurant favored by rock musicians, on Sunset Boulevard, nearby. Mariachi bands would often perform there into the early hours, and Leonard approached one of them and asked if they would be willing to come to the studio and play on his record. The band, who seemed to have no idea who Leonard was, performed on "Ballad of the Absent Mare," a song inspired in equal parts by the horse Leonard had bought from Kid Marley in Tennessee and Roshi's teachings on the Ten Bulls, illustrated poems depicting the stages along the path to enlightenment. They also played on "Un Canadien Errant" ("The Wandering Canadian"), a patriotic folk song from the 1840s, about a rebel from Quebec, banished to America and longing for home. Being sung in English by a Canadian Jew who had wandered to California of his own volition, accompanied by a Mexican band living in L.A.,

---

* Brotman, coincidentally, had joined the band the Kaleidoscope shortly after their appearance on Leonard's debut album.

brought new layers to the song's theme of exile. And Leonard, newly orphaned and divorced, did appear, despite his self-proclaimed lack of sentimentality and nostalgia, to be longing for home—or some sort of home. The nearest he had was with Roshi, to whom he wrote in the album credits, "I owe my thanks."

Leonard also thanked his late friend Robert Hershorn for introducing him to the Persian poets and mystics Attar and Rumi, "whose imagery influenced several songs, especially 'The Guests' and 'The Window,' even if the imagery in 'The Window'—spears, thorns, angels, saints, "*the New Jerusalem glowing*," the "*tangle of matter and ghost*" and "*the word being made into flesh*"—appears largely Christian.* The image of the window had long been important in Leonard's poetry and song, as a place of light and observation, as a mirror and as a boundary between different realities, between the internal and external. Leonard, talking about this song, described it as "a kind of prayer to bring the two parts of the soul together."[8]

Recent Songs teems with feasts, thorns, roses, smoke and sainthood, songs about light and darkness, and about loss and being lost. "The Gypsy's Wife" directly addresses the loss of Suzanne. Its sensual melody is paired with dark, accusatory lyrics that are biblical in tone. Leonard said it was one of the quickest songs he had ever written. After Suzanne left him, he was in a woman's apartment in Los Angeles, and the woman had a guitar, which he picked up and played while she got ready to go out. "And that is exactly what I was thinking," he said, "'Where, where is my gypsy wife tonight?' In a sense it was written for . . . the wife that was wandering away, but in another way it's just a song about the way men and women have lost one another."[9] It does seem a touch disproportionate that a man who had referred to himself in song as "some kind of gypsy boy"[10] and

---

* In the version of "The Window" published in *Stranger Music*, Leonard's 1993 collection of poetry and songs, Leonard changed the "New Jerusalem" line to the nondenominational "the code of solitude broken."

who clearly did not want for female company should be so apocalyptically stern in song about the judgment that awaited whomsoever might come between a man and his wife. But the pain of losing his family was still acute.

Recent Songs also featured three songs from the abandoned *Songs for Rebecca* album: "Came So Far for Beauty," "The Traitor" and the jazzy "The Smokey Life." The first gave John Lissauer credit as its cowriter and coproducer. "It was exactly as I recorded the demo," Lissauer says—Lissauer playing piano, John Miller on bass. "They didn't do anything to it." Lissauer received no credit on the other two songs, although he says that they too were very much as he and Leonard had done them together.

"I was so brokenhearted by this whole thing," says Lissauer. "I was doing dozens of other albums and Leonard wasn't selling a ton, so I wasn't losing big dollars or anything, I just was disappointed by how I was treated. I've always said, it's not Leonard, it's Marty [Machat]." There appeared to be no other *Rebecca* songs among the outtakes, which included "Misty Blue," "The Faith," "Billy Sunday" (an unreleased song Leonard would sing on several dates of the 1979–80 tour) and "Do I Have to Dance All Night," a dance song recorded at a 1976 concert in Paris and released as a single (backed with "The Butcher") in Europe.

Recent Songs was released in September 1979, two years after *Death of a Ladies' Man*—a quicker follow-up than fans had come to expect from Leonard. It was dedicated to Irving Layton, Leonard's "friend and inspiration, the incomparable master of the inner language." The portrait of Leonard that took up the entire front cover was based on a photo shot by his friend and onetime lover Hazel Field; the illustrated version made him look less haggard and more Dustin Hoffmanesque than in the photograph. After the incongruous rage and bombast of *Death of a Ladies' Man*, its largely acoustic style and graceful arrangements, along with the romantic gypsy-folk flavor of the violin and the Near East exoticism of the oud, were greeted by critics as a return to form. The *New York Times* placed it among its top ten albums of the year. *Rolling Stone* wrote, "There's not a cut on *Recent Songs* without something to offer."[11] Larry "Ratso" Sloman, reviewing for *High Times*, predicted it would be "Cohen's biggest LP" and said it was "sure to go silver, if not gold."[12]

But John Lissauer was correct; the album did not sell many copies. Despite the warm critical response, it barely sold at all in the U.S. and failed to make the charts in Canada. In the UK it reached No. 53—but this was the lowest position yet for a Leonard Cohen studio album; even the widely unpopular *Death of a Ladies' Man* had made it to No 35. *NME,* echoing the generally middling reviews it received in Britain, described it as "Cohen's most accomplished album in musical terms," but took it to task for its "detached, almost impersonal air" and lyrics that "tend towards a rather fey obscurity."[13] But Leonard was pleased with *Recent Songs*. "I like that album," he would say more than twenty years later. "I think I like it the best."[14]

The *Recent Songs* tour began in Sweden, in October 1979. Leonard's band for the fifty-one-date European tour was Passenger—Roscoe Beck, Steve Meador, Bill Ginn, Mitch Watkins and Paul Ostermeyer—plus John Bilezikjian and Raffi Hakopian. "It was world music before the term existed," says Beck. "Leonard and I have talked about what a unique group it was for its day." Leonard was also accompanied by two of his finest female backing vocalists, Jennifer Warnes, who had toured with him at the beginning of the decade, and a newcomer named Sharon Robinson.

Robinson had been singing and dancing in Las Vegas in the Ann-Margret revue when Warnes, who had taken on the task of finding a second backing singer, called out of the blue, asking if she would like to audition for Leonard Cohen's European tour. Robinson was not familiar with Leonard's work, but Europe sounded good. "Jennifer vetted me beforehand at her house on her own, then she brought me to audition for Leonard." Sharon remembers, "The whole band was there. I was a little nervous, but Leonard, sitting on the couch, seemed to exude a really bright kind of energy and a real warmth and friendliness that I really appreciated. I felt at home right away."

Helping make Leonard feel at home was Roshi. He traveled with the band on the tour bus, dressed in his robes, reading quietly through his big square spectacles as Europe rolled by on the other side of the glass. "He came to the concerts and he was there backstage," Beck recalls. "It's very odd, his presence was at once large and yet almost invisible at times. Not a lot of words were spoken, and he seemed to disappear into the wall of the greenroom. He is really a Zen master!" It was in tribute, perhaps, that when Leonard sang "Bird on the Wire" he changed the "knight from some old-fashioned book" into "a monk bending over a book." On the long drives between cities, Leonard and the band would sing "Pauper Sum Ego" ("I Am a Poor Man"), a monastic chant in Latin in the round. During the long bus rides, Leonard and Jennifer Warnes cowrote a song about a saint called "Song of Bernadette." Sometimes Bilezikjian would go to the back of the bus when the rest of the band were in their bunks, sleeping, and play his oud and violin, "softly so I wouldn't wake anyone up." But when everyone was up, he remembers, "all of us would sing Leonard's songs. They became like our anthem. We'd come up with a vocal arrangement, singing as if we had our instruments. I think Leonard was touched by that. I saw a big smile on his face." As on their 1972 tour, they had a filmmaker with them on the road. Harry Rasky, a Canadian, was making a documentary on Leonard for CBC. Their number increased again when Henry Lewy flew out to join them for the UK tour—a hectic eleven shows in twelve days—recording the concerts with the aim of making a live album. Despite Leonard's sounding less improvisational and significantly more cheerful on this tour than he had on his last live album, 1973's *Live Songs*, Columbia chose not to release the album recorded on the 1979 tour—at least not until two decades later, when it finally appeared in 2000 under the title *Field*

Commander Cohen.[*] The tour came to an end in Brighton in December, sixteen days before the end of the seventies. After two months off (two weeks of which Leonard spent in a monastery)—it resumed in the eighties with a successful tour of Australia.

When the band members flew back to their respective homes, according to Jennifer Warnes, they did not know what to do with themselves. "[There were] two or three divorces right after the tour, and I think they were simply because the mates couldn't understand what had happened. There had been severe altering of personalities. Roscoe started wearing Armani suits. It was a mess. We'd call each other and say, 'What do we do now?' The aperture of the heart had been broken open."[15] Beck and Warnes were now a couple, having become romantically involved halfway across Europe. Like the rest of the band, they wanted nothing more than to take the tour across America. "We couldn't mount enough interest to put one together," says Beck. Curiously though, at around this time an interview with Leonard appeared in the U.S. celebrity weekly magazine *People.*

Readers more used to stories about movie stars and the Betty Ford Center read how a Canadian singer-songwriter who could not sell records in America recovered from his "brief periods of collapse" in Roshi's "center for meditation and manual labor." Leonard explained, "When I go there, it's like scraping off the rust. . . . I'm not living with anybody the rest of the time. Nobody can live with me. I have almost no personal life." As this last statement was a concept alien to *People,* they also interviewed his former partner. Suzanne was quoted as saying of Leonard, "I believed in him. He had moved people in the right direction, toward gentleness. But then I became very alone—the proof of the poetry just wasn't there." The article reported Suzanne's claim that Leonard had not kept to their child-support agreement. Leonard in turn complained about Suzanne's "Miami consumer hab-

---

[*] The original photo of Leonard on which the *Recent Songs* portrait was based was used on its front cover.

its," adding, "My only luxuries are airplane tickets to go anywhere at any time. All I need is a table, chair and bed."[16]

Harry Rasky's documentary *Song of Leonard Cohen,* which was broadcast in Canada in 1980, made a far more dignified setting for Leonard. The film opens with Leonard sitting in the window—that most symbolic of places for him—in his apartment in Montreal. The apartment looks sparse and uncluttered—much more like Leonard's home in L.A. and his house on Hydra than the nearby cottage crammed with knickknacks and books where he had lived with Suzanne and their children. This has white walls, bare; painted floorboards; an old wooden table, and a small claw-footed bathtub. Leonard also appears to be surrounded by friends and supporters. Hazel Field, who lives in the neighboring apartment, is seen clambering over the balcony, all long limbs and ironed hair, carrying a cup of coffee for Leonard, and Irving Layton drops by, bringing a young, blond companion with him. The two sit spellbound when Leonard plays them his song "The Window" on a boom box.

"Leonard was a genius from the first moment I saw him," Layton states, adding, "[His songs have] the quality of mystery, of doom, of menace, of sadness, the dramatic quality that you find in the Scottish ballads, the English ballads" from the twelfth and thirteenth centuries. Asked by Rasky if he found Leonard's songs sad or joyful he answers, "Both. What I like particularly in Leonard's songs is what I call the depressive manic quality. If you notice, in some of his most telling and moving songs, he always begins on a note of pain, of anguish, of sadness, and then somehow or other works himself up into a state of exaltation, of euphoria, as though he had released himself from the devil, melancholy, pain."[17] Then, Jews, Layton says, "have always had the gift of anxiety and pain and alienation and solitude."[18] The Wandering Canadian tells Rasky that "he is tired of moving around" and would like to "stay in one place for a while." The problem is that "there always seemed good reasons to move.[19]

On October 24, 1980, Leonard was back in Europe for five more weeks of concerts. Jennifer Warnes chose not to join him this time, leaving Sharon Robinson as his sole backing singer. By this time Leonard and Sharon had become close. In Israel, where the tour ended, they started writing a song together, called "Summertime." Sharon, says Leonard, "had this melody that I hadn't written a lyric for but I really loved." In the lobby of their Tel Aviv hotel there was a baby grand piano, so she played it to Leonard, who liked it. "Right on the spot," she says, "he started looking for the appropriate lyric." Although Leonard did not record the song himself, their first cowrite would be covered by both Diana Ross and Roberta Flack.

The tour ended with two dates in Tel Aviv. Sharon remembers Leonard taking the band on a trip to the Dead Sea and also to visit a kibbutz. When it was over, Leonard flew to New York. In his room at the Algonquin Hotel, he prepared to celebrate Hanukkah with Adam and Lorca. He had brought candles and a prayer book with him, and also a notebook. When Hanukkah was over and the children gone, he opened it to the page where he had started to write a powerful and beautiful hymn of surrender, titled "If It Be Your Will."

———————

And so the curtain came down and Leonard stepped out quietly through the backstage door. It seemed as good a time as any to make an exit from the music business. The tour was over and, though the concerts had been good, his album had not sold well. The world had other things to occupy it; Leonard did not think he would be missed.

Had you lost interest, or simply run out of steam?

"I don't know, I suppose it reflected a certain insecurity about what I was doing. I kind of lost the handle of it, I thought. Although in retrospect, even in examining the work of other writers, that's a very common and almost routine assessment of one's work at different periods. Often one's best work is at the time considered inadequate or incompetent. I certainly struggled with those notions, and not just as a writer— but, as any man

or woman locates a large component of their self-respect in their work, it's always an issue."

Did you have any plans for how you would spend this time away?

"My children were living in the South of France and I spent a lot of time visiting them there and going back and forth. The pieces in 'Book of Mercy' were coming and I was writing the album that ended up being called Various Positions. *At a certain point my work was so slow and it became such an ordeal that I was discarding much of what I did, so I think it was legitimate for me to say that my life and my work was in disarray."*

The next four years were spent out of the public eye. If you were looking for Leonard you might find him in the monastery on Mount Baldy, in his apartment in Montreal, in his house on Hydra or in France, in a trailer at the bottom of a path leading to the house where Suzanne and the children lived. Leonard flew to France often.

Adam Cohen, speaking some three decades later, described it as "admirable, the way in which he managed to keep in touch with us, despite the . . . domestic unrest, shall we say, the post-divorce antagonisms."[20] Things between Leonard and Suzanne remained contentious, although in Suzanne's opinion, "We worked it out—over many years with many highs and lows—better than most that I've ever met and heard of since. The voyeurs and gossipers will only want to exaggerate the difficult times and the ill-willed will be suspicious of the best."

The house that Suzanne found and Leonard purchased was on a seventeenth-century farm in Bonnieux that had been owned and run by monks. The surrounding countryside was littered with old, rural churches. Sometimes Suzanne took the children there, "although," she says, "I didn't whisper sweet nothings in the children's ears about Jesus walking in the Garden." She was aware that Leonard "would have liked me to educate them with at least the knowledge of the Jewish tradition in some way," but there were no synagogues in the area, she says. Later, when she and the children lived in Manhattan, she "looked into it in earnest, but the rabbi I spoke to just didn't make it accessible to me and I gave up. And to do it without Leonard didn't make sense to me." Leonard took on the children's Jewish education himself. "I told them the stories, I told them the prayers, I showed them how to light the candles, I gave them the A to Z of the important holidays," he says, and he celebrated the holidays with them.

When he was on Hydra Leonard fell gratefully into his old rhythm of swimming, writing and socializing at the bar by the harbor. He heard from Anthony Kingsmill about a concerto that Terry Oldfield, one of the younger expat residents, was working on, and asked Oldfield if he could hear it. Having heard it, he offered to go to Athens with Oldfield and have it recorded. "A very generous guy," says Oldfield. "I was somebody trying to make it with music and really trying hard at it, and I think he identified a bit with that. Maybe it took him back to his early days on the island when he was writing." Leonard invited Oldfield to his house and showed him the room where he wrote. "It was in the basement, very dark, and looked like a kind of womb, and it had a little electronic keyboard he played around with, one of those battery-operated Casios. And this was the room where he wrote a lot of his best stuff. He said, 'This room has been very kind to me.'"

———

In early 1982 Leonard's friend Lewis Furey came to Hydra for a month with his wife, Carol Laure. With them was a friend of theirs, a French photographer named Dominique Issermann. Furey, who had made two records as a singer, was, like Leonard, "not that thrilled with the music industry and the idea of making records." He says, "I was more interested in theatrical song, song cycles that told a story." One reason for his visit was that he had the idea for a musical, a rock opera, and was hoping that Leonard would write the song lyrics.

At the time, Leonard was "working experimentally, for my own instruction, on the form of the Spenserian sonnet," he said, "which is a very complex metrical and rhyme form—just to keep my chops up in meter and rhyme." When Furey asked if he wanted to write lyrics for his rock opera, his answer was "Not particularly." But Furey was persuasive, and when the conversation turned to their releasing it on video disc—a new format the size of a record album, one not destined to survive—Leonard was intrigued. "He gave me some very elementary plot outlines," said Leonard, "and I wrote lyrics to them as an exercise."[21]

Over the next four weeks Leonard came up with "at least four or five complete lyrics," Furey recalls, "very technical and all perfectly structured," like sonnets. Furey began writing music to them. The project, which they titled *Night Magic*, was "very much a Faust story," says Furey, "only the Mephistopheles character is three teenage angels who appear at the window, and the price you have to pay is suffering joy, redemption and decay." Leonard and Furey worked on the musical on and off over the next year and a half—mostly in Paris, where Furey and his wife lived and where Suzanne was planning to move with Adam and Lorca. Dominique Issermann also lived in Paris. Leonard had begun an enduring relationship with the beautiful photographer on Hydra.

While Furey set about getting funding, Leonard started work on a short musical film for CBC television called *I Am a Hotel*, whose plot revolved around characters in an imaginary hotel. Leonard made an appearance in the film as a long-term resident of the hotel, smoking a cigarette and watching as the various characters' stories played out—with no dialogue—to five of his songs. These were "The Guests," the song that had been the inspiration for the project; "Memories"; "The Gypsy's Wife"; "Chelsea Hotel #2"; and "Suzanne." It was broadcast in 1983 and won an award at the Rose d'Or, the Montreux television festival. Leonard, meanwhile, was meeting with McClelland & Stew-

art about the new book he was writing, which he first titled *The Name*,
then *The Shield*, and finally *Book of Mercy*.

Dennis Lee, whom McClelland had quite recently hired to head
the poetry department, is a poet and essayist, author of a 1977 book
called *Savage Fields: An Essay in Literature and Cosmology*—a joint
study of Leonard's novel *Beautiful Losers* and Michael Ondaatje's *The
Collected Works of Billy the Kid*. Says Lee, "For ten or twelve months,
Leonard and I lived in each other's back pockets and got to know
each other very intensely within this one very narrow sphere of the
new book he was working on." Leonard described this new book as
"a book of prayer . . . a sacred kind of conversation." It was "a secret
book for me," he said, "meant for people like myself who could use it
at a particular time."[22] He wrote it, he said, because he found himself
"unable to speak in any other way. I felt I had been gagged and silenced for a long, long time, a number of years. It was with the greatest difficulty that I could communicate with anybody, even for the
simplest thing. And when I was able to speak it was in these terms,
an address to the source of mercy."[23]

> *In utter defeat I came to you and you received me with a sweetness
> I had not dared to remember. Tonight I come to you again, soiled by
> strategies and trapped in the loneliness of my tiny domain. Estab-
> lish your law in this walled place.*

"6," BOOK OF MERCY

"The content, the prayerful quality of what he was doing had in
some ways always been there," says Lee, "but he really took off his
gloves and went into it more directly and explicitly than he had before. I was very conscious that he was breaking new ground for himself." Lee remembers that the first draft he saw of *Book of Mercy* "was
much sketchier than what you read in the book now. A number of the

very best pieces were written later in the process. I remember we were working away in Toronto and partway through he took off for a month or two to France—he told me that he was very much on his own when he wasn't with his kids—and he told me when he got back that, while he was there, he kept hearing my voice in his head saying what I'd said before he left: 'I think there's still more.' There was no prima donna 'I'm Leonard Cohen, you shouldn't be making any suggestions.' He was the most charming and thoroughbred human being, and really focused on trying to get the book right, despite the other stuff going on in his life. In the evenings there was nothing to do but hone in on the manuscript, probing for more material. He came back with some things that really knocked my socks off."

On Leonard's last trip to Toronto before the book's publication, the main discussion between the two of them was the title. "One question Leonard had was: was there a danger of putting a title out that might sound pretentious or guilty of religiosity, that would invite suspicion from a reader even before reading it? But in the end, for Leonard it came down to a question of whether it should be called *The Book of Mercy* or just *Book of Mercy*, and we decided the 'the' should be omitted so that it didn't sound like this was the *definitive* book of mercy, or a book in the Bible. It's a more modest title. Maybe he doesn't like to appear to be making a larger claim than he wants to." (Perhaps for the same reasons, Leonard often dispensed with the definite article in titles of his albums and songs.) After their work was done on *Book of Mercy*, Leonard and Lee went to the set of *Fraggle Rock*, a children's television series made in Toronto by Jim Henson. Leonard wanted to meet the man who invented the Muppets. Says Lee, "He got a real kick out of watching him shoot the show."

Book of Mercy, Leonard's tenth book, was published in April 1984. Its front cover was illustrated with a symbol designed by Leonard that he called "the emblem of the Order of the Unified Heart." It took the form of a hexagram, the Star of David, made up of two interlinked hearts, or as Leonard described it, "a version of the yin and yang, or any of those symbols that incorporate the polarities and try and reconcile the differences." The book was dedicated to his "teacher." What Leonard had learned from studying with Roshi had also brought him a deeper understanding of the Talmud, the Torah, the Kabbalah and the Jewish prayer book. He said he had reacquainted himself with his Jewish studies after having "wrecked [his] knees"[24] and finding himself unable to sit for long periods in *zazen*—seated meditation. "I had decided to do what I had never done which was to observe the [Jewish] calendar in a very diligent way, to lay *tefillin* every day and to study the Talmud. *Book of Mercy* came out of that investigation."[25] Although there are Christian and Buddhist, as well as secular, references in the book, Leonard's aim in writing it was, he said, "to affirm the traditions I had inherited" and to "express my gratitude for having been exposed to that tradition."[26]

The book is made up of fifty short, numbered prose pieces, one for each year of Leonard's life. In them, he talks, pleads, confesses and prays—to himself, to his friend, to his teacher and to his woman, but mostly to his God—for deliverance and mercy. The pieces are written with the rhythm, tonality and implied music of psalms, and in "the charged speech that I heard in the synagogue, where everything was important." Leonard said, "I always feel that the world was created through words, through speech in our tradition, and I've always seen the enormous light in charged speech, and that's what I've tried to get to."[27] When one finds oneself "unable to function," he said, the only option is "to address the absolute source of things. . . . The only thing you can do is prayer."[28]

The review in Canada's *Globe and Mail* described *Book of Mercy* as "an eloquent victory of the human spirit in combat with itself." The Canadian Author's Association gave it the CAA Award for Poetry. Rabbi Mordecai Finley (whom Leonard would come to know later) remembers that one day, after synagogue, he said to Leonard, "So many of your poems have the feel of Jewish liturgy. Did you consciously write something liturgical?" Finley continues, "He said, 'That's what I thought I was always writing, liturgy,' meaning, something out of the heart so that, in recitation, you're brought to a deeper place. His poetry had a liturgical feel, rhythmic; it almost bypasses the brain and enters straight into us. We have a liturgical tradition in Judaism where great Jewish poets wrote poetry and then they incorporated it into the prayer book—they didn't try to write prayers—and I think Leonard is actually the greatest liturgist alive today. I read his poems aloud at high holidays, from *Book of Mercy*. I think *Book of Mercy* should be in our prayer book."

Seventeen

The Hallelujah
of the Orgasm

Psalms were meant to be sung. As soon as Leonard was back in Los Angeles, he called Henry Lewy. The two went into the studio to make an album of Leonard reading *Book of Mercy*, accompanied by a string quartet. The record was not released. Instead Leonard flew back to New York and called John Lissauer, to make another album whose content was different from, but in its own way a mirror to, *Book of Mercy*.

Leonard said that during the writing of *Book of Mercy*, "the public almost evaporated"[1]; he had written these prayers for himself. He also said that he had no intention of becoming "known as a writer of prayers."[2] Once the book was completed, the public had come sharply back into focus. One big reason for this was that Leonard was running out of money. If Leonard lived like a celebrity, if he'd had a yacht or a cocaine habit, it might be easier to understand. But though he did not spend much money on himself, he still had expenses: Suzanne, the children, Roshi's monastery and various friends whom he supported financially in one way or another. The majority of Leonard's income came from his songs, not his books, and five years had passed since his last album.

John Lissauer was "a little surprised" when he picked up the phone and Leonard was on the line, saying he was in New York and ready to record again—an understandable reaction given that Leonard had walked out on the last album and had gone on to rewrite or record the songs with two other producers. Upset as he had been, Lissauer—like Ron Cornelius, who had been uncredited for many years as the co-writer of "Chelsea Hotel #2"—blamed Marty Machat. "It was just one of those things, a lesson to watch out for managers, or for managers who were obsessed. Leonard knew that Marty was Marty, but Marty had taken such good care of him, so Leonard was in a little bit of Machat denial. He and I have joked about it since and he has admitted what Marty was really like, but at the time it was an unbroachable subject." Lissauer did not mention the aborted *Songs for Rebecca*. "What was the point of making Leonard uncomfortable? It would have put the kibosh on this, and I was happy that he was calling."

In his room at the Royalton, "Leonard had this shit-eating grin on his face—and Leonard, when he's grinning like a little boy, is something you never forget. He had this little crap Casio synthesizer which he'd bought on Forty-seventh and Broadway at one of those camera shops for tourists, where you push your finger down on a key and it'll play a dinky rhythm track. And then he sang me 'Dance Me to the End of Love.'" Leonard played Lissauer several songs in various stages of completion, and only one of them on guitar. On the others he was accompanied by the jaunty parping of the Casio. Lissauer came to the conclusion that Leonard had reached a point in his songwriting where he had "run out of ideas as a guitar player. There were certain things he could do with his guitar playing, but this dopey Casio did things that he couldn't on his guitar and made it possible for him to approach songwriting in a different way." Writing songs was certainly proving torturously difficult for Leonard again. But this cheesy little two-octave keyboard that Leonard seemed so fond of gave him a whole new set of rhythms to work with, and he found he was able to come up with things he could never have created with six strings and what he called his "one chop."

This time Marty Machat made no objection to Leonard's working with Lissauer. His only stipulation was that the budget be kept as low as possible. The impression Lissauer got from Machat was that Leonard had been spending "a ton of money unwisely and hadn't been touring." Lissauer called Quad Recording and negotiated a good deal by block-booking four or five days of studio time. Quad was on Broadway and Forty-ninth, thirteen floors above the Metropole, an upscale strip club "where a guy would stand outside with fliers under a big rotating disco ball." Lissauer put a small band together: his friend Sid McGinnis, who played guitar in the David Letterman show band; Richard Crooks, a drummer who had played with Dr. John; and Ron Getman and John Crowder, two Tulsans who would later front a successful country group, the Tractors. Lissauer himself played keyboards and Synclavier.

"Instead of basing it around Leonard and his guitar and over-dubbing things, we went in and started doing tracks as a band and tried to make a little performance out of it," says Lissauer, "which is something I don't think he'd done in quite a while. I brought in my Synclavier, a very early prototype, a phenomenally big thing, four rolling cases and computers and floppy discs, that cost around thirty-five thousand dollars. Leonard's Casio would have been ninety-nine dollars, if that much, but I couldn't get Leonard to drop his Casio." It did not even have an audio output and needed to be miked. "I tried everything, we tried recording it with real drums, but he liked the sound of the Casio, and in a way it was very charming. So we added stuff to it so that it wasn't quite so embarrassing."

Leonard had "always been interested in electronic machines and keyboards," he said. "In fact, for my first record I interviewed one or two people who were doing experimental work in electronic instruments. I tried to get a sound, a drone, that would go behind 'The Stranger Song'—I never managed to get the right kind I was looking for—but the technology had reached a sophistication by this time where I could use my little toys in the actual recording."[3] The first song to feature Leonard playing his Casio was the new album's opening track, "Dance Me to the End of Love." The seed of the song was something Leonard had read about an orchestra of inmates in a concentration camp, who were forced by the Nazis to play as their fellow prisoners were marched off to the gas chambers. As a testimonial to Leonard's way with words and a romantic melody, it would go on to become a popular song at weddings.*

Leonard named his seventh studio album *Various Positions*, a title suggestive of a Cohen Kama Sutra. But his aim with the album was to explore "how things really operate, the mechanics of feeling, how the heart manifests itself, what love is. I think people recognize that the spirit is a component of love," he said, "it's not all desire, there's something else. Love is there to help your loneliness, prayer is to end your sense of separation with the source of things."[4] The songs take a variety of positions. Different characters in different songs offer different instructions: his dead mother sends him back into the world in "Night Comes On"; the commanding officer sends him back to the battleground in "The Captain." Sometimes similar characters reappear in different songs in different contexts—"Heart with No Companion" has a mother with no son and a captain with no ship. "Hunter's Lullaby," sung in the persona of a wronged woman, the

---

* In 1995 it would also provide the title and words to an eponymous book of art and poetry, whose introduction describes "a deliriously romantic song by Leonard Cohen that is brilliantly visualized through the sensual paintings of Henri Matisse." None of the paintings depicted the Holocaust.

deserted wife and mother of his children, has echoes of Leonard's commentaries in *Death of a Lady's Man*.

The song "Hallelujah" contains a multiplicity of positions. It is a song about the reasons for songwriting (to attract women; to please God) and about the mechanics of songwriting ("*it goes like this, the fourth, the fifth . . .*"), about the power of the word and of the Word, about wanting sex, about having sex and about the war of the sexes. It is also a song about "total surrender [and] total affirmation." As Leonard explained it, "This world is full of conflicts and . . . things that cannot be reconciled, but there are moments when we can transcend the dualistic system and reconcile and embrace the whole mess. . . . Regardless of what the impossibility of the situation is, there is a moment when you open your mouth and you throw open your arms . . . and you just say 'Hallelujah! Blessed is the name.'"[5]

"Hallelujah" took Leonard five years to write. When Larry "Ratso" Sloman interviewed him in 1984, Leonard showed him a pile of notebooks, "book after book filled with verses for the song he then called 'The Other Hallelujah.'" Leonard kept around eighty of them and discarded many more. Even after the final edit, Leonard kept two different endings for "Hallelujah." One of them was downbeat:

> *It's not somebody who's seen the light*
> *It's a cold and it's a broken hallelujah*

The other had an almost "My Way" bravado:

> *Even though it all went wrong*
> *I'll stand before the Lord of Song*
> *With nothing on my tongue but*
> *Hallelujah*

Bob Dylan said he preferred the second version, which was the one Leonard finally used on the album, although he would return to the darker ending at various concerts. Leonard and Dylan had met up when they both found themselves in Paris and sat in a café, trading lyrics back and forth. Dylan showed Leonard his new song "I and I." Leonard asked how long it took him to write, and Dylan said fifteen minutes. Leonard showed Dylan "Hallelujah." Impressed, Dylan asked how long it took Leonard to write it. "A couple of years," said Leonard, too embarrassed to give the true answer. Sloman, who was a friend and admirer of both Leonard and Dylan, says, "I always had this kind of debate in my own head over who's the better songwriter. Bob had those amazing feats of imagination that I don't think anybody could ever come close to, these lines coming out of nowhere—'I wrote it in fifteen minutes in the back of a cab'—which would literally knock you over. But I think that as a formal, structural writer Leonard is the superior writer."

"Hallelujah" was the one song Leonard had played to Lissauer in his hotel room on which he did not use the Casio. "He played me some verses on the guitar in his six-eighths style," Lissauer remembers. "Kind of *chung-chiggie, chung, chung, chung-chung-chung chung*, you know, with chords that didn't really go anywhere. That song was one of the first things I started working with. I took it home and started to work on the chords to make it more gospel and give it a lift. We went in the studio right away, and I sat down at the grand piano and played and sang it for him in a big, grand, gospel way. Leonard said, 'That's fabulous.' So that's the version we did. His original version was really quite different."

Lissauer brought the band in. "I didn't want to make a power ballad out of it, so I told the drummer not to play with sticks but use brushes, nothing loud. I wanted it to be really exposed in the beginning, like the voice of God." Then Lissauer added a choir. "Not a big gospel choir but regular people, people singing 'hallelujah' like they would in church, people who weren't really singers, like the guys in the band, so that it had a feel of sincerity and it wasn't 'We Are the World.'" Among the women singers were Erin Dickins, Crissie Faith, Merle Miller and

Lani Groves (one of Stevie Wonder's backing vocalists) and a jazz singer and keyboard player making her first appearance with Leonard, Anjani Thomas. Leonard's own voice echoed as if he were singing in a cathedral. "I remember being begged by Leonard for reverb," says Leanne Ungar. "Leonard always liked reverb." There is certainly plenty of it on *Various Positions*, on which Leonard's already deepened voice sounds cavernous. When they finished recording "Hallelujah," Lissauer played it back, and everybody, he says, was stunned. "We were like, 'Whoa, this is a standard. This is an important song.'"

Dylan had told Leonard that he thought Leonard's songs were becoming "like prayers," and none more so that the album's closing song, "If It Be Your Will." It was, Leonard said, "an old prayer that it came to me to rewrite."[6] The first draft was written in the Algonquin Hotel in New York in December 1980, shortly after Hanukkah was over and his children had gone back to their mother. It is a song about surrendering, resigning completely to the will of another, whether it be to "*speak no more and my voice be still*" or "*sing to you from this broken hill.*" It is a prayer for conciliation and unity, its last verse beseeching, "*draw us near / And bind us tight / All your children here.*" And, like *Book of Mercy*, it is a prayer for mercy:

> *Let your mercy spill*
> *On all these burning hearts in hell*
> *If it be your will*
> *to make us well*

It is an intensely moving song, intimate and fragile, and sung in a voice that had deepened with age. Lissauer noted that it had dropped four semitones since he and Leonard had last worked together. "It was a heavenly recording," Lissauer says. "Jennifer Warnes came in and sang with him. Just one take." Leonard was very pleased with it. Asked in an interview in 1994 which song he wished he had written, Leonard answered, "'If It Be Your Will.' And I wrote it."[7]

The whole album, according to Lissauer, had been easy to record. "The boys in the band weren't drinking or getting high, nor was Leonard, and Leanne Ungar is very straight; I was probably doing some coke at the time at two in the morning because I was working so much and staying up longer than my body could do on its own, but it was very straight-ahead." Yet it had taken a long time, "about seven months, because Leonard would keep leaving for a couple of months." This time, unlike on *Songs for Rebecca*, Leonard would come back, and they would work on one or two more songs. One reason Leonard would leave was to write. "He was still shy a song or two for an album," says Lissauer, "and he was working at that as we went along."

Things might have been going well in the studio, but in his room at the Royalton Hotel, Leonard was tearing his hair out. "I found myself in my underwear, crawling along the carpet, unable to nail a verse, and knowing that I had a recording session and knowing that I could get by with what I had, but that I'm not going to be able to do it."[8] Part of the problem was perfectionism; it was not that Leonard literally could not write but that what he wrote was not good enough. "I had to resurrect not just my career," he said, "but myself and my confidence as a writer and singer."[9] Among the songs attempted and abandoned for the album were "Nylon and Silk"—so called, says Lissauer, "because he was playing a nylon guitar and I was playing some silky synthesizer sounds. I don't think he ever had any lyrics to it"— and also "Anthem," a very different early version of the song that would finally appear two albums later on *The Future*. Due to a technical problem, the intro to "Anthem" was accidentally erased by a technician. "I'd thought of a few different ways to fix it," says Leanne Ungar, "but Leonard decided that meant the song was not ready to be recorded yet."

When Leonard and Lissauer heard the final mixes of the album, they were both excited. Leonard was happy with the modern sound, the subtle arrangements and the smooth, high-tech production.

"There were some exquisite moments on it," says Lissauer, "'Hallelujah,' 'If It Be Your Will.' I was like, 'This is special. This is *it*. This will be the record that's going to do it for Leonard in the States.'" Leonard and Marty Machat took the tape to Columbia and played it to Walter Yetnikoff, the head of the music division. He did not like it. Leonard remembers, "Walter Yetnikoff said, 'Leonard, we know you're great, we just don't know if you're any good.'" They neglected to inform him that they had decided against releasing his new album in the U.S.

How did you learn that Various Positions *would not get an American release?*

"I happened to pick up a catalog of their recent releases and I just looked through it to see a picture of my record in the pamphlet. I couldn't locate it, so I thought there must be a typographical error. They didn't have to tell me why. From their point of view, the market was so limited that it didn't justify the distribution machinery that would have to go into operation."

Had you resigned yourself by that time to not having an audience in the U.S.?

"I thought they were making a mistake. I thought that there was an audience in the United States and Canada. What I didn't understand at that time—because I thought that if they had bothered to promote it, the work would have sold more widely—but what I understand now, very thoroughly, is that the dollar they spend on promoting me can much more profitably be spent on promoting another singer, so I completely understand their strategy and I have no quarrel with it. I don't think I suffered any sense of remorse or bitterness. Most of the energy was devoted to trying to find some little label that would put it out."

"When Leonard told me he'd had that meeting with Yetnikoff and he wouldn't release the album," says Ratso Sloman, "I was so infuriated that I literally started hounding Yetnikoff. I would go to all these Columbia events, like Dylan's, and go up to him and say, 'The nerve of you not releasing Leonard's album, shame on you.'" He wrote in a 1985 article for *Heavy Metal* magazine that Columbia had sent "Leonard's new kid straight to the showers. Aborted in the USA, as 'the Boss' would say. But, as Dylan told me a few months ago in the studio as he was finishing up his newest Columbia LP, 'Somebody'll put out Leonard's record here. They have to.'" As for John Lissauer, he was devastated, he says, "because I knew how good the whole album was. So I said, 'Okay, I've had it with the music industry, they're a bunch of idiots,' and I quit." He says he was never paid for producing the album.

In retrospect *Various Positions* can be viewed as a stepping-stone between the timelessness and guitar-ballad style of Leonard's earlier albums and the slick electronics and almost anthemic sound of those that followed. The minor-key melody of "Dance Me to the End of Love" has a familiar Old European romance and gravity but also the modernity and jarring novelty of the tinny Casio. Where once there might have been dark, Old Testament lyrics, sung by Leonard alone, there are the transcendent prayer "If It Be Your Will," sung serenely with Jennifer Warnes, and the hymn "Hallelujah," sung with a choir of voices and a synthesizer.

The album was released worldwide, excluding America, in January 1985. Unusually, it was largely ignored by the UK music press. *NME* noted the "sad gaiety" that hung over much of it, "the maidenly correctness" of Jennifer Warnes's harmonies and the album's overall resemblance to "a French movie soundtrack, or even Scott Walker in his Brel period. . . . If the title proposes another thesis of sexual sneering, the songs are complex but peaceful reports from a wearied heart."[10] *Sounds* magazine reviewed its first and only single, "Dance Me to the End of Love," describing its chorus as "inspiration copulating with commerciality" and predicting a hit.[11] It flopped. The album did not fare much better. In the UK it made it to No. 52, one of Leonard's lowest chart positions. With the exception of Norway and Sweden, Leonard's first album in five years did remarkably little across Europe, although it did make the lower half of the Top 100 in Canada.

The *Various Positions* tour began on January 31, 1985, in Germany—a lengthy tour with seventy-seven concerts. Leonard, who had turned fifty a few months earlier, had no desire to go back on the road but dutifully dusted down his suit. John Lissauer could not go with him as his new wife was expecting their first child, but he put a band together for him: John Crowder, Ron Getman and Richard Crooks, who had played on the album, and Mitch Watkins, a veteran of Leonard's 1979–80 tours. All it lacked was a keyboard player and backing singers. "I thought of Anjani," says Lissauer, "killing two birds with one stone."

Anjani Thomas, then in her early twenties, was a singer and piano player who had played in a jazz trio in her native Hawaii. She had recently moved to New York, and Lissauer was one of the first people in the music business she met. He had hired her to sing a background vocal on "Hallelujah" after the main recording was finished, and two months later invited her to audition for Leonard's tour. "So I went to John's loft on Thirteenth Street," Anjani remembers. "I got there first, then Leonard arrived. I remember John opening the door and I looked down—I was very shy then; I'd just moved to the big city from a little island in Hawaii, and I really knew nothing about Leonard or his work and stature. I saw his black shoes first. As my eyes traveled up I saw the black pants and the black belt and the black shirt and the black jacket, the black bolo tie, and I thought, 'Wow.' Where I come from the men wear aloha shirts and shorts. I'd never seen anyone so present in black like that before. He was very nice, shook my hand, and I played him a song and he said, 'Well great, now I know you can sing and play. You've got the job.'"

The European leg of the tour included, for the first time, Poland—the People's Republic of Poland was not well-known for welcoming Western pop musicians. The four dates had been a last-minute addition resulting from the efforts of an independent promoter who was a Leonard Cohen fan. Leonard's name was known in Poland largely through Maciej Zembaty, a comedian, writer and popular radio personality who had been translating and singing Leonard's songs—more than sixty of them—since the early seventies, and who had been imprisoned in 1981 for organizing a festival of songs banned by the regime. Zembaty's Polish version of Leonard's adaptation of "The Partisan" had become an unofficial anthem of the Solidarity movement. The concerts were instant sellouts (the first show was delayed by two hours while police at the front door confiscated thousands of forged tickets) and the fans so spirited that Anjani was given her own bodyguard, a man previously assigned to protect the pope.

Leonard, with his Lithuanian ancestry, appeared touched by his visit to Poland. He talked onstage about the "thousands of synagogues and Jewish communities which were wiped out in a few months" during the war. But when word reached him that Lech Walesa, the leader of Solidarity, had requested that Leonard appear onstage with him, he declined, perhaps out of concern for the promoter who had fought hard to get him there, or likely his usual disinclination to take political sides. During that Warsaw concert Leonard also said, "I don't know which side everybody's on anymore, and I don't really care. There is a moment when we have to transcend the side we're on and understand that we are creatures of a higher order. It doesn't mean that I don't wish you courage in your struggle. There are on both sides of this struggle men of goodwill. That is important to remember—some struggling for freedom, some struggling for safety. In solemn testimony of that unbroken faith which binds a generation one to another, I sing this song." It was "If It Be Your Will."

Anjani was the sole woman on the tour (there was no second female vocalist; John Crowder, Ron Getman and Mitch Watkins also sang harmonies) and also the youngest member of the band. Neither of these things was a new experience for her, but a tour of this size was. "A couple of times on that tour I'd run into Leonard at the hotel sauna, and we spoke about spiritual matters, and that was a bit of a relief, you know, connecting with a kindred soul on the path."

Anjani had started meditating when she was sixteen years old, after a couple of her friends died from drug overdoses. "I knew that if I stayed in music and kept on doing drugs that that could very well be a possibility for me. I had to go in another direction completely, so I went off on a spiritual trek. I was young enough to believe that if you put in the time, you'll become enlightened. It didn't happen, but it certainly made my life miserable on the way. I also saw that Leonard was having a tough go of it on a certain level—because everyone on that spiritual journey is having a tough go of it, for the most part."

Before leaving for the tour, Leonard had told Ratso Sloman, "Look, nobody enters a Zen meditation hall to affirm his health. You enter because you have a doubt and because you want to study how the mind arises, so they make you sit still for seven days, and finally you get so bored and fatigued with your mind that you might be lucky enough to let it drop for a second. As soon as that mind is at rest, the Mysteries manifest as reality. It ain't no mystery." Leonard also told Sloman that this was the first time in his life that he'd had to work, to support his kids, but that it was the thought of his kids that kept him going. "Other than that," Leonard said, "it's bleak, it's bleak."

When the European tour ended on March 24, they flew back to the U.S. to play a handful of East Coast concerts. At the Boston show, at a safe distance from Poland, Leonard dedicated "The Partisan" to the Solidarity movement. Crossing the border to Canada for a whirlwind tour, Leonard learned while he was there that *Night Magic*, his musical film collaboration with Lewis Furey, had won a Genie Award for Best Original Song, "Angel Eyes."* The tour continued in Australia, then returned to America, the West Coast this time, for shows in San Francisco and Los Angeles. Then it was back to Europe again for fifteen more shows, plus one in Jerusalem.

---

* The soundtrack was released as a double album in France in 1985, where the film was also an official selection at the Cannes Film Festival.

It was the midsummer of 1985 when Leonard was finally home in L.A. In his still-barely-furnished half of the duplex, he unpacked his case, opened a bottle of wine and heated up a TV dinner.

Various Positions was finally released in America in January 1986, on the tiny Passport label. It did not trouble the U.S. charts. But the Lord works in mysterious ways, and particularly so in the miraculous story of "Hallelujah." John Lissauer had told the record label that he thought it should be a single; "I thought it the best single I'd ever made for a serious artist. But they said, 'What *is* this? We don't even know what it is.' 'Well, it's kind of an anthemic thing,' I said." They told him, "It will never get off the ground." Some twenty-five years after its first appearance on *Various Positions*, "Hallelujah" would become, as *Maclean's* magazine described it, "the closest thing pop music has to a sacred text."

In recent years a number of essays and lengthy articles, as well as an hour-long BBC documentary, have appeared across the world on the subject of this one Leonard Cohen song. At the time of the writing of this book, "Hallelujah" has been covered by a remarkable assortment of artists, more than three hundred of them. Some interpretations favored one ending of the song over another. John Cale went so far as to ask Leonard for all the verses he had written so that he could compile his own version; Leonard offered him fifteen. "Subsequent covers tinkered here and there with the words to the point where the song became protean, a set of possibilities rather than a fixed text," wrote Bryan Appleyard in the *Sunday Times*. "But only two possibilities predominated: either this was a wistful, ultimately feelgood song or it was an icy, bitter commentary on the futility of human relations."[12] He forgot to mention a third category, "the hallelujah of the orgasm," as Jeff Buckley described it onstage, although arguably this might fit into the first possibility. But Appleyard was right; "Hallelujah" would become a kind of all-purpose, ecumenical/secular hymn for the new millennium. As k. d. lang remarked, "It just has so much fodder, so much density, it can be deep, simple, mean a lot of things to different people, there's so much in it."[13] Also, as with many of Leonard's songs, the melody's spaciousness was generous to people who chose to cover it.

Among them were Bob Dylan, Neil Diamond, Willie Nelson, Bono, Hawaiian ukulele master Jake Shimabukuro and San Franciscan a capella group Conspiracy of Beards. Rufus Wainwright sang it on the soundtrack album to the animated film *Shrek.*[*] Justin Timberlake and Matt Morris from *The Mickey Mouse Club* sang it in the *Hope for Haiti* telethon. Jeff Buckley's transcendent version, recorded on his 1994 album *Grace*, was used on the soundtracks of numerous American television series, including *ER*, *Scrubs*, *The OC*, *The West Wing* and *Ugly Betty*. "Hallelujah" was sung in the finale of *American Idol*, where the judge Simon Cowell declared it (specifically the Buckley rendition; fans of the song take distinct sides) one of his favorite songs of all time. In similar fashion, it made the finale—it's a song made for finales—of the UK TV talent show *The X Factor*, where the big, gospel version by the young winner Alexandra Burke became the fastest-selling Internet download in European history.

Burke's version topped the UK singles chart over the Christmas of 2008, prompting protest action from outraged Jeff Buckley fans that resulted in the late singer's "Hallelujah" taking over the No. 1 position and pushing Burke down to No. 2. In the aftershock, Leonard's original version rose to No. 36—a trinity of "Hallelujahs" in one chart at the same time. Leonard's version also resurfaced the following year in the movie *The Watchmen*, providing the background music to a sex scene between two superheroes. For most who knew the song, it brought a wry smile to the face. But one exasperated journal-

---

* John Cale's version was used during the movie itself, having previously appeared in the more sympathetic setting of *Basquiat* (1996).

ist called for a moratorium on the use of "Hallelujah" on film and TV soundtracks. "I kind of feel the same way," said Leonard in a CBC TV interview. "I think it's a good song, but too many people sing it." He couldn't help mentioning that there was also "a mild sense of revenge that arose in [his] heart" when he recalled that his American record label had refused to release it. "They didn't think it was good enough."[14]

————

Jennifer Warnes, who had signed to Arista as a solo artist, had been talking to Clive Davis, the head of the record label, about the new album she wanted to make. On Leonard's 1979 tour, on which Warnes and Roscoe Beck became a couple, they had the idea of making an album of her singing only Leonard Cohen songs, which Beck would produce. "I could hear it before it became a reality," remembers Beck. "I specifically recall watching Leonard and Jennifer doing their duet on 'Joan of Arc' every night, and visualizing it with Jennifer singing the lead." Davis, who had been the head of Columbia Records when Leonard was signed by John Hammond, seemed to hold much the same view of the marketability of Leonard's songs in America as had Walter Yetnikoff, the man who succeeded him in the job. Davis turned her down. But Warnes saw it as "a record that had to be made"—not just for herself, but for Leonard. "Leonard had years of mixed reviews and I think he had lost faith."[15] Warnes, on the other hand, had enjoyed considerable commercial success with her duets with Joe Cocker ("Up Where We Belong") and Bill Medley ("[I've Had] The Time of My Life"). Says Beck, "We would have given our dying breath to finish that record." Finally, they found a small independent label that was willing to release it and started work.

Around forty musicians appeared on Warnes's *Famous Blue Raincoat*. They included David Lindley, who had played on Leonard's first album; Sharon Robinson, who sang with Warnes on the 1979 tour; guitarist Stevie Ray Vaughan; R & B singer Bobby King; and composer, arranger and keyboard player Van Dyke Parks. As the recording progressed, Beck would call Leonard and update him on how it was going. He told Leonard they had recorded the Cohen-Warnes cowritten "Song of Bernadette" and asked if he might have any more new songs they could hear. "He played me his working copy of 'First We Take Manhattan' over the phone. I taped it and we came up with our own arrangement, a bluesier version. As soon as I heard it I knew I wanted Stevie Ray Vaughan to play on it." Beck knew the celebrated young blues rock guitarist from Austin, where Passenger was based: "Stevie and I were friends from the age of twenty; he used to sit in with Passenger quite often and I used to sit in with his band. He was in L.A. for the Grammy Awards, so I tracked him down to play on the song." Vaughan was performing at the Greek Theatre; Beck invited Leonard and Jennifer to go with him. "They had never seen him live. Jennifer was amazed, as was Leonard. I remember him commenting, 'Now that's what I've been trying to get my guitar players to do for years: make the guitar talk.'"

Beck played Jennifer Warnes's record for Leonard, and Leonard listened in silence. Impressed, Leonard began to take a much closer interest in the album. He sang a duet with Warnes on "Joan of Arc." He also gave her another of his new, unreleased songs, "Ain't No Cure for Love," whose title he had come up with after reading about L.A.'s AIDS crisis.

Famous Blue Raincoat was released in 1987. It featured nine songs,* including a few that Judy Collins had previously covered ("Bird on the Wire," "Joan of Arc," "Famous Blue Raincoat") and a few that Warnes—like Collins in the past—would release before Leonard had recorded his own versions. It was to some degree a tribute album, but really it was a Jennifer Warnes album whose songs all happened to have the same writer. Her impeccable vocal brought out the lyricism of Leonard's songs. By removing the factor that

---

* There were four more on the 2007 twentieth-anniversary reissue.

some people seemed to have problems with—Leonard's voice—
they sounded smoother, more melodious, and with Beck's polished
production, more contemporary. "She transformed grappa into
Chardonnay," said the review in *Saturday Night*. "A perfect elixir for
mid-Eighties audiences."[16]

Warnes's album sold three quarters of a million copies in the U.S.
It went gold in Canada and spawned a single, "Ain't No Cure for
Love," that was a hit in both the adult-contemporary and the country music charts. The artwork on the inner sleeve was a drawing
that Leonard had made: a hand—Leonard's—holding out a torch to
Warnes, with the caption "Jenny sings Lenny." He was happy and
grateful to pass the torch on to her. With *Famous Blue Raincoat*, he
had finally succeeded in hiding his own voice and giving his songs
entirely over to the female voice.

Leonard was writing songs for his own new album. Once again it
was a slow and painful process. Over a glass of brandy, he complained
to Roshi how difficult it was and asked him what he ought to do. Roshi answered, "You look up at the moon, you open your mouth and
you sing." So Leonard sang, recording as he went along over a span of
a year and a half, running up studio bills in three different countries
as he bounced back and forth between his lives in Paris, Montreal
and L.A., leaving a paper trail of abandoned words as he went. He
was happy to hear, as he had been before, that the songs he had managed to write in the past were getting on without him. Aside from
Jennifer Warnes, Nick Cave had covered "Avalanche" on his first album with the Bad Seeds. Leonard's children were telling him that he
had become something of a cult figure among younger musicians: Ian
McCulloch and Suzanne Vega were singing his praises in interviews,
and the British band Sisters of Mercy, having taken their name from
one of his songs, had nicknamed their drum machine Doktor Avalanche. Leonard also learned that there was another musical based on
his work being made in New York, called *Sincerely, L. Cohen*, its title
taken from the closing words of "Famous Blue Raincoat."

It was intriguing, this resurgence of a song that Leonard had always had problems with—that he had "never been satisfied with, never really nailed the lyric, always felt there was something about the song that was unclear."[17] His mother had liked the melody though. "I remember playing the tune for her, in her kitchen, and her perking up her ears while she was doing something else and saying, 'That's a nice tune.'"[18] And the song had held up and served him well, just like the old Burberry raincoat that inspired it. It seemed a lifetime ago that he had bought the coat in London, when he was a twenty-five-year-old writing his first novel and sleeping on a cot in a cold Hampstead boardinghouse. A girl Leonard had pursued during his first London winter had told him that it made him look like a spider—which might, he thought, be why she refused to go to Greece with him. "It hung more heroically when I took out the lining," he wrote in his liner notes to *Greatest Hits* (1975), "and achieved glory when the frayed sleeves were repaired with a little leather. Things were clear. I knew how to dress in those days." The coat was stolen from the loft where Marianne had lived when she visited New York, while he was recording his first album. Leonard said, "I wasn't wearing it very much toward the end."

In September 1986, while in Paris visiting Dominique Issermann, Leonard recorded a new song called "Take This Waltz." The lyrics were Leonard's English adaptation (assisted by a Spanish-speaking Costa Rican girlfriend) of a poem by Federico Garcia Lorca. It was for a compilation album, *Poetas en Nueva York*, that would mark the fiftieth anniversary of Lorca's death. It had been hard work—it took a hundred and fifty hours, Leonard said—but it was more than a translation, it was a poem in itself, and one that seemed to reflect Leonard as much as Lorca. For example, Leonard rendered Lorca's macabre image of a forest of dried pigeons as "a tree where doves go to die." After recording the song, Leonard flew to Granada to attend a gala in Lorca's honor. Then he flew back to the U.S. to take a role in the TV detective series *Miami Vice*. Over the years the program had invited an eclectic list of guest stars, such as Frank Zappa and James Brown, to make cameo appearances. Leonard's character, the French head of Interpol, was on screen for barely a minute, murmuring in a dark, French manner into a telephone, but it had the effect that Leonard desired when he took it on: it impressed his now-teenage offspring.

Leonard's relationship with Dominique, though, was going the way of all flesh. In 1987, back in Paris again, he wrote in a poem, titled "My Honor":*

> *My honor is in bad shape*
> *I'm crawling at a woman's feet*
> *She doesn't give an inch.*
> *I look good for fifty-two*
> *but fifty-two is fifty-two*
> *I'm not even a Zen master. . . .*

He was nothing more than

> *that asshole in a blue summer suit*
> *who couldn't take it any longer*

"Then I broke down," said Leonard, "and went to a monastery. . . . I thought, I don't have to do a record any more, I'll be a monk."[19]

Leonard had gone to the monastery to be nowhere and to be no one. He had gone to sit in this austere place for hour upon hour with no goal. It said in the literature that if he were able to sit goal-less for long enough, all the versions of himself would arise and, having aris-

---

* Published in the book *You Do Not Have to Love Me*, 1996, with lithographs by Josette Trépanier.

en, decide there was nothing to stick around for and take off, leaving only perfect peace. He had gone to be with Roshi, whom he loved, and who both cared deeply and deeply didn't care who Leonard was. Leonard had gone to work hard, to bang nails, to fix and mend things, at least physically. Roshi knew how much Leonard liked austerity, solitariness and work. He instructed him to go and find a tennis court, and play.

Eighteen

The Places Where
I Used to Play

Iggy Pop has a story about Leonard Cohen. Iggy was in Los Angeles, recording an album, when one night Leonard phoned. "Leonard said, 'Come over, I've got a personal ad from a girl who says she wants a lover who will combine the raw energy of Iggy Pop with the elegant wit of Leonard Cohen. I think we should reply to her as a team.'" Iggy said, "'Leonard, I can't, I'm married, you're going to have to do this yourself.' I guess he did," says Iggy. "I don't know if he got laid."

Iggy Pop was curious as to the outcome of a reply you sent a woman seeking love through a personal ad.

"[Smiles] As I remember it, I bumped into Iggy at a session being produced by Don Was, a friend of mine, and I showed him the clipping that someone had sent me from a San Francisco newspaper. We decided to reply, and to certify its authenticity, Don took a Polaroid of Iggy and myself sitting together in my kitchen. We spoke to the young woman—at least I spoke to her—on the telephone. But there was no personal involvement."

Leonard surely felt an empathy with this woman who named her-self "Fearless" and whose ideals, when it came to romantic partners, seemed almost as formidable as his own. If nothing else, answering the ad with Iggy was an exercise in making the impossible possible—if only for a moment, and for someone other than himself. Leonard had been living with impossibilities for some time, one of them being the idea that he might ever finish another album. For more than three years he had been writing, unwriting and rewriting songs, then, having finally deemed something ready to record, after listening to himself singing it, he would decide that it did not sound honest and needed to be rewritten yet again. Leonard had been serious when he spoke about never wanting to make another album, and the thought of giving it up and going to a monastery was certainly a possibility. However arduous that existence might be, it had nothing on the hard labor that songwriting had become.

Various Positions, the album he had hoped would resurrect his career and his confidence as a songwriter and help take care of his financial responsibilities, had done none of these things. It took "a great deal of will to keep your work straight," he told Mat Snow in the *Guardian*, but "with all the will in the world you can't keep your life straight. Because you're too much of an asshole. . . . As you get older, you get very interested in your work, because that's where you can refine your character, that's where you can order your world. You're stuck with the consequences of your actions, but in your work you can go back."[1] He had left behind him, he said, a "shipwreck of ten or fifteen years of broken families and hotel rooms for some kind of shining idea that my voice was important, that I had a meaning in the cosmos. . . . Well, after enough lonely nights you don't care whether you have a meaning in the cosmos or not."[2]

But still he worked. He lived alone and he recorded alone—no musicians, no producer, just an engineer—slowly and painstakingly, at a glacial pace. Leonard was spending long periods in Montreal, so several of his new songs were recorded there, in Studio Tempo. Anjani Thomas—who by coincidence was also living in Montreal at that time; her boyfriend, Ian Terry, was the studio's head engineer— added backing vocals to some of them. "It really was a solo affair," said Leonard, "because I had the conception very clearly in mind, I knew exactly the way I wanted it to sound, and I was using a lot of synthesised instruments."[3] But by 1987, Leonard had reached a point where he could use an outside pair of ears. Having been impressed by his work on *Famous Blue Raincoat*, he called Roscoe Beck and asked him to book a studio in L.A.

Beck remembers the first time he heard the song "First We Take Manhattan," which Leonard had given Jennifer Warnes for her album. What stood out was its "harmonic sophistication. It was no longer just folk songs on guitar. Now that Leonard was writing on keyboards, he was writing from a different perspective." Leonard had become used to playing his new songs alone and was keen to retain as much of that spare, unembellished feel as possible on the album. "He wasn't sure at first whether we were going to hire a band," Beck says. "I think it was a mutual decision not to and to record them as they were, just as he was playing them on his keyboard." Leonard had upgraded from his ninety-nine-dollar Casio to a Technics keyboard, but it was still a primitive synthesizer with no individual outputs, making it a challenge to record. The engineers, technicians, keyboard players and track performers listed in the credits far outnumber the conventional musicians. There were drum machines, synthesized strings and push-button cha-cha rhythms, as well as some of the most singular keyboard playing to have ever made it onto a major-label album, such as the proudly plinked one-finger solo on "Tower of Song." Toward the end they brought in "a few last people to sweeten it," says Beck, including Sneaky Pete Kleinow on pedal steel on "I Can't Forget," John Bilezikjian on oud on "Everybody Knows," and Raffi Hakopian on violin on "Take This Waltz," the song Leonard had recorded in

Paris for Lorca's fiftieth-anniversary album. Jennifer Warnes came in to sing on several tracks, including the catchy, retro-pop *"dee-do dum-dum"*s in "Tower of Song."

Eight songs had been completed, but an album that was eight songs and forty minutes long looked a good deal more undersized on compact disc than it would have done on a vinyl LP. So Leonard tried for a ninth. He recorded a new version of "Anthem" with Beck, and strings and overdubs were added before Leonard once again pulled the song. They also recorded an early, very different version of "Waiting for the Miracle." This Leonard liked. He called Beck to say how happy he was with it. Three weeks later, he called again to say that he had rewritten the lyrics and wanted to redo the vocal. In the studio, Beck discovered he had also rewritten the melody, "and it didn't match up with the track [they'd] cut." They kept working at the song, long into the night. "We cut several vocals until he got very tired. Finally he said, 'I'm done, comp it'" (meaning, make a master vocal out of the best bits of his various vocal takes). Leonard found a place to lie down and sleep while Beck worked. "Just as I had it together, Leonard woke up, walked into the control room and said, 'Well, let's hear it.' I played it for him and he said, 'I hate it.' He left and that was that."

The song went through several more changes before it was finished. At one point Leonard gave it to Sharon Robinson—although they had not worked together since the 1980 tour, they had remained close friends—who came back with "a completely different version," says Beck, "that I played guitar on. I really liked Sharon's version, but that didn't end up being the final version either" (which was the one that would appear on his 1992 album *The Future*). Another Cohen-Robinson cowrite made it onto this album. On a visit to her house, he had handed her a sheet of verses—a litany of world-weary wisdom and cynicism—and asked her if she could write a melody. She did, and it became the song "Everybody Knows."

What struck Beck most strongly when working with Leonard on the album was the change in his voice. "I thought, 'Wow, Leonard has found a whole new place to sing from.' The baritone element in his voice was always there—on the song 'Avalanche,' for instance, he's singing deep in his chest—but here he was really making use of it and his singing voice was becoming more narrative." His delivery was laconic, almost recitative, like an old French *chansonnier* who had mistakenly stumbled into a disco. It was urbane and unhurried; as one UK critic would put it, Leonard lingered on every word "like a kerb crawler."[4] His voice was as deep and dry, sly and beguiling, as his songs. His new album had everything. It was polished and mannered but very human, it was brutally honest but very accessible and its songs covered all the angles: sex, sophistication, love, longing and humor—particularly humor.

> *I was born like this*
> *I had no choice*
> *I was born with the gift*
> *of a golden voice*

"TOWER OF SONG," *I'M YOUR MAN*

The humor had always been there, but many had failed to see it—it was dark and ironic and generally aimed at himself. But the gags were never as overt as on this album.

I'm Your Man was released in February 1988 in the UK and Europe and two months later in the U.S. and Canada. The title track presents the prophet as lounge lizard, falling to his knees, howling at the sky, trying to figure out what it is that women want and ready to give it to them in whatever form they might require. While "Ain't No Cure for Love," a sing-along about love, sex and God, was inspired by reports of the AIDS crisis, it was imbued with Leonard's own take

on love: that it is a lethal wound that a man can no more avoid than
Jesus could the Cross. "I Can't Forget," which started life as a song
about the exodus of the Jews from Egypt, has Leonard moving on
once again but unable now to remember his motive, having spent so
long living in the myth of himself. "Everybody Knows" is an infec-
tious paean to pessimism. "First We Take Manhattan" is very likely
the only Eurodisco song to reference the war between the sexes and
the Holocaust. "Tower of Song" is about the hard, solitary, captive
life of a writer (going so far as to evoke a concentration camp in the
line "They're moving us tomorrow to that tower down the track") but
substitutes self-mockery for the usual self-indulgence of this type of
song: he was still "crazy for love" but now he ached "in the places
where [he] used to play" and in spite of all his hard work, none of
it was of any significance to women, to God or even to pop-music
posterity; his writing room was still a hundred floors below Hank
Williams."

The photo on the front sleeve shows Leonard dressed in a smart
pin-striped suit, wearing big French-film-star sunglasses, his hair
slicked back, his face as unsmiling and impenetrable as that of a
Mafia don. In his hand, where a gun might be, or a microphone, is
a half-eaten banana. It was shot at the former Ford Motor Company
assembly plant in Wilmington, California, a gigantic windowed room
with a vast steel-girdered indoor parking lot that is often used as a
movie location. Jennifer Warnes was there shooting the video for her
version of "First We Take Manhattan," in which Leonard had agreed
to appear. Sharon Weisz, the publicist for Warnes's record label, was
on the set, shooting stills, when the steel doors of the truck-sized elevator opened and Leonard stepped out with the banana. "I pivoted
and took one picture of him," says Weisz, "and forgot about it. When
I got back the proof sheet and saw it, I thought it was really funny and
had a print made and sent it to him. A few weeks later he called and
said, 'What would you think if I put it on the cover of my album?' I

didn't even know he was making an album. I asked him what he was calling it, and he said *I'm Your Man*, and I started laughing uncontrollably." Although the pose was a lucky accident, Leonard could not fail to recognize how perfectly it summed up the heroics and absurdity that went into the album's creation.

I'm Your Man rebranded Leonard, not least among younger fans, from dark, tortured poet to officially cool. Although it sounded different from Leonard's early albums, it had that feeling of instant familiarity, rightness and durability that makes for a classic. It was preceded in January 1988 by a single, "First We Take Manhattan"—one of the two songs on the album already familiar to many listeners thanks to the success of Jennifer Warnes's album. *Famous Blue Raincoat* had definitely helped pave the way for Leonard's eighth album (in America in particular) and *I'm Your Man* sped along it, propelled by its more upbeat songs and contemporary sound. The album was a success—Leonard's biggest since the early seventies and biggest in America since his debut. It made No. 1 in several European countries, went platinum in Norway, gold in Canada and silver in the UK, where it sold three hundred thousand copies before it was released in the U.S. It even sold well in America. Leonard waggishly attributed this to the payola he sent the marketing department of Columbia in New York.

It was a scheme he hatched up with Sharon Weisz, whom he had asked to do publicity for the album. "He had kind of an odd relationship with the record label, since they had refused to put out his previous record, *Various Positions*, and he was very cynical about it," says Weisz. "So I was trying to figure out how he was going to work with these people and how receptive they were going to be to a new record by him." They did not appear overenthused, judging by the poor turnout of people from Columbia Records at a party in his honor in New York, where the international division presented him with a Crystal Globe award for sales of more than five million albums outside the U.S. "From that point on, it sort of became the two of us against the world," says Weisz. She came up with a list of names of the various Columbia promotion reps across the U.S., and Leonard sent each of them a hand-signed letter.

"Good morning," Leonard typed on a plain, gray sheet of paper, dated April 1, 1988. "I don't quite know how this is done so please bear with me. I have a new record, I'M YOUR MAN, coming out next week. It is already a hit in Europe and I'm on my way there now for a major concert tour. I know I can count on your support for this new record in the U.S., and if you can make a couple of phone calls on my behalf, I would really appreciate it. I've enclosed a couple of bucks to cover the calls. Thank you in advance for your help," the letter concluded. "Regards, Leonard Cohen. PS. There's more where this came from." ("We went back and forth on whether the dollar bills should be brand-new or really old," Weisz remembers, "and we settled for the kind that looked really mangy.")

I'm Your Man was lauded by critics on both sides of the Atlantic. John Rockwell in the *New York Times* called it "a masterpiece"; Mark Cooper wrote in UK rock magazine *Q* that it was Leonard's best album since the midseventies. Leonard had perfected "the art of being Leonard Cohen . . . the usual gorgeous melodies and an ageing poet taking himself very seriously, until he twinkles."[5] "All the major critics of the era reviewed it," says Weisz, "and the reviews were extraordinary." Those who seemed to think that Leonard had gone away hailed it as a comeback.

On February 7 Leonard left for Europe on a promotional tour to do interviews. There was great anticipation for the concert tour, which was due to begin in April. Leonard went back to Los Angeles to prepare for it, but there was a serious problem. His manager was dying. Marty Machat was gravely ill with lung cancer, and although it was clear to almost everyone else that his condition was terminal, Machat was convinced he was going to pull through. In early March, with only weeks to go before the tour began, Leonard was getting anxious. A large sum of money had been paid into Machat & Machat's attorney account as a tour advance, and Leonard needed access to it. He called Marty. Avril, Marty's lover, picked up the phone.

Says Steven Machat, "Dad was very quiet, very shy, Leonard was very quiet, very dark, and in the middle of their relationship was Avril." Machat dismisses his father's romantic partner as "a woman who Dad gave money to, to do Leonard's PR" and someone whom he "kept around because he thought Leonard Cohen wanted her around." Steven Machat did not like Leonard either. "I never liked him from the moment go; he never looks you in the eyes, ever. He plays victim." But Marty Machat, he says, loved Leonard and would have done more for him than for anyone. Since this presumably included his son, it might not have helped relations between Steven and Leonard. "My dad would get on the phone with Leonard. My dad didn't give a fuck about anyone, he wanted the money, but Leonard he would sit there with, he'd listen to Leonard. If Leonard got sick, my dad would be upset—'Oh, Leonard's got a cold.' It was interesting. When Leonard went to Israel making believe he was going to fight in the war, all of a sudden my dad rediscovered that he was of Jewish blood."

Steven knew that his father did not have long to live. In his mind he saw vultures circling and among them he included Leonard. But Leonard, on the eve of a major tour for what was potentially the most commercial album of his career, was doing his best to take care of business. Steven Machat says that Leonard turned to him for help and that, for his father's sake, he agreed. Perhaps he did, although the evidence seems to indicate that Leonard turned to lawyers for advice and to women for help. With Marty's blessing, Avril went with Leonard to the bank to withdraw the money he needed. Kelley Lynch, Marty's secretary and assistant, stepped up and offered to take care of administrative matters for the tour. When Marty Machat died on March 19, 1988, aged sixty-seven, Lynch took various files on Leon-

ard from the offices of Machat & Machat that the lawyers said could
be taken legally, including documents relating to the publishing company that Marty Machat had set up for Leonard. Lynch took the files
to L.A., where she set up shop and began making herself as indispensable to Leonard as Marty had once been. At one point Leonard
and Kelley became lovers. Eventually she became his manager.

Meanwhile, Roscoe Beck had been putting together Leonard's
touring band. Leonard had asked him to come along as his musical
director, but Beck was scheduled to produce albums by Eric Johnson
and Ute Lemper. So Leonard went on the road with a band made up
of Steve Meador and John Bilezikjian, both of whom had played on
Leonard's 1979–80 tour; Steve Zirkel (bass); Bob Metzger (guitar and
pedal steel); Bob Furgo; Tom McMorran (both keyboards); and two
new backing singers, Julie Christensen and Perla Batalla.

They were quite a pair—Julie a striking, statuesque blonde who,
for half of the eighties, had sung with her then husband Chris D.
in an edgy L.A. punk-roots band called the Divine Horsemen, and
Perla a petite, sparkling brunette of South American ancestry, with
her own band and a background in jazz and rock. Both were stylish
and mischievous, and accomplished singers who had sung together in
the past. Christensen was the first of the two to be hired. Beck had
known her from Austin, where she sang jazz and occasionally played
gigs with Passenger. Christensen can remember seeing Passenger
when they returned from Leonard's 1979–80 tour and noticing how
"they all came back changed; everyone had some kind of aura around
them of having become citizens of the world." So there was no hesitation when Beck invited her to audition for Leonard's 1988 tour. Henry Lewy, overseeing the rehearsals with Beck, was impressed with
not just her singing but her knowledge of Leonard's songs; she had
sung them at the piano with her mother since she was a young girl.
"I didn't have to audition for Leonard," says Christensen, "but he
wanted to meet me, because being on the road is like this marriage

that's going on." Over lunch, Leonard told her, "This is going to be a very difficult tour; we'll be playing four or five nights a week in different cities." Christensen laughed and told him, "'Leonard, I had just got done doing CBGB's and the Mab and these places where I had to pee by the side of the road and change in awful restrooms.' I was like, 'Come on, let's roll up our sleeves and go.'" Leonard was charmed.

When Beck called Perla to audition, having not grown up playing Leonard Cohen songs, she went straight to the record store and bought as many cassettes of his as she could find. This being America, there were not many. But Roscoe told her not to prepare anything, "because," she says, "99 percent of this was Leonard's feelings about me as a person. Which made me nervous. I remember walking in, dressed in white from head to toe, and Leonard was there completely in black. We just looked at each other and laughed and that was it." Again, Leonard was charmed. "But the true magic happened when Julie and I started singing. We read each other's minds musically; we'd never say which part we'd take, our voices were constantly mixing. Together we were a real force as a backup singing pair, and it showed onstage." The day they left for Europe, Perla's mother and father came to the airport to see her off. "It was my first time out of the country. My dad was really an old-fashioned kind of guy, very ill, but an elegant man, who dressed in a suit—he was like Leonard in that way—and it was a big deal to him that I was leaving for Europe. He asked Leonard to take care of me and they shook hands and Leonard promised him he would."

The tour—fifty-nine concerts in three months—began on April 5, 1988, in Germany. "There was a good feeling among all the people on that tour," Julie says. "Leonard just had this way of being really like the camp counselor. We would do this thing on that tour where, if we were jet-lagged and wide-awake in the middle of the night, we would hang a hanger on the door to indicate that we were awake and it was okay to come in, and there were several times when I would go to Leonard's room and just have snacks and chat." Perla remembers Leonard seeming "very happy, and very playful. A lot of people don't know that side of him, but Leonard was one of the funniest people I've ever met, so hilarious at times you just want to crack up." When she and Julie came up with a spontaneous vaudeville routine onstage, Leonard happily played along with them. During the Spanish leg of the tour, Leonard had Perla translate for the audience what he said between songs, which, depending on his mood and his red wine intake, could be long, complex and mortifying—and terrifying for a woman who had been raised speaking English. "Every night we were on the edge of our seats to see where he was going to go," Perla says. "It was so much fun, and as risky as live theater sometimes."

In Europe, Leonard was often mobbed by fans. "Women would follow us around," Julie says, "and men for that matter, and go, 'Where is Leonard staying?'" In Sweden they had to fight their way through a crowd of teenage girls to get on the ferry to Denmark. Perla says, "If Leonard was in the street or in a café people would come up to him; there was no privacy whatsoever. But he was very happy. We'd take long walks through the streets together and he was in his element, I think, delighted with his success." In the UK, the BBC made a documentary about him, *Songs from the Life of Leonard Cohen*, and Buckingham Palace sent him an invitation to appear at the Prince's Trust concert, alongside Eric Clapton, Elton John, Dire Straits, the Bee Gees and Peter Gabriel. Julie remembers, "Peter Gabriel came up to Leonard with a couple of albums for Leonard to sign. He was like a little disciple: 'Can you sign this one? And this one's for my son.'" Prince Charles, whose charity the concert benefited, was also a Leonard Cohen fan. "The orchestration is fantastic and the words, the lyrics and everything," the prince said in a British television interview. "He's a remarkable man and he has this incredibly laid-back, gravelly voice."[6] In Iceland, Leonard was received by the president of the country.

On the eve of Independence Day they flew back to the U.S. By now Leonard had become used to the difference between the European and American tour experience. But the Carnegie Hall concert on July 6 could not have gone much better. The show was sold out and the media had come in droves. "I remember thinking that if they dropped a bomb on the place, American rock music criticism would be over," says Sharon Weisz, "because of the number of journalists who had requested tickets to this show." The *New York Post* reviewer Ira Mayer wrote, "If ever there is an award for emotional laureate of the pop world, Leonard Cohen will be the uncontested winner. He gave vent—magnificently—to all the doubts, fears, longings, memories and regrets that comprise love in the twentieth century."

Following two West Coast shows, in Berkeley and L.A., there was a three-month break before the North American tour resumed in October. At Halloween, in Texas, they performed in a TV studio for *Austin City Limits*, a popular long-running concert program that airs on PBS. On November 16 the tour ended, as it had begun, in New York, where the *New York Times* named *I'm Your Man* its album of the year. Leonard stayed on in New York. Adam and Lorca were living there now and Hanukkah was just a couple of weeks away. Leonard rented a room in a hotel in one of Manhattan's less fashionable neighborhoods and began preparing for the holiday.

The eighties had not been easy on many of the recording artists who had come up in the sixties. They tended to flounder in a decade when style took the place of substance, yuppies replaced hippies, shiny CDs made vinyl LPs obsolete and the drugs of choice were designed to boost egos, not to expand consciousness. Although Leonard had had a tough time of it during the first half of the eighties, by the end of the decade he had adapted far more successfully than most of his near-contemporaries. He had the style, the beats, the synthesiz-

ers and the videos—two excellent videos made by Dominique Issermann, to whom *I'm Your Man* had been dedicated. (Written around
a picture of a man and woman ballroom dancing were the words "All
these songs are for you, D.I.")

I'm Your Man had outsold all of his earlier albums. "In terms of my
so-called career," Leonard said, "it certainly was a rebirth. But it was
hard to consider it a rebirth on a personal level. It was made under
the usual dismal and morbid conditions."[7] Suzanne was suing him
over money, and his romantic relationship with Dominique was un-
raveling. This was a dance whose complicated steps Leonard knew
well: the intimacy and the distance, the separations and reconcilia-
tions, running on the spot and, when the music stopped, good-bye.
Romance would often be replaced by an enduring friendship; Leonard appears to have remained good friends with many of his former
lovers, remarkably few of whom seem to bear him any ill will. But
the more immediate result of the end of a long love affair would be a
rush of freedom, which gave way to depression, from which Leonard
might emerge with a poem or a song.

Leonard has claimed in several interviews—and confirmed it in
the closing verse of "Chelsea Hotel #2"—that he is not a sentimental or a nostalgic man, that he does not look back. Religion would
validate this as a healthy position: when Lot's wife looked back at
Sodom she was turned into a pillar of salt. As a writer, although he
tended to look inside himself or at his immediate environs, Leonard also looked back at lovers from whom he had parted. In *The
Favorite Game*, Leonard's fictional alter ego writes to the girl he
loved in fond anticipation of their separation: "Dearest Shell, if you
let me I'd always keep you 400 miles away and write you pretty poems and letters. . . . I'm afraid to live any place but in expectation."
As a writer Leonard seemed to thrive on this paradox of distance
and intimacy. As a man, it was more complicated. Often it seemed
to make him wretched, and, as a wretch, he turned to God. But as

Roshi told him, "You can't live in God's world. There are no restaurants or toilets."[8]

Back in L.A., with little to keep Leonard occupied, his depression reappeared. It came "in cycles," he said[9]—sometimes even when things were going well, which would make him feel ashamed. "One might think that success helps you fix up your personal problems," he said, "but it doesn't work that way."[10] When things were not going well, though, depression could send him into a serious tailspin.

"I never knew where it was coming from and I tried everything to shake it, but nothing worked."

What did you try?

"Well, I tried all that stuff, all the antidepressants before Prozac, like Demerol, desipramine, the MAO inhibitors."

Valium? The morphines?

"No, not morphine. That would have been deadly. But I tried everything right up to Zoloft and Wellbutrin. I tried everything they had. Most of it made me feel worse than when I started."

So, you're an expert in all things pharmaceutical when it comes to depression?

"I think I am. But nothing worked."

Leonard told the actress Anjelica Huston, "When I was on Prozac my relationship with the landscape improved. I actually stopped thinking about myself for a minute or two." He stopped taking it because, he said, "it didn't seem to have any effect whatsoever on my melancholy, my dark vision," and because "what it does is completely annihilate the sexual drive."[11] He had friends who had recommended psychotherapy, but, he said, "I never deeply believed. I had no conviction that this model was workable. And having observed a number of friends who for many years had undergone this treatment, it began to be clear that it wasn't terribly effective for these people, so I was never convinced in the value it would have for me."[12] It might be that Leonard felt that, as a former debating society president and a man of words, he could run rings around anyone trying to administer the talking cure. There were also his dignity and an almost British stiff upper lip to contend with. Leonard was not the kind of man to give someone else the responsibility of removing the suffering from him. Amphetamines helped, if he didn't use them too much for too long—though now that he was in his fifties he was finding them hard to take at all. Drinking was also helpful, as was sex—Leonard had become something of an expert at self-medication. But what seemed to work best of all was a disciplined routine. The long hours of meditation and study Leonard had put in with Roshi had not cured him of depression but had helped him view the situation from a more useful perspective. He had come to recognize that his depression "had to do with an isolation of"[13] himself—an isolation he had tried to address through his various spiritual pursuits. The hard part was making it work in the world of restaurants and toilets.

For the first time in a long while, the world was treating him well, as regards his work. The success of *I'm Your Man* had pushed Leonard's *Best Of* album back again onto the UK charts, and his American label had been inspired to give a belated release to his slighted last album, *Various Positions*. In Canada his poetry was being celebrated in an exhibition at the Library and Archives. Both Leonard and his music appeared in a Canadian television program called *A Moving Picture*, a dance fantasy that featured the National Ballet of Canada. In February 1989 Leonard was in New York, where he was invited to perform on the U.S. TV show *Night Music*, cohosted by David Sanborn and Jools Holland. One of its young producers was Hal Willner.

"Like they say about the Kennedy assassination," Willner says, "you remember the first time you heard Leonard Cohen. It was on WDAS in Philadelphia, I was very young, and 'Suzanne' came on the radio, and there was nothing like it. Hearing Leonard, I think even more than Dylan, I was able to see music as poetry. When I moved to New York, I had a little internship job at Warner Bros., around the time they were doing *Death of a Ladies' Man,* and I remember seeing what a controversial figure he was within the industry. They either got it or they didn't, there was nobody who was in the middle. That record had a very big effect on me, and Doc Pomus loved that record too; we used to listen to it all the time." Willner considered *I'm Your Man* a "masterpiece." He had gone to see Leonard's last show in New York at the Beacon Theatre and thought it "one of the most perfect concerts I've ever seen. Since he was doing TV for the album, I jumped at having him on the show."

Willner had become known for curating albums and performances that featured eclectic ensembles of musicians and singers performing material written by another artist. As Willner put it, he was "trying to combine things that are sort of fantasy." He took the same approach to Leonard's appearance on *Night Music.* "Leonard said he wanted to do 'Tower of Song,' but I had a fantasy in my head of doing 'Who by Fire' with Leonard and Sonny Rollins, who was another guest on the show. Usually when people jam they go with up-tempo things; that song had a spiritual aspect, but I knew that people would relate." When he mentioned his idea to Leonard, "there was this silence. Then he said—tentatively—'Will he do that?'" At the rehearsal, Leonard appeared wary. Sonny Rollins was watching him closely as if trying to read him. Leonard looked behind him: Julie and Perla were there, watching his back, and they smiled. Leonard started singing "Who by Fire." Then, Willner recalls, "Sonny Rollins, who was sitting there staring at Leonard the whole time, picked up his horn and started wailing in a different kind of understanding of the song." After the rehearsal, says Julie, Rollins—"this saxophone colossus, this master"—came up to her and asked, quietly, "Do you think Mr. Cohen likes what I'm doing?"

Back in Los Angeles, a heat wave had set in. Leonard was upstairs in his duplex, in the corner of the living room, playing his Technics synthesizer—something he spent much of his time doing when he was not needed elsewhere. He was happy enough in his cell with its bare floorboards and its plain white walls, no pictures or distractions. The windows were open, letting in the sweltering heat. He had thought about installing air-conditioning but would not get around to it until the next decade. He was interrupted by the phone ringing. It was a young woman friend, Sean Dixon, who sounded distressed and wanted Leonard to come over. They had met when Leonard was working at Rock Steady Studios on *I'm Your Man;* Dixon was the receptionist. One day Leonard had gone to the studio with Leanne Ungar to pick up the master tapes, since they planned to mix them in another studio. When they arrived, Dixon was there on her own, nursing a stray dog she had just found in the street. Leonard decided on the spot that they would stay and mix at Rock Steady. "Every day," Dixon remembers, "I would come in with this little lost dog which was very depressed. And we would just sit there when Leonard wasn't working and hold this little dog, while he talked and thought about what he wanted to do."

Dixon was actually phoning Leonard about a cat. Her roommate had gone back to Texas, leaving her with Hank, a long-haired cat of indeterminate age, which was now very sick. The vets could not figure out what was wrong with it. The enema and IV fluids they had given him on the previous two visits had not helped. Hank had crawled under the Murphy bed in her small apartment. Dixon thought he was dying. The next morning she went to take him back to the vet, but her car was gone; it had been stolen. She says, "I pleaded with Leonard, 'Can't you please just come and look at him? I don't know what to do.'"

Leonard drove over and Dixon pulled the cat out from under the bed. "He looked horrible, he was covered with all this medicine he had spit up and he hadn't groomed in days. But right away Leonard said, 'Oh, I don't think this is a dying animal.' He said, 'I'm going to chant to him.' I thought, 'Oh my God, Leonard is such a freak,' but he was, 'No, really, it vibrates all the internal organs, it's a really good thing.' I was desperate so I said, 'Okay, fine, you do whatever you want to do.' So he put Hank on the bed.

"There was a chair at the end of the bed, right up against the bed, and Leonard sat and leaned over, put his mouth right up against Hank's forehead, and he just chanted like they chant at the monastery, '*Ooooooooooooooooooom*,' very, very deeply, way lower than he sings, like a rumble. He did that for ten minutes—and he's allergic to cats so his nose was running and his eyes were running and he was getting stuffed up, but he just kept doing it. And Hank just sat there, didn't try to get away or scratch him or anything. Then finally Leonard stopped and said, 'That's it, darling, that'll fix him up,' with total confidence." He gave her $1,000, insisting that she use it to get another car, and left. Hank slunk back under the bed. "But in the middle of the night I heard him get up and wander into the kitchen and I heard a lot of strangled sounds coming from the cat box. The next thing I heard in the morning was Hank crunching away on his food. I couldn't believe he was eating, he hadn't eaten in days. Then I looked at the cat box, expecting to see something really horrible, but the weird thing was there wasn't anything—the miracle of the cat box. And the cat was fine. Apart from the odd hairball he was never sick again."

Dixon witnessed another demonstration of Leonard's skills at his house, when his kitchen was invaded by ants. "They were all over the counter and I was looking for something to spray them with, and he said, 'No. I'll get them to go. Watch.' He leaned over, pointed his finger and admonished them: 'You get out of my kitchen this instant, all of you, right now, get going!' He did that for a few minutes and, I swear, the ants all left and didn't come back. A cat whisperer and an ant whisperer."

Two miracles. Enough to qualify Leonard for sainthood. He had also, miraculously, found another love and muse—a beautiful blond actress, smart, successful and almost thirty years younger than him. "I don't think anyone masters the heart," said Leonard. "It continues to cook like a shish kebab, bubbling and sizzling in everyone's breast."[14] Or it does on the flames in the ovens in the tower of song.

Nineteen

Jeremiah in Tin Pan Alley

"Interestingly, he thinks we first met when I was five or six years old," says Rebecca De Mornay. Leonard would have been in his early thirties. It was in the late sixties, in England, when Rebecca attended a boarding school named Summerhill. A friend of Leonard had a child there and Leonard had gone to give a little concert. Summerhill was an early experiment in progressive education, a school with no rules; Leonard remembered seeing a female teacher walking about the place, topless. He also remembered seeing Rebecca. "I said, 'How could you remember me from then?' He said, 'It was something about your light.' Amazing, but Leonard would remember light, and he doesn't tend to make things up."

Rebecca was born in California and raised there until her father, the conservative talk-show host Wally George, left her bohemian mother. From then, she spent her childhood on the move, from Austria to Australia and several points in between. Rebecca's mother had been a Leonard Cohen fan and would play her his records when she was small. "I remember going to sleep listening to his music, almost as a lullaby—'Suzanne,' 'The Stranger Song,' 'One of Us Cannot Be Wrong.'" When Rebecca started playing the guitar, his were some of the first songs she learned, and when she decided to become a singer-songwriter in her midteens, his songs were an influence. In her late teens, Rebecca turned to acting and moved back to California, where she started her successful movie career at the age of twenty-two in Francis Ford Coppola's *One from the Heart*.

The first time Leonard and Rebecca met as adults was in the mideighties, at a party thrown by film director Robert Altman, another Leonard Cohen fan. Rebecca, having recognized Leonard from across the room, remembers that she went over to him "and sat down and proceeded to talk to him, which is actually very unlike me with someone I don't know. I just had this feeling I could and should talk to him. I don't know what I said, but he seemed a little skeptical. I remember a great reticence on his part—I couldn't tell if he was shy or wary of me. There's that saying, 'Trust the art, not the artist,' which is almost always true, but when I met Leonard, the person was as interesting, if not more so, than the art."

Their paths crossed again in 1987 in Los Angeles at a Roy Orbison concert that was being recorded for a PBS TV special, *A Black and White Night*. Among Orbison's guests were Bruce Springsteen, Tom Waits, Jackson Browne and Jennifer Warnes. Leonard was in the audience. So, separately, was Rebecca. "I saw Leonard and again I went up to him: 'Hey, remember we met?' And again there was the skeptical look. It was funny, as if he anticipated that making a connection with me might wind up some kind of arduous enterprise. Which maybe it did." Rebecca laughs. "I said, 'You know, I'd really like to get together and talk.' He simply said, 'All right,' and it sounded like a reluctant surrender."

So they got together and talked, and continued to do so. "We had this friendship at first that lasted two or three years. Strictly a friendship; I had a boyfriend," says Rebecca. They talked about art and work, in particular Leonard's. "I ask a lot of questions if somebody interests me and he enjoyed talking to me about his process." Slowly, imperceptibly, it became a courtship. "It started to become this meaningful relationship to me; we started talking about our real lives, our secret lives. Then at some point after all this talking, I'm not sure exactly how it happened, but it turned this corner and we were just suddenly madly, passionately in love. He gave me a very beautiful ring. Unbelievably, in a way, we were to be married."

There was a proposal—"*Ah, baby, let's get married, we've been alone too long*"—in the song "Waiting for the Miracle." A very Leonard Cohen proposal admittedly: resigned, cheerfully pessimistic and with references to nakedness and war. Leonard and Rebecca discussed moving in together, but for now it suited them to keep their separate homes. Rebecca lived with her cats in a house in the hills, two miles north of Leonard's, and Leonard shared his with his daughter, Lorca. She had taken a job working for a distress help line. He could hear her at night through the bare floorboards, downstairs, talking to would-be suicides on the phone. Of his relationship with Rebecca, Leonard said, "I find the whole thing very workable." Although he felt it "incautious to declare yourself a happy man," even he had to admit that he "couldn't complain."[1]

Those who have read this far and are not punching the air or saying "at long last" might be thinking this a curious development. Not that Leonard had a beautiful girlfriend, or even that he was happy, but that he was taking a wife. An old Eastern European adage says that a man should pray once before going to sea, twice before going to war and three times before getting married, but when it came to the last of the three, Leonard never seemed to stop praying. But marriage to Rebecca De Mornay really did appear to be workable. Movie stars are used to early starts, so they are unfazed by someone who sets his alarm for four thirty every morning to go to the Zen Center. Their work requires them to leave home for lengthy periods, so they are less likely to be bothered if you do the same. They are committed to their work. They have their own income. They are accustomed to being around people who are distracted or self-involved. To have got where they are in their business, they have to be fiercely tenacious. And, if they are Rebecca De Mornay, they are young, strikingly beautiful, very sexy and love music, and Leonard's music in particular. So, if Leonard should forget to pray for the angels, perhaps it might not be quite so perilous now that the miracle appeared to have come.

"In the midst of all this," says Rebecca, "I was doing what turned out to be so far the biggest movie of my career and he was trying to get his record *The Future* together, which also turned out to be his biggest American success. We had a very creative, inspiring impact on each other, smoking up a storm of cigarettes, drinking cauldrons of coffee—just together, living, working." Rebecca had won the starring role in *The Hand That Rocks the Cradle*, in which she plays a disturbed young woman pretending to be a nanny. The film was shot in Tacoma, a suburb of Seattle. Leonard went with her, "which very few men would feel comfortable doing," Rebecca points out. This was Leonard's first significant relationship with a woman more celebrated and successful than himself, but it appeared not to trouble him in the least. "He stayed with me at a house I rented there, and actually spent time in my trailer, happily songwriting while I was shooting, playing his synthesizer. The last track on *The Future* is called 'Tacoma Trailer,' and that was the trailer."

It is a nice image, Leonard noodling contentedly on his keyboard while Rebecca goes off to play a psychotic nanny, and playing a song to her when she comes home from work. "Tacoma Trailer" is an instrumental, but it came quickly. Rebecca was doing a good job as a muse. And Leonard needed one. Writing songs had become no less arduous. There had rarely been a time when it was easy, but sometime around 1982 something had changed in him—he couldn't say exactly what—and it had become much worse. It appeared to be some kind of acute perfectionism related to a craving for complete authenticity. He could write a "perfectly reasonable" song, he said, even "a good song," but when he listened to it sung he could hear "that the guy was putting you on."[2]

Leonard speculated that the problem might have to do with a sense of mortality, "that this whole enterprise is limited, that there was an end in sight."[3] As deadlines do, it focused him, but instead of moving things along, it kept him in the same place, going deeper, trying to find "the kind of truth that I can recognize, the kind of balance of truth and lies, light and dark."[4] He would work on the same song over and over, diligently and devotedly, for years, forever if need be, trying to make it work. Ever since he was a young poet, he had felt intensely passionate about writing, he said, and the feeling "of being in this *for keeps*."[5] When it came to his romantic relationships, he did not appear to have given that kind of dedication to staying in one place, with one person, "for keeps," and doing whatever it took to make it work. The problem with romantic relationships, though, was that they tended to get in the way of the isolation and space, the distance and longing, that his writing required. In 1993, Leonard wrote an advice page (sadly just a one-off) for the American men's magazine *Details*. He answered the question "What is the one thing men ought to know about women?" with "Women are deeply involved in a pattern of thought centered around the notion of commitment."[6] Yet he seemed at last ready to commit to Rebecca. He told journalists that his and Rebecca's was "an exclusive and highly conventional relationship,"[7] and said, "There is a formal arrangement between us, yes."[8]

The success of *I'm Your Man* had resulted in anticipation for a new album. That did nothing to speed up the process. Nor did the fact that more than half the songs Leonard was working on had been around in some unfinished form or other for a long time. He was writing the sixtieth verse for one such song, "Democracy," when he was interrupted by the phone. His son, Adam, had been in a serious car accident in Guadeloupe, where he had been working as a roadie for a calypso band. He was badly injured: fractured neck and pelvis, nine broken ribs and a collapsed lung. The eighteen-year-old was air-ambulanced, unconscious, to a hospital in Toronto. Leonard flew up to meet him as he was taken into intensive care. During the four months Adam spent in the hospital, Leonard stayed there, keeping vigil. He would sit in the room quietly, watching his son, who remained in a coma. Sometimes he would read aloud to him from the Bible. When Adam finally regained consciousness, his first words to his father were, "Dad, can you read something else?"[9] Suzanne says, "Leonard wanted to stay there by his bedside—for months—and did practically nothing else, dropped everything else to be there. Finally, if I had forgotten why I loved him even for a moment with what might have been a heart full of resentments, after Guadeloupe, to see how he was so solidly there for our children, I remembered."

Adam made a complete recovery. During the process, father and son became very tight. Leonard, having put all thoughts of work aside while he focused on Adam, had once again begun to think that, if he never got around to finishing another album, it was not the end of the world. As had happened in the past, his songs seemed to be doing all right without his direct involvement. One of them, "Bird on a Wire" was at No. 1 on the U.S. charts, a soulful version by the Neville Brothers, taken from the soundtrack of a romantic comedy of the same name. Another contemporary movie, *Pump Up the Volume*, used his song "Everybody Knows"—two versions of it, in fact, Leonard's original and a cover by Concrete Blonde. As it happened, the soundtrack of the latter also featured a hip young rock band called the Pixies, whose front man would, inadvertently, be the impetus for a Leonard Cohen tribute album.

The French rock magazine *Les Inrockuptibles* had thought up the idea of making an album of Leonard Cohen covers by artists from the more interesting end of the rock spectrum after an interview with the Pixies' Black Francis, during which he raved about *I'm Your Man*. Francis had not been a fan of Leonard's music until 1990, when, on a particularly grim European tour with his band, he happened upon a cassette of *I'm Your Man* in a French highway service station. The tape remained unopened in his bag until the bus reached Spain and the band had a few days off. "The plan," says Francis, "had been for us to all go to a beach town with nightclubs. But the band wasn't in a happy space and I really wanted to get away from everybody—in particular Kim, the bass player." He asked the tour manager to take him somewhere quiet, where he could be alone. He was dropped at a large, empty tourist hotel farther down the coast. Checking in, he saw to his chagrin that Kim Deal had had the same idea. "The hotel assumed we were the best of friends and, although there were eight hundred rooms in this hotel and no one in it, they put us right next to each other. We were both too exhausted to resist and just accepted our fate."

Francis stayed locked in his room and did not come out. He had brought with him the two new cassettes he had bought on the road, one being *I'm Your Man*. "It was summer, bright and sunny, but I had all the curtains drawn and it was very dark and black in my little room, and I played *I'm Your Man* on my boom box. It was all I listened to for three days straight, over and over. I was in the right kind of emotional state—kind of lonely, frustrated, bored, a whole combination, and alone in this empty place, this hotel at the end of the universe—and I got it. The voice, those little Casio keyboards, that kind of lush but spacious artificial landscape that frames his work on that record, just brought everything about him right to a head: everything that's sexy about him was extra sexy, anything funny about him extra funny, anything heavy was extra heavy. I was a fan."

Nick Cave was a Leonard Cohen fan too, but of longer standing. He had first heard Leonard's music in his teens, in a small country town in Australia, when a girlfriend made him sit with her in her room

and listen to *Songs of Love and Hate*. Many were the men introduced
in such fashion to Leonard's early albums. "I'd never heard anything
like it," says Cave. "It remains one of the seminal albums that completely changed the kind of music I would make. It was really the
first record that showed a way where it was possible to take some of
the kind of dark, self-lacerating visions we found in much of the European poetry and literature we were reading in those days and apply
them to a kind of rock sound. When the Bad Seeds put out our first
record we did a version of 'Avalanche' as the first track—even more
lugubrious than his—as a kind of attempt to set the tone." When
seven years later *Les Inrockuptibles* asked Cave and the Bad Seeds to
appear on the album, he declined; he despised tribute albums and
"could not think of anything worse. Then what happened was we
went to the pub and spent the afternoon there, and came back into
the studio rather intoxicated, and just started to play 'Tower of Song.'
We played it for about three hours nonstop, kind of segueing through
all the different kinds of musical styles in history, just playing around,
and then we forgot about it. Someone found it and did an edit on it,
and it sounded good, or it at least like there was a sense of humor
behind it. That was one fucked-up version of that song." It wound up
on the tribute album.

I'm Your Fan was released in November 1991, with eighteen
Leonard Cohen songs covered by, among others, the Pixies ("I
Can't Forget"), R.E.M. ("First We Take Manhattan"), James ("So
Long, Marianne"), Lloyd Cole ("Chelsea Hotel") and Ian McCulloch ("Hey, That's No Way to Say Goodbye"). John Cale, the oldest
of the contributors, gave "Hallelujah" its first cover by any artist of
substance—*NME* described his version as "a thing of wondrous, savage beauty." Leonard was "tickled pink" by the whole album. It did
not bother him so much, he said, if his books were left to gather dust
on shelves, "but the song really has an urgency, and if it isn't sung, it's
nowhere."[10] Everybody, he said, could use some encouragement, and

if you hung around long enough it was bound to happen, and Leonard's time had come. The same year, Leonard was inducted into the Juno Hall of Fame in Canada. In his acceptance speech he quipped, "If I had been given this attention when I was twenty-six it would have turned my head. At thirty-six it might have confirmed my flight on a rather morbid spiritual path. At forty-six it would have rubbed my nose in my failing powers and have prompted a plotting of a getaway and an alibi. But at fifty-six, hell, I'm just hitting my stride and it doesn't hurt at all."[11] Which was fortunate, since his countrymen gave him an even higher honor in October, making Leonard an Officer of the Order of Canada.

Perhaps to help balance the scales, Leonard agreed to Hal Willner's request to appear on a tribute album to Charles Mingus, *Weird Nightmare*. "I went over to his house in L.A. one night with a bunch of Mingus's poetry," Willner says, "and he picked out one stanza that he loved in a poem called 'The Chill of Death.' I had a little DAT recorder and he sat at his desk and repeated the poem over and over again into the microphone for half an hour. While he was doing so, someone made a phone call, and he picked up the phone, still reading the poem. They said, 'Leonard, what are you doing?' 'I am a man reading "The Chill of Death."' That's on the record too."

In March 1992, Rebecca attended the Oscars ceremony. Her escort, the immaculately dressed man who walked down the red carpet beside her, was Leonard. Cameras buzzed like mosquitoes, and photos of Rebecca and Leonard made it into a number of tabloids. "There was an English magazine that printed pictures of us and said 'Beauty and the Beast,'" says Rebecca. How mean of them to call her a beast. It brought to mind the headlines that greeted Serge Gainsbourg when he was photographed with his famous lovers Bardot, Gréco and Birkin. The difference was that Leonard, unlike Gainsbourg, had always gone out of his way in the past to avoid such attention. "The Academy Awards *was* probably the least likely place to sight Leonard Cohen," Rebecca says. "I asked him to go with me, because they asked me, and I was with him at the time, and he just went, 'Okay.' He didn't do the regular guy thing of having some reaction or anti-reaction to it, he just accepted it. It wasn't something he was looking forward to, but it wasn't something that he was going to say no to and leave me standing there without him. I think Leonard, like I am, is really in the moment with the individual he's with, as opposed to the image of what the person is supposed to be. There was just the reality of us as two people, irrespective of me being an actress, Leonard being a famous songwriter."

Leonard, as well as working at home, was writing songs at Rebecca's house on her synthesizer. Two of those songs in particular stuck in her mind. One was "A Thousand Kisses Deep," which Leonard kept writing over and over, "like a painter who paints over his original painting that you loved, and paints a whole new painting on top of it, and then he paints a whole new one on top of that, and ten years later it exists on a record* and doesn't have a single note or word that's the same as anything I heard when he first played that song." The other was "Anthem." "He got stuck on this one song. He was at my synthesizer and played it again—I'd heard it for years by now—and I suddenly said, 'Just like that, *those* words, *that's* the song.' Again he looked at me kind of skeptical; I guess I just must provoke that response in him. He said, 'You know what? You produce this song. I think you really know what this song has to be, I think you ought to produce it with me.' So he sort of launched me into this position, which I was extremely flattered by, and surprised. But I really did feel that I knew the song—in fact I just played it before I spoke to you for this interview and it still makes me cry. It has the impact of 'Auld

---

* *Ten New Songs*, 2001.

Lang Syne,' it's just immortal, it's the final statement on the subject, it's the searing authenticity that he has in his voice when you talk to him, the presence that he is in person. He is so fully present, with compassion for the underdog, as well as genuine compassion and understanding for the enemy—which is very hard to do and hard-won.

"However," Rebecca says, "within this stance it's extremely hard to be Leonard Cohen. He's on his own solo voyage, and he's lying on a bed of cactus perpetually, but somehow finding windows into infinity everywhere: '*Every heart to love will come, but like a refugee. . .; Forget your perfect offering / There is a crack in everything / That's how the light gets in.*' It's definitive. Such a unique way to describe the wisdom of compassion. I heard from a friend of mine who was in one of the established rehab places that they quoted this line in their pamphlets on recovery. He has taught me so much; he's humble but also fierce. He has this subtext of 'Let's get down to the truth here. Let's not kid ourselves.'" Early on in their relationship, Rebecca was "whining about the various pain I had, my childhood, and this and that. And Leonard is the best listener, but at a certain point he said, 'I understand, it must have been really terrible for you, Rebecca, having had to grow up poor and black.'" Rebecca laughed. "It wasn't in any way mean-spirited, there was no judgment from him; there never is. Leonard developed the tenacity and character to sit still within suffering—even though in earlier years, like many people, he tried every form of escape, be it drugs, sex, music, fame, money, all the usual things—but, early in his life compared to most people, he was brave enough to sit in the suffering, and write out of it, and live out of it, and not try to escape from it."

April 1, 1992, was Roshi's eighty-fifth birthday. Shortly after the Academy Awards, Leonard threw a grand party of his own. A hundred people gathered in one of the big hotels on Sunset Boulevard. There was a band, fronted by Perla Batalla, and Leonard asked them to end the evening by singing "Auld Lang Syne," Roshi's favorite song. By the time they got to it, the old man had nodded off in his chair. Leonard smiled. "It was a great sign if he's asleep," he said. Guests left with a book that Leonard had organized and published, with help from Kelley Lynch, celebrating the old man's life. Leonard had it bound in gold, like an Oscar.

Leonard was in the studio, working on his new album *The Future*, when the L.A. riots broke out on April 29, 1992. Four white police officers had been acquitted of the beating of a black motorist—an incident that had been caught on video by an onlooker and was frequently aired on television—and South Central L.A., a predominantly African-American neighborhood, erupted. Cars and buildings were set on fire and stores attacked and looted. A white man was dragged from his truck by a mob and severely beaten. As the violence spread, the dinner-party conversation in affluent white neighborhoods turned to buying guns. By the fourth day, the government sent in the marines. There had been fifty-three deaths, hundreds of buildings destroyed and around four thousand fires. Leonard could see them burning from his window. There was a layer of soot on his front lawn. His home was not far from South Central. The Zen Center was closer still. He had become used to hearing gunshots on his way to the *zendo* in the early hours of morning and to stepping over syringes to get through the gate. Now from his car he could see boarded-up stores and the charred remains of a gas station. It was "truly an apocalyptic landscape and a very appropriate landscape for my work."[12] He had started writing the song "The Future"—then titled "If You Could See What's Coming Next"—in 1989, when the Berlin Wall toppled, and just as he had predicted, it was all coming down.

"I said to him, 'Why do you even want to live in Los Angeles?'" says Rebecca De Mornay. "'You have a place in beautiful Montreal, and Hydra, and you've lived in New York and Paris. Why here?'"

Leonard said something like, 'This is the place. It's like a metaphor of the decline. The whole system is coming apart, I can feel it. The future is grim, and Los Angeles is at the center of it. It has the decay, and some sort of wild hope too, like weeds growing through the asphalt. I want to write from this place, from what's really going on.' So I was like, 'Wow, okay, we're living in the decay, you at the bottom and me at the top of this one street. Great.' And from within that he wrote 'The Future'—and it was very different Leonard Cohen writing from what I'd ever seen him do." Leonard renamed his new album—which he had had previously titled *Be for Real*, then *Busted*—after this apocalyptic song.

The Future was recorded with a large revolving cast of musicians and engineers whose numbers rivaled Phil Spector's on *Death of a Ladies' Man*. The credits list almost thirty female singers, including Jennifer Warnes, Anjani Thomas, Julie Christensen, Perla Batalla, Peggy Blue, Edna Wright, Jean Johnson and a gospel choir. There were string players and synthesizer programmers, an R & B horn section and various country music instruments—mandolin, pedal steel—as well as the usual rock instruments and an "ice rink organ." Perla Batalla, Rebecca De Mornay, Jennifer Warnes and David Campbell are credited as arrangers and Rebecca, Leanne Ungar, Bill Ginn, Yoav Goren and Steve Lindsey as coproducers of various tracks, but on the label it is described as "A Record by Leonard Cohen."

"It was a difficult birth," remembers Leanne Ungar, the album's chief engineer. "It was done kind of a song at a time and each song had its own specific method. A lot of the songs Leonard started at home with Yoav Goren, who was specifically working with him to program synthesizers on several songs to help him get the sounds he wanted. At the time, I was also working in another studio on another project, with Steve Lindsey, doing some overdubs and mixing for [R & B band] the Temptations. I mentioned that to Leonard and he said, 'Oh, I want to do some Motown-flavor tracks,' and he asked if I would introduce him to Steve." Leonard described Lindsey as "a man of great musical sensibilities. He's produced Aaron Neville, among others, and Ray Charles. He put together 'Be for Real' "—Leonard's cover on *The Future* of a soul ballad by Frederick Knight—"which I couldn't have done without him."[13]

Lindsey also played a key role in the album's second cover song, the Irving Berlin standard "Always." It was a favorite of Leonard's late mother. Leonard said, "He assembled those very fine musicians and organized the wonderful evening when we produced about an hour's worth of 'Always.' Basically, I prepared my drink that I invented in the city of Needles, California, during a heat wave in 1976, the Red Needle—tequila and cranberry juice with fresh fruit and lemon and lime—for myself and for everybody else who wanted communion. The session became fairly animated, and we played for a long, long time."[14] Everyone was "bombed," said Lindsey, and it sounds like it. "After doing multiple takes, we finally got the take we thought was really great. Leonard went in to do the vocals. He cut out during the solo, but when the solo was over he never came back. I found him lying on the floor in Capitol Studios' bathroom. He wanted me to get the janitor so he could thank him for cleaning up after him."[15] Said Leonard, "Several musicians told me it was the happiest time they ever spent in a recording studio."[16] Kelley Lynch, Leonard's manager, was also there for the recording. Leanne Ungar remembers seeing "sparks flying a little bit between Steve and Kelley." The two would go on to have a relationship that produced a son.

Ungar was "thrilled" to see the return, after almost ten years, of Leonard's song "Anthem." Although it was not she who had accidentally erased the version Leonard did for *Various Positions*, she says, "As the engineer of the project I always felt somehow responsible." The new version was significantly different. "Closing Time" also went through several changes. "When it first came into the studio it was this absolutely gorgeous slow, slow song with slowed-down synthesized strings," says Ungar. "I was in love with it. And Leonard came in and said, 'We're going to have to scrap the whole thing and start over.' I was, 'No, you can't!" But he came in the next day with his fast version of it, and went on not only to have a huge hit with it in Canada but the Male Vocalist of the Year award." In his acceptance speech at the 1992 Juno Awards ceremony, Leonard deadpanned, "It's only in a country like this that I could win a best vocalist award."

Rebecca, who went to Canada with Leonard for the ceremony, would also frequently drop by the recording studio while the album was being made. She was there for the recording of "Waiting for the Miracle," the song that contained Leonard's marriage proposal, and for "Anthem," for which Leonard gave her a coproduction credit. This was not a lover's indulgence, he said. "I generally designate the producer as the person without whom that particular track wouldn't exist. Rebecca happens to have an impeccable musical ear, a very highly developed musical sense. I had played many versions of 'Anthem' to her—fully completed versions with choruses and overdubs, and none of them seemed to nail it—and while I was revising it for the hundredth time, at a certain point she stopped me and said, 'That's the one.' It was quite late at night, but we managed to find a studio, and she lent me her Technics synthesizer and we produced the session that night, the basic track and the basic vocal. So her contribution was not insignificant."[17] The mixing of the album "took forever," says Ungar, but finally it was done. Four years after *I'm Your Man*, *The Future* was ready to go.

The Future was released in November 1992. Instead of a picture of Leonard on the cover, there was a simply drawn, quasiheraldic design of a hummingbird, a blue heart and a pair of unlocked handcuffs. They might have symbolized beauty, bravery, freedom, loss of freedom, S & M or all of the above; with Leonard one never knew. He dedicated the album to his fiancée with three verses from Genesis 24: "And before I had done speaking in mine heart, behold,

Rebecca came forth with her pitcher on her shoulder, and she went down unto the well and drew water. And I said unto her, let me drink I pray thee. . . ."

Almost an hour in length, *The Future* was Leonard's longest album to date, containing nine songs, seven of them originals, one of those a cowrite and another an instrumental. Following the line begun by its predecessor, it is accessible and contemporary sounding, the songs catchy, the tempos often upbeat and the melodies sung in a deep, gruff, yet seductive voice somewhere between a prophet of doom with a black sense of humor and Barry White. The title track, which opens the album, sets gleeful pessimism to a synth-pop dance groove. "*I've seen the future, baby: / it is murder,*" Leonard prophesizes—going one step farther than Prince, whose own song called "The Future" says, "I've seen the future and boy it's rough"—and name-checking Stalin, the devil, Charles Manson and Christ. Leonard catalogs the sins of the West—crack, abortion, anal sex, Hiroshima and, worse than all of these, bad poets—and takes a bow as "*the little Jew who wrote the Bible.*" ("I don't exactly know where that line comes from," said Leonard, but "I knew it was a good line when it came."[18]) It is his rap moment, his "Hoochie Coochie Man." "It's humorous, there's irony, there's all kinds of distances from the event that make the song possible. It's art. It's a good dance track. . . . It's even got hope. But the place where the song comes from is a life-threatening situation. That's why you're shattered at the end of it."[19]

In the lyrics of the stirring "Democracy," Leonard seems at his most sociopolitically direct. There are no Abrahams, Isaacs and butchers here:

> *It's coming . . . from those nights in Tiananmen Square . . .*
> *from the fires of the homeless,*
> *from the ashes of the gay . . .*
> *I love the country but I can't stand the scene*

And I'm neither left or right
I'm just staying home tonight,
getting lost in that hopeless little screen.

In interviews at the time Leonard referred to democracy as "the greatest religion the West has produced," adding, "[as] Chesterton said about religion, it's a great idea, too bad nobody's tried it."[20]

There are moments of calm amid the chaos and apocalypse: "Light as the Breeze," on the healing power of cunnilingus, and "Always"—though the latter's schmaltz is given an ironic edge by its over-the-top barroom performance, and the former's sweetness is tempered by a sense that the comfort of sex and love is fleeting, little more than a Band-Aid to get you back into the ring for another round. Leonard sings in the album's masterpiece, "Anthem":

Ah the wars they will
be fought again
The holy dove
She will be caught again
bought and sold
and bought again
the dove is never free

And yet it also has hope.

Forget your perfect offering
There is a crack in everything
That's how the light gets in.

"The light," Leonard explained, "is the capacity to reconcile your experience, your sorrow, with every day that dawns. It is that understanding, which is beyond significance or meaning, that allows you to live a life and embrace the disasters and sorrows and joys that are our common lot. But it's only with the recognition that there is a crack in everything, I think all other visions are doomed to irretrievable gloom."[21] Leonard had spoken in the past of wanting a balance of dark and light and dark, and truth and lies, in his songs, and on *The Future* he achieved it.

Reviews of the album were resoundingly positive. The album was a commercial success, doing particularly well in English-speaking countries. It made the Top 40 in the UK, went double platinum in Canada and sold almost a quarter of a million copies in the U.S. Three of its songs, "The Future," "Anthem" and "Waiting for the Miracle," were included on the soundtrack to Oliver Stone's 1994 movie *Natural Born Killers*. Leonard, meanwhile, was on the promotional treadmill, doing more interviews than he had in years, saying much the same things about America, the apocalypse and, very occasionally, his relationship with Rebecca, to scores of journalists. To the bemusement of the Toronto press, Rebecca—who happened to be in Toronto to make a movie with Sidney Lumet—joined Leonard in his interviews. When the journalist from *Maclean's* noted that she looked "demure and a little out of her element," he might have been describing Leonard at the Oscars.[22] Rebecca, taking over Dominique Issermann's previous role, directed the video for *The Future*'s first single, "Closing Time." Perla Batalla, who appeared in the video alongside a pregnant Julie Christensen, remembers Rebecca turning up on the set at the end of a day's shooting with Lumet "and she would bring bottles of Cristal, which we would drink out of Styrofoam cups." To loosen Leonard up even more, Rebecca feigned a striptease and flirted with him from behind the camera.

Leonard agreed to interview Rebecca for *Interview*, the upscale celebrity gossip magazine, founded by Andy Warhol, that had once refused to run Danny Fields's Leonard Cohen story because Leonard was not a big enough star. Their interview was a mixture of insight and flirtation, and repartee of the kind that showed either that Leonard had met his match or that Rebecca had acquired something of his style. Rebecca began it by saying that the best thing about being interviewed by Leonard Cohen was that she would not be asked "what the exact nature of [her] relationship is with Leonard Cohen." Naturally that was Leonard's first question. He asked Rebecca if she viewed acting as "a form of healing." She answered, "If you have wounds that are bleeding I don't think acting will ever get them to stop. But I find acting is a form of illumination." When he asked her what roles she would like to play, she said, "Joan of Arc." Like the softest TV talk-show interviewer, or ironist, or older man in love with a beautiful young woman, Leonard asked her, "How do you maintain your pure and rosy complexion?" Did he want a beauty tip, she asked? He said, "Yes." Rebecca said, "To be more beautiful, Leonard, you have to be happier."[23]

With the album done, Leonard returned to a long-unfinished book project: the anthology of his poems and song lyrics he had been working on since the mid to late eighties. Sorting through stacks of material, trying every method he could conceive of to arrange his work, he had compiled three different books—one small, one medium, one large—and abandoned all three. His publishers were getting impatient; Leonard's celebrity was at an all-time high, and it had been nine years since his last book and twenty-five since his last anthology, *Selected Poems 1956–1968*. Marianne had helped him choose the poems for that. Leonard asked his friend Nancy Bacal if she would help.

"He had been sitting with a huge pile of poems and lyrics for months, years," says Bacal. "It was a life's work, overwhelming, impossible for him to get to. So we took a very esoteric route. We wanted only to use the poems that were more current and sparse, more elliptical than the younger man's voice. We put together a book of those, which took quite some doing, and we were really quite pleased." One day while they were working on it, Rebecca came in. He showed her what they had done. Noticing that none of her favorite poems were there, Rebecca came up with her own list, which, like Marianne's, included his more romantic poems. "We kind of looked at each other, bewildered," Bacal remembers, "and I could feel him begin reconsidering, 'Well, maybe they should be there.' So it changed. And once the doors of possibility opened there was the chaos, and it was hard to make decisions. I remember the agony he was in. He faxed changes till the last minute. I'm sure the editors at the publishing company were going mad. At the very end I drifted away; it was far too confusing for my brain to handle."

Stranger Music: Selected Poems and Songs, dedicated to Adam and Lorca, was published in March 1993. A substantial book—some four hundred pages—its selections are arranged chronologically, concluding with eleven previously unpublished "uncollected poems" from the eighties. Although not the authoritative collection it was presented as being, it is a fairly comprehensive cross-section of his work, but with some curious choices and omissions. There are excerpts from his second novel, *Beautiful Losers*, for example, but not his first, *The Favorite Game*, and he chooses the well-known song versions of "Suzanne," "Master Song" and "Avalanche," for example, over their less familiar poetic versions. Leonard also took the opportunity to make textual changes, sometimes quite drastic, to several of the pieces. But with a new generation of music fans curious about his literary background, and with so many of the books containing the original poems out of print, *Stranger Music* sold very well.

The tour for *The Future* was due to begin on April 22, 1993, in Scandinavia. Leonard had with him an eight-piece band—Bob Metzger, Steve Meador, Bill Ginn, Bob Furgo, Paul Ostermayer, Jorge Calderon, Julie Christensen and Perla Batalla. All bar one, Calderon, were old companions of the road, and several had been with him on his successful, enjoyable *I'm Your Man* tour. Spirits were high. During the last week of rehearsals Leonard's U.S. label, marking his new status in America, had arranged for them to play a private concert in their L.A. rehearsal studio, the Complex, which was syndicated to a hundred radio stations across the country as *The Columbia Records Radio Hour Presents: Leonard Cohen Live!* In recent weeks, Leonard had also appeared in two U.S. TV shows, *In Concert* and *David Letterman*. Tickets to his sixteen U.S. concerts—which were intermingled with twenty-one dates in Canada—were selling well.

The European tour schedule included several sports arenas, stadiums and two rock festivals. As was invariably the case in Europe, the crowds were good and the critics generally favorable. A review of the Royal Albert Hall concerts in the *Independent* remarked on Leonard's new sense of showmanship and the large number of screaming women of mature years in the audience. Leanne Ungar, who accompanied her now-husband Bob Metzger on the road, recorded the shows. (Eight songs from these concerts, along with five from the 1988 tour, would make up Leonard's first live album in eleven years, *Cohen Live*, released in 1994.) Along the way, Leonard appeared on the UK TV show *Later . . . with Jools Holland*, and on TV shows in Spain and France. He recorded a duet with Elton John, for Elton's *Duets* album, choosing to sing a Ray Charles song that he knew by heart, having heard it so often on Hydra, "Born to Lose." At the concert in Vienna, Rebecca showed up with an enormous cake. It had a hummingbird as its centerpiece and the iced inscription "R. loves L. Loves R. Loves L." Whenever her schedule allowed, Rebecca traveled with Leonard and the band on the tour bus for three or four days at a time, in Europe and in the U.S.

The U.S. tour also brought positive reviews, with *Rolling Stone* describing him as a contemporary Brecht and the *New York Times* describing the audience reaction as "almost reverent, waiting for every phrase."[24] In Canada, Leonard narrated a two-part Canadian TV series on *The Tibetan Book of the Dead*, a book he had first encountered in Marianne's old house on Hydra. In the last poem in *Stranger Music*, "Days of Kindness," written on Hydra in 1985, he had been thinking about

> *Marianne and the child*
> *The days of kindness*
> *It rises in my spine*
> *and it manifests as tears*
> *I pray that a loving memory*
> *exists for them too*
> *the precious ones I overthrew*
> *for an education in the world.*

Unsentimental as he said he was, something seemed to be drawing Leonard back to the past. Perhaps it was his current preoccupation with not just *The Future*, but the future. He had spoken about having a sense of mortality in terms of his work, of the end being in sight; he had also committed to spending this future with one woman. And still he had so much work left to do.

The attention and the adulation, although he was grateful for it, were beginning to get to him. Just as he thought that Canada had at last run out of laurels to bestow—in the past two years he had been inducted into the Canadian Music Hall of Fame; made an officer of the Order of Canada; won two separate Junos for Songwriter of the Year, two for Best Video and one for Best Male Vocalist; and even been awarded an honorary degree by his old university, McGill—Leonard learned he had won the Governor General's Award for Lifetime Artistic Achievement. It is the kind of award that makes a man feel old and finished—even a man whose last album and book were bestsellers and who was last seen with a beautiful young blond fiancée on his arm.

In November 1993 Leonard flew to Ottawa, accompanied by Julie and Perla; there was to be a tribute gala performance at which the two women were to sing "Anthem," backed by an orchestra and a gospel choir.

At the presentation ceremony in Rideau Hall, Leonard, his hair shorn almost to a stubble, said, "I feel like a soldier." From the stage he could see his old comrade-in-arms Pierre Trudeau in the audience. "You may get decorated for a successful campaign or a particular action that appears heroic but probably is just in the line of duty," he continued. "You can't let these honors deeply alter the way you fight."[25] His acceptance speech was a perfect Cohenesque mix of modesty, honesty and statement of intent. Irving Layton, as ever, rose to the occasion, declaring, "He makes you think of a Jeremiah in Tin Pan Alley. He wants to be bare-knuckled and smash whatever remaining illusions people have about the time in which they're living and what they can expect."[26] Leonard also seemed compelled to smash his own.

Work was under way in Canada on another tribute to Leonard, a book titled *Take This Waltz*, with contributions from writers and personalities such as Louis Dudek, Allen Ginsberg, Judy Collins and Kris Kristofferson, scheduled for release in September 1994 to celebrate Leonard's sixtieth birthday. Leonard, meanwhile, had flown back to L.A. He unpacked his suitcase, packed a knapsack and climbed in his car and drove away from the city and from a future with a beautiful young actress. He was returning to the place where he had moved quietly, with no announcement, a few months before, not long after the last date of the *Future* tour. A small, bare hut on a mountain, where he had chosen to live as the servant and companion of an old Japanese monk.

Twenty

From This Broken Hill

The day was hot and dry but a sliver of snow still clung to the mountaintop like a broken fingernail on a worn sweater.

Leonard, dressed in a long black robe and sandals, walked briskly along the winding path, eyes cast down, hands folded in front of him. There were other black-clad figures on the path and they marched in formation, silent but for the sound of stones crunching underfoot. "People have romantic ideas about monasteries," Leonard said. Mount Baldy Zen Center was decidedly unromantic, an abandoned Boy Scouts camp sixty-five hundred feet up in the San Gabriel mountains, fifty-five miles east of L.A., where the pine trees were as thin as the atmosphere.

Leonard's new home looked like the archaeological remains of a small, civilized community cruelly reduced to rubble—a scattering of simple wood cabins, a small statue of Buddha, the stone circle where the scouts once had their campfire sing-alongs—that some kindly souls with primitive tools had done their best to fix up. It did not even offer the romance of seclusion, being just off the road that linked the university town of Claremont below with the ski slopes above. On the other side of the road was an inn, whose sign, offering cocktails, food and lodging, only served to remind the monks of the pleasures of the flesh. On Saturday nights, laughter and music would waft on the cold night air through the monks' thin wood cabin walls. In winter the Zen Center was shrouded in deep snow. On summer days there were swarms of gnats. The place seemed full of things that bite—rattlesnakes, even the occasional bear, which the monks would chase off by throwing rocks, as compassionately as possible of course.

There are a lot of rocks on Mount Baldy. The slopes are heaped with large boulders, sharp edged and ash gray. They give the appearance of having stopped midtumble, as if a vote had been taken midavalanche and they had unanimously chosen not to continue. The paths that circle the property and link the residences with the common buildings—meditation hall, refectory, outhouses and showers (no hot running water until the late nineties)—are bordered with medium-sized stones and surfaced with small crumbly ones. The place looks like a rock pile, a hard-labor camp.

It was, Leonard admits, "a rigorous and disciplined existence."[1] During *sesshin*—weeklong periods of intense Buddhist study—a three A.M. wake-up call gave the residents ten minutes to dress and trudge through the pitch-darkness (and in winter shovel through the snow) to the kitchen/dining hall, where tea was served in a formal manner and drunk in silence. Fifteen minutes later a gong signaled that it was time to file silently into the meditation hall and take their allotted place on the wooden benches around the walls, facing center. An hour of chanted meditation—"very long chants, all one note"[2]—was followed by the first of six daily periods of *zazen*, an hour or more of seated meditation, legs crossed in full lotus, back rigid, eyes pointed at the floor. Monks carrying sticks patrolled the room on the lookout for anyone who appeared to be nodding back to

sleep, whom they would return to consciousness by giving them a
sharp rap on the shoulder. After the meditation came more meditation, *kinhin*, walking meditation, outdoors, whatever the weather—
and this high up the mountain the climate was extreme; sometimes
there were hailstones the size of limes. Then came the first of several
daily *sanzen*, individual meetings with Roshi for instruction and *koan*
(riddle) practice.

There were short breaks for meals at six forty-five A.M., noon and
five forty-five P.M. for dinner, during which everybody filed into the
dining room, took their allotted plastic bowl set, wrapped in a nap-
kin, from the shelf, and sat at one of the seven long tables, where they
would eat in silence. After lunch came shower breaks and work duties; after dinner there was *gyodo*—simultaneous walking and chanting meditation—and more *zazen* and *sanzen* until nine, ten, maybe
eleven at night, depending on how long Roshi decided it should continue. But however late the day might run, the next morning at three
A.M. promptly, the whole process would start again.

The daily schedule when there were no *sesshin* was somewhat less
relentless, beginning at five A.M. and ending at nine P.M. and allowing
for some private time between study and work duties. Nevertheless,
for a man in his early sixties, for a musical icon whose last album was
the biggest seller of his career, for a sophisticate, a man of the world,
a ladies' man, none of this life Leonard had chosen was anything
but extraordinary. The first rule of celebrity is that celebrities are
to be served; but here was Leonard, chopping wood, banging nails,
fixing toilets, doing whatever the monk charged with doling out and
supervising work duties assigned him to do. Kigen, who held that
position when Leonard first moved into the monastery, says he had
"no idea at all that Leonard was a celebrity. I didn't know Leonard
from beans." Leonard was perfectly happy with this. When Kigen
told Leonard to rake out the bamboo and, having checked his work,
told him to go back and do it again, that he'd missed some, Leonard
did as he was instructed without protest.

Leonard lived in a wood cabin in the center of the monastery, close to the path. A doormat on his front step read WELCOME. A brave cluster of yellow wildflowers had forced their way through the stones to bloom beside his front door. Leonard had always been partial to small, plain dwellings and this answered the description perfectly. A white-walled room about nine feet square—between the size of a U.S. and a Canadian prison cell—held a narrow, metal-framed single bed and a chest of drawers. There was a menorah on the dresser and a tiny mirror on the wall. Its one small window was covered by a thin white curtain and a fly screen, which at nighttime was layered with dust-brown moths, attracted by the light. Leonard's cabin also had an additional room the size of a walk-in closet, in which were a desk, an old Macintosh computer, some books, a bottle of liquor or two and a Technics synthesizer. There was no TV, radio or stereo; if Leonard wanted to listen to a CD he would have to do so in his jeep, which was parked near the Zen Center entrance. His main luxuries were having his own toilet and a coffee machine. Roshi had granted Leonard special dispensation to get up earlier than the others and enjoy a solitary cigarette and coffee—sipped from a mug decorated with the album sleeve design of *The Future*—before joining the other residents in their daily tasks and observances.

Leonard's main job was working directly with Roshi, mostly as his chauffeur and cook. In the monastic tradition, the monks subsisted on lentils, lima beans, rice, split peas and pasta—there was a row of large garbage cans in the kitchen filled with them—and on food donations, which came once a week. These last made for all manner of curiosities, like the sweet wafer biscuits that appeared to have time-traveled from a 1940s English afternoon tea tray, which fortuitously arrived on the same day as a separate consignment of Indian tea marked for export to Russia. Leonard became expert at rustling up soups. At the age of sixty-one, he would earn a certificate from San Bernardino County that qualified him to take work as a chef,

waiter or busboy.* Sometimes he would ask himself what he was doing living like this, in this "land of broken hearts,"[3] as he called it, but
he knew the answer. There was nowhere else he could be.

Leonard had been coming to Mount Baldy for *sesshin* and retreats
for more than twenty years; he was familiar with everything about
the place. He knew what he was in for—this was no celebrity-friendly
Zen-lite retreat, of which California had no shortage. Rinzai monks,
Leonard liked to boast, were "the Marines of the spiritual world"[4]
with a regimen "designed to overthrow a twenty-year-old."[5] Why he
should have chosen to sign up full-time at the age of sixty, when he
was too old for the regimen and old enough to know better, is a question that has a three-part answer: Rebecca, the record business and
Roshi.

Shortly before he left L.A. for the monastic life, Leonard ran into
Roscoe Beck. He told his former musical director, "I've had it with
this music racket." He was getting out. Strange timing, one might
think. *The Future* was no *Various Positions;* it had been one of Leonard's most successful albums. But the tour that followed the album's
release had been a dislocating and debilitating experience. He hated
it and he was drinking heavily. So heavily that Roshi, a man by no
means averse to alcohol, expressed his concern.

Leonard's relationship with touring had always been complicated.
From the outset he viewed it at best as a necessary evil, foisted upon
him by his record contract, and he approached it under sufferance,
usually with the aid of alcohol, or in the early days, other palliatives.
Stage fright was a part of it, a shy man's fear of humiliating himself. Though the attention and the stage had not appeared to trouble
him as a young poetry reader, his insecurities as a singer and a musician made his fear of failure more acute. His first-ever major concert

---

* The test, taken after studying a DVD course on safe handling of food, required correct answers to forty out of fifty multiple-choice questions. Leonard's
exact score is unknown.

appearance—when Judy Collins had brought him out in 1967 at a benefit in New York—had been a "total failure."[6] Over the next few years, as he became more used to performing, the fear had mutated into a kind of public projection of his perfectionism, "that to take up people's time with anything but excellence is really too much to think about."[7] He was never able to take a concert he did casually, he said—which is believable, since Leonard had never shown any great ability at doing "casual" in any aspect of his life. If a show did not go well, "you feel you've betrayed yourself," he said,[8] which in turn evolved into a fear of betraying his art, by making it work like a prostitute night after night.

But Leonard also wanted people to hear his songs and buy his records. Given his general lack of radio attention and the geographical distance between him and his main fan base, which was not in the U.S. or even Canada, this meant going on the road and playing them. And as time passed, sometimes he would actually quite enjoy it, so long as everything ran smoothly and nothing felt out of his control. He had felt "entirely at home" on the *I'm Your Man* tour. Those who knew him well remarked how relaxed he seemed; he had even stopped drinking by the intermission. In 1993, when it came time to go out with *The Future*, Leonard rehired several crew members from the 1988 tour as well as five of its musicians for the eight-piece band he took on the road. Julie Christensen, who was on both tours, says, "I think Leonard really depends on the people around him to sustain the magic. He knows he can't do it all alone." But this time the magic didn't work.

Perla Batalla, who was also on both tours, describes the *Future* tour as "very, very drama laden." Though it might not have appeared so dramatic to an outsider, to someone as sensitive and conflicted about touring as Leonard, it was. The scheduling was more onerous than usual, with a great deal of travel and little time to catch one's breath. The North American leg, which followed almost directly on

from the twenty-six European concerts, had been particularly exact-
ing: thirty-seven shows in under two months, with meet-and-greets
arranged backstage after almost every show—Leonard's second album in succession to be well received in the U.S. seemed to have
sent his once-indifferent U.S. record label into overdrive. (The *I'm
Your Man* tour, by comparison, had twenty-five dates separated by a
fifteen-week summer break.) The routing, which doubled back and
forth across the border, was also stressful, while the tour bus, which
suffered from defective shock absorbers, was hell on Canada's curvy
mountain roads and did nothing to help with bonhomie. Spirits were
already at an all-time low. Leonard's keyboard player Bill Ginn had
an addiction problem, which other members of the band were trying
and failing to help him with. That Perla Batalla had married since the
last tour and Julie Christensen had a young baby she had had to leave
behind only compounded the feeling that this was not the carefree
tour experience it had been five years before. Leonard had more than
once expressed anxiety that he was pulling families apart.

Leonard's fiancée, Rebecca De Mornay, had shown up at various
points in Europe and North America and on occasion traveled on
the bus with them for three or four days at a time. She could see that
touring was "very rough on him. It's a terrific conflict of taking someone who really likes to spend his time in one room that he could probably not leave for three days at a time, and to suddenly thrust himself
onto a stage with thousands of people listening." Rebecca appeared
well liked by everyone, but however good her intention she was a distraction, sometimes good, sometimes not. His energy seemed to shift
when she was there, affecting band rapport, which some of the musicians believed could be felt sometimes onstage. Offstage, there were
times when Leonard seemed elated at having Rebecca there. But
other times, later on the tour, raised voices could be heard behind the
closed dressing room door. By the midsummer of 1993, when the tour
was finally over, Leonard and Rebecca's engagement was too.

One of the most public of Leonard's relationships ended privately and quietly. Neither of them spoke about it to the press. Later Leonard would say, "She kind of got wise to me. Finally she saw I was a guy who just couldn't come across. In the sense of being a husband and having more children and the rest."[9] Rebecca disagrees. "I think the real truth is that Leonard in fact did come across more than he ever had with anyone. I think that's why there's no hard feelings, because we both know we each gave it our all."

Leonard did not tell Rebecca that he was leaving for the monastery. "But," says Rebecca, "all those things are just details. The real thing is we really impacted each other's lives in incredibly positive ways. One of many things Leonard said in the course of our relationship that was very wise was, 'Look, here's what I know: marriage is the hardest spiritual practice in the world.' I said, 'What are you talking about?' He said, 'People wonder how anybody can sit on Mount Baldy for hours on end, weeks, months, even, but it's nothing compared to marriage. If you're really there, really present, for marriage, it's self-reflection, twenty-four/seven. In other words, who you are is reflected back to you in the mirror of your marriage partner, daily, minute by minute, hour by hour. Who can take that?' He's very self-aware."

Leonard, says Rebecca, "was searching all of his life to figure out what is it, where is it, or maybe just, how do I get the hell out of here? Having all these relationships with women and not really committing; having this elongated history with Roshi and Zen meditation and yet always running away from it also, and having this long relationship to his career, and yet feeling like it's the last thing he wants to be doing. I have a feeling that a lot of things came to a head for him within the context, or the time frame, of our relationship; I think we each crystallized something for each other once and for all. And after we broke up, he committed to the other thing that he'd been unwilling to commit to: he became a monk, which he'd never done, and which, by the way, has given me a fearsome reputation: 'God, after you men run off and become monks; what do you do to them?'"

With Rebecca gone from his life, and having taken his leave of the music business, there was no reason for Leonard to remain in L.A. The reason Leonard himself gave for going to the monastery was "for love"[10]—not so much love of Buddhism and the idea of living as a monk, but love of Roshi, the old man with whom he could sit in silence on this broken hill. As Leonard described it, "Something like this you can only do for love. If Roshi had been a professor of physics at Heidelberg University, I would have learned German and gone to Heidelberg to study physics. I think that one approaches a master in many various conditions. If you want a master, he becomes your master; some people want a disciplinarian, so there's a strict regime available for such people. I was more interested in friendship, so he manifested as a friend. When I finished my tour in 1993 I was approaching the age of sixty; Roshi was approaching ninety. My old teacher was getting older and I hadn't spent enough time with him, and my kids were grown and I thought it was an appropriate moment to intensify my friendship and my association with the community."[11]

Leonard had gone there ostensibly to be of service to Roshi, but the arrangement worked for him and Roshi both. He had also been drawn to the monastery, he understood a few years later, by "the sense of something unfinished, something that would keep me alive."[12] He likened the Zen Center to a mountain hospital and he and his fellow residents to "people who have been traumatized, hurt, destroyed, maimed by daily life," sitting in the waiting room, all waiting to see this small, rotund Japanese doctor. Whatever its hardships and deprivations might be, the monastic life had its own voluptuous luxury for a man with an appetite for discipline, who was harsher on himself than any punishing regime an old monk with a bagful of koans could devise. The emptiness and silence, the lack of distractions, the sense of order counteracted the confusion of words and anxieties in his head. Here Leonard was no one special. He was a cog in the machine, everyone and everything interconnected, simply one of a small and constantly changing community who all dressed alike, shared chores and ate together at the same time from identical plastic bowls. Leonard had no problem with that in the least. Right now he had very little interest in being "Leonard Cohen." What he was looking for was a kind of emptiness—something he had sought in many different ways throughout his adult life, be it through fasting, sex or Scientology auditing. It was "this emptiness" that had first attracted him to Roshi's monastery. "It's a place where it's very difficult to hold fast to one's ideas. There is this sort of charitable void that I found here in a very pure form."[13] At Mount Baldy Zen Center he had no decisions to make, he was told what to do and when and how to do it, but—unlike a record company contract or a marriage—there was an escape clause. Leonard could leave if he wanted to.

On a few occasions he did. Hanging his robes on the peg, he would drive down the mountain, past the signs that warned against throwing snowballs, and join the freeway traffic heading northwest to L.A. He was going back not for some decadent lost weekend, but to be alone. A small monastery on a mountain might sound like an isolated existence, but it did not appear that way to Leonard: "There's very little private space and private time. There's a saying in the monastery, the monks are like pebbles in a bag; one is always working shoulder to shoulder, so it has the same quality as life anywhere, the same sensations of love, hate, jealousy, rejection, admiration. It's ordinary life under a microscope."[14] Leonard's first stop was McDonald's, to buy a Filet-O-Fish; he would wash it down later with a glass of good French wine. But after a day or two at home watching television—*The Jerry Springer Show* was a favorite—having been reminded of how his life would be were he not in the monastery, Leonard drove back up the mountain and slipped back into his robes.

The days ran into one another, divided into segments of near-constant, mostly regulated activity. "You don't sleep for very long and you work many hours a day and sit in the meditation hall for many hours a day, but once you get the hang of it," Leonard said, "you go into ninth gear and kind of float through it all."[15]

This level of acceptance did not come immediately. He and Kigen, being considerably older than many of the people who came to Mount Baldy for the *sesshin*, would commiserate with each other over the severity of the place. "The landscape is austere and that altitude very challenging. Leonard said it was designed for people with a ton of energy," says Kigen. "But what a lot of the practice is about is being able to go with confidence to a place that normally you would become very insecure about, and realizing that you *can* make your home there, that you can actually live and thrive and find peace in those extreme places." Leonard felt more at peace for longer stretches of time than he cared to remember. "They just work you to death so that you forget about yourself," Leonard said, "and forgetting about yourself is another kind of refreshment. There is a strict sense of order, but I like that sort of thing. Once you overcome your natural resistance to being told what to do, if you can overcome that, then you begin to relax into the schedule and the simplicity of your day. You just think about your sleep, your work, the next meal, and that whole component of improvisation that tyrannizes much of our lives begins to dissolve."[16]

It is a popular belief that an artist or writer needs an element of disorder, misery and improvisation in order to create. As Leonard himself said, "It's true that God himself, as it relates in Genesis, uses chaos and desolation to create the order of the universe, so chaos and desolation could be understood as the DNA of all creativity."[17] But the highly structured existence, in conjunction with his desire to forget who he was and overcome his ego, appeared to free up Leonard's creativity. That last might appear paradoxical, when the urge to create would seem to come from an expression of the artist's ego. But the removal of internal distractions—anxiety, expectations—from his Zen practice was as important as the lack of external distractions in these plain, orderly surroundings. In the precious, circumscribed hours between duties, Leonard was busy writing, drawing and composing music on his synthesizer—delicate, poignant music he described as "a lot like French movie music from the fifties."[18] Some of this poetry and artwork would appear in *Book of Longing*, but that would be a decade in the future. Working in the back room of his little cabin, Leonard gave no thought to publishing a book or releasing an album. He worked for the sake of the work, with as little attachment to its outcome as a man who had not yet attained *satori* (enlightenment) could muster.

Busy as Leonard's life was on Mount Baldy, time seemed to stand still. Although the world outside went on without him, Leonard showed little interest in the details, letting it slip off the reel like an old film he had no real desire to see again. Months went by, then years, marked only by the changes in season and the periodic earlier alarm calls that signaled the start of another rigorous *sesshin*. During the many long hours Leonard sat in *zazen*, his mind would wander from the pain in his knees to the songs he was writing in his head, or even to sexual fantasies. "When you're sitting for long hours in the meditation hall you run through all your numbers. It takes a while to exhaust those things and maybe they're never fully exhausted, but after a while you get tired of running your own Top 40 scenarios about the girl you want or lost or the one you need to recover."[19] Though they were fewer in number than monks, there were nuns on Mount Baldy. They had their own quarters, and liaisons with the male residents were not encouraged. Of course, they went on. "The situation offers up certain erotic possibilities," Leonard said. "It's a lot easier than cruising the terrace cafés of Paris. For a young person with energy—since there's not much free time—it's a very promising environment." When he was younger, Leonard "had several brief, intense liaisons" at Mount Baldy,[20] but he was no longer "terribly active in that realm."[21]

He was not entirely devoid of female companionship. Chris Darrow, whose band the Kaleidoscope played on Leonard's debut album, lived in Claremont, at the base of Mount Baldy, and was surprised to spot Leonard sitting in the sun on the patio of the local Greek restaurant, Yanni's, drinking a Greek coffee, in the company of a beautiful nun. Were it not for the black robes and shaved heads, it might have been Hydra. Darrow went up to their table. "Hi, Leonard, remember me?" They had not seen each other since the *Songs of Leonard Cohen* session in 1967. "Sure," said Leonard. "You saved my record."

While Leonard showed no interest in making a new album, in September 1995, after he had been living in the monastery for two years, another tribute album was released. *Tower of Song* differed from *I'm Your Fan* in a number of ways. The first tribute had been an independent album, a labor of love compiled by a French rock magazine, on which predominantly young, edgier rock artists covered Leonard's songs. *Tower of Song*, by contrast, was a major-label album set in motion by Kelley Lynch, produced by her romantic partner Steve Lindsey, and featuring more mainstream, big-name acts. At Lynch's urging, Leonard had taken a few days away from the monastery to assist her in contacting some of the musicians on the wish list. He tackled the uncomfortable task with humor, sending a message to Phil Collins that asked, "Would Beethoven decline an invitation from Mozart?" No, Collins replied, "unless Beethoven was on a world tour at the time."

Among the lineup on *Tower of Song* were Collins's former Genesis bandmate Peter Gabriel as well as Elton John, Don Henley, Willie Nelson, Billy Joel, Tori Amos, Suzanne Vega and Aaron Neville. Sting and the Chieftains teamed up to perform a Celtic "Sisters of Mercy," while Bono took a break from U2 to record an ambient Beat poetry-gospel version of "Hallelujah."

"Nobody," the author Tom Robbins wrote in the album's liner notes, "can sing the word 'naked' as nakedly as Cohen." This was probably not the best endorsement for an album of Leonard Cohen songs not sung by Leonard Cohen. But Leonard, who had also been persuaded to do a few interviews to help promote the album, told the press he was very pleased with it. "Except for being written, this is the best thing that has happened to these songs and I am deeply grateful to these eminent artists, who could so easily have done without this project, for their kindness and solidarity."[22] Reviewers, however, were not kind. As a sales ploy, the record company sent free copies to bars and cafés (and this long before Starbucks became a music-marketing machine) that had what they referred to as the "Leonard Cohen vibe." Presumably what they had in mind were sophisticated, elegant establishments. Certainly not a small wooden cabin on a rock-strewn hill, which Leonard returned to as swiftly as etiquette allowed and which he showed no inclination to leave.

On August 9, 1996, three years into his life in the monastery, Leonard was ordained a Zen Buddhist monk. Steve Sanfield, the friend through whom Leonard first became acquainted with Roshi, drove up for the ceremony and Esther, Leonard's sister, flew in from New York. Leonard, dressed in robes, his head shaved, turned to Sanfield and whispered wryly, "You got me into this, can you get me out of it?" Leonard had agreed to the ordination not as a step toward sainthood, nor as a step away from the religion he was born to. As he wrote in his 1997 poem "Not a Jew,"

Anyone who says
I'm not a Jew
is not a Jew
I'm very sorry
but this is final
So says:
Eliezar, son of Nissan,
priest of Israel;
a.k.a.
Nightingale of the Sinai.

Yom Kippur 1973;
a.k.a.
Jikan the Unconvincing
Zen monk,
a.k.a.
Leonard Cohen . . .

He had agreed to ordination to "observe protocol."[23] Roshi had told him it was time for him to become a monk, and so that is what he did. Leonard had also recently taken on responsibilities for which official status might be deemed appropriate: Roshi had asked him to preside over his funeral. The old man, now approaching his ninetieth birthday, instructed Leonard that he wanted a traditional, open-pyre cremation. If Leonard would like to, Roshi said, he could keep one of his bones.

At the ordination ceremony, Leonard was given a new name: Jikan. "Roshi doesn't speak English very well so you don't really know what he means by the names he gives you," Leonard said. "He prefers it that way because he doesn't want people to indulge themselves in the poetic quality of these traditional monks' names. I have asked him what Jikan meant many times, at the appropriate moment over a drink, and he says 'ordinary silence' or 'normal silence' or 'the silence between two thoughts.'"[24] Dangerously poetic. And deliciously ironic for a singer and a man of words.

In all, the silence of the monastic life seemed to suit Leonard. There were occasional visitors, however. Adam Cohen, who had just signed a record deal with Columbia, came and discussed with his father the lyrics for the songs he was working on for his first album. Leonard gave his son a song that he had been "working on for years" and knew he'd "never get around to doing,"[25] "Lullaby in Blue." Sharon Robinson, who knew the Zen Center, having been there her-

---

* Leonard published a six-line edit of "Not a Jew" in *Book of Longing* (2006).

self on retreat, drove up and, over a bottle of wine, listened as he played for her on his synthesizer the latest of his countless versions of "A Thousand Kisses Deep." Among the uninvited guests, in Kigen's words, was "a beautiful young lady who came up one evening and was wearing rags and feathers, literally. 'Where's Leonard? I'm here for Leonard.'" But really there were remarkably few celebrity-seekers; Kigen says he could count them on one hand.

Two separate, small film crews also made their way up the mountain, one from France, the other from Sweden. The result was two insightful TV documentaries, Armelle Brusq's *Leonard Cohen: Portrait: Spring 96* and Agreta Wirberg's *Stina Möter Leonard Cohen.* The French film showed Leonard working in the monastery kitchen, sitting in the meditation hall, reading the chants through a large pair of tinted spectacles and marching outside with the other monks. He assured Brusq that his life wasn't one of isolation. Real life was far more solitary, he said. When a tour ended, he would return to the "tyrannical solitude" of home, where he might spend days alone, speaking to no one, doing nothing.

The Swedish presenter, Stina Dabrowski, questioned Leonard about love, and he answered like a man who'd had the time and space to think about it. "I had wonderful love but I did not give back wonderful love," he said. "I was unable to reply to their love. Because I was obsessed with some fictional sense of separation, I couldn't touch the thing that was offered me, and it was offered me everywhere." Nonetheless, at times when the world started feeling bright again, he would forget now and then that he lived "in this sixty-three-year-old body" and he would think about finding a young girl, marrying her, buying a house and getting a real job, maybe working in a bookstore. "I could do that now. I know how to do it now," he said. When he was asked the inevitable question about coming back to music he answered no, saying, "I can't interrupt these studies. It's too important for me to interrupt . . . for the health of my soul." Quoting the Jewish sage Hillel the Elder, "If I'm not for myself, who will be for

me? And if not now, when? But if I'm only for myself, who am I?"
Leonard asked his fans to please forgive him. He was trying to learn
some things, he said, that would result in "songs that are deeper and
better."[26]

In the absence of Leonard or any word of a new album from him, in
1997 Columbia Records released a compilation, *More Best Of* (1997).
Twenty-two years had passed since the first *Best Of* album—or *Greatest Hits*, as it was called in the UK and Europe, where Leonard actually had hits—and Leonard had felt "no great urgency" for another.
But it was the thirtieth anniversary of his having signed to Columbia;
he said, "Although I myself feel very little nostalgia, I went along
with it."[27] Leonard was asked to choose the songs, which he did—
enough songs to fill a double album. In the end the label decided on
a single album, which they wanted to focus on his more recent material. They also asked Leonard if he had any new songs he might give
them. Leonard had actually finished a jaunty and self-deprecating
number titled "Never Any Good." Another new song was a short,
computerized piece called "The Great Event," its melody a backward *Moonlight Sonata*, its vocal a synthesized version of Leonard's
own real voice.

Leonard had been working in the monastery on experimental
music. One idea he had come up with, but had been unable to realize on his elderly computer and synthesizer, was to create a vocal
that sounded "like some broken-down speaker that was left after the
destruction of the cosmos, just filled with some kind of absurd hope
for regeneration"[28]—the next step from "The Future," as interpreted
by a Zen monk. Around this time, Mount Baldy for the first time had
connected to the Internet—a slow, dial-up connection through the
monastery's one and only phone, but Leonard was online.

Jarkko Arjatsalo, an accountant living in Finland, was surprised
to receive a message from a monk in California, asking if he would
call him. Leonard had heard about the Leonard Cohen Files, a web-

site devoted to his work that Arjatsalo and his teenage son Rauli had created in 1995. If Arjatsalo could create a website, Leonard thought, perhaps he could answer his technical questions (this being pre-Google, and the connection being so painfully sluggish). "Leonard was looking for software that could imitate his voice—not a perfect copy, something that was obviously mechanized though recognizably him," Arjatsalo remembers. Through his website's global network he found a scientist at the University of California at Berkeley who came up with a solution. It was the start of a close association and friendship between Leonard and the man he dubbed "the general secretary of the party." LeonardCohenFiles.com would become known as Leonard's digital archive and the communications hub for the international fan community.

Leonard asked if he might add some material of his own to the website. He submitted early versions of lyrics for songs, including "Suzanne," and drafts of new songs and poems. He wanted to "make the process clear, or at least throw some light on the mysterious activity of writing," he wrote. He also sent copies of his artwork, which ranged from drawings on napkins to digital art. Leonard particularly enjoyed creating art on a computer. He just liked computers. "They say that the Torah was written with black fire on white fire. I get that feeling from the computer, the bright black against the bright background. It gives it a certain theatrical dignity to see it on the screen."[29] His interest in Macs started early on, thanks in part to the Apple company giving away free computers to select Canadian writers—among them Leonard, Irving Layton and Margaret Atwood—and sending tutors to their homes to show them how to use them.

Leonard said in an interview with *Billboard* in 1998 that he had been "posting a lot of original material on the Finnish site." He said, "I don't know what the ramifications are. Speaking as a writer toward the end of his life, where most of my work is out there, I've collected royalties on it, I've been able to live and maybe even provide for a respectable retirement. I'd be happy to publish everything on the Internet at this stage of the game."[30] His record company did not share his sentiments. When he included the website addresses of the Leonard Cohen Files and other related sites on the back sleeve of *More Best Of*, they told him to take them off, talking about "permissions" and "compliance." But Leonard insisted and the URLs remained in place.

Leonard had taken to the Internet wholeheartedly—and this some considerable time before the decline of the recording industry and the expansion of the Web made it a necessity for artists. For someone who had essentially cut himself off from the world, it allowed him to communicate with the world on his own terms. He could keep in touch with his fans around the globe without having to get out of his robes and onto a plane. He could keep his work in the public eye without having to go through an intermediary, like the record company. He was already living, to some degree, a virtual existence up there in that remote spot a long way above the ground and a longer way from heaven; in the Internet he'd found a perfectly Cohenesque way of being both not there and never more fully present.

Leonard logged off for the night. There was a good bottle of cognac on the table that he'd picked up on his last grocery run to Claremont. Tucking it underneath his arm, he crunched up the hill in his flip-flops to Roshi's cabin.

Autumn 1998. Leonard had been living in the monastery for five years. He was as thin as the air; his long black robes hung loosely on his body. During countless hours of meditation, he had had out-of-body experiences and moments when "the sky opens up and you get the word." There had been periods during his life on Mount Baldy when Leonard felt contentment and when everything seemed to make sense. This was not one of them. Pulling himself out of his bed in the middle of the night, putting the water on for coffee, fingers waxy from the cold, what Leonard felt was despair. In the meditation hall, where he sat listening to Roshi's familiar voice deliver the *teisho* from the lectern-throne at the front of the room, he realized that he no longer had any idea what Roshi was saying. "I used to be able to understand, but my mind had become so concerned with dissolving the pain that my critical faculties had become really impaired."[31] The anguish did not abate; it deepened. His doctor prescribed antidepressants, telling him they would put a floor on how low he could go. But "the floor opened up," Leonard said, "and I fell right through it."[32]

One day Leonard was taking Roshi to the airport—Roshi was flying to New Mexico to lead one of his periodic *sesshins* at his second monastery in Jemez Springs—and he needed to go back to Mount Baldy for something. Driving up the mountain's switchback roads, Leonard was suddenly seized by a panic so crippling that he had to pull over. He reached into the backseat for his knapsack and pulled out the shaving kit in which he kept his antidepressants. His heart pounding, he took out the pills, then threw them out of the car. "I said, 'If I'm going to go down, I'm going to go down with my eyes open.' There's something obscene about taking this stuff and going down. And then I went back to Mount Baldy," Leonard said, "and I *really* went down."[33]

He was unable to find his way back up. The winter months felt crueler than ever; Roshi's *teisho* sounded like gibberish. After five and a half years in the monastery and in the deepest pit of depression, Leonard felt that he had "come to the end of the road."[34] On a cold early January night in 1999, Leonard walked up the hill to Roshi's cabin. It was black and starless; there was snow in the air. Roshi, shrunken with age, peered over the reading glasses whose magnification made his eyes look profoundly deep. The two sat together in stillness, as they had so often done. Leonard broke the silence. "Roshi," he said, "I've got to go. I'm going to go down the mountain."

Roshi said, "How long?" Leonard said, "I don't know." The old man looked at him. "Okay," Roshi said. "You go."

Leonard's note of apology to Roshi for his desertion read: "I'm sorry that I cannot help you now because I met this woman. . . . Jikan the useless monk bows his head." The words were accompanied by a drawing of a female Hindu temple dancer.* Less than a week after leaving Mount Baldy, Leonard was in India. Leonard had left Roshi to be with not a woman but a man.

Ramesh S. Balsekar was eighty-one years old, a strip of a lad compared with Roshi. He had studied at the London School of Economics and had been the president of a leading bank in India until, in the late seventies, he became a devotee of Nisargadatta Maharaj, a master of the Advaita (meaning non-dual) school of Hindu philosophy. Ramesh now received students of his own in his apartment in South Mumbai. Among them, just days after having left Roshi's monastery, and "in a state of acute depression and deep distress," was Leonard.[35]

Leonard had first encountered Ramesh's teachings while living on Mount Baldy. A few years earlier, someone at the monastery had given him a book called *Consciousness Speaks*, a question-and-answer session with Balsekar, published in 1992. At the foundation of Ramesh's teaching is that there is one supreme Source, Brahman, which created everything and is also everything it created. Since there is only this one single consciousness, then there is no "I" or "me," no individual doer of any action, no individual thinker of any thoughts, no experiencer of any experiences. Once the sense of self drops away, once a person deeply understands that he has no free will, no control over what he does nor over what is done to him, when he takes no personal pride in his achievements or personal affront at what might befall him, then that person becomes one with that single consciousness or Source. When Leonard read the book that first time, he liked

---

* Later published in *Book of Longing*, 2006.

it but could not say that he understood it. He put it aside, and during "those last dark days"[36] at the monastery he found himself drawn back to it. This time when he read it, it seemed to make more sense. He even found that by applying Ramesh's teachings to Roshi's *teisho*, he could once again understand Roshi. But it was a purely intellectual understanding that did nothing to ease the intensity of his mental torment. Leonard drove to the Bodhi bookstore to look for more books by Balsekar and decided to go to India to hear him in person. He booked a flight to Mumbai.

The years Leonard had spent in the monastery had done nothing to dull his talent at sniffing out a nondescript hotel room. Kemps Corner was a two-star hotel in the south of Mumbai in a busy, built-up neighborhood. A small place—just thirty-five rooms—it was not more than a couple of hundred yards from the beach, though closer still to a highway overpass. The building was old but not elegant. There was a jaunty striped awning over the entrance door that led into a miniature, dimly lit lobby. Leonard took a small single room at the back of the building, where there was less street noise. There was a narrow bed, one side pushed up against the white-painted wall; an armchair; a wooden desk beneath a wood-framed mirror; a tiny TV; and a white-tiled bathroom.

In Mumbai Leonard once again kept to a fairly strict schedule. Every morning a little after eight he would leave the hotel, dressed in Western clothes—loose black shirt tucked into light-colored linen trousers, Leonard's formal take on casual—and walk to the *satsang*, which was a mile away. He always took the same route, which led him through the congestion of people and traffic, beggars and eternal car horns, and onto Warden (now Bhulabhai Desai) Road, the main road that ran beside the beach and the Arabian Sea. The buildings he passed—the Breach Candy Club and Gardens, the U.S. consulate—grew increasingly privileged the closer he came to North Gamadia Road, the small, quiet lane where Ramesh lived on the top floor of a five-story art deco apartment building, Sindula House. This part of town was considerably more upmarket than Leonard's, its residents a mix of old money, successful writers, well-known actors and retired bank presidents like Balsekar.

The apartment was well appointed though not luxurious. It had four rooms, the largest of which, the living room, was used for the *satsang*. It could accommodate around forty people sitting on the floor. Leaving his shoes outside the door, Leonard sought out an inconspicuous spot in a back corner and sat there, cross-legged, eyes cast down. At nine A.M. Ramesh, a small, trim man, his hair white, like his clothes, entered from the next-door room and took his chair at the front. Following a short formal reading, the question-and-answer session began, which Ramesh would start by inquiring of someone— usually a newcomer—what had brought them to India and what their background was.

"Most of the attendees were foreigners—a lot of them from Israel—with maybe three or four Indians in a group of thirty-five or forty," says Ratnesh Mathur, an Indian banker who became friendly with Leonard during Leonard's first trip to Mumbai. Mathur had not heard of Ramesh until Leonard spoke about him and invited him to a *satsang* (the first of around forty *satsang*s Mathur would attend over the next four years) since Ramesh was relatively unknown as a spiritual leader among his countrymen. "Ramesh alienated himself from the cults," Mathur says, "he didn't target the Indian mass media. He was not a big publicity seeker and he was clearly living on a pension so there was no financial motive. His articulation was in English, his mannerisms were Western, his message was rather erudite and intellectual, and his style was not part of the Ramana Maharshi legacy." Ramana was a popular guru and some of his followers had cast aspersions on Ramesh as a spiritual leader. "Really, he lived like a retired banker—he liked his occasional golf and whiskey—except that one or two hours a day he would leave it open to have people come to his home. People came mostly by word of mouth. It was a very respect-able crowd, not the traditional hippie crowd," although some seek-ers had come to Ramesh after visiting the Osho commune in Pune, two hours from Mumbai. (Its leader, Bhagwan Shree Rajneesh, had established an alternative living community in Oregon in the early eighties, before controversy and scandal, and the guru's deportation, led to its closure.)

Ramesh was a straight-talker. He dealt with his *satsang* audience much as you might imagine he would his employees at the bank, imparting information and instructions in a direct, no-nonsense man-ner. Mathur says, "Ramesh easily lost patience with folks who spoke too much and tried to involve him in some esoteric argument. He would remind them that he charged no entrance fee"—if someone wished to make a donation they could do so later—"and then show them to the exit door." When he spotted someone in the room who had been coming repeatedly for too long he would single them out and say, according to Mathur, "'Don't you have anything better to do? My main message to you is that God is everywhere, so you can't just focus on religion, you don't keep meditating your way to God.' Basically he said, 'Get a life.'" Ramesh never said this to Leonard, though, whom he had also seen privately and with whom he became friendly. "He was always very polite and nice about Leonard."

After approximately two hours Ramesh would look at his watch, which indicated that the questions and answers had come to an end. When Ramesh left the room, a *bhajan* singer, Mrs. Murthy, came in to lead the gathering in the singing of the traditional Hindu songs. A paper was passed around the room with the words written in both the original Sanskrit and the Roman alphabet. "But Leonard didn't need that," Mathur remembers. "He knew every word." When the sing-ing stopped, everyone filed out past the table where Mrs. Murthy's husband sold copies of Ramesh's books and of the audiotapes made of every *satsang*. The tapes dating from Leonard's earliest months of attendance—when he had asked Ramesh questions, rather than sit quietly, as he would do later, concentrating on what he was saying—proved a popular sales item once word started to spread about Leonard's studying with Ramesh. Mathur started noticing that some attendees seemed to be seeking Leonard more than Ramesh. No one bothered Leonard during the *satsang*, but people would come up and talk to him by the table or on his way out of the building.

"He was normally very polite," says Mathur. "He would talk to them. Occasionally if he found someone interesting, he would take them to a small tea stall," an unassuming little spot some fifty yards away, the kind of place Leonard consistently found and frequented in whichever city he happened to be living. The workers in the tea shop all recognized him, greeting him with a smile and a respectful exchange of *namaste*. They did not know him as a celebrity but as a Westerner with short silver hair, a friendly man who came in regularly and always treated them well. "He told me most people didn't recognize him on the street when he walked and he loved that about being here." Leonard, Mathur observed, "deliberately avoided spending time with the Mumbai rich and famous." People always came to him with invitations, Mathur included, to which Leonard would politely make his excuses, "but he told me once about going to some taxi driver's slum home. I remember being surprised to see how he developed these bonds with folks who knew nothing of him as a famous singer-songwriter. Perhaps the folks who spent the most time with him in India are the cleaners of Kemps hotel and the workers at the tea stall."

After tea Leonard left for the other regular item on his schedule, his midday swim. There were YMCAs with pools in Mumbai but nothing convenient, so Leonard joined the Breach Candy Club, an exclusive, private club on the seafront on Warden Road, which had a lap pool as well as an enormous outdoor pool, built in the shape of

India.* The rest of the day was usually spent alone in his hotel room, meditating, sketching, writing and reading books written or recommended by Ramesh. Mathur had offered Leonard some books on related topics but he declined them politely; he did not want distractions. Early evening he would take himself off to a restaurant for a vegetarian meal, then return to his room, light some incense, put on a CD of Indian music and meditate and read some more. He had little interest in sightseeing, but he paid a visit to the Keneseth Eliyahoo Synagogue, which served a small Jewish community. Not far from the synagogue was a large, bustling record store, Rhythm House. He asked if they had any Leonard Cohen albums. They did. He could find them, he was told, under "Easy Listening."

Leonard flew home back to L.A. in the spring. There he put the finishing touches to a song he was writing for an event in tribute to the late Canadian poet and intellectual Frank "F. R." Scott, whom Leonard had known from his McGill University days. The song "Villanelle for our Time" was a Scott poem of the same name that Leonard had set to music. Working on the song, Leonard realized it needed a woman's voice. He called Anjani Thomas, one of his former backing singers, and asked if she would come over. They completed the recording in a single afternoon.

Then Leonard drove to Mount Baldy. It had been almost four months since he had seen Roshi and he wanted to pay his respects. As they had done so many times, they sat with a cognac in the old man's cabin, the world outside swollen up in darkness, moths pressed against the fly screen on the window like dried flowers in a poetry book. They talked little but when they did it was not about Leonard studying another discipline with a different master. Nor did Leonard discuss with Roshi what he had learned from Ramesh. "Roshi doesn't discuss," not even his own teachings, Leonard said. "He's not

---

* Salman Rushdie, who grew up in the area, describes the pool in his book *Midnight's Children*.

interested in perspective or talking. You either get it or you don't. He doesn't give you any astounding truths that we come to expect from spiritual teachers, because he's a mechanic—he's not talking about the philosophy of locomotion, he's talking about repairing the motor. He's mostly talking to a broken motor. Roshi is direct transmission."[37]

Leonard did not stay in the monastery long. In June he came back down from the mountain. His close friend Nancy Bacal, who met with him in L.A., observed that "he was like a kid when he came back from Baldy; suddenly he could come and go as he pleased, do whatever he wanted. It took him a moment or two to figure that out, but when he did, it was a delight to see him so happy and so joyous. Baldy was wonderful for him. Now it was time to take the next step."

For the first time in years, Leonard went back to Hydra. He packed the notebooks he had filled during his long stay in the monastery, and, in his old study, in the white house on the hill, he went to work on poems and songs in various states of completion. He also returned to Montreal and visited his old friend Irving Layton, now eighty-seven years old, suffering from Alzheimer's and living in a nursing home. Leonard had been rereading a good deal of Layton's poetry lately and was thinking about setting some of it to music, as he had done with F. R. Scott's.

Leonard also returned to Mumbai, once again taking his old room at the Hotel Kemps Corner. In 1999 the room was his home for almost five months. He spent his last birthday of the millennium there. When Mathur met with Leonard that day, he could not fail to notice how happy Leonard seemed. Leonard celebrated after *satsang* with a birthday lunch. "There was one girl who had come along with us, a girl who had come to Ramesh's sessions and was clearly enamored of Leonard. He had picked up a flower in the hotel vase and put it in the lapel of his jacket, and he smoked a cigarette or two that day, although I think he had given them up at the time. He said that he was very happy to be here, and this happiness was evident all the way through. It was on his face and in everything he was saying, which was all very, very positive."

Something had happened to Leonard in India. Something, as he told Sharon Robinson, "just lifted" the veil of depression through which he had always seen the world. Over the space of several visits Leonard would make to Mumbai over the next few years, returning to his room at the Hotel Kemps Corner and making his daily walk to *satsang*—altogether, he spent more than a year studying with Ramesh—"by imperceptible degrees this background of anguish that had been with me my whole life began to dissolve. I said to myself, 'This must be what it's like to be relatively sane.' You get up in the morning and it's not like: Oh God, another day. How am I going to get through it? What am I going to do? Is there a drug? Is there a woman? Is there a religion? Is there a something to get me out of this? The background now is very peaceful."[38] His depression had gone.

Leonard was unable to articulate precisely what it was that had cured his depression. He thought he had read somewhere "that the brain cells associated with anxiety can die as you get older,"[39] although the general intelligence is that depression worsens with age. Perhaps this was *satori*—enlightenment—though if it was, it had come with "no great flash, no fireworks."[40] Why it had come with Ramesh and Core Hinduism rather than Roshi and Zen Buddhism he could not say. Despite the differences in their teaching methods and approaches—Roshi's strict, rigorous regimen and his repetitive *teisho*, delivered on the in-breath and the out-breath and addressed not to the intellect but to the meditative condition; Ramesh's direct, straight-talking question-answer approach and his instruction that his followers should live however they choose—there was a great deal of consistency in their doctrines: overcoming the ego, nonattachment, universal consciousness, *tendrel*, the interrelatedness of all things. Most likely it was a combination of the two and had simply happened on Ramesh's watch. Ramesh implied as much. "You got this very quickly," he told Leonard, adding that his thirty years with Roshi did not hurt.[41] Still, as Leonard's mother had always used to say to him, "Don't look a gift horse in the mouth," so Leonard didn't. What was left in the deep, dark hole left after the anguish had gone was "a deep sense of gratitude, to what or who I don't know. I focused it on my teachers and friends."[42]

The year was drawing to a close. Back in Los Angeles, Leonard once again ran into his musician friend Roscoe Beck. The last time they had seen each other had been more than five years before, just as Leonard was leaving to go live with Roshi. Beck reminded Leonard of what he'd said on that occasion, that he'd "had it with the music racket." Leonard smiled. "Ah," he said, "now I've had it with the religious racket. I'm ready to take up music again."

Of course he hadn't really had it with religion. Religion, as Leonard has said on any number of occasions, was his "favorite hobby." He still studied with Ramesh, he still meditated at the Zen Center in L.A. and he continued to read the Jewish scriptures and light the Sabbath candles at dusk every Friday. But what he had said about taking up music again was true. Leonard picked up the phone and called Sharon Robinson and Leanne Ungar, asking them to come over. It was time to record his first album of the new millennium.

Twenty-one

Love and Theft

Women. You couldn't move for them. After the largely male life of
the monastery, it was a novelty and a delight. A comfort too; Leonard
had not lived in such a female world since he was a nine-year-old boy
in Montreal. In the apartment downstairs was his daughter Lorca.
Upstairs, in the room above the garage, Sharon Robinson and Leanne
Ungar were working in the studio they had put together for Leonard to make his album at home. Sharon and Leanne would arrive at
noon to find him in the kitchen, preparing them lunch. Kelley Lynch,
Leonard's manager, would often show up at around the same time
and eat with them.

Cooking was one of the habits Leonard had brought home with
him from the monastery. Another was getting up at four A.M., having
a quiet coffee and a cigarette, then starting his day's work. Although
he had quit smoking, he had taken it up again during a visit to India;
a wise man had said to him, when he refused the offer of a cigarette,
"What is life for? Smoke." While the world still slept, Leonard recorded in the aerie above the garage, until the birds began their dawn

chorus in the grapefruit trees and the sound of the neighbors starting up their cars bled through the unsoundproofed walls. His computer screen lighting up the darkness, he would murmur softly into an old microphone linked to Pro Tools recording software, the harrowed young man playing a Spanish guitar to a sad-eyed girl in a bedroom seeming a lifetime away.

Leonard was happy. He was fully aware of the novelty of such a circumstance, but it was something he tried not to think about too much; he did not want to risk thinking himself back into his old familiar state of unhappiness. Nor did he wish to tempt fate, acknowledging, "God may take it away."[1] The depression and anxiety had been so much a part of him for such a long time that on occasion they seemed hard to separate from the depth and seriousness of his work. They had certainly been the drive behind the great majority of his pursuits in his adult life—"the engine," as Leonard expressed it, "of most of my investigation into the various things I looked into, whatever it was: wine, woman, song, religion."[2] Women and drugs, as well as mantras and fasting and all the various regimes of physical and spiritual self-discipline he had pursued, had had their pleasures, but they were also palliatives, medication, attempts to "beat the devil, try to get on top of it,"[3] or help ease the pain. Now the pain had gone. Sometimes, as he went about his work, he surprised himself with the ease with which he adapted to this new lightness of being and peace of mind.

There was also a new woman in Leonard's life. Readers will not find this surprising, although Leonard seemed to. He thought he'd had it with the romance racket, thinking perhaps that it might have vanished along with the depression and anguish. "I think one becomes more circumspect about everything as one gets older. I mean, you become more foolish and more wise at the same time as you get older," he said. In his midsixties, he had been reminded that the heart could not be mastered: "I think one is vulnerable at any moment to those emotions."[4] His first new love since leaving the monastery was, like his last love before he entered it, a talented beauty twenty-five years his junior: a singer and keyboard player from Hawaii who performed under her first name, Anjani.

Anjani Thomas had been in and out of Leonard's musical life since 1984, when John Lissauer, the producer of *Various Positions*, hired her to sing on "Hallelujah" and tour with Leonard. Although Leonard was not immune to office romances, there had been nothing between them on the 1985 tour, nor when Anjani sang on *I'm Your Man* or *The Future*—on the latter singing on "Waiting for the Miracle," the song containing Leonard's marriage proposal to Rebecca.

In the period between those two albums, Anjani had moved to Los Angeles and married an entertainment lawyer, Robert Kory. Around the same time that Leonard parted with Rebecca and the music industry and left L.A., Anjani's life took something of a similar turn; her marriage was over and her music career seemed to be heading the same way. But while Leonard chose to become closer with his spiritual teacher, Anjani had become disillusioned with hers, the Maharishi Mahesh Yogi, whose Transcendental Meditation practice she had followed for years. Making a clean break from everything, she moved to Austin, Texas, where she bought a little house and took a job as a saleswoman in a jewelry store. She was living in a city full of clubs and musicians but refused to even listen to music on her car radio on the way to work. "I was burned out," she says. "I didn't want anything to do with it." Four or five years later, while she was visiting her family in Hawaii, Anjani opened the closet in her old bedroom and saw her guitar. She took it out and started writing songs—"Two records' worth of material," she says. "I was thirty-nine at the time and I said to myself, 'I'm going to be forty. If I don't do this record I'll regret it the rest of my life.'" She sold the house and moved back to L.A. around the same time Leonard returned from Mount Baldy. Sometime later, when their paths crossed again, she played him one of the songs she had written, "Kyrie,"* which he liked and encouraged her to record. The two became musical coconspirators and lovers; later they would become musical collaborators. But for now Anjani worked on her album and Leonard worked on his.

Leonard had left the monastery with around two hundred and fifty songs and poems in various states of completion. An idea of what he might do with them came to him while he was at a classical concert in Los Angeles in late 1999. The performer was his godson, whose mother is Sharon Robinson. Leonard took Sharon aside during the intermission and said, "I've got some verses and things and I'd like for you to work on a record with me."[5] Not simply a song or two, as they had done in the past, but a whole album. Her job would be to write the melodies. It turned out to be a good deal more; *Ten New Songs*—at Leonard's insistence—was as much Sharon's album as it was his.

One might have imagined that Leonard's first album since his return to the music business would be all about Leonard—down from the mountain in a blaze of glory, imparting his wisdom on tablets of stone. It is not that Leonard had no melodies; he did. He either preferred Sharon's melodies, or he preferred collaborating; perhaps one after-effect of his studies with Roshi and Ramesh was to put ego aside and be inclusive. What's more interesting is how very female this album was. Women had always played a part in Leonard's songs, but mostly as backing singers and muses. Here he handed almost everything over to the women. Apart from an appearance on one song by Leanne's guitarist husband, Bob Metzger, and a string arrangement on another by David Campbell, Leanne Ungar engineered and mixed, and Sharon produced, arranged, played the instruments and wrote the melodies. In this supportive environment, all Leonard had to do was to sing the words over which he had labored so long.

---

* It would appear on her second album, *The Sacred Names* (2001).

"Sharon, I would say, was the person who has had the most success writing with Leonard," Leanne says. "She doesn't seem to have experienced some of the difficulties other people have had. Sharon understands a lot about what Leonard likes to sing, what he's capable of singing, then writes melodies that fit his sensibility; she comes up with the most beautiful music for him. And sometimes Sharon understands his lyrics in that he'll give her a poem he's written and she'll pick out the phrases she thinks will make a chorus and construct the song based on that. I know there's a lot of back-and-forth between Leonard and Sharon."

Leonard and Sharon did not discuss the album; they did not even refer to what they were working on as "an album." It was important "to keep it open," Sharon remembers. "'Well, we might be doing an album but maybe not, I don't know.'" Leonard was loath to introduce the expectations of other people into the exercise, particularly those of the music business. Instead they simply got together and worked at a song—"one song at a time, no pressure"—as if that was something they always did when they met up. "The first day, we sat quietly, listening to the music of an Indonesian singer that involved chants and ethnic rhythms. I think, in hindsight, that it helped set the tone for the workdays to come, which had a certain serene quality to them."

Working in Leonard's home and not in a studio also helped maintain the illusion of two close friends just hanging out and playing some music. The room above the garage, which Leonard nicknamed Small Mercies Studio, was, unlike regular studios, very bright, its windows looking out onto a small garden of grapefruit trees, jasmine and morning glories. He had furnished the room with a couple of art deco pieces from his mother's house in Montreal, and the sun streamed in on the curved-armed sofa where he and Sharon would sit, talking. They talked about the old soul and R & B records that both of them loved and whose sound influenced several of Robinson's melodies—

Sam Cooke, Otis Redding. Sometimes Leonard would have come up
with a rhythm he liked, or a few changes, which he would play for her
on the keyboard. Other times, when he handed her a set of lyrics, he
might mention that he wrote them with a specific musical style in
mind—"That Don't Make It Junk" was a country song, for example.
Mostly though, he was interested in seeing where Sharon would go
with it. She would take the lyrics home and work on them alone in
her home studio, save the melodies she had come up with onto a
hard drive, then give it to Leanne, who transferred it onto Leonard's
computer, which she had set up so that he could simply push a button
and continue to work on the song on his own in the early hours of the
morning. Leonard enjoyed this way of working—relaxed, collaborative, but also alone.

His relationship with Anjani appeared to follow a very similar pattern: they were a couple but they were also, as Leonard termed it,
"impossibly solitudinous people" and did not live together. "I like
to wake up alone," said Leonard, "and she likes to be alone."[6] Anjani
had moved into a house within walking distance of Leonard's duplex.
Leanne, who had worked with Leonard for many years, couldn't help
but notice how much happier and more secure he seemed. "I think
he had found a kind of domestic peace. Or maybe it's because we
worked at his house and, instead of being in this impersonal room
and ordering out, we were sitting in his kitchen and he was cooking.
It had a kind of intimacy that I think you can hear in the vocals."
There was no deadline, no meter running in a studio. A song might
go back and forth between Leonard and Sharon numerous times before it was finished and the next one begun. There were also breaks
between recording, three or four weeks at a time, while Leonard
wrote or rewrote lyrics.

During these absences, Leanne was busy going through tapes
from Leonard's 1979 *Recent Songs* tour. Henry Lewy, his producer,
had recorded all the UK concerts. The tapes had been gathering dust

for decades, but Leonard had not forgotten them and was curious to see if they deserved resuscitating. In February 2000, an album of twelve of these songs was released with the title *Field Commander Cohen*. Leonard's first album of the new millennium presents a polished performance with the jazz group Passenger, the violin and oud players Raffi Hakopian and John Bilezikjian, and backing singers Jennifer Warnes and Sharon Robinson, who was at that time a newcomer to Leonard and was now his songwriting partner.

During a longer break, Leonard returned to Mumbai. Reinstalling himself at the Hotel Kemps Corner, he slipped back into his old schedule, taking his daily walk along Warden Road to *satsang* with the sea breeze in his hair, then on to the Breach Candy Club for a swim. The city was a riot of color and noise, but nothing disturbed Leonard's sense of peace. So comfortable did Leonard appear with his life in Mumbai that Lorca, curious as to what kept her father there so long, flew out and stayed with him for a week or two. At Leonard's suggestion she spent some of the time hunting through Mumbai's markets for old furniture to ship back to the antiques store she now ran in L.A.

In Canada, meanwhile, where new ways of honoring Leonard were still, miraculously, being found, Stephen Scobie organized an event in Montreal in May 2000 titled *Some Kind of Record: Poems in Tribute to Leonard Cohen*. Leonard, as seemed to have become an unspoken policy, declined to attend. A cartoon in a Montreal newspaper showed a woman of a certain age, hippily dressed, with an acoustic guitar, sitting forlorn on a park bench while a policeman tells her, "C'mon now, lady, everyone else has gone home. Leonard Cohen isn't coming." Leonard did go to Montreal not too long afterward, but on private business, to visit Pierre Trudeau, who was terminally ill. Leonard returned in September, at the request of Trudeau's children, to be a pallbearer at Trudeau's funeral.

While he was in his old hometown, Leonard took the opportunity to go see Irving Layton in the nursing home. When Leonard entered his room, the eighty-eight-year-old poet, who was suffering from Alzheimer's, stared at Leonard with a blank, bewildered face. Leonard said, "It's Leonard." Irving replied, "Leonard who?" Leonard's face fell. Layton laughed uproariously. He knew who it was. The moment the nurse left the room, they had an illicit smoke, Leonard lighting his old friend's pipe because Layton's big boxer's hands shook too much to do it himself.

September 2001. It was still monsoon season in Mumbai, but the rains had started to ease up. Having finished work on his new album, Leonard had returned to India and Ramesh. One day, as he walked into the lobby of the Hotel Kemps Corner, the desk clerk offered his sincere condolences. This was how Leonard first heard of the 9/11 terrorist attack on New York. Not long after, Leonard's phone rang; a journalist from the *New York Observer* wanted his reaction to what had happened, since Leonard after all had predicted apocalypse in his last album *The Future*. Leonard was reluctant to give an opinion— "In the Jewish tradition one is cautioned against trying to comfort the comfortless in the midst of their bereavement." But, when pressed, he offered something he told the reporter he had learned from his Hindu studies: "It's impossible for us to discern the pattern of events and the unfolding of a world which is not entirely of our making."[7]

In October 2001, *Ten New Songs*, Leonard's new album, was released. The photo on the front sleeve, which Leonard took on his computer's built-in camera, pictured Leonard and Sharon, side by side. "The album," Leonard said, "could be described as a duet." She had expected, and sometimes urged, him to replace her vocals and remove the synthesizers on which she composed her melodies, "but as the sound unfolded," said Leonard, "I began to insist that she keep her voice on there and that we use these synthesizer sounds, because the songs seemed to insist that the original treatments were appropriate. Also I like the way Sharon sings."[8]

Leonard's voice on the album—so different from the voice on *Field Commander Cohen*—is a soft, dry baritone that unfurls like smoke over the translucent, skeletal, yet soulful-sounding digital keyboard tracks. The instruments make no attempt to disguise that they are not "real," giving a lo-fi charm not normally associated with synthesizers. The intimacy in Leonard's voice reflects how he recorded his vocal parts, murmuring quietly while his neighbors slept, and there's a meditative quality to how the songs seem to flow gracefully and solemnly in and out of one another. Leonard's own description of the album was "serene."

The lyrics are about wounded dawns and light, America and Babylon, about praying to God and just getting on with it. The words of "Love Itself"—which Leonard dedicated to his friend, the writer and critic Leon Wieseltier—are an account of Roshi's *teisho* on love, while "By the Rivers Dark" ("*By the rivers of Babylon we sat and wept*") is loosely based on Psalm 137, which laments the destruction of the temple and exile of the Jews. The dreamlike "Alexandra Leaving," which Leonard had been writing since 1985, was inspired by a poem by Constantine P. Cavafy, "The God Forsakes Antony." The dazzling "A Thousand Kisses Deep" has multiple layers of meaning, among them holding, letting go, creating and surrendering to the Creator. This song too had been through numerous incarnations, melodically and lyrically. Rebecca De Mornay remembers hearing various versions of it in the early nineties; in 1995 Leonard told the *New York Times* that he wanted it to feel like "an old folk song."[9] Its companion piece "Boogie Street" is, at first glance, about Leonard accepting who he is and what he has to do, even if he does not know why, and leaving the monastic life for the music business. It opens with a prayer and a kiss before moving on to the unreality of real life, the impermanence of romantic love and the permanence of desire. "Boogie Street," said Leonard, "is that place that we all live, whether you're in a monastery or down in the city."[10] It is also a real place, in Singapore. Leonard had been there once.

"During the day it's a place of bazaars and shops and booths with a lot of bootleg records. Since I didn't see any on display, I asked one of the vendors if he had any Leonard Cohen records. He went back to where he kept his inventory and came out with an entire box of my catalog—much more thorough than most of the stores that I'd been to, and a dollar apiece. Very reasonably priced, I thought. At night, Boogie Street transformed into this alarming and beautiful sexual marketplace, where there were male and female prostitutes, transvestites, extremely attractive people offering to satisfy all the fantasies of their numerous customers."

An all-service paradise, then.

"As my old teacher used to say, 'We can visit paradise but we can't live there because there are no restaurants or toilets in paradise.' There are moments, as I say in that song, when 'You kiss my lips, and then it's done, I'm back on Boogie Street'—*in the midst of an embrace with your beloved you melt into the kiss, you dissolve in the intimacy, [it's like] you take a drink of cold water when you're thirsty; without that refreshment you would probably die of boredom in a week or two. But you can't live there. Immediately, you're plunged back into the traffic jam."*

Leonard dedicated the album to Roshi.

The critics, bar a very few dissenters, were full of praise. They welcomed Leonard back, told him how much his voice, his profundity and his sly humor had been missed—even if the new album did not have all the cool, playful one-liners of *I'm Your Man*—and that *Ten New Songs* was worth the long wait. He was asked in interviews if he planned to tour behind it. Leonard demurred, saying he doubted he could still fill seats. It was a typically Cohenesque answer, modest and self-deprecating. Perhaps there was an element of insecurity after so much time had passed since his last tour, but what it really came down to was that he did not want to tour. There was clearly an audience for him in Europe, where *Ten New Songs* was a hit—Top 30 in the UK, No. 1 in Poland and Norway and gold in seven other countries. In America, reverting to Leonard's pre–*I'm Your Man* pattern, it sold poorly, failing to make the Top 100. In Canada, though, it went platinum and brought him four more Juno awards: Best Album, Best Artist, Best Songwriter and Best Video (this last one for the smooth soul single "In My Secret Life").

Leonard's fellow countrymen now seemed unable to stop with the honors and homages. The Canadian consulate commissioned a tribute concert to Leonard in New York as part of its Canada Day celebrations, hiring Hal Willner to put it together. Willner was renowned for the concept ensemble projects he produced—Nino Rota, Thelonious Monk, Kurt Weill. The last time Willner had seen Leonard was pre-monastery, on the *Future* tour. Willner had gone to the New York show with Allen Ginsberg and remembers, "You could tell there was something going on; the vibe wasn't as much fun as on the *I'm Your Man* tour. I went back with Allen to say hello, and Leonard had ducked out even then."

Willner called Kelley Lynch to make sure that Leonard had no objection to the Brooklyn concert. He was fine with it, she said, as long as he did not have to do anything, so Willner got going. Among the first people he called was Julie Christensen, looking for a contact for an artist he wanted to ask to perform. Julie told him, "If you're doing Leonard stuff, you should have Perla and me come sing backup." He thought it an interesting idea and called Perla Batalla, who told him that the date conflicted with another gig. "Then I got off the phone with Hal and I just started to cry," Perla remembers. "I can't *not* be involved." She called back and told Willner she would cancel the other show on the condition that she could sing "Bird on the Wire" and duet with Julie on "Anthem." Hal said, "'Anthem' is not in the show." He changed his mind later when Leonard, over a coffee with Perla and Hal, agreed that it might make a good addition to the set list. This would be Leonard's only involvement.

More than half the singers Willner invited to perform were women. There were Laurie Anderson, Linda Thompson, Kate and Anna McGarrigle, Kate's daughter Martha Wainwright, Perla, Julie and Rennie Sparks, of the duo the Handsome Family. "It just seemed to make sense," Willner says. "We weren't trying to imitate him, and Leonard loved women—a true, true love. They're great songs for women to sing, the way he has of taking emotion into words." Nick Cave, one of the five male singers on the bill (along with Kate McGarrigle's son Rufus Wainwright; Linda Thompson's son Teddy Thompson; Marc Anthony Thompson, no relation; and Brett Sparks, the other half of the Handsome Family), found it "really moving to hear a lot of women singing Leonard's songs. They made wonderful sense of his stuff—I think more effectively in a lot of ways than the male singers. What I hadn't always realized was that these were extraordinary songs on any level and that, although I love his voice—which is incredibly affecting and has a tone that's totally unique, something like Miles Davis's trumpet—it doesn't need Leonard's voice to carry these songs. They're just really good songs—and there's a lot of them. I'd always had a particular love for the early stuff, particularly *Songs of Love and Hate* because it's punk rock, raw as can be. But he just got deeper, more humane."

Willner decided who would sing what. "I put a show together, like a script, a play, so it's more about the cast with this material we all love than a 'tribute show.' And you don't want everyone coming out and doing their favorite song and moving on. That way you don't get a real balance of the material. I wanted to have some of the more obscure things, like 'Tacoma Trailer' and 'Don't Go Home with Your Hard-On,' from *Death of a Ladies' Man*." Willner had a particular fondness for the latter.

In February 2003, Phil Spector was arrested for the murder of Lana Clarkson, an actress and nightclub hostess he met at the House of Blues and had taken back to his mansion. Shortly after the arrest, two detectives from the homicide bureau paid Leonard a visit. They had been poring through old press clippings of stories about the eccentric producer and his guns—and there were many, involving famous names like John Lennon, Stevie Wonder, Michelle Phillips and the Ramones, as well as Leonard. "Apparently the detectives had come across some old interviews I did in 1978 or 1979 in which I spoke of the difficulties of recording *Death of a Ladies' Man:* the brandishing of guns, armed bodyguards, drunkenness and Phil's famous megalomania." Leonard told the detectives, "Even though Phil put his arm around my shoulder and pressed an automatic into my neck, except for the real possibility of an accident I never at any moment thought that Phil meant to do me harm. I never felt seriously threatened." It was "basically just a good rock 'n' roll story," he told them, that had become exaggerated over the years.

They asked him when he had last seen Spector. "Over twenty years ago," he said. "They were very surprised. They said they were under the impression we were close friends. I said no. Hearing this, they thanked me for their time, finished their coffees and left. It was clear that I was not to be considered a valuable witness. I was never approached again by anyone concerned with the case, [and] needless to say, I did not testify before a grand jury."[11]

On June 28, 2003, Hal Willner's *Came So Far for Beauty: An Evening of Songs by Leonard Cohen Under the Stars* took place in Prospect Park in Brooklyn. The stage was draped with a large maple-leaf flag and a female representative of the Canadian consulate came out during the intermission and lauded Leonard as "the sexiest man alive." The concert was a success and quickly led to offers for Willner to stage it overseas. Since it had been more than a decade since Leonard last played a concert—a situation he showed no inclination to change—this tribute concert not only helped satisfy the demand from fans to see his music performed live, it also helped to keep his songs as Willner said, "out there."

Leonard's record label was also doing its part in this enterprise. Two different, career-encompassing, double-album retrospectives were released in 2002 and 2003: *The Essential Leonard Cohen* and *An Introduction to Leonard Cohen* (the latter in the UK as part of the "*MOJO* Presents" series). There was a new, fortieth-anniversary edition of *The Favorite Game* as well, to tie in with the premiere of Bernar Hébert's film. As for Leonard, he was working on his first collection of poems since 1984, titled *Book of Longing*. Much of the material—artwork as well as poetry—he was sorting through and editing had been created when he lived in the monastery. In the Swedish documentary shot on Mount Baldy, Leonard, describing himself as "a writer who failed his promise," points to a pile of notebooks and adds, "I may redeem myself."[12]

In October 2003 Leonard was made a companion of the Order of Canada—one of the two highest civilian honors his country could bestow. Leonard sent his thanks and got back to work—not on his book but, remarkably, a new album.

Dear Heather, Leonard's eleventh studio album, was released in October 2004, two weeks after Leonard's seventieth birthday and three years after *Ten New Songs*. In Leonard Cohen terms, this was surprisingly fast; his fans and his record label had become used to four-, five-, even nine-year gaps between album releases. Since Leonard had come down from the mountain he had been working nonstop, but this was nothing new; Leonard was always working. He simply chose not to release the majority of the material he had worked on. This apparent new urgency appeared to have nothing to do with the sense of mortality he had talked about more than ten years before. If anything, at seventy Leonard appeared to be in better condition, mentally, physically and emotionally, than he had been at sixty. Thoughts of being "old" did not seem to trouble him. In fact he played on the word in the original title for the album, which had been *Old Ideas*. It was a reference to his intention to bring together various odds and ends on this album: songs he'd written in tribute to the work of other poets, recordings of him reciting his own work, little musical sketches and half-finished ideas. Some of these ideas were old—"The Faith," for example, a song based on an old Quebec folk ballad that he had recorded with Henry Lewy in 1979–80 and shelved; "Tennessee Waltz," a live recording from 1985 of the weepy country standard, for which Leonard took the liberty of writing an even darker, sadder closing verse—but the majority dated from August 2003, when he began recording the album. Leonard was persuaded to substitute *Old Ideas* with *Dear Heather* only when it was pointed out that his fans might mistake it for yet another retrospective album.

If *Ten New Songs* was Leonard's most collaborative album (*Death of a Ladies' Man* had been written with Spector as equal, but Leonard had no say in the recording, and the Cohen-Lissauer project *Songs for Rebecca* was never released), *Dear Heather* is his most experimental. Its thirteen songs, recorded once again in his home studio, make up a sort of scrapbook, a collage of word, image and sound. The CD liner-note booklet, in which the lyrics appear side by side with Leonard's sketches, might have been a pocket-sized companion for *Book of Longing*, on which he worked at the same time. His idea, Leanne Ungar remembers, had been "to put together some melodies that the songs evoked and to actually do some poetry readings"— reminiscent, perhaps, of the shows he had performed in the late fifties with Maury Kaye.

The opening song, "Go No More A-Roving," is (in the manner of "Villanelle") a poem by Lord Byron set to music by Leonard. The accompanying drawings in the booklet are of Irving Layton, to whom the song is dedicated—wide hangdog face, crushed poor-boy cap—

and the entirely Cohenesque image of a guitar by an open door. "To a Teacher" also concerns a poet who was important to Leonard, A. M. Klein, who was silenced in his later years by mental illness. This time the poem set to music is Leonard's, from his 1961 collection *The Spice-Box of Earth*:

> *Let me cry Help beside you, Teacher*
> *I have entered under this dark roof*
> *As fearlessly as an honoured son*
> *Enters his father's house*

For an avowed nonsentimentalist like Leonard, there seems to be a good deal of looking back in these songs, from absent friends to the unnamed women he thanks in the delightful "Because Of," for having been inspired to take off their clothes by *"a few songs / Wherein I spoke of their mystery."*

The sense of collage is also evident in the music, which is diverse in style: folk, beatnik jazz, waltzes and some of the French-sounding music Leonard had talked about having written on his synthesizer on Mount Baldy. The title track takes lyrics not much longer than a haiku and repeats them, deconstructs them, then folds them over the keyboards and trumpet like aural origami. "On That Day," a ballad written about the 9/11 terrorist attacks, has the sentimentality and straight-talking of a Randy Newman song. There is no lack of synthesizers, but there are real instruments too, including a Jew's harp, which Leonard plays on "Nightingale," a collaboration with Anjani, and "On That Day." On two of the collaborations with Sharon Robinson, "There for You" and "The Letters," Leonard's voice is almost a whisper; most of the singing is left for the women to do. On "Morning Glory," sung by its muse, Anjani, Leonard sounds like a ghost of himself, hovering around the beauty of her multitracked voice. On some songs Leonard lets the women sing alone; on others he speaks his words over their voices, murmuring softly, deeply and close to the microphone, like Serge Gainsbourg, or "bassing in" once in a while like a Jewish-Buddhist A. P. Carter. Although there was a very strong female presence on his previous album, on *Dear Heather* the women are given even greater prominence.

Anjani says, "That record was a turning point, for both of us." Leonard had initially called her in to sing harmony on "Undertow," then decided that he wanted to scrap the melody and use the harmony as the lead. The song was about a bereaved, lost woman; what he liked about the harmony part was that it did not get to the root note except at the very end of the song, which gave it a tension that mirrored her emotional distress. He left Anjani and Leanne Ungar to record it while he went back to the house and made some phone calls. "I went through it a couple of times," Anjani remembers, "and we ended up with this track that I thought was gorgeous, the best thing I've ever done, and Leanne loved it." When Leonard came back, she said, "Wait until you hear this." "Leanne ran the playback," says Anjani, "and he does what he always does when he listens to music, which is stare off into space, no expression—I don't care if you're playing a salsa tune, he won't move, he just sits there motionless. At the end of it he said, 'That's beautiful. Now sing it but don't sing it.'" Anjani looked at him quizzically. "He said, 'This is not an anthem. It's the song of a broken woman, so *be* the woman on the deserted beach with nothing left.' I remember feeling outraged that he didn't like the superb performance that I'd just belted out, and then I thought, 'What am I supposed to do?' and I got really nervous and kind of shaky, like every tool I had just went out the window; I really truly had nothing left. And when I sang, this really tentative, broken thing came out. At the end of it he said, 'That's it. Now you've got it,' and that's when he said he had never heard me in that way before. He later described it as 'Her voice dropped from her throat to her heart.'"

What also distinguishes *Dear Heather* from earlier albums is the gentle modesty with which it deals with the Big Subjects, like love, death, life, faith and madness. As Leon Wieseltier noted in his album review, it "revels in its own lack of monumentality."[13] There was simplicity instead of grandiosity in his song mourning the 9/11 terrorist attacks, "On That Day," while in the title track whimsy replaced the more common anguish about women and lust. "The longing persists," Wieseltier concluded, "but the slavery is over. And the evidence of inner freedom is everywhere in *Dear Heather*. It is a window upon the heart of an uncommonly interesting and uncommonly mortal man."[14]

Leonard was for the most part straightforward and unambiguous in his lyrics (although it's perfectly possible that he had attained such Zen mastery that the lack of ambivalence was actually a refined ambiguity). Whatever it is, it's a beautiful, muted, beguiling album. On its front cover is a sketch by Leonard of Anjani; on the back is a photo by Anjani of Leonard, bestubbled, crushed-capped and clutching a coffee cup. Leonard dedicated the album to the memory of Jack McClelland, his longtime Canadian publisher, who died in June 2004, the year of its release. Leonard declined to tour behind the album—not even a promotional tour, as he had done for *Ten New Songs*. As soon as he had finished it, he had left for Montreal, where he spent the summer, happily sitting in the Parc du Portugal with the other old men, watching the world go by.

The album seemed content to sell itself without Leonard's help. It made the charts just about everywhere in Europe, reaching No. 34 in the UK and going gold in Canada, Poland, Demark, Ireland, Norway and the Czech Republic. In the U.S., oddly, it made it into the Top 20 of the World Music chart, while failing yet again to make *Billboard*'s Top 100. In the absence of any word from Leonard, many journalists appeared to view the album as the Last Word of Leonard, a prelude to retirement. But, as Leonard wrote to Jarkko Arjatsalo at the Leonard Cohen Files in the summer of 2004, he saw it as closing a circle in his work before moving on to the next record, which he was "deep into," he wrote, "six or seven songs already sketched out, and, g-d willing, it will be done over the next year. Also the B of L [*Book of Longing*], or something resembling it, seems to be about to step out under a new name and form."[15] Leonard clearly had no plans for retirement. Which was fortunate, since a strange and unexpected set of circumstances dictated that he could not have retired if he had wanted to.

In October 2004, the telephone rang in Leonard's Montreal apartment. It was his daughter, Lorca, calling from L.A. She had just had an enigmatic conversation with the boyfriend of an employee of Kelley Lynch, who had come into her shop. He told her that Leonard needed to take a look at his bank accounts, and quickly. It was as puzzling to Leonard as it had been to Lorca. Kelley took care of Leonard's business affairs—good, reliable Kelley, not simply his manager but a close friend, almost part of the family; he even employed Kelley's parents. Leonard, who took little interest in such things, had given Lynch broad power of attorney over his finances. He trusted her enough to have named her in his living will as the person responsible in an extreme medical circumstance for giving the order as to whether he should live or die. Lynch had been there almost continuously during the making of *Dear Heather* and they had been in regular contact since the album was completed, just as they always were, and Kelley had said nothing about any financial problems. But Lorca was uneasy, so Leonard agreed to fly back to L.A. He went straightaway to his bank—he had been there so infrequently he could barely remember the address—and they pulled up his accounts. Apparently, it was true; just a few days earlier Leonard had paid an American Express bill of Kelley's for $75,000. As the clerk scrolled through his earlier statements, it became clear that this was not an isolated incident. Almost all of Leonard's money was gone.

Back at the house, Leonard lit a cigarette. He dialed Kelley's office number. Her voice on the phone was bright and friendly. Leonard told her that he had removed her name as a signatory on his accounts, and he fired her. Kelley. Of all the women in his life to do him wrong. Leonard knew that Lynch—like Marty Machat, his previous manager and Lynch's previous employer—had her faults, but like Machat she knew Leonard's business and had taken care of it. In 1998 Leonard had told *Billboard* (in a special feature celebrating Leonard's thirtieth year as an artist), that in matters of business he had been "taken many, many times," but then "I found Kelley and set my house in order and I've been making a living ever since . . . almost exclusively because of Kelley. Kelley, bless her heart, organized me and my son."[16]

Kelley, also like Marty Machat, loved Leonard—or had given every appearance of loving him for years. They had been lovers some fourteen years earlier, but it was "a casual sexual arrangement," Leonard said; he "never spent the night, and it had been mutually enjoyed and terminated"[17] giving no appearance of having damaged their close friendship. To have had almost all the money he had made stolen out from under him was difficult to take in, but also remarkably easy. It was the oldest story in showbiz. Hadn't his mother warned him about it when he left for New York in the sixties with his guitar? "You be careful of those people down there," she had told him. "They're not like us." To which Leonard responded with an indulgent smile before going on to unwittingly sign away the rights to several songs. But losing a few songs was a drop in the ocean compared to the epic financial impropriety this would turn out to be. That it appeared to have dated back to the time when Leonard left the material world to live in a monastery added more than a touch of irony. That it continued after Leonard came down from the mountain proved only what many already know, or at least suspect: musicians and monks tend to have few skills in matters of finance. Leonard had been happy to let his manager Kelley take care of the business and money, but now Kelley was gone, and so was the money, leaving Leonard with a monumental mess to take care of, and no manager or money with which to do it. If not quite a koan, it was a hell of a conundrum, and a debilitating distraction. "It's enough to put a dent in one's mood," Leonard told his friends. He repeated the same understatement to the media once the lawsuits began and the story went public. And what a strange story it would turn out to be, one with a tangled plot whose cast of characters included a SWAT team, financiers, a tough-talking parrot, Tibetan Buddhists and Leonard's lover Anjani's ex-husband.

Twenty-two

Taxes, Children, Lost Pussy

Death by a thousand paper cuts. To have been redeemed from depression in his old age only to have to spend it in an eternity of legal and financial paperwork was a cosmic joke so black as to test even Leonard's famous gallows humor. His temptation had been to simply let the whole thing go. He had been broke before, he did not need much to live on and he had a roof—roofs, in fact—over his head. If, on balance, he would have preferred having money in the bank to not having it—and when he did have it, he tended to spend it on other people and on Roshi's monasteries, in his own personal version of his ancestors' philanthropy and synagogue-building—there was very little evidence in his lifestyle or his career, apart from the initial move into songwriting, that money was anywhere near the top of Leonard's motivations.

When he had unknowingly signed away the rights to "Suzanne" in the sixties, his response had reportedly been sanguine; it was appropriate somehow, he had said, that he did not own a song that he felt had become beyond ownership. Admittedly that is what he told the press; in private he might well have expressed a different view, since it is unlikely that a man in his thirties, renowned in the Canadian literary world and unused to being treated dishonorably, would feel anything but incensed at having been duped of his first known—and for years best-known—and most successful song. But what Leonard said both publicly and privately about the business with Kelley Lynch suggested that it meant less to Leonard to lose his fortune than his songs. Though as the story continued to unfold, it appeared he might have lost them too.

Leonard's relative calm in the face of financial disaster might have reflected his long, hard Zen training with Roshi, or the perspectives he learned from his studies with Ramesh, but his survival instinct may have also played a part; to risk becoming too engaged might have invited the return of his anxiety and depression. Leonard had wanted to walk away from the whole thing, but the lawyers said he couldn't. They told him that lot of the missing money had been in retirement accounts and charitable trust funds, which left Leonard liable for large tax bills on the sums withdrawn and no money with which to pay them. It was no good telling the IRS that he had not been the one who had made the withdrawals; they needed proof. Which was why Leonard was sitting at his desk with Anjani and Lorca, in the house he had been forced to mortgage in order to pay his legal bills, grimly going through stacks of financial statements and e-mails. It was a complicated business. Since Kelley Lynch, with his blessing, had dealt with his finances on his behalf, he knew few details himself about the various accounts, trusts and companies set up in his name. His lawyers had spent the past month trying to make sense of it and still Leonard seemed to be getting nowhere except deeper in debt.

Then something occurred to Lorca. Wasn't Anjani's ex-husband a music industry lawyer? Perhaps he might have some ideas. Robert Kory was indeed a lawyer. He had worked with the Beach Boys for ten years, although he had since sworn off the music business in favor of a practice in entertainment and technology finance. "But when Leonard Cohen shows up at your office," Kory says, "what are you going to do? Close the door?" He had opened it to see his ex-wife standing hand in hand with a man whose poetry books he had read as a student at Yale. "Hello," Leonard said. "I may have lost a few million dollars."

Kory agreed to help. Deferring his fees, he set about "trying to get a basic understanding of Leonard's affairs, to understand the history, understand what money he had and what happened to it, the magnitude of the loss, and figure out legally what they had done." Quite a challenge, since Kelley Lynch had the records. "I started making contacts in a very delicate way with bankers and with Leonard's accountant, who was also Kelley's accountant, and lawyers that represented Leonard in the sale of his music publishing and his future record royalties." Three months later, after Kory's then litigation associate and now partner Michelle Rice had conducted a comprehensive review of the available documents, along with bank records that had been subpoenaed, Kory and Rice explained to Leonard that a case could probably be made that between ten and thirteen million dollars had been improperly taken. "That stunned him," says Kory. "It stunned me."

Rice's analysis suggested it possibly dated as far back as 1996, the year Leonard was ordained as a monk. Around that time, Lynch, with the aid of Leonard's other financial advisers, made the first of two separate sales of Leonard's music publishing to Sony/ATV—127 songs. In Kory's opinion there had been no need for Leonard to sell his songs because he had money in the bank and income from royalties. Much of the proceeds from the sale, less Lynch's 15 percent commission, had been deposited in Leonard's bank account, over which Lynch had control, and some had been deposited in charitable trusts. To manage the investments, Lynch had brought in a friend, a Tibetan Buddhist financier named Neal Greenberg, who was the head of a securities company in Colorado. Greenberg had studied since the early seventies under the late Chögyam Trungpa Rinpoche. Lynch herself was a longtime student and friend of Trungpa, as was Doug Penick, the father of the older of her two sons, Rutger. (Penick had been involved in the 1994 Canadian documentary *The Tibetan Book of the Dead*, for which Leonard provided the narration.) Greenberg in turn brought in a lawyer and tax professor from Kentucky named Richard Westin. In 2001, Kelley, Greenberg and Westin orchestrated the sale of Leonard's future record royalties to Sony/ATV for $8 million. After various cuts, Leonard apparently netted $4.7 million, according to documents later filed in Los Angeles Superior Court. The money from this second sale of Leonard's intellectual property went into a company account, which had been set up with the intention of paying Leonard a pension when he retired and to provide an inheritance for his children. What went wrong, according to Rice's analysis and what was alleged in later litigation, was that the plan only worked if Leonard's children owned 99 percent of the company and Leonard 1 percent. At the last minute, Rice alleged, they gave Kelley 99 percent ownership instead of his children, and Leonard had no idea about the last-minute change in the documents.

Since Leonard had expressed a strong desire to avoid the ordeal of litigation, Kory, after consulting with the former L.A. district attorney Ira Reiner, wrote to Lynch, Greenberg and Westin. Greenberg's response was to file a preemptive lawsuit which accused Leonard and Kory of attempted extortion. Westin agreed to go into mediation, and a confidential settlement was reached. Lynch's lawyers insisted at first that their client had been given the authority to do what she did, though later they advised her to mediate. At that point, Lynch fired them. She made a phone call to Kory herself and asked him to meet her for lunch. This surprised Kory, but he accepted, and they agreed on a place.

At that meeting, Kory held out the possibility of a reasonable settlement if Kelley would disclose what had happened to all the money. The alternative, he said, would be serious litigation and ultimately the destruction of her life as she knew it. Her response, Kory said, was "Hell will freeze over before you find out what happened to the money. It was my money."

So in August 2005 the first of the lawsuits began. That same month, somewhat ironically, a short film titled *This Beggar's Description*, in which Leonard made an appearance, premiered on Canadian TV. It was a documentary about a schizophrenic Montreal poet named Philip Tétrault. Leonard had been his longtime supporter and friend. We see Leonard sitting on a park bench in Montreal with Tétrault, chatting about frostbite and Kris Kristofferson, while the soundtrack plays Leonard Cohen songs Leonard no longer owned.

Back in Los Angeles, the letters and lawsuits, accusations and counteraccusations continued, becoming ever more convoluted and bizarre. A particularly sorry and surreal episode occurred at Lynch's home in Mandeville Canyon. Looking out of her front window, she could see police officers cordoning off the road. Several police cars pulled up on her lawn. As Lynch described it, twenty-five armed men jumped out—a SWAT team—and aimed weapons at her house. The police had been called about an alleged hostage-taking. They were told there were guns in the house. Lynch, who had kept the younger of her two sons, Ray Charles Lindsey, home from school because he felt unwell, assumed that he must be the alleged hostage and that the call had been made by the boy's father, her estranged partner Steve Lindsey—the producer and musician Lynch had met when he worked on Leonard's album *The Future*. The boy was at that moment with his half brother, Rutger; Lynch had asked her older son to take Ray out of the house and down the road to where the actress Cloris Leachman, apparently, was waiting for them in her car.

Lynch came out of the front door, dressed in a bikini and holding a dog on a leash. As she walked toward the policemen, she said, several trained their guns on her and the dog while other officers ran into the house. When they entered, they were greeted by a voice screeching, "I see dead people! I see dead people!"—it was Lou, Lynch's gray African parrot. Lynch ran to the swimming pool and jumped in. She was removed by officers, handcuffed and taken away in a squad car, still in her wet bathing suit.

By Lynch's account, the police took her on a long drive, interrogating her en route about her friendship with Phil Spector (who had been freed on $1 million bail while awaiting trial for murder). The journey ended at a hospital across town, where Lynch was taken to the psychiatric ward. She claimed that she was involuntarily drugged and held in the hospital for twenty-four hours, and that during this time Steve Lindsey filed for and subsequently won custody of their son. Lynch believed that Leonard and Kory were behind the whole episode, as well as several other strange things she claimed had happened to her following the hostage incident, such as being rear-ended by a Mercedes and threatened by a mysterious man.[1]

Lynch's subsequent accounts, related in thousands upon thousands of words she posted on the Internet, involved long, elaborate conspiracies, in which Phil Spector's murder trial seemed to feature frequently and in which Lynch claimed to be a scapegoat in a scheme devised to hide Leonard's lavish spending and tax fraud. Rather than fight Leonard in court, Kelley did so in cyberspace. Wherever Leonard was mentioned online and there was a space for comments, she left them, and not in brief. She sent innumerable lengthy e-mails to Leonard and his friends, family, musicians, associates and former girlfriends, as well as to the police, the district attorney, the media, the Buddhist community and the IRS.

Leonard, who had been obliged to stay in L.A. while the litigation continued, kept his head down and tried to work. For such a private man, having his confidential affairs made so distastefully public was a real test of his Buddhist nature. It was hard to work under these conditions, but at the same time, focusing on work kept his mind off it. There was also the matter of having to try to make some money; at this point in the game, Leonard had no idea how things might turn out. Thanks in good part to this urgency, in the space of a few months Leonard had written and recorded almost an entire new album—not the album on which he had started work immediately after *Dear Heather*, but a collaboration with Anjani, titled *Blue Alert*.

Leonard also finally completed *Book of Longing*—which his friends had started calling *Book of Prolonging*, Leonard having spent so long working on it. The one thing that was missing was some artwork, which had been in one of the thirty boxes of sketchbooks, notebooks, journals and personal papers that Leonard had left in Lynch's office for safekeeping. Lynch, with her source of income cut off, had given up the office, so presumably they were in her house. Lynch wasn't saying. With her house now heading toward foreclosure, there had been reports that she had been looking into selling Leonard's archives.

Leonard, who had become close to Rice, called her about the pending foreclosure. Although she and Kory had engaged another law firm by then to assist in the litigation, Rice felt the situation was too pressing to wait for the slow resolution of the lawsuits. She employed a writ of possession, a rarely used self-help legal procedure in which someone can make a claim that another person has his or her property and refuses to give it back. Lynch had ignored Leonard's lawsuit, including requests for discovery, and he was frustrated by her ability to avoid any accountability, even in litigation. But once a court issues the writ, Rice explained, the person who filed it can take it to the sheriff's office and ask for officers to go with him to where his property is being held and take it back.

On a rainy October morning at nine A.M., Rice and her paralegal showed up, unannounced, at Lynch's house in Mandeville Canyon with two armed sheriffs in riot gear, to search the house and garage and take possession of Leonard's documents per the court order. The sheriffs emerged with one box after another. The process took nearly two days and required a moving truck, but they recovered a treasure trove: "precious notebooks, the history of 'Hallelujah' and how it got written, letters from Joni Mitchell, Dylan, Allen Ginsberg and all the drawings," Rice says. There were tears in Leonard's eyes as he opened the boxes and found what he thought had been lost. Among them was the sketchbook containing Leonard's drawing of a bird that would become the cover design of *Book of Longing*.

In December 2005, Lynch lost her home. For a while, she slept on the beach in Santa Monica, before setting off in a van across the U.S. In May 2006 a superior court judge granted a default judgment against Lynch for $7,341,345. Once again, she ignored it, and anyway, to all appearances she was penniless. Rice also prevailed in the lawsuits against Greenberg, insofar as she obtained dismissal of all Greenberg's claims against Leonard and Kory, and obtained an order that awarded Leonard the last $150,000 under Greenberg's control, even though Greenberg claimed these funds were owed to him for his legal fees. Through the various legal proceedings, Leonard had recovered some of his lost money, though nothing like all of it. Lynch, who continued her ceaseless assault of blogs and e-mails full of accusations and invective, also began to make threatening phone calls—to Leonard, to Kory and to friends and associates from various places across the U.S. State by state, Rice led an effort to obtain a series of restraining orders against Lynch. And so the ugly business dragged on.

Came So Far for Beauty, Hal Willner's Leonard Cohen tribute concert, had taken on a life of its own. Staged in New York in 2003 and commissioned as a one-off by the Canadian consulate, it had been adopted by other countries—"We kept getting asked to do it," says Willner—and had become something of an annual international event. First it went to England, as part of the 2004 Brighton Festival, surviving the transatlantic crossing with its spirit and almost the entire cast intact. Two more performers were added to the lineup, Beth Orton and Jarvis Cocker, and, to keep it fresh, some new songs.

Says Nick Cave, "Hal told you what songs he wanted you to do; you didn't get a choice. Nobody knows what's going on or gets time to rehearse, so it's done on a wing and a prayer, which was one of the great things about it." Between them the cast, each channeling their own inner Leonard Cohen, conjured up his humor ("I'm Your Man"), piety ("If It Be Your Will"), melancholy ("Seems So Long Ago, Nancy") and libidinous machismo ("Don't Go Home with Your Hard-On"). Willner says, "It became a team, all these artists who would never be in the same room, collaborating, watching each other at the side of the stage and cheering each other along."

"Those concerts started to become a parallel universe to all of our lives," says Rufus Wainwright. "We would meet up again in all these locations and it took on this mystical aura, like some exotic family get-together." Wainwright was already something of an extended Cohen family member. He and Leonard's daughter, Lorca, who had met in their teens in Montreal, had become close friends. When he moved to Los Angeles they became roommates, living in Lorca's half of Leonard's duplex. The first time Lorca took Rufus upstairs to meet her father, "I walked in and Leonard was in his underwear—boxers, nothing too risqué, and a T-shirt, kind of a Billy Wilder morning outfit—and he was chewing a boiled hot dog into tiny little bits and spitting it out and putting it on a toothpick and feeding this little bird that he'd rescued from the front yard that had fallen from a nest. He was very nice and he made me noodles and we talked for a while. We didn't necessarily connect—it was sort of right before the crash and he was going through some stuff, and I'm a pretty brash character, very extroverted, and he's very introverted, and I would be trying to tap-dance all the time around his soft-shoe. That's what struck me the most: how shy he is and how unassuming. But I think we've figured each other out since."

In 2005, the cast reconvened in Australia, for the Sydney Festival. Among them was a newcomer, Antony Hegarty, a New York singer with an otherworldly voice. "Before we met Antony," Julie Christensen remembers, "Hal was saying, 'Wait until you see this guy, he sounds like a cross between Janis Joplin and Tiny Tim.' We kind of wondered what this would be like." A big, cobwebby sweater draped over his rotund body like a worn tarp on a Volkswagen Beetle, Antony sang a soulful version of "If It Be Your Will" that earned a standing ovation. "I'm an Australian," says Cave, "I know what Australian audiences are like, and it was incredible to me to see their response to this guy." Says Rufus Wainwright, "It was boiling hot, an insane summer day; we were playing the Opera House and I almost felt like we'd gone to the Krypton palace to summon Superman, and we did this amazing show. Thank God, it got filmed."

Hal Willner had met Australian filmmaker Lian Lunson at a party in Los Angeles. After saying how much he had enjoyed her documentary on Willie Nelson, which had been broadcast on a public television station, he complained "that it was a shame these Leonard shows aren't going to be on film. So she did it." The only way she could do something with the footage, she told him afterward, was if she could interview Leonard on camera. With some persuasion, Leonard agreed. Lunson also filmed him in a New York nightclub playing a secret performance with U2. They sang just one song together— "Tower of Song," the title track of the 1995 Leonard Cohen tribute album on which Bono did his beatnik-soul version of "Hallelujah"— and there was no audience, but for a man who since 1993 had been content to let other people sing his songs onstage, it was not insig-

nificant. Lunson's film, titled *Leonard Cohen: I'm Your Man*, was first
screened in September 2005 at the Toronto International Film Festival. That same month, Leonard was awarded a plaque on the Canadian Folk Music Walk of Fame. Leonard, as had become his custom,
sent his thanks and his apologies and stayed home in L.A.

Leonard flew to Montreal in January 2006 for a very different kind
of ceremony. Irving Layton, at the age of ninety-three, was dead. At
the funeral, his big white coffin was wheeled out to the strains of
Beethoven's "Ode to Joy," while around seven hundred people, including ex-wives, former students, family, friends and media, looked
on. Leonard, dressed in a thick overcoat with a fur collar and a crushed
cap, slipped into the chapel quietly, taking a seat at the back, where
he tapped his toe to the music. In his eulogy Leonard said, "What
happened between Irving and me is between us and doesn't bear
repeating. But what does bear repeating, and will be repeated, are his
words." He read Layton's poem "The Graveyard," which ended with
the lines "There is no pain in the graveyard, or the voice / whisper-
ing in the tombstones / 'Rejoice, rejoice.'" Layton was "our greatest
poet, our greatest champion of poetry," Leonard said. "Alzheimer's
could not silence him, and neither will death." When Leonard tried
to slip out just as quietly, he was requisitioned as a pallbearer. Layton,
Leonard thought to himself, smiling, would have heartily approved
of the whole event.

It felt good to be back in Montreal, even in midwinter, and even
for an occasion such as this. Leonard was going stir-crazy in L.A.
For some time he had been thinking—as he often did—about moving back to Montreal, and Anjani seemed to agree that it was a fine
idea. Leonard had recently hired a Canadian manager, Sam Feldman, whose clients included Joni Mitchell and Diana Krall. When,
five months after his last Canadian award, Leonard was inducted into
the Canadian Songwriters Hall of Fame in February, at Feldman's
urging, since there were a new album and a new book both scheduled
for release in May, Leonard agreed to attend.

"I'm not really drawn to these kind of events," Leonard said. "It's a very tricky occasion, being honoured. In one sense, it feels like an obituary and you don't really feel [that] about yourself."[2] The gala featured yet more tributes from artists performing Leonard's songs onstage—Rufus Wainwright once again; Willie Nelson, dressed for the occasion in a suit; and k. d. lang, whose rendition of "Hallelujah" moved Leonard to tears. There were more tears when Adrienne Clarkson, the former governor general, presented the award. "One of the reasons one avoids these things is because they summon some really deep emotional responses," Leonard told the *National Post*. "This happens to an artist or a writer very rarely, where you have in front of you the unconditional acceptance of your work."[3] In his acceptance speech he said, "We shuffle behind our songs into the Hall of Fame."[4] Leonard, Clarkson said in her speech, "changed all of our lives with the complexity of his sadness, the breadth of his love. . . . He gets inside your brain, your heart, your lungs. You remember him, you feel him, you breathe him. He is our connection to the meaning of ecstasy, our access to another world we suspected existed but which he puts into song." She thanked the millions of her fellow countrymen who failed to buy his early poetry books and novels, "because without that he might not have turned to songwriting."

In the various interviews he gave in Canada, Leonard appeared upbeat and lighthearted, even on the unavoidable question of his ex-manager and his missing money. There was no vitriol or attacks, just some self-reprobation for not reading his bank statements and that line about its being enough to put a dent in his mood, to which he added "Fortunately it hasn't."[5] Among these interviews was one with *CARP* magazine, the publication of the association for Canadian retirees. At Leonard's apartment journalist Christine Langlois found the septuagenarian who could not afford to retire sitting in a sunbeam at the kitchen table with Anjani, smiling and eating bagels. Surprised at such a picture of domestic bliss, she

asked how it squared with his reputation. "Everything changes as
you get older," Leonard said. "I never met a woman until I was
sixty-five. Instead, I saw all kinds of miracles in front of me." In
the past, he had always viewed women through his own "urgent
needs and desires," he said, and "what they could do for me." But
in his midsixties—which roughly coincided with Leonard leaving
the monastery and his depression starting to lift—"that started to
dissolve and [he] began to see the woman standing there." Anjani,
laughing, pointed out, "I was the one standing there when that
idea occurred to him." By this point she and Leonard had been
together seven years. Leonard was quoted as saying that "old age"
was the "best thing that ever happened to me." Despite the business with Kelley Lynch, he felt light and peaceful. "The state of
mind I find myself in is so very different than most of my life that
I am deeply grateful."[6]

Book of Longing, Leonard's first new volume of poetry in twenty-
two years, was published in May 2006 and dedicated to Irving Layton. Like *Dear Heather*, it is something of a scrapbook: a 230-page
miscellany of poems, prose pieces and artwork. There are as many
drawings as there are poems—among them sketches of Roshi and
Leonard's fellow monks; of Irving Layton and Pierre Trudeau; of
women, more often than not undressed; and several self-portraits, in
which his expression ranges from hangdog to glum, and which are accompanied by wise, comic, morbid and/or mordant marginalia:

> *I never found the girl*
> *I never got rich*
> *Follow me*

or elsewhere,

taxes,
children
lost pussy
war
constipation
the living poet
in his harness
of beauty
offers the day back to g-d.

(Throughout the book, Leonard, in the respectful Jewish tradition, uses "g-d" in place of "God," and also hyphens in place of sexual expletives.)

The literary content is wide-ranging, from formal to pop cultural, from long, lyrical ballads to short, whimsical doggerel, prose pieces to songs, or poems that became songs—the quite different words of both the poem "Thousand Kisses Deep" and the song "A Thousand Kisses Deep" set side by side on opposing pages. Many of the poems—particularly those written on cold, dark nights or in snatched moments in a mountain monastery—are about death: anticipated, contemplated, mourned and recalled. "Who Do You Really Remember" catalogs various deaths—his dog, his uncles and aunts, his friends—that occurred between his father's death, when Leonard was nine, and his mother's, when he was forty-three. The prose poem "Robert Appears Again" describes a conversation with the ghost of a dead friend, conducted while Leonard was on the twenty-year-old speed he'd found in the pocket of an old suit. In "I Miss My Mother," Leonard wishes he could take Masha to India, buy her jewelry and tell her that she was

right about everything
Including my foolish guitar

And where it got me . . .
She'd pat my little head
And bless my dirty song

Often on Friday nights, when he lit the candles to mark the Sabbath and Adam, Lorca and Anjani came over for dinner, Leonard would imagine that his mother was there too and her reaction to "seeing how I've finally stabilised my life."[7]

But it is the *Book of Longing,* not the book of the dead, and these losses are only one of the "various forms of longing: religious, sexual, just expressions of loneliness," that Leonard addresses.[8] He berates himself for his failings as a Buddhist monk, from his inability to understand his teacher ("Roshi") to the "enormous hard-on" he has under the robes when he dresses for the morning meditation ("Early Morning at Mount Baldy"). In the abbreviated, six-line version of his poem "Not a Jew" he asserts that he remains unswervingly Jewish. In "One of My Letters" he signs off not with "L. Cohen" but with his Jewish and his Buddhist names, Jikan Eliezer.

He addresses the decline of his powers with age and his failures as an artist ("My Time") and as a ladies' man ("Never Once"). In the honest and erotic "The Mist of Pornography," he discusses his relationship with Rebecca De Mornay and why it had to end. In "Titles" he writes,

I had the title Poet
and maybe I was one
for a while
Also the title Singer
was kindly accorded me
even though
I could barely carry a tune . . .
My reputation
as a Ladies' Man was a joke

It caused me to laugh bitterly
through the ten thousand nights
I spent alone.

But despite these protestations, in "Other Writers," having extolled the virtues of his poet friend Steve Sanfield and of Roshi, he brags, "I prefer my stuff to theirs," and describes a sexual encounter with a young woman in the front seat of his jeep. Irving Layton, Leonard recalls in "Layton's Question," would always ask him: "Are you sure you're doing the wrong thing?" Layton would have been proud.

"As a person of Jewish ancestry," Leonard said in an interview with the Buddhist magazine *Tricycle*, "I find it deeply satisfying that the description of God's creative activity as it appears in the Kabbalah is remarkably parallel to that of my teacher Joshu Sasaki Roshi, contemporary Japanese Zen master."[9] Leonard and Anjani had begun to regularly attend a synagogue in Los Angeles led by Rabbi Mordecai Finley.

Finley, a martial artist, former military man and professor of liturgy, Jewish mysticism and spirituality at the Academy for Jewish Religion in California, founded the Ohr Torah congregation in 1993. Leonard and Anjani first encountered Finley at the wedding of Joni Mitchell's producer Larry Klein. "The rabbi gave an inspiring, extemporaneous speech about love and how to stay together as a married couple," says Anjani. "I looked at Leonard and said, 'I want to hear more from him.'" There was a moment's hesitation, then Leonard said, "I'm going to go with you.'" Finley remembers that he had talked about marriage "as an opportunity to be of service to another human being, an opportunity for the deepest human transformation, because you're so deep in the presence of another human being. Which takes work, it takes mindfulness, it takes commitment, it takes discipline. It probably resonated with Leonard's understanding of spirituality. A while later he just started showing up at the synagogue." He would often see Leonard sitting there, his back straight, his eyes cast down, as if in seated meditation in Roshi's monastery, but with Anjani by his side. It seemed to the rabbi that Leonard was taking in the mood and the energy as much as the meaning of the words.

In his first conversation with Leonard, the rabbi had asked him, "You're a Buddhist priest, how does that square with Judaism?" It was the same question Leonard had been asked by the press when he was ordained a monk; he had answered it in his poem "Not a Jew."

Leonard answered Finley that it did not have to square; Buddhism was nontheistic and Roshi was a great man with a great mind. "Leonard made it very clear to me that it had nothing to do with his religion, nor his beliefs. As we got to know each other better, I was delighted to see that he is a very learned Jew. He's deeply well-read, very committed to understanding Kabbalah and—in a very similar way that I do—is using the Kabbalah not so much as a theology but as spiritual psychology and a way to mythically represent the Divine. If you understand that human consciousness is basically symbolic, then one has to find some kind of symbol system that most closely articulates one's understanding of all the levels of reality."

Finley, being nearer to Anjani's age than Leonard's, and an American, did not grow up with any great awareness of Leonard and his work. He started to investigate; everything he read felt "like a prayer. He always operates in the metaphysical realm; even anything that he writes about on the material realm has the metaphysical echoing into it, an echo of the cosmic even in the most mundane of things." On one occasion, Leonard showed him the book his grandfather Rabbi Klonitzki-Kline had written. "It's a very fine volume, a substantial, learned book. It's tragic that it has not been translated and put out in wide circulation." They opened the book—which was written in Hebrew—and talked about various passages in it, and Finley was impressed by Leonard's scholarship. "He grew up in an ambience of deep, serious, Jewish study. He was up-to-date, he knew who the great Jewish thinkers were and understood their arguments. There are obscure parts of Kabbalah that we actually differed on and sometimes we would be talking about one thing and come back to that thing, 'Here we are again.' He could be a great teacher of Judaism. If that were his thing, to be a rabbi, he had it in his power to have been one of the greatest of our generation.

"By the way," Finley adds, "modern students of Kabbalah are very interested in Leonard's work, because they see Leonard as not a professor of Kabbalah, not a theologian, but someone who really understands Kabbalah from within, [and his poetry as] the best poetry on the Kabbalah they've ever read. He gets the inner ethos of brokenness and healing and the tragedy of the human condition, in that we're not particularly well suited for this life but you still have to find your way through."

On May 13, 2006, in Toronto, Leonard gave the closest thing to a public musical performance in more than a decade. It was at a bookstore, where he was signing copies of *Book of Longing*. Three thousand fans showed up—the book was already on its way to the top of the bestseller list—and the police had to close off the street. On a small stage, Anjani, Ron Sexsmith and Barenaked Ladies provided the entertainment. Leonard had not planned to sing, but during her set Anjani asked him to join her and would brook no refusal. After duetting with her on "Never Got to Love You," Leonard went on to sing solo "So Long, Marianne" and "Hey, That's No Way to Say Goodbye." The response was rapturous.

Blue Alert, the album Leonard and Anjani had worked on together, was released, as was *Book of Longing*, in May 2006. Like *Ten New Songs* it was a full collaboration—Leonard's words, Anjani's music.

But unlike *Ten New Songs* it was not a duet album, it was an Anjani album. Her picture adorned the front cover. Underneath her name, in much smaller letters, was written "Produced by Leonard Cohen." It was as if this man who so loved women, who so often wrote songs about women (or, as he had often claimed, wrote to attract women), who believed, as he said, that women "inhabited this charged land-scape that poetry seemed to arise from, and that it seemed to be the natural language of women,"[10] had finally achieved with this album what perhaps he had been working toward since his debut, which he had experienced once with Jennifer Warnes's *Famous Blue Raincoat* and which, on the albums he had made since leaving the monastery, he had come ever closer to achieving: to hand his songs over to the female voice to sing.

It was a first for Leonard to make an album whose muse was not only his current romantic partner but his cowriter. The fact that it would be Anjani's album, not his, seemed to speed up the writing process. Anjani had found the words for what would become the title song on Leonard's desk—it was a new poem he had written for *Book of Longing*. She asked if she could try to make a song from it and when he consented, and told her he liked what she did with it, she moved on to another one. She took an old poem, "As the Mist Leaves No Scar," from *The Spice-Box of Earth*—a volume published when Anjani was two years old—and set it to music, unaware that Phil Spector had already done so with "True Loves Leaves No Traces" on *Death of a Ladies' Man*. Anjani's melody for the song, which she titled "The Mist," was very different though, with the feel of an old folk song. The ballad "Never Got to Love You," a noir short story of love, regret and moving on, was put together from unused verses for the song "Closing Time." Sometimes, as she went through Leonard's note-books, Anjani would find small scraps of lyrics that she liked, and she would tell him, "Just finish the song." "Thanks for the Dance" started out as a few lines in one of Leonard's journals: "*Thanks for the dance, I hear that we're married, one-two-three, one-two-three, one.*" "I said, 'Finish that; I could really sing *that* song,' which is like telling Leonard to write 'Hallelujah' in a couple of weeks. But he enjoyed the task, because it was very freeing—he didn't have to sing it, he was writing it for me now, and the standards of what he would write for himself didn't apply, so it came quite easily. It also happened for 'No One After You.' It was funny because I said, 'Okay, it's almost there, it's almost good,' and then I remember there was one night when I was going in the studio the next day and I said, 'You've got one hour to come up with that last line.' He said, 'Okay, well give me some chocolate.' So he's nibbling at a bar of chocolate and he's wandering back and forth until he shouted, 'I'm a regular cliché.' I thought, 'Thank you, you *can* write under pressure.'"

The recording process was not so easy. "There were some moments when it really wasn't pretty," Anjani remembers. "I was crushed, especially early on. Don't get me wrong, he's wonderfully gracious, he's generous, he's everything that he appears to be, but nobody's perfect, myself included, and we both definitely have strong ideas. On *Blue Alert* I really started to get independent about what I wanted to do. In 2004, when we were making songs for his record *Dear Heather,* a friend of mine had died and I was really sad about it, and Leonard walked into the room and said, 'Here, maybe this will make you feel better,' and it was the lyric to 'Nightingale,'" a song that appeared on both *Dear Heather* and *Blue Alert.* "But the sections were reversed. It started off, '*Fare thee well, my nightingale.*' When I was reading it, the melody came into my head and I immediately thought, 'This should go here and that should go there.' It was like a puzzle I was solving. I took it home and I didn't change the words but I rewrote the structure and I recorded it and I played it for him. And I could see his eyes open wide, because I'd actually fucked with his song. It didn't even occur to me that he might react that way. He kept listening intently and afterward he said, 'Well of course it starts with "*I built my house.*" '" At some point, though, it became clear that they needed a referee. Leonard called John Lissauer, his old producer, and the man who had first brought Anjani into Leonard's life.

Lissauer describes what he witnessed in the studio as "a tug-of-war." As he saw it, when Leonard had worked with Sharon Robinson on *Ten New Songs*, it had been Leonard's record, but although *Blue Alert* was Anjani's album, "Leonard was still expecting it to be Leonard's record. Leonard would want one thing and Anjani would want another, and I was sort of in the middle of that because I knew them both and I was trying to answer to both of them." When he listened to the demos, Lissauer thought the songs beautiful but was not impressed with all the synthesizers and drum machines they played them on. "I said, 'Let me at least get some organic instruments and add some colors here and there.'" Taking six songs away with him, Lissauer added instrumental touches, much as he had done on Leonard's albums *New Skin for the Old Ceremony* and *Various Positions*. He thought they sounded "lovely," as did Leonard and Anjani, "but they were bickering quite a bit, like they were trying to get custody. And—this was the most bizarre thing—their trade-off was 'I'll throw that thing of John's out but you have to . . . ,' and one by one, in order to settle their arguments and to spite each other, they threw out the improvements and wore away all the colors and stripped it back down to the demo sound." All that remained of his work, Lissauer says, "was the baritone saxophone solo on 'Blue Alert' and the waltz song 'Thanks for the Dance' that we did together."

The album was ultimately recorded on neutral territory, with engineer and coproducer Ed Sanders in his analog studio in L.A. Sanders had worked with Anjani on her last album, *The Sacred Names*, and, ever since she introduced him to Leonard during the making of *Dear Heather*, he had also been working as Leonard's administrative assistant. No one had been killed in the making of the album, although Lissauer, as often seemed to happen, was left a little bruised by the experience. Still, it did not prevent him from describing *Blue Alert* as "one of the great albums of the decade." It is certainly fascinating to hear the erotic desires of an old man and lyrics about memories, fatigue and valedictions expressed in the voice of a young woman and couched in elegant folk-jazz melodies. In the liner-note booklet, Leonard is photographed sitting alongside the youthful, beautiful Anjani, his face out of focus, fading, as if he were in the process of becoming a ghost.

In October 2006, *Came So Far for Beauty* took its final bow in Ireland as part of the Dublin Theatre Festival. The lineup included many of the previous participants and others including Lou Reed, Mary Margaret O'Hara and Anjani, the last of these three at Leonard's request. Willner was happy to oblige. Anjani broke with the tradition of singing whatever Willner allotted and performed two songs from *Blue Alert*. Lou Reed also selected his own songs—two from *Songs of Leonard Cohen*, the album that Leonard was in New York recording when Reed met him for the first time. Willner asked Reed if he would also sing "Joan of Arc" as a duet with Julie Christensen. "First of all I don't do *la-las*," said Reed, but he agreed. Nick Cave, who this time had been given two songs from *Songs of Love and Hate*, his favorite, remembers Reed's treatment of "The Stranger Song" as "extraordinary, so irreverent. It was a Lou song that happened to sound like Leonard Cohen had written it before Lou."

That autumn, Lian Lunson's film *Leonard Cohen: I'm Your Man* started to do the rounds of independent U.S. cinemas. Leonard slipped into a movie theater in L.A. to watch it with Anjani. It is a curious film, part concert movie, part biographical interview. Selected stage performances from the tribute concerts and testimonies from

participants—"This is our Shelley," says Bono, "this is our Byron"—
are interspersed with artily shot black-and-white footage of Lunson's
conversation with Leonard. As the filmmaker and her subject tread
gently through the touchstones of Leonard's past—his father's death,
the Montreal poetry scene, the stories behind "Suzanne," the Chelsea Hotel, Phil Spector and the monastery—Leonard offers up old,
familiar lines as if they have just occurred to him: "I started writing
poetry trying to get girls interested in my mind"; "The less I was of
who I was, the better I felt." For his newer fans, those who came to
his songs through the famous cover versions that kept turning up on
film and TV and in Willner's tribute concerts, it was an intriguing introduction. If Leonard, wise, dapper and self-deprecating, said nothing that his old fans did not already know, they were still happy to
hear him, and especially see him, saying it, since few outside of Canada had seen him in years. And the scene in which he sings "Tower
of Song," backed by a doting U2, showed he still had the chops. A
soundtrack album was released, with sixteen Leonard Cohen covers
recorded live at the Sydney and Brighton concerts. "Tower of Song"
made it on, but one song that did not was the rousing "Don't Go
Home with Your Hard-On." Phil Spector, Leonard's cowriter, refused
to give his permission.

Leonard Cohen: I'm Your Man certainly helped pique and revive
interest in Leonard. But another effect of the film was to prompt
the question, why was everyone except Leonard singing his songs? A
Canadian journalist asked Leonard directly if he ever intended to go
back on the road. Leonard answered that it was "becoming more and
more attractive to me as we drink," but he failed to mention that he
rarely drank much anymore. In *Book of Longing* he had captioned one
of his drawings with the verse

*the road
   is too long*

> *the sky*
>> *is too vast*
> *the wandering*
>> *heart*
> *is homeless*
> *at last*

But as the year drew to a close, Leonard showed no inclination to be anywhere other than home.

Twenty-three

The Future of Rock 'n' Roll

On the table were a slab of beef tongue and bottle of good cognac. Leonard knew what Roshi liked. He poured a large glass for Roshi and a small one for himself and they sat with their drinks in easy silence, Leonard and the old man who had named him Jikan but usually called him Kone (not quite "koan," but close). In a few weeks' time Roshi would be one hundred years old, and yet here he still was, the constant in Leonard's life, the good friend, the wise father figure who disciplined and indulged him and never left, not even when Leonard had left him. Life, aside from "the pesky little problem of losing everything I had,"[1] was treating Leonard kindly in his old age. He had Roshi, he had Anjani and he had a grandson, Cassius Lyon Cohen—two good names, Leonard's boxing hero and his grandfather—Adam's son, born in February 2007.

Leonard wore his own seventy-two years lightly. Still, he had noticed some changes, like losing his capacity for alcohol for one, as well as his taste for tobacco. When he quit smoking, Leonard had promised himself he could start again when he reached seventy-five. He blamed his abstinence from cigarettes for the loss of the two lowest notes in his vocal range, even if in truth they had only ever been audible to certain mammals and devoted female fans. His voice now was deeper than it had ever been. It was like old leather, soft and worn, a little cracked in places but for the most part supple, and hung suspended somewhere between word and song. Since Leonard's return from the monastery, it seemed to have been leaning more toward the word. Of course there was always music in the word, but when it came down to actual melodies, Leonard seemed as content to leave them to others to write as he had been to let others sing his songs.

Another project was about to come to fruition, which featured his words set to music that Leonard neither wrote nor sang. Unlike *Blue Alert*, this was a stage production, with music by Philip Glass—among the most distinguished, influential and prolific composers in postmodern American music. Almost a quarter of a century earlier, between writing his avant-garde opera *Einstein on the Beach* and scoring the Martin Scorsese film *Kundun*, Glass had taken a poem of Leonard's from *The Spice-Box of Earth*, "There Are Some Men," and turned it into an a capella hymn, which was performed as part of *Three Songs for Chorus a Cappella*, a work commissioned for the celebration of the 350th anniversary of Quebec. At that time, he and Leonard had never met. But having been introduced backstage at a concert somewhere along the way, they had talked about spending some time together and eventually, fifteen years later, they did, in L.A. They spent the day together, Glass recalls, "talking about music and poetry," by the end of the day, they had agreed to work together on something, though neither knew what or when.

Glass had collaborated over the years on diverse projects with orchestras, rock musicians and filmmakers, but he particularly enjoyed working with poets. One of his favorite collaborators was Allen Ginsberg, with whom he worked for ten years, until Ginsberg's death in 1997. Not long after, Glass tried to get in touch with Leonard again, but he says, "I discovered he had gone into the monastery." It would be several more years before Leonard e-mailed to say, "I'm out of the monastery, so we can go back to that project." Glass, who "was missing having that in-depth relationship with a poet that was *alive*," was delighted. "I kind of went from Allen Ginsberg to Leonard Cohen—a pretty good transition, don't you think?"

When Glass visited Leonard at his L.A. home, Leonard was still working on *Book of Longing*. He handed the composer a stack of loose pages, poems and illustrations, in no particular order. Sitting at the wooden table, Glass leafed through them, relishing the randomness. He started formulating categories into which he divided the contents: ballads, "the long poems I thought would be the pillars of the work"; rhymes and limericks, "the little ones"; dharma poems, "spiritual meditations"; love/erotic poems; and personal poems, about Leonard. He picked five or six from each category to write music for. Among them were some that Leonard had already recorded as songs. Tentatively, Glass asked Leonard if he would like to be involved in the music. "I was terrified that he might say yes, but he said, 'You write the music.'"

Glass composed a series of song cycles to be performed by four voices and a small ensemble made up of strings, oboe, horn, percussion and keyboards. To retain the sense of randomness he had felt and to give the theater audience a sense of "flipping through a book of poetry," he included in each song cycle a poem from each of his five categories. He also wanted to hear how the poems sounded in their author's voice, so he asked Leonard if he would record himself reading a few. Leonard recorded the entire book and sent that. "When I heard the quality of this reading," Glass says, "I thought I would put his voice into the piece itself. I said, 'Though you may not be there to perform it, may I use your voice?' He said, 'Yes.'" Leonard also gave Glass use of his artwork as a backdrop. When the composition was finished—ninety minutes, twenty-two poems—he played it for Leonard, who sat and listened quietly. "He said almost nothing. There was one vocal part that he felt was a little bit high and I eventually brought it down an octave, but that was the only thing, and it did work better."

The world premiere for *Book of Longing: A Song Cycle Based on the Poetry and Images of Leonard Cohen* was set for June 1, 2007, in Toronto, coinciding with the opening there of *Leonard Cohen: Drawn to Words*, a traveling exhibition of Leonard's drawings and sketches. Glass flew to Canada to conduct the final rehearsals. To his surprise Leonard flew there too and spent a week working with him and the cast. As with *Blue Alert*, Leonard was not without opinions on how his words ought to be sung. Glass remembers, "He met the singers and said, 'Well here I am, you can ask me anything you like.' They talked for hours. He had powerful insights into the approach to singing that worked with his words. He began talking about the 'voice' that they should employ in singing the work—I don't mean the *kind* of voice, I mean the aesthetic. At one point he said, 'You start by singing and make it simpler and simpler and simpler and where you reach the point where you're actually speaking, then you're finished.' He didn't actually literally mean they would be speaking, I believe he meant it would be *as if* you were speaking, that the affectations of singing were absent. And they followed that advice and they simplified their vocal style until it became almost like speech." Leonard had said much the same thing to Anjani.

Leonard stayed and joined Glass in a public discussion of the work. When he was asked whether he considered what Glass had done to be classical or musical theater, Leonard's answer, "Glassical," was wry but accurate. Although originally labeled minimalist for their haunting, repetitive rhythms and motifs, Glass's musical compositions were also earthy and erotic and drew on any number of different musical styles, all of them evident in this work. The *Toronto Star*'s reviewer's description was "a confusing work of considerable importance."[2]

Following three successful nights in Toronto, the show left on a small tour, and in December 2007 the album *Book of Longing: A Song Cycle Based on the Poetry and Images of Leonard Cohen* was released, making it to No. 17 on the U.S. classical music charts. Over the next two years, the production would be staged in a number of U.S. and European cities and at a festival in New Zealand. In 2009 it returned to America for a five-night stand in Claremont, the university town at the bottom of Mount Baldy. The theater in which it was staged faced the mountain. A college building nearby hosted an exhibition of Leonard's art. Both events had been arranged by Robert Faggen, a writer and professor of literature at Claremont Graduate University who had a cabin on Mount Baldy, a short walk from the monastery. He and Leonard had become good friends since their first encounter in Wolfe's Market—the store at the bottom of Mount Baldy where Leonard would go to buy treats for Roshi. On the occasion of their meeting, Leonard was standing in the deli aisle, dressed in his monk's robes, meditating on the merits of buying some potato salad.

Faggen took Glass, who flew out for the Claremont shows, to the monastery to meet Roshi. Glass, like Leonard a Jew of Lithuanian-Russian descent, also shared his deep involvement with Buddhism; he had himself been on long retreats (where, in his case, he was given special dispensation to take his piano) and had been a contributing editor to the Buddhist magazine *Tricycle*. At Mount Baldy Zen Center, Glass sat for a *teisho* with Roshi. Although the old teacher declined to come down from the mountain to go to the concert, the audience included a number of monks.

There were now three productions featuring Leonard's work without Leonard making the rounds: *Book of Longing: A Song Cycle*, *Came So Far for Beauty*, and *Leonard Cohen: Drawn to Words*. It was an invisible kind of visibility that suited Leonard just fine. "If you hang in there long enough, you begin to be surrounded by a certain gentleness and invisibility," he once told an interviewer. "This invisibility is promising, because it will probably become deeper and deeper. And with invisibility—and I am not talking about the opposite of celebrity, I mean something like The Shadow, who can move from one room to another unobserved—comes a beautiful calm."[3]

With age had come a greater degree of serenity than Leonard had ever felt in his adult life. With age too had come homages and awards without end. He had to stop counting how many tribute albums there were—more than fifty by this point, from twenty different countries. A couple had caught his eye. One, because it was recorded by his first and most stalwart champion, was *Democracy: Judy Collins Sings Leonard Cohen*—from 2004, the year Leonard turned seventy—on which Collins had gathered all her interpretations of his songs under one roof. Another that had delighted Leonard was *Top Tunes Artist Vol. 19 TT–110*, an instrumental album of his songs (packaged with an album of Enya songs) made specifically for karaoke bars. "At last," Leonard said, "somewhere to go in the evening,"[4] though in reality he was still happiest at home, "an old man in a suit . . . delicately talking about his work to somebody."[5] Then Sony decided to reissue *Blue Alert*.

On its original release the previous year, Anjani's album had reached No. 18 in the U.S. jazz charts but had had little impact anywhere else. For the new edition the record label added a DVD of videos and a documentary by Lian Lunson on the making of the album. The label also put together a short tour. In March 2007, shortly before Roshi's one hundredth birthday, Leonard flew with Anjani to Europe. The first three shows, in London, Oslo and Warsaw, were invitation-only events, media mostly, and Leonard Cohen fans who had won tickets through radio and website contests. Journalists who wanted to interview Leonard—and there were many—were told that they would have to talk to him and Anjani as a pair. As far as Leonard was concerned, the tour and the album were Anjani's, not his.

To a UK newspaper, Leonard described his work with Anjani as more than mere collaboration, "an expression of some kind of deep mutuality, some kind of marriage of purpose."⁶ Picking up on the "marriage" aspect, the host of a Norwegian television talk show asked Leonard to talk about their "love story." Leonard's answer— that he "found it's best not to name a relationship"—demonstrated that he had lost none of his skills at deflection. However, Anjani did appear to be wearing an engagement ring. In an interview with the Buddhist magazine *Shambhala Sun* Leonard elaborated, "The woman is saying, 'What is our relationship? Are we engaged?' . . . and my disposition is, 'Do we really have to have this discussion, because it's not as good as our relationship?' But as you get older, you want to accommodate, and say, 'Yeah, we're living together. This is for real. I'm not looking for anyone else. You're the woman in my life.' Whatever terms that takes: a ring, an arrangement, a commitment, or from one's behavior, by the way you act."⁷

During the *Blue Alert* tour Leonard had restricted his role to making the introduction, then taking a seat in the audience to watch the show. But one night, partway through a concert in a nightclub in London, Anjani invited Leonard to come up and sing with her, an invitation he accepted, shyly. His appearance was greeted by rapturous applause. When the tour arrived in the U.S., Leonard would show up on occasion and duet with Anjani on the song "Whither Thou Goest." As word of this spread, the small venues where Anjani had been booked to play started to attract large crowds—people who were hoping to see Leonard. The question was, did Leonard want to see them?

Leonard had never much enjoyed touring, however good the concerts might have been. He toured simply because if you were in the music business that was what you did. You made an album and when it was done you went on the road to check in with your fan base and sell it. This ritual was of particular importance to an artist like Leonard, whose records were not all over the radio. It had been almost fifteen years since Leonard had last toured, with *The Future*, and it had been such a disagreeable experience that it was one factor in Leonard's decision to leave the music business and go live in the monastery. Since his return to the music business, none of his albums had sold a fraction as well as *The Future*, so there seemed even less point in going out on tour.

But the music business had changed drastically during Leonard's absence. As the Internet grew and people increasingly wanted music for free, or at best to buy it online one song at a time, even big-name, established artists were no longer selling albums in the large numbers they had before. Musicians were starting to look for new ways to sell their music and themselves, coming up with all manner of solutions. Joni Mitchell, for example, had signed a deal with the coffee shop chain Starbucks, which played her CD as background music and sold it alongside lattes and croissants. Joni had been on Leonard's mind lately; Herbie Hancock had asked him to appear on a tribute album, *River: The Joni Letters* (2007); Leonard recited "The Jungle Line."

Major artists were increasingly making their money from touring, charging considerably higher ticket prices than under the old system, when concerts existed to promote album sales. Although Leonard refused to consider himself a major artist, he also knew that the tributes, the collaborations, the signed limited editions of his artwork and even the lawsuits had done little to refill his empty retirement account. Of all the options available to him for making a living, the only one that appeared even remotely feasible was going back on the road. But Leonard was almost seventy-three years old, and it had been so long since he had last toured, it seemed to him, that to expect that he would still have an audience would be like making a sandcastle and going back a decade and a half later and expecting it to be there waiting for him.

Still, he thought, it was not going to be any easier when he was seventy-five or eighty. And due to the combined publicity from the film and the tribute concerts, Anjani's album, Glass's production and the media interest in his financial problems, Leonard was as much in the public consciousness as he was likely to ever be again. Tenta-

tively and ambivalently—very ambivalently—Leonard began to consider the idea of a tour. Since he had no manager to look into setting
one up, having parted company with Sam Feldman some time ago,
Leonard asked Robert Kory if he would do it.

As it happened, Leonard was not the only one considering the
possibility. Steven Machat had heard from Leonard's old European
promoter, asking if he would help him talk Leonard into touring. Machat knew Leonard had financial problems; he had first read about
the business with Kelley Lynch in the *New York Times*, and though he
was not entirely sympathetic—he had not forgotten that Lynch, who
had once been his father Marty Machat's assistant, had, as he saw it,
purloined Leonard's files, with Leonard's support, as his father lay
dying—he was curious. He put in a call to Leonard, as he had promised the promoter he would. Leonard invited him to his house for
lunch. Standing at the stove in his small kitchen, cooking, Leonard
conceded to his guest that he might indeed have to tour, since he had
no money. "I said to Leonard, man to man, why would any human
being allow someone else to have the access to his fortune for five
years? But Leonard is an extremely fearful man," Machat says. "Kelley Lynch played that to the hilt."

If Leonard was going to tour, it certainly would make sense to
start in Europe, where he had his most loyal following. Robert Kory
had thought as much and had already put in a call to AEG Live, a
London-based promoter. He asked what they knew about Leonard
Cohen and the response was "Not much, but there's a man in the
company who is a big fan." That man was Rob Hallett. Hallett had an
impressive record in the business. In the eighties he had been Duran
Duran's worldwide promoter, and he had been behind Prince's recent sold-out twenty-one-night stand at the twenty-three-thousand-
capacity O2 Arena in London. Kory called Hallett, who flew to L.A.
to meet with him and Leonard and make his pitch. "I've got every album you've ever made," Hallett told Leonard. "I've read every novel,

every poem, I bore all my friends regularly with quotations from your songs, and I've lived my life by a couplet from a poem that you wrote in 1958, 'He refused to be held like a drunk / under the cold tap of fact.'"

Leonard listened soberly. The more he heard, the more he saw the potential for humiliation. "He wasn't sure he could do it," says Hallett, "and he wasn't sure if anyone cared. I said, 'I'm a cynical old bastard and I don't want to see anything, but I want to see Leonard Cohen, so there must be others.' I was convinced there were hundreds of thousands of people out there who wanted to see him. His biggest concern was that he didn't want to embarrass himself. But also, he didn't have any money left. So I said, 'I'll tell you what, do some rehearsals, do as long as you want, audition as long as you want, and I'll pick up the tab and pay for everything. If at the end of it you say, "Thanks, but this isn't working for me, I can't go out there and perform," I'll go, "Well, we tried," and you won't owe me anything.'" It was an offer Leonard couldn't refuse. There were no strings and it had an escape clause, two of his favorite things. "That sounds like a reasonable deal," Leonard said. They shook hands on it. Kory began putting together a touring plan, while Hallett set about convincing the industry that Leonard Cohen concerts would be a going concern.

When Sharon Robinson opened her door one day soon after, she saw Leonard on her doorstep with a worried look on his face. "Darling," he said, "I think I'm going to have to go on tour again." He didn't want to do it, he said, but all the signs were pointing that way. He did not ask Sharon to come on the road with him. Nor did he ask Anjani. He thought—because the tour for *The Future* had soured him on working with old friends, perhaps, or because he did not want to let old friends down or let them see him fail—that he should take all new people with him, musicians he'd never worked with before. The one exception was Roscoe Beck, whom he asked to be his musical director.

"Leonard was very apprehensive about the entire enterprise," Beck remembers. "He didn't even want to talk on the phone about it. He flew down to Austin to talk to me in person. He said, 'I'm thinking about touring again. Would you help me put the band together and would you go?' I said, 'Yes, of course, I had already promised myself if I ever heard from you again I would go.'" (Beck had put together Leonard's *I'm Your Man* touring band but had been unable to join himself.) "Leonard said, 'Look, I don't know if I'm really going to do this. I hope you won't hold it against me if I decide to back out.' He really wasn't sure he could go through with it. He said, 'I'm 92.7 percent sure'—the numbers would change all the time—'I'm 82 percent sure, I'm 93 percent sure.' He said, 'I have the option of backing out at any time if I don't like the way it's developing, and if I do go I'm only committed to do six weeks. But if the whole thing doesn't happen would you forgive me?' I said, 'Of course.'"

Leonard had begun to feel less concerned about the actual touring—as long as his vocal cords didn't give out, he felt confident he could keep up the pace—than about the band. It had been so long since he'd played with one, he had no idea what kind of band he wanted-ed. He was used to working at home with Anjani and Sharon, but an old man with two women and two synthesizers would not really cut it onstage. In January 2008, Beck started making calls and holding auditions. The first person Beck hired was actually someone Leonard knew well—Bob Metzger, Leanne Ungar's husband, who had played on the *I'm Your Man* tour and on the album *Ten New Songs*—though the next two recruits were new to Leonard, Neil Larsen, a keyboard player whose résumé ranged from Kenny Loggins to Miles Davis, and Javier Mas, a Spanish bandurria, laud and twelve-string-guitar player. Mas had been the musical director of a Leonard Cohen tribute concert in Barcelona, in which Leonard's son, Adam; Jackson Browne; and Anjani had performed. Leonard had seen a DVD of the concert and Mas had impressed him.

Beck was also trying to work out exactly what kind of show Leonard had in mind. Over the years, as Leonard's voice became increasingly deeper and his musical approach more refined, the bands and the volume level had changed accordingly. It appeared to Beck that this band he was putting together was "more like a chamber group." Six weeks into rehearsals they still had no drummer. Eventually they hired Mexican-born Rafael Gayol, another newcomer to Leonard; Beck had worked with Gayol in Austin. At one point Leonard decided he wanted a violin player, and a female violinist joined the band. Then Leonard realized he did not need a violin, and she was let go, and once again Leonard began to doubt himself—to regret, as he put it, "that I had started the whole process."[8] Instead, Beck brought in a multi-instrumentalist, Dino Soldo, to play saxophone, woodwind and keyboards.

All that remained to find were the backing singers. Beck asked Jennifer Warnes, but she declined. Anjani had dropped by for some of the early rehearsals, but no mention was made of her joining the tour. Says Beck, "I just wasn't sure what was going to happen in that regard because of the personal relationship between Anjani and Leonard." Anjani herself attributes it to "a difference of opinion" in their approach to the concerts. "I had in mind a revolutionary approach to Leonard's music; I wanted to showcase it in ways that hadn't been done before, with arrangements that were innovative and unexpected. The other approach was to re-create the past tours. In the end he went with what he felt comfortable with, and I understand the decision." Beck called Sharon Robinson, who expressed interest. But Leonard wanted two backing singers, and the search went on.

It was March 2008; the tour, if there was going to be one, was just two months away. Leonard meanwhile was in New York, being inducted into the Rock and Roll Hall of Fame—the American hall of fame, the big one, the greatest honor the once-dismissive U.S. music industry could bestow on him. Lou Reed was there to introduce

Leonard and present his award. In an odd little ceremony-within-a-ceremony Reed, dressed in a black leather suit and fuchsia shirt and carrying a stack of typewritten notes and a copy of *Book of Longing*, gave a reading instead of an introduction. Now and then he paused to interject his own comments like an enthusiastic college professor: "He just gets better. . . . We're so lucky to be alive at the same time Leonard Cohen is."[9]

Leonard, silver haired and dignified in his tuxedo and black bow tie, came out onstage, bowed deeply to Reed and thanked him for reminding him that he had written a few decent lines. This was "such an unlikely event," Leonard said, and it was not just modesty; he meant it. It brought to mind, he said, "the prophetic statement by Jon Landau in the early 1970s: 'I have seen the future of rock 'n' roll, and it is not Leonard Cohen.'"[10] Leonard was making a joke; what Landau, the head of the Hall of Fame's nominating committee, had actually said back in the days when he was a journalist for *Rolling Stone* was that he had seen the future of rock 'n' roll, and it was Bruce Springsteen. But *Rolling Stone* magazine had certainly dismissed Leonard's early albums, describing *Songs from a Room* as "depressed and depressing"[11] and *Songs of Love and Hate* as "unlikely to make you want to shake your little body."[12] As Lou Reed had, Leonard gave a recital in place of a speech—a solemn reading of the first five verses of "Tower of Song." He declined to follow the Hall of Fame tradition of performing with the other inductees; he was not ready to perform yet. But he was getting there. Leonard left the stage to Damien Rice to sing "Hallelujah," a song that at that time was No. 1 on the iTunes chart—the late Jeff Buckley's version. That it had been propelled back into the national consciousness had nothing to do with Leonard's finally taking his official place among the popular music pantheon, but through the sheer number of online discussions that followed Jason Castro's performance of "Hallelujah" on *American Idol*.

Back in Los Angeles, Beck was pulling out his hair. None of the women singers he had auditioned had worked out. He asked Sharon Robinson if she could think of someone—anyone. Sharon mentioned Charley and Hattie Webb. The Webb Sisters were in their early twenties. Born in England two years apart, they had sung and played as a duo since their teens, Charley on guitar, Hattie on harp. They had come to L.A. to work on an album and, during the process, their record label asked them to write some songs for a children's album they planned to release. Sharon, who had a publishing deal with the same company, was also brought in on that project. All three women remember how well their voices blended when they sang together.

Since that time, the Webbs had lost their record deal and were on the point of giving up and going home to the UK when Sharon called, telling them that Leonard was looking for a singer. They replied that they did not know many Leonard Cohen songs; although they had grown up on their parents' record collection of sixties and seventies singer-songwriters, their hairdresser father had banned Leonard's albums from their home because a colleague at the salon played nothing but Leonard Cohen albums all day long. They also told Sharon what she already knew: that they came as a pair and would not separate.

The whole band was in the rehearsal studio at SIR when the Webb Sisters arrived. Beck played a recording of "Dance Me to the End of Love" and told the three women to work out some parts. After singing them, the Webbs took their harp and guitar out of their cases and played two of their own songs, "Baroque Thoughts" and "Everything Changes." When Beck had first checked the sisters' Myspace page, he thought they looked too young, but the moment he heard them sing, this changed to, "Here are our singers." When they left, he called Leonard in New York. "I said, 'I've got good news and bad news. The good news is I think I've found our singers.' Leonard said, 'Great.' 'The bad news is now there's three.' We arranged for the sisters to come back when Leonard returned from New York, and it was a no-brainer. We knew we had our vocalists, and at last, our band."

Rehearsals resumed in earnest; there were less than six weeks left to go. "It was an interesting way of rehearsing," Charley remembers. "There wasn't a strong direction, Roscoe wasn't turning around and bossing anybody, and Leonard wasn't." "I felt that they were both allowing everyone to come to the song," says Hattie. "We would rehearse a few songs and then people would stop for tea and sandwiches, and while we were pottering Leonard would go back up just with his guitar, and play 'The Stranger Song' or 'Avalanche.' I felt he was just getting his bearings at this new time and in this environment." At the end of the week the sisters were dispatched to England to pick up work visas. They stayed the weekend, then flew straight back again for the next rehearsal on Monday.

In these last few weeks of rehearsal, Beck began noticing a change in Leonard's attitude to the tour. "The band really started taking shape and Leonard was able to conduct the rehearsals, fine-tune the band to his specifications and get exactly what he was looking for musically." He was also working on his showmanship, "falling to his knees even in rehearsal. It wasn't just an effect for the audience, it's for the band in a way, because if he goes down on one knee and cups his microphone, he's giving us a signal which we will interpret as, 'Play softer.' It's becoming more intimate."

Rob Hallett was getting anxious. Leonard had been rehearsing for at least four months now and all he had was bills. "About a million dollars later, I started panicking. Then Leonard said, 'Okay, come and see the rehearsals.'" They set up a sofa just for Hallett in front of the instrument-and-equipment-laden rehearsal-room stage. "I was blown away," says Hallett. "It was sublime." The show was ready to go. "And then Leonard insisted that before doing anything serious he wanted to do all these shows in the wilds of Canada—tiny places; he named some towns I'd never heard of." As the tour began to look like a reality, Leonard had asked Kory to set up what he called a "pre-tour tour," eighteen small, low-key warm-up shows in the Maritimes, away from the eye of the world. The kind of places where it was less likely there would be people waiting to see him fall. He also asked Kory if he would be his manager.

The very first concert took place on May 11, 2008, in Fredericton, New Brunswick. "The joke at the time," Hallett remembers, "was, 'First we take Fredericton, then we take Berlin.'" Leonard, the band and crew, and Kory and Hallett arrived several days early so that they could rehearse some more in the theater, five, six hours a day. The show couldn't have been better prepared. The tiny playhouse theater—just 709 seats—sold out in minutes; they could have sold it out ten times over, Hallett thought to himself, if Leonard had not insisted on such a small venue and Kory had not done his best to keep the show quiet.

Standing in the wings on opening night, his double-breasted suit hanging on his slight frame, Leonard still couldn't have sworn on the Scriptures that he was 100 percent sure about this tour. "He was nervous," says Hallett. "You wouldn't have known it on the outside, but he was incredibly nervous." If Leonard's mother had been there she would have advised him to have a shave. A few stiff drinks and a smoke would have helped as well, but this was going to be Leonard's first tour without alcohol and cigarettes. He took a deep breath; one lesson he had learned from his years at the monastery was to "stop whining."[13] Taking off his hat, he bowed his head and mumbled a little prayer. The house lights went down. Straightening his spine and pushing his fedora back firmly on his head, Leonard stepped out onto the stage.

Twenty-four

Here I Stand, I'm Your Man

The applause was deafening. It bounced off the walls of the small theater and resounded in Leonard's ears. The whole room was on its feet. A minute ticked by, then another. Leonard had not sung a word and no one had played a note, but still they applauded. Leonard smiled shyly. He took off his hat and held it over his heart, in a gesture of humility, but also as armor. The response was gratifying—whatever they told him, he had never been entirely confident as to what the reception might be—but also worrying, having such expectations to fulfill. Though in reality there were no expectations. It was the opening night. The audience had as much of an idea of what to expect of Leonard as he had of them. For all they knew—which was not very much, because, at Leonard's insistence, the whole thing had been kept as low-key as possible—it might be some broke and broken old man with a nylon-string guitar, singing them through their memories, accompanied by a female vocalist or two if he could afford them. Everyone had read about Leonard's money troubles and how they had forced the old monk back on the boards with his begging bowl.

But here he stood in the spotlight in his sharp suit, fedora and shiny shoes, looking like a Rat Pack rabbi, God's chosen mobster. He was flanked by three women singers and a six-piece band, many of whom also wore suits and hats, like they were playing in a casino in Las Vegas. The band started up. Leonard pulled his fedora down low on his forehead, and cradling the microphone like it was an offering, he began to sing, "*Dance me to your beauty with a burning violin*," his voice a little rough at the edges, but deep and strong, "*Dance me through the panic till I'm gathered safely in*" ("Dance Me to the End of Love"). On this small, crowded stage, shoehorned with musicians and instruments and equipment, the women so close to him that if he felt the need he could reach out and hold on to them so he would not fall, Leonard sang as if he had come to this place alone to tell all these people in the seats, individually, a secret. He sang as if he had brought nothing with him onto the stage but this life of songs.

He told the audience, as he would go on to tell hundreds more, that the last time he had done this he was "sixty years old, just a kid with a crazy dream." He admitted to being nervous but chatted and joked with the audience, commiserating with them over the town's recent floods and paying tribute to its local poets—among them Fred Cogswell, who, more than half a century earlier, had published a review of Leonard's first book in his magazine *Fiddlehead*. The songs Leonard had selected for the show ranged across his career, while bypassing his darkest and most brutal material. (An exception was made for "The Future," although its "anal sex" was changed to something less anatomically specific.) While Roscoe Beck was putting the band together, Leonard had been going back through songs he had not listened to in years in search of those he felt he could still "live in."[1] It surprised him he had found so many—and that he remembered the words. That his choices leaned toward the more stirring, later songs than the naked early ones was perhaps in part an old man's delicacy, but more likely because they worked better with a large band, and Leonard needed a large band to drown out the noise of doubt. Equally important was that those early songs were largely solo guitar based. As relatively easy as it had been to reenter his songs, he found it much harder playing the guitar; it had been so long since he had played it that it needed to be restrung. He had to practice long and hard, he said, "to get [his] chop back," the one on "Suzanne," one of the few songs he played without adornment. Mostly, on the occasions when he did play an instrument, it was his synthesizer, acknowledging with a humble bow the applause for his mock-solemn, one-finger solos. But more often Leonard just sang, sometimes like a supplicant, his head bowed low over the microphone cupped in his hands, other times like a showman, the microphone cord draped casually over his arm, falling to his knees, working the crowd with meticulously choreographed moves—an intricate dance between self-awareness, irony and emotional honesty that he pulled off gracefully and well.

His band was smooth, elegant, note-perfect, its sound brush-stroked, its volume turned way down. "We called ourselves the world's quietest band," says Beck, "or at least the quietest with electric instruments. The focus was finely tuned to Leonard's voice and to making sure that the audience heard every word." But Leonard also gave the musicians solo spots. Stepping away from the light, he would watch them, rapt, his hat over his heart, marveling along with the audience when Javier Mas played the laud or twelve-string or Sharon sang him into "Boogie Street," as if he too was hearing this excellence for the first time and was humbled by it. They played for almost three hours that night, with a short intermission—and no one played three-hour shows, certainly not a man in his seventies who had not sung more than a handful of songs in succession on a stage in a decade and a half. Leonard's son, Adam, had tried to persuade him to keep it to an hour and a half, but Leonard was having none of it. And, remarkably, he seemed to be enjoying it. It was not simply relief that the rehearsals had paid off, the band worked and people were thrilled to see him. It was something deeper. There was some necessary rite that was being performed here, some gift being exchanged and something important being shared.

"I saw people in front of the stage, shaking and crying," remembers Charley Webb, "not just one person and not children. You don't often see adults cry, and with such violence." Says Hattie Webb, "The audience reaction from that first night was, 'This is hugely momentous.' It was for us too." With the first show behind them, everybody relaxed, even Leonard, as they headed in the bus to the next tiny Canadian venue. These shows had been booked at Leonard's insistence. His response to the tour schedule his manager had shown him was, "What have you gotten me into?"[2] "He set out a series of conditions," says Robert Kory. "I said, 'Leonard, this is a no-compromise tour, we will do it exactly the way you want to do it or we won't do it.' Every element of the tour articulated his vision, from three months of rehearsals to the warm-up dates."

There were eighteen of these dates in Eastern Canada. "You pick up a rock," says Rob Hallett, "and there's a town under it. One place I remember had a sign with those clip-on letters, advertising a local brass band on Monday, Leonard Cohen Tuesday and on Wednesday an Elvis Presley impersonator." At another of the concerts, two young women rushed the stage, prompting Leonard to comment wryly, or wistfully, or both, as security gently led them off, "If only I were two years younger." Kory also instituted a policy of no one being allowed backstage who did not need to be there, meaning no meet-and-greets, nor even visits from celebrity friends, before or after shows. This tour, Kory declared, would be "fueled on silence and deep rest and providing the level of support that helps him to do these performances night after night." This was quite a change from Leonard

Cohen tours in the past, which had been fueled by cigarettes and alcohol or the drug du jour. (By the end of his last tour, with *The Future*, Leonard had been smoking two packs a day and drinking three bottles of Château Latour before every show.)

The official starting date of the tour was June 6 in Toronto, where Leonard had sold out four nights at the three-thousand-seater Sony Centre. This time Leonard skipped onstage—literally skipped, like a little child—the very picture of gaiety and delight. Although the Toronto crowd had a better idea than Fredericton of what to expect, they had not anticipated this. "It was a surprise to me too," says Roscoe Beck, laughing. Leonard had also taken to dancing a light-footed shuffle during the song "The Future" whenever it reached the words "white man dancing." The set list had also lengthened. Among the four additional songs were "A Thousand Kisses Deep," whose words Leonard recited as a poem over Neil Larsen's hushed keyboard playing, and "If It Be Your Will," which was sung by the Webb Sisters, accompanying themselves on harp and guitar. The room was so completely silent during the performances of the songs that you could hear the hairs stand up on people's arms. But when the music ended, there were standing ovations—so many that the *Toronto Star* reviewer described the concert as "a love-in."[3]

This time the international press was welcomed to the concerts. The critic from *Rolling Stone*, having confessed to trepidation at the prospect of a comeback show by a man "older than Jerry Lee Lewis" trying to make enough money to retire on, called it "stunning."[4] Leonard told *Maclean's* magazine that he had decided—100 percent now—that the tour would go on. "As the Irish say, with the help of God and two policemen, [it] may last a year and a half, or two."[5] Four days after their last Toronto show, Leonard and the band were in Ireland, playing three consecutive nights in Dublin. There was a day off for travel, then four more concerts in a row in Manchester, followed by an appearance at the Montreal International Jazz Festival and, immediately afterward, another transatlantic flight back to Britain to play at the Glastonbury Festival. This was a punishing schedule by anyone's standards, let alone a man in his midseventies. Leonard had known what he was taking on and held up without complaint. Still, he was not looking forward to Glastonbury.

Michael Eavis was. The dairy farmer who founded the UK's biggest and best-loved rock festival had been trying to get Leonard to agree to play there, he said, "for almost forty years."[6] The Webb Sisters were so looking forward to it that they showed up two days early and melted into the crowd. When Leonard and the band arrived on the day of their performance, they were stunned at what they saw. Only seven weeks after having played to seven hundred people in Fredericton, they would be playing to a hundred thousand. "It was so . . . ," says Sharon Robinson, searching for a word to describe the magnitude of it and settling for "huge. And very exciting." Leonard did not share the excitement. He had never much enjoyed festivals, however successful his performances had been. It was not his crowd, one never knew who one was playing to, he could not spend a couple of hours sound-checking, and they had been instructed to shorten their usual set by almost half, which drastically altered its rhythm. None of these would please a perfectionist, a creature of habit or a man who needed to feel in control, in particular when it came to performing. Leonard peered out at the audience from the side of the stage. It was still daylight. A blanket of people stretched back from the stage as far as he could see. Those at the front all seemed to be youngsters. He slipped farther back into the wings and bowed his head. He might have appeared to be praying, but he was singing— "Pauper Ego Sum" ("I Am a Poor Man"), the Latin song-in-the-round he used to sing with his band on the tour bus half a lifetime ago. The Webb Sisters and Sharon, who were beside him, took up the song, and the rest of the band joined in. They were still singing it when they came out onstage, to be met with a roar of applause.

"There will never be anything better than Leonard Cohen's performance that night, for me," said Michael Eavis. The sun was starting to set when Leonard started singing "Hallelujah," and "people were just lifting off the ground."[7] Some of the young people singing along appeared to be wondering what this cool-looking old guy was doing up there singing a Jeff Buckley/Rufus Wainwright/*American Idol/X-Factor* song, while at the same time marveling at what a great job he did of it. The response from the audience was ecstatic, and reviewers agreed with Eavis, calling Leonard's performance the highlight of the festival. Leonard and the band did not have a chance to read the reports in the next morning's newspapers before they were on their way to Scandinavia for a whirlwind tour of Europe—at one point playing three-hour concerts in three different countries on three consecutive days. Everywhere they played, they were buoyed by this massive wave of love from the audience.

In July, still only two months into the tour, and back once again in England, Leonard headlined his first big arena show. The twenty thousand tickets to London's O2 Arena, a large, round, permanent marquee by the river Thames, sold out quickly. The vast stage had been strewn with Turkish rugs, to make it appear more homey, but it still looked like Leonard was playing inside a gigantic, sterile, skewered contraceptive cap. "It's wonderful," Leonard deadpanned, "to be gathered here on the other side of intimacy." The *London Evening Standard* reviewer described an audience "overpowered by a magnificent performance," and the closing song, "Whither Thou Goest," as "the most final of farewells."[8] Except the tour showed no sign of stopping anytime soon.

There were more concerts scheduled in the same arena in November. Meanwhile Leonard was on another lap around Europe, including a headlining appearance at the UK's Big Chill Festival and a tour of Eastern Europe. Sharon Robinson remembers everyone feeling like they were "on this ever-expanding, growing magic carpet, where it's, 'Okay, they love us in Northeast Canada, great,' but then we'd get the same thing again and again in bigger places. It was a kind of a curious, gradual acceptance of being involved in something very special." Leonard himself said, "I'm being sent like a postcard from place to place." Given his statements in the past on such a circumstance, it was not insignificant that he should add, "It's really wonderful."[9]

The bookings kept coming; Leonard was playing to the biggest and most age-diverse audiences of his career, and every show was a sellout. Following a six-week break for the holidays, during which Leonard spent Hanukkah with Adam and Lorca, and "Hallelujah" spent Christmas dominating the UK charts (three different versions, including one by Leonard), the tour resumed in January 2009 in New Zealand and Australia. Again Leonard triumphed. But he had always done well in these countries, just as he had in the UK, where even his bleakest albums made the Top 10, and in Europe, where he was feted for the very things that had turned the North American music industry off: his dark humor, old-world romance, existential gloom and poetry. North America was the next stop—his largest U.S. tour to date, interspersed with shows in Canada. Most of the American shows were in smaller venues, theaters, but he had also been booked to play at the Coachella festival and the Red Rocks Amphitheatre. Sensibly, Leonard started the tour on familiar ground, in New York City, with a show at the Beacon Theatre whose audience was crammed with media and hard-core fans alerted through the fan sites.

Rolling Stone reported a scene of "absolute chaos" outside the theater, "with hordes of people desperately looking for tickets. The few scalpers were getting upwards of five hundred dollars a seat";[10] *Billboard* said seven hundred.[11] In honor of the place he had once called home, Leonard added "Chelsea Hotel #2" (which he had been practicing in his room, privately, surprising the band by picking up his guitar and launching into it onstage). The show was now more than three hours long. "Fortunately there are curfews in most places," Robert Kory says, "or he would sing more." Both the critics and the audience were fulsome with praise—a response that would continue through the rest of the tour, with its sold-out shows, scalpers and standing ovations. It seemed as if suddenly everyone, everywhere, was talking about Leonard, asking themselves and each other, was he always this good, this wise, this droll, this cool.

Following the first leg of the U.S. tour, Leonard and the band flew back to Europe for forty more shows, some in new locations such as Serbia, Turkey and Monaco, but many in places they had already played but could still sell. There were ten dates booked in Spain, all in large venues, all sold out, and the majority in September, the month in which Leonard would turn seventy-five years old. During the September 18 concert in a cycling arena in Valencia, while singing "Bird on the Wire," Leonard collapsed. His bandmates, shocked, rushed over to him. His small limp body was carried gently off the stage, as fans near the front held up their mobile phone cameras to capture what looked like Leonard Cohen having sung himself out of the world, and having chosen the country of his beloved Lorca in which to do it. Farther back in the crowd, there was confusion. After some time Javier Mas came back onstage and explained in Spanish that Leonard was okay, he had regained consciousness and was on his way to the hospital, but the show was over and they would get their money back. The doctors diagnosed food poisoning. Several members of the band had apparently also been affected, but none of them was a gaunt seventy-five-year-old front man. Two days later, Leonard was back on the bus. Looking frail but unbroken, he celebrated his seventy-fifth birthday playing a three-hour performance in a packed sports arena in Barcelona.

In Montreal, his birthday was marked with a book launch. *Leonard Cohen You're Our Man: 75 Poets Reflect on the Poetry of Leonard Cohen*—the most celebrated of these poets being Margaret Atwood—was a fund-raising project by Jack Locke, founder of the Foundation for Public Poetry, to establish a Leonard Cohen Poet-in-Residence program at Leonard's old school, Westmount High. In New York, it was celebrated with the unveiling of a plaque on the wall by the entrance to the Chelsea Hotel. This project, spearheaded by Dick Straub, was funded by donations from Leonard Cohen fans across the world, and the ceremony was attended by Leonard's former producer John Lissauer, his writer friend Larry "Ratso" Sloman, and Esther, Leonard's ever-loyal sister. The plaque put Leonard in good company—Dylan Thomas, Arthur Miller, Brendan Behan, Thomas Wolfe—though none of these great writers' plaques could boast a quotation that alluded, as Leonard's did, to a world-famous blow job performed within the hotel's walls.

Three days after his birthday, Leonard was in Israel, playing his first concert in that country in more than twenty years. Ramat Gan Stadium, near Tel Aviv, held fifty thousand people and had sold out. Proceeds from what was billed as "A Concert for Reconciliation, Tolerance and Peace" were to go to Israeli and Palestinian organizations and charities promoting peace. "Leonard decided that if he was going to play there, he wanted the money to stay there," Robert Kory says. Still, there was controversy. When the show was announced, there were letters in the press and protests on the Internet by those urging a cultural boycott of Israel. In Montreal, a small demonstration was held outside one of Leonard's favorite Jewish delis. Leonard responded by adding a smaller show the next night in Ramallah, on the West Bank. But the organizers, the Palestinian Prisoners Club, pulled out, as did Amnesty International, who were to distribute the proceeds; both felt under pressure, that the event had become too politicized. So Leonard founded his own charity to allocate the almost two million dollars that the Tel Aviv concert made.

It was a warm summer night; the air shimmered with the glow sticks that the crowd held aloft like thin green candles. There were screens displaying translations of the songs Leonard sang through the three-and-a-half-hour show, the words in Hebrew of "Who by

Fire" reading like a page from the prayer book. Leonard dedicated "Hallelujah" to all of the families who had lost children in the conflict and expressed his admiration for those who in spite of this had resisted "the inclination of the heart to despair, revenge and hatred." When he told the audience, "We don't know when we'll pass this way again," they seemed visibly moved. Coming from a man of Leonard's age, his words had that sense of valediction that reviewers had also noted in his last album and his last volume of poems. When the last song was sung, Leonard raised his hands to the sky. Speaking in Hebrew, the descendant of Aaron gave the crowd the "Birkat Kohanim," the "Priestly Blessing."

Back in the U.S., with a few days off before the next leg of the tour, Leonard learned that Ramesh Balsekar was dead. His teacher died at the age of ninety-two on September 27, 2009, in the Mumbai apartment where Leonard had so often gone for *satsang*. Although his concert schedule had prevented him from spending much time with Ramesh, they had kept in touch by e-mail. "Just before he passed away," Ratnesh Mathur remembers, "I had a conversation with Ramesh, who mentioned that he was in correspondence with Leonard and said that it was good to see that he was performing again." The tour resumed in mid-October—fifteen more dates, including a return visit to New York to play Madison Square Garden.

It was getting to where past and present seemed to constantly bump into each other. While Leonard was writing and trying out new songs onstage (the first of them being "Lullaby") his record label re-released two old compilation albums from different periods—*Greatest Hits*, also known as *The Best of Leonard Cohen* (1975), and *The Essential Leonard Cohen* (2002)—as well as his first three studio albums from the late sixties and early seventies. *Songs of Leonard Cohen* came with two old songs released for the first time: "Store Room" and "Blessed Is the Memory," which were recorded during the 1967 sessions and shelved.* The reissued *Songs from a Room* also had two additional songs, the previously unheard versions of "Bird on the Wire" (titled "Like a Bird") and "You Know Who I Am" (titled "Nothing to One") that Leonard recorded with David Crosby before making the album with Bob Johnston. As its sole bonus track, *Songs of Love and Hate* had one of the many early outtakes of "Dress Rehearsal Rag." Still, it was one too many for Leonard, who disliked these additions and had not given his blessing for their inclusion. Feeling they ruined the integrity of the original album, he put a stop to the label's doing it again.

One remarkable temporal overlap was the release within weeks of each other of two new live CDs and DVDs. *Live in London* was recorded in 2008 at Leonard's first triumphant London O2 Arena show. *Live at the Isle of Wight 1970* contained recently unearthed recordings and footage of a 1970 performance. Watched side by side, these two UK concerts from each end of Leonard's touring career make for fascinating viewing. The 1970 show, outdoors, before a crowd of six hundred thousand in the early hours of a rainy morning, has Leonard—bestubbled, stoned and dressed in a safari suit—playing guitar backed by his small band, the Army; it is a spontaneous, edgy and seductive performance, with an intimacy that seems unfeasible in such a vast, inhospitable space. Four decades later, playing indoors in an arena, Leonard—silver haired, sober and in a smart suit—plays synthesizer with a nine-piece band; the show is as planned and rehearsed as a military operation, yet it is still magnificent, and once again Leonard makes a cavernous, anonymous space as small and intimate as a bedroom.

It was a reflection of Leonard's growing confidence onstage that he premiered more new material on the 2009 U.S. tour, "Feels So Good" and "The Darkness." The set list, remarkably, had continued to expand, now featuring more than thirty songs. Even "So Long,

---

* A *Songs of Leonard Cohen* tribute album by the rock musician Beck and friends, including Devendra Banhart, was also released in September 2009.

Marianne" came with an additional verse. Leonard's showmanship had also become more polished—the skipping on- and offstage, the falling to his knees, the playful dance during "The Future," to which the Webb Sisters had long ago added synchronized cartwheels. In November 2009, at the last show of the year in San Jose, California—which many in the audience took to be his last show, period—in "I'm Your Man" Leonard added the wearing of "an old man's mask" to the full services he offered the women gazing up at him from the metal folding chairs of the soulless Silicon Valley arena. During the extended encores, some of these women threw flimsy garments onto the stage in a mock Tom Jones tribute.

A year and a half had gone by since that first small show in Fredericton; Leonard had celebrated his seventy-fourth and seventy-fifth birthdays on the road. His 2008 tour had been named by business magazines as one of the year's most successful, and the rock press had designated the 2009 tour the best of the year. Between them, these two years of concerts had grossed well over $50 million. Not all of it went into Leonard's pocket—a band, crew and tour that size was an enormous expense—but as the promoter Rob Hallett put it, "I think it's safe to assume the garden's rosy again." Leonard had earned back all he had lost and more. He could stop now, hang up his guitar and never set foot onstage again. But it had gone beyond a moneymaking exercise a long time ago. Leonard wanted, perhaps even needed, this tour, and—remarkably, in a business and at a time where attention spans were not long—people continued to want to see him. A 2010 tour was scheduled, due to start in Europe in May, followed by another trip across Australia and shows in Cambodia and Hawaii, before ending in a victory lap of North America.

But for now Leonard had three and a half months to himself. Very much to himself; Leonard was once again a single man. Whether it had been the distances put between them by two years of touring or that the age difference between a fifty-year-old and a seventy-five-

year-old seemed more daunting than that between a forty-year-old
and a sixty-five-year-old, Leonard and Anjani were too discreet to
say. "Relationships are not stagnant, they change and grow," says Anjani, who remains Leonard's close friend and collaborator. "Rather
than me explaining it to you or him explaining it, I should send you
something he wrote, called 'I'm Always Thinking of a Song for Anjani
to Sing.' All there is to know about our relationship is in that poem. I
told him I cried when I read it. And he answered, "I cried too."

> *I'm always thinking of a song*
> *For Anjani to sing*
> *It will be about our lives together*
> *It will be very light or very deep*
> *But nothing in between*
> *I will write the words*
> *And she will write the melody*
> *I won't be able to sing it*
> *Because it will climb too high*
> *She will sing it beautifully*
> *And I'll correct her singing*
> *And she'll correct my writing*
> *Until it is better than beautiful*
> *Then we'll listen to it*
> *Not often*
> *Not always together*
> *But now and then*
> *For the rest of our lives*[12]

It felt good to be back in Montreal, trudging through the December
snow with Mort to the deli on the Main for bagels and beef tongue—
Mort's old favorite before it was Roshi's—and listening to his oldest

friend complain about the new coffee bars and boutiques that had sprung up in their old neighborhood. "He and I have been here longer than most of the people around here," says Rosengarten. "We're the old fogies. He seems to be spending more time here now." Leonard, as he often did, thought about staying in Montreal. It had changed a little, in ways other than Mort had mentioned—people would recognize him and approach him on the street or in restaurants in a way that they had not done in the past. Being Canadian, most were very polite about it, and Leonard had also come up with some evasive tactics, such as going for dinner in the afternoons when no one was there. One person in particular, who had come up to him in the park and introduced herself—a beautiful young singer named NEeMA—became his protégée; Leonard coproduced her album *Watching You Think* and drew a portrait of her for the front sleeve.

But once again Leonard was drawn back to Los Angeles. His children and his grandchild were there, and Roshi. In his 103rd year now, Roshi still presided over the Zen Center, and Leonard still went there to meditate when he was in town. Earlier in the year, when the tour came through L.A., Leonard had taken several members of the band to one of Roshi's early-morning teachings. When he had finished, Roshi gave Leonard a bottle of *ng ka pay* to open, and at eight in the morning, they all sat around enjoying a glass of the old man's favorite liqueur. It was one of the few times Leonard took a drink. Though on the road he was happy to mix drinks for the band, he made chocolate whey protein shakes for himself. He meditated in his dressing room, in the hour and a half of quiet time he liked to take between the sound check and the show. He meditated on airplanes too, back straight, eyes cast down, hands cupped in his lap, thankful that, if he fell asleep—which in truth he did, more than once—there was no one wandering the aisle with a stick, ready to prod him back to consciousness.

Ten years had passed since Leonard's life as a monk and yet, in this equally (perhaps from Leonard's perspective, more) unexpected incarnation as the hardest-working man in show business, there were many parallels, one of which was the strange quality of timelessness that time had taken on. His life was a blur of busy-ness, with one day, one year even, barely distinguishable from the one before. The new decade began with "Hallelujah" at the top of the iTunes download charts in 2010—the version Justin Timberlake and Matt Morris sang on the *Hope for Haiti* telethon—and the first of a new slew of awards. In January Leonard was presented with a Grammy Award for Lifetime Achievement. "I never thought I'd get a Grammy Award," Leonard said in his acceptance speech. "In fact, I was always touched by the modesty of their interest as to my work." (The only recording of his the Academy apparently deemed worthy was his recitation of his ex-lover's lyrics on Herbie Hancock's Grammy-winning Joni Mitchell tribute album.) But America was doing its best to make up for lost time. At a party thrown by the Canadian consulate in L.A. in honor of its Grammy-nominated countrymen, Leonard made a speech in honor of his native land. "My great-grandfather Lazarus Cohen came to Canada in 1869, to the county of Glengarry, a little town in Maberly. Because of the great hospitality that was accorded my ancestor who came here over a hundred and forty years ago, I want to thank this country, Canada, for allowing us to live and work and flourish in a place that was different from all other places in the world."

Leonard had been off the road for less than two months, but he was counting the days until spring, when the tour was due to resume. Then, while doing a Pilates exercise, he threw out his back—a spinal compression injury, the doctors told him, that would take four to six months of physical therapy to fix. Leonard insisted he was fine. His friends say he was not, that he was in great pain and could barely move. The tour was postponed. Since he was stuck in one place, Leonard thought he might as well do something. He began recording a new album.

In June Leonard flew to New York for another American award ceremony—induction into the Songwriters Hall of Fame. He was dressed in an identical tuxedo to the one he wore to the Rock and Roll Hall of Fame two years earlier but looked several years younger. As before, he quoted one of his songs in his acceptance speech— "Hallelujah" this time—and k. d. lang, as she had in Canada, serenaded him with the song. Judy Collins was there too and sang him "Suzanne." "A sublime experience," said Leonard, staying just long enough to have his photograph taken with an arm around Taylor Swift and to tell *Rolling Stone* that his new album, "God willing, will be finished next spring."[13]

The 2010 tour began in Croatia on July 25, followed by thirty-four European and Eastern European concerts and one in Russia. The eight-month break appeared to have no ill effect on the performances. The shows were long, the band a well-oiled machine, and Leonard, despite his back injury, still skipped on and off, fell to his knees and held his hat over his heart while his musicians soloed or sang or cartwheeled. His voice sounded softer and rougher at the edges now, a little cracked, but no matter, that was how the light got in.

A few of the critics, particularly those who had seen multiple shows, made mention of how it had become a kind of smooth-jazz traveling theater, with the same production, the same choreography, night after night. In the beginning, this kind of military precision and discipline, leaving nothing to chance, knowing what was going to happen and when, was the only way that someone so anxious about performing was going to be able to do it after so long away. "You never know what's going to happen when you step on the stage, whether you're going to be the person you want to be, or if the audience is going to be hospitable," as Leonard told Jian Ghomeshi, who interviewed him for CBC. "Even when you've brought the show to a certain degree of excellence," he said, "there are so many unknowns and so many mysteries."[14] But as his anxiety subsided somewhat over time, there were subtle changes to the blueprint, with Leonard frequently adding or replacing a song, sometimes during the show. For the 2010 tour they devised a communication system, whereby Leonard would whisper a song title to Beck, and by pressing a foot pedal, Beck would convey it quietly to the rest of the band and crew. Among the songs added to the set list was "Avalanche," one of the dark songs Leonard had eschewed in the earlier shows, and another new song, "Born in Chains," which Leonard recited, then sang, in an almost Tom Waits growl:

> *I was taken out of Egypt*
> *I was bound to a burden*
> *but the burden it was raised*
> *Oh Lord I can no longer keep this secret*
> *Blessed is the Name*
> *the Name be praised.*

September 2010 saw the release of a second live CD/DVD from the tour, the first having given Leonard a top 10 hit in twelve countries. *Songs from the Road*, like its predecessor, was produced by Ed Sanders, who had been recording the entire tour from the first concert in 2008. The gatefold sleeve opens up onto photos of Leonard with his hand wrapped variously around a glass of whiskey, a wineglass and a microphone. In another he stands silhouetted in a doorway, the bright sky behind him. Aside from the fedora, one imagines this must have been how Leonard had first appeared to Marianne on Hydra when he asked her to join him. Leonard no longer went to Hydra. He still had his little white house on the hill, but his son and daughter used it mostly. Marianne, ever loyal, had come to the show in Oslo, though she did not go backstage. "Because I know he is working, I try not to impose," she says, "but I believe he somehow knows I am there." At other stations on the way there were other muses—Joni, Dominique, Rebecca.

This new live release, as it had the year before, coincided with the appearance of something else from the past: a DVD of *Bird on a Wire*, Tony Palmer's long-lost documentary of Leonard's 1972 European tour, which Leonard had rejected as too confrontational and had had remade. Steven Machat had somehow managed to get hold of two hundred reels of film footage that Palmer had long thought lost. Using the soundtrack as a guide, Palmer painstakingly pieced his original movie back together. Even if the film was not to Leonard's taste, it is a remarkable account of the intense, often improvised, sometimes chaotic concerts in Europe and Israel, a tour beset by equipment problems and riots, journalists wanting to interview him, women wanting sex with him and Leonard trying desperately to deal with fame, trying to retain the purity of his vision as a poet and stay true to himself and his songs. "Although I didn't think this at the time," says Henry Zemel, the friend Leonard had hired to help reedit the film, "you could see his life to a large extent as an effort to recapture a purity."

The 2010 tour was heading toward the finish line. In its closing weeks there were concerts as far apart as Slovakia, New Zealand and Canada, before Leonard worked his way back down the west coast of America toward home. The last two dates of the tour, December 10 and 11, were to be held in, of all places, a Las Vegas casino. The soaring, fake Corinthian-capitaled billboard outside Caesars Palace displayed an image of a small, white-haired Leonard, clutching his fedora, beneath a large gold sign reading JERRY SEINFELD.

There was a rodeo in town when Leonard arrived and, farther along the Strip, the American Country Music Awards. Sin City was teeming with Stetsons and men as big as beef cattle. There was a photo of a country singer on the backstage pass for Leonard's show too—Hank Williams, part of a collage Leonard had made of his heroes, who included Ray Charles and Edith Piaf; the poets Lorca, Yeats and Irving Layton; Leonard's parents; Saint Kateri Tekakwitha; Ramesh; and Roshi. Standing on the stage of the Colosseum theater, Leonard looked around him. "So strange a place, so unmagical, and with such great effort to achieve the unmagical," he told the audience with a lopsided smile, "you've really got to love." He looked old and frail, thinner than three years ago when the tour began, and he was thin enough then. He also looked unstoppable. "We seem to have come to the end of a chapter," he said. When it began, he "was seventy-three, just a kid with a crazy dream." As he reworked his old joke, there was emotion in his voice. He assured the audience that he and the band would give them "everything we've got." At the end of the first half of the four-hour set, a woman ran onstage while Leonard was on his knees and held on to him like a crucifix. During the intermission, a group of fans gathered at the front and sang a song Leonard was filmed singing in *Bird on a Wire*, "Passing Thru." When Leonard came back out onstage, he joined in the singing.

The band struck up "Tower of Song." Leonard stood to one side, watching as the women sang the *"da doo dum dum"*s. He refused to come in, making them sing their part over and over again, with a big smile on his face like a child, or like a voyeur, or somebody who really had just seen the light. "Listening to you," he said, "all the unimaginable mysteries are unraveled. I understand it now; it is a matter of your generosity. It has taken three years, I have found the answer to the riddle. It was so simple I should have known from the beginning. Here it is, the answer: *da doo dum dum dum, da doo dum dum*." He had spent a lifetime trying to get to the bottom of the big, timeless subjects, going back over them again and again, digging deeper, trying to come up with some answer, or at least some beauty, or at the very least a gag. It had been hard work. Leonard had no problem with hard work.

These past three years on the road, with their three-hour shows and two-hour sound checks, sometimes barely a day off in between, had been more than rigorous, but much as Leonard had said of Roshi's monastery, "once you get the hang of it, you go into ninth gear

and kind of float through it all." Leonard was floating. The parame-
ters of this life, like his life on the mountain, had paradoxically given
him a kind of freedom. The falling to his knees and the bowing—to
the musicians who did him the honor of delivering his words, and to
the audience who did him the honor of accepting them—satisfied a
sense of rite that was rooted deep in him. More than one reviewer
had likened Leonard's concerts, the quiet, the jubilation, the sense
of grace, the reverence for the beauty of the word, to religious gatherings. One or two went so far as to compare them to papal visits,
but most alluded to some nondenominational yet authentically pure
spiritual fellowship of the faithful. Leonard could joke onstage—and
he did, frequently, as he settled into these tours—but at the same
time he was intensely serious about his work. Always had been. It
was evident when he was a nine-year-old boy, burying the first words
he had written, to his dead father—words never revealed—in a secret
ceremony. It was there too when he moved to the U.S. and took his
first steps into pop music, and dissolved all boundaries between word
and song, and between the song and the truth, and the truth and
himself, his heart and its aching.

   All the heavy labor, the crawling across carpets, the highs, the
depths to which he had plummeted and all the women and deities,
loving and wrathful, he had examined and worshipped, loved and
abandoned, but never really lost, had been in the service of this. And
here he was, seventy-six years old, still shipshape, still sharp at the
edges, a workingman, ladies' man, wise old monk, showman and
trouper, once again offering up himself and his songs:

   "Here I stand, I'm your man."

Twenty-five

A Manual for
Living with Defeat

So the stage was dismantled one last time, the rabbit was put back in the hat, the equipment was loaded on the truck and everyone, Leonard included, was sent home. There were tears and emotional farewells; it had been quite a ride. As to the financial transgressions that had forced Leonard back on the road, there is an interesting footnote, and one that might indicate that the laws of karma might be more efficient than the courts of law.

In 2008, as the tour was about to begin, the U.S. Securities and Exchange Commission brought its own case against Neal Greenberg, the financier whom Kelley Lynch engaged to manage Leonard's investment accounts, charging him with fraud and breach of fiduciary duty related to more than a hundred clients. Says Robert Kory, "According to the reports, his clients apparently lost a great deal of their money, tens of millions. The irony is that if Kelley had not taken the money, [leading to the] discovery earlier, which then prompted Leonard to re-examine what he was doing in his life and to go on tour, Leonard might well have lost all that money anyway, because it was invested with Neal Greenberg. And he would have lost it at a time when [because of the market crash] it would have been impossible for me to persuade promoters to finance Leonard's tour."

The tour not only restored Leonard's lost funds, it improved on them considerably. But it also brought Leonard something more important: vindication as an artist. Even in parts of the world where he had spent almost his entire career undervalued, he had been playing to packed crowds in enormous venues, received universally with acclaim and love. If this were a Bible and not a biography, Kelley would have the Judas role, since it was her betrayal that set in motion the course of events that led to this remarkable resurrection. Lynch, after losing her house in Mandeville Canyon, continued to move around America, blogging, e-mailing and leaving offensive and threatening messages on answering machines as she went.* Greenberg, prohibited from working in investment as a result of the Securities and Exchange Commission case, moved to Leonard's hometown, Montreal, where he was last reported working as a Buddhist teacher.

Back in his Los Angeles duplex, Leonard hung up his stage suit and put on a pin-striped suit, the old-fashioned kind with wide lapels

---

* Lynch was living in Berkeley, California, when on March 1, 2012, shortly before this book went to press, Michelle Rice led a team effort with private investigators and the LAPD Threat Management Unit to have her arrested. Lynch was charged with violating a permanent protective order that forbade her from contacting Leonard, which she had ignored repeatedly. After her arrest, she was transferred to a detention facility in L.A. County to await trial. On April 13, the jury found her guilty on all charges. On April 18, she was sentenced to eighteen months in prison and five years' probation. "It gives me no pleasure to see my onetime friend shackled to a chair in a court of law, her considerable gifts bent to the services of darkness, deceit and revenge," said Leonard in his statement to the court. "It is my prayer that Ms. Lynch will take refuge in the wisdom of her religion, that a spirit of understanding will convert her heart from hatred to remorse."

that you find in thrift shops, as Leonard did. Along with the white-stubbled five o'clock shadow and the rakish tilt of the fedora he wore indoors, he looked less like a showman with connections than a private detective, retired, but should his services be required, still ready for the game. At home, Leonard was dressed for work. As soon as the tour ended, he picked up where he had left off on the album begun in 2007 and put on hold by the ever-expanding tour. Eager to finish it, he could not blame the urgency on his finances this time, so he rationalized it as being in "the homeward stretch"[1] and the sense that time was running out. From a seventy-six-year-old this sounds plausible, although Leonard had said much the same thing when he was fifty-six.[2] In truth, Leonard was in excellent shape—better shape, in many ways, than he had been twenty years earlier. Besides the food-poisoning incident and the exercise injury, he had breezed through the previous three years and the three-hour shows. More than anything, it appeared that he was so keen to complete this new album because he wanted an excuse to tour again.

After his initial reservations, Leonard had come to love this life on the road, the small, closed community of supportive fellow travelers and the almost military regime. Being in service and being of service both held enormous appeal for a poet who had so often seemed born to be a soldier or a monk. It is possible too that the rush of such an intense, heightened existence had become addictive—Leonard, after all, had for many years been inordinately fond of amphetamines. Having given up his last two vices, cigarettes and alcohol, for the tour, he was probably in no mood to quit cold turkey. But the most important thing about the tour, for a man of Leonard's age and temperament, was the feeling of full employment: of doing what he had spent a lifetime training to do and doing it successfully and well. There had been times before the tour—and even farther back, times before his financial troubles—when he felt to some degree like he was treading water or even withdrawing. He had felt, he said, as he imag-

ined Ronald Reagan had felt "in his declining years"—remembering
that once upon a time, he'd "had a good role, he'd played the President in a movie, and I felt, somewhat, that I 'had been' a singer."[3]
Although Leonard had never stopped writing and drawing, and likely
never would, the desire to engage in the business of making his work
public had become less and less urgent. Touring, he said, "really re-
established me as being a worker in the world. And that was a very
satisfactory feeling."[4] Through his own hard work, Leonard had won
back his lost retirement fund. Now that he had it, he did not want to
retire.

***

In Leonard's half of the duplex, the living room, which doubled as
a dining room, had been temporarily requisitioned as an informal
music room, with two full-sized synthesizers squeezed between the
three-piece suite, large dinner table, small marble-topped table and
potted bamboo plant. Leonard went to one of the synthesizers and
pressed the power switch.

*"There's one song that I've been working on for many, many years—
decades. I've got the melody and it's a guitar tune, a really good tune, and
I have tried year after year to find the right words. The song bothers me so
much that I've actually started a journal chronicling my failures to address
this obsessive concern with this melody. I would really like to have it on the
next record, but I felt that for the past two or three records. Maybe four. It's
a song I'd really like to complete. So, these are hard nuts to crack."*

*And when you do crack them after all these years, sometimes is there
nothing in there but dust?*

*"My father kept a bottle of champagne downstairs in a cabinet in the
cellar. He died when I was quite young, but as soon as I got the keys to the
cabinet, which my mother finally gave me when I was a little older, when
we broke out this bottle that my mother had been keeping since maybe their
wedding, it was undrinkable. So you have to develop a perspective about*

the whole thing. I mean it's not the siege of Stalingrad. In the great scheme of things it's not terribly important, but it bothers me a lot."

The puzzle of the song?

"Yeah, the puzzle of the song. You know that. I'd like to finish my work; still in the back of my mind is: 'What is the groove for that song?' I've got the words and the tune but I don't know the groove or the arrangement, and that's going on in my mind as we speak; that's what I'm thinking about."

He pressed a button that struck up an electronic rhythm track, and over it he played a melody.

"I'm in this key."

The music floated along serenely, hypnotically, until Leonard hit an unexpected chord. He stopped short, like he had hit a wall. His face had a quizzical expression that seemed to say, "Where the hell do I go now?"

"So, that's what my work is right now and that's what I think about. My mind is not given to philosophy, it's given to a kind of prayer, a kind of work. But mostly it's about that problem of getting back to the key I started off in."

In reality the problem seemed mostly about Leonard's pitilessness toward his songs when it came to judging them done. He already had enough material for an album. Prior to the tour he had amassed a small stack of songs, which included "The Captain," "Puppets" and "Different Sides," a cowrite with Sharon Robinson. There was "Lullaby," an early version of the song he premiered on tour; "Treaty," a song he had been tinkering with for at least fifteen years; and the even older "Born in Chains," which he began writing in 1988, the year he released *I'm Your Man*, and which he described when trying it out onstage as having been based "on some general appetite for prayer."[5] Leonard had also been trying his hand at writing blues songs. "I've always loved the blues and I've always loved the musical construction of the blues," he said, but he had never felt he had the right to sing the blues. "Somehow the right was granted me, I don't know by what authority, and a number of songs came to me in that way now that I have permission to sing the blues."[6] Two of these songs, "Feels So Good" and "The Darkness," also made their way onto the tour's expanding set list. Since his return from Las Vegas, he had been working with Anjani on new versions for his album of three songs they cowrote for her album *Blue Alert*—"Crazy to Love You," "Thanks for the Dance" and "Whither Thou Goest"—as well as on a song they wrote together in 2001 called "The Street." Anjani, who continued to live around the corner, came by often; they were still close. The second synthesizer was for her.

His life was busy and full, but he missed touring. On tour, "you know exactly what to do during the day and you don't have to improvise—as you do here, especially now, in the midst of composing. There's always something to draw you away."[7] Some distractions were less galling than others. Less than two months after the last date of the tour, the household had a new member, Viva Katherine Wainwright Cohen. Lorca, who still lived downstairs, gave birth to her first child—Leonard's second grandchild and first granddaughter—in February 2011. The tiny girl was the progeny of two Canadian musical dynasties, her father being Rufus Wainwright, the singer, Lorca's close friend and, in the period when he shared Lorca's apartment, Leonard's downstairs neighbor. When fans of Rufus referred to Lorca as a "surrogate mother" online, the whole family, including Leonard, stepped up to correct them. The baby would be raised by Lorca, Rufus and "Daddy #2," as Wainwright referred to his fiancé Jörn Weisbrodt. Leonard doted on the baby. When Lorca came upstairs with Viva or Adam came by with Cassius, Leonard would happily spend all day playing with them. Smiling, he said, "I feel I'm off the evolutionary hook. I've done my bit." This, he said, was the legacy that mattered. "As to my own work, inhabiting the great scheme of things and knowing you're going to leave pretty soon, you know that whatever you're doing is tiny as hell, but on the other hand it's your work, so you treat it with respect."[8]

On April 1, as he donned his monk's robes to visit Roshi, who was celebrating his 104th birthday, Leonard learned that he had won the prestigious Glenn Gould Prize. The award, given to a living artist for a lifetime contribution to the arts, came with a $50,000 purse. Previous winners had included Pierre Boulez and Oscar Peterson. The chairman, Paul Hoffert, told a press conference in Toronto that Leonard Cohen had been the unanimous choice of all seven members of the international jury, which included the filmmaker Atom Egoyan (whose 1994 film *Exotica* featured "Everybody Knows" on its soundtrack) and actor and writer Stephen Fry (who deadpanned, "I thought we agreed on Justin Bieber"). Hoffert praised Leonard's poetry and song for transcending boundaries and cultures and "touching our common humanity. His unique voice is nonetheless the common voice of people around the globe telling our stories, expressing our emotions, reaching deeply into our psyches."[9]

Leonard had met Glenn Gould in the early sixties, when *Esquire* sent him to interview the celebrated Canadian pianist. The piece was never published. Leonard had been so enraptured by what Gould said that he stopped taking notes, believing it "indelibly imprinted in [his] mind." When he got home, he "could not remember a single thing" Gould said to him.[10] Leonard did not mention this mishap in his letter to the award committee, in which he thanked them for "a great honor, sweetened by [his] love of the work of Glenn Gould." Leonard continued to work on his album, which now had a title— the same title his last studio album had, before he was persuaded to change it to *Dear Heather*—*Old Ideas*.

Adam Cohen was also working on a new album, his fourth, which, at his father's suggestion, he had titled *Like a Man*. The album, Adam said, was an homage to his father, "a fusion of elegance and humour, of eloquence and effortless casualness" and "the consummate gentleman."[11] Adam had written some of its songs more than a decade earlier but had shelved them because he felt that they bore too much of his father's influence. His sister, Lorca, did not appear to share

Adam's need to distance herself from their father and his work. She had joined Leonard at several points on the tour, making videos and shooting photos for his CD sleeves; in April 2011, she staged a series of short films by artists and experimental filmmakers, inspired by *New Skin for the Old Ceremony*, the album Leonard released the year she was born. But finally, a year away from turning forty, Adam felt ready to "come out" as Leonard Cohen's son. "Despite my efforts to carve out a different identity," he said, "really I belong to a long line of people who have embraced their father's business."[12]

Delighted with his son's album, Leonard was also taken with the album's producer, Patrick Leonard, a piano player, composer and songwriter who had a long history of working with Madonna, with whom he cowrote "La Isla Bonita" and "Like a Prayer." Adam introduced them, and Leonard and Leonard started to meet for coffee. Before long they were writing together. "Pat saw the lyric for 'Going Home' and he said, "This could be a really good song.' I said, 'I don't think so.' He said, 'Can I have a shot at it?' I said, 'Sure.' He came back with the music—I don't know if it was the next hour or the next day, but it was very fast. He was working quickly and I was working quickly, and, very quickly, we wrote several more songs."[13]

———

Leonard revealed the existence of his new album in the late summer of 2011, at almost the same time that his U.S. record label was preparing to release yet another career retrospective, *The Very Best of Leonard Cohen*, a single CD whose songs were selected by Leonard. The compilation was put on hold, but not the far more copious retrospective CD box set, *Leonard Cohen: The Complete Columbia Albums Collection*, which contained all of Leonard's albums, studio and live, from *Songs of Leonard Cohen* in 1967 to *Songs from the Road* in 2010.

The imminent arrival of another album did rather spoil the title, but in fairness, his record company was not alone in taking the end of Leonard's triumphant tour for the end of his career as a recording artist. Leonard himself appeared to be leaning that way at the beginning of 2010 when, in his acceptance speech for the Lifetime Achievement Grammy Award, he referred to making his way toward "the finishing line." He was more likely talking in veiled terms about death, which he did often enough, than about the last dates of the tour. But in September 2011, as he celebrated his seventy-seventh birthday, sharing his cake with Roshi, even Leonard had to admit that he was "in good form."

In October, Leonard was in Oviedo, Spain, to receive his second major honor of the year. The Prince of Asturias Award for Letters came with a fifty-thousand-euro purse and a Joan Miró sculpture. It had not gone unnoticed that this was an award for literature; past laureates, who included Günter Grass and Arthur Miller, were not known for their songs. But as the statement from the jury read— mirroring in many ways what the Glenn Gould Prize jury had said— Leonard had been chosen for "a body of literary work in which poetry and music are fused in an oeuvre of immutable merit." It was another vindication. Although it often seemed to fall on the deaf ears of academics and literary critics, this is what Leonard had been saying all along.

Leonard had always been good with an acceptance speech, but at the Prince of Asturias ceremony he excelled himself. His address to the distinguished audience, among whose number were the Spanish royal family and Federico Garcia Lorca's niece, was at once personal and a polished piece of prose (despite his claim of having sat up all night in his hotel room, scribbling notes, none of which he consulted). It was also a performance—as accomplished, practiced, dignified, humble, intimate, graceful and grateful a performance as any of the concerts on his last tour. It opened with the usual expression of gratitude and followed with his habitual self-deprecation, protesting how uncomfortable he felt being honored for his poetry when "poetry comes from a place that no one commands, no one conquers, so I feel somewhat like a charlatan." As if to underline the "charlatan" claim, he tossed in a line he had used countless times in countless interviews: "If I knew where the good songs came from, I would go there more often." His unease had led him, he said, to seek out the old Spanish guitar he had bought some forty years ago. He took it out of its case and held it to his face, inhaling "the fragrance of the cedar, as fresh as the day that I acquired the guitar." "A voice seemed to say to me, you are an old man, and you have not said thank you, you have not brought your gratitude back to the soil from which this fragrance arose . . . [and] the soul of this land that has given me so much."

Leonard talked about the tragic young Spaniard he had encountered in his teens, playing a guitar in Murray Hill Park, at the back of his family home on Belmont Avenue. Girls had gathered around to listen, and Leonard listened too. When he stopped playing, Leonard urged him to teach him how to play like that. Over the course of three lessons, he taught Leonard the "six chords" and the flamenco guitar pattern Leonard called "the basis of all my songs and all my music."

Leonard spoke even more eloquently about the impact on his life of another Spanish man. When he had begun playing guitar, he said, he was also writing poems. He had been copying the styles of the English poets he had studied at school, but he "hungered for a voice." He said, "It was only when I read—even in translation—the works of Lorca that I understood that there was a voice." Leonard said that he did not copy that voice—"I wouldn't dare"—but he listened closely to what it said. It gave him permission "to locate a self, a self that is not fixed, a self that struggles for its own existence." It also told him "never to lament casually, and, if one is to express the great inevitable defeat that awaits us all, it must be done within the strict confines of dignity and beauty."

The ceremony was followed by a tribute concert. It began with a short video Leonard's daughter had made. There were filmed interviews with Leonard's band. A member of the prize jury, Andrés

Amorós, recited Spanish translations of Leonard's poetry and lyrics, accompanied by the Webb Sisters. Laura Garcia Lorca thanked Leonard for being "the best ambassador" her late uncle could have had. Musicians, including the flamenco singer Duquende, the Irish singer-songwriter Glen Hansard and Leonard's comrade of the road Javier Mas, performed his songs. Leonard was a veteran of tributes. He had sat through more heartfelt covers of his songs these past ten years than he could count. Yet there were tears in his eyes. During the closing song, "So Long, Marianne"—just as he had when he sang the same song in Jerusalem on the last night of a tour almost forty years before—he let them run freely down his face.

At the long wooden desk in his small study, Leonard searched through numerous icons on the oversized computer monitor. Now and then he stopped and clicked on one; it usually turned out to be a photograph of one of his grandchildren. He was looking for a linernote booklet. Unable to locate the digital version, he got out of the typing chair to look for the mock-up. He found it on the bookshelf, where it was keeping company with three volumes of the Zohar, Bukowski's *The Pleasures of the Damned*, Braque's *Lithographie*, a small row of Leonard Cohen books, *The Language of Truth*, a book on the Greek poets and an Allen Ginsberg bobblehead.

Leonard returned with the *Old Ideas* booklet, whose pages were stuck together with glue, like a child's arts and crafts project. On the cover is a photograph of Leonard, sitting, reading, on a garden chair downstairs on the small front lawn. The shadow of the woman who shot the picture (Leonard's assistant) takes up as much space as Leonard himself. He is dressed formally in a black suit, black fedora, black shoes, black socks and black sunglasses, but his black tie is awry and the top of his white shirt is undone. Inside the booklet, along with the words of the songs, are earlier versions of the lyrics, reproduced from pages of Leonard's pocket-sized notebooks and illustrated with his artwork. There is a self-portrait—crushed cap, grim face. There is a naked woman with long black hair, posing next to a skull.

Leonard clicked on a file on the computer screen and leaned back in the chair. The album began to play. Leonard straightened his spine a little and lowered his eyes; he might have been meditating. Now and again, his lips barely moving, he silently mouthed the words. By the middle of the third song his eyes had closed, and remained closed for the rest of the album. Which meant that he did not notice when his computer went into screen-saver mode and a parade of news flashes started a stately procession across the monitor—Republican party candidates, the UK phone-hacking scandal, the controversy over the sale of emergency contraceptives—adding random and sometimes oddly apposite captions to the music.

The album had gone through a number of changes since Leonard had resumed work on it at the beginning of the year. Of the new songs he introduced on tour, only two are included: "Darkness," still largely recognizable as the song he played onstage, and "Lullaby," with drastically rewritten lyrics. Leonard's cowrite with Sharon Robinson "Different Sides" is here, but his cowrite with Anjani "The Street" is not. There is just one of the three reworked *Blue Alert* songs, "Crazy to Love You," which has some minor lyrical changes but, far more significantly, is now a guitar, not a piano, song. After a long stretch of contentment with his synthesizer, Leonard found himself returning to the guitar, playing it on four of the tracks. His guitar on "Crazy to Love You" takes the listener back to his earliest albums, in particular to *Songs from a Room*. There are keyboards on the album too, and violins, horns, drums, banjo and archilaud, and Jennifer Warnes, Dana Glover, Sharon Robinson and the Webb Sisters on backing vocals. The credits name as producers Leonard Cohen, Ed Sanders, Anjani, Dino Soldo and Patrick Leonard, who cowrote four songs.

When the tenth and final song ended, Leonard opened his eyes.

This was the first time he had heard the album since they mixed it almost two months ago. He had been listening, intently, "for any false steps, or if there's anything that could have been done another way, or if somehow the reverie were interrupted." If it were, he said, he would have taken it back into the studio and worked on it some more. Smiling, he said, "I didn't find any traitorous elements. I had not misjudged its readiness."[14]

Old Ideas was released on January 31, 2012. The accompanying press release described Leonard as "a spiritual guy with a poetical streak" and the album as his "most overtly spiritual." But though the first single, "Show Me the Place," does have churchlike qualities— the slow piano, the deep, solemn voice intoning, *"Show me the place / Where you want your slave to go . . . For my head is bending low"*—anyone in the least familiar with a Leonard Cohen album would recognize that the words might as easily be addressed to a naked woman as to an Old Testament God. (The first press release was quickly replaced with one from which the unfortunate phraseology was deleted. Perhaps by way of compensation, the record label erected a giant billboard of the album sleeve in New York's Times Square.)

Leonard's flair for fusing the erotic and the spiritual remains unparalleled on his twelfth studio album. Even in "Amen," where, in perfectly biblical fashion, *"the filth of the butcher"* is *"washed in the blood of the lamb,"* the angels at Leonard's door are *"panting and scratching,"* and the *"lord"* to whom *"vengeance belongs"* has a lowercase "l." It would probably be a safe bet that the lines *"Dreamed about you baby / You were wearing half your dress,"* in "Anyhow," are not directed at Jehovah. And though "The Darkness" might arguably be about depression, disease or the darkness of the grave, the words *"You said: Just drink it up . . . You were young and it was summer / I just had to take a dive"* seem just as unarguably about cunnilingus.

The album has levity as well as gravity. It skips and it cartwheels, falls to its knees, bows its head in prayer, hat over its heart, and flirts with the women in the front row. The protagonist of the album's opening song "Going Home"—God, presumably, or some kind of higher power concerned with giving Leonard orders and pulling his strings—is less than pleased with this lighthearted attitude to the job he wants Leonard to do. Which is throw off his burden, go home behind the curtain, sing himself off this earthly stage and on to a better place, like an old man ought, like an old icon certainly should, like Bob Dylan did in "Beyond the Horizon," and Glen Campbell with *Ghost on the Canvas*, and Johnny Cash on almost all of his late-life recordings. But Leonard Cohen, this so-called "*sage*," this "*man of vision*," is nothing more than a "*lazy bastard living in a suit*" who wants to write about the same things he has been banging on at forever: "*a love song, an anthem of forgiving, a manual for living with defeat*"; the same old ideas that were on his first album, *Songs of Leonard Cohen*, and that have been on every Leonard Cohen album since. Something as insignificant as old age was not going to change that. And, anyway, Leonard always was old. He was old on his first album—thirty-three, a decade older than the other singer-songwriters making their debuts. He did not need age to give him authority; he already had it. Instead, the passing of the years appeared to have given him a lightness—the same lightness we saw on the last tour, when he skipped out from behind the curtain and onto the stage, night after night.

As Greg Kot noted in his *Chicago Tribune* review, "*Old Ideas* is not another of the dreaded winter-of-my-years albums that have become a cottage industry in recent decades. [Cohen is] still feisty after all these years, his entanglements with love and aging documented with wicked wit and an attitude that is anything but sentimental."[15] Kitty Empire wrote in the *Observer*, "*Old Ideas* is not all about death, betrayal and God, juicy as these are. As the title suggests, it is more of the stuff that has made Cohen indispensable for six decades: desire, regret, suffering, love, hope, and hamming it up."[16] The reviews were almost universally positive, although some critics focused more

on the "ultimate defeat" than on Leonard's "manual for living"—
Rolling Stone saw him "staring down the eternal with unblinking
honesty"[17]—and treated the album as if it were a last farewell, a bone
of the saint that was still just a little warm. "It is difficult, albeit a little
ill-mannered, not to regard *Old Ideas* as possibly Leonard Cohen's
final recorded testament," wrote Andy Gill in the *Independent*. "But
if it is to be his last communiqué, at least the old smoothie's going
down swinging."[18]

For now, the old smoothie packed his good suit and left for a short
promotional tour—New York, Paris, London. There were countless
requests for interviews, which he turned down, having appeared to
have entirely lost interest in the interview process. Perhaps he had
never had much interest in the first place, but he had been happy
(or courteous enough, or curious enough) to participate in the game
and proffer exquisitely structured, perfectly worded bons mots.
Instead he held a few press conferences—theatrical affairs, with a
handpicked media audience. He played his album, then invited a few
questions. A master of deflection, with great charm he parried almost
every one. He recycled old lines and gags into new column inch upon
column inch in major publications. "How is it for you to listen to your
own records?" asked Jarvis Cocker, the Britpop star who moderat-
ed the London event. "I wasn't listening," Leonard replied. Cocker
asked him how he felt about his latest award. PEN New England,
an American literary association whose jury included Bono, Elvis
Costello, Rosanne Cash and Salman Rushdie, had named Leonard
Cohen and Chuck Berry as joint winners of their inaugural prize for
Song Lyrics of Literary Excellence. Leonard replied, "The thing I
liked about this award was that I'm sharing it with Chuck Berry. 'Roll
over Beethoven and tell Tchaikovsky the news': I'd like to write a
line like that."[19]

At the press conference in Paris (which Leonard's old lover Dominique Issermann attended), when someone asked him about death

he answered, in a perfect imitation of solemnity, "I have come to the conclusion, reluctantly, that I am going to die." As to the follow-up question, of what he would like to be in his next life, Leonard the Jew answered, "I don't really understand that process called reincarnation," while Leonard the Buddhist monk said without hesitation, "I would like to come back as my daughter's dog."[20]

Back in Los Angeles, Lorca's dog was at the vet's and Leonard was heading back from the doctor's. He had just taken Roshi for his checkup. Leonard had returned, at least part-time, to his old job of driving Roshi around, running errands and taking him food; Roshi had become quite fond of Leonard's chicken soup. Roshi, weeks away from his 105th birthday, was still working; Leonard had recently gone to the *sesshin* he led in New Mexico. It was as tough as it had ever been. Tougher, in fact. "Roshi has ratcheted up his schedule a few degrees," Leonard said, the smile on his face indicating that he was not displeased with this adjustment. "He's at the top of his game; it's like he's digging in. All the monks feel it and they're making the most of him." With customary modesty, Leonard shrugged off any mention that much the same might be said about him, despite having followed the most successful tour of his career with what was starting to look like his most successful album. *Old Ideas* debuted in the Top 5 of the charts in twenty-six countries, reaching the No. 1 spot in seventeen of them, including the UK and Canada, and topping *Billboard's* folk chart in the U.S.

Leonard had been asked at the press conferences whether he was going to tour. He answered ambiguously that he planned to tour but that he had no touring plans. Meanwhile, negotiations were under way for another very lengthy tour, which Leonard remained very keen to do. But it was complicated. Given Roshi's age, Leonard was loath to commit to spending lengthy periods a long way away from him. He did not say so because it would have been ungracious, and he knew what the old man's reaction would have been. Back when they sat drinking cognac in Roshi's cabin on Mount Baldy, Roshi, then in his midnineties, would apologize to Leonard for not having died; Leonard had moved to the Zen Center when Roshi was eighty-seven, wanting to spend time with the old man while he still could. Instead, Leonard reasoned that, rather than go back on the road and enjoy himself, he should follow Roshi's lead and ratchet up his schedule, and dig in and do his work, saying, "One does have a sense that this is not going to last forever, that one's health is going to become more of a consideration at a certain point, so I would like to bring as many things to completion as possible."[21] Leonard had begun a new album.

Epilogue

It is beautiful winter's day in Los Angeles. Leonard suggests we
make the most of it and sit outside. Since the sun is losing the battle
against the nip in the air, he urges me to wrap up and invites me to
borrow a hat. There are four on the hall stand: two crushed caps and
two fedoras besides the one he has on his head. He is dressed almost
exactly as he was in the *Old Ideas* sleeve photo, except that his tie is
straight and the top of his shirt is buttoned. On his wrist he wears a
cheap metal bracelet, the kind they sell in Mexican stores: twelve
tiny cameos of Jesus, Mary and the saints strung together with elas-
tic. He is slight as a jockey and lean as a runner, and has more than
a touch of Fred Astaire. That slight stoop he'd had since he was a
young man, as if deep inside he felt himself much taller than he was,
appears to have vanished, along with whatever else had been weigh-
ing him down.

The brightest, most sheltered spot is the balcony, which is off his
bedroom. It is a small balcony, just big enough for two chairs, a little
table and a plant in a terra-cotta pot. It overlooks a small neat garden
with two grapefruit trees, one sun lounger, and two dogs—Lorca's—
that are padding idly about the lawn. Beyond them is the garage-
turned-studio where Leonard is working on his new album. He is

already four or five songs into it. It's remarkable, I say, that little more than a year ago he was still on the last leg of the tour. "Was it really just a year ago?" he asks. His face has one of those smiles little boys make when they're caught doing something they shouldn't, but of which they are secretly rather proud. "I don't know if it's a function of the imminent departure, or just a habit of work, or having very few distractions now. Before the tour, I was very busy with trying to sort out my economic and my legal life, and once the tour started I got back into the mode that I'm very familiar with, and which I like, which is working and writing. And I would like to finish my work. You don't feel like wasting too much time at a certain point."

Time speeds up, they say, the closer it gets to the end of the reel. "It is odd," Leonard says. "There are metaphysicians who tell me that time actually has collapsed. Although I don't understand the mechanism and I think they may be putting me on, it certainly feels that way." Is there one piece of work that he is dying to finish, I ask, before noticing the morbid choice of word. "Oh, please," Leonard says, smiling, "do get morbid. There's that [nameless] song I'd like to complete that bothers me a lot, and I would really like to have it on the next record. But I've felt that for the past two or three records, maybe four." He doesn't think too much about the future, he says, other than looking forward to the promise he made himself to take up smoking again on his eightieth birthday. He thinks, or hopes, he will be touring when he's eighty and is looking forward to the prospect of sneaking outside the bus for a quiet cigarette. One thing he does know is that he has "no sense of or appetite for retirement."

A leaf-blower starts up in a garden down the street. It almost drowns out Leonard's voice, which is already soft—softer still when he is asked to talk about himself. There were times as I tried to retrace his life, I tell him, when he wore me out with all his worrying and hard work—times when I wanted to say to him, "For heaven's sake, what are you doing? What is it that you want?" "Right, right," he says, nodding sympathetically. "But this conversation for me is part of another world because I'm not in it anymore. I have little or no interest in any of these matters. I never talk about them to myself." He is not, he says, much of a self-examiner. "I suppose it's violating some Socratic imperative to know thyself, if that's who it was, but I've always found that examination extremely tedious. Sometimes elements of my life arise and an invitation to experience something that is not mundane arises, but in terms of a deliberate investigation of my life to untangle it or sort it out or understand it, those occasions rarely if ever arise. I don't find it compelling at all."

What is going through his mind right now is a song. "One of my mother's favorite records was 'The Donkey Serenade.' Have you heard the song?" He sings, *There's a song in the air, yet the fair senorita, doesn't seem to care, for the song in the air.* "My mother seemed to love that song," he says. "I think she was learning a dance step to go with it. The dance teacher would come to the house—it's very touching—and she did this step. I saw the diagram once. It looked like a square." Leonard gets up out of the chair. In a neat little square of sunlight, against the backdrop of a solid blue sky, quietly humming the melody, he dances alone the dance of "The Donkey Serenade."

Coming to the
end of the
book
but not
quite yet
maybe when
we reach
the bottom[1]

Author's Note

The sun was starting to set, so we moved indoors to the kitchen, where Leonard set about plying me solicitously with food and drink: tea, cognac, wine, a hot dog, perhaps some scrambled eggs? We finally shook on lattes, which he served in two of the coffee mugs his record company made some twenty years before to promote his album *The Future*. While we sat drinking at the small kitchen table, which was pushed up against the wall, by an open window through which a cool breeze blew, he asked how things were going with the book—a book, I should add, that he did not ask me to write and did not ask to read, neither of which appeared to inhibit his support. He was just making conversation, really. I gathered his only interest in the book was that it wouldn't be a hagiography and that its author shouldn't starve to death, at least not on his watch. "Think about this seriously before you answer," he said in that solemn voice. "Would you like a scoop of ice cream in your coffee?"

To write a biography, particularly of a someone still living, is to immerse yourself in that person's life to a degree that would probably get you locked up in any decent society. Without the tolerance, trust, candor, generosity and good humor of Leonard Cohen, this book would not be what it is. The same can be said for his manager, Rob-

ert Kory. I am deeply grateful to them both. I also owe a great debt
to the more than one hundred people—friends, family, associates,
musicians, muses, writers, record producers, publishers, lovers, rabbis and monks—who kindly granted me interviews. Their names—
some well known, others people who were speaking to a biographer
for the first time—can be found at the head of every chapter to which
their stories and insights contribute.

Several went way beyond the call of duty and offered, along with
ongoing encouragement, access to their personal archives, letters, diaries, address books and photographs. Special thanks to Marianne Ihlen,
Aviva Layton, Rebecca De Mornay, Suzanne Elrod, Julie Christensen,
Perla Batalla, Anjani Thomas, Judy Collins, Steve Sanfield, Roscoe
Beck, Bob Johnston, Chris Darrow, Dan Kessel and Steve Sanfield; to
Thelma Blitz for her diaries and contacts; to Ron Cornelius for copies
of the journals and short stories he wrote while touring with Leonard;
to Ian Milne for playing me the rare reel-to-reel recording he made of
one of Leonard's mental hospital concerts; and to Henry Zemel for
the CD he made for me from an even earlier reel-to-reel recording of
Leonard and his friend playing music in the midsixties.

Biographies also have a lot in common with detective stories, the
lack of corpse aside. An enormous amount of time is spent on foot-
work, knocking on doors, looking for fresh information, double- and
triple-checking that information, establishing motives and checking
alibis. Since Leonard moved around so much—geographically, spiri-
tually, in all sorts of ways—it made for an enviable air-mile balance,
but also presented challenges. I was extremely lucky to have found
so many people around the world who were ready and able to help.
In Montreal, my thanks to Rabbi Shuchat and Penni Kolb at Shaar
Hashomayim; Honora Shaughnessy at the McGill Alumni Association; Leonard's cousin, the late David Cohen; Mort Rosengarten; Arnold Steinberg; Erica Pomerance; Penny Lang; Suzanne Verdal; Phil
Cohen; Jack Locke; Janet Davis; Dean Davis; Sue Sullivan; Rona
Feldman; Melvin Heft; Malka Marom; Gavin Ross; and journalist

Juan Rodriguez, who generously handed over his Leonard Cohen newspaper archive. In Toronto: Greig Dymond, who unearthed a mighty stash of Leonard Cohen interviews from the CBC archives; Steve Brewer, president of the Westmount High Alumni, for his copy of the school's 1951 yearbook (Leonard's graduation year); Dennis Lee; and at Thomas Fisher Rare Book Library Jennifer Toews and the late Richard Landon, who were an enormous help in negotiating a path through the mountain of file boxes that constitute the University of Toronto's Leonard Cohen archives.

In California I am very grateful to writer-producer Harvey Kubernik, who generously offered memories, contacts and old interviews; to photographer Joel Bernstein, who shared his stories and pictures; to Robert Faggen, who took time away from writing his Ken Kesey biography to lead me (via a shooting gallery, where he showed me how to use a handgun) to the monastery on Mount Baldy; to Andy Lesko, Arlett Vereecke and Colleen Browne, who between them kept me sane; and to my interviewees Ronee Blakely, David Crosby, Hal Blaine, Rufus Wainwright, Jackson Browne, Rabbi Mordecai Finley, monks Daijo and Kigen, Jac Holzman, Sharon Robinson, Sharon Weisz, Larry Cohen, Paul Body, Sean Dixon, Peter Marshall, Chris Darrow, Chester Crill, David Kessel, Nancy Bacal, Suzanne Verdal and David Lindley. (Biographers always lament the ones who got away, and I was sad not to have added Joni Mitchell, Jennifer Warnes and Phil Spector to this list. I tried.)

In New York I had the excellent company and assistance of Randy Haecker at Sony Legacy; Tom Tierney, director of the Sony Music Archives Library—their artist's cards from Columbia Studio gave invaluable clues to the recording of Leonard's first seven albums; Danny Fields; Dick and Linda Straub; my East Coast interviewees John Simon, John Lissauer, Hal Willner, Bob Fass, Terese Coe, Liberty, Larry Cohen, Larry "Ratso" Sloman and Philip Glass; and my manager, rock and longtime friend Steven Saporta. In Nashville, I was grateful for the help of John Lomax III, Charlie Daniels, Kris

Kristofferson and Christian Oliver, and in various other U.S. cities not yet mentioned, of interviewees Leanne Ungar, Black Francis, John Bilezikjian and Murray Lerner.

In the UK and Europe I was blessed with the assistance of Helen Donlon, friend, researcher and book editor, who tracked down the people whose interviews helped me fill the gaps in Leonard's early days on Hydra, and in London and New York: Barry Miles, Richard Vick, Terry Oldfield, Jeff Baxter, Ben Olins, Don Wreford and George and Angelika Lialios. Thanks also to Kevin Howlett at the BBC, Richard Wootton, Kari Hesthamar, and to Tony Palmer, Joe Boyd, Tom Maschler, Rob Hallett, Ratnesh Mathur and Charley and Hattie Webb for the interviews.

They say you can judge a man's character by the company he keeps, and the same might apply to a musician's fans. I've been around a lot of fans in my many years writing about musicians, but there are few as erudite and informed as Leonard's or as generous with their expertise. A round of applause for my unofficial international team of Cohenologists, who were always there to answer the stickiest questions and pull rare acetates out of hats: Jarkko Arjatsalo, founder and overseer of LeonardCohenFiles.com—Leonard calls him "the General Secretary of the party"—to whose website Leonard contributes; Allan Showalter, psychiatrist, wit and webmaster of 1heckofaguy.com, a site Leonard is known to frequent; Tom Sakic of LeonardCohenCroatia.com; Marie Mazur of Speaking Cohen; writer John Etherington; Hebrew scholar Doron B. Cohen; and Jim Devlin, author of three books on Leonard Cohen, though that did not stop him from helping me with mine.

I was also helped by a great many music journalists, who from start to finish stepped up at all the right moments with clippings, alcohol, commiseration and words of advice. A couple volunteered, without me being forced to use my new shotgun skills, to read and critique the entire book in draft form. Another leapt in to help with an eleventh-hour subedit. Yes I'm biased, I love music journalists, and I fully intend to go back to being one soon (in tandem, of course, with my illustrious career as a ukulele-playing singer-songwriter, performing to crowds that on a good day you can count on two hands). I would like to salute, for their various services rendered, Phil Sutcliffe, Johnny Black, Fred Dellar, Peter Silverton, Joe Nick Patoski, Lucy O'Brien, Paul Trynka, Rob O'Connor, Jonathan Cott, Fred de Vries and Phil Alexander and all at the world's best music magazine, *MOJO*, reserving a very special thanks to Brian Cullman, Michael Simmons and Neil Spencer.

Thanks to my agent, Sarah Lazin; her assistant, Manuela Jessel; and the unflappable Julian Alexander in the UK. My book has three different English-language publishers—Ecco in the U.S., McClelland & Stewart in Canada and Jonathan Cape in the UK—and it could not have found better homes. I count myself extremely fortunate to have as my publisher and lead editor Dan Franklin at Jonathan Cape in London. I'm deeply grateful to Dan and to his assistant, Steven Messer, for their care and support and all their hard work. My sincere thanks and appreciation also to Daniel Halpern and Libby Edelson at Ecco and Ellen Seligman at McClelland—and a hearty round of applause to all the tireless copyeditors and proofreaders.

Most of all, thank you, Leonard Cohen, for being so considerate as to choose the second I hit puberty to release your first album, for continuing to move and enlighten me with your music and words ever since, for permitting me to out you as a ukulele player, and for living a remarkable life that has run me ragged these past few years. What can I say; it was a swell party. Now if you'll excuse me, I've got to go empty the ashtrays and take the bottles out. I hear you're heading back on the road any day now. Good. We need you out there. Hope to see you somewhere along the way.

Sylvie Simmons
San Francisco, 2012

Afterword

Traveling Light

And what if it had been a mistake all along, this life in word and song, paradoxes and koans, love sought and abandoned, all the sinning, all the prayers? These old ideas he'd pursued and documented with discipline, depth, courage, despair, laughter, and seriousness ever since that day in January 1944, when a nine-year-old boy wrote some words to his dead father and buried them in the snow. What had driven it all? What was the design? Did he know?

It was 2012, Leonard's seventy-eighth year, and we were talking—or mostly I was talking; at this kind of questioning, Leonard's voice tended to trail off in the direction of his gaze, which was somewhere middle distance or maybe nowhere at all—about how to end a biography whose subject and work had not ended, and the kinds of conclusions a reader might feel his or her due after almost six hundred pages. Leonard considered this for a while before answering allegorically. "This house we're in, I never put this house together. I never designed it. I never thought about it much at all. I bought it with two other guys who were students of Roshi, and we bought it because it was close to

[Roshi's] zendo. I liked it when there wasn't much in it, when I just bought it. And I don't care if it represents me. There are moments when I've thought, 'Oh I've got to do something with this, I want it to represent me,' but I don't care anymore, I don't care what's in here."

He agreed that his work "was driven, but," he said, "I was never conscious of a choice. I don't really know what the choice was. It just seemed to be what I was doing from the beginning and I was doing it all the time. And there's something about keeping a record of the thing, the idea that it might help if you kept a record of the approach to sanity, that somehow it could all become clearer. I was totally preoccupied with these matters. And my work, well you know that all that you're doing, whatever you are doing, is tiny as hell in the great scheme of things. But on the other hand, it is your work. So you treat it with respect. Outside of that, there's not really much going on, and it's fine, you don't really want too much going on. You're just trying to finish a song. You know that you're going to leave pretty soon. This is not going to last forever; your health is going to become more of a consideration, so I would like to bring as many things to completion as possible."

There were piles of notebooks, boxes of papers overflowing with loose ends. Leonard did not like loose ends; by his own account he was "a tidy kind of guy." In the years that led up to his return to the stage he said he had felt at loose ends himself. He had not forgotten the work he had to do but the urgency wasn't there, or more important, the structure. "I need structure. My capacity for disorder is abundant. Like every writer, I've spent a lot of my life improvising the day, trying to find some self-respect, which is something you're only going to get from a day's work. Which isn't always easy to arrange, because the work is so hard and the distractions are so abundant." He had found that structure living as a monk on Mount Baldy, cooking, driving, and working for Roshi. "I know what I'm doing all day, and if I have a moment left to work, I work." The next time he found it was on the 2008–2010 tour: "At the end of a day's work, you're in your hotel room,

you have a guitar, there's no distraction, and your life has a certain purpose that civilian life doesn't always imply. I've always liked those situations."

He said that the band and crew were calling him all the time,
asking when they might go back out again. "And I share that feeling
with them. Because I think anybody would say there was an unusual
dynamic in the actual relations between the musicians and the crew
and the audience and the work. It had a very special quality to it."
Following the success of that tour, there was no shortage of venues
in many countries offering him a lot of money to play. And Leonard
wanted to be back on the front lines. It was only his duties to Roshi—
which now regularly included driving him back and forth to doctors'
appointments—that kept him off the road. Roshi, by this point, was a
hundred and five years old.

When Roshi had turned ninety, three years after Leonard left Los
Angeles for the monastery to care for his friend and teacher in what appeared to be his final years, Roshi told him, "Excuse me for not dying."
Leonard borrowed Roshi's words to apologize to me for robbing the
book of a tidy ending by not having died at the end of the triumphant
tour. Leonard had no problem at all talking about death. Death was
never a stranger to his conversation, his humor, or his work. Death had
haunted Leonard's songs and poems from the beginning, and they had
come to some kind of amicable-enough agreement decades ago.

I asked Leonard if he still carried a notebook, if he was still keeping
some kind of record. He did and was. I suggested that the last thing he
wrote in it should be the ending of my book. He took the little notebook from his pocket, turned to the last page he'd blackened and read
it to himself. Then he leafed back a few pages and this time read aloud.

*Dream last night. I heard we were allowed to go into the women's
room. I opened one door. It was the women's bathroom. I saw a
woman putting on, no taking off, her makeup. I wasn't allowed in*

*there and I had no interest in staying. I hurried away. Another door.
I opened it and slipped into a small room. Behind a separation I could
hear a young woman talking to her therapist. I wasn't really sure I was
allowed in there, but I thought the rules were somewhat ambiguous
and, if discovered, I could justify my presence. There was a narrow camp
bed close to the door with fresh sheets and a light blanket. I snuggled
into the bed and began to listen intently to the confession the young
woman was making to a therapist. I don't remember what she was
saying, but she stopped abruptly and said, "Leonard Cohen is listening
to us." They both came over to the bed. I pretended that I had been
sleeping, not listening. I pretended to slowly come awake. And I woke
up in my hotel room, 4904 in the Melbourne Sofitel.*

Some months after relating this dream from the road, Leonard
called to say that his new album was done, so the biography's first
ending was put on hold. Back at his house, he played me *Old Ideas*
and I watched him as he sat there, head bowed, eyes closed, the poet
laureate of the broken and imperfect, listening for imperfections.
When none were found, or at least nothing to challenge the record's
release, we celebrated with wine and ice cream on the balcony, where
Leonard decided to dance us out of the first edition of the book with
his mother's favorite song, "The Donkey Serenade."

He did go back on the road with his band. A year and a quarter of
three hours–plus concerts in Europe, the US, Canada, New Zealand, and Australia, from August 2012 to December 2013. There really had been nothing like those two tours: the unwavering quality
of the performances, the hushed attention, the elegance and fierce
humility, the mischievous black humor, the intimacy—or rather
the illusion of intimacy in often the least intimate of venues—and
also that camaraderie, the sense of fellow feeling that was always

so present, that we were all in this together, all in the same rickety boat making our way through the dark, every one of us broken but maybe all of us holy too. Leonard knew his way around darkness. He had faced it head-on from the beginning and mined it for his work. But if these two extraordinary tours showed anything, it was that he was all about finding the light.

Among the biggest-grossing of their time, the tours produced four live albums: *Live in London* (2009), *Songs from the Road* (2010), *Live in Dublin* (2014*)*, and *Can't Forget: A Souvenir of the Grand Tour* (2015). Leonard continued to premiere new songs at this second round of shows and, as before, when the last concert was over, he went straight back to work on another new album with Patrick Leonard. Once again it was completed at remarkable speed: nine months. *Popular Problems*, Leonard announced, would be released on his eightieth birthday. With his usual mix of darkness and glee, he described it as setting "a new tone and speed of hope and despair, grief and joy."

There was a clear difference in tone from the soft-focus production of *Old Ideas*, whose autumnal glow had many music critics treating the album as Leonard's last farewell. *Popular Problems* sounded leaner, wryer, more energized. On the album, as onstage, Leonard seemed renewed. In the opening number, "Slow," a sensual, down-tempo blues song, he dismissed any talk of age with "*I never liked it fast / It's not because I'm old / Slow is in my blood.*" The opening lines of "Born in Chains," a gospel-blues song about the exodus of the Jews, dated back to the eighties as an early draft of "I Can't Forget." "The Street," which had been published as a poem in the *New Yorker*, was a song Leonard had written in 2001 with his ex-fiancée, Anjani. The lyrics spoke of betrayal, war, and loss but also of endurance. "Almost Like the Blues," another song published as a poem in the *New Yorker*, set torture, rape, the Holocaust, and "all my bad reviews" (an ironic dig at narcissism) to a rhythmic Latin beat. The epic "Nevermind," which started out as a poem in *Book of Longing*, was about oppression and peoples displaced by war. On "Samson in New Orleans," a hymn to a flooded city and a divided country, a violin played a slow elegy. But *"even though the news is bad,"* he sang in the album's closing song, *"You got me singing / That Hallelujah hymn."* Leonard, as his friend Leon Wieseltier observed, "had an unusual inflection for darkness: he found in it an occasion for uplift. His attitude of acceptance was not founded on anything as cheap as happiness."

Leonard dedicated *Popular Problems* to Roshi, who had died in a Los Angeles hospital on July 27, 2014, age one hundred and seven. "We became close friends," Leonard said, "and that association just deepened over the years." He described Roshi as "someone who really cared about—or deeply didn't care about—who I was; therefore, who I was began to wither, and the less I was of who I was, the better I felt." This made him "a very helpful friend" as well as a multipurpose patriarch. When a sex scandal regarding Roshi's longtime behavior toward a number of his female students became public, Leonard stayed silent on the subject. It had been the flaws in the holy man, the sinner in the savior, that had attracted him to Roshi in the first place, and Leonard would have been the last person to claim he was without flaws himself. The state of being cracked or broken was one of his deepest studies and might have been his battle cry.

There was another big loss that year. Two weeks before Leonard's eightieth birthday, his sister, Esther Cohen, died at age eighty-four. So many goodbyes, even for one who said that he was drawn to the valedictory. All the space that's left when the passing of time takes away everything—friends, family, libido, his taste for alcohol, his health—there's nothing left to fill it but work. So Leonard lit a cigarette and worked.

He had come to terms with growing old. He called it "one of the most compassionate ways there is of saying goodbye." He joked about it onstage, warning the audience against looking in magnifying mirrors in hotel bathrooms after a certain age, just as he'd joked about lost friends and aching in places where he used to play "Tower of Song" in decades before. When he talked about it seriously, it was to express gratitude that the Divine Voice he had always heard, even if he couldn't always understand it, was now telling him to just get on with the things he had to do. "It's very compassionate at this stage. More than any time in my life," he said, "I no longer have that voice that says, 'You're fucking up.' That's a tremendous blessing."

Old age suited Leonard. The man in the suit and fedora seemed much more at home with himself than the young Leonard. Where so many stories of the lives of musicians and poets have unhappy endings, Leonard found himself happier, more productive, better off, and more successful than he had ever been. He was at the top of his game. *Old Ideas* had topped the charts in eleven countries, *Popular Problems* in ten, and the awards continued to pile up: four Junos from Canada, a Brit Award from the UK, and—the only one that seemed to pique his interest—the 2012 inaugural PEN New England Song Lyrics of Literary Excellence Award, a prize Leonard shared with Chuck Berry. An e-mail from Bob Dylan was read aloud at the ceremony, in which he called Berry "the Shakespeare of rock n roll" and Leonard the "Kafka of the blues," concluding, "Chuck, you have indeed written the book with a capital B, and congratulations to Leonard, who's still writing it."

There was another new album underway. But though his mind was still sharp, Leonard's body betrayed him. Time and touring had taken their toll. No more skipping onto a stage or falling to his knees; he had multiple compression fractures of the spine. He was also fighting cancer. Immobilized by pain, in the words of a man of soldierly habits, he was "confined to barracks." His children worried about his deteriorating health. "Adam sensed that my recovery, if not my survival, depended on my getting back to work," Leonard said. "He took over the project, established me in a medical chair to sing, and brought these songs to completion." With Leonard unable to climb the stairs to the studio where he had recorded all his albums since *Ten New Songs*, Adam set up a makeshift studio in the living room—computers, speakers, a microphone on the dining table. He also took over as the album's producer.

"I was dealing with an ailing old man," Adam said, "but an ailing old man who was showing paranormal levels of devotion and focus, and that rubbed off on everybody. The encounters were urgent and sweet and meaningful. It was as if we were riding some kind of mysterious wind." There were days when Leonard could only work for an hour or two. But on one occasion Adam saw his father lift himself out of the medical chair and dance in front of the speakers. "There were hilarious, esoteric arguments fueled by medical marijuana," Adam said, "episodes of blissful joy that sometimes lasted hours, where we'd listen to one song on repeat like teenagers."

In July of that year, word reached Leonard that Marianne Ihlen was in a hospital in Oslo, dying. She too had cancer and, like Leonard, had kept her illness private. Leonard wrote her at once, and tenderly. "Well Marianne, it's come to this time when we are really so old and our bodies are falling apart and I think I will follow you very soon. Know that I am so close behind you that if you stretch out your hand, I think you can reach mine. And you know that I've always loved you for your beauty and your wisdom, but I don't need to say anything more about that because you know all about that. But now, I just want to wish you a very good journey. Goodbye old friend. Endless love, see you down the road." Two days later, Marianne lost consciousness and quietly slipped away.

"I am ready to die," Leonard told the *New Yorker*. He had said such things before, but at eighty-two years old it did seem more of a possibility. A number of newspapers ran with the quote and started preparing obituaries. Leonard was actually putting the finishing touches on his new album. At a press conference held at the Canadian consulate in L.A., he denied the reports of his imminent demise. "I think I was exaggerating. One is given to self-dramatization from time to time," he said. "I intend to live forever." He expressed his gratitude to his son and daughter, "an incredibly sustaining force, especially during this recent bad patch." Adam sat on the stool beside him for support. Leonard was visibly frail and short of breath, but he handled the questions with a mix of charm, self-deprecation, and deflection, recycling old answers here and there, generous with what little time and energy he had, yet at the same time not giving much away. No, he didn't know where the songs came from or he would go there more often; no, he had no idea why ideas continued to come; no, he had never thought of himself as a religious person and didn't have a spiritual strategy: "I kind of limp along like so many of us do in these realms." Yet he had told his rabbi, Mordecai Finley, that he thought everything he wrote was liturgy.

"How do we produce work that touches the heart?" Leonard said back in the nineties. "We don't want to live a superficial life. We want to be serious with each other, with our friends, with our work. Serious has a kind of voluptuous aspect to it. It is something that we are deeply hungry for." Leonard's fourteenth and final studio album was the perfect example of that voluptuous seriousness, perhaps the richest, most intense album in a lifetime of rich and intense work. *You Want It Darker*, it was called—there was no question mark; it was a statement. The somber sleeve pictured Leonard at the window—windows had always held a special place in his songs—smoking a cigarette. There were songs about endings and reckonings and taking leave—of everyone, everything, everywhere; the bar, the card table, the temple, the bloody hill. There was one heart-tugging ballad on the album, "If I Didn't Have Your Love," but barely a trace of romantic love or consolations of the flesh. As he sang, with no real acrimony, in "Leaving the Table," *"The wretched beast is tame"* and in "Treaty"—some twenty years in the writing—sounding wise and weary he appeared to apologize to his muses: *"I'm sorry for the ghost I made you be / Only one of us was real and that was me."* But there was an intimacy to the album, a tenderness to the voice, perhaps a by-product of working so closely, for the first—and last—time with his son.

Layers melted into layers; the same images reappeared in different songs and guises: angels, devils, candles, flames, dealers, prisoners, Jesus. Water turned to wine and back to water again. Things that were once embraced were relinquished. There was righteous anger at the material world but also nonattachment. There was anger too at the God he had conversed with so deeply and for so long; nevertheless he was ready to do His will. *"Hineni"*—"Here I am"—he sang in the title track, which featured the cantor and choir from Congregation Shaar Hashomayim in Montreal, the synagogue that Leonard's great-grandfather Lazarus Cohen had founded. "That *'hineni,'*" Leonard explained, "that declaration of readiness no matter what the outcome, that's a part of everyone's soul. We all are motivated by deep impulses and deep appetites to serve, even though we may not be able to locate that which we are willing to serve. So this is just a part of my nature, and I think everybody else's nature, to offer oneself at the critical moment when the emergency becomes articulate. It's only when the emergency becomes articulate that we can locate that willingness to serve."

Leonard died at home in his sleep on November 7, 2016, following a fall in the middle of the night. He was buried three days later, according to his wishes, in a plain pine box next to his parents in the Shaar Hashomayim Cemetery in Montreal. It was a small, private ceremony; he didn't want a fuss, just family and a few close friends. Leonard had known his time was running out. But right to the end

he was out there on the front line—his work demanded that of him—
making notes on what he could see, "keeping a record of the thing,"
like he said, "that somehow it could all become clearer."

> *I've worked at my work*
> *I've slept at my sleep*
> *I've died at my death*
> *And now I can leave.*

—"MISSION," *Book of Longing*

Sylvie Simmons
San Francisco, May 2017

Notes

Unless otherwise stated, all extracted quotes in the form of a Q & A are taken from the author's interviews of Leonard Cohen. These interviews are indicated in the sources by the initials SS and the date of the interview.

Prologue

SS, 2001.

One: Born in a Suit

Author interviews with: Leonard Cohen, David Cohen, Mort Rosengarten, Arnold Steinberg, Rabbi Wilfred Shuchat

Books and documents: Miriam Chapin, *Quebec Now*, Ryerson Press, 1955. L. S. Dorman and C. L. Rawlins, *Prophet of the Heart*, Omnibus, 1990. Leonard Cohen, *The Favorite Game*, Secker & Warburg UK, 1963 (Viking U.S., 1964). Leonard Cohen Archive, Thomas Fisher Rare Book Library, University of Toronto, Canada ("Archive"). Ira B. Nadel, *Various Positions*, Bloomsbury, 1996. Harry Rasky, *The Song of Leonard Cohen: Portrait of a Poet, a Friendship and a Film*, Souvenir Press, 2001.

Chapter heading: Leonard Cohen to SS, 2001.

1. SS, 2001.

2. Rasky, 2001.

3. Ibid.

4. Christian Fevret, *Les Inrockuptibles*, August 21, 1991, reproduced in *Throat Culture*, 1992, trans. Sophie Miller.

5. Ibid.

6. William Ruhlmann, "The Stranger Music of Leonard Cohen," *Goldmine*, February 19, 1993.

7. SS, 2001.

8. SS, 2011.

9. Chapin, 1955.

10. Fevret, 1991.

11. Archive (undated, likely late 1950s).

12. Dorman and Rawlins, 1990.

13. Pamela Andriotakis and Richard Oulahan, *People*, January 14, 1980.

14. Fevret, 1991.

15. Arthur Kurzweil, "A Conversation with Leonard Cohen," *Jewish Book Club*, 1994.

16. Fevret, 1991.

17. Archive (undated, likely late 1950s).

Two: House of Women

Author interviews with: Leonard Cohen, Mort Rosengarten, David Cohen, Steve Brewer, Rona Feldman, Phil Cohen, Nancy Bacal

Books and documents: Anonymous, *25 Lessons in Hypnotism: How to Become an Expert Operator*, undated, Archive. Miriam Chapin, *Quebec Now*, 1955, Ryverson Press. Leonard Cohen, *The Favorite Game*, Secker & Warburg UK, 1963 (Viking U.S., 1964). Leonard Cohen, "The Juke-Box Heart: Excerpt from a Journal," unpublished, undated, Archive. Ira B. Nadel, *Various Positions: A Life of Leonard Cohen*, Bloomsbury, 1996. Mordecai Richler, *Home Sweet Home: My Canadian Album*, Chatto & Windus, 1984. Mordecai Richler, *Oh Canada! Oh Quebec!*, Penguin Books Canada, 1992. Summer camp reports, Archive. *Vox Ducum*, Westmount High School Yearbook, issues 1950 and 1951.

Chapter heading: SS.

1. Anonymous, *25 Lessons in Hypnotism*, Archive.

2. Cohen, 1963.

3. Brian D. Johnson, *Maclean's*, December 7, 1992.

4. Richler, 1992.

5. Archive.

6. Cohen to Bruce Headlam, *Saturday Night*, December 1997.

7. Archive.

8. Cohen, 1963.

9. Archive.

10. Federico Garcia Lorca, "Gacela of the Morning Market," *Divan Del Tamarit*, 1936, published in *The Selected Poems of Federico Garcia Lorca*, ed. F. G. Lorca and Donald M. Allen, New Directions Publishing, 1955, 2005 edition, trans. Stephen Spender and J. L. Gili.

11. Marco Adria, *Aurora*, July 1990.

12. Arthur Kurzweil, "A Conversation with Leonard Cohen," *Jewish Book Club*, 1994.

13. Christian Fevret, *Les Inrockuptibles*, August 21, 1991, reproduced in *Throat Culture*, 1992, trans. Sophie Miller.

14. Cohen, Prince of Asturias Award speech, October 21, 2011.

15. Fevret, 1991.

16. SS, 2011.

17. SS, 2001.

18. Ibid.

19. Cohen, Asturias Award speech.

20. Cohen, 1963.

Three: Twenty Thousand Verses

Author interviews with: Leonard Cohen, Mort Rosengarten, Nancy Bacal, Arnold Steinberg, David Cohen, Steve Brewer, Dean Davis, Janet Davis, Melvin Heft, Rabbi Wilfred Shuchat, Aviva Layton

Books, films, publications and documents: *CIV/n*, 5, 1954, and 6, 1955. *The Forge*, March 1955 and March 1956. Irving Layton, *The Love Poems of Irving Layton: With Reverence and Delight*, 1984. Leonard Cohen Archive, Thomas Fisher Rare Book Library, University of Toronto, Canada ("Archive"). Lian Lunson, *Leonard Cohen: I'm Your Man*, Lionsgate, 2006. Hugh MacLennan, *Two Solitudes*, 1945. McGill University alumnus archives. McGill University Rare Books Library. Ira B. Nadel, *Various Positions: A Life of Leonard Cohen*, Bloomsbury, 1996. Harry Rasky, *The Song of Leonard Cohen*, documentary film, 1980. *Vox Ducum*, Westmount High School yearbook, 1951. Ruth Wisse, "My Life Without Leonard Cohen," *Commentary*, October 1995.

Chapter heading: Mort Rosengarten to SS, 2009.

1. *Vox Ducum*, 1951.

2. Archive.

3. Christian Fevret, *Les Inrockuptibles*, August 21, 1991, reproduced in *Throat Culture*, 1992, trans. Sophie Miller.

4. Rasky, 1980.

5. Wisse, 1995.

6. Fevret, 1991.

7. Ibid.

8. Cohen, speech given at Irving Layton's funeral, January 2006.

9. Cohen in Lian Lunson, 2006.

10. Fevret, 1991.

11. Rasky, 1980.

12. Ibid.

Four: I Had Begun to Shout

Author interviews with: Leonard Cohen, Aviva Layton, Mort Rosengarten, Arnold Steinberg, Phil Cohen, Henry Zemel, David Cohen

Books, documents and publications: Leonard Cohen, *A Ballet of Lepers*, Archive. Leonard Cohen, *The Favorite Game,* Secker & Warburg, 1963 (Viking U.S., 1964). Leonard Cohen, *Let Us Compare Mythologies*, 1956. Leonard Cohen, *The Spice-Box of Earth*, 1961. L. S. Dorman and C. L. Rawlins, *Prophet of the Heart*, Omnibus, 1990. Letters, Archive. Ira B. Nadel, *Various Positions*, Bloomsbury, 1996. Georgianna Orsini, *An Imperfect Lover: Poems and Watercolors*, Cavankerry, 2002.

Chapter heading: Leonard Cohen, "Rites," in Cohen, 1956.

1. Cohen, from "For Wilf and His House," in Cohen, 1956.

2. Dorman and Rawlins, 1990, p. 79.

3. Cited anonymously in ibid., p. 80.

4. Milton Wilson, review of *Let Us Compare Mythologies*, in *Canadian Forum* 36, March 1957.

5. Allan Donaldson, review of *Let Us Compare Mythologies*, *Fiddlehead* 30, November 1956.

6. Christian Fevret, *Les Inrockuptibles*, August 21, 1991, reproduced in *Throat Culture*, 1992, trans. Sophie Miller.

7. *Let Us Compare Mythologies*, McClelland & Stewart, 2006 edition.

8. SS, 2001.

9. Ibid.

10. Ibid.

11. Ibid.

12. "Synergie, Jean-Luc Esse and Leonard Cohen," radio program, France-Inter, October 1977, trans. Nick Halliwell.

13. Fevret, 1991.

14. Archive, file 5.

15. SS, 2001.

16. Ibid.

17. Ibid.

18. Fevret, 1991.

19. Orsini, 2004.

20. Archive, boxes 1 and 3.

21. William Ruhlmann, *Goldmine*, February 19, 1993.

22. Archive.

23. Gavin Martin, *NME*, January 1993.

24. Irving Layton, interviewed by Ian Pearson, *Saturday Night*, March 1993.

Five: A Man Who Speaks with a Tongue of Gold

Author interviews with: Leonard Cohen, Nancy Bacal, Mort Rosengarten, Steve Sanfield, George Lialios, Angelika Lialios, Marianne Ihlen

Book: Kari Hesthamar, *So Long, Marianne: Ei Kjaerleikshistorie*, Spartacus, 2008.

Chapter heading: Marianne Ihlen to SS, 2010.

1. Ira B. Nadel, *Various Positions*, Bloomsbury, 1996, p. 110.

2. Jack McClelland, *Imagining Canadian Literature: The Selected Letters of Jack McClelland*, ed. Sam Solecki, Key Porter Books, 1998.

3. Cohen, letter to McClelland & Stewart associate editor Claire Pratt, July 21, 1959, in Archive.

4. SS, 2001, for the article "Heroes' Heroes," in *MOJO*, March 2002.

5. SS, 2001.

6. Richard Goldstein, *Village Voice*, December 28, 1967, reproduced in *Goldstein's Greatest Hits: A Book Mostly About Rock 'n' Roll*, AbeBooks, 1970.

7. SS, 2011.

8. Arthur Kurzweil, "A Conversation with Leonard Cohen," *Jewish Book Club*, 1994.

9. SS, 2001.

10. Cohen, letter to Layton, April 21, 1963, in Archive.

11. Cohen, Kari Hesthamar, Norwegian radio interview, 2005.

12. Cohen, letter to Marianne Ihlen, December 24, 1960.

Six: Enough of Fallen Heroes

Author interviews with: Leonard Cohen, Steve Sanfield, Marianne Ihlen, Aviva Layton, Nancy Bacal, Richard Vick, George Lialios, Barry Miles

Books, films and documents: Donald Brittain and Don Owen, *Ladies and Gentlemen . . . Mr. Leonard Cohen*, documentary film, 1965. *The Canadian Encyclopedia* (online). Leonard Cohen, *Beautiful Losers*, 1966. Leonard Cohen, *Flowers for Hitler*, 1964. Leonard Cohen, *The Spice-Box of Earth*, 1961. Leonard Cohen Archive, Thomas Fisher Rare Book Library, University of Toronto, Canada ("Archive"). Ira B. Nadel, *Various Positions*, Bloomsbury, 1996.

Chapter heading: Leonard Cohen and Irving Layton, *Enough of Fallen Heroes*, unpublished work for TV, 1961.

1. Cohen, letter to Desmond Pacey, February 23, 1961, Archive.

2. Cohen, letter to Jack McClelland, October 12, 1960, Archive.

3. Lorca, letter to his parents, April 5, 1930, cited in Nadel, 1996.

4. Brittain and Owen, 1965.

5. Interview in Nadel, 1994.

6. Ibid.

7. Christian Fevret, *Les Inrockuptibles*, August 21, 1991, reproduced in *Throat Culture*, 1992, trans. Sophie Miller.

8. Ibid.

9. Cohen, *Spice-Box of Earth*, first edition, dust jacket.

10. Robert Weaver, *Toronto Daily Star*, June 10, 1961.

11. David Bromige, *Canadian Literature*, Autumn 1961.

12. Cohen, radio interview with Kari Hesthamar, 2005.

13. Cohen, letter to Layton, October 15, 1962, Archive.

14. Robin Pike, *ZigZag*, October 1974.

Seven: Please Find Me, I Am Almost 30

Author interviews with: Leonard Cohen, Erica Pomerance, Suzanne Verdal, Marianne Ihlen, Aviva Layton, Dennis Lee, Allan Showalter, Mort Rosengarten

Books and publications: Leonard Cohen, *The Favorite Game*, Secker & Warburg, 1963 (Viking U.S., 1964). Leonard Cohen, *Flowers for Hitler*, 1964. Ira B. Nadel, *Various Positions*, Bloomsbury, 1996. Michael Ondaatje, *Leonard Cohen*, McClelland & Stewart, 1970. Jack McClelland, *Imagining Canadian Literature: The Selected Letters of Jack McClelland*, ed. Sam Solecki, Key Porter Books, 1998. T. F. Rigelhof, *This Is Our Writing*, Porcupine's Quill, 1998.

Chapter heading: Leonard Cohen, "Marita," in *Selected Poems 1956–1968*.

1. Ondaatje, 1970.

2. Rigelhof, 1998.

3. Danny Fields, *Soho Weekly News*, December 1974.

4. Sarah Hampson, *Globe and Mail*, May 25, 2007.

5. Ibid.

6. Ondaatje, 1970.

7. Cohen, letter to McClelland, August 1963, Archive.

8. Cohen, quoting a 1984 conversation with Walter Yetnikoff, to SS, 2001.

9. Cohen, letter to McClelland, July 1963, Archive.

10. Cohen, letter to McClelland, March 1964, Archive.

11. Cohen, letter to McClelland, September 9, 1963, published in McClelland, 1998.

12. Cohen, letter to McClelland, September 2, 1964, published in McClelland, 1998.

13. Cohen, letter to McClelland, September 9, 1963, published in McClelland, 1998.

14. Sandra Djwa, *Ubyssey*, February 3, 1967.

15. Ibid.

16. Milton Wilson, *Toronto Quarterly*, July 1965.

17. Paul Kennedy, *The Story of Suzanne*, CBC TV Canada, 2006.

18. Ian Pearson, *Saturday Night*, March 1993.

19. Interview with Kevin Howlett, *Leonard Cohen: Tower of Song*, BBC Radio One, August 7, 1994.

20. Brian D. Johnson, *Maclean's*, June 11, 2008.

21. Richard Goldstein, *Village Voice*, December 28, 1967.

22. Susan Lumsden, "Leonard Cohen Wants the Unconditional Leadership of the World," September 12, 1970, reproduced in Michael Gnarowski, *Leonard Cohen: The Artist and His Critics*, McGraw-Hill Ryerson, 1976.

23. Cohen, letter to editor at Yilin Press, China, regarding the foreword to a Chinese edition of *Beautiful Losers*, February 2000, Archive.

24. Ibid.

25. Cohen, letter to McClelland, March 20, 1965, Archive.

26. Lumsden, "Leonard Cohen Wants."

27. Jon Ruddy, *Maclean's*, October 1, 1966.

28. Goldstein, *Village Voice*.

29. Christian Fevret, *Les Inrockuptibles*, August 21, 1991, reproduced in *Throat Culture*, 1992, trans. Sophie Miller.

30. Cohen, letter to McClelland, August 1965, Archive.

Eight: A Long Time Shaving

Author interviews with: Leonard Cohen, Judy Collins, Bob Fass, Jac Holzman, Marianne Ihlen, Penny Lang, Tom Maschler, Henry Zemel

Books and films: Donald Brittain and Don Owen, *Ladies and Gentlemen . . . Mr. Leonard Cohen*, National Film Board of Canada, 1965. Leonard Cohen, *Beautiful Losers*, 1966. Leonard Cohen, *Parasites of Heaven*, 1966. Kari Hesthamar, *So Long, Marianne: Ei Kjaerleikshistorie*, Spartacus, 2008. Jack McClelland, *Imagining Canadian Literature: The Selected Letters of Jack McClelland*, ed. Sam Solecki, Key Porter Books, 1998. Ira B. Nadel, *Various Positions*, Bloomsbury, 1996. Michael Ondaatje, *Leonard Cohen*, McClelland & Stewart, 1970. Harry Rasky, *Song of Leonard Cohen*, documentary film, 1980.

Chapter heading: Leonard Cohen, in Brittain and Owen, 1965.

1. Sandra Djwa, *Ubyssey*, February 3, 1967.

2. Interview for CBC with Phyllis Webb, cited in Ondaatje, 1970.

3. Jack McClelland, letter to Cohen, June 1965, reprinted in McClelland, 1988.

4. Jack McClelland, letter to Cohen, May 1966, reprinted in McClelland, 1988.

5. Nicolas Walter, *Times Literary Supplement*, April 23, 1970.

6. Irving Layton, in *Chatelaine*, September 1983.

7. Barbara Amiel, *Maclean's*, September 18, 1978.

8. Paul Zollo, *Songwriters on Songwriting*, 1992, revised edition, Da Capo, 2003.

9. Nadel, 1996.

10. Ondaatje, 1970.

11. Cohen, interview with Adrienne Clarkson, *Take 30*, CBC TV, 1966.

12. Robert Fulford, *Toronto Daily Star*, 1966.

13. Jon Ruddy, *Maclean's*, October 1, 1966.

14. Interview on *The John Hammond Year*s, BBC, September 20, 1986.

15. Leonard Cohen, *The Best of Leonard Cohen* liner notes, 1975.

16. Zollo, 2003.

17. Cohen, letter to Marianne Ihlen, December 4, 1966, reprinted in Hesthamar, 2008.

18. Christian Fevret, *Les Inrockuptibles*, August 21, 1991, reproduced in *Throat Culture*, 1992, trans. Sophie Miller.

19. Harry Rasky, *The Song of Leonard Cohen: Portrait of a Poet, a Friendship and a Film*, Souvenir Press, 2001.

20. Cohen, letter to Marianne Ihlen, December 1966, published in Hesthamar, 2008.

Nine: How to Court a Lady

Author interviews with: Leonard Cohen, Judy Collins, David Crosby, Danny Fields, Lou Reed, Jackson Browne, Bob Johnston, John Simon, Jac Holzman, Aviva Layton, Thelma Blitz, Larry Cohen, Bob Fass, Marianne Ihlen, Juan Rodriguez, Joel Bernstein, Nancy Bacal, Erica Pomerance

Books, films and documents: Artist's cards, Columbia Records Archive. Patti Smith, *Just Kids*, Ecco, 2010. John Hammond and Irving Townsend, *On Record*, Ridge Press/Penguin US & UK, 1981. Kari Hesthamar, *So Long, Marianne: Ei Kjaerleikshistorie*, Spartacus, 2008. Mary Martin televised interview, Louise Scruggs Memorial Forum, Country Music Hall of Fame, November 17, 2009.

Chapter title: Leonard Cohen, at Henderson Hospital Concert, UK, August 1970.

1. Leonard Cohen, Henderson Hospital concert, UK, August 1970, taped by Ian Milne.

2. Reed, interview with the author, 2005.

3. Browne, interview with the author, 2008.

4. Ibid.

5. Ibid.

6. Ibid.

7. Ibid.

8. John Walsh, *MOJO*, September 1994.

9. Prologue to live performance of "Joan of Arc," Paris, October 20, 1974, leonardcohen-prologues.com.

10. Ibid.

11. Prologue at Henderson Hospital concert, UK, August 1970.

12. Smith, 2010.

13. Hammond and Townsend, 1981.

14. Cohen, letter to Marianne Ihlen, February 23, 1967, Ihlen private collection.

15. Cohen, letter to Marianne, April 9, 1967, Ihlen private collection.

16. Ibid.

17. Cohen, letter to Marianne, April 12, 1967, Ihlen private collection.

18. John Hammond and Leonard Cohen, BBC radio interview, September 20, 1986.

19. Ibid.

20. Harry Rasky, *The Song of Leonard Cohen: Portrait of a Poet, a Friendship and a Film*, Souvenir Press, 2001.

21. Layton, interview with the author.

22. Robert Enright, *Border Crossings* 7, February 2001.

23. Mark Ellen, *Word*, July 2007.

24. Enright, *Border Crossings*, 2001.

25. Robert Fulford, *This Was Expo*, McMaster Libraries, 1968.

26. Leonard Cohen, liner notes to *Greatest Hits/The Best of Leonard Cohen*, 1975.

27. Simon Houpt, *Globe and Mail*, February 27, 2009.

28. Hammond and Townsend, 1981.

29. Susan Nunziata, *Billboard*, November 28, 1998.

Ten: The Dust of a Long Sleepless Night

Author interviews with: Leonard Cohen, John Simon, Marianne Ihlen, Danny Fields, Steve Sanfield, David Lindley, Chris Darrow, Chester Crill

Books, documents and films: Artist's cards, Columbia Records Archive. Armelle Brusq, *Mount Baldy, Spring '96*, documentary film, 1997. Kari Hesthamar, *So Long, Marianne: Ei Kjaerleikshistorie*, Spartacus, 2008.

Chapter heading: Leonard Cohen, "One of Us Cannot Be Wrong," *Songs of Leonard Cohen*, 1968.

1. SS, 2001.

2. Leonard Cohen, "This is for you," later published in *Stranger Music: Selected Poems and Songs*, 1993.

3. Brusq, 1997.

4. SS, 2001.

5. Paul Grescoe, *Montreal Gazette*, February 10, 1968.

6. John Hammond and Leonard Cohen, BBC radio interview, September 20, 1986.

7. Prologue at concert in Antwerp, April 1988, leonardcohen-prologues.com.

8. Arthur Schmidt, *Rolling Stone*, September 2, 1971.

9. Donal Henahan, *New York Times*, January 29, 1968.

10. Karl Dallas, *Melody Maker*, February 17, 1968.

11. Ibid.

12. Ibid.

13. Jacoba Atlas, *Beat*, March 9, 1968.

14. William Kloman, *New York Times*, January 28, 1968.

15. *Playboy*, November 1968.

Eleven: The Tao of Cowboy

Author interviews with: Leonard Cohen, David Crosby, Bob Johnston, Marianne Ihlen, Terese Coe, Liberty, Thelma Blitz, Danny Fields, Kris Kristofferson, Steve Sanfield, Richard Vick, Terry Oldfield, Henry Zemel, Bill Donovan, Ron Cornelius, Charlie Daniels

Books, films and documents: Artist's cards, Columbia Records Archive. Leonard Cohen, *Selected Poems 1956–1968*, Jonathan Cape, 1969. Bob Dylan, *Chronicles: Volume One*, Simon & Schuster, 2004. Lian Lunson, *Leonard Cohen: I'm Your Man*, documentary film, Lionsgate, 2005. Michael Ondaatje, *Leonard Cohen*, McClelland & Stewart, 1970.

Chapter heading: SS.

1. Prologue at concert in Paris, June 6, 1976, leonardcohen-prologues.com.

2. Prologue at concert in Nuremberg, May 10, 1988, leonardcohen-prologues.com.

3. Lunson, 2005.

4. Dylan, 2004.

5. Rainer Blome, trans. Nick Townsend, *Sounds*, 1969.

6. Prologue at Henderson Hospital concert, UK, August 1970.

7. Leonard Cohen, *Selected Poems 1956–1968*, dust jacket of U.S. first edition, Viking, 1968.

8. Ondaatje, 1970.

9. SS, 2001.

10. Blome, 1969.

11. Michael Harris, *Duel*, Winter 1969.

12. Ibid.

13. SS, 2001.

14. Alec Dubro, *Rolling Stone*, May 17, 1969.

15. William Kloman, *New York Times*, April 27, 1969.

Twelve: O Make Me a Mask

Author interviews with: Leonard Cohen, Suzanne Elrod, David Cohen, Steve Sanfield, Danny Fields, Bob Johnston, Charlie Daniels, Ron Cornelius, Mort Rosengarten, Bill Donovan, Ian Milne, Kris Kristofferson, Jeff Dexter, Murray Lerner

Film and documents: Artist's cards, Columbia Records Archive. Murray Lerner, *Leonard Cohen: Live at the Isle of Wight 1970*, CD and documentary film, Columbia Legacy, 2009.

Chapter heading: Dylan Thomas, "O Make Me a Mask," 1938.

1. Paul Saltzman, "Famous Last Words from Leonard Cohen," *Maclean's*, June 1972.

2. Archive.

3. Pamela Andriotakis and Richard Oulahan, *People*, January 14, 1980.

4. Archive.

5. SS, 2001.

6. Gavin Martin, *NME*, October 19, 1991.

7. Harvey Kubernik, *Melody Maker*, March 1, 1975.

8. Robin Denselow, *Guardian*, May 11, 1970.

9. Archive.

10. Nancy Erlich, *Billboard*, August 8, 1970.

11. Steve Turner, *NME*, June 29, 1974.

12. Lerner, 2009.

Thirteen: The Veins Stand Out Like Highways

Author interviews with: Leonard Cohen, Suzanne Elrod, Charlie Daniels, Ron Cornelius, Joe Boyd, Chris Darrow, Chester Crill, David Lindley, Henry Zemel, Brian Cullman, Bob Johnston, Bill Donovan, Peter Marshall, Steven Machat, Liberty, Steve Sanfield, Tony Palmer

Books, films and documents: Artist's cards, Columbia Records Archive. Leonard Cohen, *The Energy of Slaves*, McClelland & Stewart, 1972. Tony Palmer, *Bird on a Wire*, documentary film, 1974. Henry Zemel, *Bonds of the Past*, documentary film, 1972.

Chapter heading: Leonard Cohen, "Dress Rehearsal Rag," *Songs of Love and Hate*, Columbia, 1971.

1. SS, 2001.

2. Roy Shipston, *Disc & Music Echo*, November 14, 1970.

3. John Walsh, *MOJO*, September 1994.

4. Martin Walker, *Guardian*, November 8, 1972.

5. SS, 2001.

6. Karl Dallas, *Melody Maker*, May 22, 1976.

7. Paul Saltzman, "Famous Last Words from Leonard Cohen," *Maclean's*, June 1972.

8. Leonard Cohen, "I have no talent left," *The Energy of Slaves*, June 1972.

9. Cohen, "The poems don't love us anymore," Ibid.

10. Cohen, "How we loved you," Ibid.

11. Cohen, "You are almost always with someone else," Ibid.

12. Cohen, "The 15-year-old girls," Ibid.

13. *Times Literary Supplement*, January 5, 1973.

14. Stephen Scobie, *Leonard Cohen*, Douglas & McIntyre, 1978.

15. Saltzman, 1972.

16. Palmer, 1974.

Fourteen: A Shield Against the Enemy

Author interviews with: Leonard Cohen, John Lissauer, Lewis Furey, Mort Rosengarten, Bob Johnston, Suzanne Elrod, Tony Palmer, Henry Zemel, Marianne Ihlen, Terry Oldfield, Leanne Ungar, Malka Marom, Danny Fields, Harvey Kubernik, Paul Body, Richard Vick, Aviva Layton, Larry "Ratso" Sloman

Book, films and documents: Artist's cards, Columbia Records Archive. L. S. Dorman and C. L. Rawlins, *Leonard Cohen: Prophet of the Heart*, 1990. Ira B. Nadel, *Various Positions*, Bloomsbury, 1996. Tony Palmer, *Bird on a Wire*, documentary film, 1974. Larry "Ratso" Sloman, *On the Road with Bob Dylan*, 1978; reprinted by Three Rivers Press, 2002.

Chapter heading: Leonard Cohen, "Lover Lover Lover," *New Skin for the Old Ceremony*, Columbia, 1974.

1. Archive, "The Woman Being Born/My Life in Art," 1973.

2. Robin Pike, *ZigZag*, October 1974.

3. Ibid.

4. Roy Hollingworth, *Melody Maker*, February 24, 1973.

5. Leonard Cohen, "My Life in Art," unpublished manuscript, Archive.

6. Ibid.

7. Pike, *ZigZag*, 1974.

8. Gavin Martin, *NME*, October 19, 1991.

9. Leonard Cohen, "The Final Revision of My Life in Art," unpublished manuscript, cited in Nadel, 1996.

10. Article marking the twentieth anniversary of the war, *Maariv*, 1993, trans. Doron B. Cohen.

11. Cohen, "The Final Revision."

12. Leonard Cohen, prologue to live performance of "Lover Lover Lover," Frankfurt, Germany, October 6, 1974, leonardcohen-prologues.com.

13. Pike, *ZigZag*, 1974.

14. Harvey Kubernik, *Melody Maker*, March 1, 1975.

15. Leonard Cohen, liner notes to *Greatest Hits/The Best of Leonard Cohen*, 1975.

16. Michael Wale, *ZigZag*, August 1974.

17. Kubernik, *Melody Maker*, 1975.

18. Cited in Dorman and Rawlins, 1990.

19. Clipping from *NME*, 1974 (author and date unknown).

20. Paul Nelson, *Rolling Stone*, February 26, 1975.

21. Prologue at concert in Melbourne, Australia, March 1980, leonardcohen-prologues.com.

22. Barry Coleman, *Guardian*, September 13, 1974.

23. Harry Rasky, *The Song of Leonard Cohen* (documentary film), 1980.

24. Larry Sloman, *Rolling Stone*, November 1974.

25. Kubernik, *Melody Maker*, 1975.

26. Archive, "My Life in Art."

27. Leonard Cohen, "The End of My Life in Art," unpublished essay, Archive.

Fifteen: I Love You, Leonard

Author interviews with: Leonard Cohen, Dan Kessel, David Kessel, Harvey Kubernik, Suzanne Elrod, Hal Blaine, John Lissauer, Steven Machat, Malka Marom, Ronee Blakley

Books, films and documents: Artist's cards, Columbia Records Archive. Leonard Cohen, *Death of a Lady's Man*, 1978. Mick Brown, *Tearing Down the Wall of Sound: The Rise and Fall of Phil Spector*, Knopf, 2007. *Leonard Cohen Under Review 1934–1977*, documentary film, Chrome Dreams, 2007. Steven Machat, *Gods, Gangsters and Honour*, Beautiful Books, 2010. Richard Williams, *Phil Spector: Out of His Head*, 1972; Omnibus reprint, 2003.

Chapter heading: Phil Spector, quoted by Leonard Cohen to Kevin Howlett, *Leonard Cohen: Tower of Song*, BBC Radio One, August 7, 1994.

1. Cohen, interview with Harvey Kubernik, 1977, later published in *LA Phonograph*, January 1978.

2. Brown, 2007.

3. Leonard Cohen, prologue to live performance of "Memories," Tel Aviv, 1980, leonardcohen-prologues.com.

4. Cohen, interview with Harvey Kubernik, 1977.

5. Ginsberg in *Record Collector*, February 1995.

6. Cohen, interview with Harvey Kubernik, 1977.

7. SS, 2001.

8. Kevin Howlett, *Leonard Cohen: Tower of Song*, BBC Radio One, August 7, 1994.

9. *Leonard Cohen Under Review*, 2007.

10. Brown, 2007

11. *Leonard Cohen Under Review*, 2007.

12. Brown, 2007.

13. Stephen Holden, *Rolling Stone*, January 26, 1978.

14. Ibid.

15. Janet Maslin, *New York Times*, November 6, 1977.

16. Cohen, interview with Harvey Kubernik, 1977.

17. Maslin, *New York Times*, 1977.

18. Paul Nelson, *Rolling Stone*, February 9, 1978.

19. Sandy Robertson, *Sounds*, November 26, 1977.

20. SS, 2001.

21. William Ruhlmann, *Goldmine*, February 19, 1993.

Sixteen: A Sacred Kind of Conversation

Author interviews with: Leonard Cohen, Suzanne Elrod, Rabbi Mordecai Finley, Nancy Bacal, Steve Sanfield, John Lissauer, Lewis Furey, Roscoe Beck, Harvey Kubernik, John Bilezikjian, Terry Oldfield, Dennis Lee, Sharon Robinson

Books and films: Leonard Cohen, *Book of Mercy*, 1984. Harry Rasky, *Song of Leonard Cohen*, documentary film, 1980. Harry Rasky, *The Song of Leonard Cohen: Portrait of a Poet, a Friendship and a Film*, Souvenir Press, 2001. Howard Sounes, *Down the Highway: The Life of Bob Dylan*, Grove, 2001.

Chapter heading: Leonard Cohen to Robert Sward, 1984.

1. Barbara Amiel, *Maclean's*, September 1978.

2. Columbia Records press release, 1979.

3. Nick Paton Walsh, *Observer*, October 14, 2001.

4. SS, 2001.

5. Sounes, 2001.

6. SS, 2001.

7. Ibid.

8. ZDF TV, Germany, October 31, 1979.

9. Rasky, 1980.

10. Cohen, "So Long, Marianne," *Songs from a Room*, Columbia, 1969.

11. Debra Cohen, *Rolling Stone*, February 21, 1980.

12. Larry "Ratso" Sloman, *High Times*, February 1980.

13. *NME*, 1979.

14. SS, 2001.

15. Brad Buchholz, *Austin American-Statesman*, March 31, 1979.

16. Pamela Andriotakis and Richard Oulahan, *People*, January 14, 1980.

17. Rasky, *Song of Leonard Cohen* film.

18. Ibid.

19. Ibid.

20. Nick Duerden, *Guardian*, October 7, 2011.

21. SS, 2001.

22. Robert Sward, "Leonard Cohen as Interviewed by Robert Sward," 1984.

23. *NME*, March 2, 1985.

24. Bruce Headlam, *Saturday Night*, December 1997.

25. Ibid.

26. Christian Fevret, *Les Inrockuptibles*, August 21, 1991, reproduced in *Throat Culture*, 1992, trans. Sophie Miller.

27. Sward, "Leonard Cohen."

28. Peter Gzowski, *Leonard Cohen at 50*, CBC, 1984.

Seventeen: The Hallelujah of the Orgasm

Author interviews with: Leonard Cohen, John Lissauer, Leanne Ungar, Larry "Ratso" Sloman, Anjani Thomas, David Lindley, Roscoe Beck

Chapter heading: Jeff Buckley, in *OOR*, 1994.

1. Robert Sward, "Leonard Cohen as Interviewed by Robert Sward," 1984.

2. SS, 2001.

3. Ibid.

4. Nigel Williamson, *Uncut*, October 12, 1997.

5. Cohen to John McKenna, RTÉ, May 9, 1988.

6. Paul Zollo, *Songwriters on Songwriting*, 1992, revised edition, Da Capo, 2003.

7. *Q*, September 1994.

8. Zollo, 1992.

9. Williamson, *Uncut*.

10. Richard Cook, *NME*, February 9, 1985.

11. *Sounds*, January 26, 1985.

12. Brian Appleyard, *Sunday Times*, January 9, 2005.

13. *Word*, July 2007.

14. Cohen, interview with Jian Ghomeshi, CBC TV, 2009.

15. Warnes, interview with Kevin Howlett, BBC Radio One, August 7, 1994.

16. Ian Pearson, *Saturday Night*, March 1993.

17. Cohen, interview with Kevin Howlett, BBC Radio One, August 7, 1994.

18. Ibid.

19. Marc Rowland, *Musician*, July 1988.

Eighteen: The Places Where I Used to Play

Author interviews with: Leonard Cohen, Iggy Pop, Roscoe Beck, Sharon Robinson, Sharon Weisz, Perla Batalla, Steven Machat, Sean Dixon, Julie Christensen, Hal Willner

Chapter heading: Leonard Cohen, "Tower of Song," *I'm Your Man,* Columbia, 1988.

1. Mat Snow, *Guardian,* February 1988.

2. Mark Rowland, *Musician,* July 1988.

3. SS, 2001.

4. Mark Cooper, *Q,* March 1988.

5. Ibid.

6. Prince Charles, interviewed on *Ant & Dec,* ITV1, May 20, 2006.

7. SS, 2001.

8. Ibid.

9. Ibid.

10. Christian Fevret, *Les Inrockuptibles,* August 21, 1991, reproduced in *Throat Culture,* 1992, trans. Sophie Miller.

11. Anjelica Houston, *Interview,* November 1995.

12. SS, 2001.

13. Elena Pita, *El Mundo,* September 26, 2001.

14. SS, 2001.

Nineteen: Jeremiah in Tin Pan Alley

Author interviews with: Leonard Cohen, Rebecca De Mornay, Anjani Thomas, Black Francis, Nick Cave, Hal Willner, Julie Christensen, Perla Batalla, Nancy Bacal, Leanne Ungar, Suzanne Elrod

Book: Leonard Cohen, *Stranger Music,* McClelland & Stewart, 1993.

Chapter heading: Irving Layton to Ian Pearson, *Saturday Night,* March 1993.

1. Brendan Kelly, *Financial Post,* December 12, 1992.

2. Paul Zollo, *Songwriters on Songwriting,* 1992.

3. Ibid.

4. Ibid.

5. Ibid.

6. *Details,* July 1993.

7. Brian D. Johnson, *Maclean's*, December 7, 1992.

8. Alan Jackson, *Observer*, November 22, 1992.

9. Agreta Wirberg and Stina Dabrowski, *Stina Möter Leonard Cohen*, TV documentary, 1997.

10. Barbara Gowdy, November 19, 1992, reprinted in *One on One: The Imprint Interviews*, ed. Leanna Crouch, Somerville House, 1994.

11. Cohen, Juno Canadian Music Hall of Fame induction speech, March 3, 1991.

12. SS, 2001.

13. Ibid.

14. Ibid.

15. *Billboard*, November 28, 1998.

16. Gowdy in *One on One*.

17. SS, 2001.

18. Gavin Martin, *NME*, January 9, 1993.

19. Anthony De Curtis, *Rolling Stone*, January 1993.

20. Gowdy in *One on One*.

21. Ibid.

22. Johnson, *Maclean's*.

23. Leonard Cohen and Rebecca De Mornay, *Interview*, June 1993.

24. Jon Pareles, *New York Times*, June 16, 1993.

25. Cohen, induction speech, Governor General's Award, Canada, 1993.

26. Ian Pearson, *Saturday Night*, March 1993.

Twenty: From This Broken Hill

Author interviews with: Leonard Cohen, Kigen, Robert Faggen, Roscoe Beck, Rebecca De Mornay, Daijo, Sharon Robinson, Steve Sanfield, Jarkko Arjatsalo, Perla Batalla, Julie Christensen, Ratnesh Mathur, Chris Darrow, Nancy Bacal, Leanne Ungar, Anjani Thomas

Books and films: Armelle Brusq, *Leonard Cohen: Portrait: Spring 96*, documentary film, 1997. Leonard Cohen, *Book of Longing*, Ecco, 2006. Agreta Wirberg and Stina Dabrowski, *Stina Möter Leonard Cohen*, TV documentary, 1997.

Chapter heading: Leonard Cohen, "If It Be Your Will," *Various Positions*, Columbia, 1985.

1. SS, 2001.

2. Ibid.

3. Gilles Tordjman, *Les Inrockuptibles*, interview with the author, October 15, 1995.

4. Robert Hilburn, *Los Angeles Times*, September 24, 1995.

5. SS, 2001.

6. Cohen, letter to Marianne Ihlen, February 1967.

7. Billy Walker, *Sounds*, October 23, 1971.

8. Wirberg and Dabrowski, 1997.

9. Pico Iyer, *Buzz*, April 1995.

10. SS, 2001.

11. Ibid.

12. Wirberg and Dabrowski, 1997.

13. Gilles Tordjman, *Les Inrockuptibles*, March 15, 1995.

14. SS, 2001.

15. Ibid.

16. Ibid.

17. Ibid.

18. Ibid.

19. Bruce Headlam, *Saturday Night*, December 1997.

20. Tordjman, *Les Inrockuptibles*, 1995.

21. Neva Chonin, *Rolling Stone*, December 11, 1997.

22. *NME*, September 1995.

23. SS, 2001.

24. Ibid.

25. Ibid.

26. Wirberg and Dabrowski, 1997.

27. SS, 1997.

28. Ibid.

29. Paul Zollo, *Songwriters on Songwriting*, 1992.

30. Susan Nunziata, *Billboard*, November 28, 1998.

31. SS, 2011.

32. Ibid.

33. Ibid.

34. Ibid.

35. Ibid.

36. Ibid.

37. Ibid.

38. Ibid.

39. SS, 2001.

40. SS, 2011.

41. Ibid.

42. Ibid.

Twenty-one: Love and Theft

Author interviews with: Leonard Cohen, Robert Kory, Rufus Wainwright, Nick Cave, Hal Willner, Anjani Thomas, Leanne Ungar, Sharon Robinson, Ratnesh Mathur, Julie Christensen, Perla Batalla, Robert Faggen, Richard Landon

Books and films: Armelle Brusq, *Leonard Cohen: Portrait: Spring 96*, documentary film, 1997. Leonard Cohen, *Book of Longing*, Ecco, 2006. Agreta Wirberg and Stina Dabrowski, *Stina Möter Leonard Cohen*, TV documentary, 1997.

Chapter heading: Leonard Cohen, "To a Teacher," *The Spice-Box of Earth*, 1961.

1. Christian Langlois, *CARP*, June 2006.

2. SS, 2001.

3. Ibid.

4. Ibid.

5. Robinson, interview with the author, 2009.

6. Sarah Hampson, *Shambhala Sun*, November 2007.

7. Frank DiGiacomo, *New York Observer*, February 22, 2002.

8. SS, 2001.

9. Jon Pareles, *New York Times*, October 1995.

10. SS, 2001.

11. SS, 2011.

12. Wirberg and Dabrowski, 1997.

13. Leon Wieseltier, *Arts & Opinion* vol. 4, no. 2, 2005.

14. Ibid.

15. Cohen, e-mail to Jarkko Arjatsalo, June 2004.

16. Susan Nunziata, *Billboard*, November 28, 1998.

17. Katherine Macklem, Charlie Gillis and Brian D. Johnson, *Maclean's*, August 22, 2005.

Twenty-two: Taxes, Children, Lost Pussy

Author interviews with: Leonard Cohen, Robert Kory, Anjani Thomas, Hal Willner, Nick Cave, Rufus Wainwright, Julie Christensen, Perla Batalla, John Lissauer, Rabbi Mordecai Finley

Chapter heading: Leonard Cohen, self-portrait in *Book of Longing*, 2006.

1. Ann Diamond, "Whatever Happened to Kelley Lynch," riverdeepbook.blogspot.com, July 3, 2008.

2. J. Kelly Nestruck, *National Post*, February 7, 2006.

3. Ibid.

4. Cohen, speech at induction into the Canadian Songwriters Hall of Fame, February 5, 2006.

5. Angela Pacienza, *Toronto Canadian Press*, February 4, 2006.

6. Christine Langlois, *CARP*, June 2006.

7. Ibid.

8. Phoebe Hoban, *New York*, May 14, 2006.

9. Sean Murphy, *Tricycle: The Buddhist Review*, August 2007.

10. Biba Kopf, *NME*, March 1987.

Twenty-three: The Future of Rock 'n' Roll

Author interviews with: Leonard Cohen, Philip Glass, Robert Faggen, Hal Willner, Anjani Thomas, Robert Kory, Steven Machat, Rob Hallett, Sharon Robinson, Roscoe Beck, Charley Webb, Hattie Webb

Chapter heading: John Landau, *Rolling Stone*, 1974.

1. SS, 2011.

2. Greg Quill, *Toronto Star*, June 3, 2007.

3. Mireille Silcott, *Saturday Night*, 2001.

4. Leonard Cohen Files, April 29, 2002.

5. Mireille Silcott, *Saturday Night*, 2001.

6. Neil McCormick, *Telegraph*, May 26, 2007.

7. Sarah Hampson, *Shambhala Sun*, November 2007.

8. SS, 2011.

9. Lou Reed, Rock and Roll Hall of Fame speech introducing Cohen, March 10, 2008.

10. Cohen, Rock and Roll Hall of Fame induction speech, March 10, 2008.

11. Alec Dubro, *Rolling Stone*, May 17, 1969.

12. Arthur Schmidt, *Rolling Stone*, September 2, 1971.

13. Geoff Boucher, *Los Angeles Times*, February 27, 2009.

Twenty-four: Here I Stand, I'm Your Man

Author interviews with: Leonard Cohen, Sharon Robinson, Tony Palmer, Robert Kory, Rob Hallett, Anjani Thomas, Hal Willner, Roscoe Beck, Charley Webb, Hattie Webb, Henry Zemel

Chapter heading: Leonard Cohen, "I'm Your Man," *I'm Your Man*, Columbia, 1988.

1. SS, 2011.

2. Ibid.

3. Ben Rayner, *Toronto Star*, June 7, 2008.

4. Andy Greene, *Rolling Stone*, June 9, 2008.

5. Brian D. Johnson, *Maclean's*, June 11, 2008.

6. Johnny Black, *Audience*, September 2008.

7. Ibid.

8. John Aizlewood, *London Evening Standard*, July 18, 2008.

9. Johnson, *Maclean's*.

10. Andy Greene, *Rolling Stone*, February 20, 2009.

11. Lavinia Jones Wright, *Billboard*, February 20, 2009.

12. Leonard Cohen, "Now and Then."

13. Patrick Doyle, *Rolling Stone*, June 18, 2010.

14. Cohen, interview with Jian Ghomeshi, CBC TV, April 16, 2009.

Twenty-five: A Manual for Living with Defeat

Author interviews with: Leonard Cohen, Robert Kory

Chapter heading: Leonard Cohen, "Going Home," *Old Ideas*, Sony, 2012.

1. Simon Houpt, *Globe and Mail*, February 27, 2009.

2. Paul Zollo, *Songwriters on Songwriting*, 1992, revised edition, Da Capo, 2003.

3. Cohen to Jarvis Cocker, *Guardian*, January 19, 2012.

4. SS, 2011.

5. Cohen onstage, Las Vegas, December 11, 2010.

6. Cohen, press conference, Paris, January 16, 2012.

7. SS, 2011.

8. Ibid.

9. James Adams, *Globe and Mail*, April 1, 2011.

10. SS, 2011.

11. Adam Cohen, interviewed by Rebecca Ecker, *Maclean's*, October 6, 2011.

12. Ibid.

13. SS, 2011.

14. Ibid.

15. Greg Kot, *Chicago Tribune*, January 24, 2012.

16. Kitty Empire, *Observer*, January 21, 2012.

17. Jon Dolan, *Rolling Stone*, December 7, 2011.

18. Andy Gill, *Independent*, January 20, 2012.

19. Cohen to Jarvis Cocker, press conference, London, January 2012.

20. Cohen, press conference, Paris, January 16, 2012.

21. SS, 2011.

Epilogue

Author interview with: Leonard Cohen

1. Leonard Cohen, calligraphy, liner note artwork, *Old Ideas*, 2012.

Permissions

Index